COMPARATIVE
ECONOMIC ORGANIZATION

COMPARATIVE

ECONOMIC ORGANIZATION

by

ARTHUR ROBERT BURNS

Professor of Economics
Columbia University

New York

PRENTICE-HALL, INC.

1955

PRINTED IN THE UNITED STATES OF AMERICA

Preface

For many millenia differences in levels of living throughout the world were comparatively small. Differences there were, but population increase kept the mass of the people in most groups on a somewhat comparable level. There were also differences in levels of living within groups, a few being better off than the majority of the population. Then some three hundred years ago this picture began to change. Some countries began to improve their economic position and, in time, that of a large part of their populations. The new methods of raising levels of living also spread, but most unevenly. Some social groups have remained economically stable and some have even lost ground. At the same time the more advanced have the means to continue to advance rapidly and the gap between the richest and the poorest groups is wider than ever before, and still widening.

The resulting inequality in economic conditions among national groups has had a serious impact on politics and economics. In politics it is the source of our most desperate international problems. Inequalities among nations are more sharply realized now than formerly, and the widespread belief that they can be reduced is an obdurate political fact. Enquiry into the causes of this growing inequality is a first step towards effective action to reduce present fears and frustrations.

In economics these international differences raise questions whether past methods of analysis are equally applicable to societies differing in social attitudes and methods of economic organization. Adam Smith directed attention to comparative economic study (and to the importance of economic organization) nearly two hundred years ago when he entitled Book III of the *Wealth of Nations*, "Of the different progress of opulence in different nations." But after the time of John Stuart Mill this aspect of the subject attracted little attention until the present century, except perhaps from Alfred Marshall. During the present century comparative economic study has been influenced by broad changes in political organization relocating economic power within societies. Studies of "economic systems," such as capitalism, socialism, communism and the like, rest

v

upon a recognition of the variety of ways of organizing economic life. But such studies have yielded little information as to the outcome of different "systems." These studies have relied mainly on general assumptions concerning the consequences of different forms of organization. This failure to compare results is largely due to the difficulty of fitting countries into the classification used. Many countries embody elements of various "systems," and the relative importance of the elements is changing. Also influences other than the broad system of economic organization affect the performance of an economy. Many now underdeveloped countries would presumably have to be classified as capitalist, yet their performance differs so markedly from that of more developed capitalist countries that the classification serves no useful economic purpose. Information concerning the performance of various economies is, however, now becoming available in rapidly increasing volume. It is often faulty but it permits us to begin with what we know about performance and to try to explain it.

The present book begins, therefore, with a summary of the presently available information as to relative well-being in different national economies. This summary merely defines the problem. The remainder of the book is an attempt to provide a systematic explanation of international differences. Levels of living depend partly on economic potentials and partly on the extent to which human organization achieves full use of them. Economic potentials rest partly on gifts of nature, but I have restricted the facts of economic geography for the most part to broad generalizations. Economic potentials at any time depend also on past human behavior, for example, behavior affecting exhaustion of the land or minerals or additions to capital goods facilitating production. The extent to which countries use their means of production depends wholly on human conduct. The economic well-being of a group depends also on its position in the world economy, and particularly on the terms on which it can transact business with the rest of the world. These matters cannot be wholly ignored, but they must be a minor part of a book primarily focussed on the internal resources and organization of various groups.

The explanation is chiefly concerned with the influences affecting average output because the amount of production is the major, although not the only, cause of differences in economic welfare. But production adjusted for the impact of international transactions furnishes only part of the explanation of differences in levels of living. Consumption is the immediate source of economic welfare. Production may exceed consumption because the economy is devoting part of its effort to increasing the means of future production. Some countries are now rapidly increasing their production but are leaving consumption on a low and almost unchanging level. Finally, explanation cannot rest solely on average consumption. Within economies there are almost always groups with widely differing levels of consumption. These differences depend not only on differences in incomes from property and labor but also on the activities of governments, which influence consumption by subtracting from, or adding to, these incomes. General tax policies and social security arrangements are merely outstanding examples of increasingly elaborate patterns of government action bearing upon the material welfare of the individual.

The comparisons run chiefly in terms of national economies. These national groups are far from ideal units for economic study but much of the available information is about such groups, and there is greater uniformity of organization within them than among them. I have not, however, attempted a series of rounded pictures of national economies. Instead I have sought to isolate the major economic problems facing any economy, such as the selection of the framework within which individuals shall participate in production, the regulation of the relative supplies of the different means of production, the arrangements affecting the extent to which they are utilized, and the devices affecting the distribution of the produce among individuals. Comparison of a wide sample of economies in each of these aspects seems to me to be more helpful in building up a method of comparative economics than a series of total national comparisons. It is true that the categories used represent forces that impinge on each other, especially in a developing society. This difficulty can be surmounted, at least in part, by avoiding too rigid and isolated a discussion of each factor. The resulting duplication of discussion, while regrettable, merely reflects the reality that the forces operating on the economic life of a group are interdependent rather than separate. As Chapter 2 contains a more detailed description of the argument of the book, there is no purpose in repeating it here.

Comparison restricted to present conditions is meagre and inadequate. Any enquiry into differences in the wealth of nations must lead to questions about when and how the present inequalities came to be. Economic history has followed different paths in different countries because of differences in opportunity, in propensities to take advantage of opportunity, and of changes in this propensity. Capitalism provided the social framework for the most notable economic development for some two hundred years, but the socialist government of Russia has achieved rapid development in the past thirty years. Evidently some social frameworks are more hospitable to innovation than others, but they can change in this respect in the course of time. But improvements in productivity have resulted as much from changes in resources as from changes in methods of using them. The economists of the nineteenth century were predominantly concerned with the most economical use (or the best allocation) of given resources. In retrospect, this emphasis suggests a failure to appreciate contemporary economic conditions. These economists lived in societies which were developing rapidly, not only because methods of production were changing, but also because economic resources (especially capital equipment) were growing. Indeed, the changes in methods of production depended largely on these changes in resources. The economists did discuss changes in the supply of capital and labor but failed to bring the factors influencing their change within an ordered body of economic theory.

Towards the end of the century, studies of cyclical fluctuations in production in the more advanced economies pointed up the spasmodic quality of economic growth. Only recently, however, have economists turned to the trend of economic growth and the forces which regulate it. I have attempted no general theory of economic development, but the attempt to explain present conditions has compelled me to direct considerable attention to past trends in different countries. The forces impinging on production differ greatly in relative importance, for instance, in the small economically static "primitive society," the capitalist economy, and the socialist economy. But they also differ notably in different countries operating in general within a capitalist framework. It is therefore necessary to enquire how far these differences are due to differences in the relative value societies place on the material and the non-material aspects of life. How far has the availability of resources accelerated change in some but retarded it in others? Many of the new techniques of the progressing societies were available to be copied by others, but why has diffusion been so spotty? Not all these questions can be answered, but they will never be answered if they are not asked. And they lead us from comparisons over space to comparisons over time. For this reason I have tried to look behind the present to its historical background.

I hope that students of economic theory can be persuaded to make use of the book. Comparative study of the economic organization and operation of various groups can bring economics nearer to the implications of its name. On the one hand, this approach illumines economic problems that are universal and, on the other, focusses attention on the variety of ways in which man has attempted to solve these problems. It also gives a new stimulus to the appraisal of the economic organization in which the student himself lives. One is always in danger of accepting the ways of one's own country as too obvious for fundamental appraisal. Knowledge of the interior workings of countries of different types appears to me to be essential also to the study of international relations, more particularly in view of the increasing importance of economic forces in this field. And the time has come to replace the study of "economic systems" by studies placing more emphasis on operating results and their causes. Lastly, I trust that various parts of the book will be useful as comparative supplements to courses on particular aspects of economics, such as agriculture, industrial organization, labor, public finance, and social security.

Convinced as I am of the necessity for making a beginning with systematic economic comparison, I have many times been almost overwhelmed by my foolhardiness in trying to meet the need. The field is too wide to be adequately covered by one person, and I confess to the unevenness of my competence in different aspects of economic life and of my knowledge of the various countries mentioned. Many readers with special knowledge of particular countries will find errors and omissions. I can only ask them to give me the benefit of their criticism. My ultimate purpose is to set out by example a method of comparative study and I shall be rewarded if such study is stimulated.

My acknowledgments of indebtedness should be many. The staff of the United Nations has made the greatest contributions in this field and I have drawn liberally upon them. I am deeply grateful to the Council for Research in the Social Sciences of Columbia University, which financed extended field work in a number of countries with which I had previously had no first-hand acquaintance. I am also grateful to the many public officials, representatives of labor and industry, and academic colleagues in many countries for their help and hospitality. Their number is too great to permit particular acknowledgment. I am especially indebted to my wife and colleague Eveline M. Burns for her help with the material on social security. I hasten, however, to add the conventional, but nevertheless proper, statement that I alone am responsible for omissions and errors of statement or emphasis. Finally, I thank the stenographers, too numerous to specify, who have labored over successive editions of the manuscript.

ARTHUR ROBERT BURNS

Contents

COMPARATIVE

ECONOMIC ORGANIZATION

Part One

Introduction

Chapter 1

Comparisons of Economic Welfare

Societies organize the production and consumption of economic goods
in various ways. By discovering the similarities and differences we may
not only increase our knowledge of one important aspect of human behavior, but also appraise the extent to which various methods of economic
organization contribute to human welfare. Such appraisal is difficult because welfare depends on more than the supply of economic goods.
Nevertheless it is possible to make some comparisons of levels of economic well-being in different societies.

A. National Income[1]

The amount of goods and services available to a society has a considerable bearing on its level of living. On the basis of national income per
head, levels are highly unequal. The richest 7% of the people in the world
enjoy about 42% of the world's income while 66% of the people subsist
on 15% of the world's income (Table 1), the average income in the first
group being about 30 times that in the second. A study of countries with
more than 90% of the world's population, and a considerably higher proportion of the world's income, indicates that in 1949 income per person
in the United States of America was about 70% higher than in any other
single country, and nearly 60 times higher than in the poorest country.

---

[1] See Kuznets, S., "National Income," in *Encyclopedia of the Social Sciences;* Kuznets, S., *National Income: a summary of findings;* Shoup, C. S., *The Principles of
National Income Analysis;* U.N., *National Income Statistics* 1938-48, 1948.

1

TABLE 1

DISTRIBUTION OF THE POPULATION OF SEVENTY COUNTRIES BY SIZE OF
PER CAPITA INCOME IN 1949*

Size of per capita income per year	Population as % of world population	National incomes as % of world total
Less than $ 50	31	4
" " 100	54	9
" " 200	66	15
" " 400	85	38
" " 600	89	44
" " 900	93	58
" " 1500	100	100

* U.N., *National and Per Capita Income in Seventy Countries* (1949), 29.

Average incomes in New Zealand, Australia and Northwest Europe were 35 to 60% as high as in the U.S.A. ($1,453), (in Britain about 50%). Average income in Russia[2] was less than a quarter of that in the U.S.A., and in 40 countries it was less than $200 a year (Table 2). The greatest concentration of low incomes was in Asia,[3] Africa and parts of the Middle East[4] (Table 3). Thus the highest average incomes are obtained by the more industrialized countries.

This great inequality among countries has appeared during the past two or three centuries and is still increasing. In Britain, income per person has increased, probably since the 18th century. More recently the index rose from 57 in 1870 to 100 in 1900 and 134 in 1938.[5] In the U.S.A. ag-

---

[2] National income as calculated in Russia has not included services (such as passenger transport and many government services) regarded as "unproductive" in Marxist terms, but important in the national income of many (especially the more developed) countries. The estimated income originating in these industries has, however, been included in the above figure to make the Russian figure more comparable with that of other countries. In 1952, moreover, Premier Stalin announced the abandonment of this distinction between productive and unproductive labor and stated that "all types of labor satisfying the working class needs are equally indispensable" (*Cit.* N. Y. Times, Oct. 4, 1952). The money value of Russian national income also differs from its real value because of the turnover or sales taxes (which affect the valuation of industrial output), the method of valuing agricultural output, of treating profit and interest and allowances for depreciation. (Bergson, "Soviet National Income and Product in 1937," *Quar. Jour. of Econ.*, Aug. 1950.) Indirect taxes have been deducted to arrive at the average income. But, as these taxes provide most national saving in Russia (Ch. 21), this procedure omits from the Russian figure most savings, which the figures for other countries include. After allowing for the allocation to net investment of a proportion of the national product, 50 to 75% higher than in western countries, and to defense a proportion about twice as high as in Britain and the U.S.A., civilian consumption expenditures per person in Russia have been estimated to be about 30% of those in the U.S.A. in 1948. (*Economist*, Dec. 18, 1948, and Baran, P. A., "National Income and Product of the U.S.S.R. in 1940" in 29, *Rev. Econ. Stat.*, 226, 1947.)

[3] *U.N. Econ. Surv. of Asia and the Far East in 1948*, 9.

[4] U.N. Conciliation Commission for Palestine, *Final Report of Economic Survey Mission for the Middle East*, 34. Issawi, *Egypt: An Economic and Social Analysis*, 50.

[5] Prest, A. R., "National Income of the United Kingdom, 1870 to 1947," LVIII *Econ. Jour.*, 31 (1948). See also Rostas, L., *Comparative Productivity in British and American Industry*, 43.

TABLE 2

AVERAGE INCOME PER HEAD OF POPULATION
IN SEVENTY COUNTRIES IN 1949*

Country	Average Income in U.S. Dollars of 1949 Purchasing Power	Country	Average Income in U.S. Dollars of 1949 Purchasing Power
United States	1,453	Costa Rica	125
Canada	870	Turkey	125
New Zealand	856	Lebanon	125
Switzerland	849	Mexico	121
Sweden	780	Brazil	112
Great Britain	773	Southern Rhodesia	101
Denmark	689	Egypt	100
Australia	679	Japan	100
Norway	587	Syria	100
Belgium	582	Peru	100
Luxembourg	553	El Salvador	92
Netherlands	502	Nicaragua	89
France	482	Iran	85
Iceland	476	Iraq	85
Ireland	420	Paraguay	84
Israel	389	Honduras	83
Czechoslovakia	371	Guatemala	77
Finland	348	Dominican Republic	75
Argentina	346	Ceylon	67
Uruguay	331	India	57
Venezuela	322	Bolivia	55
Germany (Western Zone)	320	Pakistan	51
Soviet Union	308	Afghanistan	50
Poland	300	Philippines	44
Cuba	296	Ecuador	40
Hungary	269	Saudi Arabia	40
South Africa	264	Yemen	40
Portugal	250	Haiti	40
Italy	235	Ethiopia	38
Austria	216	Liberia	38
Chile	188	Burma	36
Panama	183	Thailand	36
Yugoslavia	146	Korea (Southern)	35
Colombia	132	China	27
Greece	128	Indonesia	25

* Source: U.N., *National and Per Capita Income in Seventy Countries—1949*, 14.

gregate income has risen greatly, owing in part, however, to increases in population. Income per person in terms of current prices rose 200% from 1799 to 1938.[6] Between 1850 and 1940 output per head in terms of 1940 prices rose 333%.[7] In Japan real income per head rose about 2 to 3% a year between 1868 and 1895; 3.5% between 1896 and 1913; 4.9% between 1914 and 1919, and 6.13% between 1920 and 1929. The national income

[6] Calculated from National Industrial Conference Board, *cit. U.S. Bureau of Census. Historical Statistics of the U.S.*, 14.
[7] Dewhurst *et al., America's Needs and Resources*, 23.

TABLE 3

Countries Classified by Size and Per Capita Income in 1949 and by Continental Division*

Income per Capita in U.S. Dollars	Population		Africa	America, North	America, South	Asia	Europe and U.S.S.R.	Oceania
	Number (million)	Per cent						
Under $100	509	34	Kenya, N. Rhodesia	Dominican Republic	Ecuador, Paraguay	Burma, Ceylon, India, Iran, Pakistan, Philippines, Thailand		
$100–200	284	19	Egypt, S. Rhodesia	Mexico	Brazil, Chile, Colombia, Peru, Surinam	Japan, Syria, Turkey	Bulgaria, Greece, Spain, Yugoslavia	
$200–300	82	6	Union of S. Africa	Cuba, Puerto Rico			Austria, Hungary, Italy	
$300–450	305	20			Argentina, Uruguay	Israel	Czechoslovakia, Finland, Germany (Western), Ireland, Poland, U.S.S.R.	
$450–600	69	5			Venezuela		Belgium, France, Iceland, Luxembourg, Netherlands, Norway	
$600–900	89	6		Canada			Denmark, Sweden, Switzerland, United Kingdom	Australia, New Zealand
$900 and over	149	10		U.S.A.				
Total	1,487	100						

General Note: The countries are listed alphabetically in each group. The concept of income used to calculate the per capita data is national income produced within the territorial boundaries of the country or net geographical product at factor cost.

of Russia fell by 60% between 1913 and 1921 but has risen rapidly since 1926. Production per head of the whole population probably increased 250% to 300% between 1913 and 1950.[8] This overall average, reflecting increases in the proportion of the population at work and shifts from less to more productive work, provides, however, no indication of consumption per person, which has in fact risen little (Ch. 30).

Between 1939 and about 1950 real incomes per person increased about 40% in the U.S.A., Canada, U.S.S.R., Poland, Czechoslovakia and Puerto Rico.[9] Most European and Latin American countries had higher incomes than before the war. In these countries industrial production increased relatively to agricultural production, and in most of European industry, capital goods were a larger proportion of total output than before the war. Thus consumption per person[10] increased less than income per person. Government consumption rose and the distribution of income also changed; generally wage-earners' shares increased and inequalities in income were reduced. Statistical information regarding the Middle East is unsatisfactory, but income per person probably rose in Turkey, it probably fell 39% in Egypt between 1913 and 1951.[11] In many Far Eastern countries (with the notable exception of Ceylon) incomes were lower in 1950 than in 1913 (markedly lower in Burma). In African countries making statistics available, incomes were generally higher in 1950 than in 1939. Nevertheless, the median income of the world population has probably declined since 1913. "A shrinking proportion of the world population has been rapidly raising its standard of living, while the living standard of an increasing majority of the world population has been rising much more slowly or has remained stationary. The improvement within the first group and the very slow improvement in the second group are, however, swamped by the shift in relative numbers from the first group to the second."[12]

---

[8] Calculations of national income in Russia excluded consumer services, thus making it lower than it would have been if calculated in the same way as in capitalist countries. But the inclusion of much of the industrial output (which has greatly expanded as a proportion of national income) at the high values of 1926-7 (until recently) exaggerates the official figures for income. The income planned for 1950 is estimated to be 5 to 6 times that in 1913 rather than 8 to 9 times as estimated by Russian authorities. (*Economist*, Dec. 18, 1949, and A. Gerschenkron, "The Soviet Indices of Industrial Production," 29, *Rev. Econ. Stat.*, 217, 1947.)

[9] U.N., *Econ. Surv. of Europe in 1949*, 20, U.N. *Prelim. Rep. on the World Social Situation*, 1952, 132. U.N. *National Income Statistics 1938-48*, passim., U.N. *Monthly Bulletin of Statistics*, June 1950, 147. In the U.S.A. real income per head in 1948 was 152% of 1938 (U.N. *National Income Statistics 1938-48*, 245).

[10] U.N., *National Income Statistics 1938-48*, 245. Consumption per person was above prewar only in the Scandinavian countries, about equal to prewar in France and the United Kingdom, and considerably below in Austria, Germany (Western Zone) and Italy. (*Ibid.*)

[11] *La Revue d'Egypte Economique et Financière*, Dec. 1952.

[12] Singer, H. W., "Economic Progress in Underdeveloped Countries," 16 *Social Research* 1. (1949).

The broad interpretation of these data is inescapable. There is ample supporting evidence that levels of living differ widely throughout the world. But the data do not accurately measure economic welfare—indeed, we are not yet able to measure it. The meaning of national income figures depends on how they are calculated. They all rest on measurements of flows of goods and services. These flows must be measured in a single unit so that a total can be obtained. Money units are used because more things are quoted in money than in any other medium. Three bases of calculation all give the same result. The bases are (a) the aggregate net values added[13] in all branches of economic activity[14] *plus* net income from abroad, (b) the aggregate income payments accruing to all factors of production (i.e., wages, salaries, interest, dividends, profits, rent, etc.), or (c) aggregate expenditures on consumption goods and services *plus* net domestic and foreign investment. Systematic calculations of this sort date from the 1930s and, since different countries do not all calculate in the same way, the results are not always entirely comparable.[15] For many countries there are no figures, or only doubtful estimates.

The use of money values results in a figure for national product, but it has a deceptive precision. Government services such as military and police service are usually included at cost although their addition to the social welfare is in fact difficult to measure. Some government payments (such as payments of interest on government debt not covered by productive assets) are not included in the total because they are regarded as transfers of income rather than additions to national income. The distinction between transfers and additions, however, is not made on the same basis everywhere, notably in regard to contributions for social security. Where goods and services do not pass through a market, their values are estimated (e.g., goods produced and consumed on the farm and payments in kind). This imputed component is about 60% of the total national product in China, 45% in India, and 9% in Italy, but 2% or less in the more

---

13 The "value added" by an enterprise consists of the difference between the sales value of the product and the products of other industries (but not labor) consumed in the production process. Professional activities are usually valued at the price paid for them.

14 Where goods and services are valued at market prices, the resulting national income is stated to be "at market prices." Where goods and services are valued net of indirect taxes but after inclusion of subsidies (so as to reflect the payments received by the factors of production), the resulting national income is said to be "at factor cost."

15 These problems are described in U.N. *National Income Statistics, 1938-48*, 4 ff. Goods and services not purchased may be difficult to measure in physical terms, and also to value. The services of housewives are typically excluded. The imputed annual value of owner-occupied houses is often included but not that of other durable consumer goods such as clothing, furniture and automobiles. Payments in kind (e.g., to members of armed forces) are usually valued. Goods produced and consumed by the same family unit present serious problems but must be valued in order to arrive at any useful estimate of income.

developed industrial countries. Estimation is difficult in underdeveloped countries because the physical quantities of goods consumed is uncertain and their valuation is arbitrary because such countries are usually so poorly organized that market prices for the same product vary widely in different parts of the country. In socialist countries like Soviet Russia, the prices at which all the various components of national income are valued are determined by the government. Finally, no monetary value can be placed upon the fatigue, strain and hardships of economic life.

International comparisons of national income are possible only if national figures are converted into a common unit. Even where governments do not control rates of foreign exchange, these rates do not reflect accurately the relative purchasing power of different monetary units. Tourists and pensioners long ago discovered that some countries are cheaper to live in than others. Government-controlled exchange rates are likely to be farther than ever from useful indexes of the relative purchasing power of monetary units.[16] The United Nations arrived at the figures above quoted by converting national figures into United States dollars essentially by using pre-1939 exchange rates adjusted on the basis of "suitable price index numbers."[17] Other methods of conversion based on direct comparisons of purchasing power are devised to take account of differences in the composition of the national product in different countries.[18] But all these methods of conversion contain unavoidable elements of arbitrariness affecting the resulting figures.

Because the national incomes of different countries vary widely in composition, it is questionable whether equal average incomes in two countries indicate equal material well-being, and whether differences in average income indicate proportionate differences in well-being. Where consumers are free to choose how to spend their income, and the production of various goods is adjusted to consumer choice and to costs of production, the composition of national income depends on the distribution of incomes and on consumer needs and desires. Each individual aims to maximize the satisfactions obtained from the expenditure of his income. But the satisfactions of individuals with equal money incomes are equal only if their needs and desires are equal. These needs and desires depend on age, sex, health, number of dependents, and the effectiveness of want-creating mechanisms like advertising. These conditions differ even more widely among nations than within them. There are marked differences among countries in the size of families, climate, mores, and the effectiveness of sales promotion. But even if needs and desires are equal, as well as money incomes, productive systems respond differently to effective de-

---

16 U.N., *National Income Statistics, 1938-48* (1948), 111.
17 U.N., *National and Per Capita Incomes in Selected Countries* (1949), 17 ff.
18 Clark, *Conditions of Economic Progress* (2d), Ch. II.

mand. Differences in resources and in the efficiency with which they are used cause differences in price patterns for goods and, therefore, differences in the ways in which people with similar money incomes spend them, and in the satisfactions they obtain. International trade releases the people in a country from sole dependence on national resources, but this relief is limited by transport and other costs of trade, and government restrictions.

In socialist countries like Russia the "product and services mix" in the national product is not controlled by consumer choice and the relative cost of producing different goods. The demand for consumer goods is held down to the supply by holding the prices of consumer goods well above the cost of production. Presumably if the production of different goods were adjusted to consumer choice and costs, consumers would get more nearly "what they want," and a given money income in Russia would yield more satisfactions than it now does. Consequently, even when average Russian income is converted into an international unit, it is still not comparable with similar income in a free-market economy. But the satisfactions obtainable from income in non-socialist societies also often differ from those in a free-market economy, owing to monopolistic pricing and to governments taxing away part of individual incomes and spending the proceeds in ways the taxpayer would not have chosen. Such government spending may, however, increase satisfactions, which suggests that the perfectly free market economy does not always maximize the satisfactions obtainable with given resources.

Differences in personal income are not proportionate to differences in satisfaction if marginal utility diminishes with increasing supply. For this reason, although average national income in the U.S.A. is said to be 60 times that in Indonesia (Table 2), it is unlikely that people in the U.S.A. are 60 times as well off in a material sense as those in Indonesia, even apart from differences in felt needs. Insofar as well-being is affected by comparisons of income, however, the rapid spread throughout the world of knowledge of inequality has probably reduced well-being, even where supplies of goods and services have not fallen. The gap between aspiration and achievement has widened.

The composition of national incomes is affected also by economic relations with other economies, capital formation, and the interpersonal distribution of incomes. If national income is calculated to reveal income produced in a country, it includes net payments to foreign investors, government transfers abroad, and export goods, but excludes net receipts from foreign investments, government transfers from abroad and import goods. A better indication of well-being is obtained by adding visible imports and net receipts from abroad and deducting visible exports and net payments abroad. The resulting figure shows the market value of goods consumed or invested within the country.

Capital formation causes immediate well-being to diverge from average gross national income. Two countries may have the same average income but in one a larger proportion may be in the form of capital goods. A smaller proportion is therefore available for consumption. In Soviet Russia and its satellite countries, for instance, increases in average national income have meant little or no increase in consumption. But the increase of capital goods will presumably permit increases in future production (and possibly consumption).

The distribution of incomes influences the composition of the national product and presents the question whether countries with similar average incomes but different interpersonal patterns of income distribution are equally well off.[19] The mass of the population in one may be considerably worse off than in the other. On the other hand, where average national incomes differ, a country with a relatively high average may nevertheless have a number of very poor people, and in a country with a low average the above-average incomes of some may be offset by the very low incomes of others.

Information regarding income distribution is very inadequate, especially for underdeveloped countries, and methods of measurement differ. Nevertheless, there are indications that incomes are more unequally distributed in the poorer countries than in the richer. In Canada, Denmark, Sweden, the U.S.A., and Britain, the richest tenth of the population has received about 30% of total income in recent years, whereas in several less developed countries, this tenth has received 40% or more. Similarly the poorer half of the population seems to receive a higher proportion of total income in the richer than in the poorer countries. There are also indications that the proportion of total income received by the richest tenth of the population has declined since about 1936, partly because taxes have taken an increasing proportion of higher incomes.[20]

If the poorer half of the population receives a smaller proportion of total income where national income is small than where it is larger, the average incomes of this lower half of the populations are clearly farther apart than is suggested by the over-all national averages. But the idea of group welfare is too vague to permit a comparison of the welfare of national groups with different distribution patterns.

Comparisons of welfare in a single economy at different times present almost all the same problems as international comparisons. The problem of devising a common measurement unit, however, takes a somewhat different form. The purchasing power of the monetary unit changes with time. Attempts to base calculations on the purchasing power of money in a selected period by the use of a general index of prices is only par-

---

[19] Ch. 27.
[20] U.N., *Prelim. Rep. on World Social Situation*, 1952, 130.

tially satisfactory because of changes in the nature of many commodities (and the satisfactions they yield) as well as in the relative importance of each commodity to buyers.

B. Specific Components in National Consumption

Material welfare may also be appraised in terms of consumption per person of specific groups of goods or services. These indicators necessarily ignore capital formation, and present special problems of interpretation. The location and shape of individual demand curves summarize demands at different price levels, assuming constant income. A rise in income generally increases demand at each price (moves the curve to the right). But this income-elasticity of demand varies greatly at different levels of income and for different goods. Expenditures for the same goods in different countries depend, therefore, on general factors affecting the utilities attached to the goods, levels of income, and the relative cost of different goods. If meat is cheaper in relation to other products in Argentina or Australia, meat consumption per person is likely to be higher than elsewhere. But the tendency for very low incomes to be spent on basic necessities—and for successive increments to be spent, in increasing proportions (within a certain range of incomes), on less necessary goods—means that expenditures on one product or class of products are rarely proportionate to total income. In fact, as incomes rise, the proportion spent on some classes of goods falls and that spent on others rises faster than income.

1. Food

Food consumption per person is difficult to measure because nutritional needs can be met by a variety of foods. Food consumption in calories per day are quite unequal (Figure 1) as is the proportion of food calories obtained from foods other than grain and potatoes (Figure 2). But the physical intake of food is not proportional to total income and well-being because the income elasticity of demand for food falls with progressive increases in income, although for a time expenditures on food rise because of improvements in quality and variety. As incomes rise, vegetable carbohydrates are partly replaced by meat and dairy products (Figure 2). In general the proportion, but not the absolute amount, of income spent on food is highest where incomes are lowest although relative prices and national taste have some influence.[21] Although about 30% of personal consumption expenditures in the U.S.A. are for food,[22] the percentage is about 50 in India.[23]

---

[21] Clark, *Conditions of Economic Progress* (2d ed.) 362 ff. U.N., *Econ. Surv. of Europe in 1949*, 36.

[22] U.S., *Mid-Year Economic Report of the President.* July 1951, 228.

[23] India: Famine Inquiry Commission, *Final Report*, 111.

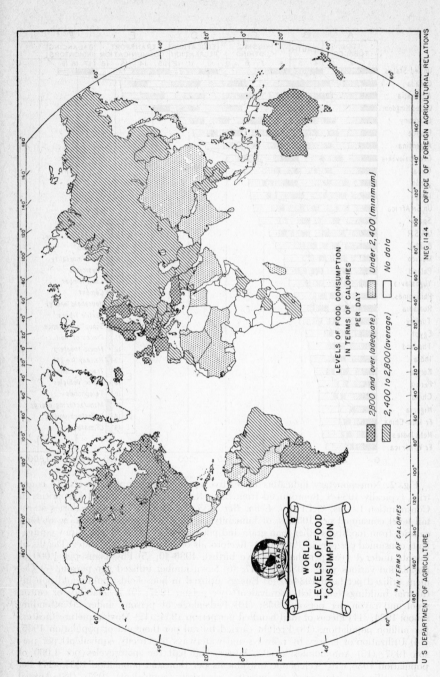

Fig. 1. From *A Graphic Summary of World Agriculture*, p. 13.

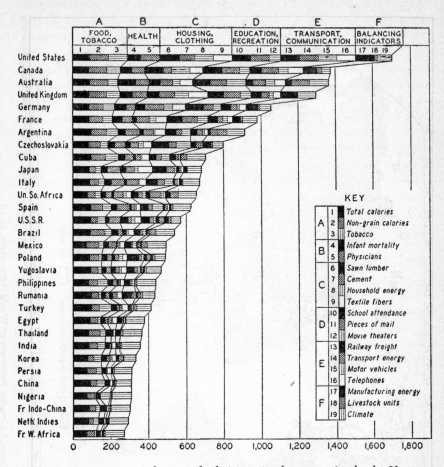

Fig. 2. Non-monetary indicators of relative national consumption levels, 31 countries, typically 1934-8. Reproduced from Bennett, M. K., "International Disparities in Consumption Levels." XLI *Am. Econ. Rev.* 635 (1951) *Key:* (1) Food calories at retail level consumed per 100 lbs. of humanity per day 1934-8; (2) Percentage of food calories from foodstuffs other than grain and potatoes 1934-8; (3) Tobacco (raw equivalent) consumed per person 1934-8; (4) Reciprocals of Infant Mortality Rates (Deaths of infants under 1 year per thousand live births), 1936-40; (5) Physicians per 1,000 of population various years 1938 to 1947; (6) Sawn lumber utilized per person; (7) Cement utilized per head 1934-8; (8) Energy utilized in households, public and non industrial buildings (electricity equivalent) per person 1937; (9) Availability of cotton wool and rayon per person, 1938; (10) Percentage of persons under 20 attending school 1934; (11) Pieces of mail handled per person 1934; (12) Moving picture theaters per million population; (13) Freight carried by rail per thousand of population 1935; (14) Utilization of energy by railways and waterways (electricity equivalent) per person 1937; (15) Automobiles, trucks, busses, and half the motorcycles per 1,000 of population 1936; (16) Telephone instruments per thousand population 1935; (17) Per capita utilization of energy in industry (electricity equivalent) 1937; (18) Animal units per person 1938; (19) Number of days per year with temperature over 41°F.

Food expenditures are also appraised in terms of biological requirements. The crudest test is whether people die for lack of food. Over the
long sweep of history, death from starvation has been fairly common.
The 19th century was the first in which the eternal fear of famine was, in
the main, removed from Europe. Even the serious shortages of food in
Europe at the end of the war in 1945 did not result in widespread starvation. Improvements of transport make it easier to move food from surplus
to shortage areas, and governments have become more concerned with
preventing death from starvation. But death from famine has persisted
in many parts of the world, in North Africa, for instance (where many
Arabs died in 1945 owing to drought), the Middle East, and parts of Asia.
In India, seventeen famines between 1860 and 1900 caused the death
of some 20 million people.[24] As late as 1943, a famine in Bengal caused
1.5 to 2 million deaths.[25] People still die of starvation in Burma and
China,[26] more particularly where areas of shortage are cut off by poor
transportation from areas of surplus.

Even if people stay alive, their satisfactions may be few because of
disease and debility. Measures of food deficiency in this sense rest on
measures of the food needs of the human body. There are no general
statistics of malnutrition, however, because there are no general standards
of food requirements, which vary with climate, methods of house heating,
size of the individual body (especially its surface area), and, possibly,
with metabolism. All observers testify, however, to widespread malnutrition in much of the Far and Middle East (even in Egypt, where agricultural methods are advanced and there is large capital investment).[27]
Per person consumption of food in the Middle East declined during
World War II, and the small increases in supply after the war did not
compensate for the growth in population.[28] In India about 30% of the
families in typical urban and rural groups "do not get enough to eat."[29]
Although it is doubtful whether standards of nutrition are declining, "un-

---

[24] Lille, W. S., *India and its Problems.* Wadia and Merchant, *op. cit.,* 58.

[25] India: Famine Inquiry Commission, *Report on Bengal.*

[26] More than 50 million persons were "affected" through malnutrition by food
shortages in China in the winter of 1949-50 but no estimate of deaths is available.
(*N.Y. Times,* Oct. 15, 1950)

[27] The consumption of major food products in Egypt showed a marked down-
ward trend between 1920 and 1938 in spite of a 25% increase in population. The *per
capita* consumption must, therefore, have fallen disastrously. (Issawi, *Egypt: An
Economic and Social Analysis,* 50, 55). (Keen, *The Agricultural Development of the
Middle East,* 40). In 1947-8, the *per capita* consumption of cereals and potatoes in
Egypt was 120% of that in U.S.A., but of milk and cheese, 28%, and meat, 14%.
(Food and Agriculture Organization *Food Balance Sheet, 1948.*)

[28] U.N., *World Econ. Rep. 1948,* 172.

[29] Famine Inquiry Commission *Final Report,* 1945, 107, 112. Also Thakurdas *et al.,
A Plan for the Economic Development of India* ("Bombay Plan"), Part 1, Para. 10.
Even cereal production falls short by 10% of what is needed in a balanced diet. (India,
Advisory Planning Board *Report,* 7).

dernutrition and malnutrition are widespread."[30] Even where diets are quantitatively adequate, they are ill-balanced—consisting preponderantly of cereals, markedly deficient in protective foods.[31] Indeed, abject poverty is characteristic of much of the East.[32] By the crop year 1949-50, although agricultural production had increased in India and the Far East, it was not keeping pace with the increase of population. Food supplies per person available for consumption were about 88% of prewar in quantity and were deficient in quality. Consumption per person was falling. Even the attainment of prewar consumption levels remains a "distant goal."[33] Much of the native population of Africa, North,[34] central, and South,[35] suffers from malnutrition.

During World War II, the world output of food fell 10 to 15% while world population increased about 7% (even after war casualties, direct and indirect). Thus food supplies per person fell 15 to 20%. But supply and population both changed unequally in different areas. Food supplies rose about 26% in the U.S.A. and Canada and 19% in Latin America, but fell 8% in the the Fast East and 23% in Europe. Food supplies per person rose about 12% in the U.S.A. but fell in all other major regions (16% in the Far East and 27% in Europe (except U.S.S.R.). By 1950 food supplies in calories per person in the world were about 6% lower than prewar, the reduction having fallen most heavily upon the less well-nourished. The proportion of world population receiving over 2700 calories fell only from 30 to 28% but the proportion receiving less than 2200 calories rose from 39 to 60%. The proportion of world population receiving over 30 grams of animal protein fell from 22 to 17; the proportion receiving 30 to 15 grams rose from 19 to 25. Evidently the proportion at low levels of animal protein consumption changed little.[36] It is evident that considerably

---

[30] Famine Inquiry Commission, op. cit., 90. The net area under food crops in 1945 was about 60% of that estimated to be necessary to produce even an "emergency restricted diet" under American conditions. (Ibid., 80, 102). The area of land used per person for the production of food crops has been declining since 1880 because the population has increased faster than new land has been brought into cultivation. Heavy food imports have been necessary in recent years.

[31] The Famine Inquiry Commission thought it possible that the population was adapting to the low diet by reduction in the height and weight of individuals, although it found no adequate evidence of such an adaptation. (Ibid., 90, 110).

[32] U.N. Econ. Surv. of Asia and the Far East 1948, 8. The rice output of South and East Asia increased 10% between 1918 and 1939 but the population increased 20%. (Food and Agriculture Organization Rice Report.)

[33] U.N. Econ. Surv. of Asia and the Far East 1949, 8, 9, xviii.

[34] In Algeria the amount of cereals per person (the staple diet of the native population) fell about 20% between 1870 and 1900, and 60% between 1870 and 1948. The food supply of the nomadic population in Tunisia has also been falling.

[35] Kenya, The Kikuyu Report, 33; Development Commission Report II, 1954; Uganda, Report for 1946, 56; Franklin, N. H., Economics in South Africa, 31, 50; Union of South Africa: Interdepartmental Committee, Report on the Social, Health and Economic Conditions of Urban Natives, 1942, 1, 7.

[36] U.N., Prelim. Rep. on World Social Situation, 1952, 41.

increased supplies will be needed in 1960 to enable the population of the world to meet modern standards of nutrition.[37]

In summary, some people are so near to the minimum biological requirement that they die in years of poor crop, and the survivors take a large part of their income in food often inadequate to maintain full health. But in other regions, notably Western Europe and North America, food supplies have risen above this minimum level, and food has increased greatly in variety since about 1800. Nevertheless, medical authorities tentatively concluded in 1935 that nearly half the population of England existed to a greater or lesser extent below the safe level of nutrition. Too, there are inequalities in diet in different parts of the United States (especially between the South and the North).

2. CLOTHING

Comparative information about per capita supplies of clothing is very inadequate, but supplies are generally low in the less developed areas (Figure 2). The proportion of consumption expenditure for clothing is not closely correlated with national income. Income elasticity probably remains higher somewhat farther up the income scale than for food. Need varies with climate and methods of house heating, but at higher income levels the social aspects of clothing increasingly affect demand. The war of 1939-45 left a serious legacy of clothing shortages. Even in 1948 the shortage of textiles was one of the major causes reducing the incentive to work in many parts of Africa, Malaya, India, and Java.

3. SHELTER

At low income ranges, housing is a small part of personal expenditure, but the proportion rises as income rises. Social considerations increasingly affect demand at higher income levels. There is, however, no standard by which the differences in the quantity and kind of housing can be translated into differences in human well-being. Types of housing differ because of differences in climate and in the materials available. The extent of urbanization also affects the housing needs of the population, more particularly in regard to sanitary provisions.

In northwest Europe and North America there is a shortage of housing,

---

[37] Food and Agriculture Organization of the United Nations.

	Food Requirements in 1960 as a Percentage of Output in 1939
Cereals	121
Roots and tubers	127
Sugar	112
Fats	134
Pulses	180
Fruits and vegetables	263
Meat	146
Milk	200

but the standard of housing even in the poorer-housed parts of these regions is higher than in the rest of the world (Figure 2). The climate necessitates more protection, but housing has been improved as part of the general rise in standard of living. It has improved also because housing conditions influence frequency of crime, the productivity of workers, and their attitudes toward work and society. In many other parts of the world, however, housing is far less adequate.

In Russia, housing facilities generally provide little space (about 4 square meters per person), and are of low quality, but, being heavily subsidized, they cost only 2 or 3% of average incomes.[38] In South America generally, urban housing is overcrowded and lacks the ordinary amenities.[39]

The poorer parts of most eastern cities consist of slums inferior to the accommodation provided for animals in many western countries. Urbanization without the adaptation of housing to urban needs has increased the risk of epidemics and generated social unrest. Even the public housing provided in some Indian cities falls far below any West European or North American standard.[40] The African slums created by natives unable to live in the reservations because of overcrowding, and unable to pay for respectable housing in the cities (particularly around Johannesburg), have now become notorious.[41] In many rural areas, especially in parts of the Middle East[42] and in Africa, roofs are often barely adequate. Lack of light and ventilation are common, with serious effects on health.[43]

4. EDUCATION

Because education can be provided only after the food, clothing and shelter necessary for survival, inequalities in economic conditions are magnified when reflected in levels of education (Figure 2). No general measures of education are available but literacy is a crude test of elementary education. Illiteracy does not indicate lack of intelligence, but literacy vastly widens the mental and economic horizon of the individual.

The percentage of illiterates over ten years of age is very low in North-

---

[38] U.S.S.R., *Information Bulletin*, Feb. 10, 1950; Bergson *et al.*, "Post War Reconstruction and Development in the USSR," *Annals Amer. Ac. Pol. Sci.*, 1949, 64.

[39] U.N., *Econ. Surv. of Latin America 1948*, 55.

[40] Thakurdas *et al.*, *A Plan for the Economic Development of India*, I, para. 14.

[41] See Paton, A., *Cry the Beloved Country*. Also Union of South Africa: Interdepartmental Committee on the Social, Health, and Economic Conditions of Urban Natives *Report*, 1942, 13, 15.

[42] "To speak of housing conditions is to exaggerate: In the Egyptian village there are no houses. The fellaheen inhabit mud huts built by making a framework of sticks, usually cotton sticks, and plastering it with mud. The hut is a small enclosed yard where the family and the buffalo live together with a small inner room with a roof but no windows and a sleeping roof where chickens, rabbits and goats are kept." Warriner, *Land and Poverty in the Middle East*, 43.

[43] African children suffer from tuberculosis and sometimes die from suffocation owing to the absence of chimneys in houses. Dirt floors cause fly and worm diseases as well as general filthiness.

west Europe and North America, but higher in Southern and Eastern Europe (Table 4). In Asia (except Japan), Africa, and among the native populations of South America, few are literate. In China in 1930, about 70% of children between the ages of seven and 16 never attended school. Literacy is generally highest where non-agricultural production is more developed. In about 1947, in countries where 50% or more of all gainfully occupied males were employed in agriculture, 69% of all the population 10 years of age and over was illiterate, but in other countries the percentage was only 3.5.[44]

These international differences are also largely a phenomenon of the past hundred and fifty years. The speediest increase in literacy in recent

TABLE 4

PERCENTAGE OF THE POPULATION OVER TEN YEARS OF AGE WHICH IS ILLITERATE
IN SELECTED COUNTRIES[*]

	Percent		Percent
Sweden	0.1	Porto Rico	31.5
Finland	0.9	Panama	35.3
France	3.8	Greece	40.8
Canada	3.8	Ceylon	42.2
Czecho Slovakia	4.1	Colombia	44.2
U.S.A.	4.3	Jugo Slavia	45.2
Belgium	5.6	Portugal	48.7
Hungary	6.0	Mexico	51.6
Virgin Islands	13.4	Peru	56.6
Mozambique	13.5	Venezuela	56.6
Hawaii	15.1	Brazil	56.7
Alaska	20.1	Guatemala	65.4
Italy	21.6	Honduras	66.3
Cuba	22.1	Korea	68.6
Poland	23.1	El Salvador	72.8
Romania	23.1	Turkey	79.1
Spain	23.2	Egypt	85.2
Chile	28.2	India	90.9
Bulgaria	31.4		

[*] U.N., *Statistical Year Book 1948*, 429. The figures are not precisely comparable. They relate to different years (1930 and subsequent), and the accuracy of recording and the tests of literacy vary. (No figures are given for the United Kingdom.)

years has been made in Russia. About 78% of the population was illiterate in 1900. Lenin pronounced that without literacy there could be no politics and by 1926 only some 43% of the Russian population was illiterate and by 1950 adult illiteracy was small.

C. Indirect Indicators of Welfare

There is a great variety of possible indirect indications of relative well-being, average length of life and frequency of sickness being among those more frequently used.

---

[44] Davis, "Population and the Further Spread of Industrial Society," *Proc. Am. Phil. Soc.*, Feb. 13, 1951, 16.

1. Average Length of Life

For the world as a whole the average expectation of life of a newborn child is 35 years,[45] but national averages range from 65 to 27 years. Most of the countries with an expectation of more than 55 years are in North America, northwest Europe, and Australia. Expectation is lower in southern and eastern Europe, still lower in Japan, Russia, and China, and less than 40 years in parts of Asia and the Far East, the Middle East and Latin America (Table 5). The expectation of 27 years in India is about 40% of that in the Netherlands. For many countries where expectation is believed to be low, there are no statistics.

TABLE 5

Expectation of Life of Males at Birth in Selected Countries*

	Years		Years
Netherlands	65.7	Austria	54.5
Denmark	65.62	Finland	54.45
New Zealand	65.46	Italy	53.76
Sweden	64.3	Czecho Slovakia	51.92
Australia	63.48	Jamaica	51.7
Canada	62.96	Panama	50.54
Switzerland	62.68	Greece	49.09
U.S.A.	61.6	Spain	48.74
Iceland	60.9	Portugal	48.58
Norway	60.68	Poland	48.2
Germany	59.86	Hawaii	47.79
Ireland	59.01	Japan	46.92
Union of S. Africa (European)	58.95	Bulgaria	45.92
England & Wales	58.74	USSR (1926-7)	41.93
N. Ireland	57.8	China	41.08
Belgium	56.02	Chile	37.9
Scotland	56.0	Brazil (both sexes)	37.43
France	55.94	Guatemala	35.97
Hungary	54.92	Egypt	35.65
		India	26.91

* U.N., *Statistical Year Book 1948*, 52. The periods to which the figures apply vary, but relate mostly to periods in the decade 1929-39. The expectation of life of males is typically 2 to 6 years less than that of females.

Because human beings are most susceptible to malnutrition and disease at the beginning of life, average duration of life is short in countries with high infant death rates. Indeed, infant death rates are a good (though rough) indicator of general economic welfare. The highest infant death rate is about five times as high as the lowest (Figure 3). Before 1939 the rate was between 150 and 250 per thousand live births in Africa, Latin America,[46] and Asia, about 150 in eastern Europe, 114 in southern Europe,

45 U.N., *World Econ. Rep. 1948*, 223.
46 U.N., *Econ. Surv. of Latin America 1948*, 145, 150.

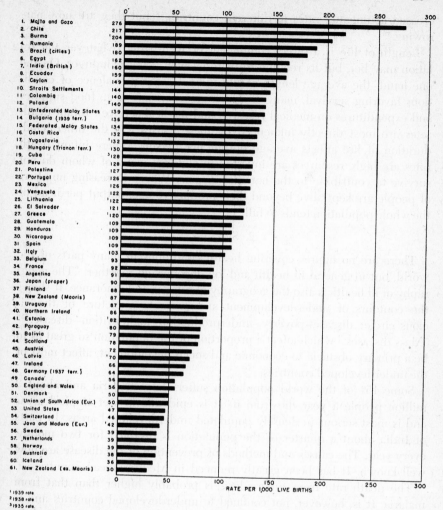

	Rate per 1,000 live births
1. Malta and Gozo	276
2. Chile	217
3. Burma	204[2]
4. Rumania	189
5. Brazil (cities)	180
6. Egypt	162
7. India (British)	160
8. Ecuador	159
9. Ceylon	149
10. Straits Settlements	144
11. Colombia	140
12. Poland	140[2]
13. Unfederated Malay States	139
14. Bulgaria (1939 terr.)	136
15. Federated Malay States	134
16. Costa Rica	132
17. Yugoslavia	132[1]
18. Hungary (Trianon terr.)	130
19. Cuba	128[3]
20. Peru	128
21. Palestine	127
22. Portugal	126
23. Mexico	126
24. Venezuela	122
25. Lithuania	122[1]
26. El Salvador	121
27. Greece	120[1]
28. Guatemala	109
29. Honduras	109
30. Nicaragua	109
31. Spain	109
32. Italy	103
33. Belgium	93
34. France	92
35. Argentina	91
36. Japan (proper)	90
37. Finland	88
38. New Zealand (Maoris)	87
39. Uruguay	87
40. Northern Ireland	86
41. Estonia	82[1]
42. Paraguay	80
43. Bolivia	79
44. Scotland	78
45. Austria	72
46. Latvia	70[1]
47. Ireland	66
48. Germany (1937 terr.)	64
49. Canada	56
50. England and Wales	56
51. Denmark	50
52. Union of South Africa (Eur.)	50
53. United States	47
54. Switzerland	46
55. Java and Madura (Eur.)	42[1]
56. Sweden	39
57. Netherlands	39
58. Norway	39
59. Australia	38
60. Iceland	36
61. New Zealand (ex. Maoris)	30

[1] 1939 rate.
[2] 1938 rate.
[3] 1935 rate.

Fig. 3. Deaths within the first year of life (per thousand live births) for selected countries. (Federal Security Agency. U. S. Public Health Service; *Summary of International Vital Statistics*, 35.)

110 in Japan, 63 in Oceania, 61 in northwest-Central Europe and 54 in Canada and the U.S.A. These differences are due not to absence of medical knowledge, but to lack of medical services springing from deficiences of resources or the will to use them for social improvement.[47] International differences in these death rates began to widen when levels of living in-

---

[47] Even in Britain the infant death rate from environmental diseases is highest in the lowest income groups and in the poorest parts of the country. (Titmuss, R. M., *Poverty and Population*, Ch. IV). The relation between death and birth rates is discussed in Chapter 18.

creased at unequal rates in different countries,[48] but they are now narrowing.[49]

Length of life is a direct component of well-being (whatever the relation may be), but its relation to material well-being is indirect. On the one hand, the average length of life indicates the prevalence of conditions favoring survival, many of which are economic (e.g., food supplies and expenditures on medical research and medical service). Infant death rates are most directly influenced by these causes. On the other hand, duration of life affects average output per person. Where infant death rates are high, resources are invested in children many of whom do not survive to contribute to the national income. Where increasing numbers of people are kept alive beyond their productive age, output per head of the whole population tends to fall.

2. SICKNESS

There are no figures covering health conditions in many parts of the world, but in general ill health and low incomes go together. "The geography of ill health is also the geography of hunger and ignorance. It shows the contours of underdevelopment and presents a picture of the vicious circle: disease—poverty—underproduction—malnutrition—disease."[50] "Mass diseases," which affect a proportion of the population so great as to be a primary obstacle to economic and social development, affect most of the underdeveloped countries.

Some 15% of the world population suffers from malaria and about 3 million people a year die from it. It is epidemic in wet tropical areas and is most serious in densely populated underdeveloped areas. In parts of India about a quarter of the population is disabled for two months every year. The causes and methods of prevention of the disease are now well known. It has been greatly reduced in Mediterranean countries.

The death rate from tuberculosis is probably higher than that from malaria. It is, however, not confined to underdeveloped countries and is more closely associated with urbanization and industrialization. Syphilis is world wide, the incidence being especially high in many underdeveloped countries. Bilharziasis (a debilitating disease transmitted by a

---

[48] In the U.S.A. the average length of life probably increased from about 35 to about 65 between 1800 and 1940. In Britain the death rate began to fall in the 18th century and after 1870 the mortality in almost every five-year period was less than in the previous one. (U.K. Royal Commission on Population *Report*, 1949, 19, Cmd. 7695.) In Sweden the expectation of life about doubled between 1750 and 1940. But the expectation in Greece during the Fifth Century B.C. and in the early Roman Empire (about 30 years) was probably higher than in India between 1881 and 1931. (Usher, "The Balance Sheet of Economic Development," *Jour. Econ. Hist.*, 1951, 331.)

[49] Data regarding population and death rates are fragmentary for the underdeveloped regions. In countries with reasonably complete statistics death rates have fallen markedly since 1930, especially markedly where death rates were high. (U.N., *Monthly Bull. of Stat.*, March 1952, X).

[50] U.N., *Prelim. Rep. on World Social Situation*, 1952, 32.

water snail) is widespread in parts of Africa, the Middle East, South America and China. In Egypt, it is believed to reduce productivity about 33%.[51] Yaws, hookworm, and trachoma also are serious in many underdeveloped countries. Diseases like cholera, smallpox, bubonic plague,[52] typhus, typhoid and yellow fever are serious in epidemic form but in endemic form are now localized and under somewhat more control than the other diseases mentioned.

International differences in the incidence of disease occur partly because of differences in knowledge of methods of preventing particular diseases, and partly because some diseases occur more frequently in some countries than in others. But the international differences are mainly due to differences in resources available for combating disease and the willingness to use them for this purpose. There are some 900,000 doctors in the world[53] or one to about 2,600 people, on the average, but they are very unequally distributed. In countries like Nigeria, Indo-China, and Indonesia there is one doctor to more than 50,000 people, in Pakistan, 1 to 10 per 50,000 people, while in all the more developed countries there is one doctor to less than 2,000 people.

D. Combinations of Components and Indicators

Information regarding components of consumption and indirect indicators of well-being may be combined to compare well-being. One study of this sort[54] covering 31 nations comprising 85% of world population in 1935, and relating to the years immediately before 1939, showed the U.S.A. at the top of the list and French West Africa at the bottom (with a score about 7% of that of the U.S.A.) (Figure 2). These results depend, however, on what is included in the combination and how the resulting single score for each country is obtained. All the items are measured in nonmonetary terms. The food figures, being calculated in calories per 100 pounds of humanity, allowed for differences in need due to differences in the proportion of children in the population, and in the size of the average adult. They also took some account of the quality of food intake in the form of the percentage of calories obtained from grain and potatoes.

Although the comparisons relate to consumption, some of the components included goods used both for consumption and for production (e.g., lumber, cement, railroad freight, trucks, telephones, and industrial energy) that are influenced by methods of production as well as by levels of consumption. These, however, are usually related. Services provided

---

[51] U.N., *Prelim. Rep. on the World Social Situation*, 1952, 25.

[52] In the decade 1901-11, 5.3 millions died of plague in India and in 1911-21, 2.9 millions (Wadia and Merchant, *op. cit.*, 60).

[53] U.N., *Prelim. Rep. on World Social Situation* (1952), 24, 28.

[54] Bennett, M. R., "International Disparities in Consumption," XLI; *Amer. Ec. Rev.*, 632 (1951).

by military and police are excluded. Infant mortality rates are the principal indirect indicator.

Such a variety of figures clearly cannot be added. For each category the figure for each country was expressed as a percentage of the highest figure for any country for that category, and the percentages for all categories were added for each country to obtain its score. The results were not intended to, and do not, measure relative well-being. They merely rank countries in respect to their consumption levels. They yield results differing little from figures based on national income.

Chapter 2

The Analysis of Comparative
Economic Welfare

A. The Order of Analysis

The attempt to analyze the influences affecting economic welfare can start off with the quantity and nature of consumption. But societies do not, over long periods, generally consume more than they produce (although they may consume less). With minor exceptions production sets a ceiling on consumption. Explanation can begin, therefore, with production. The amount of production depends upon the productive resources and the use made of them. Decisions on these matters are made at various levels, from the production unit to the state. In view of the marked differences among agriculture, mining, and manufacturing, the organization of each calls for separate discussion.[1] These decisions are made within a framework of arrangements affecting the use of the major types of resource (minerals, land, water, labor, and capital goods). These arrangements, in varying degree, affect the supply of these resources and the extent and direction of their utilization. The allocation of resources among different uses affects the composition of the national product and, therefore, its effect on economic welfare.[2]

Finally, it is necessary to examine the arrangements for coordinating the various activities making up the production process. Conflicts, duplication, bottlenecks, and the like reduce total output. Such harmony as is achieved (both within and among nations) may result from over-all social control and planning, or from the operation of the market. Both depend upon, and are influenced by, monetary institutions.[3]

A society's consumption is rarely identical with its production. Most

---

[1] Ch. 3 to 13.
[2] Ch. 14 to 22.
[3] Ch. 23 to 26.

23

groups produce some goods and services which they exchange with foreigners for other goods and services. Some groups lend or borrow from others, and there may be uncompensated surrenders or receipts of goods and services in the way of war booty, reparations, or international gifts. The consumption of a group may also differ from its production because of saving or dissaving. Consumption falls short of aggregate production if part of the output consists in aids to future production, in addition to those necessary to replace existing aids to production which are wearing out or becoming obsolete.

Production, after adjustment for international transactions and saving and dissaving, gives total group consumption. Individual consumption, or that of homogeneous sub-groups, depends on the pattern of individual incomes. The explanation of this pattern lies in the actions of the family, private groups, and the state, which may directly fix incomes or may protect property and acquiesce in the distribution of income resulting from the operation of the labor, capital, land, and consumers' goods markets.[4]

This explanation runs in terms of the operations of political groupings of people partly because most general information is on this basis. These political units are used also because within each there is a number of influences affecting the well-being of most of the members of each group. But, on the one hand, it is sometimes necessary to consider sub-groups within national units (such as wage earners, agriculturists, or property owners). On the other hand, some influences affect many national units; it is possible to generalize in terms of regions ("Western Europe" or "the Middle East"), basic types of economic organization ("predominantly agrarian," "capitalist," or "socialist"), or levels of economic development. Comparisons over periods of time are necessary because the explanation of present conditions lies partly in the past, sometimes the past of countries from which ideas have been taken over.

A series of "country" studies, each giving a comprehensive view of an economy, would provide one way of comparing economies. But it would involve repetition where countries follow similar policies, and the final comparison is not easy. Economies might also be grouped according to some broad characteristic—such as whether they are capitalist, socialist, or communist. But in fact countries do not fall comfortably into such a classification. It seems preferable, therefore, to set out from the fact that the most basic economic problems of adapting environment to the satisfaction of human desires are the same everywhere and at all times. Each of the major economic functions can, therefore, be discussed in terms of the various ways in which peoples have dealt with it. This approach facilitates comparison of like with like; it emphasizes differences in ways of dealing with the same problem and it throws into relief the diffusion of ideas about social organization.

---

[4] Ch. 27 to 32.

B. The Nature of Organization

The basic economic problems that are common to all societies arise out of disparities between the material satisfactions people would like to enjoy and those they can enjoy without effort. The gregariousness of mankind (whatever the reasons for it) provides occasion for conflict over goods or the means of providing them (such as land, boats, or tools). Imitation and emulation focus interest on similar objects and, combined with gregariousness, increase the possibility of conflict. Without scarcity (or assumed scarcity), however, people living in groups have no primarily economic source of friction, nor would imitation and emulation lead to economic conflict. But scarcities are evident everywhere and at all times. Consumer goods are scarce at least at the place and time for consumption. The means of production are often, but not always, scarce. Even where "there is plenty of unoccupied land," differences in location or fertility cause scarcities of the "best" land. Tools and equipment are also scarce.

"Arrangements" or "organization" to prevent friction and, possibly, civil war, consist of rules regarding economic goods. These rules may rest upon the coercive power of the state, represented by a chief, a dictator, a democratic government, or a combination of these. In primitive societies convention, rather than state regulation, may be the major force bringing uniformities into the conduct of individuals. But there is frequently some means of enforcing conventional behavior. If ostracism of nonconformists is the chief coercive force, there is usually some set of social institutions to keep alive notions about the things that "are not done" and to give driving force to attempts to maintain conformity. Furthermore, in times of disaster, or rapid change, the community may discover that it has no appropriate conventions. In more ordinary times, it may need to amplify existing conventions to meet unforeseen situations.

Whoever makes new general rules or amplifies old ones is acting as an embryonic state. The mere existence of the state introduces some uniformities. In many primitive societies and in socialist countries, the state may directly control most of the means of production, and decide what shall be produced and who shall enjoy it. In capitalist countries, individuals are free to obtain control over most of the means of production, determine their use, and dispose of the produce on any terms they can enforce. But even in these countries the state defines property rights and enforces them. States change property rights when they regulate prices, ration supplies, tax owners of property, or prohibit some kinds of production. The ownership of land in these countries is also partly traceable to direct government distributions of land in the past.

Private property systems, unlike others, provide that the person who controls a resource may use his control to influence his share of the production of the group. This linkage has been held to be the principal stimulus to production in countries where private property is important. Disputes between property owners and workers as to the payment for labor, and criticism of monopoly profits, indicate, however, that this system can generate internal tensions. The linkage of control and reward does not invariably result in the pursuit of maximum personal income, on the one hand, and efficiency of use of resources, on the other. In some underdeveloped countries, for example, private landowners do not ensure the full use of their land and the maximization of their incomes from it.

The operation of an economy may be influenced also by widely prevalent patterns of behavior. These may result from formal organizations other than the state. Religious institutions (which, however, have not always been, and are still not everywhere, separate from the state) have exerted great influence. Guilds of craft workers, industrial corporations, large units for agricultural production (such as plantations and *haciendas*), labor unions, political parties, and manufacturers' associations all exercise power varying in the nature of their conduct and the number of people within their field of influence. The family influences behavior by the decisions made within concerning the rate of reproduction, and because of its influence upon the developing young. It often influences marriage and occupation, and in many parts of the world is still a production unit with relatively little contact with others. Within the family are made decisions about the contributions of the members to, and the shares which the members receive, of the welfare of the family group. Some types of behavior of primary importance, such as the value attached to material things, the desirability of economic activity, rates of human reproduction, and attitudes to saving and investment, are not traceable to any one formal organization, and indeed their ultimate source is not fully understood.

There are, of course, limits to the kinds of rules that can be made. The rules must at least permit the group to survive by enabling it to meet external attack or internal revolt. True, states do not have to, and do not all, survive; but if they collapse or are submerged for economic reasons the rules are changed. The ability of the group to meet these tests depends upon the effect of the rules upon the internal distribution of well-being and upon the volume of production.

The distribution of income may be a source of internal tension, which, if not released, may cause the society to succumb to attack from without.[5] For three or four centuries, feudal systems have been giving place to other forms of organization. The internal tensions in highly capitalistic societies have been due partly to the distribution of incomes within them,

---

[5] The popular revolts of the 14th and 15th centuries in Europe were probably attributable to the prevalence of doctrines of social equality and the belief that existing property systems were indefensible, combined with only meager outlets for expression by the mass of the people. (Cheyney, E. P., *The Dawn of a New Era*, 111). Turner, R. E., "Economic Discontent in Medieval Europe," *Tasks of Econ. Hist.* 1948, 85, 94, 96.

but in recent years sharp changes have occurred.[6] Whether the rules are changed depends upon the degree of tension and the techniques used to maintain the system in the face of opposition. Religious teaching has often been a means of reducing tensions, and police systems a means of preventing their translation into revolt.

The volume of production affects the ability of the group to survive because the greater its production the greater the ability of the group to set aside resources to meet external attack, and itself to attack without so lowering the level of living as to undermine loyalty to the state. The importance of economic organization in relation to military strength has never been more evident than it is today. But large production is also important because it makes inequality of distribution more tolerable if the poorest are less poor than they would otherwise be. During the period of most rapid development of the capitalist countries, internal tensions were somewhat eased in this way.

Human action in economic matters must also operate within the limits of available resources. In discussing periods too short to permit much change in the supply of resources, they can properly be taken as "given." But over longer periods, resources change, and most changes are the result of human action (the principal exceptions being uncontrolled natural phenomena like earthquakes and changes in climate). In fact, human action not only controls the utilization but also in considerable degree the supply of resources. The supply of labor depends on decisions affecting birth, death, migration, and the distribution of incomes. The supply of equipment is subject to human volition. Even the supply of land is subject to some control. The mineral supply depends on human action in seeking deposits and ways of using them, and on past decisions regarding the rate of utilization. Although lack of natural resources such as fertile land or sources of power limit the increase of production in an area, well-being depends on how many people live in the area—this number depends on human decisions regarding migration. Individuals may not move because they do not wish to or because they are prevented.

<hr>

[6] Ch. 31.

Chapter 3

Production per Head of All Goods and Services

A. Comparative Productivity in Fact

Aggregate world production must have increased fairly continuously to enable increasing numbers of human beings to keep alive. But over the major part of human history, average production increased, if at all, very slowly and unequally among different economies. Between 1938 and 1948, however, average world production of goods (but not services) increased somewhat over 10%.[1] But a world average is subject to a wide margin of error in calculation and gives no indication of the inequality among countries.

Production of goods per person in 1948 was over three times as high in the U.S.A. as in Europe generally (Table 6). Within Europe production was about four times as high in the northwestern group of countries as in the south and southeastern group. In Latin America, Argentina and Uruguay produce about 66% as much per person as Britain; Venezuela and Cuba about 33% as much; most of the remainder is on an Asiatic level.[2]

Calculations of production per worker in work (Table 7) allow for the part of the population not normally at work and for the persons normally

---

[1] U.N., *World Econ. Rep.*, 1948, 220.
[2] Queensland *Rev. of Econ. Prog.*, May 1949.

TABLE 6*

NET VALUE OF COMMODITY (AGRICULTURAL AND INDUSTRIAL) PRODUCTION PER HEAD
OF POPULATION IN SELECTED EUROPEAN COUNTRIES AND THE U.S.A. IN 1938 AND 1948

	U.S. Dollars of 1938 Purchasing Power	
	1938	1948
United States	225	331
Sweden	203	237
Switzerland	185	233
United Kingdom	182	200
Denmark	167	179
Belgium—Luxemburg	147	154
Norway	133	148
France	136	139
Ireland	115	131
Netherlands	132	124
Czechoslovakia	103	115
Finland	108	110
Poland	62	87
Austria	101	73
Hungary	63	59
Italy	71	58
Rumania	38	45
Other European Countries	36	38
Total ex. Germany	97	104
Germany	189	90
Total including Germany	113	101

* Econ. Surv. of Europe for 1948, 21.

at work who are unemployed. Such calculations give about the same comparative results.[3]

These inequalities in production per worker in work are largely the outcome of unequal rates of change in the past two centuries. For most countries, measurement of such changes does not go far back. In the first half of the 19th century, real product per worker in work per year appears to

[3] Total national product is obtained, where possible, from national income produced at factor cost after deductions for depreciation and maintenance. Where possible, interest on unproductive debt and other transfers, as well as net receipts from overseas investments, are excluded. Imputed income from owner-occupied houses and farm products consumed on the farm is included, but not imputed income from other consumers' durable goods. The real value of goods and services consumed is adjusted for the real value of imports and exports in order to arrive at national income produced in the country.

Values in local currency are converted to "international units" (the purchasing power of a U.S. dollar on the average from 1925-34) by valuing each of the major components in the national income (food, rent, clothing, fuel, car and gasoline, and "other" but not investment goods and government services) in American prices in the base period. They are also revalued in American prices but giving each component a weight based on American distribution of expenditure among the components. The geometric average of the two results gives the value of the national currency in international units. Conversion rates for years before or after 1929 are the 1929 rate adjusted on the basis of each country's own price indexes. (Clark, op. cit., Ch. II and III.) (Conversion rates for 1929 are given, ibid., 27, and for 1946, ibid., 36.)

have declined a little in Britain, risen a little in the U.S.A., and risen about 20% in France. For other countries there is little information. In the second half of the century output increased in the U.S.A. about 50%, Britain over 20%, France some 80%, Germany over 100%, but little in Belgium. During the 20th century output continued to increase in the older industrialized countries, 100% in the U.S.A., 50% in Britain, and 30 to 40% in France. But it also increased markedly in a number of the other countries such as

TABLE 7

PRODUCT PER PERSON IN WORK IN SELECTED COUNTRIES*
(In International Units)

	Per Year		Per Hour	
	1938	1947	1938	1947
U.S.A.	1998	2566	1.011	1.186
Canada	1696	2247	.697	.964
U.K.	1396	1383	.573	.588
France	715	....	.362	
Belgium	812	791	.325	.316
Netherlands	1070	....	.445	
Switzerland	879	....	.364	
Norway	842	930	.365	.372
Denmark	985	823	.394	.330
Sweden	961	1500	.398	.406
Finland	792	....	.327	
Hungary (frontier of 1919-38) (1938-9)	408	....	.165	
India (1931-2)	231	....	.083	
China (1933)	138	....	.033	
Japan	582	....	.192	
Australia (1938-9 & 1947-8)	1473	1511	.668	.690
New Zealand (1938-9 & 1947-8)	1779	2281	.833	1.067
South Africa (1938-9)	478	....	.192	
Brazil (1946)	....	297	....	.110
Argentina (1945)	....	1002	....	.43
Cuba (1945)	....	500	....	.202
Czechoslovakia (1947)	....	445	....	.18
Turkey	....	419	....	.164

* Source: Colin Clark, *Conditions of Economic Progress* (2nd Ed.), 46, 54, 63, 80, 84, 85, 87, 103, 124, 136, 151, 158.

Norway (100%), Sweden (200%), Netherlands (20%), Switzerland (50%), Canada (40%), Australia (65%), New Zealand (55%), Japan (350%), and India (50%).[4] As a result the gap between the most and the least developed countries widened and it is still widening. The U.S.A., for example, produced about twice as much per capita as the average European country in 1938 and over three times as much in 1948. (Table 6.) Within Europe,

[4] Clark, *op. cit.* (2nd Ed.), 46, 71, 80, and Ch. III.

the countries of higher productivity per head (mostly in N.W. Europe) have been increasing productivity faster than the lowest.[5] The highest sustained rate of increase in output per employed worker that has been achieved seems to have been about 1.5% per year compound (which was utilize these things?

Output per man hour takes account also of changes in hours of work. In progressing countries generally, hours of work have been shortened and, therefore, output per man hour has increased more than output per man week or year. In the first half of the 19th century output per man hour rose little in the countries for which there are figures, with the exception of France and Germany. But in the second half of the century there were increases of 50 to 100% in the countries in Table 8, except Australia and India. Increases accelerated in the first half of the 20th century and ex-

TABLE 8

INCREASES IN OUTPUT PER HOUR WORKED IN SELECTED COUNTRIES
IN THE NINETEENTH CENTURY*

Country	Period	Output Per Man Hour (International units)	
		Beginning of Period	End of Period
U.S.A.	1800 to 1850	.229	.241
	1850 to 1894-1903	.241	.418
United Kingdom	1860-9 to 1894-1903	.230	.301
France	1789 to 1800-12	.051	.069
	1800-12 to 1850-9	.069	.118
	1850-9 to 1890-9	.118	.181
Belgium	1846 to 1895	.091	.113
Germany	1805 to 1854	.034	.121
	1854 to 1894-1903	.121	.259
Sweden	1861-9 to 1894-1903	.107	.172
India	1867-8 to 1895	.035	.045
Japan	1887 to 1914	.026	.047
Australia	1886 to 1901-3	.358	.377

* Source: Clark, *Conditions of Economic Progress* (2d Ed.), 46, 63, 80, 84, 100, 103, 124, 134, 136, 140.

tended to more countries in Europe as well as in Oceania and Japan (Table 9). Production per man hour was about equal in the U.S.A. and Britain in 1880 when Canada, Australia, and New Zealand all had higher produc-

[5] U.N., *Econ. Surv. of Europe for 1948*, 21.
[6] Rostas, L., *Comparative Productivity in British and American Industry*, 1948.

tivity than the U.S.A. (probably because small populations were exploiting
the cream of their resources). Between 1899 and 1950 output per man hour
increased 2.2% a year in the U.S.A.[7] and by 1947 was about twice that in
Britain; Canada and New Zealand fell somewhat behind the U.S.A. and
Australia to 66% of the U.S.A. Germany rose from a poverty level in 1800
to about the same level as Britain in 1913. Sweden had exceeded German

TABLE 9

INCREASES IN OUTPUT PER HOUR WORKED IN SELECTED COUNTRIES
IN THE TWENTIETH CENTURY*

Country	Period	Output Per Man Hour (International units)	
		Beginning of Period	End of Period
U.S.A.	1894-1903 to 1947	.418	1.186
United Kingdom	1894-1903 to 1947	.301	.588
France	1890-9 to 1938	.181	.362
Belgium	1895 to 1947	.113	.316
Germany	1894-1903 to 1933	.259	.380
Norway	1891 to 1947	.138	.372
Denmark	1913 to 1947	.300	.330
Sweden	1894-1903 to 1947	.172	.406
Netherlands	1900 to 1938	.259	.445
Switzerland	1899 to 1943	.160	.285
Canada	1903 to 1947	.545	.964
Australia	1901-3 to 1947-8	.377	.690
New Zealand	1901 to 1947-8	.521	1.067
Russia	1913 to 1940	.166	.178
Japan	1887 to 1944	.026	.181
India	1895 to 1944-5	.045	.094

* Clark, *Conditions of Economic Progress* (2d Ed.), 46, 63, 80, 84, 100, 103, 106,
108, 85, 87, 54, 140, 191.

productivity by 1939. Between 1900 and 1939 Japan increased productivity
about 500%, from almost a Chinese level in 1900, but in 1939 it was still
about one-fifth of the level of the U.S.A.[8] Russian productivity per man
hour in 1940 seems to have been less than 10% above 1913 and to have increased about 10% between 1940 and 1950.[9] In India productivity per man
hour doubled between 1867 and 1921 and by 1944 was about 160% above
1867. It is alleged, however, that real wages in India were 150% higher in
1650 than in 1938.

7 Mills, F. C., *The Role of Productivity in Economic Growth.*
8 Queensland *Rev. of Econ. Prog.*, April 1949.
9 National income in 1950 was claimed to be 160% of 1940 and man hours worked
increased 45%. (*Economist*, Feb. 24, 1951).

B. General Influences Affecting Productivity

The foregoing figures of productivity depend on methods of calculation. Many countries have no figures and in the remainder definitions of production vary. Leaving aside these imperfections in the data, productivity is influenced by the availability of resources for production and methods of using them.

1. THE AVAILABILITY OF RESOURCES

The amount of possible production everywhere depends partly on the proportions in which different resources are available for use. The principal means of production in very broad terms are labor, land, and, usually, equipment and improvements to land. In any given state of technology, a greater input of a resource would rarely result in a proportionate increase in output. If output increases proportionately more than the input of the resource, there are increasing returns to the resource. If output increases proportionately less than the input of the resource there are decreasing returns.

Increasing returns result from labor applied to a given amount of land and capital in agriculture so long as the soil responds more than proportionately to increased applications of labor to it. These responses are a matter of biological fact. Increasing returns also may result because larger numbers of workers can take advantage of differences in the qualities of different pieces of land. Returns in production in general may increase because larger numbers of people permit more specialization of labor, and labor gains in productivity as a result of specializing. This increased productivity may occur because some people are better at some jobs than others, or because repetition results in greater skill and even greater knowledge of the job. Greater numbers of workers permit the more general services, such as transport and the production of capital goods, to be more effectively performed, again largely due to specialization. Decreasing returns occur at the point at which the operation of these influences in some activities is more than offset by diminishing returns in others. In general, there is a range within which returns per unit of labor increase and beyond which they decrease. The turning point represents the economically "optimum" labor force.[10]

The importance of the supply of land to a group depends largely upon the nature of its activities. Land is more important in its effect upon agricultural than upon industrial production. Returns from different amounts of capital goods, assuming a given supply of land and labor, and a fixed technology, generally diminish. Any given amount of capital is applied to the most productive purposes and a slightly larger amount would have taken in some less productive uses. But larger amounts of

[10] Ch. 18.

capital generally increase production per worker, although at a diminishing rate—other things, including technology, being unchanged.

Even where knowledge of methods of production is similar, therefore, productivity may differ because the relative quantities of resources differ. The amount of land per worker in agriculture often differs widely in different countries. The amount of capital also differs, but the use of widely differing amounts of capital necessitates a change in technology.

The widening differences in productivity that have appeared in the last century or two have, however, been due to inequalities in technological change. These changes call for new "mixtures" of resources. Some countries have responded to this call more than others, the most notable change in the relative supplies of resources being increases in capital per head in the developing countries.

2. METHODS OF ECONOMIC ORGANIZATION

Societies may fail to realize the full production potential of their resources. They may also fail to expand their resources in order to increase production. Achievements in these directions are the outcome of organization.

Productivity depends partly on decisions by individuals. Everyone makes decisions of this sort, but decisions vary widely in scope. A state may establish or change laws of property or plan the use of resources. An individual may decide to save or to increase the size of his family. There are, however, certain foci of important decisions affecting production, namely the primary production unit, the group of production units, and the state.

The primary production unit is the group within which resources are brought together and physical production is organized and achieved. These production units may be responsible for only part of the process necessary to make goods and services available for final consumption. The farmer may produce goods which require processing, transport, and treatment in the home before they can be consumed. Some organizations are responsible only for transport, and some for making only producers' goods, some merely for distributing consumers' goods, and many for a variety of services. This concept of the primary production unit derives from Western capitalist economies, but something like it appears in every society. The unit may consist of one man (such as a farmer or craftsman), or it may consist of groups of various kinds.

The primary production unit is important in its effect upon the volume of production because of its internal organization. Is it organized so that it determines upon and uses the means of production in their most effective combinations? Does its range of activities in respect to products and services permit and induce the best use of resources? Is it large enough to utilize the best current knowledge of production methods (especially technology) and equipment of the most efficient size—or is it too large to utilize these things?

Groups of production units, such as trade associations, cartels, agricultural marketing cooperatives and the like, consist, in the main, of representatives of primary units, all producing similar products. The influence of these groups depends upon the sorts of decisions they make. The internal organization of such groups affects these decisions because it determines who makes the decisions and in what setting they are made. What is the scope of the decisions of such organizations?

The state, being the organization with the widest field of influence, can not only define the scope of action of the primary and secondary groups already mentioned, but can also consider the effectiveness of the allocation of the resources of the group as a whole. How, then, is the state organized in this respect? Who makes decisions, and within what setting? What types of decisions are made? The state may make decisions regarding production directly, for most branches of production (as in Russia), or it may set out a few ground rules and leave the ultimate determination of volume and kind of production to the operation of the market (as in the typical free enterprise economy).

The nature of the decisions made at these various levels depends upon the way in which people achieve economic power, large or small, and the setting in which they decide. Individuals may be selected for their position by heredity. Chiefs in many primitive societies, those who control large blocks of land, and some of those controlling large industrial units are so selected. Individuals may achieve their power through the competitive process. In competitive capitalist societies, entrepreneurs achieve or retain power to control sets of resources insofar as they succeed in competition. Civil servants may be selected by competitive examination. Different methods of selection might be expected to have different results.

The setting in which the selected individuals make decisions consists largely of social traditions, which express the basic values of the society. These values vary widely. Although they are not usually very clear, they have marked effects on production. They find expression in the law, in group activities, and in personal attitudes. In some societies, there is more emphasis upon the importance of material things than in others. Capitalism, for instance, has placed great emphasis on material values, partly, perhaps, because of the appearance of great opportunities for increasing material satisfactions. But nationalism, which has grown contemporaneously with capitalism, has induced a diversion of resources from the pursuit of material interests toward the might of the nation. Russia and the socialist countries in this respect resemble the capitalist ones. In the Middle East, Asia, and the Far East, the pursuit of material ends has been far less vigorous, which partly explains slowness of these regions to develop. Primitive peoples are also typically less intense in their pursuit of material things. Religion may divert people from material interests. The religious attitude, for instance, toward the cow in India, which cannot be killed or eaten by Hindus, prevents much improvement of stock and adjustment of the numbers of stock. There are prohibitions upon usury in many religious codes, although they do not in fact seem to be of great practical importance. But religion may also facilitate production by inducing among the working population resignation in the presence of poverty and hard labor.

Chapter 4

The Chief Components in National Production

National production consists of various goods and services in differing proportions. National outputs can be analysed in terms of agriculture, manufacturing, and services; capital goods and consumption goods; goods for export and those for the internal market; and many other ways. The most significant, in terms of productivity differences, is analysis in terms of agriculture, manufacturing, and services. Others will be later discussed in other connections.

A. The Composition of National Production in Fact

Until a few centuries ago production consisted mainly of agricultural activities and a few crafts and personal services. Manufactures and the related production of capital goods have relatively recently increased as a proportion of national output, but only in some countries.

Comparisons of the proportion of national income derived from each of the main sectors are dangerous because some countries do not classify the same activities within the same sectors. But there is a general pattern as to the relative importance of different sectors which is too striking to be explained away in terms of statistical methods.

Information concerning the proportion of national product derived from the major sectors is available for relatively few countries. The proportion of national income contributed by agriculture is notably low in Britain (6%), in the U.S.A. (7.5%), and in Israel (9.5%). It is around 15% in Canada, Chile, France, the Netherlands, Norway, and the Union of South Africa. In Europe it rises to about 40% in Greece and 54% in Turkey. In Egypt it was about 30% in 1948. In Latin America the proportion was Argentina 24% (1945), Chile 16% (1950), Colombia 31% (1940), Dominican Republic 41% (1946), Mexico 17% (1946), Peru 33% (1942) and Honduras

59% (1950).[1] In India agriculture accounted for 53% of the national income in 1931-2 and 47% in 1948,[2] and in Japan agriculture contributed about 63% in 1860[3] but only 29% in 1950. In Russia the proportion was 21.5% in 1937.

The proportion of national income from manufacturing and construction was over 50% in western Germany, and ranged from 40% to 49% in Britain, Canada, Denmark, Finland, France, the Netherlands, and Norway. It was about 43% in Russia in 1937, 38% in the U.S.A. in 1950, and

TABLE 10

NET GEOGRAPHICAL PRODUCT BY INDUSTRIAL ORIGIN IN SELECTED
COUNTRIES IN 1950*

Country	Percentage of Net Geographical Product Derived from:		
	Agriculture and Fishing	Manufacturing and Construction	All Other (Including Trade, Transportation, Communication and Government)
Canada	14	40	46
Chile	16	31	53
Colombia (1949)	39	22	39
Denmark	22	40	38
Finland	29	40	31
France (1949)	16	40	44
Western Germany	12	52	36
Greece (1949)	39	25	36
Guatemala (1949)	45	21	34
Honduras	59	14	27
India (1948)	47	17	36
Ireland	30	25	45
Israel	9.5	36	54.5
Italy	30	33	37
Japan (1948)	29	34	37
Kenya	44	17	39
Netherlands	13	42	45
Norway	15	43	42
Peru (1949)	35	28	37
Porto Rico (1948)	24	14	62
Turkey	54	14	32
Union of South Africa	18	36	46
United Kingdom	6	45	49
United States	7.5	38	54.5

* Calculated from U.N. *Statistics of National Income and Expenditure*, 1952, 25-31.

less than 20% in Turkey, India, Kenya, and Puerto Rico (Table 10). These percentages, however, are influenced by the wide variations in the proportion of national income from the remaining activities (trade, transport and communication and government services) which are due partly to

[1] U.N., *Econ. Surv. of Latin America*, 1948, 86.
[2] Rao, V.K.R.V. *National Income of British India 1931-2.*
[3] Clark, *op. cit.* (2d), 134.

differences in classification and partly to actual differences in the importance of service and government activities.

The proportion of the working population engaged in agriculture (Table 11) is the only indication of the relative importance of agricultural production in many countries. As output per worker in agriculture is usually lower than in industry, the proportion of workers in agriculture is usually greater than the proportion of national income contributed by agriculture. For instance, in the U.S.A. in 1950 about 13% of the population was dependent on agriculture, but agriculture contributed only 7.5% of the national income.

The lowest proportion of the labor force in agriculture is in Britain (6%) and the next lowest in the U.S.A. (about 13%), Australia, and New Zealand. The other low percentages are in Western Europe and Canada. In Russia the proportion of the total population employed in agriculture

TABLE 11

PROPORTION OF POPULATION ENGAGED IN AGRICULTURE
BY REGIONS

Region	Proportion of Population Engaged in Agriculture in 1949[*]	Proportion of Population Living in Countries with more than 50% of Gainfully Occupied Males Engaged in Farming, Fishing, Hunting and Forestry in about 1940-1947[**]
North America (Canada and U.S.A.) ..	20	0
Europe	33	30[***]
Oceania	33	16
South America	60	77
Central America (including Mexico) ...	67	88
Asia	70	93[***]
Africa	74	100
U.S.S.R.		100
World	59	76

[*] U.N. Food and Agriculture Organization *Year Book of Food and Agriculture,* 1950, 15.
[**] Davis, "Population and the Further Spread of Industrial Society," *Proc. Am. Phil. Soc.,* Feb. 13, 1951, 9.
[***] ex. U.S.S.R.

is about twice as high as in the U.S.A. Dependence on agriculture is high in Central and South America (where the lowest figure is 36% in Chile), Africa, and Asia (Figure 4). In Asia and the Far East generally 60 to 70% of the working force is in agriculture, 10% in industry, and 20 to 30% in transport, public service, professions, and domestic service,[4] although in Japan only 49% of the population is dependent on agriculture. The highest proportions of the labor force in industry, mining, and construction in

---

[4] U.N., *Surv. of Asia and Far East, 1948,* 110.

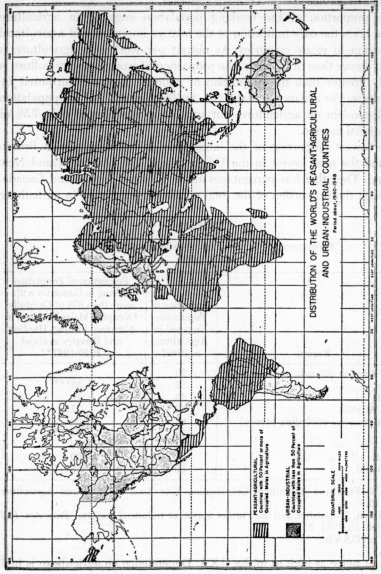

Fig. 4. Reproduced from Davis "Population and the Further Spread of Industrial Society," *Proc. Am. Phil. Soc.*, Feb. 13, 1951, 9.

recent years are in Belgium (44%), Switzerland (45%), Britain (42%), France (38%), and Canada and the U.S.A. (29%) in 1940.[5]

The relatively low proportion of the labor force in agriculture in some countries is due to agriculture expanding slower than the total labor force during the past two centuries. In Britain the proportion fell from 66% in 1760 to 12% in 1880 and 6% in 1939. In the U.S.A., it fell from 59% in 1860 to 43% in 1890 and 13% in 1948.[6] In a few countries the proportion in agriculture has *increased*, because other employment has grown more slowly than the total population. In India, for instance, the percentage of the population engaged in industry was 12.3 in 1880, but only 9.7 in 1931.[7] The proportion of the active population in industry has increased considerably in Europe, mostly in Denmark, Norway and Sweden, but in most countries where population has been increasing relatively fast, agriculture, trade and services have absorbed most of the increase.[8]

B. The Factors Affecting the Composition of National Production

The composition of the national product is influenced by the pattern of internal demand, conditions of international trade, the resources available for production, and the effectiveness with which they are used.

Demand within a society depends on techniques of production, the amount of investment, and the level of consumption. Increased industrialization generates an expanded demand for producers' goods, notably capital goods of industrial origin. Differences in consumption demand among countries (and changes within the same country) are strongly influenced by levels of income. At the lowest income levels a large part of all consumption consists of food and a few other essentials (as, for example, in China and India). But as living standards rise, the proportion spent on these products falls and that on more elaborate versions of essentials, and on products not previously consumed, rises. In the U.S.A., for instance, the proportion of the national income spent on farm products (not exclusively food products) was 34% in 1870, but only 11.6% in 1939. In much the same way, a redistribution of incomes in favor of lower income groups reduces the proportion of the total spent on essentials. But as incomes continue to rise, the proportion spent on industrial goods may level out as an increasing proportion is spent on services. It has been suggested that in the most advanced countries the demand for farm products falls to 10% of national income and may fall lower, the demand for manufactured goods tends to settle at 20 to 25% of the national income and that for services (including building and handicrafts and the

[5] Clark, *Conditions of Economic Progress* (2d), 397.

[6] Dewhurst *et al.*, *America's Needs and Resources*, 621; Clark, *op. cit.*, 47.

[7] Subsequent censuses have not provided comparable information. (Famine Inquiry Commission, *Final Report*, 80.)

[8] U.N. *Econ. Surv. of Europe Since the War.* 1953, 150.

products of small scale manufacture) to 70% or more.[9] The expansion of some services (such as transportation and trade) may, however, be necessary before income can be raised from low levels. Moreover, this category includes small business, and reflects in addition to demand, methods of organizing business.

Changes in consumption pattern do not necessarily cause similar changes in production pattern. International trade permits a country to consume either more or less food than it produces. In New Zealand and Denmark, agriculture is more important in the production than in the consumption pattern, but less important in Britain and Belgium. The production pattern depends, therefore, upon each country's comparative advantages in foreign trade, and upon the freedom of trade. International trade in services, however, although not unimportant, is somewhat restricted.

The resources available determine, on the one hand, the extent to which incomes can rise and influence demand, and on the other hand, each country's advantages in foreign trade. The effectiveness with which resources are used is in part a matter of allocation among sectors. Even if each economy made the best possible allocation, overall average production per person would differ. But actual differences are also affected by differences in the nearness of their approach to an ideal allocation.

The best allocation is that in which any shift of resources from one sector to another will reduce overall output (i.e., marginal value products of all resources are equal in all sectors). But there is practically no information concerning marginal value products. What data do exist relate to average products, and, even if marginal products in all sectors are equal, average products need not be equal. For instance, if agriculture is subject to diminishing returns, the withdrawal of a marginal worker reduces output by less than the average products in agriculture. Indeed, it has been suggested that marginal products in agriculture are only about half the average while in manufacturing the two may be equal. With an ideal allocation, therefore, average product in agriculture would be twice that in industry.[10]

Overall average product does depend, however, on average product in each sector and on the proportion of resources in each. Countries with a large proportion of their labor in agriculture generally have a low overall average product (Figure 5). In general, a country with 55% of its population in agriculture has an average income twice as high as one with 80% and a country with 30% in agriculture an average income twice as high as one with 55%. But there are exceptions. Canada, Sweden, Norway, and Denmark have similar proportions in agriculture but different average national incomes. So do Mexico, Brazil, Peru, Pakistan, and

---

[9] Clark, *op. cit.* (2d), 366.
[10] Clark, *op. cit.* (2d), 452.

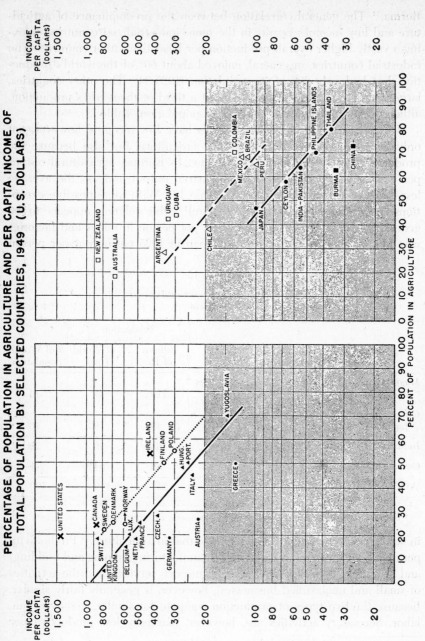

PERCENTAGE OF POPULATION IN AGRICULTURE AND PER CAPITA INCOME OF TOTAL POPULATION BY SELECTED COUNTRIES, 1949 (U.S. DOLLARS)

Fig. 5. From *Foreign Agriculture*, June 1951, p. 131.

Burma.[11] The general correlation between the predominance of agriculture and low incomes results in the more industrialized countries enjoying a vastly higher overall production per head than other countries. The industrial countries, in general, enjoyed about 66% of the world's production, but had only 29% of its population (1925-34). The other countries, largely unindustrialized, enjoyed about a third of the world's production, although they had over two-thirds of its population (Table 12).[12]

Most primarily agricultural countries have low incomes, however, not only because they are dependent on agriculture, but also because the productivity of agricultural labor is low. In Europe, agricultural output per worker is everywhere below industrial output and, on the average less than 30% of industrial output (Table 13). With some possible exceptions (e.g., Australia, and New Zealand[13]) this relation appears to be general. In India in 1948-9, net output per person in mines and factories was 340% of that in agriculture. In Japan in 1925 net output per person

TABLE 12

PRODUCTION IN RELATION TO DEGREE OF INDUSTRIALIZATION*
1925-1934

| | Production | | |
Region	Billions of IU	% of World Total	% of World Population
Major Industrial Countries (U.S., U.K., Germany, France)	119	47	13
Other Industrial Countries (incl. Russia & Japan)	49	19	16
Industrial Countries	168	66	29
Other Countries	86	34	71
WORLD	254	100	100

* Source: Colin Clark, The Conditions of Economic Progress (1st), 3.

in non-agricultural activities was 170% of that in agriculture.[14] Productivity per man hour in secondary activities (manufacturing, mining and building) and in tertiary activities (commerce, transport, services, and the activities of small and unclassified businesses), however, is generally fairly similar, because the two types of production compete for similar, mainly urban, labor. Secondary activities are, however, markedly less productive per

---

[11] For. Agric., June 1951.

[12] In 1939 the average per capita income for 30 countries with more than 50% of gainfully occupied males engaged in farming, fishing, hunting, and forestry was $76 per annum and for 22 "industrial countries" $287, or four times greater. (Davis, op. cit., 16).

[13] Clark, op. cit. (2d), 316.

[14] Clark, op. cit., 134.

TABLE 13*

PRODUCTION PER WORKER IN INDUSTRY AND IN AGRICULTURE
IN SELECTED EUROPEAN COUNTRIES AND THE U.S.A. IN 1938

	U.S. dollars of 1938 Purchasing power	
	Industry (including small scale)	Agriculture
U.S.A.	1730	580
Sweden	950	470
United Kingdom	910	560
Denmark	900	440
Norway	890	200
Ireland	830	310
Germany	790	290
Netherlands	790	500
France	580	280
Czechoslovakia	450	200
Italy	450	130
Poland	400	130
Finland	360	110
Hungary	340	150
Bulgaria	300	110
Rumania	290	180
Europe (ex. U.S.S.R.)	645	175

* U.N., *Economic Survey of Europe for 1948*, 225.

man hour than tertiary in Britain, Holland,[15] and Australia, but more productive than tertiary in Norway, Hungary, Rumania, India, New Zealand, and Japan.

The large numbers in agriculture in some countries are in fact a partial cause of the low productivity there. Where the proportion of workers outside agriculture is high, productivity in agriculture is likely to be high (notably in Australia and New Zealand, but not in the U.S.A.).[16] High proportions of labor in non-agricultural activities usually accompany high productivity in these activities. This causes competition for labor with primary activities in an effort to enlarge the secondary ones, and tends to raise the productivity in primary activities. In short, a high proportion of the labor force in low productivity sectors means a low overall average productivity, but the expansion of secondary and tertiary activities generally raises productivity in all sectors. Thus productivity per worker is about three times greater in the U.S.A. than in the average European country, in both agriculture and industry.

Overcrowding persists in agriculture in some countries because of shortages of the means of expanding industry, especially capital. But the

[15] In Britain and Holland, shipping and banking services are an important part of tertiary activities.

[16] Clark, *op. cit.* (2d), 316.

shortage of capital is partly due to the poverty resulting from overcrowding. Thus overcrowding continues and may become worse. General poverty also provides too poor an internal market for industrial goods to induce investment to supply such goods. But in the more industrialized countries increasing productivity per agricultural worker has reduced the number of workers necessary to feed a given population at a given level. In practice such increases have somewhat offset the effect of increases in population on the demand for labor in agriculture (and magnified the effect of reduction in rates of population increase).

Chapter 5

Productivity in Agriculture

Total agricultural output has increased and the variety of agricultural products has widened since neolithic times, and especially in recent years. Almost half of all cropland is devoted to cereals for human and animal consumption,[1] but there are no measures of the importance of different products in world agricultural output.

Agriculture is more widely distributed throughout the world than industry. It has been conducted nearly everywhere people live; it provides essentials of life which are rarely wholly obtained by foreign trade owing to the cost of transport and the wide distribution of the means of agricultural production. But the cultivated acreage of the world is distributed unevenly among countries. Of the cultivated land in the world, 17.6% is in the U.S.A., 16.8% in the U.S.S.R. and 15.5% in India. (Table 14 and Figure 6). Particular crops are still less evenly distributed. The distribution of the production of wheat, rice, cotton, and dairy products is shown in Figures 7 to 10.

A. The Productivity of Labor in Agriculture

Information about agricultural output per unit of labor is not available on a comprehensive basis for particular crops. Efforts have been made, however, to calculate output per worker in agriculture in general in a number of areas. Physical output per person in North and Central America combined appears to be about twenty times as high as in Africa, five times as high as in South America, and three times as high as in Europe. (Table 15). Value of output per year per worker (Table 16) was nearly twenty-five times as high in New Zealand as in India. Much of this inequality in agricultural productivity has appeared in the last two centuries. Output per worker per hour increased some 450% in France from the last half of the 18th century to 1946, and in Britain about 150% from the later 17th century to 1938. In the U.S.A., output per hour increased 170% between 1870 and 1939; in Sweden nearly 500% between 1869-71

---

[1] U.S. Dept. of Agric., *A Graphic Survey of World Agriculture*, 1.

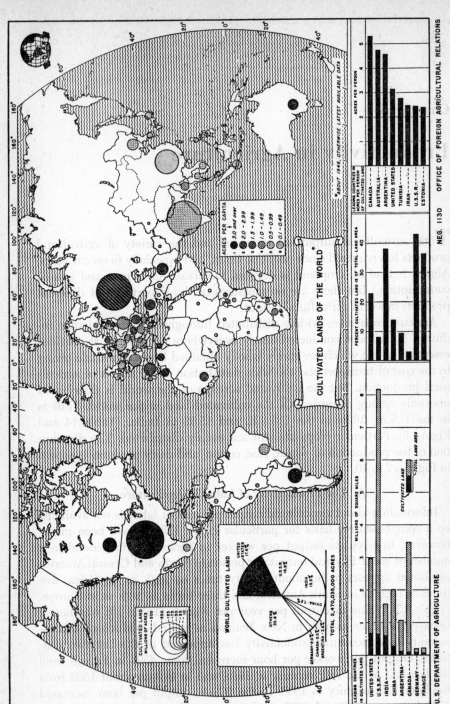

Fig. 6. From *A Graphic Summary of World Agriculture*, p. 14.

CULTIVATED LANDS OF THE WORLD

ACRES PER CAPITA

1 3.0 and over
2 2.0 - 2.99
3 1.5 - 1.99
4 1.0 - 1.49
5 0.5 - 0.99
6 0.1 - 0.49

*ABOUT 1946, OTHERWISE LATEST AVAILABLE DATA

WORLD CULTIVATED LAND

UNITED STATES 17.4%
U.S.S.R. 14.8%
INDIA 15.5%
CHINA 7.8%
OTHERS 35.9%
GERMANY 2.0%
CANADA 2.5%
ARGENTINA 2.5%

TOTAL 2,470,035,000 ACRES

CULTIVATED LAND IN CULTIVATED LAND MILLIONS OF ACRES

LEADING COUNTRIES IN CULTIVATED LAND

MILLIONS OF SQUARE MILES

UNITED STATES
U.S.S.R.
INDIA
CHINA
ARGENTINA
CANADA
GERMANY
FRANCE

CULTIVATED LAND
TOTAL LAND AREA

PERCENT CULTIVATED LAND IS OF TOTAL LAND AREA

ACRES PER PERSON OF CULTIVATED LAND

LEADING COUNTRIES IN ACRES PER PERSON

CANADA
AUSTRALIA
ARGENTINA
UNITED STATES
TUNISIA
IRAN
U.S.S.R.
ESTONIA

U.S. DEPARTMENT OF AGRICULTURE

NEG. 1130   OFFICE OF FOREIGN AGRICULTURAL RELATIONS

U.S. Dept. of Agric., A Graphic Summary of World Agriculture. 1

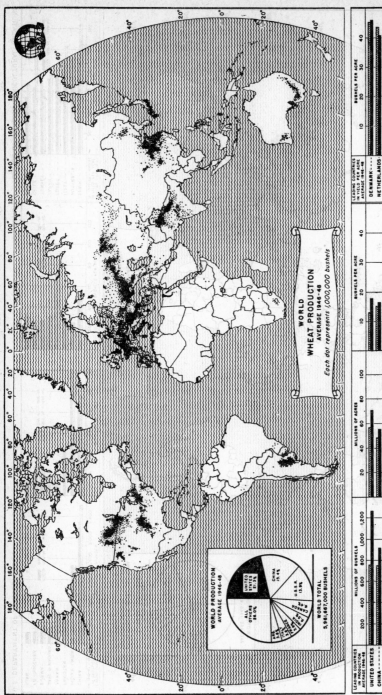
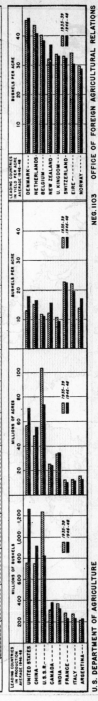

Fig. 7. From *A Graphic Summary of World Agriculture*, p. 16.

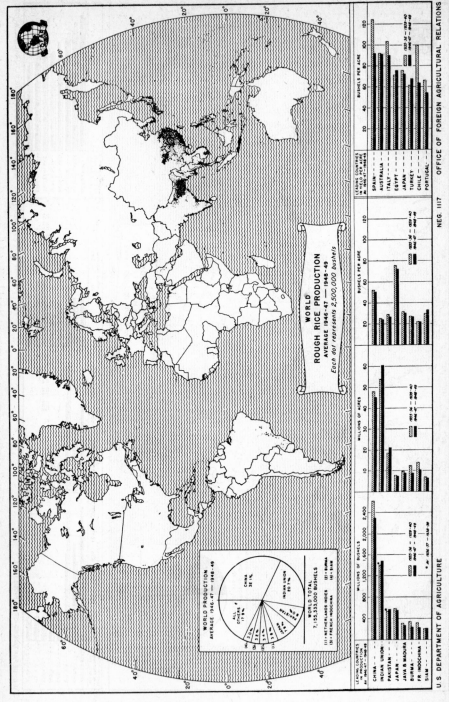

Fig. 8. From *A Graphic Survey of World Agriculture*, p. 21.

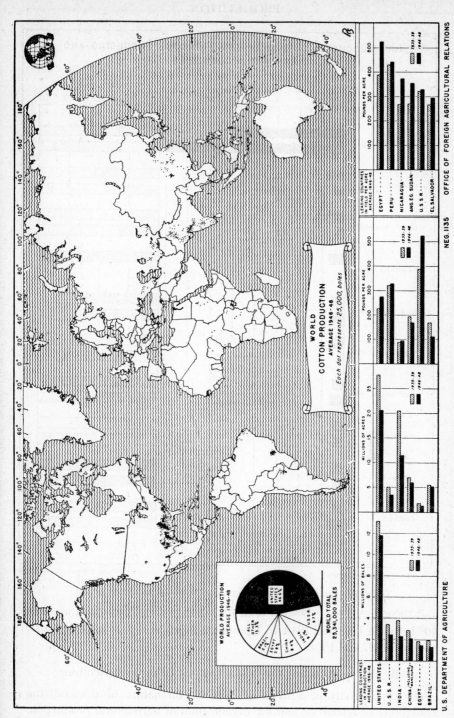

Fig. 9. From *A Graphic Summary of World Agriculture*, p. 31.

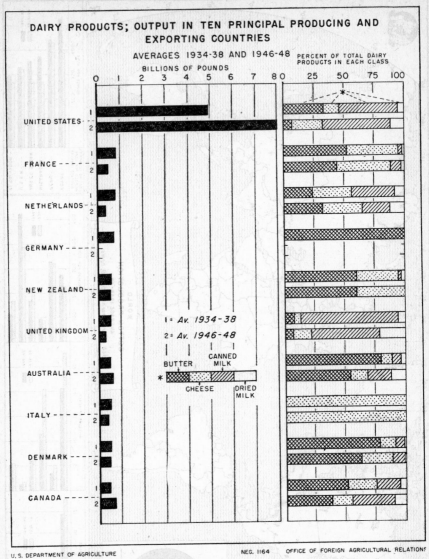

DAIRY PRODUCTS; OUTPUT IN TEN PRINCIPAL PRODUCING AND EXPORTING COUNTRIES

AVERAGES 1934-38 AND 1946-48   PERCENT OF TOTAL DAIRY PRODUCTS IN EACH CLASS

BILLIONS OF POUNDS

1 = Av. 1934-38
2 = Av. 1946-48

BUTTER   CANNED MILK
*
CHEESE   DRIED MILK

U. S. DEPARTMENT OF AGRICULTURE   NEG. 1164   OFFICE OF FOREIGN AGRICULTURAL RELATIONS

Fig. 10. From *A Graphic Summary of World Agriculture*, p. 38.

and 1929; in Australia, 50% between 1911 and 1939; in New Zealand about 40% between 1928 and 1940. In Japan output per man-year increased 130% between 1897 and 1934.[2]

B. Factors Affecting the Productivity of Labor in Agriculture

The productivity of agriculture depends on nature of demand, the availability of resources, and the organization of agricultural production.

[2] Clark, *op. cit.* (2d), 209, 212, 213, 216, 217.

TABLE 14

Country	Acres Cultivated (Millions)	Cultivated Land as Percentage of Total Land	Cultivated Land Per Capita (Acres)	Percentage of World Cultivated Land
United States	435	22.8	3.13	17.6
Soviet Union	414	7.9	2.43	16.8
India	382	37.9	.98	15.5
China (ex Sikiang and Sinkiang) ..	178	13.8	.29	7.2
Argentina	64	9.3	4.56	2.6
Canada	63	2.9	5.29	2.5
Germany	50	42.8	.72	2.0
France	49	36.3	1.22	2.0
Poland	47	49.2	1.47	1.9
Spain	44	35.6	1.65	1.8
Iran	41	10.2	2.47	1.6
Manchuria & Jehol	38	11.9	.89	1.5
Italy	35	47.9	.77	1.4
Australia	35	1.7	4.71	1.4
	1,875			75.8

* U.S. Dept. of Agric., *A Graphic Summary of World Agriculture*, 2.

TABLE 15

	Yield per hectare (Metric tons)		Yield per person in agriculture (Metric tons)	
	Pre-1939	1947-8	Pre-1939	1947-8
World Average:	1.24	1.30	0.42	0.42
North and Central America .	1.07	1.50	1.80	2.57
South America	1.28	1.39	0.58	0.48
Europe	1.51	1.34	1.04	0.88
Oceania	1.06	1.20	1.94	2.38
Asia	1.26	1.20	0.24	0.22
Africa	0.77	0.73	0.12	0.12

* U.N., Food and Agriculture Organization, *Monthly Bulletin of Food and Agricultural Statistics*, Vol. 2, No. 9, Sept. 1949 (excluding Soviet Russia).

1. THE DEMAND FOR AGRICULTURAL PRODUCTS

The demand for agricultural products affects the value productivity of agriculture (as well as the amount of resources in agriculture). Short-term changes in demand influence value productivity through their effect on

TABLE 16

NET AGRICULTURE AND PASTORAL OUTPUT* PER MALE WORKER
AND PROPORTION OF LABOR TO LAND IN SELECTED COUNTRIES
IN 1934 AND 1935†

	Net Agricultural and Pastoral Output per Male Engaged in Agriculture *Per Year* (International Units)	Occupied Males Engaged in Agriculture Per Square Kilometer of Land of Standard Climate⁰
New Zealand	2,006	0.54
Australia	1,329	0.33
Argentina	1,115	1.77
Uruguay	815	1.22
U.S.A.	623	1.87
Denmark	592	10.00
Canada	531	0.89
Great Britain	531	5.00
Netherlands	489	17.00
Belgium	466	17.90
Iceland	461	0.63
Switzerland	460	—
Germany	416	10.70
France	414	8.56
Sweden	354	4.27
Estonia	292	4.96
Czechoslovakia	287	12.40
Eire	273	7.79
Hungary	242	21.00
Brazil	239	1.02
Palestine	232	145.0
Poland	189	14.50
Syria	165	43.3
Cyprus	159	10.0
Italy	154	25.50
Japan	146	17.35
U.S.S.R.	127 (1938)	11.8
Turkey	119	14.3
Iraq	108	31.6
Egypt	92	74.3
India (ex Native States)	83	26.8
Philippines	83	7.70

* Output is net after deduction of agriculture and non-agricultural products used up in agricultural production and of other non-labor costs (i.e., it is "value added").

† Clark, *Conditions of Economic Progress* (2d Ed.), 200.

⁰ Land of standard climate excludes uninhabitable land and adjusts the remainder for differences in humidity and temperature.

prices. The amount of these price changes depends on the speed with which resources in agriculture are adjusted to the change in demand. If the price falls, value productivity is reduced until contraction of output raises the price again. But over longer periods, changes in demand may affect the costs of production. Increased output may be profitable only at higher prices. If the increased costs include increases in average incomes from labor in agriculture, the value product of labor rises. Reduced production, however, may be possible at a lower cost owing partly to lower wages reflecting a lower value product.

For many centuries the demand for agricultural products was almost entirely a consumer demand for food and clothing. Agriculture still produces practically all human food and drink (excluding salt), most clothing material, and many medicines. But it also produces some fuel, building materials, and many industrial products, notably rubber.

Past changes in this demand pattern reflect rising levels of living, changes in methods of agricultural production, and the expansion and changing methods of manufacturing. Rising standards of living in some countries have taken the form of increasing consumption per head of animal products, such as meat, milk, butter, and poultry, which has especially benefited New Zealand, Australia, Argentina, and Denmark. Most of these improvements in levels of living have occurred in temperate countries that have also increased their consumption of tropical vegetable products. The consumption of spices is ancient, but in the past two or three centuries trade in coffee, tea, cocoa, sugar, bananas, and citrus and other fruits has grown rapidly.

Changes in methods of agricultural production have influenced the pattern of agricultural output mainly because animal power "fuelled" with agricultural products has given place to machinery fuelled with petroleum. The fall in the number of horses and mules in the United States from a peak of 26.7 millions in 1918 to 8.3 millions in 1949 freed about one-seventh of the harvested cropland for production for human instead of animal consumption.[3]

The growth and change in methods of manufacturing has influenced and been influenced by the pattern of agricultural production. Industry has demanded increased quantities of fibers (such as wool, cotton, sisal, and hemp), rubber, industrial adhesives, and cellulose (for paper and some plastics). Although industry has hitherto relied mainly on exhaustible supplies of minerals for fuel and structural materials, research is now being directed to the discovery of agricultural substitutes for metals and petroleum. Vegetable alcohol is substituted for gasoline in some countries, and plastics for metals in a few uses. But some industrial developments have been competitive with agriculture—for example, the production of synthetic substitutes for fibers (nylon and rayon, the latter of which is, however, based on agricultural raw materials), rubber, quinine, camphor, (from turpentine, another agricultural product), vegetable dyes, and flavorings like vanilla. By 1947 about 30% of the world production of rubber was synthetic, although the production of natural rubber was about 5% greater than in 1937. Cement is now an important substitute for lumber.

---

[3] U.S. Statistical Abstract, 1949. 708; Cooper. M. R. and Barton. G. T., "A Century of Farm Mechanization," 32, The Agricultural Situation, 9 (1948).

The growth of manufacturing in capitalist countries has destabilized the demand for agricultural products. Production for consumption within the producing family is undertaken in response to a fairly stable demand. But where agricultural production is for the market and manufacturing activity fluctuates, the power of industrial workers to purchase agricultural products, and of manufacturers to purchase agricultural raw materials, also fluctuates.

These changes in demand do not necessarily generate increased output in the country where demand changes. They may stimulate imports from other countries where output expands. While most countries produce a good deal of the food they consume, international trade in food has for long been important. It existed in classic times; Greece and Rome were considerable importers. But since 1800, the cheapening of transport, the suppression of piracy, and the improved organization of foreign trade have greatly increased international trade in agricultural products. This causes divergencies between the production and consumption of agricultural products in particular countries (Figure 11). In some countries populations have grown beyond the capacity of the local food supply (e.g., Britain, France, Belgium, Germany, Norway, Finland, and Iceland (which imports almost all its food supply). Other countries have developed their agriculture beyond the capacity of their local markets (notably Canada, Argentina, Australia, New Zealand, Denmark, Siam, and Indo-China).

Changes in demand have a marked effect on the value of output in the short run because the conditions of supply affect the extent to which output responds to price. The weather typically imposes a seasonal pattern upon agriculture. Decisions on what to produce must be made simultaneously by all producers in an area. Each of the various productive operations must usually also be performed simultaneously by all producers (whereas in industry decisions on output can frequently be made almost continuously, and all processes of production be carried on simultaneously). If demand in fact diverges from what was anticipated when production commitments were made, the price will differ from the anticipated price. Production can be changed only when the time comes for the next commitment. Unless price falls below the cost of harvesting and marketing, all output is likely to be sold. But fluctuations in weather cause variations in crop from season to season in response to a given input of resources which contributes to price fluctuations. It may be possible, however, to reduce these fluctuations by irrigation or the use of drought-resistant strains of plant or animal.

The period of adjustment to changes in demand depends on the length of the production cycle, which depends on weather cycles and the behavior of animals and vegetables and of the labor force. The production cycle consists of a period of maturation and a period of yield. Some crops have a less than annual cycle and yield more than one harvest a year. Two

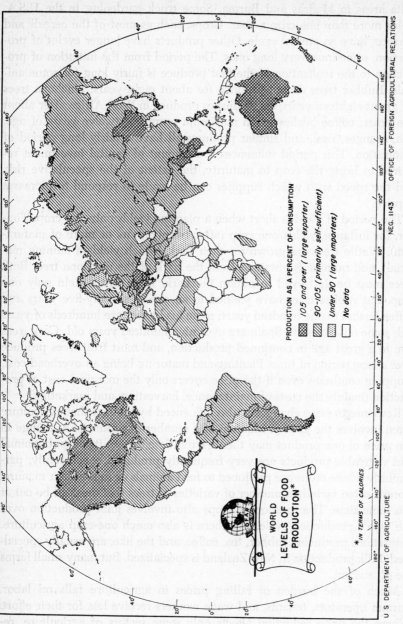

Fig. 11. From *A Graphic Survey of World Agriculture*, p. 12.

and sometimes three crops of rice are produced in parts of Java and the delta areas in Madras and Burma. Some truck gardening in the U.S.A. yields more than one crop a year. Crops, such as most of the cereals and tobacco, have an annual cycle. Other products have longer cycles of production, sometimes very long ones. The period from the initiation of production to the realization of the first produce is fairly long for some animals. Rubber trees do not produce for about eight years; cinchona trees for about eighteen years; cocoa bushes produce in West Africa after about five years; coffee bushes reach maximum output at twelve years of age. Tea, oranges, sisal, and similar products all have a fairly long period of maturation. This period influences the amount of capital investment required to bring the crop to maturity, the extent of the speculative risk, and the speed with which supplies can be made to respond to increases in price.

The period of yield is short when a planting yields only one crop. Timber, for instance, yields one crop (after twenty years or more of maturation). Wattle trees are grown for their bark (which yields a tanning material), and quinine is obtained from the bark of the cinchona tree. Both trees must be destroyed to obtain the bark. Meat cattle yield only one crop. But rubber trees have yielded to an age of seventy-five years and coffee bushes to one hundred years; some tea bushes are hundreds of years old; some olive trees in Spain are over nine hundred years old. Cork trees live to a great age in continued production, and most fruit trees produce over a long period of time. Planting and maturing being an overhead cost, cropping continues even if the price covers only the marginal cost of production (mainly the costs of maintenance, harvesting, and marketing).

Response to price changes is also influenced by the fact that agriculture often involves the joint production of a number of products. A change in the price of one product may then have little effect on its output. Animal and vegetable products are very frequently produced concurrently, particularly where crops are produced to feed animals or to use their manure. Forests often include a number of varieties of trees that must all be cut at the same time. The rotation of crops also involves joint production over the whole production cycle. But there is also much one-crop agriculture. Plantations producing rubber, tea, coffee, and the like, are usually specialized. Milk production in New Zealand is specialized. But many small farms are diversified.

Much of the burden of falling prices in agriculture falls on labor. Farmer operators, tenants, and wage workers receive less for their effort. Where the price reduction affects only some sectors of agriculture, resources may be shifted to other sectors. But where a large part of all agriculture is affected, and there is little opportunity to move to non-agricultural sectors (as in the typical underdeveloped country), production may not be greatly reduced for a long time. Prices may cover costs because costs have been reduced by reducing the remuneration of labor. Thus the value product per worker is reduced. If demand increases, higher prices may be necessary to maintain output in the long run. The benefits may take the form partly of higher land rents and partly of higher wages (if they are necessary to attract additional labor).

2. The Availability of Resources

Agriculture typically requires more land than other activities, land being measured in terms of productivity. Productivity depends not only on area but also on topography, structure of the soil, weather, and location.

The amount of land per worker is therefore somewhat correlated with output per worker. The number of agriculturally employed male workers per square mile of cultivated land is:[4]

U.S.A. and Canada	10
Oceania	17
South America	57
U.S.S.R.	62
Africa	64
Europe (ex. U.S.S.R.)	74
Caribbean and Central America	129
Asia (ex. U.S.S.R.)	182
World	88

Cultivated land per worker is highest in sparsely settled areas like Canada, Argentina, and Australia. It is low in Italy and Germany, but lowest in Asia, where it is nearly four times as high in India as in Japan and China (in terms of total population in relation to cultivated land) (Tables 14 and 17). It is six times as high in the U.S.A. and Canada as in the U.S.S.R. There is a closer relation between output and amount of land per worker after the land has been "adjusted" for differences in humidity and temperature. Recently settled lands like New Zealand, Australia, Argentina, the U.S.A., and Canada have a high output per worker and generally a high ratio of land to workers. The extent to which land responds to increasing applications of labor depends, however, on the amount of capital in use, the quality of the worker, differences in soils, and land-use patterns (especially the amount used for agriculture) (Ch. 16).

The availability of capital varies widely, partly because the amount of capital for all uses differs and partly because agriculture varies in its attractiveness as a field for investment compared with other uses. Its attractiveness depends partly on the availability of labor, as indicated by its cost. Competing demands for labor (e.g., from industry) maintain the cost of agricultural labor. Where agricultural wages have risen, as they have in recent years in the Scandinavian countries, Britain and the Netherlands,

---

[4] Davis, "Population and the Further Spread of Industrial Society," *Proc. of Am. Phil. Soc.*, Feb. 13, 1951, 11.

TABLE 17

POPULATION PER SQUARE KILOMETRE OF CULTIVATED LAND IN
INDIA AND THE FAR EAST IN ABOUT 1947[*]

Country	Population Per Square Kilometre of Cultivated Land
Japan	1300
Formosa (Taiwan)	645
Korea	629
Philippines	494
Java and Madiera	452
Indo-China	451
Ceylon	444
China proper	425
Pakistan	408
Siam	347
India	345
Manchuria	245
Burma	240
India and Far East	404

[*] U.N. *Econ. Surv. of Asia and the Far East*, 1948, 7.

the margin of substitution between labor and machinery has changed and the use of machinery has greatly increased.[5] In the 40 years to 1953, the man hours of labor to produce wheat have been reduced 66% in the U.S.A., and those to produce cotton 50%. But in many countries the inflow of capital is blocked by labor reserves and low wages that diminish the inducement to substitute capital for labor.[6]

The availability of knowledge of methods of production is a matter of the nature of existing knowledge, the extent to which producers in various countries have access to it, and methods of organizing production.

Knowledge of production methods increased slowly over a long stretch of history. The Romans improved intensive agriculture under the empire, and there were slow improvements during the "dark ages" in Europe. The modern period of improvement was initiated in Britain in the 17th century since when the rate of progress has accelerated notably during the 20th century.[7] The utilization of this knowledge has been very uneven. While Australia, New Zealand, and the countries round the north Atlantic have rapidly improved production methods, the countries where productivity is low have made little change for centuries.

Increasing knowledge of plant nutrition has made it possible to raise output per man and per acre. For centuries practice developed slowly out of experience. The most primitive device is that of resting the land from time to time by conducting "patch agriculture," that is, cultivating small

[5] U.N., *Ec. Surv. of Europe Since the War*, 1953, 157.
[6] Schultz, *op. cit.*, 78.
[7] Keen, *Agricultural Development in the Middle East*, Ch. IV.

patches of land but shifting from year to year from one location to another. This practice is common for example in parts of North, Central, and East Africa, the Caribbean and Latin America, and many other tropical areas. Cattle raising is often conducted also by moving herds over wide areas. About 15% of the population in the Middle East is nomadic and supplies most of the livestock products. The Masai in East Africa also range widely. Rather more organized agricultural systems often provide for a period of fallowing for each plot. This practice has declined in Europe where only 5% of the arable land lies fallow each year except in the Mediterranean area. But it persists in India, the hotter parts of Mexico,[8] in Iraq (where it is standard practice for half the land to lie fallow each year), and among Arab tribes in North Africa.

The introduction of a crop rotation (including a soil building element) reduces the waste of land in fallow and increases the output of the major crops. The enclosures in England in the 17th century replaced the three-field system of the feudal period (with a cycle of production which included fallowing) with a four-crop cycle (mainly wheat, barley, clover, and turnips) without fallowing. Crops were increased, fodder was insured for stock throughout the year, and the fertility of the soil was increased. This system survived until the latter part of the 19th century, when it was virtually demolished by imports of wheat and meat from America and Australasia.[9] But the crop rotations of the temperate regions are usually not applicable to other areas. The long, hot, dry season of much of the Middle East, for instance, prevents the adoption of British or American practice.

Plant nutrition has also been provided by animal manures, which were used in ancient Greece and Rome. But they are little used by many peasant producers, for example in Mexico and many parts of East Africa, where governments are endeavoring to induce manuring. In India and much of the Middle East,[10] animal manure is burned for lack of any alternative fuel. This loss of organic material for the soil is a primary cause of low agricultural productivity. Countries like Denmark and Britain, on the other hand, have indirectly imported animal manure when they imported animal feeds and engaged in animal husbandry in their own countries. The mechanization of agriculture, however, has reduced the supply of animal manure by reducing the number of power animals on the land. In recent years there has been greatly increased emphasis on mulching, which maintains the supply of organic material holding water in the soil. This practice began in the temperate parts of the world, and is now spreading to tropical areas, for example, in rubber and tea plantations. But there is still some question whether the effects are the same in tropical areas (where the soil is subjected to high temperatures) as in temper-

---

[8] *The World Today,* March 1949, 109; Keen, *op. cit.,* 29.

[9] Keen, *op. cit.,* 12.

[10] U.N., *Final Report of Economic Survey Mission for the Middle East,* II, 4.

ate zones. Chemical fertilizers, mainly nitrates and phosphates, have increased greatly in importance, but only since about 1850; they are essentially a product of the industrial revolution. Their intensive use is confined mainly to the more highly developed countries (especially the U.S.A., Britain, Denmark, and Japan, but also Egypt) partly because of their high cost of transport.

The adaptation of plant and animal strains has also been accelerated. Selecting the best specimens of plant and animal for breeding is an ancient practice. But since the publication of Darwin's *Origin of Species* in 1858, breeding has become systematized to increase yields, improve resistance to disease and weather, and facilitate harvesting and processing. Here again knowledge is very unevenly used. Improved wheat strains permitted a 300% increase in wheat acreage in Canada, Australia, and Argentina between 1898 and 1930. In the U.S.A. the output of eggs per hen increased 50% between 1925 and 1950. On some land the output of corn has increased over 300%. Milk yields per cow in Europe in 1950 ranged from 3,800 litres a year in the Netherlands, 3,500 in Denmark, and 3,400 in Belgium, to 1,200 in Spain and 0.900 in Greece.[11]

The control of pests has also increased output in some countries, notably since about 1850. The chemical industry, utilizing biological research, has developed devices for pest control. They are used intensively in the U.S.A. and Western Europe, but very little in countries of low productivity outside plantations.

Some of the principles of modern manufacturing have been applied to agriculture, although in the world as a whole it remains predominantly on a craft basis. Mechanization was greatly accelerated in the U.S.A. after the middle of the 19th century. Power-driven agricultural machinery based on the same mechanical principles as industrial machinery (but generally using smaller and more mobile power units) has been substituted, mostly since 1920, for animal power in plowing, cultivating, harvesting (though not of fruit), transportation on the farm, milking, and many types of processing. Mechanization has spread in recent years in Canada, Northwest Europe, Australia, New Zealand and Russia. Of the 4.6 million agricultural tractors in the world in 1948, about 71% were in North America, 9% in Soviet Russia, 5% in Britain, 2.4% in France and 2.4% in Germany.[12] In Russia in 1950 tractors were used for 90% of the plowing and sowing of grain and more than 50% of the crop was gathered by harvester-combines. In the U.S.A. productivity has also been raised by the increased farm use of electricity.

Mechanization in general increases output per worker. For instance: the output of rice per worker on large mechanized farms in Louisiana, Texas,

---

11 U.N., *Econ. Bull. for Europe*, Vol. 3, No. 2, (1951) 35.
12 Food and Agricultural Organization, *Year Book of Food and Agricultural Statistics, 1949*, 178.

and Arkansas is 20 to 50 times greater than in India, Thailand, or Indo-China.[13] Mechanization lightens the burden on the worker and increases the proportion of output sent to market. Part of the land previously used to produce feed crops for the animals that provided the power has been released to produce milk, pork, beef, eggs, and other animal products. But little mechanization is to be found in the Middle East, India, the Far East, and among primitive peoples, where most agricultural production is based on human power (mostly that of women wielding a hoe).

Specialized plantations, mostly in tropical areas, produce long-cycle crops such as rubber, tea, coffee, sisal, cinchona, and palm oil, in what are almost agricultural factories. Management control is centralized, considerable bodies of routine labor are employed, and frequently considerable capital (to finance the period of maturation and, often, processing equipment) is used.

These wide differences in technology among countries persist in spite of the relatively cheap and easy access of every country to knowledge of improved methods developed in others. But not all improvements in agricultural technology are applicable in all parts of the world.[14] Most agricultural research has been conducted in temperate countries and practically none, for instance, in the Middle East.[15] But there is a tremendous fund of knowledge in China and Japan concerning the technology for an over-crowded agriculture that may be transferable to countries in which there is similar over-crowding. Access to knowledge depends partly on literacy and partly on specialized channels for the communication of knowledge—such as the Agricultural Extension Service in the U.S.A.[16] This access depends also on the organization of agriculture.

3. The Organization of Agricultural Production

The framework of agricultural production affects productivity according to its compatibility with the most effective methods of production. The feudal system with its open fields had to be replaced by enclosed agriculture before much improvement could be made. The tribal organization of many native peoples, or land ownership of the type prevalent in the Middle East and India, is incompatible with great agricultural improvement. Yet it may be in the interest of many members of these societies to oppose social reorganization. Competitive individualism has applied considerable pressure to introduce new methods. Obsolete techniques of production and kinds of equipment cannot be maintained in use against the competition of producers who adopt new ideas. A few innovators can compel others to come up to their standards. But even in these countries

---

[13] Schultz, op. cit., 152.
[14] Warriner, Land and Poverty in the Middle East, 123, 124; Keen, op. cit., 47; U.S. Administrator of Agricultural Research Report, for 1949.
[15] U.N., Conciliation Commission for Palestine, Rep. Econ. Com. II, 6, 34.
[16] Ch. 8.

the acquisition of new knowledge is more a matter of government activity than competitive individual effort. Custom and religion may also retard the introduction of more efficient methods. In India, for instance, religion is responsible for the sickly race of cattle because the killing of cattle is prohibited. The Indian cow produces 5% as much milk as the Danish, and there are more cattle per square mile in India than anywhere else in the world. In parts of East Africa cattle are a means of indicating personal wealth and of obtaining wives (who are a means of agricultural production). Consequently there is considerable pressure to maintain an excessive number of cattle, which causes soil erosion. In less developed colonial areas, in many parts of Africa and Malaya, for instance, workers apply relatively few hours of labor to agricultural production, as a part of a way of village life that may be difficult to change.

It is necessary, therefore, to turn to the nature of the production unit in agriculture (Ch. 6), to that of private groups of production units (Ch. 7), and to government policies (Ch. 8). But productivity also depends on the arrangements regulating access to land, water, labor, and capital (Ch. 16 to 22), and on the arrangements for coordinating production in general and, therefore, the place of agriculture in relation to other sectors of production (Ch. 23).

Chapter 6

The Production Unit in Agriculture

Production units influence production chiefly through their decisions on the use of resources, the pattern of their activities, and their size.

A. The Structure of Production Units

The form of organization of the production unit chiefly affects the incentives of the participants in production to be efficient and progressive.

The simplest type of organization is that of the individual producer who makes a production policy, gets together the means of production (although he need not own the land), and manages production. He and members of his family may work, and he may employ wage workers. These units may be, but are not necessarily, small. Disregarding relations between landowners and producers,[1] such units have predominated over all other types almost until the 20th century. Because the income of the producer, in kind or in money, depends on the efficiency of his operations, he has an incentive to use resources efficiently. But the vigor with which he pursues efficiency depends on his attitude toward material gain, and the extent to which landowners and the state facilitate or hinder improvement (Ch. 16). In Russia and eastern Europe, socialist governments have actively sought to eliminate farming based on the profit motive. After the revolution in Russia, the land was nationalized but the number of individually operated farms increased as a result of the breaking up of large land holdings. The total collapse of production caused famine and peasant uprisings, and the government relied mainly on individualist farming during the period of the New Economic Policy (1921-7). But the high price of industrial products, compared with that of agricultural, discouraged agriculture. It continued on a low technological level. Output in 1927 was only about 88% of that in 1913.[2] Even in 1933, at the end

---

[1] See p. 76.

[2] Baykov, A., *The Development of the Soviet Economy*, 135, 190, 327.

of the first Five Year Plan, individual peasant farming accounted for 85.3% of agricultural production, but it has since withered away. Most of the countries in eastern Europe are now passing through the earlier stages of a similar elimination of individual farming.

Partnership occurs in agriculture, but is not common, and there is no information as to its frequency. In principle it differs from individual operation in that no one individual makes all the decisions necessary in production and takes the consequences.

The proportion of all workers who are individual or partnership proprietors or independent workers (as against members of the family assisting the proprietor and salary and wage earners) is far greater in agriculture than in industry. During the 1930s the proportion varied widely from over 60% in Italy, India, France, and the U.S.A., to less than 40% in Germany, Portugal, Hungary, Britain, and Chile.[3]

The corporation as a means of organizing agricultural production has appeared primarily during the 20th century, and is increasing in importance. It typically involves a wage labor force under centralized control, some separation of control from ownership, and the distribution of profits according to contributions of property to the enterprise. The corporation was first used to organize plantations that had previously often been family concerns, but not all corporate agriculture is in plantations and not all plantations are corporate. Corporate plantations are significant in the production of rubber and palm nuts in Malaya; coffee, tea, cinchona, and tobacco in Java; tea in India; bananas in Central America; sugar in Natal (Union of South Africa); edible oils in central and west Africa; sisal and coffee in Kenya; oranges in Rhodesia; and pineapples in Hawaii. Corporations like the United Africa Company, the Société Financière of Paris, and the United Fruit Company operate a number of plantations.

Plantations are often distant from the headquarters of the corporation, and engaged largely in export (which involves special knowledge of the organization of the export trade). The directors of many plantation companies have therefore delegated part of the management to the agents for shipping and insurance companies, trading concerns, and banks operating in the areas of production. These managing agents have special knowledge of local problems, of the branch of agriculture concerned, and of exporting produce and importing the supplies necessary for production. Such firms frequently manage a number of plantations producing similar products, presumably in competition with each other. They are important in the conduct of tea plantations in India, rubber plantations in Malaya, pineapple and sugar plantations in Hawaii, and of many of the plantations in Java.

The effect of this shift of control depends upon the conditions under

---

[3] Clark, *Conditions of Economic Progress* (2d Ed.), 434.

which managing agents operate. They are typically appointed for a period of years. If they are remunerated by a percentage of gross receipts, they are less concerned with profit than with volume of output and are, therefore, under less pressure than an individual producer to maximize efficiency. Furthermore, their interest may conflict with that of the corporation (e.g., when they buy its produce or sell it supplies). Although the effect of this system on efficiency has not been sufficiently appraised, the efficiency of Malayan rubber plantations has been seriously questioned.[4]

Corporate organization is much less common in the production of short-cycle crops. It exists in the U.S.A. more particularly in the production of wheat in Montana, where farms from twenty to fifty thousand acres are operated by corporations. Corporations working chains of small farms have also developed in the Middle West as a result of the increasing complexity of problems of cultivation, management and machinery and of foreclosures by banks during the depression after 1929. Large corporate farms also exist in the Nile delta in Egypt.[5]

Producers' cooperatives resemble the corporation in requiring the unified control of a number of workers in production, but differ from it in principle in vesting control and profits in the workers.[6] This type of organization has been most extensively used in Russia[7] and territories under Russian control.

The organization of the producers' cooperative (artel) in Russia is prescribed by a basic law passed in 1935. The land is the property of the people through the state, which allots it to cooperatives. Cooperatives have the right of permanent use, but not of sale or lease. Members are allotted a limited amount of land for individual use as houses, gardens, orchards, and the rearing of a limited number of cattle. The law regulates entry into cooperatives, and provides safeguards against arbitrary expulsion. The labor is supplied by the members. If they refuse to carry out a task assigned by the manager, they may be fined and, on repetition of the offense, expelled from the cooperative. Workers are usually organized in brigades that take charge, under a foreman, of particular sections of the cooperative land. When a task is completed, members are credited with a number of labor-days based on the estimated period of labor necessary to complete the work, the skill required, and the efficiency with which it was performed.

---

[4] Bauer, P. T., "The Working of Rubber Regulations," LVI Ec. Jour., (1946) 401.

[5] Bonné, State and Economics in the Middle East, 129.

[6] "Agricultural cooperatives" for marketing and providing credit are not producers' cooperatives, but organizations of individual producers and are discussed later (Ch. 7).

[7] Collective farms (kholkoz) include (1) agricultural communes, (2) societies for joint cultivation (toz), and (3) producers' cooperatives (artels). All collectives involve consolidation of the means of production and a single planned process, and all are subject to vigorous control by the state. In addition to collective farms there are state farms (Ch. 8).

The more important management decisions, within the power of the cooperatives, are made at a general meeting of all members or their elected delegates. A managing committee, elected by the general meeting, controls productive operations in accordance with the decisions of the general meeting, but also with the policies of the government (which very considerably limit the power of the cooperatives) (Ch. 8). Day-to-day operations are controlled by a manager.

The returns from the cooperative activities are distributed in kind and in cash. In the distribution of produce, the first charge is for deliveries to the state. Thereafter part of the produce is set aside for seed and fodder and for food funds for the relief of invalids, for children's nurseries, and similar purposes.[8] In 1938, 36.1% of the produce of grain and legumes was marketed (15% as compulsory deliveries to the government and 16% for work by tractor stations, both at fixed prices, and 5.1% at market prices). A little over 25% of the total gross produce went in kind to the members of the cooperatives in payment for their work in proportion to the number of labor-days credited to each member. The cash obtained by the cooperatives is subject first to charges for taxes, insurance and debts. Thereafter it is allocated to providing machines, livestock and investments; for distribution as rewards for exceptional work; for contributions to cultural funds and for support of members under special training. The remainder, distributed in cash in proportion to the labor-days contributed by each member, was about 53% of all cash obtained by the cooperatives from the sale of grain and legumes in 1938.[9] The distributions in the form of produce are, however, more important to the members because the purchasing power of cash is often low and uncertain. Collective farms which produced little more than 0.5% of agricultural output in 1927-8 produced 63% in 1938. During the German invasion some 98,000 collectives were partly or wholly destroyed, but the government has largely restored them.

The Russian government also relied for a time on Associations of Peasant Farmers for the Joint Cultivation of the Land (*toz*) consisting of members who often carried on considerable production outside the *toz*, but who contributed land and draft animals and cooperated in production. Part of the proceeds of the operation were shared according to property contributions. In 1929, 62% of all collective farms were *toz*.[10] Resting in part upon a capitalist principle, the *toz* was accepted during the New Economic Policy, but subsequently virtually eliminated. But such associations have also been introduced in Poland and Hungary for collective plowing and sowing.

Producers' cooperatives now account for the bulk of agricultural pro-

---

[8] Baykov, *op. cit.*, 311.
[9] *Ibid.*, 312.
[10] Baykov, *op. cit.*, 191n, 495.

duction in all the areas taken over by Russia, e.g., in Latvia, Estonia, and Lithuania, and in the areas taken over from Finland, Czechoslovakia, and Rumania. The countries in eastern Europe under Russian political control since 1945 all aim at the collectivization of agriculture, the Cominform having prescribed the elimination of the *kulak* class in 1948, after the dispute with Yugoslavia. Policy in Yugoslavia, moreover, has been similar to that in Russian controlled areas. The methods of forming peasants into collectives follow in general a common pattern, namely, lower income taxes than for individual farmers, loans to collective farmers, lower charges for the hire of state tractors, cancelling past obligations for deliveries of produce to the state, relatively high pay in produce per labor hour and, finally, the deportation of resisting "kulaks." But disastrous Russian experience with speedy collectivization and peasant resistance in many countries has somewhat moderated the pressure and induced resort to temporary conciliatory devices. In Poland, Rumania, Czechoslovakia and Albania the government promised not to collectivize the land it distributed among the peasants when the large estates were subdivided. But in Yugoslavia such land must be farmed collectively. Some east European governments have provided that members contributing land to collectives may receive rents or a share of produce for the land (above their share for their labor) (e.g., Bulgaria, Poland, Hungary, and Yugoslavia). Bulgaria, Hungary and Yugoslavia have provided that members may withdraw from cooperatives after a few years (in 1950 a number were seeking to withdraw in Bulgaria). But members cannot recover their former holdings and run the risk of receiving less productive land. These countries provide tractors and place great emphasis on the use of labor-days as a basis for distributing produce. But the percentage of tillable land in collectives at the end of 1950 remained small: Bulgaria 50%, Yugoslavia 22%, Czechoslovakia 14%, Hungary 7%, and Rumania 23%, and little in Poland,[11] where serious resistance induced less stringent sanctions than elsewhere. Since 1950 the campaign to collectivize has been intensified and collective farms have rapidly increased, but these countries remain at different points along the road to collectivization.

The Chinese Socialist government is also committed to ultimate collectivization. In 1953, 42% of the peasant population belonged to temporary or year-round "labor mutual aid" organizations pooling labor, capital and equipment, but less than 1% to producers' cooperatives. The government aimed, however, at bringing 20% of rural households into producers' cooperatives by the end of 1957.[12] The members of these cooperatives retain ownership of their land, animals, and equipment and receive a share of cooperative output for their use as well as for the member's labor. Similar cooperative farms are being established in Formosa.

[11] *For. Agric.*, April 17, 1951; U.N., *Progress in Land Reform*, 248.
[12] U.N., *World Econ. Rep.*, 1952-3, 53.

Wherever land holdings are too small to permit economical cultivation, because of recent redistributions of land or for other reasons, governments seeking increased productivity are compelled to look for ways of increasing the size of operating units. Some have considered the producers' cooperative. In Puerto Rico the government, having taken over land from large corporations, has established farms of 100 to 500 acres, each under a manager. The workers each have an individual plot of one to three acres, but work on the land for wages and a share of profit. In 1949 there were some 48 farms under this "Proportional Profits Farms Scheme," almost all of which were successfully producing sugar.[13] In Mexico, as a result of the land reforms prescribed in the constitution of 1917, land was granted to village communities (*ejido*), and where the land is irrigated, it is farmed collectively. Some such collective farms exist in Saskatchewan, Sweden, Italy, British Guiana, Jamaica,[14] and India.[15] In Israel, however, cooperative farms (*Moshav Shitufi*) very similar in organization to the Russian, cultivated over 3% of the cultivable land in 1951 and were increasing in number.[16] A few similar experiments in South Africa have been unsuccessful.[17]

The producers' cooperative permits a larger scale of organization than individual farming and may, for this reason, be more efficient. But the incentive to individual work is diminished because the reward of the individual depends more on the effectiveness of the work of the members as a group than upon any one of them.[18] Where, however, as in the Russian and east European cooperatives, the produce is allotted somewhat on the basis of piecework, incentives are somewhat strengthened. But agricultural output in Russia is probably more influenced by state action (Ch. 8) than by the producers'-cooperative type of organization.

Consumers' cooperatives appear never to have engaged in agricultural production. Communal organization of agricultural production also has made little progress even in Russia. It is regarded as the highest form of collective production, but too high to be acceptable to the rural population at present. There is, however, a small number of communes. All their members are pledged to complete collectivization of their individual property. They work and consume on a basis of equality, irrespective of their contributions of property or labor. In Israel, however, there were some 213 communes (*kibbutz*) in 1951 containing about 67,000 persons and cultivating about 49% of the cultivable land. There were also 82

---

[13] U.N., *Land Reform*, 23, *Progress in Land Reform*, 86.

[14] U.N., *Land Reform*, 59-82. *For. Agric.*, Sept. 1951, U.N. *Progress in Land Reform*, 244.

[15] India: Cooperative Planning Commission *Report*, 27, 30; Famine Inquiry Commission, *Final Report*, 513, 517.

[16] Keen, *Agricultural Development of the Middle East*, 25; Warriner, *op. cit.*, 68.

[17] Union of South Africa: Director of Native Agriculture, *Annual Report*, 1944-5, 17.

[18] U.N., *Rural Progress through Cooperatives*, Ch. 9.

cooperative villages (*Moshav Ovdim*) cultivating 15% of the cultivable land, but the land was operated on a family basis, although produce was sold and supplies were bought cooperatively. In primitive societies land is often owned communally (Ch. 16), but in many, cultivation is individual, crops being the property of the individual cultivator subject to family obligations (e.g., the duty of the wife or wives to supply the husband with food).

Governments have nowhere socialized all agriculture, not even in Russia. Many operate experiment stations and model farms, but with the object of improving agriculture in general, even where it is individualistically organized. In Russia, farms operated by managers appointed by the state, using wage labor, have never produced a large proportion of all agricultural produce (9.3% in 1938). After the Revolution some such farms were established on large estates taken over from the previous government, the church, and private owners. They have produced chiefly meat products, sugar beets, cotton, tea, hops, and grain. In general their yield has been less than on the previous estate and on producers' cooperatives and not above that on peasant farms. But they have contributed to increasing grain output by using new land for grain crops. Their output has been held down by the quality of their land and their management.[19] Their total acreage fell during the 1930s, some being reduced in size and others liquidated.

Governments have operated agricultural enterprises in other countries. The Netherlands East Indies government owned cinchona plantations. Turkish state farms produce tobacco and figs. The British government, through the Overseas Food Corporation (financed and operated by the Ministry of Food), experimented in the large-scale mechanized production of peanuts in East Africa. But after producing an initial crop worth £100,000 at a cost of £600,000 in 1949-50, the operation was sharply curtailed and converted in part to cattle production.[20] Another British government enterprise, the Colonial Development Corporation, attempted to develop a large poultry farm in Gambia, West Africa. The British government also formed a corporation to take over former German-owned banana, rubber, palm oil, cocoa, coffee, and tea plantations in the Cameroons, the profits from which go to the development of that country.[21]

Governments operate a large and increasing proportion of all forest lands. Britain suffered a serious timber shortage during the war of 1914-

---

[19] Ladejinsky, "Soviet State Farms," *Pol. Sci. Quar.* March 1938, 65. Baykov, *op. cit.*, 327, 332.

[20] U.K., *The Colonial Empire, 1939-47* (Cmd. 7167), 83; U.K., *A Plan for the Mechanized Production of Ground Nuts in East and Central Africa*, 1947 (Cmd. 7030); U.K., *The Future of the Overseas Food Corporation* (Cmd. 8125), 1951.

[21] U.K., *The Colonial Empire 1939-47* (Cmd. 7167) 83. A similar corporation has been set up in the trust territory of Tanganyika.

18, and the government established a Forestry Commission which planted some 370,000 acres of timber from 1919-39. After 1945, it was authorized to plant a further 500,000 acres by 1955, and to aim at 5 million acres by 1989. A yield of 3% is expected on the investment, but planting has been slower than was planned.[22] In the U.S.A., the federal government parcelled out much of its timber in land grants to railroad and other corporations, states, and individuals, and the states allowed much of their public domain to pass into private hands. But this policy has now been reversed: by 1930 about 21% of the forest lands of the country were owned by the federal, state, county, and municipal governments, 90% of this publicly held land being in the hands of the federal government. Lands have been abandoned to governments as the timber has been cut.

Agricultural activities are only occasionally undertaken by mixed government and private bodies. In the Gezira, south of Khartoum in the Sudan, the government constructed a dam on the Nile and an irrigation system to make land cultivable. Individual cultivators came to work, but under the supervision of two private corporations which ginned and marketed cotton. Of the cotton produced, the government received 40% (the proceeds of which went to defray the cost of the dam), the cultivators 40%; and the managing corporation 20%. Other crops in the rotation, however, belong wholly to the cultivators. But in 1950 the government took over the functions of the corporations.[23]

B. Combinations of Functions within Agricultural Production Units

The variety of functions performed by a production unit affects its efficiency and often the prices received for its produce. The variety of functions differs according to (1) the combination of agricultural and non-agricultural activities, (2) the variety of agricultural products, and (3) the extent of vertical integration.

1. COMBINATION OF AGRICULTURAL AND OTHER PRODUCTION

Agricultural and non-agricultural production are combined within a single unit when the family is self-sufficient. Though such independent families exist in some remote areas, they are rare. Usually some things must be obtained from outside the household and often outside the local group (particularly salt and metals). In this modified form, self-sufficiency occurs in large parts of India and China, Central and East Africa, and among the Indian populations of Latin America. This organization limits the scale of production to what the family can handle. If it produces all it needs and there is much variety in its needs, the scale of production of each product must be small. Typically, it uses little equipment, and pro-

---

[22] *Economist,* July 16, 1949.
[23] Keen, *Agricultural Development of the Middle East,* 18; U.N., *Land Reform,* 35.

duction is likely to be inefficient in relation to larger, more specialized units. But in some remote regions the cost of transportation offsets the advantage of lower cost of production on a larger scale, at distant points.

Agricultural and non-agricultural production, both for the market, are combined where the rural population spends part of its time in craft production or home industry (as it does in a few parts of the U.S.A., in Sweden, Russia, Germany, China, Japan, Czechoslovakia, and many other countries). The combination may result from some members of the family producing craft goods, or from most of the family doing so in periods of low demand for labor in agriculture. In countries in the early stages of development, workers may leave their families on the land and depart to work in factories or mines, returning to the land for seeding and harvesting (e.g., in India, South Africa, and parts of Latin America). Where the demand for agricultural labor fluctuates seasonally the labor of workers who would otherwise be unemployed during some seasons is thus utilized. Furthermore, some members of the family who might be underemployed in agriculture thus add to national income. Where agricultural methods cannot be changed, and land holdings are not large enough to permit efficient use of existing technology, these arrangements increase national income. Although productivity may be low in both agricultural and non-agricultural work, supplementation of income from agriculture by income from craft production permits the family to survive with less land or less efficient use of it than if the family specialized in agriculture.

But the combination may be incompatible with more efficient production both in agricultural and in other pursuits. If industrial products begin to compete with craft products they destroy not only craft production but the agricultural production dovetailed with it. This happened when industrially produced textiles appeared in Britain in the late 18th century and in India in the 19th century.[24]

2. Variety of Agricultural Products

The combination of single product agriculture with the self-subsistent family or group is possible only where the family can subsist on a single product. However, the Masai in East Africa produce only cattle and live on a diet consisting mostly (but not wholly) of milk, blood, and meat. Most specialized farming is for the market. There are almost single-product units among the dairy farms in New Zealand, where the climate, permitting the growth of grass for almost eleven months in the year, makes it unnecessary to combine the growth of fodder crops with dairy farming. Lamb producers, however, produce meat and wool. Dairy farmers in Holland are fairly highly specialized, although many produce pork as well as butter. Some chicken farms in the U.S.A. are in effect specialized factories, and most plantations specialize on a single crop. Such specialization

---

[24] India: Famine Inquiry Commission, *Final Report*, 81.

is efficient only for certain types of crop; even then producers may diversify to minimize the fluctuations of income due to fluctuations in the output or price of one crop.

Mixed farming combining arable farming and animal husbandry is typical of much of the U.S.A. and western Europe. It reduces costs when the farm is a long distance from the market because low-value grass and fodder crops can be converted at the farm into higher-value meat and dairy products, which can more easily carry high freight costs to distant markets. The use of animal manure as a fertilizer also increases yield of other crops. Such mixed farming requires, however, a market with sufficient purchasing power to buy meat and dairy products. Mixed farming is possible only in some climates; not, for instance, where there is a hot rainless season (as in much of the Middle East).[25] Finally, it calls for considerable skill in management.

Variety of vegetable products is necessary in the economically self-contained family if it wishes to enjoy variety in consumption, but many such family units have sought little variety, e.g., in the Far East, or Latin America. The African native villager produces very little but maize in the southern part of Africa and millet in the north in spite of strenuous government campaigns to induce increases in garden produce. Producers for the market may be forced to diversify, however, if the same crop cannot be continuously grown on the same land and if they wish to reduce costs by avoiding fallowing.

3. Scope of Vertical Integration

The full sequence of processes involved in agricultural production includes the assembly of means of production, cultivation, harvesting, processing, and distribution (including transport and marketing). Only in self-sufficient households is the whole range, as well as consumption, performed within one group. Most agricultural units undertake only some of the activities in the sequence. They then operate, in capitalist countries, within limits set by markets for means of production and for produce. Their efficiency depends not only on the organization of their own operations but on the limitations placed on them by these markets.

a. Production Restricted to Harvesting

Some primitive peoples obtain a fair amount of their subsistence by gathering cocoanuts, berries, and herbs, and by hunting. But such activities are sometimes aimed at supplying a market. Until about 1905, for instance, practically all the rubber marketed was obtained by native workers who tapped wild trees in Brazil, Peru, and the Congo, and brought the latex to collecting centers. The corporation operating in the

---

[25] Keen, B. A., *The Agricultural Development of the Middle East*, vii; Warriner, D., *Land and Poverty in the Middle East*, 4. Twentieth-century techniques of dry farming may, however, be more appropriate.

Congo is said to have practiced incredible cruelties upon the natives to force the collection of rubber—in Peru, natives were virtually enslaved. But soon after 1905 rubber began to be cultivated in Ceylon, Malaya, and the Dutch East Indies, and now virtually none of the normal supply is wild. Gum arabic is collected in the hot season in the southern Sudan by tapping a variety of acacia tree. It is then sold to dealers in the towns. Somewhat similar activities survive on a small scale in most countries. Wild rice and berries are collected in the U.S.A., where there is also hunting. These activities involve the minimum of resort to the market for resources. The collector typically supplies his own labor and simple tools and may pay a fee for access to the crop. If he has a pecuniary interest he will produce if the proceeds of the crop, less his costs, provide a better income than any other available use of his labor. But the quality and quantity of the crop (collected or not) is subjected to no human control.

b. Production Involving Cultivation

When agricultural units engage in cultivation their production is influenced by the terms on which they obtain the means of production and those on which they sell their product.

i. The Acquisition of the Means of Production

Knowledge of methods of production is a matter of tradition and slow change over much small-scale agriculture (Ch. 5). In the more advanced countries, however, it results from research, much but not all of which is financed by governments and made available without charge. Plantations and large agricultural enterprises pay for knowledge as part of the remuneration of managers.

Access to capital varies widely with the total supply of capital, the means of channelling it into agriculture (Ch. 22), and opportunities for using it. In the Middle East, India, the Far East and much of Latin America, little capital is used in small-scale agriculture. But in North America and northwest Europe, more capital is used because it is cheaper and the means of channelling it into agriculture more efficient. Equipment may be purchased on mortgage, and much is owned by production units. Although they cannot always keep it in full use, they are sure of access to the equipment at all times. Equipment which is expensive and less frequently used may, however, be rented for the period of use, as combine-harvesters are in the western parts of the U.S.A. and Canada. Some farm equipment is similarly rented in New Zealand and Australia. Cooperative ownership of equipment by a group of producing units is feasible, but uncommon, because the demands of the members for the use of the equipment often conflict. It has, however, recently developed in France, Denmark, Finland, Sweden, Norway, the Netherlands, Belgium, Italy, West Germany, and Britain.[26]

In Russia and eastern Europe and on a small scale in China, governments provide equipment as a central feature of the organization of agriculture. Mechanization was necessary in order to free labor for industry, but the shortage of industrial facilities for producing equipment necessitated arrangements for economical use. As producers' cooperatives are frequently not large enough to keep equipment in full use, the government established tractor stations that maintain tractors and provide mechanical personnel, the tractors being operated by the members of the cooperative. The stations (now some 9000) participate in formulating the production programs of the collectives (partly to ensure that they are compatible with the equipment available). The collective must carry out improvements specified by the station, and the collective may not sell farm animals without the permission of the station. In return for full service, the stations take some 25% of the gross output of grain and a proportion of other crops serviced.

Access to labor influences agricultural production through the cost and efficiency of the labor. The producer may rely on his own labor. But on larger individually controlled farms in the U.S.A. and western Europe, and on plantations, labor is hired. Assembling and supervising labor is not costly in small units, but comes to be important in large ones. On plantations and in the cooperatives in Russia and eastern Europe, a gang system is usually used (with an element of piecework on the cooperatives). But in many parts of the world large land holdings are rented in small plots on a share-cropping system that gives some incentive to workers.

Land is of such central significance in agriculture that the terms upon which primary producers obtain access to land have a serious effect on agricultural efficiency.

Communal ownership of land means that the terms of access are decided by the chief, the tribal council, or the government. Where land is plentiful, access may be relatively free and "patch agriculture" prevail. Where the land supply is small in relation to population (as on some of the native reserves in East and South Africa) the general objective in allocating land is equity. Government ownership of land is the modern version of communal ownership in larger societies. The government in Russia, for instance, allocates land and prescribes the conditions under which it may be used as the king did in feudal societies (Ch. 16).

Private ownership of land prevails over much of the world. Production units may then obtain access to land by buying, renting, or inheriting it. The combination of ownership and cultivation is characteristic of most plantations and *haciendas* (in Spain and Latin America), large estates in

---

[26] "Cooperative Mechanization in France, the Netherlands and England and Wales," *Farm Economist*, Aug.-Dec. 1949; U.N., *Progress in Land Reform*, Ch. 10.

eastern Europe in the 19th century, and large estates in the ancient world. Owner-operation is not, however, confined to large units. Many small-scale farmers in Europe and North America cultivate land which they own, although the land may be mortgaged. In the U.S.A. 61.3% of all farms were cultivated by their owners in 1940 (compared with 71.6% in 1890). Of all the farms, 34.5% were mortgaged in 1940, the total mortgages being about 30% of the total value of all land excluding buildings. In England, 33% of the land and 35% of the farms were owned and cultivated by the same person in 1941.[27] Practically all farms are owner-operated in Denmark, Finland, and Ireland, and 92% in Norway. In the western part of Germany free land-owning peasants have frequently owned and operated 50 to 250 acres. There is some small scale owner-operation in Egypt[28] and India.[29]

Owner-operation generally maximizes the inducement to improve the land and equipment, since the resulting benefits accrue to those who make the improvements. But opportunity to improve is also necessary; in Egypt and India many owner-operated holdings are so small, and their proprietors so poor, that they cannot improve.[30] Ownership also reduces the mobility of the cultivator where land is not quickly salable. Opportunity to borrow on land permits owner-operation when the owner does not have enough capital to pay for the land, but the resulting fixed financial obligations for interest, and possibly principal, render him more vulnerable to financial pressure than the full owner.

Owners of land may, however, lease it to others for use. The terms of leases affect the way land is used. But where landowners are self-interested, they might be expected to maximize their probable income from the land by charging the highest possible rent and designing the other terms of the lease so as to maximize the tenant's ability to pay. Large landholders might be expected to be more skilled in these matters than small. The method of setting the payment for the use of land directly affects the incentives of the tenant, the chief types of payment being labor rents, produce rents, cash rents, and sharecropping tenancies.

Labor rents require the tenant to work for a prescribed period on the landowner's land without wages in return for permission to cultivate some land for his own use. A relic of the feudal system, such tenancies survive mostly in Latin America (in Bolivia, Chile, Colombia, Ecuador, Peru, and Venezuela), and are not generally associated with agricultural efficiency or progress. Produce rents requiring payment of a fixed amount of specified produce have been customary in Burma, Japan, many parts of India, and in the rich rice areas of central and south China, mostly where annual

[27] British Information Service, *Britain Speeds the Plough.*
[28] Bonné, *op. cit.,* 122.
[29] India: Famine Inquiry Commission, *Final Report,* 258-264.
[30] Keen, *op. cit.,* 13; U.N., *Rural Progress through Cooperatives,* 19.

variations in crop are not large (as with wet rice cultivation). The landowner is protected against inflation. All increases in output would go to the tenant but tenancies are usually too short for this aspect to be important.

Cash rental tenancies require the landowner to provide only the land and fixed improvements, the tenant being expected to maintain the productivity of the land. Tenancies are not common among plantation companies, which typically own their own land. In the Netherlands East Indies, however, the colonial government prohibited land purchases by non-natives. It took title to unsettled land and rented some of it for 75 years to plantations. But plantations also rent land for short periods from private owners for sugar and tobacco (the rents being regulated by the government). Among smaller farmers, cash tenancies are common in the western world. In the U.S.A., tenant farming was relatively unimportant until about 1880, but has increased since then: in 1940, 23% of all tenants were paying cash rents.[31] In England, about 66% of the land is cultivated by tenants most of whom pay cash rents, although tenancy declined as a result of high farm profits from 1914 to 1920. In Sweden, about 27% of the arable land is cultivated by tenants, in Belgium about 67%, and in Spain 22%. Cash rentals are unimportant (although they exist) in Asia, India, and the Far and Middle East, but are common in Egypt (partly owing to the expansion of cotton production), and in Arab Palestine.[32]

Cash tenancies stimulate efficient production. Once the rent is set, the tenant takes all risks of fluctuation in the amount and price of the produce, but is free to make his own production decisions within any limits set by the state, provided he does not exhaust the land. The inducement to improve the land depends not on whether the tenancy is for a cash rental, but on the length of the lease and any provisions in the lease, or in the general law of the country, requiring the owner to compensate the tenant for improvements unexhausted at the end of the tenancy.

A large proportion of all the cultivators throughout the world obtain access to land through share tenancies. The landowner supplies the land, and, sometimes, part of the seed and part of the motive power (horse, mule, bullock or tractor). The cultivator provides all the labor and usually the seed, and any motive power and fertilizer used. The owner receives a prearranged share of the crop, depending upon what he provides, the demand for the use of land in relation to the supply of it, and local tradition.

In the U.S.A., sharecroppers are share tenants to whom landowners furnish all work animals or tractor power, but they are officially reported only for the southern states. In 1940, 13% of all owners and tenants were

---

[31] U.S., *Graphic Survey of Farm Tenancy in the U.S.* 1948, 3.
[32] Bonné, *op. cit.*, 128-134.

share tenants and another 9% were sharecroppers. The typical sharecropping arrangement in the southern states is for the tenant to obtain one-half of the crop unless he supplies some equipment, in which case he may obtain as much as two-thirds. Sharecropping is unimportant in Britain, but occurs in New Zealand and Australia, mostly, however, as a stepping stone to owner-operation in dairy and wheat farming.

Share tenancies appeared in continental Europe (mostly in the south) when the feudal system began to disintegrate in the 12th and 13th centuries. Tenants received one-half to one-tenth of the crop.[33] Almost 75% of the land in western and central France was held on share tenancies (*métayer*) in the 18th century, rents ranging from half to one-third of the crop, but they had almost all been replaced by cash tenancies by 1900. The system has survived in Spain, and in Italy (*comparticipazione*, *mezzadria*) in the Po Valley and in the central and southern provinces, rents ranging from one-half to four-fifths of the produce.[34]

Sharecropping is also prevalent in the Middle East (in Egypt, Turkey, Arab aPlestine, Syria, Lebanon, Iraq, and Iran). Leases are typically for one year; rents range from one-half to four-fifths of the crop. In Egypt, if the farmer provides the working capital he gets one-half the crop; but if the land owner provides the working capital, the cultivator may obtain only one-fifth of the crop. Land is often leased only for one crop cycle and never for more than two or three years. Sometimes the landlord takes all the cotton crop, and occasionally as much as three-quarters of the wheat crop. Landowners are responsible for regulating water, drainage, and rotation of crops, although the expense is often met by the tenant. The landowner supervises the gathering of the crop and deposits it in his own warehouse to make sure of his rent, and "usually takes full advantage of his knowledge of price fluctuations in dealing with his tenants."[35] In India there are no statistics of sharecropping, but it has predominated in Sind, applied to about half the land in Punjab (where some small landowners also work the land of others on shares), and to about 20% in Bengal, but has been relatively uncommon in the United Provinces, the Central Provinces, and Bihar. The cultivator usually retains half the crop, except on land irrigated from wells, where he keeps one-third.[36] In Japan in the time of the Shogunate (until 1868), individual farmers delivered from one-third to two-thirds but usually one-half of their produce to local lords.[37] In 1939, 70% of cultivators were tenants,

---

[33] Turner "Economic Discontent in Medieval Western Europe," *Tasks of Economic History*, 1948, 85.

[34] *The World Today*, June 1949, 255.

[35] Issawi, *Egypt: An Economic and Social Analysis*, 75; Bonné, *op. cit.*, 129, 130, 134; Warriner, *op. cit.*, 107; *For. Agric.*, Dec. 1950.

[36] India: Famine Inquiry Commission, *Final Report*, 265 ff.

[37] Allen, G. C., *A Short Economic History of Modern Japan*, 11.

compared with only about 20% in 1867, paying 50-60% of their crop in rent. In China share-renting was formerly most common in the northern wheat region, the landlord's share being usually more than 50%, although over 75% of the peasants were full owners, compared with less than 40% in the rice areas of the center and south.[38] In the Philippines, 30 to 60% of all farmers have been tenants, and hemp has been produced under sharecropping leases.[39] The majority of the 2 million farms in Brazil are also held on a sharecropping tenure, especially in cotton-producing areas. In Argentina (1937), much wheat and corn was produced under similar tenures.

Share-renting as such protects the landowner against inflation and the tenant against shrinking crops or prices (to some extent). But it reduces the incentive to improve the land because only part of the reward goes to the person making the effort or investment. Landowners who improve could raise their share in the crop without hurting the tenant, but usually do not. The system persists because of a general lack of a progressive spirit among cultivators (due to their poverty), the relative prosperity of landowners (due to the relative scarcity of land), and often a generally conservative tradition. The system applies production incentives to workers while minimizing demands on owners for active land management. But the system has very different results where farming is more prosperous. In the eastern half of the U.S.A. and in New Zealand and Australia, like any renting arrangement, it often provides an opportunity for the cultivator with little capital to make a start.

The relations between landowners and tenants influence production also through the influence exerted by the landowner on the choice of crop, methods of cultivation, the sharing of the benefits of improvements to the land, the provision of capital, and the length of leases. Where land is held in quantities large in relation to the size of the typical producing units, landowners might be expected to have advantages in these respects over the owner-operator. Some such advantages have been achieved in the U.S.A., where in 1934, 124 owners held 97,618 farms.[40] Some have provided capital and managerial help, and in general farming has been progressive. In Britain, large holdings were not uncommon in the 18th and 19th centuries, and many were rented. Many landowners supplied capital (for buildings, drainage and the like) and improved farming practices. Leases were frequently long (typically seven, fourteen, and twenty-one years). Since the influx of cheap food from the American continent in about 1870, however, the number of large private estates has declined and gross rentals are substantially lower than in 1870, while the proportion of rent necessary for maintenance has risen greatly. There are now

---

[38] Lee, "The Heart of China's Problem," *Jour. Farm Econ.* (1948), 259.

[39] *For. Agric.*, Nov. 1949, 250.

[40] *Payments Made Under the Agricultural Adjustment Program*, 74th Congress, 2nd Session, Sen. Doc. 274, 1936.

more annual leases, but they carry general assurance of fixity of tenure, freedom of cultivation, and compulsory compensation by the landlord for the unexpired value of improvements made by the tenant. Large land holdings are common neither in France nor Belgium. But in many other countries large landowners have not devised relations with tenants calculated to improve efficiency.

In Italy 0.5% of landowners own 36% of all privately held land. Some owners in the north, particularly in the Po Valley, have made heavy investments in land (often for irrigation), some of which is cultivated by tenants, some under the supervision of managers. But in central Italy, where the large landowners typically rent land in very small pieces, agriculture is technically backward, and the landowner is generally a reactionary force, and, consequently, the target of political opposition and of proposals to divide the land among the peasants. Worse conditions prevail in south Italy and Sicily.[41] In the Middle East,[42] especially in Egypt and Iran, landowners are passive rent receivers. The British introduced the large estate in some parts of India in the 18th century in the hope that a class of larger landowners would become as actively interested in agriculture as the corresponding group in Britain.[43] But landowners in general have become rentiers[44] as they have in Pakistan, Burma, and Japan (prior to the redistribution of land after 1946), and in Argentina and the West Indies. In these countries leases are frequently too short to give the tenant much assurance that he will reap the benefit of any improvements, although tenancies are more secure in fact than in law (e.g., in India).[45] Land is leased in plots too small to be cultivated except by primitive methods. Sharecropping tenancies being the commonest type in these areas, and rural poverty prevalent in all of them, the form of tenure has been blamed for the inefficiency of agriculture.[46] But the underlying cause is usually pressure of population upon the land, which causes high land rents and the intensive use of labor rather than capital. Share rents are generally lower in Latin America than in the Middle East, India, and the Far East, where the pressure of population on land is greater.[47] The substitution of cash for share rents would not improve conditions much; indeed, if full economic rents were charged, the tenants might be worse

---

[41] *Economist*, Dec. 21, 1946.

[42] Bonné, *State and Economics in the Middle East*, 122.

[43] Sir Thomas Munro (1761-1827) as Governor of Madras actively opposed this policy. He successfully defended the *ryotowari* system which kept land in small plots, the same person being landlord, farmer and worker (Wrench, *The Restoration of the Peasantries*, 51).

[44] Famine Inquiry Commission, *Final Report*, 254 to 277, 450.

[45] Famine Inquiry Commission, *Report*, 266, 370.

[46] Keen, *The Agricultural Development of the Middle East*, 37; Warriner, *Land and Poverty in the Middle East*, 120.

[47] U.N., *Land Reform*, 16.

off than they were as share croppers.[48] But efforts to improve methods of production would be frustrated unless present tenures were abolished.

There is, however, some experimentation with more appropriate relations between owners and tenants in the West Indies and the Philippines. In Trinidad, the government controls the annual contracts between the sugar growers and the mills. In Fiji, the sugar mills, which own the land, developed partnerships with the cultivators. This, however, caused difficulty during the war of 1939-45, with the result that the government stepped in to control them. Some owners of land in the Philippines strictly regulated the seeds used and methods of cultivation of hemp before 1939. The share of crop taken as rent was reduced but incomes from rent rose.

ii. The Disposal of the Produce

The value of the net output of primary units depends not only on the prices paid for the means of production but also on the price received for the produce, unless the produce is consumed within the family producing unit (as it is in many underdeveloped countries). The produce may be sold for local consumption after little or no processing in village or town markets, where prices depend on the extent of competition and sometimes on custom. Where processing is necessary, it may be done by small producers if it is simple. But more complicated processing requiring a larger scale of operations is combined with production where it also is on a fairly large scale, as on plantations producing tea, coffee, palm oil, sisal, and rubber. Small rubber producers processing their output usually receive low prices because of poor processing. Otherwise small producers sell to independent processors. Cotton is usually sold to independent ginners in the U.S.A. and Pakistan, wheat and rice to independent millers, sugar if grown on a small scale is sold to *centrales*, and some small-scale rubber production to separate processors.

Where produce is assembled for sale at a distance, it may be bought by a local merchant for resale (e.g., from smaller plantations and share croppers in the U.S.A. and most small producers in Africa, the Middle East, India, Malaya, and China). These merchants may also conduct other activities. In the sharecropping areas of the U.S.A., some are landowners. They may be processors: merchants operate rice mills in Malaya and cotton gins in some areas. Merchanting is also frequently combined with the retail distribution of consumer goods, which requires a scattering of small establishments at points at which produce can be collected. The merchants frequently give consumer credit, particularly to finance the cultivator through the season, thus supplying the working capital for agricultural production. In the Belgian Congo, however, peasants have been required to sell export crops to the concession companies for process-

---

[48] India: Famine Inquiry Commission *Report*, 266.

ing and export.[49] Larger producers whose crops are sold at a distance typically sell on commission (e.g., many producers in North America and western Europe, and the larger plantations, coffee *fincas,* and the like). Where the product is quoted on an organized market (coffee, tea, rubber, cotton, and cocoa, for instance), there is an easy check upon the operations of the agent. But some plantation production is further integrated with manufacturing. Some tire companies in the U.S.A. own rubber plantations in Liberia, Sumatra, and Latin America. The United Africa Company, a subsidiary of Unilever Ltd. in England, operates plants in England which utilize the produce from its vegetable oil plantations in West Africa. The United Fruit Company exports bananas and distributes them at wholesale.

The effect of these various arrangements depends on the extent to which they provide for economical performance of each function, and on the way in which rewards are distributed among the various functions. If economical performance calls for marked differences of scale in production, processing, and marketing, integration within a single unit is uneconomical. But even if each operation is conducted on an economical scale, the markets through which produce passes from one operation to the next are often not competitive. Monopoly profits at any level cause no rise in price of the ultimate product, if price is competitively determined, unless the reduced price paid by the oligopolist when he buys reduces output. Furthermore these monopolistic buying prices may persist although monopoly profits are eliminated by high costs due to inefficiency or an increase in the number of dealers. These problems are not serious for sellers on organized markets or even in many village markets. But merchants often enjoy local monopolies and deal with small producers unskilled in marketing. The seller in debt to the merchant for supplies cannot, moreover, take advantage of such competition as exists. Where the merchant is of a different national origin from the producer, frictions are intensified (e.g., between native producers and the Indian merchants in east and central Africa, Syrians in west Africa, and Chinese merchants in Java and Malaya). But it is not clear how many such merchants exploit small producers, or how much. Their profit margins or their costs may be excessive although they often incur considerable bad debts through advance financing of small poverty-stricken producers. There is often, however, considerable indication of prosperity among merchants. In some areas attempts are being made to solve the problem—by organizing periodic controlled markets to increase competition among buyers, by establishing marketing cooperatives, or by providing for marketing

---

[49] Pendered, *A Report on a Visit to Certain African Colonies to Study Native Production and Cooperation,* Part I, 1948 (Southern Rhodesia) (hereinafter referred to as *"Pendered Report"*) 5.

by the state (Ch. 8). Processors, however, sometimes exert pressure on producers to increase their efficiency. Sugar mills frequently buy cane on the basis of its sucrose content and control the kind of cane grown and its cultivation and harvesting.

C. The Size of Production Units

The scale of production in agriculture affects the cost of production. The most economical scale varies with climate, the nature of the crop, and methods of production.

The only information about the size of production units in many countries is in terms of acreage of land used (not necessarily owned), and it is not all in comparable form. Statistics may show the majority of all holdings to be small but also that most of the land is in large holdings (Tables 18, 19). Although the data are incomplete, the broad outline of differences in the size of farming units is fairly clear. In most tropical and subtropical areas the high ratio of population to land, and the small importance of non-agricultural activities, result in large numbers of very small-scale agricultural operations. In the U.S.A., Britain, Canada, Australia, New Zealand, and South Africa the family farm predominates, but holdings of semi-arid land may be large. In northwestern and central Europe, peasant

TABLE 18

SIZE OF LAND HOLDINGS OF ABOUT 50% OF
LANDHOLDERS IN SELECTED COUNTRIES IN
VARIOUS YEARS FROM 1938 TO 1950*

	Size of Holding (acres or less)	Percentage of holders accounted for
Australia	299	51.7
New Zealand	100	43.7
U.S.A.	100	55.9
Cuba	62.5	69.6
Brazil	50	51
U.K.	20	44.0
Denmark	12.5	42.9
Germany (federal republic)	12.5	61.0
Sweden	12.5	54.5
Switzerland	12.5	57.7
Yugoslavia	12.5	69.1
Mexico	12.5	76.2
Ecuador	12.5	76
Porto Rico	9.0	52.3
Philippines	7.5	71.1
Finland	5.0	43.9
Norway	2.5	45.0
Italy	1.25	53.9
Japan	1.25	40.8
Belgium	1.00	74.6
Egypt	1.00	72.0

* U.N., *Progress in Land Reform,* 3 sq. (Hectare converted at 2.5 acres.)

TABLE 19

SIZE OF LAND HOLDINGS ACCOUNTING FOR ABOUT
50% OF TOTAL FARM AREA IN SELECTED COUNTRIES
IN VARIOUS YEARS FROM 1938 TO 1950*

	Size of Holding (acres or less)	Proportion of farm land accounted for
Australia	100,000	41.4
New Zealand	10,000	69.0
Mexico	1,000	20.5
Brazil	1,000	51.6
U.S.A.	500	46.5
U.K.	500	89.1
Ecuador	500	34.7
Cuba	500	53.0
Porto Rico	260	58.1
U.K.	100	31.5
Denmark	75	60.2
Italy	62.5	55.2
Sweden	50	57.0
Finland	25.0	44.2
Germany (federal republic)	25.0	46.8
Norway	25.0	64.0
Switzerland	25.0	51.2
Belgium	25.0	48.8
Yugoslavia	20.0	57.6
Egypt	20.0	54.0
Philippines	12.5	48.9
Japan	2.5	42.3

* U.N., *Progress in Land Reform*, 3 sq. (Hectare converted at 2.5 acres.)

proprietorship, a smaller version of the family farm, is predominant. But in parts of eastern and southern Europe where land ownership is somewhat concentrated, agricultural operations are very small-scale and often on a sharecropping basis.[50] In Russia, collectivization has enlarged the unit of operation and is now doing the same thing in eastern Europe.

In the Middle East most producing units are small. In Egypt, 72% of all holdings are less than one acre, and 94% less than 5 acres (but account for only 35% of the farm area).[51] In Turkey most units are also small, but many own their land. In Syria, Iraq, and Lebanon, small tenancies are common.[52] In most Indian states, 50% to 80% of holdings are five acres or less, and 30% to 50% two acres or less. In East Bengal in Pakistan the average tenancy is 1.89 acres and the average holding per family 3.4 acres. In Japan in 1950 only 8% of the farm area was in holdings of over 12.5 acres[53] and in China most holdings are small, especially in the wet-rice areas. In Korea, family farms average three acres and in Formosa less than

[50] U.N., *Progress in Land Reform*, 17 ff.

[51] U.N., *Progress in Land Reform*, 30.

[52] Warriner, *op. cit.*, 14, 34, 57, 63, 77; Bonné, *op. cit.*, 129.

[53] U.N., *Progress in Land Reform*, 25, 185.

four.[54] In Java, practically all rice, 90% of the kapok, an increasing part of the rubber, and about 30% of the tea is produced on a small scale, although plantations produce some of the same crops. Similar conditions prevail in Malaya, where most food crops are produced on holdings of two or three acres. In 1929, 45% of all rubber and most copra was also produced by small native producers. Smaller farmers produce rubber with little capital and with labor that would otherwise be unemployed. In Africa, native agriculture is small-scale. In parts of East Africa individual units depend on the amount a woman can cultivate with a hoe; production by the family depends on the number of wives. In French West Africa, Nigeria, and the Gold Coast, agriculture is mostly along the coast and in the hands of small peasant cultivators.[55]

In many parts of Latin America there is no shortage of land, but there are many very small holdings, although a large proportion of the land is in large holdings. In Chile 43% of all holdings are 12.5 acres or less, in Ecuador 76%, in Panama 52%, but in Cuba only 20%. In Haiti there is extreme pressure on the land, and small holdings are numerous. In Mexico, apart from the *ejidal* holdings, 84% of all the farm area was in holdings of over 1250 acres in 1940.[56] In Argentina, 66% of the land is cultivated by small tenants. In Italy and eastern Spain there is much small-scale share cropping. In some parts of Italy, Spain, and Portugal large families operate small farms which they own: in northern Portugal the average land holding is less than 1.25 acres.[57]

The family farm existed in the Roman Republic before wars ruined the cultivators by taking them away from their farms to fight, getting them into debt, and increasing the supply of slaves to compete with them. In Britain, medium-sized and large holdings emerged when the open fields of the feudal system were enclosed in the late 16th and early 17th centuries and again in the late 18th and early 19th centuries. By 1949, 21% of all holdings were of 100 acres or more and accounted for 68% of the farm area in England and Wales.[58] Over 40% of farmers work their land with only their own and their wife's labor. In New Zealand, 31.4% of all holdings are 100 to 320 acres and account for 11.6% of the land, 65% of the area being in holdings of over 1,000 acres (mainly upland used for sheep). In Australia the average wheat farm has 500 to 1,000 acres but only 5% of the farm land was in holdings of less than 1,000 acres in 1948, 80% being in holdings of over 10,000 acres mainly semi-arid and used for sheep and cattle. In South Africa, European farmers operate medium-sized farms which, however, are declining in size owing to the

---

[54] *For. Agric.*, June 1950, Oct. 1950.
[55] U.N., *Progress in Land Reform*, 33.
[56] *Ibid.*, 39, 46, 186.
[57] *Ibid.*, 14.
[58] *Ibid.*, 12.

high rate of multiplication among Afrikaans farmers and their practice of dividing their land among their sons. In the U.S.A. in 1950 the average farm was 215 acres which is 50% larger than in 1910 (and in 1880); 38.4% of all holdings were 100 or more but under 500 acres and accounted for 36.4% of the farm area. But 2.3% of holdings were 1,000 acres and over and accounted for 42.6% of the farm area, farms of under 30 acres being only 1.5% of the total area. In the dairying area of New England the average is 100 acres; in the corn and hog area in the mid-west, 160 acres; and in the wheat-growing area of the great plains, 400 acres. About 75% of the total labor in agriculture is provided by the farmer and his family. In Canada in 1951 47.2% of all holdings were 70 or more but under 240 acres and 2.7% were 1,120 acres and over, the largest farms being in the grain-growing prairie provinces.[59]

Smaller scale operations appeared in western and central Europe when feudal land holding was eliminated by enclosures in the early and middle years of the 19th century (e.g. in Russia and Rumania). In about 1950 90% or more of all farm land in Belgium, Finland, western Germany and Norway and 80% in Sweden was in holdings of less than 125 acres. In Belgium, 75% of all holdings were less than 2.5 acres in 1950, but accounted for only 5% of the farm area. In Denmark, 67% of holdings were 12.5 to 75 acres and accounted for 56% of the farm area. In Norway, 45% of all holdings were less than 2.5 acres, but accounted for only 3.6% of farm area. In Switzerland 97.3% of all holdings were less than 75 acres and included 93% of all farm land. No figures are available for France, but holdings, which were shrinking in the earlier 19th century owing to the inheritance law requiring distribution of land, ceased to shrink after the middle of the century because of (a) the decline in the rate of multiplication of the population and (b) migration to the towns.

Cultivation of 200 acres or more, involving a centrally controlled process and a considerable number of workers, is not new. Large estates existed in Asia Minor and Syria before the 3rd century B.C. and spread thence to Sicily and to Carthage in North Africa. There were fairly large-scale operations in ancient Italy during the 7th and 6th centuries B.C., producing grapes and olives. They gave place to small peasant farming in the 4th and 3rd centuries B.C., but after about 200 B.C. senators debarred from commerce bought land which was reconcentrated in the hands of the aristocracy and worked often by slaves (an important product of the wars). Distant farms were often rented to tenant farmers (*coloni*). In Africa and Egypt senators and imperial freedmen cultivated, employing dispossessed tenants. Large Junker estates were established east of the Elbe in Germany in the early Middle Ages. These *rittergut* were cultivated as centrally managed estates first by serfs, then, after their emancipation, by most of the same people. After about 1880, growth of towns and the improvement of transport sapped their labor supply, and the Junker

[59] *Ibid.*, 2 sq., 186.

families relied increasingly upon foreign (mainly Polish) workers. In 1945 this part of Germany passed under Russian occupation, or to Poland. The Allied Powers declared in Potsdam in 1945 that these estates were to be broken up because their owners had been an essential part of the military class. Subsidies on their crops had enriched them and enabled them to assist the military machine, and they had supported the aggressive, expansionist policies of Germany. The estates have since been redistributed and are in process of collectivization. In the northern U.S.A. large-estate cultivation proved unsuccessful in the colonial period because of the difficulty of attracting a labor supply. Half-servile indentured labor was tried, and wage labor was used in Dutch New York. At present some wheat cultivation is large-scale: there were 260 farms over 100,000 acres in 1945 compared with 160 such units 25 years earlier. 1.2% of all the farm units produced 21.2% of all products,[60] and in 1949 22% of farms accounted for 73% of the value of crops marketed.

Plantations are often large units producing a single crop. In general, they developed to import capital and technical knowledge into tropical and semi-tropical areas to produce export crops, for which a demand was generated by rising incomes in more developed countries, and by cheapening transport and changing industrial technology. They survive in many countries although under considerable adverse criticism. A number have passed under local control. The plantations producing tobacco, indigo, rice, and later cotton in the southern U.S.A. largely disappeared after the emancipation of the slaves, although some continued to be operated with Negro tenants. Plantations still exist mainly in the warm areas of fertile level land in the Mississippi delta (where they produce mostly cotton and sugar), on the Gulf Coast (rice), in the delta of the Colorado River, and in California. Cane sugar plantations are numerous in Florida, Louisiana, Puerto Rico, and Hawaii. Some 11 million acres were cultivated by 39,000 plantations in 1910. The contemporary American plantations do not, however, produce mainly for export. Plantations exist also in the West Indies (particularly Cuba, Puerto Rico, and Jamaica), in Mexico (on the Caribbean coast), in Brazil and Colombia, in East and West Africa, in Hawaii, Ceylon, India, Indo-China, Malaya, and the Dutch East Indies. In Jamaica, Barbados, and the other British islands in the West Indies, most of the land was originally in plantations, but the system declined owing to the increasing price of slaves, insurrections, and, later, the abolition of slavery.

Plantation products are somewhat restricted. Sugar is plantation-cultivated in the U.S.A., Cuba, Puerto Rico, Jamaica, Mexico, Brazil, British and Portuguese Africa, Hawaii, and the Union of South Africa; tobacco in Mexico and British and Portuguese Africa (particularly South-

---

[60] S. E. Johnson and K. L. Bachman, "How Many Farms: How Big?" *The Agricultural Situation*, Vol. 32, 2-3 (1948); Vol. 33, p. 14 (1949).

ern Rhodesia); bananas mainly in Central America; coffee in Brazil and Colombia (but a considerable quantity is also grown on small holdings), Indonesia, Kenya, and Tanganyika in Africa; cacao in Brazil; maguey and hennequin in Mexico; cocoanuts in British and Portuguese Africa (although in many countries they are a small-scale native-crop product); pineapples and rubber in India, Malaya, and the Dutch East Indies (although much is also produced on a small scale); citrus fruits in Southern Rhodesia; and tea in India, Ceylon, and East Africa. Rice is a mechanized plantation crop in the U.S.A., but, typically, not elsewhere. Cacao, formerly a plantation crop, is now almost wholly produced by small farms in West Africa. The large British chocolate manufacturers, disturbed in 1908 by charges that forced labor was used in St. Thomas and Principé, promoted small scale production in Nigeria and the Gold Coast. The state farms in Russia are virtually large nationalized plantations although not always with a single crop, nor producing for export. In 1938 the average state grain farm had 58,000 acres, the dairy and meat farm 71,500 acres and the average sheep farm 270,000 acres.[61]

The *hacienda* in Latin America is a large farming unit usually engaged in mixed farming. Such large units have been common in most parts of South America but are declining somewhat in importance (e.g., as a result of land reforms in Chile). In Argentina there are large cattle- and sheep-raising enterprises. In 1937, 70% of all farm land was in holdings of 3087 acres or more. The largest holdings are on sheep lands in Patagonia; these are usually over 1560 acres, some over 480,000 acres. Less than 2% of the cattle owners owned half the cattle.[62]

In the Middle East a few large-scale, modern agricultural operations exist in the Nile delta; and there are some large estates in Turkey.[63] In Iraq a company (Latifiyah Estates)—holding some 60,000 acres of irrigated land producing cereals, sesame, millet and some cotton and sheep—formerly operated on plantation lines, but has turned to tenant farming, owing to a deficiency of capital and to the apathy of workers unused to daily-wage employment and requiring too much supervision. The company now provides mechanical threshing and cultivation to tenants, who pay about 50% of their produce as rent for the land. Large estates produce part of the date crop in Iraq.[64]

In Tunisia some 3000 land owners own about 2.4 million acres of land (about 10% of all the cultivable area). A little less than half this area is owned by French colonists practicing large-scale dry farming to produce cereals. Their yields are about twice as high as those of the Arab culti-

---

[61] Baykov, *op. cit.*, 333.
[62] U.S. Tariff Commission: *Agricultural, Forest and Pastoral Industries in Argentina*, 12.
[63] Bonné, *State and Economics in the Middle East*, 130.
[64] Keen, *The Agricultural Development of the Middle East*, 29-30.

vators, possibly because the large holders have the richer land and use better methods. Large estates also produce wheat in Algeria, side by side with poor, badly exploited farms and a large landless proletariat. In Libya (Tripolitania and Cyrenaica) after about 1920, the Italian government granted some large sections of land to individual Italians. At first operated in the main as plantations, they were turned over, after 1932, to the settlement of small owners.[65] The large holdings in Australia and New Zealand have already been mentioned (p. 86).

The scale of agricultural operations has been influenced in some countries by government action allocating government land, redistributing private land, establishing settlement schemes with holdings of a standard size, and promoting producers' cooperatives.[66]

Government redistributions of land have frequently resulted in an increase in the number of small units, although where large land holdings had previously been worked by a number of small tenants, there was no necessary change in the scale of production. But the scale of operation was reduced by redistribution in the Baltic states created after 1918. In Russia when the land was nationalized, the size of units often was greatly reduced, but medium-sized units accounted for much of the production until collectivization. Redistributions in Rumania and Bulgaria after 1918 substituted small for large operating units, and those in eastern Europe after 1945 had a similar effect in Hungary, Finland, Yugoslavia, and Czechoslovakia. In Hungary 65% of all land was in holdings of less than 27.4 acres in 1945, and in Yugoslavia 80% of all holdings were less than 15 acres in 1950. But after a few years governments began to collectivize farming in eastern Europe. The land reforms in Mexico have established small-scale farming in place of some of the large centrally-run estates. In Japan the redistribution of land ownership reduced tenancy but increased holdings of 1.25 acres or less from 34% to 41% of all holdings.[67] Most of the land reform laws in the Indian states do not yet limit the size of holdings farmed by their owners. In the main they provide for transfers from owners to existing tenants without change in the size of tenant holdings. But some governments are pressing the combination of small holdings into larger ones.[68]

Few governments have attempted to adjust agricultural operations to an economical size (which is often not known with any certainty). In Europe, some of the Scandinavian countries and Ireland have taken steps in this direction. The Australian state governments in controlling land use divide excessively large farms and consolidate excessively small ones. Leases on crown lands (the predominant form of tenure) are withdrawn when de-

---

[65] *Ibid.*, 30.
[66] U.N., *Progress in Land Reform*, Ch. 6.
[67] Feary, *The Occupation of Japan: Second Phase, 1948-50*, 91.
[68] U.N., *Progress in Land Reform*, 183.

velopment necessitates closer settlement or a change in land use. The state governments have also scheduled marginal wheat lands to be combined to provide holdings of a size economical for mixed farming, with sheep-raising predominating.[69] In Canada, the Prairie Farm Rehabilitation Act, passed in 1935 after a series of drought years, provided that land previously used for grain production but poorly suited to it be converted into larger holdings to be used as community pastures.[70]

The most notable increases in the scale of cultivation have been introduced by the Russian government. The average collective farm in Russia contained about 80 homesteads in 1940, although 25% had 30 families or fewer.[71] In 1950, however, the government eliminated the smaller collectives and reduced the total number by 50% (from 252,000 to 123,-000), more than two-thirds being merged into 60,000 large farms. The government emphasized the need to improve management, reduce administrative costs, and facilitate the use of larger labor brigades. It contemplated collectives of 3,000 farmers living in "agro-towns," which would have reduced the individual plots of the members and made their position very similar to that of the workers on the state farms.[72] Administrative costs have apparently not yet fallen. The government may in fact be concerned with ensuring that managers are politically reliable. But poor progress in agriculture and peasant resistance caused the plan to be abandoned (Ch. 8).

This variety in the scale of operations in itself indicates neither inequalities in efficiency nor adjustment in each country to the optimum scale for each economy and crop. Crops differ in the most economical scale of production. In particular, mixed farming presents problems of management that militate against large operations. Differences in the availability of capital, labor, and knowledge call for different scales of operation for the production of similar crops, capital-intensive operations usually having a larger optimum scale than labor-intensive. But in some countries it would be uneconomical to invest the capital necessary to obtain output per worker as high as is obtained in other countries for the same crop, even if climatic and soil conditions permitted such a level of productivity. The maximum efficiency of which a country is capable may be less than that of another country with different conditions of relative supplies of capital and labor. Much of the small-scale production in poverty-stricken areas is capable of some improvement without fundamental changes in resource supply, but the amount of potential improvement is limited unless these basic conditions can be changed. The production of the same crop in the same country on both a large and a small scale does not neces-

---

[69] U.N., *Progress in Land Reform*, 188.
[70] *Ibid.*, 181.
[71] Baykov, *op. cit.*, 327.
[72] *For. Agric.*, May 1951, 95.

sarily indicate that one is less efficient. Different methods of organization can be equally efficient although it is stated that many of the rubber plantations in Malaya have higher costs than the smaller producers.[73]

The scale of production is, however, not always determined by considerations of productive efficiency. Government action has only occasionally moved the scale of operations toward the optimum. Workers on large enterprises have sought relief from their poverty in ways which may increase their share of output while reducing total output. The large estates in eastern Europe were often efficiently run, but when the land was divided among many small producing units, efficiency fell, notably in eastern Europe after each of the World Wars. Skilled estate managers were replaced by relatively uneducated, unskilled peasants lacking stock and implements (partly due to the war). In Hungary (where the size of holdings was greatly reduced) the acreage of tilled land in 1946 was about equal to that in 1938, but the harvest was less than 50% as great and the government had to import wheat and flour to feed the population. But anticipation of redistribution had already discouraged investment by estate owners, and the decline in efficiency might have been subsequently overcome if the land had not been collectivized. In Hungary, moreover, the great estates organized to produce wheat and timber had been suffering increasingly from the competition from new lands in Canada, Argentina, and Australia, and were temporarily rescued by wartime demands. The distribution of the land and its reorientation to the production of livestock, poultry and dairy products, as in Denmark and Holland, put the land to a better use, which happened incidentally to require a smaller scale of production. Plantation workers have often also objected to working in a large, centrally-organized force. Changes in the distribution of political power increase the opposition to plantations. This is intensified where ownership is foreign and the foreigner can be charged with "milking" the weaker countries in which the plantations are located. Yet the plantation has been one of the few vehicles for introducing capital into the agriculture of underdeveloped areas. Wages have been low, but often because of the relation between the supply of labor and the supply of land. The remuneration of capital has sometimes been high, but partly because of the risks involved, and the risks are increased by political opposition.[74] Collectivization in Russia has increased the scale of agricultural operations but not entirely for the purpose of increasing efficiency, and it is impossible to discover how nearly they have approached the optimum scale; in fact the large state farms are said to have produced at excessive cost.

---

[73] Bauer, P. T., "The Working of Rubber Regulation," LVI *Ec. Jour.* 401, (1946).
[74] Pim, *Colonial Agricultural Production*, 2, 27, 90.

Chapter 7

Cooperation Among Production Units in Agriculture

Agricultural production units sometimes join together to acquire the means of production, to undertake processing and marketing, to regulate prices and production, or to promote the interests of agricultural producers in general. A single association may undertake one or more of these activities. In 1946-7 there were some 180 million members of cooperatives of all sorts, of which less than 1% were in Africa, about 10% in the Americas, 25% in Asia, 30% in Europe, 30% in the U.S.S.R. and 0.3% in Oceania.[1]

A. Cooperation to Acquire the Means of Production

Agricultural cooperatives frequently purchase implements, fertilizer, seed, and similar farm needs for resale to their members. They somewhat resemble consumer cooperatives in this respect. Such purchasing is usually combined with other cooperative functions. In the U.S.A. nearly 3000 associations with about 2.26 million members made purchases valued at $1.44 billions in 1947-8.[2] In western Europe urban consumers' cooperatives in the 1860's provided a model for rural purchasing cooperatives. By 1939 Danish cooperatives supplied farmers with 44% of their feedstuffs and 37% of Danish fertilizers. In Switzerland they supplied 50% of implements, foodstuffs, and seeds, and 70% of fertilizers. In Finland they supplied 50% of the fertilizers and feed, 75% of the seed, and 75% to 90% of machinery. In Sweden a specialized cooperative sold 27% of all farm machinery in 1948.[3] In Hungary cooperatives test seed and rent machinery,[4] and cooperatives

---

[1] U.N., *Rural Progress through Cooperatives,* 17; *Progress in Land Reform,* 240.
[2] U.S., *Statistical Abstract,* 1950, 598.
[3] *For. Agric.,* Sept. 1950.
[4] I.L.O. *Ind. and Lab.,* Feb. 1949, 157.

93

purchase for their members also in France, Poland,[5] and Japan.[6] In China there were (in 1950) 45,000 cooperatives, most of which purchased for their 25 million members.

In Denmark, Britain, and the U.S.A. cooperatives provide artificial insemination services for cattle raising. They provide machinery service for ploughing, threshing, and pest control in Egypt, India, and the Sudan, and manufacture agricultural machinery in Saskatchewan and Norway. They provide irrigation (Ch. 17) in the U.S.A., Switzerland, Korea, and India. They distribute electricity in Sweden and the U.S.A. (where they are assisted by the Rural Electrification Administration).[7] They provide insurance in the U.S.A., Denmark, and France, and in a number of countries they obtain capital for agriculture (Ch. 22).

The effect of purchasing operations depends on the relative efficiency of cooperative and private trading. In western Europe and the U.S.A. cooperatives usually compete with private traders, and are presumably at least as efficient. But there is no evidence that either method of trading is the more economical. Cooperative trading has, however, probably restricted the profits of some private dealers who would otherwise enjoy local monopolies.

B. Cooperative Processing and Marketing

Cooperatives may engage in processing and marketing[8] when these activities cannot be efficiently undertaken by individual producers. Cheese and butter making are among the oldest and are still the commonest processing operations undertaken by cooperatives. The first cooperative cheese plant was established in Switzerland in 1815, and the first cooperative dairy in Denmark in 1882. In both countries these activities have greatly expanded. By 1944 cooperative dairies received over 90% of all the milk delivered to dairies in Denmark. The first cooperative dairy in Holland was established in 1887, and over half the production of the country now comes from such plants. As early as 1921, 40% of the population in Holland were members of some 4000 cooperatives, the average farmer belonging to about ten. In France 2200 cooperative cheese societies produced about 14% of the national cheese output in 1936, and there was a number of cooperative butter plants. The first cooperative dairy in the U.S.A. was established in Wisconsin in 1841. In New Zealand, cooperatives produce over 90% of all dairy products, but cooperative slaughtering of cattle, organized after 1918, failed for lack of capital and good management, and the plants were sold to private slaughterers. In Australia cooperative dairies are less important than in New Zealand.

Cooperative bacon-curing is now important in Holland and Denmark.

[5] U.N., *Econ. Devel. in Sel. Countries*, 1947, 208.
[6] *For. Agric.*, June 1952.
[7] U.N., *Rural Progress through Cooperatives*, 1954, Ch. 7.
[8] U.N., *Rural Progress through Cooperatives*, Ch. 8.

Cooperative wine presses, wine-making associations and distilleries are common in France. In South Africa the Cooperative Wine Growers Association (K.W.V.) was established in 1927 to assist winegrowers suffering from low and fluctuating prices for their product. K.W.V. is prohibited from selling in the home market, but is responsible for about 90% of all exports of wines and spirits. There are also cooperative oil presses in France. In Queensland, Australia, farmers mill their sugar cane cooperatively, selling the raw sugar to a privately operated refinery. In Poland, *Spolem,* the largest central cooperative in the country (including consumers' cooperatives) had some 4193 plants in 1949, engaged in processing foodstuffs, producing building materials, textiles, clothing and paper, and building houses. But in 1949 the cooperatives were absorbed into the socialized sector controlled by the state. In Hungary cooperatives have engaged in wine and sugar production. Cooperative processing is unusual outside Europe, North America and the British Commonwealth, but two African cooperatives have successfully processed and marketed coffee produced by the Kikiyu people on the slopes of Mount Kilimanjaro in Tanganyika.

Where products are cooperatively processed, they are cooperatively marketed.[9] But they are also cooperatively marketed where little or no processing is necessary, or the marketing cannot be economically done by the producing units. Many marketing cooperatives standardize, and raise the grades of produce to raise its price. The Danish cooperatives have been especially effective in grading bacon, butter, and eggs, and the citrus and other fruit and vegetable cooperatives in the U.S.A. have been similarly active. Some cooperatives also pack the produce for market to reduce spoilage and increase its appeal to the consumer. Many ship produce to the market and arrange for its sale. Cooperatives dominate the trade in agricultural products in Denmark, the Netherlands and Finland and are important in France, Italy, South Germany, Sweden, Switzerland and Norway[10] (where the government consults cooperatives regarding agricultural policy).[11] In the Netherlands they have successfully operated auction markets for fresh vegetables. But in Britain only 2% of farm produce was cooperatively marketed in 1945: the establishment of the marketing boards in the 1930's (Ch. 8) did not encourage marketing cooperatives.

In eastern Europe cooperative marketing has been important partly as a result of the redistributions of land (e.g., in Hungary, Bulgaria and Yugoslavia).[12] In Hungary the government decreed in 1945 that agricultural cooperatives must be set up wherever more than 411 acres of land

---

[9] U.N., *Rural Progress through Cooperatives,* 72 ff.
[10] *For. Agric.,* Sept. 1950.
[11] *Ibid.,* March 1952.
[12] *For. Agric.,* July-Aug. 1952.

was redistributed, and by 1947 more than 800 such cooperatives were operating. In Poland *Spolem* not only collected agricultural produce and delivered it, but also operated most of the road transport system and conducted most of the export trade in agricultural produce (under the direction of the state). The Polish cooperative movement was well established in 1939, and was one of the largest in the world. But in all these countries cooperatives are now merged into the state trading organization.

In the U.S.A. the Grange fostered cooperating marketing in the 1870's but few cooperatives survived to 1880. In the next decade the Farmers Alliance made similar efforts with similar results, but the movement has grown rapidly during the 20th century, particularly where there is local specialization in agriculture (except for wheat). In 1947-8, 159 marketing associations had 3.63 million members and business amounting to $7195 millions a year (which was about 30% of all farm produce).[13] The American Farm Bureau (founded in 1919) made a large but unsuccessful experiment with the marketing of grain. There remain many local cooperatively-owned elevators, but efforts to federate them for cooperative selling have failed. In Canada cooperatives were assembling half the grain from the prairies in 1938, but attempts to hold prices above the world level failed in the early 1930's. For a time they also marketed tree fruits from British Columbia and general produce from the Maritime provinces.

Where agricultural goods are produced on a small scale for distant markets, the producer must resort to an independent marketing organization, unless there is an organized market. In Australia, New Zealand, and South Africa, auction markets handle most of the wool and privately owned stock, and station agents in these countries handle much of the cattle. Cooperatives handle dairy products in New Zealand and Australia and specialized crops in South Africa and Australia. Danish cooperatives export most of the butter sold abroad, 86% of the hogs and bacon, and 28% of the eggs. In 1949 Finnish cooperatives exported all the butter, 60% of the cheese, and 18% of the eggs, and French cooperatives engaged in export. In Canada federations of local cooperatives have at times exported over half the wheat of Canada.

In the Middle East cooperative marketing is largely confined to Israel, Cyprus, Greece, and Turkey. In Israel the majority of Jewish capitalist farmers market cooperatively. *Tneuva*, the cooperative of the Agricultural Workers Association, markets about 60% of the Jewish output. Practically all the Jewish citrus plantations market cooperatively although the Arab plantations (which produced about half the fruit before the war of 1939) sold mostly through dealers and middlemen. The wines produced by Jewish vineyards are also marketed cooperatively.[14] In Cyprus (where most farms are small and owner-operated), marketing cooperatives have

---

[13] U.S., *Statistical Abstract* 1950, 597.
[14] Keen, *op. cit.*, 27, 35.

been growing since 1935.[15] In Egypt cooperative marketing has made little progress because of the low status of the *fellah*, the opposition to, or domination of, cooperatives by large landowners, and government supervision. In 1950 however, the government offered loans and grants to agricultural cooperatives in an effort to reduce the cost of living.[16] But the government is proposing to develop cooperatives as a supplement to its redistribution of land. There are also numerous societies in Greece and Turkey. In India there are no statistics separating the various activities of cooperatives (provision of credit, marketing, and the like). But the movement has developed slowly and has been most successful in the few areas where the tenant enjoys security of tenure. In general, cooperatives affect a very small proportion of the agricultural population: the poverty of the agriculturalists drives them to mortgage their crops to moneylenders, who do not favor cooperation. Skillfully run cooperatives could often obtain better prices for farmers, but many cooperatives have been poorly managed.[17] There is now some cooperative marketing in Ceylon,[18] but efforts to establish cooperatives in the Philippines have, in the main, failed. In Malaya small quantities of rubber and eggs have been cooperatively marketed.[19] In China many of the 45,000 cooperatives in 1951 were marketing as well as supply cooperatives. In many of the villages in northeast China where land has been redistributed, 60 to 80% of the villagers are members. Many of these cooperatives are urban consumer cooperatives which trade with rural cooperatives. In Japan cooperatives developed after 1900, first mainly as credit cooperatives dominated by merchants and village landlords. In 1943, membership was made compulsory, and the government controlled agriculture partly through the cooperatives. But after the passage of a cooperative law in 1947 as part of the agrarian reform initiated by the military occupation authorities, independent cooperatives spread widely. By 1952 virtually every farm family belonged to one or more of the cooperatives that together market about half of all farm produce and nearly all staple crops.[20] In Latin America only scattered cooperative marketing associations exist; those in Chile are the most successful.

The British government has made some efforts to encourage cooperative marketing in colonial areas, but without much success. In Nigeria the government has encouraged cooperative marketing of cocoa since 1922, and cooperatives now handle about 12% of the cocoa crop. But Britain's efforts to organize similar marketing of palm oil have so far been

---

[15] Keen, *op. cit.*, 37.

[16] Issawi, *op. cit.*, 79; I.L.O. *Ind. and Lab.*, Jan. 15, 1951, 70.

[17] India Famine Inquiry Com. *Report* 292, 316; India Cooperative Planning Committee *Report* 5, 19, 46, 57; Keen, *op. cit.*, 35.

[18] Pim, *Colonial Agricultural Production*, 68.

[19] Pim, *op. cit.*, 58.

[20] *For. Agric.*, June 1952.

unsuccessful. In the Gold Coast, the internal marketing of agricultural produce is almost wholly in the hands of African traders and a few Syrians, but the government has achieved some success in organizing cooperative cocoa marketing. The local governments and marketing boards for West African cocoa are under a special obligation to encourage and assist cooperatives acting as buyers for the Boards. In Uganda there are small cooperatives marketing cotton, coffee, and milk, but there is little cooperative marketing in Kenya.[21] Registrars of Cooperative Societies have now been appointed in a number of areas to promote the movement, but progress is slow. In the Belgian Congo, monopolistic concession companies have undertaken all processing and marketing. But as the concessions expire, the government intends to replace them with semi-cooperative forms of organization. Outside the concessions, European and African traders are licensed by the government. The latter, however, is said to be interested in cooperative marketing; "methods of production containing elements of cooperative practice are already in operation."[22] In South Africa only two cooperative marketing societies for native producers are reported, since

> The native is not particularly cooperative as an individual, although the greater part of his land—the Veld—has always been used on a communal basis. There is no reason to assume, however, that the native will not become more cooperative in spirit as the advantages become more apparent. Indeed, there are clear indications that he is becoming alive to the benefits of cooperation.[23]

The organization of cooperatives of production units for processing and marketing differs from that of the producers' cooperative (Ch. 6) (in which the members unite in cultivation). The processing or marketing cooperative is controlled by its members, who usually have one vote each, and the association is usually open to membership by any producer. It pays interest to its members on any capital they subscribe. The members frequently make enforceable contracts to deliver their whole or a specified amount of their produce to the association, and can withdraw only at the expiration of their contract. The proceeds of the sale of each product, and sometimes each grade, are pooled and distributed among the members according to their produce deliveries to the association. Frequently part of the anticipated proceeds is paid on delivery of the produce and the remainder when the accounts for the season are closed. Special legislation is usually necessary to endow such associations with a legal personality and exempt them from taxes on profits.[24]

Cooperative activity is most feasible where the scale of cultivation is smaller than the most economical scale of processing or marketing. Plan-

---

[21] *Pendered Report*, 10, 13; U.K., *The Colonial Empire 1939-47* (Cmd. 7167), 92, 23.

[22] *Pendered Report*, 15, 21.

[23] Director of Native Agriculture, Department of Native Affairs, *Annual Report, 1944-45*, 15; Department of Native Affairs, *Report for Years 1945-47*, 5.

[24] U.N., *Rural Progress through Cooperatives*, 233.

tation operators are often able to process and market for themselves, especially when their produce can be sold on an organized market (e.g., rubber). They often form associations, but mainly for collective representation and advertising, the organization of research, and sometimes the control of production and prices. But where economical marketing calls for a larger scale of operation than production, either private enterprise or cooperative marketing is likely. Thus redistributions of land which result in a reduced scale of production usually result in a reorganization of marketing. Cooperative processing and marketing is not necessarily more economical than the capitalist middleman. The cooperative may, however, operate at a smaller margin between the buying price and the selling price of produce because its costs are lower, or it may maintain the former margin but annex monopoly profits obtained by private middlemen. Producers of tobacco leaf in the U.S.A. and cattle in Argentina and the U.S.A. have criticized concentration on the buying side of the markets in which they sell. Similar concentration of buying often exists in beet and cane sugar areas. Cooperation in these situations (if complete among sellers) would result in a monopoly of sellers facing one or a few buyers. But, more frequently, middlemen have local buying monopolies (Ch. 6). Even so, cooperatives have not hitherto engaged very often in processing operations requiring large capital and presenting complex problems of management. Butter and cheese making and bacon curing, being relatively small-scale operations, are well-suited to the cooperative of moderate size. But cooperative meat packing failed in New Zealand. Cooperative wine making has, however, succeeded on a large scale in South Africa.

Cooperatives do not always appear where they could raise the income of the producer. In many countries the absence of cooperatives is chiefly due to severe poverty among farmers, who are thereby compelled to finance themselves through dealers, through whom they must market their crop (especially in the Middle East, India, and the Far East). Sharecropping, which gives the landowners an interest in the crop, also impedes cooperative organization. The landowner often collects and markets the crop. In theory the tenant could dispose of his part cooperatively, but it is difficult for him to do so in fact, and insecurity of tenure prevents a continuing interest in a cooperative. Poverty and insecurity frequently also impede comprehension of the methods of operating cooperatives,[25] and inexperience in the marketing of cash crops provides a further obstacle to cooperation in Africa.[26] Moreover native cooperatives are impeded in making firm contracts to deliver produce to white buyers. The cooperative can deliver only if its members deliver to it, and its members may fail. A non-native buyer making contracts of this kind is unable to enforce them wherever the cooperative or the members have little property. If they have land, the land is frequently reserved by law to the natives and

---

[25] India: Cooperative Planning Committee *Report*, 11 and Chapter V.
[26] *Pendered Report*, 76.

cannot in any form be conveyed to white owners. But it is not clear why cooperatives have made so little progress in the past in Britain, where consumer cooperation has been relatively successful and farmers have so long complained of the charges made by middlemen. After 1939, however, many of these middlemen were either replaced by the government or controlled by it, until private trading was restored in 1954.

Governments frequently assist cooperatives not only by providing the necessary legislation but also by encouraging them (in the U.S.A., Canada, Norway, Ecuador, the Philippines, and parts of Africa,[27] India, Pakistan, and Egypt). They subsidize or provide low-cost loans to cooperatives in Belgium, Norway, Portugal, Spain, Brazil, India, Britain, Sweden, and Canada.

C. Cooperatives to Regulate Prices and Production

There is a limit to the benefits cooperatives can offer their members through operating at lower costs than middlemen or through annexing the latter's monopoly profits. The cooperative may attempt to override this limit by raising the price of produce in the same way as industrial cartels or some labor unions. But to succeed they must control most of the supply. If the product is also imported, imports must be restricted, which typically means that they must obtain the help of the government. Producers may, however, seek the cooperation of competing producers in other countries. In some plantation activities such cooperation has been achieved, but for most food products there are too many producing countries for controls to be successful, at least without the active government help (Ch. 26).

The cooperative may attempt to influence prices by reducing sales, but the unsold product then presents a problem. The association may advise the farmer the amount of product that he may deliver for marketing, leaving him to dispose of the balance. But if he sells in competition with the cooperative he undermines its price policy. The cooperative may take delivery of all the produce, and divert some of it into other than the principal use at a lower price. But these lower prices reduce the average price and in the longer run, the cooperative may endeavor to reduce the total produce to be marketed. It may control planting and, to speed up results, it may uproot existing trees (as has been done in the California peach area). Success depends on comprehensive control and there is always a danger that outside competition will develop, the outsiders gaining from the price-raising activities of the cooperative, without being limited by its sales restrictions. Should outsiders become active, members leave the cooperative to share the gains of the non-members and the cooperative collapses. In general, a cooperative endeavoring to control prices is forced into much the same policies as an industrial cartel pursuing the same objectives.

---

[27] U.N., *Progress in Land Reform*, 236, 269.

D. Cooperation to Promote the Interests of
Agriculturalists in General

Cooperatives for the foregoing purposes are restricted in their membership to producers of one or a few products. In recent years there have also emerged in the more developed countries organizations of agricultural producers in general that influence public policy regarding agriculture.

General farm organizations in the U.S.A. (until 1933) expanded in depressed times and contracted in good times. The National Grange was at the height of its power in the 1870's, the Farmers Alliance (now defunct) in the 1880's and 1890's, the Farmers Union in the early 20th century, and the Farm Bureau Federation after 1918. There are now four important organizations. The National Grange (in the 1870's a radical organization in the midwest) is now most powerful in the Northeast and Northwest, and of a conservative flavor. The National Farmers Union (in 1913 concentrated around the Gulf of Mexico and primarily concerned with cooperative marketing) has for twenty years been concentrated in the plains wheat areas. It has been in general a supporter of the "New Deal" and "Fair Deal" policies of the government. The American Farm Bureau Federation has been influential in the corn-hog Middle West, the cotton-tobacco South and among commercial farmers in California and New York. The National Council of Farmer Cooperatives is a federation of 111 cooperative associations.[28] Nearly half of all farm operators belong to one or more of these organizations. In Britain the National Farmers Union, including about 80% of all farmers, influences legislation and cooperates with the Ministry of Agriculture in the administration of government policy. Similar organizations exist in western Europe. In most predominantly agrarian countries, however, no such organizations exist, but the dominant political party performs similar functions.

These agricultural organizations have developed for the same general reasons as overall organizations of manufacturers and workers in the more developed countries (Ch. 12, 30). Farmers generally lost economic and political influence during the 19th century, even where there was little industrialism. But they have achieved more political power in democratic countries during the 20th century than they previously had. Their power increased after the war of 1914-1918 in Europe (particularly in eastern Europe) and even more notably during the depression years after 1929. In Russia and eastern Europe, however, while agriculture is centrally organized, this organization is not intended to enable farmers to influence the government, but the reverse. Where general farm organizations are powerful, it is largely because of improved organization that has encouraged and been encouraged by active state intervention in agriculture. They are usually among the most property-conscious groups.

---

[28] *Economist*, Jan. 13, 1951.

Chapter 8

The State and Agricultural Production

A. Influences Affecting State Policies

The attitude of the state toward agriculture depends on the interests of the various groups in the society and their political influence.

Those whose incomes are directly derived from agriculture are generally (but not always) interested in the enlargement of those incomes. Landowners might be expected to favor government action increasing the incomes of agricultural producers because it increases the demand for the use of land and, therefore, landowners' share of the produce of the land in rent or profits. Industrialists in capitalist countries have often been interested in low prices for food because they minimized upward pressures on wages. Such was the argument of British industrialists for the repeal of import duties on wheat in the 19th century. But in the 20th century they have recognized the agricultural sector as a part of the market for manufactured goods. A decline in the purchasing power of the agricultural sector depresses the industrial sector. Where the agricultural sector is small, its influence is correspondingly weak, as in Britain. But in the U.S.A., half the country's total business is said to depend in some way on farm consumers.[1] In underdeveloped countries most purchasing power derives from agriculture. New industries are unlikely to be able to compete in export markets at the outset, but may displace imported manufactured goods. Thereafter their sales of mass-produced goods depend on domestic incomes from agriculture until they can compete abroad or until industrial production grows large enough to generate a considerable purchasing power. But new industrialists in such countries often find themselves in conflict with agriculturalists who oppose industrialization because industry is expected to compete for agricultural labor and raise wages (this happened formerly in Germany, and to some extent in Britain).

---

[1] *Economist*, April 16, 1949.

Workers in general are interested in low prices for agricultural products because the latter account for all food, most clothing, and much housing material. Agricultural labor, however, is interested in high gross revenue from agricultural operations, and low rents. Industrial labor is interested in prosperous conditions in agriculture because depressions in agriculture may, while reducing the cost of food, also reduce the market for industrial products and industrial employment.

The state must take account not only of sectional but also of general social interests, more particularly defense and social stability. A country dependent for a vital part of its food on foreign countries, especially distant or hostile ones, has great difficulties in time of war. England became thus dependent in the 19th century and in the war of 1914-18. In the war of 1939-45, it had even more serious difficulty in feeding its population. The state may also regard agriculture as a source of military manpower, because the rural population often multiplies faster than the industrial. It is also believed to supply better soldiers than the urban (which is open to much doubt). The state may regard stability of agricultural purchasing power as part of the price of economic and political stability if agricultural depression causes political unrest or the agricultural population is a conservative political force. In politically centralized countries like Russia there are virtually no land-owning or industrial profit-receiving interests, but there are conflicts of interest between agriculturalists and industrial workers, and between agriculturalists and the government.

The relative effectiveness of different interests in securing government help varies widely. In Britain industrialists became the dominant political power during the 1830s, but the spoils of victory came mainly in the withdrawal of previous government stimulation of agriculture and the application of a policy of *laissez faire*. In Germany and France, however, agricultural interests were never so decisively defeated, and continued to receive help. The 20th century revived the threat of war and increased the fear of depression. Organization of the agricultural interests has also increased their political power, not only in western Europe but also in the U.S.A.

In most underdeveloped countries landowners have maintained political dominance, although occasionally they share power with large merchants. Relative prosperity among inactive landowners exists side by side with chronic depression among agricultural workers (e.g., in Egypt and most of the Middle East, India, and the Far East and Latin America). But there are signs of change. In eastern Europe, Egypt, and China the redistribution of land signalled the collapse of the political power of landowners. In parts of Latin America (particularly in Argentina) governments supported by labor organizations have cut into the political power of landowners since 1945 and sharply reduced their incomes.

In the socialist states, policies cannot be formulated in complete opposition to public opinion, but it is difficult to trace the influence of economic groups. It appears, however, that the resistance of agriculturalists has set limits to the policies of the Soviet government and even (in 1953) induced modifications.

State action is also influenced by knowledge of devices available for directing agricultural production. Import duties and subsidies are the older devices. But during the 20th century the list of instruments has been lengthened to include quantity controls of imports and exports, exchange controls, internal taxation and subsidies (directly, or for transport or the provision of credit), internal production controls, price controls, and others.

B. The Scope of State Activities

1. ACCESS TO THE MEANS OF PRODUCTION

The state invariably influences agricultural production through its policies regarding the means of production. It influences access to land (Ch. 16). It may, but often does not, influence access to capital (Ch. 22) and labor (Ch. 20). Where agriculture depends on large-scale irrigation, the state has had great influence over agriculture since the beginning of human history (Ch. 17), and it still exercises dominant power in Egypt.[2]

Governments have varied widely in the scope of their activities in acquiring new knowledge of agriculture and making it accessible to producers. Modern agriculture sprang from experiments by private individuals in 17th- and 18th-century Britain. But in the 20th century, governments have been responsible for most agricultural research even in capitalist countries (e.g., the U.S.A., Britain, Germany, Denmark, Norway, and much of western Europe,[3] New Zealand, Australia, and South Africa).[4] The principal exceptions concern agricultural implements, chemical fertilizers and insecticides, in connection with which considerable research has been conducted by private enterprise interested in providing these products through the market. The development plans for a number of Latin American countries provide for considerable research. But government research into the agricultural problems of colonial areas is recent. The governments in the Belgian Congo and East Africa[5] now finance research. The Russian government engages actively in research.

Governments leaving most industrial research to private enterprise nevertheless engage in agricultural research partly because it is economically carried on on a large scale while agriculture is often small-

---

2 Warriner, *op. cit.*, 49.

3 *For. Agric.*, Feb. 1952, March 1952.

4 Union of South Africa Industrial and Agricultural Requirements Commission, *Third Interim Report*, 1941, 1.

5 *Pendered Report*, 19.

scale. In fact, government research facilitates the continuance of relatively small-scale agriculture. Some plantations conduct research (more particularly companies like the United Fruit Company), but many rely on research by governments or trade associations. Government research results, instead of being immediately available only to the firm paying for the research, are available to all producers, with the result that none has any temporary advantage in using new knowledge.

The application of the results of research is as important as the research itself. Governments engage in propaganda to ensure the application of new knowledge in the U.S.A.,[6] Britain, France, Germany, Denmark, Norway, and the Netherlands Indies, and Japan,[7] and these activities are spreading. The rapid rate of population increase in Latin America, leading to periodic reliance on imports of some foods, threatens to reduce this region's capacity to import capital goods for development. Most of them have, therefore, revised their development plans to give higher priority to increasing agricultural output by extending areas of cultivation (partly by irrigation), and by providing credit and agricultural implements (e.g., in Mexico, Argentina, Brazil, Uruguay, Peru, Venezuela, Chile, and Colombia).

The success of these plans rests, however, on the effectiveness with which technical knowledge is brought to producers, and whether they can be induced to adopt it.[8] Colonial governments have hitherto made little effort to bring to cultivators in their areas knowledge of methods used elsewhere. But increasing population pressure and rising economic demands by colonial peoples are impelling these governments to take action. In Southern Rhodesia an active Department of Native Agriculture has vigorously urged the native population to use cattle manure (which previously had been burned or allowed to rot), to practice contour plowing and crop rotation, to concentrate cultivation on the best lands, leaving the second-grade lands for pasture, and to consolidate plots of land. But only about 10% of the Africans on the reserve are believed to have adopted the new methods, although the latter increase yields from 100 to 900%. The government of the Belgian Congo has established peasant farming communities in which the government allocates land, controls crop rotation, and sets minimum cultivation quotas. Since 1946 the French government has been establishing "Sectors of Rural Modernization" in Morocco, in part to increase output directly, but mainly to stimulate local peasants to improve their methods. The sectors are intended to be exploited entirely for the native population, and schools, houses, hospitals, and technical assistance are provided. Five settlements were operating in 1945, but subsequent progress has been slow. In Algeria co-

---

6 *For. Agric.*, Nov. 1951.

7 *Ibid.*, Nov. 1952.

8 U.N., *Progress in Land Reform*, 271.

operatives are being established, with power to control the methods of cultivation by their members. During the war of 1939-45, the governments of some territories producing export products endeavored to insulate their territory from outside inflationary pressures by paying out to producers less than the total amount realized for their product. They placed the balance in a fund to be used later partly or wholly to finance either the improved culture of the product from which the surplus was obtained or the general betterment of the native population. In the Belgian Congo, for instance, "offices" have been set up for coffee, quinine, and pyrethrum to provide seeds and plants, technical advice, grading produce inspection, market studies, and propaganda.[9]

2. Activities Increasing the Rewards of Agriculture

Most governments interested in helping agriculture in the developed countries have found that facilitating services do not go far enough. They have moved on to more positive action. Often they first facilitate marketing, in order to raise the prices received by the producer without any necessary increase in prices to consumers. Later, however, they raise prices and reduce output.

a. Facilitation of Marketing

Governments may regulate or operate market facilities. Most developed countries regulate weighing devices, provide legal remedies for deception and fraud. They provide grading officials where products are sold on organized exchanges (e.g., cotton, wheat, coffee) in order to facilitate the operation of a competitive market and speculative transactions. Governments also grade export products, to raise or maintain the price and the reputation of the country's product and encourage producers to increase the proportion of the crop which can be classified in the highest grade. Since 1906, only butter reaching standards set by cooperative creameries may be exported from Denmark.[10]

In colonial areas, however, such activities have not been very successful until recently. Native producers claim that their produce is under-graded and under-weighed, and that they receive less than they are entitled to, even on the grade and weight recorded. Sometimes the producers are too weak in arithmetic to be able to check the payments made by traders. Where the trader is of a different national origin from the native seller (which is not uncommon), friction between them sometimes generates considerable heat. Consequently, colonial governments in some parts of Africa are adopting devices common in medieval Europe when markets were developing. In Kenya the government seeks to concentrate trade at

---

[9] *Pendered Report,* 19.
[10] *For. Agric.,* Feb. 1952.

places and times where it can be supervised and competition stimulated. Public weigh-masters are provided at these markets, and sometimes public graders. In Uganda and Tanganyika any commodity may be scheduled as "native produce," to be bought only at prescribed buying centers by licensed dealers. The reputation of dealers is investigated, their number is limited, and they pay a tax, the proceeds of which go into a fund for development or inspection of the produce on which the tax is collected. In Nigeria, the government standardizes, and endeavors to improve, the quality of export produce. Cotton may be sold only in authorized markets, where the native administration appoints graders. In the Gold Coast, cocoa, palm kernels, and copra for export are inspected by government officials. In the Belgian Congo coffee is officially graded, but official weighing is optional.[11] Such efforts, however, are often partly frustrated by corrupt officials and dishonest traders.

Some governments regulate or operate processing industries, in order to increase the prices received by producers. Regulation is uncommon in the more advanced countries in peacetime, but it is increasing in colonial areas because of the poor bargaining position of native sellers and the monopolies of buying traders. In Uganda the processing margins on cotton and coffee (robusta) have been controlled since 1939; by 1950 the Lint Marketing Board had accumulated a fund of seven million pounds. In the Belgian Congo the minimum price to be paid by the concession companies to the cultivator for cotton is regulated by the government. Any returns on dealing in ginning, grading, and baling of cotton in excess of a prescribed rate of return on capital are paid into a government betterment fund, part of which may be used to stabilize the purchase price of cotton.[12]

Governments may themselves operate processing plants to reduce processing costs or eliminate monopoly profits. In eastern Europe and China, governments have nationalized processing plants as part of their general policy regarding industry. There is little government operation in the Middle East outside of Turkey and Iran. The Iranian government owns and operates processing plants, especially sugar-beet factories and wheat cleaning and fumigating plants, but also some flour mills, canneries, tobacco plants, glycerine and vegetable oil refineries, cotton ginning plants, jute, silk, tea and insecticide plants.[13] There are few such government plants in India or the Far East, except for China. But governments have begun to process cattle for meat in Africa. In Southern Rhodesia the Cold Storage Commission, which is government owned, operates packing houses which are intended to make neither a profit nor a loss, any profits being used to increase the price paid for stock. In Tanganyika the government

[11] *Pendered Report*, 20.
[12] *Ibid.*, 20; *Economist*, May 12, 1951.
[13] Keen, *op. cit.*, 16.

has taken a 50% interest in a packing plant near Dar-es-Salaam. In Uruguay, also, the government has established a meat packing concern.

b. Price Raising Activities

Dissatisfaction with the amount of aid, to be obtained by eliminating unnecessary costs and monopoly profits in processing and marketing has induced many governments to seek to raise prices.

Obstructing imports is one way of helping agriculture, but it is not usable in predominantly exporting countries (e.g., the U.S.A., Argentina, Canada, Australia, New Zealand, Holland, Denmark, and Russia). Import controls are used even in the U.S.A., however, to assist domestic producers of wool and sugar. Such countries are more likely, however, to urge other countries to lift restrictions on imports. But import duties and quota controls have been widely used in importing or potential importing countries especially since about 1880 when both France and Germany rejected the British free trade policy. France began increasing import duties to protect agriculture in 1880 and increased them further in 1897, 1899 and 1903. It also placed quotas on imports and revised trade treaties. Germany began to restrict agricultural imports about 1879, to ensure supplies in time of war. The Junkers opposed the development of industry because it drew laborers from the land and raised agricultural wages. They opposed lower railroad rates and the extension of canals because they cheapened imported food. Nevertheless, in 1914 nearly 20% of Germany's sustenance was imported. The import duties necessary to keep low-grade lands in cultivation raised the internal prices of products to twice or three times their world price. Agriculture in Germany after 1920 suffered in much the same way as it did in the U.S.A. Subsidies were granted that were not altogether successful, and import duties were increased. Agriculture appeared to be regarded as a permanently deficit enterprise. South Africa has protected wheat production since 1826 but increased the protection after 1921,[14] and Australia and New Zealand also protect wheat growers.

The depression that began in 1929 caused a general shrinkage in demand for agricultural products, and many importing countries gave their domestic farmers preference in their home market. France increased its import duties further in 1929, and again on wheat in 1931. In Germany the Junkers pressed successfully for more protection. Duties on sugar, rye, wheat, and other grains were raised (those on wheat to 300% of the world price in 1933). Import quotas were imposed, and in 1933 the Nazi Food Estate controlled all imports and production. Japan, which had largely solved its food problem when it seized Manchuria, raised import duties on rice and millet in 1933 in response to a drastic rise in imports and fall in price. In 1931 Britain abandoned its almost

---

[14] South Africa: Wheat Commission, Report 1941, 2.

century-old policy of free imports of agricultural products. Britain was then profiting from the fall in the price of imports that supplied over two-thirds of its food, and agriculture had shrunk to only about half its size in the U.S.A. in terms of the proportion of the labor force in agriculture. But the government imposed duties on all important agricultural imports to be able to give preference to imports from within the Commonwealth, thus shifting its sources of supply. These efforts to assist agriculture imposed great hardships on exporting countries. Some directed agriculture away from export products to commodities previously imported (e.g., the Netherlands, Denmark, Sweden and Switzerland).[15]

The war of 1939-1945 seriously obstructed international trade and induced efforts to expand agriculture to meet domestic needs. Many of these efforts were continued after the end of the war. In Britain the government stimulated domestic production and monopolized imports. In France, too, the government stimulated domestic agriculture, and in 1948 revised the Monnet Plan for economic rehabilitation. This plan, which had previously placed major emphasis on industry, was reoriented towards expanding of agriculture to a size at which it could export. Sweden has taxed imports and aimed at producing about 90% of its food needs. Norway uses import duties and licenses to prevent dairy production from exceeding domestic needs and to encourage grain production to reduce dependence on foreign food. (Half of Norway's food is nevertheless imported.) In Denmark imports are controlled by license.[16]

The methods of protecting agriculture from foreign competition have been greatly elaborated during this century. The most ancient devices are import duties and sanitary regulations. Some states have imposed fixed quotas on imports (set the maximum amount of a particular product which may be imported from a particular country). Mostly since 1929, exchange restrictions have been used to control imports, e.g., in Denmark, Greece, Italy, Norway, Bulgaria, Czechoslovakia, Rumania, and Spain.[16a] Foreign exchange to pay for agricultural imports may be rationed, or it may be sold at a higher price than foreign exchange to be used for other purposes. Lastly, the government may, as it does in Russia, monopolize imports and directly decide what goods it will import. State grain import monopolies have been used to encourage domestic grain production in Norway and Denmark. The Netherlands government under the Agricultural Crisis Act of 1933 established a series of semi-government monopolies with power to regulate imports and exports, fix prices, tax imports, and control domestic production.[17]

These devices differ in their effect on prices. A rate of import duty

---

[15] *For. Agric.*, June 1951, Feb. 1952.
[16] *For. Agric.*, Dec. 1949, Feb., March 1952.
[16a] Brandt, *Reconstruction of World Agriculture*, 83.
[17] *For. Agric.*, June 1951.

prohibitive at one time may permit considerable imports at another time because the margin between domestic costs and the foreign price changes. Quantity controls of imports determine the maximum import, but the effect on price depends upon the extent to which the quotas fall below the amount that would be imported without controls, and on the elasticity of domestic agricultural supply and demand. But any controls that keep out imports encourage domestic agriculture and attract resources into it. The extent to which they do so depends on the extent of the restriction on import, and the relative costs of production abroad and at home. But such restrictions also raise the cost of agricultural products and, thereby, the cost of living. A less than the most economical allocation of resources is paid for partly in lower living standards, but the diversion may be justified on other grounds (e.g., defense demands or economic stability). But such policies often shift the terms of trade in favor of importing countries and against exporters of agricultural produce. Import restrictions to help local farmers during depression periods throw the burden of the depression predominantly upon exporting countries in the short run. They may be compelled to accept, for a time, a price fall so drastic that existing import duties of other countries may not reduce imports or assist domestic agriculture to any extent. But even if imports are reduced in favor of domestic agriculture, exports are likely also to be reduced. If the country is interested in industrial exports (e.g., Britain), the reduction in imports indirectly reduces industrial activity.

Governments of exporting countries have sometimes maintained or raised domestic prices by assisting producers to withdraw part of the supply from the domestic market for export at lower prices, the domestic price being protected, if necessary, by import duties. It is often more economical to export the surplus that cannot be sold at the domestic price than to destroy it. But producers cannot usually dump produce abroad in this way without state aid because all producers prefer to sell at the higher domestic price. The government may, as in Queensland, Australia, provide for compulsory cooperative marketing and permit the cooperatives to engage in discriminatory selling. The marketing board grades and sells the whole product for the benefit of the members, but has no legal control over production. Producers receive the weighted average price received in all markets. In Australia agricultural producers contended that the tariff discriminated against them and in favor of industry. When they failed to prevent tariff increases, they sought to raise domestic prices of agricultural products. Australian state governments are not legally empowered to regulate exports, and there is doubt as to their authority to regulate interstate trade (which is important only in some products). The federal government cannot legally regulate intra-state trade in peacetime, but complementary state and commonwealth legislation has been used to establish Boards which administered discriminatory price schemes. Such

Boards operated mostly in New South Wales and Victoria for sugar, dried vine fruits, butter, cheese, and rice, at an aggregate cost in 1938-9 of £12 millions. These arrangements tended to stimulate output and increase the proportion exported, sometimes reducing the average price received. Sugar output increased 160% between 1922-3 and 1938-9, and the proportion exported rose from 1 to 54%. Both domestic and export prices fell, and the average price fell 24%. Production of dried fruits rose 400% from 1920 to 1939 and the proportion exported rose from 52% to 98%. Butter production rose 50% between 1926 and 1939 and the proportion exported from 36% to 50%.[18] These policies were abandoned during the war of 1939-45, and after the war the relation between home and foreign prices was reversed. No equalization funds have been established for meat and wool which are the more prosperous and individualistic branches of Australian agriculture. In the Union of South Africa the Marketing Act of 1937 provided for Marketing Boards (consisting of representatives of those interested in agriculture), to whom the Minister of Agriculture may give monopoly powers over the disposal of a product. By 1946 wide powers had been given to 12 Boards regarding wheat and wheat products, dried fruit, tobacco, corn (maize or mealies), corn products, dairy products, deciduous fruit, and chicory. The Boards for corn, wheat, and citrus fruits before 1939 held up domestic prices and exported at lower prices. Because a rebate was given to those feeding corn to cattle, the principal burden was borne by human consumers of maize and maize products (which are the staple food of the native population).[19] Denmark achieved somewhat similar results between 1932 and 1934 by a tax on domestic sales of butter, which assisted exports. The defense institutes for sugar alcohol, rice, and maté in Brazil pursued similar policies. In Colombia the government authorized the Federation of Coffee Growers to fix domestic coffee prices, purchase surplus coffee, and control exports.[20]

Schemes of this sort which do not depend on a government subsidy present complex pricing problems. Raising the domestic price reduces home sales and increases sales at lower world prices. The best financial results are obtained when the marginal revenue from internal and export sales is the same.[21] The price differentials that achieve this result depend on differences in the elasticity of demand in the two markets. The existence of alternative sources of supply on the world market means that elasticity will be higher there (and prices lower). Governments seeking to help producers in these ways are facilitating a policy of discriminatory

---

[18] Australia: Rural Reconstruction Commission, *Commercial Policy Relating to Agriculture*, 30, 163.

[19] Franklin, N. N., *Economics in South Africa*, 1948, 116; Union of South Africa Industrial and Agricultural Requirements Commission, *Third Interim Report*, 1941, 33; *For. Agric.*, July-Aug. 1953.

[20] *For. Agric.*, Dec. 1948.

[21] Robinson, J., *The Economics of Imperfect Competition*, Ch. 15.

monopoly. Of course, the inclusion of government subsidies increases the aid to farmers.

Exporting countries unable to help agriculture by import and export controls often use other methods. Even potentially import countries may find that the exclusion of all imports may not assist agriculture as much as the government desires. During the decade after the First World War, a number of governments sought to raise prices by devices known as valorization or stabilization schemes, although such schemes were aimed more at raising than stabilizing prices. After 1929, these efforts multiplied in almost all countries except Denmark and Holland (e.g., in Brazil for coffee, Canada for wheat and fruit, Germany for rye and later all grains, Japan for rice and silk). In the U.S.A. the Federal Farm Board was established in 1929 to solve the problem of agricultural surpluses and depressed prices through "orderly marketing."

If the government merely prescribes a minimum price for a product, above the free market price, some produce will not be sold at that price and there is no reason to expect the unsold surpluses to be distributed among producers on any acceptable basis. Consequently, governments frequently offer to buy all produce offered to them at the stated minimum price (i.e., to "peg" the market). Such action makes the minimum price effective and avoids inequity among producers, but leaves the government with the surplus. The government may dispose of this surplus (1) by selling it later (which can be done without disturbing its minimum price only if the price equates supply and demand over the long run), (2) by selling it abroad at a world price less than the domestic price and less than the price paid for produce, the loss being met by the taxpayers; (3) by disposing of the produce at home in a way that does not undermine the domestic price, for instance, by selling to a group that would not otherwise buy (as was attempted under the "Stamp Plan"[21a] for relief recipients in the U.S.A.); (4) by letting the purchased produce rot or destroying it. If the country is not an exporter of the product and the price is kept in the longer run above the supply and demand price, those in the main domestic market pay higher prices and consume less than without the scheme. The remaining part of the burden of assisting the agricultural producers falls on the taxpayers, who meet the losses from the destruction of produce and from the government sales at below cost in special markets. If the country is the world's only exporter of the product, it can raise the world price to a monopoly level. But it must deduct from its monopoly profit the price paid for the produce it cannot sell. The high price may, too, bring out supplies from new sources. If the country is one of a number of exporters, it can raise the world price only by carrying the

---

[21a] Under the "Stamp Plan" some three to seven million families on relief were given additional purchasing power earmarked for particular commodities, but the scheme was discontinued in 1942.

whole burden of the restriction of supply, which may be very costly indeed.

. The government of Brazil has sought over many years to maintain the price of coffee,[22] of which it exports about two-thirds of the world's supply. In 1906 the state of São Paulo borrowed money to enable it to hold coffee off the market, and it prohibited new planting from 1902 to 1912. The stocks were finally sold and the loan repaid, but Brazil's share of world exports fell from 80% in 1906 to 70% in 1909-13. This action was repeated in 1917, and again the stocks were eventually sold. In 1922 the government organized the Coffee Defense Institute to administer a continuing program based on this experience. Institute stocks of coffee rose at one time to 4.5 million pounds but were disposed of by 1924. But in 1929 the price of coffee fell 50% in four months, and the government again borrowed to finance the holding of coffee off the market. Between 1931 and 1942 it taxed production and exports (imposing punitive taxes on exports above specified quotas) and regulated shipments from the interior to the ports. But it also destroyed one-third of the output between 1931 and 1942. Subsequently, however, prices have risen and all accumulated stocks have been sold. Brazil not only wasted part of its resources; it also stimulated production elsewhere. But it benefitted from parallel attempts to maintain the price of cotton in the U.S.A. and expanded its acreage under cotton (so greatly that the government had bought and was holding 200,-000 tons of cotton in 1944 to maintain its price). A government "Institute" in Brazil has also sought to stabilize the price of cocoa.

In Argentina the government established, in 1933, a Board to purchase all wheat, corn, and flaxseed offered to it at an announced minimum price, and to export them at world prices. The minimum prices were more than once suspended and restored. In 1940 and 1941 the Board endeavored to reduce production but in 1943 the government reversed its efforts and encouraged increased output, partly because of the need of grain for fuel. In 1944 the Board was empowered to deal in all agricultural products,[23] but by 1948 it was restricting price increases. A National Meat Board has set minimum prices to be paid by packing houses (frigorificos) for livestock.

In Japan the price of rice fell 50% in a year, and the Rice Control Act of 1921 empowered the Minister of Agriculture to buy and store rice when the price fell and to sell when the price rose. Four successive large crops between 1927 and 1930, and increased imports, more than offset the increasing demand for rice caused by the growth of the population, and the price fell after 1927 because government purchases were inadequate. By

---

22 Wickizer, V. D., *The World Coffee Economy* (Food Research Institute, Stanford University) and Spiegel, *The Brazilian Economy*, 169 sq.

23 U.S. Tariff Comm., *Agricultural, Pastoral and Forest Industries in Argentina*, 21 ff.

August 1930 the price was about 33% of that of January 1920,[24] and the government taxed imports of rice and millet, set maximum and minimum prices and quotas to be withheld from market, and continued to buy and sell, with the result that the price rose about 75%. Similarly, after the price of silk fell in 1930 the government initiated the Silk Valorization Scheme. This, however, failed to stabilize the price of silk.[25]

Some European governments also bought produce to maintain prices during the depression after 1929. The Dutch government bought half a million pigs and canned them in 1933, and the Swiss government bought and stored butter, some of which was resold at a loss.[26]

In the U.S.A. free markets for agricultural products were restored after 1918, but there was a long sustained depression in agriculture after 1920. Acreage had been expanded during the war of 1918, but after the war European production revived and some countries increased their exports. Increased output per man reduced the amount of labor needed per unit of output, and the replacement of draft animals on the farm reduced the demand for fodder. Population did not leave the farms in sufficient numbers to adjust output to changes in demand, and prices fell. Plans for government aid appeared after 1924, some of which were patterned on those of other countries. They provided for the government to maintain prices at home and export surpluses at lower world prices. In 1929 the government established the Federal Farm Board, which raised prices by buying produce until all its funds were invested. The higher prices relieved pressure on farmers to reduce output and they ignored the exhortations of the Board to do so; the Board lacked control of output. By 1932 agriculture received 5.2% of the national income, compared with 16.6% in 1919.

Since 1933 the U.S. government has held up the prices of major crops except in war years. Between 1933 and 1941, and since 1945, farmers have been able to borrow from the Commodity Credit Corporation stated amounts on cotton, wheat, corn, and tobacco. When the loan rate is higher than the price at which the farmer can sell the product, the Commodity Credit Corporation takes over the produce, making no claim for principal or interest. Thus the loan rate is in effect a minimum price at which the government will purchase. The Agricultural Adjustment Act of 1933 gave the Secretary of Agriculture wide discretion in the amount of the loans to be made on each product, but Congress later specified these amounts, usually in terms of "parity." Full parity support meant that the price would be supported at the average price during the years 1909-14 (for most crops), raised or reduced by the percentage by which the main cost of living items of farmers and their equipment had risen or fallen since

---

[24] Allen, op. cit., 109.
[25] Ibid., 93, 98, 111, 132.
[26] Brandt, Reconstruction of World Agriculture, 103, 105.

the base period. But the support price was fixed in legislation at 52 to 75% of parity in 1938, 85% in 1941 and 90% in 1942 (except for crops affecting the feeding of livestock, and cotton, which was to be supported at 92.5% of parity). These supports, however, did not apply to crops and livestock accounting for 56% of gross cash farm income in 1953. By 1941 the Commodity Credit Corporation had made loans and purchases amounting to $3 billion and had heavy commitments for cotton, corn, and wheat (in spite of controls on production). But rising prices owing to war permitted successful liquidation, and support prices were used to expand output during the war of 1939-45.

After 1945 support prices were reinstated on many products. Output was maintained, and the government was taking over large amounts of produce. The European Recovery Program (Marshall Plan) enabled the Commodity Credit Corporation to sell some of its grain to European countries in 1948. But by 1950 the government had incurred net losses of $517 million since 1933 and had set aside $620 million to cover possible further losses on the $4,039 million at that time committed in loans, inventories, and crop purchase contracts. Although government transactions involved profits during the war years, losses mounted rapidly from 1946 to 1949. In 1948 and 1949, new legislation substituted adjustable price supports (75-90% of parity) for rigid 90% supports. When supplies were above normal, price supports were to be lowered by specified amounts to induce greater consumption and smaller output, but the application of the new principle to wheat, corn, cotton, peanuts, and rice was postponed. In 1949 new legislation also changed the parity base to the average price of a farm product in the most recent ten years in relation to the prices of other farm commodities. This modification provided for a relative price structure more consistent with current consumer preferences, export demand, and production costs. But support prices still failed to reflect adequately changes in cost of production, with the result that output exceeded foreseeable needs and the Commodity Credit Corporation was committed to spend $4.3 billions on wheat, corn, and cotton in January 1954, and demands on it were still rising.[27] This policy raised prices to domestic consumers, who also (as taxpayers) met the losses incurred by the government on exports at world prices and on the destruction or deterioration of its holdings. Farm organizations opposed proposals in 1949 by the Secretary of Agriculture to subsidize farm incomes without maintaining prices at the expense of consumers: they objected to the regulation necessary to keep the subsidy under control.

In Canada wartime exports of food under inter-government contracts set minimum prices for a wide variety of products. But at the end of the war in 1945, purchases were reduced and also prices. The Agricultural Prices Support Act of 1944 (made permanent in 1950) provided for gov-

[27] U.S., *Econ. Rep. of the President*, Jan. 1954, Ch. 8.

ernment price supports, but for only particular products under unusual pressure and without any parity formula. An Agricultural Prices Support Board, when it decides on support, purchases at a stated price all of the produce offered to it, and resells to consumers at a loss. Subsidies have been provided in this form for milk, cheese, and hogs.[28] The Prairie Farm Assistance Act of 1939 virtually provides a crop insurance program for the most important agricultural region. The Canadian Wheat Board Act 1935 established a government agency through which farmers might, if they wished, market wheat, and the Wheat Board was given a monopoly of the marketing of wheat in 1943, when the monopoly was extended to July 31, 1953. In 1948 the Board was made the sole marketing agency for oats and barley produced and sold in Manitoba, Saskatchewan, and Alberta. The board makes initial prices each season which operate as support prices. Most of the proceeds of sale above these prices are later distributed among sellers to the Board. Also various provincial governments had prior to 1948 authorized marketing boards or schemes regulating production and marketing within the province. The Dominion Agricultural Products Marketing Act of 1949 permitted such boards, approved in their own province, to extend their controls to inter-provincial and export trade, and the power has been used by a few boards.[29]

The British government has also set minimum prices for all major agricultural products since 1939 primarily to increase output. Thus its objective is very different from that of the U.S.A. But until 1954 it was also the principal buyer of agricultural produce, both imported and domestic. Prices are announced by the Minister of Agriculture every February "in the light of all the relevant factors." The government has usually granted increases in price to cover increases in costs thus placing farmers on a "cost plus" basis. Prices are reviewed when costs rise in the middle of the year, particularly when the wage rate for agricultural laborers is increased (which is held to justify a similar increase in farm profits). In principle falling costs also justify a fall in prices except reductions in cost due to increased efficiency (an uneconomical policy in the long run). Even where production targets have been reached the government has not reduced incentives to increased production. The net income of farmers was £59 million in 1937-8, £184 million in 1946-7, and £293 million (estimated) in 1950-1.[30] Until 1954 the government resold agricultural produce at prices aimed at keeping down the cost of living. The taxpayers met the resulting losses (which amounted to £246 millions in 1950-1), but domestic consumers benefited from subsidized prices.

In Denmark the government supports the prices of butter and sugar. In Norway and Sweden the government sets minimum prices. In Sweden it

---

[28] U.N., *Progress in Land Reform*, 269.

[29] *For. Agric.*, Nov. 1950, 253.

[30] *For. Agric.*, Jan. 1950.

aims to maintain the same relation between total farm income and costs as in 1938-9,[31] and in Norway to keep farm profits in a constant relation to industrial wages.[32] In the Netherlands, price supports are administered by semi-government agencies. The Egyptian government has supported the price of cotton; in 1952 it took over all cotton future contracts and offered to buy cotton at a stated price.

Government subsidies to agriculture are fairly general in developed capitalist countries. Government purchases to maintain prices result in subsidies when the operation results in losses. The losses of the Federal Farm Board after 1929, of the Commodity Credit Corporation after 1933, and those of the British and French governments, represented subsidies on a changing variety of products at changing rates. The U.S.A. has attempted to control these subsidies by payments to producers to limit their acreage, which are further subsidies. In Britain since 1907 and in the U.S.A. and Canada since the 1930s the government has provided school meals free or below cost. This program has been regarded in the U.S.A. as a means of disposing of surpluses to a class of the population that would not otherwise buy or would not otherwise buy so much. But it is also a means of increasing the returns from expenditure on education.

Governments also subsidize particular agricultural products. The U.S.A. subsidizes sugar production. Britain has also subsidized beet sugar production since 1925. The government has also subsidized wheat since 1933 by paying wheat producers each year the difference between the average price received and an announced "standard price." These "deficiency payments" were paid out of a tax on flour; that is, by consumers. The maximum wheat production that could participate in this scheme was set. In New Zealand, since 1935, the government has purchased wheat from farmers and sold it to millers at a loss. In 1939 the price of wheat was about 50% above the world price. In Australia the government paid £89 million in subsidies during the 25 years to 1944-45, of which £29 millions was for wheat.[33] In South Africa, subsidies were introduced in 1930 to increase national self-sufficiency in food. They amounted to £25 million during the next ten years. In 1939-40 farmers were aided by increases in the prices paid by consumers for food amounting to £6.6 million, by direct subsidies of £7.5 million (paid almost wholly to white producers) and by subsidized railroad rates. The efficiency of subsidized producers has not been controlled with the result that inefficient farmers and processors have been supported and soil has deteriorated.[34]

---

[31] *For. Agric.*, Dec. 1949, Feb. 1952, March 1952.

[32] *For. Agric.*, March 1952.

[33] The above figures do not include aid through domestic price raising schemes (Australia: Rural Reconstruction Commission, *Commercial Policy in Relation to Agriculture*, 159, 160, 254, 286, 308).

[34] Union of South Africa, Industrial and Agricultural Requirements Commission, *Third Interim Report*, 1941, 30, 32, 60.

Switzerland subsidized grain production during the depression, when the government guaranteed a price which was two or three times the world price. Holland paid similar subsidies in the early 1930s.[35] Butter and sugar production were subsidized in Denmark and cattle feeds in Norway. Spain has subsidized industrial crops notably cotton, the output of which has increased, but at a cost 50% above that in the U.S.A.

The war of 1939-45 resulted in subsidies to stimulate output where imports were impeded, or likely to be, or to insulate the internal cost of living from inflationary pressures in world markets. The British subsidies since 1939 had both objectives; those in the U.S.A., neither. British subsidies on home-produced food were about 44% of cost and those on imported food about 16%. Canada paid subsidies during the war to encourage production, and in 1949 to assist the sale of crop surpluses. Norway subsidized butter, milk and grain to damp inflationary pressures, and Portugal, Australia, New Zealand, Sweden and the Netherlands have followed similar policies. Australia subsidizes fertilizer sales and wheat and milk delivered to butter and cheese plants when the estimated cost of production falls short of average receipts from domestic and foreign sales. By setting the maximum domestic price for wheat below the world price, it subsidizes poultrymen and dairymen. New Zealand raised the wheat subsidy in 1942. But the Netherlands in 1948, and many other countries in the next few years, reduced their subsidies[36] (Ch. 31). In the colonial areas, subsidies are unusual, particularly on native products. Subsidies on white agricultural production, however, occur and may be important (e.g., in Kenya).

Subsidies on exports (or bounties) provide a way of maintaining domestic prices above foreign prices. Losses on government trading due to such price differences in the U.S.A. and many other countries are in fact export bounties. Bounties may also be provided for specific products but they are likely to draw retaliation from competing exporting countries. In 1938 only the Danubian countries were subsidizing exports of wheat and flour, but following an announcement that the U.S.A. would pay such subsidies in the 1938-9 season, similar subsidies were granted by Canada, Australia, Argentina, and Uruguay. In France, wheat exports were subsidized in 1931. In Australia, exports, mainly of fruit, were subsidized until 1939. In Holland exports were subsidized after 1929. Egypt subsidized exports of wheat and corn during the 1930s. Although it thus offset to some extent the effect on landowners of a fall in cotton prices, it raised the cost of living at a time when the incomes of cultivators were falling.[37]

The effect of subsidies is to increase the allocation of resources to the products subsidized at the expense of taxpayers. But benefits accrue to

---

[35] Brandt, *op. cit.*, 102, 105; *For. Agric.*, June 1951.
[36] *For. Agric.*, Dec. 1949, July 1950, June 1951.
[37] Warriner, *op. cit.*, 32, 49.

consumers if domestic prices are kept down (as in Britain) or to foreign buyers if produce is exported below the domestic price (as in the U.S.A.). Resources are misallocated by reference to the ideal in a peaceful world with free international trade and stable relations between agricultural and industrial production. But it is far more difficult to say that there is misallocation in relation to conditions in the real world.

c. Restriction of Output or Sales

If government aid succeeds in raising the returns to farmers, it maintains or increases output. But, as the cost of aid depends on output, governments commonly try to control the cost of aid by regulating output, unless they are aiming at expansion of production (as in Britain). Some have allowed producers considerable power over output and others have assumed control themselves.

Britain sought, under the Agricultural Marketing Act of 1931, to assist agriculture through virtual cartels. Agricultural producers were authorized to organize compulsory marketing schemes operated by registered boards, which were producer-controlled, four-fifths of the members being producers and one-fifth appointed by the Minister of Agriculture. These Boards were empowered to set the price at which the producers, but not wholesalers or retailers, could sell, and the quantity to be sold by any producer. From 1931 to 1933, such Boards were established for all the more important agricultural commodities (wheat being subsidized out of a tax on flour), but they became inactive when the government began to encourage the expansion of agriculture. In 1948, the boards for bacon and potatoes were in abeyance, the board for milk was operating in accordance with government policy, and the board for hogs was in operation.[38] And although the government was itself buying 75% of all farm produce at government-guaranteed prices, and was urging expansion of output, it authorized the continuance of the Boards under producer control. Neither the Ministry of Food (representing consumers more than farmers) nor the Treasury (which was responsible for subsidies on food) was represented. The Minister of Agriculture, however, was authorized to overrule a board if he believed it to be regulating output or prices against the public interest.

A number of European governments reduced output in response to a shrinkage of foreign demand. In Holland during the depression, semi-government monopolies were set up for a number of products, with power to control output. Production was stimulated, however, where it would reduce imports (e.g., grains and feed).[39] When the foreign market for cheese declined after 1928, the Swiss government reduced production and imports of butter, cheese, oil seeds, vegetable fats, and foodstuffs. It also

[38] *Economist*, Dec. 11, 1948; *For. Agric.*, Jan. 1950.
[39] *For. Agric.*, June 1951.

compelled the margarine and shortening industries to mix 5 to 15% of butter with their vegetable product, and prohibited non-farmers from fattening pigs and restricted the import of pigs.[40] Denmark restricted exports to maintain their price, and also the production of bacon. The British import quota for bacon was divided among individual farmers.[41] In Germany, the large estate owners successfully demanded assistance from the Nazi government. It restricted the processing and acreage devoted to sugar beets, and regulated grain production and consumption. Finally, it established a highly centralized government "Food Estate" (*Reichsnährstand*), which controlled all production, handling, and distribution of food mainly through its power to fix prices at the farm and at all subsequent stages. Its chief purpose was to assist agriculture to minimize dependence on imports.

In the U.S.A., the government sought to reduce output between 1933 and 1936 in order to reduce surpluses, and between 1936 and 1938 to conserve the soil (corn, cotton, tobacco, and wheat being among the crops most likely to cause soil erosion). Acreage goals were set for major crops; goals were below what the farmer was expected to plant without control; they were based upon demand, the prospective carry-over, and the objective of maintaining price parity. The goals were broken down into quotas for states, smaller areas and, finally, farms. Farmers received cash and other inducements to limit acreage accordingly. In the first two years of the program, more than half the farmers in the country thus increased their incomes, benefit payments amounting in 1934 to about $600 million. The necessary funds were obtained from processing taxes, until 1936, when this system of taxation was held unconstitutional, and thereafter from general taxation. As further inducements farmers were offered reduced prices for fertilizers and other materials, participation in crop insurance (for a time and mainly for wheat), and the opportunity to borrow on crops. Indirectly, however, farmers hoped for higher prices if all farmers participated. A storage program promised to reduce price fluctuations, and a conservation program to maintain the value of farm land. In order to obtain immediate results at the outset of the program, in 1933 crop acreage was reduced by plowing under crops already sown, and livestock was reduced by destroying about 6.2 million pigs and 200,000 brood sows. The government established market quotas for cotton, tobacco, and to some extent, wheat, and penalized farmers marketing in excess of their quota.

Following on these measures the acreage of the four major crops fell 20% between 1933 and 1942. But the output of corn, wheat and tobacco (but not cotton) increased because output per acre increased more than the number of acres was reduced. Farmers concentrated on their more

---

[40] Brandt, *Reconstruction of World Agriculture*, 105.
[41] *Ibid.*, 104.

productive acres and cultivated them more intensively than before. Acres excluded from some crops were diverted to other crops, the output of which increased. The separate effect of restriction on prices is difficult to measure. Prices rose but did not reach "parity." But they would doubtless have risen from their low point in 1932 without government action. The major effect of restrictive efforts probably was to hold down increases in output without preventing them altogether, to improve production methods, and to protect the land by restricting the most erosive crops. Net farm incomes in current dollars fell from $5.7 billion in 1929 to $1.7 billion in 1932, and rose to $4.5 billion in 1939. Between 1935-9 and 1953 it rose over 20% in dollars of 1935-9 purchasing power.

In Japan the Silk Redundancy Scheme in 1935 provided for removing excess capacity from silk raising and from reeling mills, and for assistance in establishing cooperative reeling mills to free farmers from the influence of the big reelers. In Cuba the government sought, in 1926, to raise the price of sugar by setting maximum production, providing output quotas for mills and regulating the annual period of grinding, but these controls were removed in 1928 when production in other countries increased. Authority to control was restored in 1936, provided international controls were established.[42]

Some colonial governments have restricted export crops. The price of rubber has fluctuated widely. The demand has been inelastic, because 75% of it has been used for automobile tires, which are essential to the automobile but represent a small part of its total cost. Supply is inelastic in the short run in response to rises in price owing to the length of time (about 8 years) necessary to grow a tree to the point at which it can be tapped. Supply is inelastic downward because plantations have considerable overhead investment in organization, investments in clearing the land and maturing the trees, and in labor recruited from a distance. When prices fall, production continues unless they fall below the direct cost of production, at which level they cover none of the overhead costs. Furthermore, as prices fall producers may even increase their output to maintain their income. Consequently the British Parliament in the Rubber Restriction Act of 1922 imposed a prohibitive tax on exports of rubber from Malaya by any producer beyond a percentage of his "standard production" (in principle, his actual production for the year ending October 31, 1920). The percentage of standard production permitted could be raised or lowered quarterly as the price fell below or rose above a "pivotal price," and in fact ranged between 50% and 100% of standard production. Prices rose for a time but fell after 1926 in spite of export restrictions to the maximum permitted by the law. The scheme lapsed in October 1928, partly, if not largely, because the growers in the Dutch East Indies did not co-

[42] U.S. Tariff Commission, *Agricultural Pastoral and Forest Industries in Cuba*, 1947, 25.

operate, and the higher prices resulting from Malayan restrictions stimulated increased output in the Dutch areas. The percentage of rubber in the Far East coming from British possessions fell from 72.5% in 1921 to 57% in 1927, and the reclaiming of rubber expanded in the U.S.A.

The governments of Nigeria and the Gold Coast have considered restricting the planting of cacao to the most suitable areas and encouraging other agricultural crops. High prices for cacao are said to have unduly raised the price of other products presumably because of shortages of imports or failure of other agricultural production to respond to price increases.[43] In Southern Rhodesia the government has been reducing the supply of cattle on native reserves to their carrying capacity, which is based on rainfall.[44]

3. Activities Stabilizing the Rewards of Agriculture

At least since the time of the Pharaohs in ancient Egypt, governments have tried to protect themselves against fluctuations in food supply due to the weather by carrying over stocks from years of high output to years of low output. Such a program might be aimed at stabilizing the price. If so, the government must estimate the price for the product at which its losses and profits will balance over long periods. But the price must be changed in response to long-run changes in demand and supply (the latter due to changes in the cost of production or in competition from other countries). And in any event, stability of price will not stabilize the incomes of producers if the crop fluctuates in size.

Many marketing schemes have involved an element of price stabilization, but few have been restricted to it. Furthermore, government schemes of this sort, aimed at redistributing the physical supply over periods of time, are restricted to products that can be stored. Consequently, governments have tried to redistribute over time the monetary proceeds of sale at fluctuating prices. These prices may change because of (a) fluctuations in purchasing power generated in non-industrial sectors or (b) fluctuations in supply. The government levies some form of a tax in years of high price, and pays a subsidy in years of low price, thus establishing a fund comparable to a contributory unemployment insurance fund for workers. If the government aims at a stable money income per unit of output after allowing for payments to and from the fund, it must again estimate the prices that can be so maintained in view of the conditions of demand and supply. Even so, fluctuations in output cause fluctuations in farm incomes. Finally, as a practical matter, it has often been difficult to induce farmers to forego a good time when it is possible, particularly where they distrust the people who hold the stabilization fund.

In the U.S.A. the operations of the Federal Farm Board were intended

---

[43] *Pendered Report,* 13.
[44] Southern Rhodesia, *Report of the Secretary of Native Affairs for 1946,* 7.

to stabilize farm prices, after first raising them. Since 1933 government actions have resulted in some physical carryover, but also considerable subsidy. In New Zealand marketing boards for meat and dairy products were established before 1939 to hold back part of the price of the product in good years and pay it out in years of low price (but not to carry over stocks of the products). But the boards restricted themselves mainly to propaganda to promote sales, although they established guaranteed prices for dairy products in 1936 and had a balance of £9.5 million in the dairy fund and a small balance in the meat fund in 1938. During and after the war of 1939 to 1945 a number of governments used stabilization funds to protect their economies from external inflationary pressures. They withheld from producers part of the high export prices, promising to distribute the money in later periods of depressed prices. In New Zealand the government allowed farmers to receive in wartime only those increases in price believed to be necessary to cover increases in cost, and the policy was continued during the postwar inflation. In 1950 the government and the Woolgrowers Association agreed to freeze, in the woolgrowers' own bank accounts, one-third of the proceeds of the sale of wool at the then high prices. The proceeds bore no interest, but were exempt from income and social security taxes. Some of the Australian marketing boards pursued similar policies.

Part of the proceeds of high wartime prices for cotton from the Gezira (Sudan) were held back by the government in a stabilization fund, but by 1948 the cultivators were claiming their money and were unconvinced by the government's contention that more money would not at that time enable the cultivators to buy more goods. The government of Uganda retained part of the proceeds of exports of cotton for the same reason; the growers reacted in the same way as they had in the Sudan.[45] The Nigeria and Gold Coast cocoa growers (who are small producers) have in the past been very critical of the price of cocoa, because only 13 European firms bought 98% of the crop in 1939 and it was believed that buyers agreed among themselves to depress the price. Such agreements appear to have been made, but also to have broken down. But in 1937, the farmers on the Gold Coast so resented buying agreements that they refused to sell cocoa for a whole season, and almost completely boycotted European import goods. Consequently the West African Produce Control Board was established in 1939 with a monopoly of export in Nigeria and the Gold Coast (it extended its activities to other crops in 1942). Lack of shipping space and other hindrances to export caused difficulty during the war, but by 1947 the Board had an accumulated profit of £25.8 million, because it had regulated its payments to cocoa farmers by reference to the prospects of export sales and "the volume of cash required by producers to cover costs and purchases of the limited supplies of con-

---

[45] *Economist*, May 12, 1951.

sumer goods available under wartime allocation."[46] In 1947 separate boards were established for the Gold Coast and Nigeria (each board consisting of representatives of cacao producers, merchants and government officials) and took over the accumulated profits of the previous joint board. The cacao boards have endeavored since 1947 to improve cocoa production and marketing and assist the cocoa farming community generally, and by 1951 they had accumulated £50 million, of which £35 million was regarded as a stabilization fund and £15 million as available for regional development. In 1951, the Nigerian government set up boards for palm produce, ground nuts, and cotton. All the boards are to stabilize prices paid for produce and finance three regional development boards that have begun to stimulate domestic food production.[47] But the cocoa growers, who have been receiving about 50% of the world price, have been critical of the withholding policy.[48] The Uganda government has fixed a price for cotton for the whole season, since 1939, aiming at a "fair price" to the producer. If processors and exporters achieve profit margins higher than those set by the government, the surplus is paid into a government fund which can be used to stabilize prices, although part of it was diverted in 1947 to the general revenue because the fund was unexpectedly large. Similar arrangements have been introduced for *robusta* coffee.[49] In the Belgian Congo the proceeds of an export tax on coffee are paid into a fund which has been used to buy pyrethrum for spraying coffee trees, but which can be used to stabilize the price of coffee. In Indonesia the government has kept down the internal price of copra when world prices have risen, paying the resulting profits into a copra fund out of which it has financed losses in years when the export price has fallen below its purchase price.[50]

In Sweden export taxes on lumber and lumber products have recently been linked with export prices, the proceeds of the tax being paid into a stabilization fund, 70% of which is to be paid out to the industry at the rate of 20% a year beginning in 1958, the remaining 30% being used for various social purposes. This arrangement, by stabilizing part of the proceeds, also reduces the inflationary pressures resulting from high export prices.

4. Activities Restricting the Rewards of Agriculture

A government may hold down the prices of agricultural products and, thereby, the cost of living. In a country which does not export, it may set maximum prices by law or subsidize imports. In an exporting country

[46] U.K., House of Commons *Fifth Report from the Select Committee on Estimates: Colonial Development*, 1948, xi.

[47] (London) *Times Review of the British Colonies*, Winter 1951.

[48] *Economist*, May 12, 1951.

[49] *Pendered Report*, 28.

[50] U.N., *Ec. Surv. Asia and Far East*, *1951*, 157.

it may allow restricted private exports or monopolize exports and take the resulting profits.

Medieval European governments sometimes sought to maintain domestic food supplies by restricting or prohibiting profitable exports. The British government prohibited wheat exports in 1361. At the beginning of the 17th century, however, this policy was modified to permit exports when domestic prices fell below a prescribed level (which set a floor under domestic prices when there were exports). At the beginning of the 18th century the government began to subsidize exports when prices fell below the prescribed level. Thus shortages abroad were prevented from drawing supplies from Britain and raising prices there above the stated level. Plentiful British harvests were allowed to drive domestic prices down only to the "floor" price. In general price fluctuations were kept within limits and the impact of extreme fluctuations in supply was felt by other countries.

Inflationary pressures during the 1939-45 war revived efforts to restrain increases in food prices in food exporting countries. Rising world prices would have encouraged exports from New Zealand, Australia, and South Africa, and pulled internal prices up towards world prices. But these governments set maximum internal prices and retained sufficient internal supplies to meet demand at these prices. While they had exported some products at prices below domestic prices before 1939, export prices were above domestic thereafter. Producers profited from rising prices to the extent that they were allowed to export.

Governments holding down domestic prices, prohibiting private exports, and exporting at world prices annexed the gains from price increases. The schemes for government retention of part of the rising prices of export crops in African colonial areas (p. 123) were of this type, except that governments often prescribed the subsequent use of the proceeds (e.g., for subsidies in bad years, improvement of the crop, or general development). The governments of Burma and Thailand monopolize rice exports and keep the domestic buying price considerably below the export price.[51] In Turkey the most important crops, and all export crops, are purchased by a state monopoly. Between 1939 and 1945 there was a considerable margin between the price paid to the producer and the export price.

The government of Argentina in 1946 created the Argentine Institute for the Promotion of Trade (IAPI) with an almost complete monopoly of foreign trade, especially exports. The Institute bought produce internally and sold externally at world prices. Producers may sell internally at any price (except that IAPI controls the price of grain to flour mills). Crops, part of which are exported, sell at the prices set by IAPI, but other crops

---

[51] U.N., *Ec. Surv. Asia and Far East, 1952*, 2, 5.

may sell at prices above those announced by IAPI.[52] In 1947 internal purchase prices were about 30% of export prices, but rose to about 60% in 1951 as export prices fell. The profits of IAPI (from both its import and export business) which were intended to be used for economic development were high in 1946 ($247 million) and 1947 ($500 million) but fell thereafter—there was a loss in 1949 and a small profit in 1950 and 1951.[53]

The amount of profit that a government can thus obtain depends partly on its power over the world price. If a country provides most of the world supply of a product, competition among many exporters will result in competitive prices. But a government export monopoly could pay the same price to producers as previously but export a reduced quantity at a monopoly price. In the longer period, however, the higher prices may bring out supplies from new sources or encourage substitution. But in the main Argentina was taking advantage of, but not raising, world prices. Its profit depended, therefore, on the quantities it could sell and on the margin between buying and selling prices (after allowing for trading costs). Low prices to producers increased the profit margin per unit of product, but discouraged production and exports (and somewhat affected world prices). The acreage planted to export crops fell 35% between 1939 and 1949, and output fell because of failure to supply farm machinery, legislation increasing the cost of farm labor, industrialization which diverted labor from agriculture, drought, and locusts. Some land was diverted to cattle but cattle growing was also discouraged by rising labor costs and labor shortages. Meat exports fell in 1948. Furthermore, low internal prices for food at a time when wages were being raised diverted an increasing proportion of output to domestic consumption (especially meat). Finally, high export prices for linseed (due partly to the fact that supply was discouraged by keeping the purchase price down to 25% of the export price) induced the U.S.A., which had bought half the Argentine output, to increase its own production. Consequently, the program proved to be only a temporary source of development funds, and the government revised its policy in 1950. A new Argentine Livestock Institute was established to control the livestock industry from producer to consumer, with power to control prices, domestic consumption, the operation of packing plants and their export quotas.[54] Buying prices were raised, thus increasing the cost of living and reducing export profits. The exchange rate for meat exports was raised to increase the peso proceeds of exports 50%. The government agreed to allocate exchange for imports of farm equipment. It raised prices for the 1952-53 season 30 to 50% over the previous year, and

---

[52] *For. Agric.*, Aug. 1951.
[53] *Ibid.*
[54] U.S. Dept. of Agric., *Foreign Crops and Markets*, Oct. 30, 1950.

promised to share export profits with farmers, although little profit was in sight unless production expanded greatly.[55]

Taxes can be used to restrict agriculture, just as subsidies can be used to expand it, but such taxes are unusual. In Britain, Holland, and the U.S.A., taxes have been levied on the processing of agricultural produce, but the proceeds have been used to assist agriculture. But a reduction of import duties may have a similar effect. When the new industrial class achieved political power in Britain in the early 19th century, it found itself in sharp conflict with landowners interested in high agricultural rents, because it desired low food prices to reduce upward pressures on wages and costs. England had ceased to be a grain exporter in about 1792 and thereafter usually imported in spite of import duties. The 1815 Corn Law prohibited imports of wheat when its price was below 10 shillings a bushel. In 1844 the import duties on wheat were removed. By 1939 Britain was dependent on imports for over two-thirds of its food, and only 5% of the labor force was in agriculture (compared with 23% in 1841).[56]

Governments in Russia, eastern Europe, and China require agricultural production. Since they choose not to rely on price incentives, they seek to obtain production with less reward than if they relied on free enterprise. Denmark has required deliveries of grain since 1943,[57] but such deliveries are unusual outside the socialist countries. The primary purpose of the Russian government (and later of the other socialist governments) was to increase the production of industrial goods without reliance on foreign capital. It was therefore necessary to divert labor from agriculture. The urban population increased from about 30 millions in 1926 to 70 millions in 1950.[58] The government had to support this increase in urban population by transfers of food from the agricultural sector. It has therefore sought to increase agricultural production and to arrange for the necessary transfer of produce. Between 1929 and 1940 it emphasized increases in the production of grain, but in 1934 it initiated attempts to increase the livestock supply which were resumed after 1945.

The five-year overall plans for production made by the State Planning Committee (*Gosplan*) (which are revised at shorter intervals) include output targets for grain, cotton, flax, beets, horses, cattle, sheep, goats, pigs, and other products, acreage yields for crops and related targets for tractors and other implements and fertilizers. Other products of more local significance are dealt with by the governments of the constituent republics and some of the production of minor crops has been left to individual initiative.

[55] *For. Agric.*, Aug. 1951.
[56] Clark, *op. cit.* (2d), 408.
[57] *For. Agric.*, Feb. 1952.
[58] *Economist*, March 10, 1951.

To realize its objectives the government has reorganized agriculture. It established state farms, mostly for grain and commercial crop production (Ch. 6). The managers of these farms are responsible for achieving the targets given them.

The chief change in organization, however, has been the collectivization of agriculture,[59] achieved with much difficulty and suffering primarily as a matter of political objectives. Farmers producing as individuals for the market gravitated back to capitalism rather than towards other workers whom the government was endeavoring to convert to socialized industry. Increased efficiency of production, partly by mechanization, was a secondary motive. Nevertheless, collectivization has permitted larger-scale farming; many private holdings would have been too small to utilize tractors efficiently. But collectives that sell part of their produce on the market are still regarded as a transitional form impeding the achievement of full Communism. Stalin stated that the realization of Communism requires that collective farm property be raised to common property and that the sale of produce on the market be replaced by direct exchange of agricultural for industrial products.[60] But this transformation cannot be speedily achieved.

The government announced its intention to encourage the collective working of the land in 1919. But even the first Five-Year Plan provided that only 39% of all marketable grain be provided by collective farms in 1932-3. Early in 1930 attempts to accelerate collectivization produced disastrous results. Cattle was slaughtered to avoid confiscation or socialization at low prices, or because the peasants believed that the cattle could not survive, or because mechanical power was expected to replace cattle. Failure of the tractor supply also caused peasants to leave collectives which they had recently joined. Consequently, Stalin condemned forceful collectivization that disregarded the diversity of conditions in agriculture. The total number of *kolkhoz* was reduced from 110,200 on March 1, 1930, to 83,200 on May 1, 1930.[61] Pressure was released for a time, but later the regional governments were authorized to use "all necessary measures" against the *kulaks* (including deportation). *Kulak* property was confiscated and distributed among poor peasants, to enable them to contribute to the collectives that are now the major organizations for agricultural production. These cooperatives receive production targets. The basic pressure to achieve them is the requirement of delivery of a portion of their output to the government at low prices before any other sales are made. The 9,000 government tractor stations are the collecting agents for the govern-

[59] W. Ladejinsky, "Collectivization of Agriculture in the Soviet Union," *Pol. Sci. Quar.*, March and June 1934.

[60] *Bolshevik, cit. N.Y. Times*, Oct. 4, 1952.

[61] Ladejinsky, *op. cit.*

ment and also receive part of the produce for their services. They may refuse to serve farms raising crops which are not in accordance with government policies, or make higher charges to such farms than to others. Loans by the government may be refused or high interest charged to non-conforming agricultural units.

The amount of compulsory deliveries and the method of their calculation were frequently changed before 1933, but thereafter the rules were more stabilized. The amount of crop deliverable depended on the acreage sown and the fertility of the land; adjustments, however, did not offset all differences in fertility.[62] Livestock deliveries depended on the number of livestock on the farm. This arrangement, however, increased the compulsory deliveries when acreage was extended or herds were enlarged which diminished the incentive to increase output in such ways. Consequently since 1940 compulsory crop deliveries have been based on total cultivable land and livestock deliveries on total agricultural land. In 1939 the government also prescribed, in great detail for each collective, the crops, timing of operations, use of fertilizers, and improvements to be made. During 1940, the sown areas of collective farms increased by 7.5 million acres and the number of livestock by 12 million. Compulsory deliveries were five million tons more in 1940 than in 1939. Considering the grain problem largely solved, the government then restored to each collective discretion in distributing the crops according to its own judgment "within the framework of their sowing program." But it continued to require deliveries of prescribed kinds of grain. In 1949 when effort was again concentrated on increasing livestock production, the compulsory deliveries were again adjusted to increase incentives. If a *kolkhoz* exceeded the official targets for animal output, its minimum compulsory deliveries to the government of meat, milk, and wool were reduced 10%; but those of cooperatives failing to reach their targets were raised 10%.

The incentives to agricultural production depend on the extent to which increased effort brings increased reward to the agricultural workers. These rewards are partly in kind and partly in cash. After making compulsory deliveries and paying for tractor service both in kind, part of the grain is distributed among the members. The remainder of the grain and all cotton, flax, and sugar beets are sold to the government at a price some 25% above the compulsory delivery price.[63] Other crops are sold in village or other markets, and provide cash income to the members. The total net income of households in agriculture (in 1937) came 52% from payments received in kind, 25% from money received for sale of farm products, 13% from money payments on the basis of labor days, salaries of managers, and premiums, and 10% from wages (on state farms and trac-

---

[62] Bergson, *op. cit.*, 417.
[63] Bergson, *op. cit.*, 417.

tor stations).[64] The payments to the state are, however, comparable to land rents in non-socialist societies. They also provide much of the mechanism for transferring food and industrial materials from the agricultural to the industrial sector. In 1940 the government acquired one-third of the grain crop by compulsory deliveries and purchases. The state also uses non-economic rewards and coercion to reinforce its control of production. Various decorations are offered for outstanding performance by individuals.[65] At the other end of the scale is a series of punitive devices for failure to cooperate such as were used in the elimination of the *kulaks*.

The half- to two-acre plots of land allocated to members of cooperatives are islets of individual operation in a sea of collectivism. In 1937 about half the productive livestock was privately owned, and 21% of agricultural output was produced on these homesteads. But members have been tempted to neglect work on the collective farm to intensify work on their homesteads, and to encroach on collective land, with the result that the government in 1939 prescribed a minimum number of days of work in collective operations and provided criminal penalties for encroachment. But during the war of 1939-45 there were further diversions of labor, and sometimes of collective land to individualist operation.

The war of 1939 to 1945 devastated about 40% of all the collective farm land. The loss of practically all their tractors and most of their harvester-combines deprived the collectives in the west of their technical base, and in 1945 many were relying on the cow as the principal source of draft power. The government began to re-equip the collectives in 1946, but the pre-war level of mechanization had not been achieved by 1950. It also endeavored to restore their administrative efficiency, which had been seriously undermined during the war. It established the Council for Collective Farm Affairs to eliminate corruption and petty fraud by local officials, restore discipline, protect public lands, increase progressive management and improve democratic procedure within the collectives. The Council supervises compliance with the collective charter and with decisions of the government and party regarding collective farms. It can punish officials guilty of violating the charter of the collective, either prosecuting them or recommending their removal.

Under this system the cotton crop was reported to have increased more than 300% between 1913 and 1939, the sugar beet crop about 100%, and grains about 20%, both by improving methods of production and by increasing the area of land utilized.[66] But part of the increase after 1932 is apparent and not real, because the crop previously measured by what was put into the barns was thereafter measured by what had grown in the

---

[64] Bergson, "Soviet National Income and Product in 1937," *Quar. Jour. of Econ.*, May-August 1950, 214.

[65] Ch. 19.

[66] Schwartz, *op. cit.*, Ch. 9.

fields (the "biological crop"), which was apparently about 20% above the amount of grain actually harvested, owing to incomplete harvesting and other losses (estimated at 10% to 30% of the crop). Before the Revolution, peasants had widely scattered plots of land, one-third had no iron plow, and one-fourth no horse or ox. They produced with little manure and no artificial fertilizer; many harvested with a sickle and a flail. By 1938, 71% of all plowing was done by tractor, compared with 4% in 1929, and 48% of all harvesting by combines.[67] But it is not clear that the substitution of mechanical for animal power was economical within the conditions prevailing in Russia, particularly since tractors have not always been available at the best times. Mechanization has also made agriculture dependent on the industrial sector for equipment and power. It is estimated that after allowance for depreciation of equipment and non-farm materials used in agriculture (e.g., petroleum products, fertilizers, and insecticides), the net income from agriculture in 1932 was about 75% of that in 1928, and in 1937[68] about 115%. The major rewards from the reorganization and investment during the 1930s were expected in the next decade. But much of the result of previous efforts was destroyed between 1940 and 1945, and the next five years were devoted to recovering from these losses. The gross agricultural output planned for 1950 was 125% greater than that of 1932, but the plan included the new lands annexed at the end of the war in 1945, production on the prewar area being only about 10% greater in 1950 than in 1940.

The major efforts of the government have been aimed at increasing the output of grain and livestock. By 1939, after collectivization had been consolidated and basic technical improvements had been made, grain output (after allowance for the change in methods of reporting) appears to have been 15% higher than in 1928, and to have been obtained from 10% more acres. Any marked increases in efficiency must therefore have been largely offset by the taking in of inferior land. Nevertheless, the increase in grain output (especially the unprecedented crop of 118 million tons in 1940) permitted the government to accumulate the emergency food stocks that enabled it to survive the war. But some subsequent crops were 50% below the 1940 level that was again attained in 1947 and 1948. Agriculture had recovered from previous droughts, a part of the lost equipment had been replaced, the fertilizer supply had improved, an incentive wage system had been introduced (in 1947), and the weather was favorable. But these large crops (which cannot be expected every year) were only about 50% above those of 1913, whereas the population had increased about 43%. If it is true that grain yields in 1950 were 25% to 33% above those in Czarist Russia,[69] progress has been considerable, but in 1933-7, the

[67] Baykov, op. cit., 331.
[68] Jasny, op. cit., Schwartz, op. cit., 309.
[69] U.N., Econ. Surv. of Europe Since the War, 1953, 46.

wheat yield was about 40% of the average in Germany and 55% of that in France at the same time.[70] And apparently the acreage devoted to intensive food and industrial crops has increased more than the total acreage, with the result that the proportion of acreage devoted to grain has fallen. The planned grain output for 1955 is about 152% of the actual output in the present area in 1940, the sown area about 96%, and the output per acre about 158%. But it is doubtful whether the planned increase in output will be achieved.[71]

Government efforts to increase livestock have been less successful. The two great slaughters (the first during the period of collectivization and the second during the war of 1939-45) were disastrous. By the middle of 1932, during the campaign for collectivization, the number of cattle and horses was 40% below 1928, of hogs 50%, and of sheep and goats 66%. After the consolidation of the collectives and the decision to permit individual farmers to own livestock, the number of hogs recovered to the 1928 level, but not that of other animals. As a result of war, in 1946 cattle were about 15% below 1941, hogs 60%, and sheep and goats 25%. The minimum planned numbers for 1955 were 24% above 1937 for cattle, 20% for pigs, and 120% for sheep and goats (all for the present area.)[72]

In 1953, after the death of Stalin, the government announced that the output of agriculture had not increased in proportion to its technical equipment or to the potentialities of the collective farm regime. Grain was not fully harvested, livestock production had increased too slowly, and the output of potatoes and vegetables was too small. The rewards to agricultural workers in cash and produce were inadequate. The government, therefore, required the collective farms to abandon the practice of measuring their produce on the basis of apparent yields and to substitute actual quantities harvested. To "heighten the economic interest" of collective farmers and farms in increasing the output of potatoes, vegetables, and livestock products, the government increased the prices paid for compulsory deliveries of meat, milk, wool, potatoes, and vegetables, and raised the prices it would pay collective farms and farmers for these products beyond the compulsory deliveries. It promised improved marketing arrangements. The government noted that production on the individual homesteads of the members of the collective farms had been declining and the number of cows thereon had fallen. It therefore reduced the compulsory deliveries from the produce of these homesteads, reduced the monetary tax on them, and wrote off arrears of such taxes. Thus it reemphasized individual interest in agriculture. Finally, the government promised more mechanization and electrification, more fertilizers, and more technical assistance. Evidently the government has realized that

[70] For. Agric., Oct. 1953.
[71] U.N., Econ. Surv. of Europe Since the War, 1953, 46.
[72] U.N., Econ. Surv. of Europe Since the War, 1953, 47.

the pace of industrialization depends on progress in agriculture. The agricultural output for the enlarged territory in 1950 was planned to be about double that of 1932—a rate of increase which would permit a quadrupling of industrial output as measured by Russian statistics.[73]

The agricultural policy of all the eastern European countries is similar to that of Russia. All have accepted collectivization in principle, and the process has been accelerated since 1950 (Ch. 6). All require compulsory deliveries to the state. In Yugoslavia, after 1945, compulsory delivery quotas were high and independent of the size of crops. Bonuses were offered for deliveries in excess of quotas, both in cash and in coupons that permitted the purchase of industrial products at lower prices. State farms and collectives receive prices about 30% higher than those for individual farmers.[74] But compulsory deliveries were abolished by 1952 (except for wool). In China also agriculture is in process of collectivization and producers are under great pressure to deliver to the state.

In Britain the government was empowered to direct planting of the principal crops in wartime, but it refrained from coercion. The Ministry of Agriculture transmits production targets for major products to the county agricultural executive committees and local branches of the Farmers' Union, and relies upon persuasion to reach the targets. By regulating its purchase prices, it has stimulated great increases in output, but there are no compulsory deliveries.

---

[73] Speech by Premier Malenkov, cit., N.Y. Times, Aug. 10, 1953.
[74] For. Agric., Aug. 1951, July-Aug. 1952.

Chapter 9

Mineral Production

A. The Growth and Distribution of Mineral Production

Mineral production, which includes mining, quarrying, dredging, the drilling of wells (e.g., for petroleum, natural gas, sulphur, and salt), and the distillation of sea water, is an ancient form of production. In fact, the larger changes in the use of minerals constitute landmarks in human history in the spheres of economics and war. Gold and copper were in use in 4000 B.C., and silver nearly as early. Iron, probably of meteoric origin, was used in 3000 B.C., but the iron age dates from about 1300 B.C., and iron was in general use throughout civilized Europe by the 1st century B.C. Mineral production accelerated in Europe after the 11th century, but it began to rise to vast proportions towards the end of the 18th century, and is still increasing. The enormous production of the last 200 years has provided not only structural materials, but also the major sources of energy that have made possible the revolutionary increases in production during the period.

Mineral production, like industrial production, is less evenly distributed throughout the world than agriculture, but for different reasons. Mineral production responds to demand, but it can respond only where supplies of minerals are available. Consequently the pattern of distribution differs for each mineral. About 40% of the world output of coal (excluding the U.S.S.R.) is in the U.S.A. In 1952 Britain produced about 20%, Germany 11%, Poland 7%, France (including the Saar) 5%, Japan and India each about 4%, Belgium 3% and South Africa about 3%. Coal was also produced in Australia, Canada, the Netherlands, and Spain. Of the crude petroleum produced outside Russia in 1952, about 53% was produced in the U.S.A. and 13% in Canada, about 20% in Latin America (16% in Venezuela alone), about 23% in the Middle East,[1] and some 2% in Indonesia and

---

[1] There was little production in Iran in 1952, but the 1950 production has been included above.

134

Brunei. Nearly 90% of the natural gas is produced in the U.S.A. Uranium, is produced mainly in the Belgian Congo, Canada, South Africa, and Australia.

The minerals used for structural and electrical purposes are especially concentrated in the U.S.A. and Russia, although little reliable information is available about Russian mineral production.[2] Of the rest of the world's output of iron ore in 1952, 46% was produced in Canada and the U.S.A., 47% in Europe, and the remainder in North Africa, South Africa, and the Far East.[3] Both the U.S.A. and Britain have been rapidly using up their richest iron ore supplies, and are relying increasingly on imports. Of the world output (except Russia) of copper, about 33% is produced in the U.S.A., 20% in Chile, 10% each in Rhodesia and Canada, and 7% in the Belgian Congo. The production of tin is relatively concentrated, none being produced in the U.S.A., which is the largest consumer. In 1952 Malaya produced 36% of the output of concentrates (metal content) outside Russia, Indonesia 22%, Bolivia 20% and Thailand 6%. Over half the lead outside Russia is produced in Canada, the U.S.A. and Mexico, and 16% in Australia. Zinc and silver production are somewhat similarly distributed. In recent years about half the world output of gold (outside Russia) has been produced in South Africa, 14% in Canada, and 10% in the U.S.A. Of the world output (except Russia) of bauxite (aluminum ore), about 23% is produced in each of Surinam and British Guiana, 20% in the U.S.A., and 10% in France.[4] The production of minerals important as steel-alloying materials (some of which also have other uses) is scattered.[5]

Russia is reported to have the largest coal resources in the world (1654 billion metric tons in 1937), and also the largest petroleum resources. In 1938 the U.S.S.R. claimed 53.5% of the world's iron ore reserves, and is the leading source of manganese and chromium. It also has reserves of copper, lead, zinc, bauxite, nickel, uranium, and is one of the largest producers of gold.[6]

The present distribution of mineral production reflects in part the increased production of minerals generally. Rising demands exhaust existing sources of supply and necessitate a search for new ones. Between 1810

[2] Schwartz, *op. cit.*, 14 ff.

[3] The above figures do not allow for differences in the iron content of ores, which range from 25 to 65%. Of the European output about 40% was produced in France and about 15% in each of Sweden, Germany, and Britain. (U.N., *Monthly Bull. Stats.*, April 1953.)

[4] U.N., *Stat. Year Book*, 1948, 147.

[5] Of the nickel, 90% (outside Russia) is produced in Canada. Of the manganese, 33% is produced in the Gold Coast, 16% in India, 13% in the Union of South Africa, and about 8% in each of Brazil and the U.S.A. Of the chrome over 30% is produced in the Union of South Africa and about 15% in each of the Philippines, Southern Rhodesia, and Cuba. Of the tungsten, 60% is produced in China, Portugal, U.S.A., and Bolivia. Of the vanadium, over 50% is produced in the U.S.A., and 25% in Peru; and most of the molybdenum in the U.S.A. (U.N., *op. cit.*, 136, 148, 149, 150, 151.)

[6] Schwartz, *op. cit.*, 18 ff.

and 1910 the output of minerals increased about one hundredfold. But the distribution also reflects differential increases in demand for different minerals. Between 1800 and 1929 the output of coal increased 14,700%; of pig iron, 218,000%; of copper, 10,500%; and of lead, 7,300%. Even between 1890 and 1930, the world used more coal and metals than in all previous time. The output of petroleum increased nearly 400% between 1914 and 1943. The output of lead and zinc is still increasing. The output of copper changed little between 1934 and 1948, but the production of gold, silver, and tin has fallen in recent years. In the U.S.A. the output of minerals increased from a base of 100 in 1889 to 2220 in 1929, a rate of increase greater than in any other sector of the economy.[7]

B. The Productivity of Labor in Mineral Production and the Factors Affecting It

1. THE PRODUCTIVITY OF LABOR

There is little information on the comparative productivity of labor in particular branches of mineral production, or in mineral production in general in different countries. There are probably great inequalities among countries and some tendencies for inequalities to increase. In the U.S.A., output per man hour in mining generally rose some 400% between 1902 and 1949. Between 1902 and 1939 it rose about 483% in oil and gas wells, and 758% in phosphate rock, but 204% in bituminous coal and 172% in anthracite.[8] The decline in the grades of ore has been more than offset by mechanization and an increase in open-pit mining. In coal mining, physical output per man shift in 1884 was about 1.20 tons in the U.S.A. and Britain, but only about half as much in France and Belgium.[9] By 1938 it was 4.37 tons in the U.S.A. (bituminous), 2.4 tons in New South Wales, 1.83 in Upper Silesia, 1.79 in Poland, 1.62 in the Netherlands, 1.15 in Britain, 0.82 in France, and 0.74 in Belgium. Thus, by 1949 output per man shift in western Europe other than the Netherlands was not far above the levels 40 years previously, whereas in the U.S.A. it had risen nearly 80% and notably increased after 1945.[10] In Britain the amount of deep-mined coal produced per man-year in the period 1947-51 (averaged) was about 23% above that in 1922-25.[11]

Wherever the marginal product of labor in mineral production is higher than in other sectors, the average national product is raised when mineral production expands, although in underdeveloped countries expansion of mining has often merely postponed a decline in average product, owing to increasing population. The whole contribution of mineral production

---

7 U.S., *Minerals Year Book*, 1945, 33.
8 Clark, *op. cit.* (2d), 313; U.S., *Minerals Year Book*, 1949, 7.
9 Clark, *op. cit.* (2d), 313.
10 U.N., *Econ. Bull. for Europe*, Vol. 2, No. 2 (1948), 28.
11 U.K., National Coal Board *Report and Accounts* for 1951, 7.

to national income is a net gain only where the resources employed in mining would not otherwise be utilized. But even this contribution is relatively small in most countries. In the U.S.A. mineral production represents about 2% of the national income (about 25% of the contribution of agriculture).[12] Of this contribution, about 75% is from coal, oil, and gas. In South Africa, however, mining provided 27.5% of the national product in 1912 but 11.4% in 1948 (when manufacturing contributed twice as much as mining).[13] In Latin America, mineral production accounts for 14% of the national income in Peru, 12% in Mexico, 10% in Chile, and 2% in Argentina.[14] Petroleum production has hitherto provided only a small part of the national product even in the Middle East countries (although it is important in their government budgets and balance of payments). In Venezuela, however, it provides 30% of national income.

The proportion of the labor force in mining is small in most countries. It is highest in South Africa, Chile, Belgium and Britain. In South Africa about half the population obtained its livelihood directly or indirectly from gold mining in 1943, and in Kuwait and Bahrein 20 to 25% of the population is dependent on petroleum production. In all other countries the proportion is less than 3%, and in many less than 1%. Because of this relative unimportance there is little correlation between the proportion of the labor force in mining and national income. The proportion of workers in mining is relatively small in countries not only with the highest but also with the lowest national incomes.

Mineral production may, however, increase general productivity by providing cheap materials and energy for other branches of production. Large coal resources facilitated industrialization in Britain after 1750; this happened later in France, Germany, Belgium, the U.S.A., and Russia. Latin American countries, however, have been handicapped by lack of coal. Since the energy of coal was transformed into steam and harnessed in engines made of iron (later of steel), the nearness of iron resources to coal facilitated industrialization, especially in Britain and the U.S.A. More recently, however, Belgium, Germany, and Japan (and still more recently, Britain and the U.S.A.) have supported steel industries partly or wholly on imported ore. Changes in energy sources, however, change the relative importance of particular minerals. Especially during the 20th century, production has shifted somewhat from a coal-iron base to a petroleum-light metal-chemical-hydroelectric base. The U.S.A. and Russia are able to take advantage almost as well of the new as of the old base; but Britain is less well endowed with these materials. The principal mineral assets of Britain and Germany are coal. France, however, has iron ore, bauxite, and hydroelectric power, but no oil. Latin American countries have oil

---

[12] U.S., *Minerals Year Book,* 1949, 5.
[13] U.N., *Econ. Devel. of Selected Countries, 1950,* 243.
[14] U.N., *Econ. Surv. Latin Am.,* 1948, 64.

and hydroelectric power, and about 20% of the iron ore deposits of the world (mainly in Brazil and Cuba).

Mineral production may also make possible (or cheaper) the supply of services to other sectors of the economy. Gold mining stimulated the establishment of railroads and engineering works in South Africa,[15] the first hydroelectric works in New Zealand, and general development in California and Australia. Anthracite mining induced railroad building in Pennsylvania. Mining may also attract population. This may contribute to general productivity by bringing new skills, or by raising the population of a relatively underpopulated area to a more efficient size (as in parts of the U.S.A., New Zealand, Australia and Canada).

The effect of mining on local production in other sectors depends upon the way in which the outpayments of mining enterprises are distributed, and the way the recipients dispose of their incomes. In the more developed countries, much of the value of minerals has passed into the hands of individuals, who may save and invest. But where all mining capital is imported and all profits are exported, and where the skilled workers and management spend most of their incomes on imports, demands for other local products expand only insofar as (a) the producers buy local transport and other services and materials, (b) the incomes of local workers are increased, and (c) other employees buy local products. But in some countries the beneficiaries of mining operations have purchased local products, or invested in local activities in other fields. Australian and South African agriculture have been stimulated by gold mining. About half the dividends of gold mining, for instance, remain in South Africa, and profits from diamond mining provided some of the initial capital for gold mining.[16] Governments frequently take over part of the proceeds of mining (in royalties or taxes on production or export). They can use such proceeds to develop the country (e.g., by investing in railroads) or to reduce taxes paid by people with little propensity to invest (Ch. 31).

Gold mining differs from other types of mineral production in that it provides a stabilizer of national income over business cycles so long as governments buy gold at a fixed price. In a depression, the cost of mining falls and output increases. As prices rise the cost of mining rises, but the price of gold does not, and output falls. South Africa has benefited greatly in this way. More recently, raising gold prices in depression has further stimulated output.[17]

---

[15] Frankel, op. cit., 383. "Ever since the opening up of the Rand, the economic history of the Union is very largely a history of the gold-mining industry. . . . In the main, other industries and the railways have developed around it." (Union of South Africa: Industrial and Agricultural Requirements Commission, Third Interim Report, 1941, 27.)

[16] Frankel, op. cit., 75.

[17] De Kiewiet, History of South Africa: Social and Economic, 155; Union of South Africa: Industrial and Agricultural Requirements Commission, op. cit., 29; Social and Economic Planning Council, Report No. 11, 15, 27.

2. Factors Affecting Productivity

Productivity is affected by the nature of demand, the availability of resources, and the organization of mineral production.

a. The Nature of Demand

Labor in mining would be unproductive in the absence of demand at a price covering more than the non-labor cost of mining. The higher the price, the greater the value of the product and the greater the inducement to expand production.

The demand for minerals was relatively small prior to the 11th century, and arose mainly out of demands for weapons, tools, coins, and ornaments, and little from demands for fuel and power. Lead was used for missiles and weights, and later for pipes and roofing. Coal was used for heating only on a small scale in China before the Christian era, and by the ancient Britons. After the 11th century, the demand for metals was chiefly for weapons, coins, copper roofs for large buildings, and jewelry. The enormous increase in demand throughout the period of industrialization has not been due mainly and directly to increases in standards of living, although these have induced rising demands for electricity for home use, better housing, transport, and personal durable goods, most of which call for minerals as sources of energy or for structural purposes. The main changes in demand have come from changes in methods of production and the resulting changes in the volume of production, and ultimately from the increased use of non-biological energy in production and changes in the structural materials used in equipment and buildings.

Mineral sources of energy, almost unexploited until two centuries ago, now provide all non-biological energy other than wind and water. Coal supplies about 75% of the energy used in production. Petroleum and asphalt were used in very ancient times, but as medicines and waterproofing and embalming materials. Even when the first petroleum well was drilled at Titusville, Pa. in 1859, the oil was used mainly for illumination. Its use for motive power awaited the development of the internal combustion engine by Daimler in 1887. In the 20th century, natural gas has increased in importance, especially in the U.S.A. Finally, atomic energy, first used for destruction, holds promise of use in production. Use of non-biological energy increased about 25% between 1937 and 1948, but the increase is uneven among countries. In the U.S.A. the proportion of all energy obtained from minerals and water power rose from 5.8% in 1850 to 90% in 1940, the use of animal and human power having correspondingly declined. Over 50% of all electricity is generated in Canada and the U.S.A., and about 8% in Britain.[18] The relative importance of different mineral

---

[18] U.N., *Major Econ. Changes in 1948*, 4, 41; Dewhurst *et al.*, *America's Needs and Resources*, 787.

sources of energy is also changing. The use of coal is expanding less than that of other sources because of increases in the efficiency of its use and increased competition from hydroelectric power, natural gas, and petroleum.[19]

New methods of production have also increased the demand for structural materials of mineral origin. The first machines made of wood have been replaced by machines of iron and, later, steel. Railroads, steamships, and general construction have called for increasing quantities first of iron and later of steel. Late in the 19th century the increasing use of electricity expanded the demand for copper and lead (for storage batteries), and their prices rose considerably in relation to those of other minerals. The use of the internal combustion engine for air transport generated a demand for lighter structural materials and stimulated the production of aluminum, and later, magnesium. The development of food canning in the U.S.A. during the Civil War greatly increased the demand for tin. Increasingly specialized demands for steel have generated demands for relatively small quantities of alloying materials of great importance, such as manganese, chrome, nickel, vanadium, and molybdenum.

These changes in demand, due to changes in income levels but mostly to changes in methods of production, do not necessarily induce increases in output in the countries where demand expands. In ancient times Greece and India exported silver and Britain tin. The demand increases have been greatest in the rapidly developing countries, but they have been compelled to meet an increasing proportion of the expanded demand by foreign trade. Some have exhausted their own supplies and others have none of workable grade. Britain imports iron, petroleum, copper, bauxite, and steel alloys. Germany (before 1939) imported most minerals other than coal. Japan possessed supplies of coal and some copper, but few other minerals. The U.S.A. and Russia are best supplied with minerals. The U.S.A. produces all its own coal, almost all its own petroleum, and much but not all of its own iron, copper, and zinc. It produces some bauxite and a little chrome, nickel, and tungsten, but no tin.[20] But no country is completely independent of the rest of the world in the matter of minerals. If a country has low-grade domestic resources, it can use them in preference to cheaper imported supplies. It may synthesize oil if it has coal supplies and is willing to pay the price. Atomic fission opens up the possibility of transmuting the elements. Less developed countries, on the other hand, obtain foreign purchasing power by exporting minerals. Some have become heavily dependent on sales of a single mineral, Chile being largely dependent on exports of copper, Bolivia and Malaya on tin, South Africa on gold and diamonds, and Venezuela and a number of countries in the

19 U.S., *Minerals Year Book*, 1949, 271, 277.
20 U.S., *Minerals Year Book*, 1949, 10.

Middle East on petroleum (which is more widely traded internationally than coal).

b. The Availability of Resources

The product per worker depends on the price of the mineral and on non-labor costs. A rise in the price of the mineral increases the value product of labor. Non-labor costs depend on the economic quality of the mineral resource. Low-grade resources result in low physical output per worker and continue to be mined only where wages are low. Or such resources may be worked with higher wages but larger capital investment, which raises the productivity of labor. The economic quality of mineral reserves depends on the concentration of the ore, which determines the quantity of material to be handled and the cost of separation. It depends also on the location of the deposit. The cost of mining increases with depth. Scattered small deposits may not justify the sinking of a shaft to each, or the cost of pumping and of separation. Inaccessibly located mineral deposits involve high costs of importing workers, equipment, and food, and of getting the mineral to market.

Access to capital has increased in importance with changes in technology. The most notable changes in the past two centuries have been those permitting deeper mining, cheaper separation processes, and the mechanization of underground transport and mining. Pumps for water and air, mechanical elevators, and machinery for cooling deep mines, all require capital. Physical flotation and chemical processes for concentrating minerals have permitted the exploitation of low-grade deposits. Mechanical cutting, loading, and underground transport were rapidly developed in the coal industry in the U.S.A. after 1918, somewhat later in France[21] and Germany, and only recently in Britain where, however, over 80% of coal was mechanically loaded in 1949. Capital has been attracted into mining only partly as a substitute for labor. Capital also makes it possible to work very deep deposits that could not be worked at all without it (irrespective of the amount of labor available).

In the past, capital has flowed fairly readily into mining in response to the prospect of profit. Changes in technology have required larger production units than formerly, and these have been able to acquire capital and export it to countries where local capital has been scarce. External capital has financed the production of copper in Chile, gold in South Africa, tin in Malaya and the Netherlands East Indies, and much of the production of bauxite, petroleum, and uranium. Coal, on the other hand, is more likely to be dependent upon local capital; little capital flowed into the British coal industry from 1920 to 1948, largely because profit prospects were poor. In recent years, however, governments have begun to invest in mining, mostly in Britain and France (in coal mining) and

---

[21] U.N., *Econ. Surv. of Europe in 1949*, 205.

Latin America (mainly in petroleum in Argentina, Mexico, Chile, Brazil, and Bolivia).

The inflow of capital is, however, influenced by the nature of mineral production, which involves very considerable risks. The period of maturation of a mine (from the first investment to the beginning of income) varies greatly according to the method of production and the depth of the mine. Consequently, a rise in the price of a mineral cannot increase output beyond the capacity of existing mines until sufficient time has elapsed to bring new mines into production, even if economical reserves have been located and made accessible to producers. The period of yield also varies with the size of the deposit, the market for the mineral, and changes in technology. Some mines have continued in operation for centuries, sometimes operating intermittently. Tin attracted Phœnician traders to Britain before the beginning of the Christian era, and continues to be produced there (in diminishing quantities). Within this period of yield, output usually responds fairly quickly to an increase in price—up to the capacity of existing mines—although it takes longer to reactivate closed mines than to expand output in those operating. But when prices fall, the response of producers depends on the conditions of mining. Mines can reduce the rate of operation, but partial or complete cessation of production may involve high costs of maintenance (including pumping) if the mine is to be kept available for reopening. Where rock pressures are high, the mine may cave in unless considerable sums are spent for maintenance. For a time, therefore, mines may produce for inventory rather than close down. And in deep, long-lived mines, since a considerable part of all costs is "sunk," prices may not cover much more than operating costs for long periods.

The yield of a mine is rarely known in advance with any certainty, although trial borings now provide more information than formerly. The length of the period of investment increases the risk of changes in the price of the mineral during the life of the operation. This price may be influenced by the discovery of new ore supplies or the exhaustion of existing mines, the discovery of new processes making known, but unworked, reserves profitable, and by increases or reductions in demand.

During the 20th century the increasing use of secondary supplies has affected the demand for some virgin metals. In fact, the reuse of metals makes the supply of them above ground somewhat of a revolving fund that continues to be fed by virgin supplies. The demand for minerals also fluctuates more widely than that for industrial products, largely because it is derived from the demand for manufactured products. Fluctuations in the mineral stocks of manufacturers and processors cause the demand for minerals to fall more severely than the output of manufactured goods, and to rise more rapidly with increasing demand for finished products. Demands for energy, however, fall less and rise less than the demand for finished products during cycles of production. Wars also cause considerable fluctuations in the demand for minerals because so much of the implements of war are industrial or mineral products. Finally, foreign investments involve risks of taxation, exchange control, and nationalization. But although these risks are considerable, investors attracted by the chance of large gains may underestimate the risks they take. It has been estimated that over the whole period from 1877 to 1932 the net return on investments in gold mining in the Union of South Africa was 4.1% per year.[22]

The differential availability of labor has had little effect on the productivity of mining. Although the higher skills have often been absent, they have been imported with the capital. Recently, however, many countries have required the local population be trained during the early years of operation. The remaining labor force, usually small in relation to the total labor supply of the country, has been easily secured. The cost of native labor has, however, virtually determined the extent of gold mining in South Africa. There is an almost continuous gradation in the gold content of ores and production costs determine which can be worked with profit. The industry has been greatly assisted by cheap native labor. "But for this fortunate circumstance the industry could never have reached its present state of development."[23] Increasing economic pressure on the native population maintains this supply, although the large gold producers restrict bidding for labor and hold down native wages with the result that "the industry has seldom, in recent years, had a fully adequate supply of native laborers."[24]

In most countries labor conditions in mining have been harsh. They have improved more slowly than in manufacturing (until recent years), with the result that the amount of coal production in Britain has been greatly influenced by the availability of labor. The economic quality of labor varies among countries. In India, Africa, and parts of Latin America, poor health reduces output per man.

Access to knowledge of methods of production has differed among countries much less in mining than in agriculture. Methods of producing the same mineral differ somewhat among countries, but these differences are not so much the causes of differences in costs as the effect of differences in engineering problems. Tin is mined in Bolivia and dredged in Malaya and Indonesia. Differences in geological conditions partly explain differences in the cost of coal mining in Britain and the U.S.A. In fact, there may be fewer differences in methods of producing minerals than in agri-

---

[22] Frankel, *Capital Investment in Africa*, 91.

[23] Union of South Africa: Mine Natives' Wages Commission, *Report*, 1943, 5.

[24] Union of South Africa: Social and Economic Planning Council, *Report No. 11*, 27. Keeping wages down, and the consequent sharing of available labor among mines, "tends to maintain production on the poorer mines and reduce the rate at which the richer ore is extracted."

culture and manufacturing, after allowance is made for differences in the qualities of deposits in different countries. The mounting demand for minerals in the more developed countries has caused them to reach out for minerals in other parts of the world, taking with them, in addition to capital, this knowledge of methods of mining.

C. The Organization of Mineral Production

Productivity depends on the extent to which the organization of production is compatible with efficiency.

1. THE PRODUCTION UNIT

The organization of production units resembles that of manufacturing units. Small individual producers persist in many countries, e.g., gold producers in the U.S.A. and tin producers in Malaya. Even fairly large-scale operations were undertaken by large landowners in medieval Europe, especially coal mining in Britain and Germany. Partnerships have been especially important, because legal provision has been made for forms of organization blending the corporation and the ordinary partnership (in Britain, Germany, and the U.S.A.) that facilitate the acquisition of the considerable but uncertain amounts of capital needed. Tin mining and much coal mining until the end of the 17th century was in the hands of partnerships in Britain.

Heavily capitalized operations appeared earlier in mining than in industry. Some of the earliest corporations in 17th-century Britain and Holland were formed for mining purposes. Since that time the increased cost of exploring, acquiring mineral rights, and exploiting them has encouraged the corporate organization of mining. The shares of many mining companies are publicly held, and companies in Britain, France, Belgium, Holland, and the U.S.A. have financed much mining in other countries. Consumers' cooperatives produce coal for consumption by their members in a number of countries including Britain, but producers' cooperatives are uncommon. Government mining enterprises have existed from ancient times and have multiplied during the 20th century, organized usually as government-owned corporations.

Mining enterprises vary in the variety of functions they perform. The composition of their deposits and the prices of the different minerals determine the variety of the products they sell. Subsidiary minerals are sold if their price exceeds the cost of making them available for sale. Mineral enterprises also vary in the length of the chain of their operations. Some are little more than collectors of minerals, like the individuals who wash river mud for gold or tin or pick up diamonds on the surface in Africa. The evaporation of sea water for salt in regions with a long hot dry season is little more than collection. Where mining or quarrying is necessary, the enterprise may own as well as operate the deposit. Coal and gold mining companies, for instance, often purchase full rights to land to avoid damage suits for subsidence of the surface due to mining. But the enterprise may exploit a deposit which it does not own. It operates like a tenant paying, in cash or in kind, a royalty on output, but may also pay a capital sum to the mineral owner. The lease must be long enough and in other respects favorable enough to induce investment in the necessary shafts, galleries and working equipment.

Mining and subsequent processing are integrated in the same enterprise where the economical scale for processing is not markedly greater than for mining, and where the economies of separate large-scale processing are not offset by the cost of transporting often low-grade material. But even where the economical scale for smelting or refining is large in relation to that for mining, the two are often integrated under the control of smelters or refiners to ensure continuity of supplies. Where the numbers of smelters and of mining enterprises are both small, integration is likely, because operations in such a market resemble a poker game in which either side may be squeezed by the other.

The smelting companies generally control copper production. A considerable amount of lead was smelted by independent smelters in Germany before 1914, but since 1918 lead from the Australian mines has been smelted in Australia, and smelting and production are generally integrated. Zinc production and concentration were generally organized separately from mining until 1914, but subsequently mining, concentration, and refining have been increasingly combined under common control, smelting being shifted to the countries in which zinc is mined. Tin smelting is usually large-scale, and in Malaya the mines and dredges produce concentrate under separate ownership. Canadian nickel mining and refining are combined under a single concern, the International Nickel Company of Canada. The typical gold mine in South Africa produces gold about 90% fine that is further purified in a refinery cooperatively owned by the gold mining companies. Coal mines have usually cleaned and sorted their coal. Crude petroleum producers very frequently also operate pipe lines and refineries, and distribute their products (e.g., in the U.S.A. and the Middle East). In the U.S.A. some 80% of the gasoline was distributed by refining companies in 1928. But there are also independent producers who sell to middlemen or to integrated refining companies.[25] Exporting countries may have refineries (e.g., Iran) and export both refined products and crude oil.

Iron ore is often produced by steel-making enterprises. U.S.A. steel producers not only produce most of the iron ore in the U.S.A., but also operate deposits in Cuba, Brazil, Chile, Venezuela, and Canada. The Tata Iron and Steel Company produces its own ore in India, and so does the

---

[25] U.S.A., Fed. Trade Com., *Petroleum Industry, 1926,* 35, 59, 293; Baine, *Pacific Coast Petroleum Industry,* Vol. III, 17 ff.

Broken Hill Proprietary Company in Australia. Swedish and French companies control the iron mines in North Africa. But German steel producers have purchased Swedish ore on long-term contracts.

The marketing of minerals is often relatively simple. Gold mining companies merely pay their produce into the bank. Many other metals are traded in organized markets. Some are sold by negotiation between large producers and large users, and some through specialized dealers and brokers. Coal marketing is more complex because of the large number of producers and the heterogeneity of the product. Users of mineral products occasionally acquire interests in production. Railroad companies, steel producers, and other large users operate about 20% of the coal mining in the U.S.A. In the Pennsylvania anthracite field, railroads built as an adjunct to hard-coal mining control (through subsidiaries) about 73% of the coal output, largely to secure their coal transportation business.[26] Before coal mining was nationalized in Britain, municipal electrical systems, railroads, textile producers, and other large users owned mines. In Germany steel and chemical producers pursued a similar policy. Producers of structural minerals occasionally integrate mining with subsequent fabrication. Steel producers in the U.S.A. and elsewhere often fabricate heavy products, and in Germany also light products (Ch. 11). In the U.S.A. the chief copper fabricators are controlled by copper producers.[27]

The size of mining enterprises affects their efficiency. In many branches of mining, new and more highly capitalized methods of mining have made larger-scale operations than before both feasible and economical, but little is known regarding the relation between their actual size and the most economical size. Differences in mining conditions make the idea of an optimal size even less helpful than in manufacturing. There is, however, much evidence that many British coal mines are too small to be efficient, and the British Coal Board is attempting to remedy this condition. During the war of 1939-45, differential prices were paid in the U.S.A. and Canada to bring back into production relatively high-cost (and often small) mines whose product was urgently needed.

The size of mining enterprises, (not mines) is especially important in its effect on the number of sellers in the market, and, therefore, on its competitiveness. This number depends on the number of local producers plus the number of foreign sellers under separate control. Many minerals are the subject of international trade, but those whose cost of transport is high in relation to their value are less likely to be transported over long distances. A large number of sellers is more frequent in coal mining than in that of other minerals. Unfortunately, most figures relate to collieries rather than to enterprises. Before nationalization in 1947, there were about

---

[26] Burns, *Decline of Competition*, 123.
[27] U.S. Fed. Trade Commission, *The Copper Industry*, 54.

980 British collieries, compared with 3089 in 1900,[28] and conditions were similar in France before nationalization. The number of coal mines has fallen about 50% in the U.S.A. since 1920, but there were about 8000 (excluding those producing less than 1,000 tons a year) in 1951, of which 2.9% produced 38% of the output.[29] But eight companies controlled 78% of the recoverable anthracite in 1923.[30] In Germany there were 161 collieries in the Ruhr in 1938, and in Poland 60 in 1938. Ownership was much more concentrated in Germany and Poland than in Britain and the U.S.A. In the Ruhr 20 undertakings were responsible for 90% of the output in 1926, and in Poland, 12 companies produced about 70% of the total.[31]

Petroleum production is generally large-scale. In Rumania, however, producers of crude oil were numerous until 1945 because the government had auctioned oil concessions in small lots. In Mexico, also, producers were numerous because surface owners were allowed to exploit oil, and surface rights were in small lots. But in Rumania the industry was nationalized in 1945, and in Mexico finally in 1930. There is also a large number of producers in the U.S.A., again because oil rights are vested in surface owners. In 1926 Standard Oil Companies produced 24% of all crude oil, three foreign-controlled companies 6.7%, and 29 "independent" companies 32.4%, the remainder being in the hands of small producers.[32] The sale of refined oil was highly concentrated until 1911, but the number of sellers has increased considerably and there is a number of small firms at most stages of production in most regions. In countries where petroleum is produced under government concession, producers are usually few. In the Middle East the Anglo-Iranian Oil Company has operated in Iran, and a corporation owned by a group of American companies in Iraq and Saudi Arabia. In the Far East (Borneo, Java, Sumatra, and New Guinea) the Royal Dutch Shell Company is predominant, although two-thirds of the petroleum industry in New Guinea is owned and operated by American companies. In Latin America private production has been shared between the Royal Dutch Shell Company and American companies, but government monopolies of production are increasing. Much of the production in the world, however, is in the hands of large U.S.A. and British-Dutch groups.

The production of non-ferrous metals is also fairly concentrated. Three companies produce 83% of the copper produced in the U.S.A., and ten groups control about 70% of the world's available copper.[33] About 12 concerns produce much of the world's lead, and about ten produce much of

---

[28] U.K., National Coal Board, *Annual Report for 1951*, 231.

[29] U.S., *Minerals Year Book*, 1949, 293.

[30] Burns, *op. cit.*, 39.

[31] U.K., Ministry of Fuel and Power, Technical Advisory Committee on Coal Mining, *Report*, 16, 23.

[32] Federal Trade Commission, *Petroleum Industry*, 1926, 76.

[33] Fed. Trade Comm., *The Copper Industry*, 38, 245.

the zinc. One company produces 90% of the nickel. Of the tin produced in Malaya, about two-thirds is produced by large dredges, but the remaining third comes from small producers and individuals engaged in hand washing. There are few producers in Indonesia. Until 1952 there were three major producers in Bolivia (whose properties are now nationalized). Most of the economically usable bauxite is reported to be controlled by three groups (one in the U.S.A., one in Switzerland, and one in France). Gold is produced by a considerable number of companies, but most of those in South Africa are controlled by one of ten holding companies through stockholding, management contracts, prestige, and access to resources.[34] But concentration in this market has little direct effect on the price, which has been pegged by governments (although premium prices appeared for a time after 1949). The production of iron is so widely integrated with steel production that the iron ore market is narrow.

The smallness in number of mining enterprises has been influenced by changing methods of production that require large operations to be economical. Coal mining has been the major exception. But concentration has been increasing, if account is taken of the number of mines controlled by a single enterprise. But mining enterprises may be expanded beyond the most economical size in order to acquire monopoly profits or to avoid the uncertainties of oligopoly. An enterprise operating mines or oil wells in a number of regions is clearly influenced by more than economical mine operation. The small number of sellers of some minerals in the world as a whole is important because minerals provide the basis of modern technology.

2. PRIVATE GROUPS OF PRODUCTION UNITS

Mineral producers do not in general cooperate for the same reasons that agriculturalists do. They do not cooperate to acquire the means of production or to process their output (the cooperative gold refinery in South Africa being a notable exception). Mineral producers are usually large enough to be at no disadvantage in purchasing supplies. The managing groups in African gold mining achieve economies in purchasing stores, raising capital, and providing management and engineering services for the constituent companies. Where they face a small number of buyers (often smelters, refiners, or pipe line companies), the two operations may be integrated. But where sellers are few, they may seize the opportunity to control output and prices. Where the number of firms in the market is very small, informal unpublished arrangements that leave little trace may suffice.

Overt private control of prices and output has been most frequent in coal mining, where the number of enterprises is usually too large to be

---

[34] Union of South Africa: Social and Economic Planning Council, *Report No. 11*, 37; Franklin, *op. cit.*, 154.

controlled without explicit organization. Private understandings have, however, been arrived at in the past in the U.S. anthracite industry.[35] The first modern cartel agreement in any industry appears to have been the "limitation of the vend" of coal from Newcastle in Britain from 1665 to 1842. The Newcastle area monopolized "sea coal" shipped by water to the London market, and production was controlled and allotted among mine owners. But the margin of monopoly profit was successively narrowed by canal shipments from the Midlands after 1820, later shipments from Scotland, and, finally, by shipments by rail, and the cartel collapsed.[36] Monopolistic controls of tin were also organized in Britain and Germany. In modern times the production and sale of coke were partially controlled in Germany as early as 1882, when an association set minimum prices. As a result larger buyers in the metallurgical industries bought coal mines. In 1888 the National Mining Association attempted to control the output of the whole Westphalian field, but the agreements were loose and unsuccessful. The Rhenish Westphalian Coal Syndicate, established in 1893 to control the coal market, set an output quota for every member. Each was required to deliver this quota at an agreed price to a cooperative marketing agency, whose profits were distributed in proportion to the quotas delivered. The agreement was renewed in 1903, although with considerable modification, and remained in force until 1916 when, fearing that it would not be renewed, the government decreed that the German states could establish compulsory coal syndicates, unless syndicates were voluntarily established by producers of at least 97% of the output. The syndicate agreement was renewed.[37]

In France the whole coal output of the Nord and Pas de Calais areas, producing two-thirds of the total French output, was sold by a central selling agency that cooperated with other coal districts to maintain considerable stability of price. In Britain, after the passage of the Coal Mines Reorganization Act in 1930, coal producers were authorized to establish centralized control of production, and controls were set up in some fields. In Japan before 1938, 75% of all coal produced was marketed by the Showa Coal Mining Company, and an association of the producers restricted production and maintained prices until the beginning of the war with China, when restriction was dropped. In South Africa, associations of coal producers in Natal and the Transvaal are coordinated through the Transvaal Chamber of Mines. Price competition is apparently controlled without explicit price agreements. Such controls can succeed, however, only if the association policy is accepted by most producers in the country and, where imports are influential, by foreign producers as well. Asso-

[35] Burns, op. cit., 166.

[36] Levy, Monopoly and Competition, Ch. VI.

[37] Stockder, A. H., Regulating an Industry: The Rhenish Westphalian Coal Syndicate, 1893 to 1929.

ciations of enterprises producing similar minerals frequently also represent their members in dealing with labor organizations, again most notably in the coal industry.

Associations of mining enterprises are, in general, uncommon. The Transvaal Chamber of Mines in the Union of South Africa, however, represents gold, diamond, and coal mining enterprises. It influences the government because gold mining is so important to the economic life of the country and to the government as a source of revenue and foreign exchange. It has been especially concerned with native wages because they affect the grade of ore that can be worked. But since native wages at the mines are closely related to native wages in general, the Chamber of Mines has had considerable influence on the general level of native wages.

3. THE STATE

The pressures on the government in relation to mining are analogous to those regarding agriculture. Owners of deposits oppose measures that increase the cost of mining, including taxation. Mine operators oppose measures likely to increase costs (especially labor and transport costs). Mining labor is interested in high wages. But royalty owners and mine operators can exert effective influence only where mining contributes a large part of the national product, as it does in South Africa. Coal mine operators were also influential in making British coal mining policy until after 1914. Mining labor also usually exerts little influence. Its wages depend on wages in alternative occupations, and on access to those occupations, and because miners are often physically and economically isolated from the rest of the community, their wages have been relatively low until recent years.

The general social interest in mining depends on its potential contribution to national income, to the income of the state, and to national defense. The direct contribution to national income is small in most, but not all, countries. But governments may encourage mining, in order to attract capital and workers and to provide an energy or material base for other industries. Governments are also especially interested in minerals as a source of revenue, and they have increasingly concerned themselves with the terms on which minerals are exported, partly because of the difficult adjustments necessary when the deposits are exhausted (Ch. 15).

Governments assist mining by influencing the conditions of access to minerals or by increasing returns from mining. Some colonial governments prospect for minerals (e.g., in parts of Africa) to accelerate the development of the country. They have also stimulated the supply of mining labor by enforcing labor contracts of considerable length (e.g., in the South African mines), imposing taxation which compels native workers to leave the reserves to earn money and, occasionally, by giving special police protection for valuable mineral products (like gold and diamonds). Governments have not generally found it necessary to facilitate access to technical knowledge or capital. A few Latin American governments, however, have established small mining banks to provide capital. Also, the British government nationalized the coal mines to improve their efficiency. In 1950 the National Coal Board planned to increase efficiency by investing the equivalent of $1.778 billion over 15 years, to increase output per man hour about 37.5%.[38] Governments also encourage mining by extending transport facilities (e.g., in South Africa).

Governments have not so generally attempted to increase the rewards of mining as those of agriculture. Import duties are infrequent, partly because they raise the cost of energy or materials and discourage industry. Moreover, they encourage mining only if domestic deposits are known and if a domestic market for their output exists. Nevertheless, the U.S.A. protects its copper mining by taxing imports (which provide over 20% of its demand). Mining subsidies are more common, and high depletion allowances (for tax purposes) favor mining. During the 1939-45 war, governments subsidized low-grade mines in the U.S.A. and Canada to increase supplies of base metals. Since 1945 gold mining has been subsidized to increase supplies of dollar exchange in Canada and Southern Rhodesia. A number of governments have come to the rescue of coal mining. The Japanese Mineral Production Law of 1938 authorized the government to direct, and bear the cost of, the improvement of production facilities, to exempt from taxation new mines and increases in output from old mines, and to subsidize prospecting for new mines. The New Zealand government virtually placed coal mining on a "cost plus" basis by guaranteeing pre-1939 profits. After the failure of compulsory arbitration and repeated strikes and an attempt to repress inflation, the Commonwealth and New South Wales governments in Australia in 1947 established a joint commission which may issue directives to private operators, purchase pits, or open up new areas. It may replace colliery managers (compensating the owner for any resulting losses). It may lend to mine operators on mortgage, or purchase their stocks or bonds. In general, the private owners continued to operate the pits while the commission controlled prices and distribution and paid subsidies varying with the cost of production at each mine, although in 1948 it had taken over four pits. Subsidies may also take the form of losses by nationalized coal industries.

Government purchases to maintain prices, common in agriculture, are uncommon in mining in capitalist countries. During the 1939-45 war, the U.S. government bought metals abroad to prevent delays in arms production and to prevent competition among American buyers from driving up prices. The British government made similar purchases abroad and continued them after the war. Its selling prices have apparently lagged behind

---

[38] U.K., National Coal Board: *Plan for Coal, 1950.*

world prices, both when they were rising and when they were falling. After the war the U.S. government purchased minerals for stockpiling, but for military reasons. The resulting increase in prices has been unwelcome and has mostly benefited foreign producers. Government establishment of metallic standards for money pegs the price of gold, or gold and silver (under bimetallic standards). Since 1949, however, the South African and South Rhodesian governments have permitted sales at above the pegged price. Such sales were possible because governments holding monetary gold were unwilling to sell it and permit the exports necessary to make the official price also the market price (Ch. 26). The U.S.A., although on neither a silver nor a bimetallic standard has maintained the price of domestically mined silver by government purchases after 1939 at $0.71 an ounce and since 1946 at $0.905. In consequence, cheaper foreign silver has met most U.S. needs, and the Treasury has stockpiled American silver.

Governments have occasionally helped producers to raise prices by restricting output. Such aid is usually not necessary where producers are few, but they are often numerous in coal mining. The German government in 1919 authorized ten compulsory coal syndicates and one coke syndicate which, with the mines of the state governments, constituted the *Reichskohlenverband*, which fixed output quotas and prices. A *Reichskohlenrat*, consisting of representatives of owners, workers, and important coal-consuming industries, set the general policies for the *Verband*, supervised it, and had power to make recommendations to the Minister of National Economy in regard to its policies. Output was in fact raised, and production was concentrated in the lower-cost mines that were modernized (some becoming coal-using factories producing coke, by-products, and power). After 1945 the syndicate continued for a time under military-government control while the German socialist party sought nationalization and the U.S.A. sought decartellization. In 1951 the Allied High Commission divided the national sales organization into six separate regional organizations, as a prerequisite to the adoption of the Schuman Plan (Ch. 26). The Polish Coal Commission, established in 1925 when Germany deprived the Polish mines of their market in southeast Germany, assigned output quotas and raised prices.[39]

The British government attempted to improve the efficiency of the coal industry by passing the British Coal Mines Reorganization Act of 1930, which authorized local commissions to draw up schemes for the compulsory amalgamation of collieries in order to reduce costs and eliminate inefficient mines. But the coal owners refused to cooperate and the courts would not enforce amalgamation. Parliament had established almost impossible conditions for compulsory amalgamation: namely, that it would lower the cost of producing or disposing of coal, would not harm

---

[39] U.K., Ministry of Fuel and Power, Technical Advisory Committee on Coal Mining, *Report*, 23.

any owner affected, and would be fair and equitable to all persons concerned. As recompense for reorganization, Parliament authorized selling schemes to restrict competition. Mine operators took advantage of this authority and established a number of schemes. A few (as in Lancashire) were cooperative selling agencies. Some were agreements setting minimum prices, and a few were agreements pooling profits. But there was no provision for the coordination of the price policies and output controls of the various schemes. In Japan, where some 75% of all coal had been marketed through a central agency, the government placed all coal distribution under the Japan Coal Company in 1940.

The potash industry was almost a German monopoly until 1914, and was controlled by a series of cartels led by the Prussian government. But by 1909, high cartel prices had encouraged excessive opening of mines and new sources had been discovered, with the result that private cartel control was breaking down. A Potash Law of 1910 authorized control of prices and output and prohibitive taxes on production in excess of quota. But capital continued to flow into the industry and excess capacity increased. In 1918-19 a State Potash Council (*Reischskalirat*) was set up to fix prices and act as an economic parliament for the industry, but the potash resources passed into the hands of a French government monopoly. In Chile capacity to produce nitrates increased sufficiently to depress prices soon after 1900. The government encouraged cartels to fix prices and output. These were not wholly effective, but after 1918 the fixation of nitrogen from the air introduced serious new competition. The Chilean Nitrate Producers Association, formed in 1919 (and reorganized in 1924 and 1928), tried to stabilize output and restrict price competition. The government urged producers to join and appointed four of the eighteen directors. It granted special railroad rates on fuel and other materials, and on nitrates, and paid bonuses to compensate for price reductions. But between 1917 and 1930, Chilean nitrate sales fell 40% and their share of the world market fell from 47% in 1913 to 15% in 1931. In 1930, therefore, a corporation (briefly known as "Cosach") took over 40 of the 45 producing companies, and the government lands bearing nitrates. The government held 60% of the common stock of the company, and bonds to insure for three years the equivalent of its previous revenue from export taxes. But private holders of stock were empowered to appoint eight of the twelve directors. After 1933 no export taxes were levied, but the government was to receive profits in place of these taxes. Costs fell, unemployment rose, and the government was criticized for participating in a trust dominated by foreign capital. In 1932 the company defaulted in payment of the interest on its bonds, and in 1933 the government ordered its liquidation and the return to the previous state of affairs—the government taking back its land and reimposing export taxes. The Italian government has also regulated output and prices in the sulphur industry.

Most of these arrangements were attempts to use monopoly power to increase profits or reduce losses by restricting output. The German coal cartel, however, reorganized the industry and increased its efficiency. The British failed in this respect, and from 1940 to 1946 were compelled to maintain output without too much regard for cost. The government, therefore, established a Coal Charges Account into which was paid a levy of 12 shillings a ton on all coal sold commercially, and out of which payments were made to coal producers on the basis of their payments under the guaranteed-work-week scheme, their compensation payments and expenditures on the health plans, and their wages and profits. In fact, about 30% of the cost of coal production during this period was borne, not by each undertaking, but by the industry as a whole, the more efficient subsidizing the less efficient. But on January 1, 1947, the mines passed to the National Coal Board. A somewhat similar scheme for pooling profits prevailed in the Belgian coal industry from 1945 to 1949, but this scheme did encourage production in the low-cost mines more than in the high-cost.

In the U.S.A., state legislation originally aimed at control of production practices that wasted petroleum (owing to the flooding of wells), and natural gas has evolved into state and federal legislation restricting output to reduce "waste" resulting from "low" prices. Oklahoma began to control output by wells in 1931, when large new supplies from Oklahoma and east Texas threatened a drastic fall in price. This control was held to be within the legal power of the state, but it failed to prevent excessive drilling. State laws passed to regulate the spacing of wells have not been very effective.[40] The Secretary of the Interior, however, regulates the development of oil pools on public lands. But since 1927 the federal Bureau of Mines has issued monthly estimates of petroleum production "required" in each producing area, calculated mainly to stabilize the price of oil rather than conserve the supply. State governments may, if they so desire, adopt these quotas established by the Bureau of Mines and break them down into quotas for fields and then for individual wells. Most states do so, but California has relied on private cooperation rather than on legislation. State policies are coordinated through an interstate compact accepted by Congress in 1935, and supported by the Connally Act, 1935, which prohibits the interstate shipment of petroleum produced in excess of any quotas imposed by the state.[41]

The only important attempt to stabilize the rewards of mining has been the arrangement for central banks to buy and sell gold at a price that has been stable over long periods. But the price has been changed, and stable prices do not stabilize the profits of mining because costs change although the price of gold is fixed. (Ch. 15).

---

[40] Baine, *The Pacific Coast Petroleum Industry*, III, 27.
[41] Baine, *op. cit.*, II, 60; Rostow, E. V., *A National Policy for the Oil Industry*, 23.

State action reducing the rewards of mining is not uncommon. Rewards from the exploitation of privately owned minerals are often regarded as more "unearned" than most incomes, and as originating from the sale of a natural resource in which the nation can claim a special interest. In consequence, special taxes are often imposed on minerals in countries where minerals are private property. States also require royalties and sometimes impose taxes where the state claims minerals (Ch. 15).

Government mining operations have a long history. The city of Athens owned the silver mines at Laurium, but they were operated by contractors using free hired labor, slaves leased in gangs from Athenian capitalists, and penal labor.[42] The Prussian state engaged in mining, as did the Russian under Peter the Great. During the 19th century, the great expansion of mining was mostly achieved by private enterprise. But in the 20th century, government mining has increased. The socialist governments operate virtually all mines through administrative machinery similar to that used to operate manufacturing. In Russia all mining was nationalized after the revolution, and in eastern Europe after 1945. Socialist China has similarly nationalized mining enterprises. In western Europe, government mining is principally, but not wholly, restricted to coal. States and municipalities in Germany have for long engaged in coal mining. The spectacular development of coal mining in Holland during the 20th century has been achieved by government operation, partly to avoid domination by foreign capital. By 1930 Holland was largely self-sufficient in coal; 70% of the total output was produced by state mines. These mines, said be the most modern in Europe, were assisted by rebates of from 10 to 25% on normal freight rates from the Limburg area, where the mines are. Before 1939 the Polish government controlled one of the largest coal mining companies.

Early in the 20th century, British coal miners began to demand nationalization, which was achieved only on January 1, 1947. A National Coal Board operates the industry through eight regional controllers, under each of whom is a number of pit production committees of workers and supervisors. The Minister of Fuel and Power is the final judge of the "public interest" in coal, may give the Board directions in matters that appear to him to affect the public interest, and must approve of reorganizations of mining that require substantial capital. The Minister authorized the adoption of the five-day week in 1947, and can deny or authorize changes in price.[43]

In France all coal mining was nationalized in 1946; the *Charbonnages de France* directs a regional company for each coalfield. The company is controlled by directors equally representing the state, consumers, and

---

[42] Welles, "The Economic Background of Plato's Communism," *Tasks of Econ. Hist.*, 1948, 101.

[43] Beacham, A., "The Present Position of the Coal Industry in Great Britain," LX *Ec. Jour.*, 9, 1950.

employees. A *Chambre de Comptes* makes an annual report on the accounts of the national and regional companies. If any company operates at a financial loss, the directors are automatically removed, unless confirmed in office by the government.[44]

The government of New Zealand, in taking control of coal mining during the war of 1939-45, announced that it intended eventual nationalization.[45] The government of Nigeria operates coal mines. In other countries, such government coal mining as exists is usually in connection with government steel production, which also involves government iron mining (e.g., in South Africa, Southern Rhodesia, and Brazil). The government of India also is establishing a steel company.

Government operation of the petroleum industry is becoming increasingly common in Latin America. Government petroleum undertakings exist in Argentina, Bolivia, Brazil, Chile, and Mexico.[46] In Mexico oil rights were nationalized in 1917, but preconstitutional interests were again recognized in 1928. In 1930, however, oil rights and oil producing enterprises were nationalized. "Pemex," the government oil corporation, has been criticized as inefficient and unprogressive. Output fell until 1932, after which it rose until 1937, fell again until 1942, and rose again thereafter. Pemex is said to be operating at a profit, although there is doubt whether it has maintained its properties and explored effectively for new sources. In 1947 it contracted with a U.S. enterprise to explore and drill test wells on a cost-plus basis, the compensation being payable in Pemex bonds redeemable out of the proceeds of the oil discovered. In Brazil existing private refineries may continue, but not expand. All added production will be by a corporation 51% owned by the government. In 1951, the Iranian Parliament nationalized the petroleum industry, previously operated under a government concession by the Anglo-Iranian Oil Company. The French government has operated potash deposits since 1918. The government of Sweden has a considerable interest in iron ore deposits. The mercury deposits in Spain have been owned by the government for centuries, and those in Italy (the next largest source of supply) were taken over by the government during the war of 1914-18. The South African government has interests in diamond, gold, platinum, tin, copper, and other mines.[47] In 1952 the Bolivian government took over all three of the major tin mining companies.

When governments operate mining enterprises, they determine production and prices. The socialist governments set mineral output as part of

---

[44] Pinkney, D. H., "The Nationalization of Key Industries and Credit in France after the Liberation," LXII, *Pol. Sci. Quar.*, 368, 1947.

[45] U.N., *Econ. Devel. in Selected Countries*, 1950, 120.

[46] U.N., *Econ. Surv. Latin America*, 1948, 80.

[47] Union of South Africa: *Annual Report of Commissioner for Inland Revenue*, 1946-7, 15; Union of South Africa: Agricultural and Industrial Requirements Commission, *Third Interim Report*, 55; de Kiewiet, *op. cit.*, 163.

the general production plan. In Russia, heavy investments in mining were called for to achieve the speedy increase of military power and rapid industrialization with early emphasis on heavy industry. Consequently, coal output in 1949 was 800% of 1913, petroleum output 360%, pig iron 460%, and steel 600%.[48] In partly socialized societies, however, nationalized mining must be coordinated with other public activities and with private activities dominated by consumer choice.

In Britain the government indicated that the National Coal Board was to follow consumer choice when it required the Board's income and expenditure to balance, taking an average of good and bad years. But the Act also required it to ensure the efficient development of the industry, and make supplies of coal available in quantities and at prices that may seem to them best calculated to further the public interest. The Board took over a very sick industry. Only about a third of the mines were reasonably efficient, labor relations were unusually bad, and the labor force was aging. Increased output was urgently necessary at lower costs without lower wages. At the same time the need to expand exports in general impeded efforts to improve mining equipment. The need to maintain output has compelled the Board to keep in production a sizable fringe of high-cost pits. But it plans to reconstruct some 250 collieries to provide 70% of all output.[49] At the end of its first five years (1951), the output of all salable coal was about 22% over 1946. Average output of deep-mined coal per man year from 1947 to 1951 was 23% over 1922-5. The pithead price of coal rose 27% while prices in general rose 70% between 1947 and 1951. This policy of holding down the price tends to increase demand (which has been held down by rationing) and to reduce profits. Colliery operations resulted in a loss of 1s/0d per ton of coal in 1947, but from that year until 1951 there was a profit varying from 2s/11d to 1s/8d. Although the Board incurred a loss of £23.5 million in 1947, its accumulated loss was reduced to £4.0 million by the end of 1950, but it had risen to £13.6 million at the end of 1953 (after all interest charges).

---

[48] Schwartz, op. cit., Ch. VI.
[49] U.K., National Coal Board, A Plan for Coal, 1950.

Chapter 10

Productivity in Manufacturing

A. The Growth and Distribution of Industry

Manufacturing, which originally meant "made with the hand" now usually refers to products made by machine. In this and succeeding chapters, however, manufacturing is used to include both craft and industrial products.

Handicraft production dates back to the fashioning of the first stone axes and arrow heads, and was for many centuries the major type of production, other than agriculture. In medieval Europe, the growth of a wealthier class caused it to expand greatly (particularly in the manufacture of textiles and weapons) partly for export and partly for local markets. It remains the major non-agricultural activity in many underdeveloped countries in the Middle and Far East. In Japan, craft production was expanding before the Meiji restoration in 1868[1] and it remains important. Craft production is also common among the indigenous population of Latin America, but is less important in many parts of Africa. Handicrafts persist also in most developed countries in continental Europe. In Russia 60% of all non-agricultural workers were in handicrafts in 1929. Work in the home—preparing food, making and cleaning clothing, and the like, are virtually craft activities that, however, are passing into the sphere of industrial production in the more developed countries. General statistical measures of craft production are not available.

Industrial production is much less uniformly developed throughout the world, over 70% being located in Europe and North America in 1952 (Figure 12). World industrial and mining production increased about 130% between 1928 and 1952 and about 80% between 1937 and 1952.[2] Some of

---

1 Nobutaka, I., *Pacific Affairs*, 1949, 185.
2 U.N., *Month. Bull. Stats.*, April 1953, XVIII.

the principal expanding activities are pig iron 60%, crude steel 71% and electricity 64%.[3]

The present geographical distribution of industrial production is the outcome of past inequalities in the rate of introduction of industrial methods. These methods began to spread in Britain in the latter part of the 18th century. The output of British manufactures and mining increased from a base of 100 in 1713-19 to an index of 260 in 1800, 2000 in 1869, 3750 in 1900, and 8450 in 1938.[4] Industrial production began to expand in Belgium in the first half of the 19th century and in France, Germany, and the U.S.A. mostly in the second half. Net income from manufacturing in France increased about 100% between 1870 and 1900, and another 100% between 1900 and 1938. In Germany the increase was about 800% between 1832 and 1900, and 140% between 1900 and 1938.[5] In the U.S.A. the net output of factories and hand and neighborhood industries increased about 1100% between 1849 and 1899.

In the 25 years from 1890 to 1914, manufacturing production increased in all west European countries, Italy, and Czechoslovakia, by more than 100%, with the exception of Britain. But in the 25 years from 1914 to 1939 a similar rate of increase occurred only in Finland and Sweden. Expansion slowed notably in Belgium, France, Germany, and Britain, which were already highly industrialized by the end of the 19th century. Changes in the structure of world trade, barriers to trade, rigidities in internal organization and lack of coordination, both intranational and international, all contributed to this slowing up.[6] But in the U.S.A. the net output increased about 430% between 1899 and 1939. In recent years production has increased less rapidly in Europe and North America than in other countries (notably Russia, Australia, Argentina and Brazil) which raised their share of world industrial output from 11% in 1928 to 27% in 1952 (Figure 12). Since 1947 the most rapid rates of increase have been in countries whose economies had been most dislocated by the war, notably Germany and Japan (Figure 13). They could increase output by restoring war-damaged facilities and reducing unemployment. In other countries where the means of production were fully employed, increases could be achieved only by increases of facilities or in productivity.[7]

The present geographical distribution of particular industries reflects in part the sequence in which industries have developed. In Britain the first developments affecting industry were in transportation (roads and canals) textiles, mining, and machinery. Later, the development of the engineering industries improved the type of machinery available and the speed

---

[3] U.N., *Month. Bull. Stats.*, April 1953, XVI.
[4] Calculated from Clark, *Conditions of Economic Progress* (2d), 255, 258.
[5] Clark, *op. cit.*, 256, 258.
[6] U.N., *Econ. Surv. of Europe*, 1949, 202.
[7] U.N., *Month. Bull. Stats.*, April 1953, XI.

GEOGRAPHICAL DISTRIBUTION OF INDUSTRIAL PRODUCTION

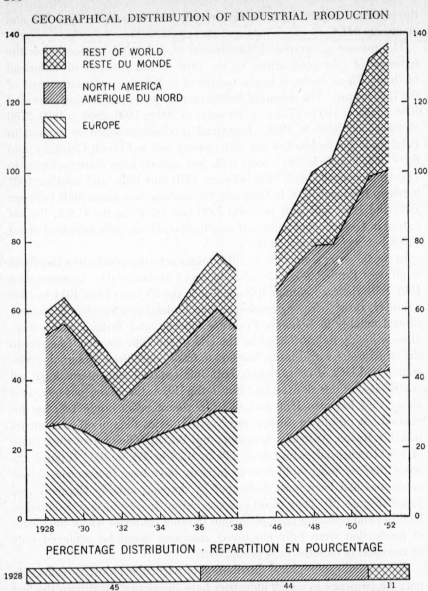

Fig. 12. From UN *Month. Bull. Stats.* April, 1953, p. viii.

at which it could operate. In the third and fourth decades of the 19th century major emphasis was upon railroads and later upon chemicals, and still later on consumer durable goods. Until 1918, other countries, building in the early stages of their development upon British experience, typically

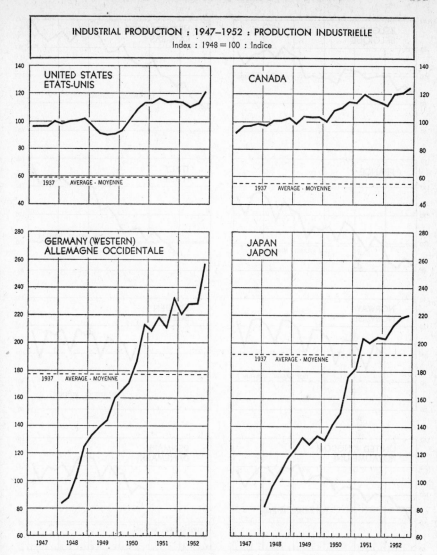

Fig. 13(a). Reproduced from UN *Month. Bull. Stats.* April, 1953, p. xii.

developed first transportation and light consumer goods industries (notably Japan). Industries like textiles required small capital and could serve the local market. In fact, the relative importance of textile production has been suggested as a rough index of the recency of industrialization. But Russia did not follow the traditional sequence. Initially it emphasized the heavy industries at the expense of the light industries, which was consistent with a policy of holding down the standard of living to accelerate development from internal resources. The eastern European countries under Russian control are following a similar sequence. Emphasis on light

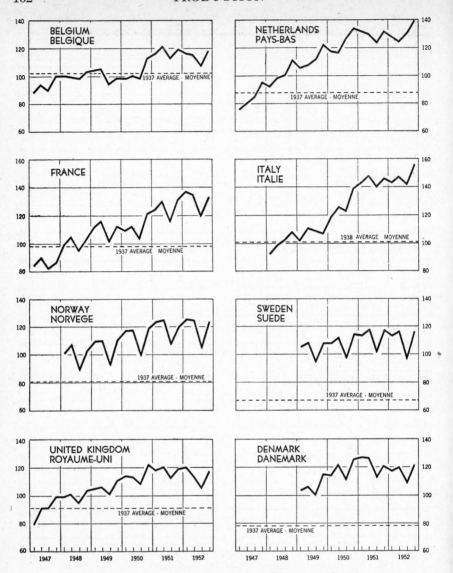

Fig. 13(b). Reproduced from UN *Month. Bull. Stats.* April, 1953, p. xiii.

industries would have exposed Russia to continued dependence on foreign supplies of raw materials and producers' goods, which for political reasons (if for no other), the government was unwilling to accept. Furthermore, the early development of textiles and light consumer goods would have provided no armament industry. The countries now beginning to develop are planning to increase cotton textile production (most Latin American countries, the Middle East, Africa, India, Australia, Canada, New Zealand,

and the Union of South Africa).[8] But more than formerly they are establishing iron and steel industries. Steel production in Africa, the Middle East, the Far East, and Latin America increased about 85% between 1925-9 and 1945-8.[9] It is still increasing, but accounts in total for less than 3% of world steel output. In 1952 the production of steel ingots and castings in the U.S.A. was five times greater than in Britain or Russia, and more than ten times greater than in any other country. Plans for European steel production provided for an increase of 35% between 1935-9 and 1953.[10]

B. The Productivity of Labor in Industry

Measures of real product per worker are not available for most industries in most countries. Such figures would, moreover, be difficult to compare, because of differences in the scope of industries with similar names in different countries and in the factors affecting prices.

Calculations of product per worker in industry in general are available for some countries, although they are approximate. In 1948 product per worker in manufacturing (after deducting depreciation) was about three times as high in the U.S.A. as in Britain, and about four times as high as in Europe generally.[11] The relationship was similar in the period prior to 1939, when productivity in New Zealand was little below that in the U.S.A., but in Japan only 20% of that in the U.S.A. (Table 20).

These relations are the historical outcome of different rates of progress in the past. Product per man hour increased about 160% in Britain between the later 1830s and 1894-1903. In France it is said to have increased about 100% from 1840-5 to 1861-5, and 1080% from 1840-5 to 1938. In Germany it is reported to have doubled between 1890 and 1907. But in the U.S.A. it increased only 65% from 1869 to 1900. After the war of 1914 to 1919, output per man (although not always per man hour) rose little in many European countries, or even declined. In France, Italy, and Poland output per man was lower in 1937 than in 1929. In Germany, however, output per man increased about .5% per year from 1907 to 1929, and between 1.0 and 1.5% per year during the 1930s. In Britain, output per man increased .5% per year from 1907 to 1924, but about 2.4% per year during the 1930s. In Russia it apparently declined 87% between 1913 and 1921, but increased 30% between 1913 and 1936.[12] But in the U.S.A. output per man hour increased 210% between 1900 and 1938 (Table 21). By 1948 output per man year had fallen below prewar (1935-8) average in France, the Netherlands, and Norway, but had risen in Sweden, Britain, Hungary, Finland, and notably in the U.S.A. (27%).[13]

---

8 U.N., *World Econ. Rep.*, 1948, 19.
9 U.N., *European Steel Trends*, 1949, 9, 96.
10 *Ibid.*, 7, 67.
11 U.N., *Econ. Surv. Europe*, 1948, 226.
12 Clark, *op. cit.* (2d), 277.
13 U.N., *Econ. Bull. for Europe*, Vol. I, No. 2, 33 (1949).

TABLE 20

NET PRODUCT PER MAN-HOUR IN MANUFACTURING IN SELECTED COUNTRIES*

Country	Period	International Units
U.S.A.	1939-41	1.070
New Zealand	1940-1	.955
Canada	1934-5	.687
Norway	1938	.506
Australia	1938-9	.454
Sweden	1930	.380
Germany	1934-5	.378
Britain	1937	.353
Hungary	1934-5	.340
France	1938	.319
Netherlands	1934-5	.305
Poland	1938	.294
Japan	1934	.200

* Clark, *Condns. Econ. Prog.* (2d), 318.

C. Factors Affecting the Productivity of Labor in Industry

The productivity of industry depends on the nature of demand, the availability of resources, and the organization of industry.

1. THE NATURE OF DEMAND

The demand for manufactured goods primarily affects the amount of resources in manufacturing. Because labor is usually more productive in manufacturing than in agriculture, an increase in the relative importance of manufacturing raises over-all average product. But an increase in the absolute size of an industry often increases physical output per worker. As demand increases, up to the amount which can be produced by a plant of the most economical size, unit costs fall. Increases beyond this point permit more plants of economical size and may also allow more economical production of raw materials, transport, power, and production equipment. General expansions of industry have a similar effect on the efficiency of those industries serving manufacturing in general. But, insofar as these economies lead to price reductions, they partly or wholly offset the tendency of expansions in manufacturing to increase value product per worker unless productivity in current money units is adjusted for price changes.[14]

For many centuries the demand for "manufactures" has been small, and it is still small in many countries where it is met largely by craft production, which is small-scale production yielding few economies as demand expands. But when incomes rise (often because of expansion of industry), expenditures on manufactures increase as a proportion of income. To the extent that the preparation of food and drink and the pro-

---

[14] Clark, *op. cit.* (2d), 295.

TABLE 21*

ESTIMATED REAL PRODUCT PER MAN HOUR IN MANUFACTURING
IN BRITAIN, FRANCE, AND THE U.S.A.

Britain	International Units
1836-45	.062
1870-6	.119
1894-1903	.161
1911-3	.195
1920	.226
1930	.296
1938	.356
France	
1840-5	.027
1861-5	.057
1930	.248
1938	.319
U.S.A.	
1869	.209
1900	.343
1910	.408
1920	.571
1930	.765
1938	1.065

* Clark, *Conditions of Economic Progress* (2d), 266, 269, 271.

duction of clothing are taken out of the home into industry, the value of the output of such activities partly displaces utilities previously produced but not counted in the national income. But the supply of shelter, transport, communication, electric power, domestic equipment, and recreation, increases in quantity and often improves in quality. Because increases in income have been unequal among countries, increases in the demand for manufactures have also been unequal.

But, at the same time, changes in methods of industrial production have created a demand for industrial goods. Methods of production have become more "roundabout," and much manufacturing is concerned with goods that affect consumption indirectly by reentering production (mainly materials and productive equipment). The more complex the industrial system, the larger the proportion of these goods in manufacturing output (such as steel and other metals, building materials, machine tools and chemicals).

In underdeveloped countries, however, low stable incomes inhibit the development of industry. In Africa and much of the East, countries are poor because they have no industry, and have no industry because they are poor. Except in a socialist country, sales of industrial consumer goods depend at the outset on spending by the wealthier, the displacement of craft goods, and increases in income. If incomes increase slowly, the market for industrial consumer goods and, therefore, for industrial producers goods, increases slowly unless the country can export. And if industry expands slowly, average incomes rise slowly. Even if money incomes are rising, the market for consumer goods does not necessarily expand at the same rate if the country saves part of the increase in incomes (through taxation, government borrowing, or inflation). But when the savings are invested, the demand for producers' goods (or for goods with which to pay for them) expands. Loans from abroad may be used to acquire producers' goods, but servicing the loan diverts some of the resulting increase in product away from consumption. Finally, even where levels of living begin to rise, increases in population, although permitting increases in the aggregate demand for consumer goods, may restrict the increase to the kinds previously consumed. More people may survive at the former level of living.

These changes in demand with rising incomes do not necessarily stimulate increased industrial output in the country where demand increases. Increased demands for internal transport and power must usually be met within the country. But industrial goods may be more cheaply imported than produced at home. During the 19th century, when international trade was relatively free, Britain, Belgium, and Germany developed manufacturing beyond their own consumption, and often beyond their own resources in materials (thus becoming processors of imported materials). Other countries supplied materials and food in return for manufactured goods. The priority of some countries in industrialization gave them cost advantages in manufacturing that were further increased by expanding exports yielding increased economies in the scale of production. The relative immobility of capital among countries further retarded development in the countries producing primary products. When they did begin to industrialize, they had to buy producers' goods from the developed countries, contributing again to the productivity of those countries. But, during the 20th century, war and depressions have induced efforts towards increased national independence through the development of an increased variety of manufacturing. This, from the world point of view, means increasing dissemination of manufacturing, and, from the point of view of the older countries, the loss of markets for their former products.

Export markets may provide an outlet for production expanding beyond the growth of the domestic market (as in Britain in the 19th century and later in Japan). But such markets decline as industrialism spreads and international trade is increasingly restricted. The British cotton industry, for instance, lost 75% by volume of its exports between 1914 and 1939. Consequently, exporting countries have been under pressure to adapt the structure of their industrial organization to such changes, and adaptation has not been easy (e.g., in Britain since 1918). Furthermore, dependence on foreign trade has hampered the modernization of British industries committed to earlier methods of production. New investment must be based on estimates of future markets, but foreign markets have become increasingly unpredictable owing to depression and the commercial policies of importing countries.

The demand for industrial goods has also fluctuated from year to year in capitalist countries. Handicraft production is free from these fluctuations except insofar as they are caused by industrial and agricultural fluctuations. Industrial production has, however, been spasmodic in capitalist countries. Purchases of durable producers' goods have fluctuated. The demand for all goods and services is equal to the disbursements of the whole system in the form of payrolls, interest and profits, after deducting amounts not spent because they are accumulated in holdings of currency or bank balances, and after adding any reductions in these holdings. Fluctuations in purchases of durable producers' goods affect immediately the steel, machinery, building, and dependent industries. But since these industries reduce their disbursements (particularly on payrolls), expenditures on durable and non-durable consumers goods, and the volume of production in these industries, decline, and secondary repercussions follow through the reduction of total purchasing power. These fluctuations are associated with societies that rely upon private decisions as to the rate at which durable producers' goods shall be replaced or increased. They have a secondary impact not only upon the production of industrial consumer goods, but also upon agriculture, and upon countries in which industrial production is relatively unimportant. But in centrally directed socialist economies like the Russian, fluctuations of this type do not occur. The output of producers goods is determined by the over-all economic plan of production, and governments do not plan for unemployment of men and resources. Even so, however, unemployment occurs, as a result of failure to coordinate various activities, causing shortages of materials, transport, or power. But it does not accumulate for a time in the same way it does in capitalist countries. These fluctuations necessarily reduce the productivity of the labor force normally employed in industry, because part of it is always periodically unemployed. They may also result in reduced productivity per person at work, in plants unable to operate at an optimal rate of output.

These fluctuations may be attributed to the methods of organizing industry. Manufacturing, unlike agriculture, is typically little dependent upon weather, so that production can often be continuous; at any one time there are products in all stages of production. If production becomes less attractive, the input of new resources into manufacturing can be quickly reduced, thus reducing output. If there is unused capacity, input and output can be quickly increased.

The length of the production cycle is independent of biological factors. It depends on the physical complexity of each type of manufacturing, which depends on the nature of the product and on whether handicraft or industrial processes are being used. In handicraft production a long time may elapse between the decision to begin a job and its final completion, but the period depends on the type of product. If the total output of a product is to be increased, the cycle is longer if all existing capacity (which means trained labor) is in use, because it will take time to train more workers. Industrial production, on the other hand, although it varies considerably among industries, utilizes mainly inanimate sources of energy and depends on machines instead of tools. It typically involves greater division of labor and, in consequence, less skill on the part of most of the individuals involved, although those who design equipment and products may have greater skill than many craftsmen. As a result of the greater division of labor and the large capacity of many machines, the output of a typical industrial production unit is much greater than of a craft unit.

The time from the decision to introduce additional resources until the first products are available may be long. In industry (as in agriculture) there is a period of maturation in economic organization. Time is involved in designing and erecting buildings, and in designing and obtaining equipment, although the period for labor training may be relatively short. The persistence of high profits during this period of delayed response to increased demand is apt to induce excessive expansion of capacity causing temporarily sharp increases in the demand for producers' goods. Subsequently, it may be difficult to keep all capacity in full use, and the demand for producers' goods may fall sharply.

There is also (as in agriculture) a period of yield that begins with the first output obtained from machinery and continues until it is no longer profitable. During this period, prices may be too low to yield any return on capital or permit its depreciation. But the typical production process involves the use of a number of machines, all of which are replaced at different times, so that there is often no observable end to the total process, except when a business is terminated. In some industries, the process in use compels the output of a number of products in fairly fixed proportions (e.g., the chemical industry). More commonly, however, industrial units turn out a variety of products, from choice rather than from compulsion, and can vary the proportion of each.

2. The Availability of Resources

The availability of land rarely has an important influence on the productivity of industry, except where an industrial raw material is of agricultural origin. But the availability of other natural resources (coal, petroleum, hydroelectric power) determines the cost of power, which greatly affects productivity.

The availability of capital varies greatly, and the amount of capital per worker directly affects productivity. The cost of capital influences the extent to which modern industrial methods are used. Craft production, using, in addition to materials, human power and skill but little capital, typically results in low product per man. In underdeveloped countries, even such industries as exist often involve more hand and less power-machine production than in more developed countries. The wide differences in product per man among the industrialized countries are mainly due to differences in industrial methods and organization, and often accompany differences in the amount of capital per worker. Much European production involves the use of less capital than American and, at least in part, the smaller usage of capital in Europe offsets the larger usage of labor.

Capital is especially important as a means of substituting non-biological power for human and animal power, which greatly increases productivity. The horsepower per person employed in manufacturing ranges from 5.0 in Sweden in 1948, 4.9 in Norway in 1947, 4.8 in the U.S.A. in 1939, and 4.4 in Finland in 1947, to 2.4 in Britain in 1930, 2.4 in Germany in 1933, 2.2 in France in 1931, and 1.6 in Italy in 1937-40. Unfortunately these figures are for different periods (in which great changes have occurred) and they are influenced by the relative importance of different industries in the different countries. But after allowance for such differences, there is a high correlation between horsepower per worker and output per worker.[15] As inanimate energy is obtained with a far smaller use of resources than animate energy, the countries with the greatest consumption of energy plus the greatest proportion of that energy from inanimate sources, are those with high productivity. The proportion of physical work performed by mechanical devices in the U.S.A. increased from about 27% in 1850 to 48% in 1900, and 94% in 1948. In 1937, 75% of all fuel and power was consumed in Europe and the U.S.A., per capita consumption being over three times as high in North America as in Europe, where it was about twice the world average. Some of this power was used for consumption (house heating and lighting) and some in agriculture, in the more developed countries.

The labor supply affects productivity by way of both its quality and its quantity. Underdeveloped countries naturally lack workers accustomed to industrial conditions of work. All countries have suffered from low productivity due to this cause in the early stages of industrialization (e.g., Britain in the late 18th and early 19th centuries, and Russia in the 20th century). Lack of experienced management is especially serious in the early stages of industrialization. In parts of Latin America the textile industry has lower productivity than in other countries using similar machinery. Manpower and equipment are poorly utilized because of poor organization.[16] But there is yet no evidence that such differences in productivity are more than a transitional phenomenon. The quantity of labor

---

[15] U.N., *Econ. Bull. for Europe*, Vol. 3, No. 1 (1951), 27, 30, 31.
[16] U.N., *Econ. Surv. of Latin America*, 1949, 71.

in relation to the demand for it affects wages, and low wages tend, as in agriculture, to discourage highly capitalized methods of production and, to hold down productivity.

The availability of knowledge of methods of industrial production is a matter of the nature of existing knowledge, the extent to which producers in different countries have access to it, willingness to innovate, and methods of industrial organization.

Knowledge of methods of production accumulated slowly for many centuries, but began to accelerate during the 17th century, and has gathered speed since. Research is, however, mainly confined to the more highly developed countries. Expenditures on research and development in the U.S.A., for example, increased from $166 million in 1930 to about $4,000 million in 1953, the federal government being responsible for over 60% of the expenditures in 1953.

Access to knowledge of methods of production is necessarily unequal. Handicraftsmen for long endeavored to restrict knowledge of their methods to members of the craft. The early British industrialists also endeavored to keep their methods secret, especially from foreigners. Patents give some temporary protection to methods of production. But, in the main, inequality is due to lack of experience or "know how." But less developed countries can import technical knowledge, either in packages with capital, or in packages with skilled technicians bringing "know how" with them. Such technicians assisted in the early stages of industrialization in Soviet Russia. In this form, knowledge involves some cost, but typically less cost than research.

Differences in production methods are due mainly, however, to differences in willingness or ability to accept innovations. Societies develop attitudes that are expressed in their religion and their political and social organization. Where there is little change in methods of production these attitudes become deeply embedded and obstruct change. Much knowledge was acquired in the ancient Mediterranean world, and later rediscovered, when it contributed to industrialization. But in ancient times there was little concern for the utilization of knowledge for improvement of material conditions. In medieval Europe, the church handed down beliefs concerning the nature of the physical and biological world, and often severely discouraged inquiry and verification. And work and trade were not in the aristocratic tradition, work being associated with a slave status and trade with attempts to get the better of others (which was permissible only in dealings with foreigners). But inflation, the import of South American silver, and coinage debasements upset rent and other obligations in money. Improvements in transport and a commercial revolution also opened up possibilities of profit. The resulting disintegration of the social structure led to adaptations of Christian doctrine, which removed hindrances to individual profit seeking and encouraged efforts to change methods of production. Dissenters from the Catholic Church emphasized the individual relation between man and God. But they elevated the pursuit of gain from a sin to a virtue; God provided man with opportunities, and it was man's duty to God to be able to render a good account of his stewardship of the resources entrusted to him. These dissenters, moreover, not only emphasized the industrious adaptation of means to ends, but also sanctified ends that were new and mainly material. But asceticism continued in a new form: man must be frugal in the enjoyment of worldly resources. The combination of frugality and assiduity in the pursuit of material ends provided a hospitable environment for efforts to increase efficiency in production and maximize accumulation (facilitating the expansion of production). Emphasis on honesty and dependability established the contract as the basis for integrating economic activity. These new attitudes also contributed to the emergence of an honest and industrious labor force, and social stability in a society of great inequality. Inequality of wealth, a dispensation of providence, was not to be exploited as a source of pleasure on earth. Real happiness was attained only in the next world, and then only after a faithful stewardship in this.[17]

Although modern capitalism developed in this religious environment, neither protestantism nor capitalism is essential to the use of industrial technology. Socialist Russia has taken over all the materialism of capitalism, but neither its religious background nor its emphasis on individual choice. Many underdeveloped countries' religious doctrines continue to reflect conservative attitudes. Mohammedanism, Buddhism, and Hinduism support economic attitudes similar to those of early Christianity and early Judaism. Fraternal dealings with one's fellow men preclude acceptance of interest and limit the pursuit of individual gain. By calling for resignation in the presence of earthly misery they diminish pressures for its amelioration. But trading (often sharp) and the disguised acceptance of interest have persisted under all these religions. The gospel of resignation supported the opposition of interested classes to industrialization (as well as to the improvement of agricultural technology). Landowning groups observed how their counterparts in developed countries have been superseded by industrial classes, and saw the effect of industrial development on agricultural wages or their equivalent. But the mass of the people in these countries are becoming increasingly aware of their comparatively low standards of life. They press for industrialization. Yet the social framework must be rendered more hospitable to innovation. These countries may choose the capitalist or the socialist solution, or a blend of the two.

Capitalist societies do not necessarily continue to be hospitable to innovation. Productivity in a number of west European countries is considerably less than in the U.S.A. In Britain, this lower productivity impeded efforts to expand exports after 1945. Yet such exports were necessary

---

[17] Weber, Max, *The Protestant Ethic, passim.*

to replace the income from foreign investments lost during the war, which in pre-war years had provided part of the means of paying for imports of food and raw materials. A series of working parties investigated the major industries, and reported ancient equipment and inefficient organization. In the cotton textile industry, the adoption of American practices was estimated to save 38% of the labor in spinning and 80% in weaving. In the pottery industry, firms were mostly too small to use modern equipment. Plants needed to be completely redesigned and the number of designs was excessive. Consequently the industry had lost most of its export and part of its home market to Japanese producers. In the building industry, low productivity was attributed to the low degree of mechanization and poor planning of the flow of supplies. In the shoe industry, output per operative was about half that in the U.S.A.; plants were smaller, and runs were short because of the large number of styles. Much obsolete equipment persists also in France and Belgium.[18] War damaged and destroyed equipment, and caused disorganization.[19] Increasing controls of foreign trade and the spread of industrialism reduced export markets. Evidently these capitalist systems were not flexible enough to adjust to these changes and to digest improvements in methods of production.

3. The Organization of Industrial Production

The general framework of industrial organization affects productivity according as it is compatible with the most effective methods of production. It is therefore necessary to turn to the structure and size of production units in industry (Ch. 11), private groups of primary producing units (Ch. 12), and the state (Ch. 13). Productivity is also affected by the arrangements influencing the supply and utilization of resources (Ch. 14-22), and coordinating productive activities in general (Ch. 23-26).

---

[18] U.N., *Econ. Surv. of Europe*, 1949, 203.
[19] *Ibid.*, 3.

Chapter 11

Production Units in Manufacturing

A. The Structure of Production Units

The structure of manufacturing units consists, in the last resort, of relations among the people who make up a primary manufacturing production unit. These relations are chiefly important because of their effect upon decisions on what to produce, how to produce, and how to give effect to these decisions.

1. Private Organizations

The individual enterprise operated by an "entrepreneur" was a central feature of economic writing for the first 150 years of the industrial revolution. The entrepreneur combines in one person the functions of making decisions on production, and receiving the resulting profits or bearing the resulting losses. This combination was assumed to maximize the efficiency of the unit and, under competitive conditions, of the economic system as a whole.

Individual entrepreneurship has been common in craft manufacturing, and still is in the Middle and Far East, and wherever craft activity is the dominant type of manufacturing. There were ten times as many handicraft workers as factory workers in China in 1933. Cottage industries in India employed over four times as many workers as large-scale industry in 1931. In Burma handicraft workers in the textile industry alone were over six times as numerous as factory workers.[1] The entrepreneur may employ a considerable number of workers, sometimes, but not always, brought together in a workshop. There is then division of labor, at least to the extent that the employer typically provides the capital and markets the goods, while the workers do the physical work of production. The workers may, however, also specialize on particular (often skilled) parts of the produc-

[1] U.N., *Prelim. Rep. on World Social Situation*, 1952, 105.

173

tion process. In industrial production, individual entrepreneurs are far less important.

The conduct of sustained activity by a number of individuals requires that the power of control and the rights and obligations of each of the members be defined. Where property is involved, the relations between people and property are fundamentally different from those of individual ownership. In a partnership a small group typically supplies the capital, takes the risks and makes the major production decisions. There were partnerships among the Jews in about the 3rd century B.C., with property separate from that of their members. In Roman and Greek times the *commenda* provided for a number of persons to contribute money or goods for a voyage and to commend these goods to one person who went with them to dispose of them and purchase a return cargo. The profit on the whole operation was shared on an agreed basis. This *commenda* was one of the chief vehicles of commerce in medieval Italy. All operating decisions were made by one member (known as the "commendatory"), the inactive partners usually being undisclosed. Partnerships are still numerically important, but each is usually small, and together they account for a relatively small proportion of all manufactures in developed countries. In France, however, much manufacturing is in the hands of small family firms, many of which are unincorporated.

The location of control in a partnership may be difficult to find. The partners must often compromise in order to arrive at a policy and agree how the proceeds of the operation will be shared, and how far each partner is liable for dealings with the outside world. Partnerships are legal entities in France, continental Europe, and countries which have adopted Napoleonic law (and also in Scotland). They can be constituted without legal formalities like registration, and some partners may be dormant— they do not participate in management. In France a partnership with a firm name (*Société en nom collectif*) must be established by a written contract. If it has dormant partners, it is a *société en participation*. In Germany a partnership is known as a *Geselleschaft*, but where some partners are silent and entitled only to fixed interest, as a *Stille Geselle-schaft*. But in Britain a partnership is not an entity in law, which recognizes only the individual members and the partnership contract. The Companies Consolidation Act of 1906 restricted the number of persons who may belong to a partnership to twenty (ten in a banking partnership).

Most countries now provide that some partners may limit their liability for the obligations of the partnership to the capital they contribute, or agree to contribute, provided they are not held out to the public as partners, and do not participate actively in management. In France such a partnership is known as a *Société en Commandite*, and dates back to 1673. In 1807 such partnerships were authorized to issue shares to the limited partners. Such an association is then known as a *Société en Commandite sur Actions* and some of these partnerships have issued their shares to bearer since 1832. In Germany partnerships with some inactive partners with limited liability and some active partners with unlimited liability are known as *Kommanditgeselleschaft,* or if they issue shares, as *Kommanditgeselleschaft auf Aktien.* Provision was made for similar partnerships in Britain in the Limited Partnership Act of 1907, which provided that there must be one or more unlimited partners and that a partner's liability would be limited only if he was registered as such. Provision was made for limited partnerships in the U.S.A. in New York in 1922, and subsequently in most states. But legal decisions that a person may lend to a partnership and take a share in the profits without becoming liable for partnership debts or a member of the partnership, make the limited partnership somewhat unnecessary. Limited partnerships are numerous in England (there were 1200 in 1930) and France, but less so in the U.S.A. The Creusot steel works in France, for instance, is organized as a partnership with shares, members of the Schneider family having been the active partners for 100 years.

The corporation is usually, but by no means always, a larger group than a partnership, with more formal and public relations among its members. Most of the elements of the modern corporation were in use in the Roman Republic and Empire where the fictitious corporate person was accepted in law. The relations between the members of the group were represented by shares of capital, and liability to the outside world was limited.[2] These devices were redeveloped in western Europe with the growth of commercial capitalism, particularly for the conduct of foreign trade.

The "regulated companies" were more comparable to trade associations or chambers of commerce than to the modern corporation. They developed out of the adaptation of the craft guild to foreign trade. The company negotiated with the government of the foreign country, maintained trading stations, and regulated competition, but its members typically operated as individual traders. The company often obtained monopolies from the Crown to conduct foreign trade with particular areas. Such companies were at the height of their power from about 1550 to early in the 17th century, and controlled the British trade with Europe for a century or more. The most famous of them was the Merchant Adventurers, established soon after 1500; the Muscovy Company and the Levant Company were started in this form. But they were unsuited to seize the opportunities presented by the opening of trade with Asia and America.

The modern corporation was put together by combining already existing devices for organizing group activities. Corporations for holding property separately from their members existed for charitable, religious, and governmental purposes. The guilds and regulated companies contributed the idea of a common purse and perpetual succession. The Dutch East

---

2 *Encyclopedia of the Social Sciences:* "Corporation."

India Company (formed in 1602) pioneered in the development of corporate forms, but the British East India Company (formed in 1600) carried the process farther, and the high dividends of the two companies made the corporate device known and popular throughout Europe.[3] These and other early companies at first organized a series of financially separate ventures by changing groups of individuals. Members were invited to subscribe to each venture, and capital plus profit (or minus loss) was returned at the end of each venture. This practice was superseded by a continuing fund of capital (or joint stock), the first issue of which was made in 1693. Upon these innovations subsequent elaborations have been built.

The modern corporation made its first appearance in foreign trade because the need for large capital first appeared there. This need was due not so much to the necessity for equipment (because the companies frequently hired their ships), but to the necessity of building fortified trading posts and maintaining a defense force. Investments were sometimes also needed to pave the way for trade. But, after considerable experimentation, companies declined in this field. They were used in the 17th century as a device for land development and colonization, aimed at encouraging trade. James I set up the Virginia Company, the Massachusetts Bay Company, and the Hudson's Bay Company. Until recently, a chartered company was responsible for the development of Southern Rhodesia, and another for North Borneo. Groups lending to the state on the security of taxes sometimes sought the privilege of incorporation, and, in Italy, of note issue. The Bank of England was incorporated on this basis in 1694. Some mining was organized in corporate form in the 16th century. The Company of Mines Royal was formed in England in 1568 to finance mining and trading and coal mining companies became fairly common in 18th-century England.

The corporate device was used after 1819 in Belgium for organizing insurance, investment banking (the *Société Generale* was formed under Royal patronage in 1822 to promote corporations), banking, mining and metallurgy and railroads. But the corporation played little part in the organization of industry during the first century of the industrial revolution. Turnpike roads, canals, and insurance provided new fields for corporate activity, but the railroad after the 1830s provided a far wider field.

Until the last third of the 19th century, manufacturing in the modern sense was chiefly organized by individuals and partnerships in England and the U.S.A. In 1852, the *Crédit Mobilier*, itself in corporate form, was formed to promote the formation of other corporations in France. Similar banks were established in most continental European countries (Ch. 21 and 24). The device was applied to commercial banking in England after 1833 and at about the same time in the U.S.A., but not until about 1870

---

[3] Hamilton, "Prices as a Factor in Business Growth," XII, *Jour. Econ. Hist.*, 332.

in Germany. The investment company, another type of financial corporation, dates from about 1860 in England and the early 1920s in the U.S.A. In the 20th century the corporation has been extended to wholesale and retail distribution, particularly the operation of department and chain stores, and to new industries such as air transport and radio. In Egypt in 1937 about half all industrial activity was incorporated. Even in socialist countries something approaching the corporate form is used, although it lacks the capitalist element of private stockholders. What is known in the U.S.A. as the corporation is more commonly known in Britain as the Joint Stock Company; in France, as the *Société Anonyme;* in Germany, as the *Geselleschaft auf Aktien,* and in Spanish countries, as the *Sociedad Anonima.* Japan adopted the joint stock principle as early as 1869.

The chief significance of the corporation in relation to the structure of manufacturing units lies in its arrangements for assembling capital. Non-managerial labor is assembled in much the same way as it is by entrepreneurs. The large size of many corporations has, however, widened the gap between employer and worker. Capital is attracted by offering investors a variety of rights to income from, and control of, the corporation. Rights to income have been designed to take account of differences in the willingness of investors to take risks. Those who prefer a minimum of risk and a stable, if relatively low, income are offered bonds, and do not become members of the corporation. Their debt may be secured by a mortgage, or it may be unsecured. Others willing to take more risk in return for a higher prospective income may be offered preferred stock (which may or may not be preferred as to capital in liquidation). Others willing to take still more risk may be offered common stock, whose returns depend upon what is left after paying all debts and any prior stockholder claims, and upon the decisions of the directors as to the amount of profit to be distributed. In the U.S.A. a number of companies have also issued stock purchase warrants, the holders of which are not members of the corporation at all, but have an option to become members under prescribed conditions.

The distribution of profit depends on the arrangements made with each class of contributors in the articles of incorporation and the charter of the corporation, and to some extent on the general law. Bondholders are merely creditors for the interest due to them and for the repayment of their principal. Preferred stockholders have a preferred right to profits up to a prescribed amount, if any profits are distributed, but the directors are not usually compelled to distribute profits even though they are made. Some preferred stocks are cumulative—if their dividends are not paid in one year, the preferred stockholders have a prior claim to all accumulated dividends before any distribution is made to the common stockholders. Holders of non-cumulative preferred stock have no such right to payment of arrears of dividend. Preferred stocks may also be participating—the holders participate in any funds distributed after the common stockholders have received a prescribed amount. Dividends are always distributed among holders of any one class of stock according to the number of shares held.

The distribution of control over management compromises between the necessity for attracting investors on the one hand, and for ensuring effective operation on the other. Individuals do not hand over their property to others unless they are satisfied with the inducements offered. The attractiveness of a share in corporate profits depends upon the probability of profit, which depends upon management and luck. But not all property owners can manage. The use of corporate resources can be restricted, especially as to the type of business undertaken, in the charter and by-laws or articles of incorporation of the company. The directors are personally responsible for uses of property outside any objectives stated in the charter and by-laws, which can be changed only with the consent of the stockholders. Within these limits stockholder control is exercised through representatives. Those who risk their property elect directors to manage the pooled property. The stockholder who disapproves of the management, but cannot muster sufficient support to eject the directors, may leave the corporation, selling his interest to another, usually through a stock exchange. But he may find that the management of the corporation has deteriorated the terms upon which he can sell his rights. The early corporations with a permanent capital fund accepted new members only with the approval of existing members, but such restrictions are now rare.

The practice of representative government in corporations departs considerably from the theory. In the U.S.A., where the corporation has developed most vigorously, management has become increasingly independent of ownership, owing to competition among states to issue charters, and increases in the size of corporations. The stockholders have the legal power to appoint directors, but the boards of directors of large corporations are becoming almost self-perpetuating bodies, appointing new members by co-option. The proxy machinery, intended to enable stockholders to appoint others to vote for them, has become an important instrument in the hands of the controlling group of many corporations. The larger the number of stockholders the more costly it is for any dissenting group to mobilize a majority and induce them to give proxies to those who will turn out the existing management. The directors, on the other hand, can pay the cost of a proxy campaign out of the corporate funds.

The responsibility of directors differs somewhat among countries. In the U.S.A., directors not also involved in management are typically not paid high salaries and are not expected to control the day-to-day operations of the corporation. They select the management and deal with matters of general policy at periodic, and not always frequent, meetings. They are legally responsible for acting with reasonable business prudence, not acquiring interests adverse to those of the corporation, and not acquiring property to resell to the corporation at a profit. The definition of the activities of the corporation in its charter or articles of incorporation often has little restrictive effect, because the objectives of the corporation are so widely defined. The charter frequently prescribes a number of specific purposes, but adds that the corporation may pursue any other objectives which the directors deem desirable, in any part of the world. Directors have also obtained increasing power to change the relations between the classes of stockholders. As early as 1865 in the U.S.A., directors had power to vary the rights of the different participants in the corporation by issuing new securities (for instance, preferred stocks) ranking ahead of the common stock, or by decisions not to pay dividends on non-cumulative preferred stock. Because these dividends, if not paid in any year, do not accumulate, such a decision diverts part of any subsequent profits to the common stockholders. Some states also permit corporations to place a fairly large proportion of the proceeds of new capital issues in "paid-in surplus" available for dividends. Thus, some stockholders may receive dividends out of capital contributed by others. But there is a vague doctrine that these powers must be exercised in the interests of all.

Corporate practice in Britain is generally similar to that in the U.S.A. But there has been more use of dummy directors ("guinea pigs"), sometimes titled people or members of the clergy. Directors have typically received higher payment than in the U.S.A., although many of the directors in large corporations in Britain are also active in management. The average remuneration per director for twelve large corporations for 1948 ranged from £30,946 to £2940, the average for all companies being £10,440. The cost of the salaries of the board in terms of thousands of pounds of corporate assets ranged from £15.8 to £1.37, and averaged £6.42 for the twelve companies. In general, the cost of directors seems to be higher in the distributive trades than in industry, and the cost is somewhat less per unit of assets in large than in small companies.[4] Directors have also generally been compensated for loss of office, for instance, when companies are merged with others. Recent discussion of the age of directors indicates a problem in Britain that has perhaps been under-emphasized in the U.S.A. Finally, if the directors do not nominate the existing auditors for reappointment, they must report the reasons to the annual meeting of the stockholders.

In France, Switzerland, Luxemburg, and Holland, share certificates are issued entitling the bearer to vote and receive dividends. Such bearer shares are not permitted in the U.S.A. They make it impossible to know who are the members of a corporation at any time. Intercorporate relations have also become very elaborate in these countries, again widely separating ownership and control, especially in Germany. Directors are usually

[4] *Economist*, July 24, 1948.

not permitted to change the profit participation of the various classes of members. Both in France and Germany there is provision not found in Anglo-Saxon countries for a board of managers in addition to a board of directors. The Board of Managers is known as the *Vorstand* in Germany and the *Comité de Direction* in France. The Board of Directors is known as the *Aufsichtsrat* in Germany and the *Conseil Administratif* in France. The Board of Managers is responsible for active management and is appointed by the Board of Directors, which is the guardian of the interests of the stockholders, and its members may not be managers. These directors are elected by the stockholders and loans to the officers require the consent of the directors who must also approve of the annual financial statement.

The separation of ownership from control in the large corporation is not due essentially to the usurpation of power by directors or managers, but is an inevitable result of methods of production requiring the assembly of large quantities of capital under unified control. The individual entrepreneur is, in fact, incompatible with much modern industrial technology. But the profit-seeking entrepreneur making decisions and taking his consequences was the kingpin of the 19th century theory that a capitalist system achieves a more efficient use of resources than any other. The relegation of the individual entrepreneur to a somewhat minor role raises the question who now makes important production decisions, with what motivation, and within what setting.

If we continue to assume that individuals in business will act to maximize their personal profit, directors may profit at the expense of the corporation, which does not necessarily make for an effective manufacturing system. In most countries directors have taken advantage of this opportunity, most notably when the corporation is first coming into use and, perhaps, when the temptations are unusually great. But persistent behavior of this kind would reduce faith in the corporation and discourage investors. Most governments have now placed legal barriers in the way of this sort of behavior. Directors may, however, be motivated by loyalty to the corporation, although those who defend corporate business criticize socialist industry on the ground that the lack of the profit incentive results in inefficiency, if not corruption. Adam Smith,[5] moreover, doubted whether corporations should be established in any but activities reducible to a strict routine. In countries in which corporate organization is familiar, directors are probably dominated by concern for their own good name. They want corporations with which they are associated to be successful, and may appraise success in terms of profit or increase in size. But lack of knowledge on this subject, and the emergence of very large corporations in the most developed capitalist countries, causes continuing concern about the extent to which directors shall account to the community at

[5] *Wealth of Nations*, Book V, Ch. I (Cannan ed.), II, 246.

large for the power they exercise over so large a proportion of the assets of the community. This matter is discussed in Chapter 13.

The managers who control the day-to-day operations of the corporation have a more direct financial interest in the success of the corporation than the directors, although less than an entrepreneur. Where they are paid salaries, the retention of their jobs and increases in income are partly dependent upon the success of the enterprise. Furthermore, in the past twenty years or so, in the U.S.A. there has been an increasing tendency to give the managers a share in profits either as a discretionary cash payment based on profits at intervals of time, or as part of a more systematic arrangement involving the award of stock free or at special prices, or the distribution of a share in profit according to a prearranged plan. Profit sharing between management and the corporation has been less important in Britain, but in France and Germany it has been almost conventional to set aside a proportion of the profits (typically 5%) as a *tantième* for distribution among the executives.

Management has sometimes been widely separated from both stockholders and directors through the appointment of managing agents similar to those managing plantations. Such management agreements exist in the U.S.A., particularly in some public utilities. They have played a predominant part in developing industry in India (e.g., jute mills, cotton mills, cement mills, and automobile plants). The agents often buy materials and sell products. The British private merchant investment houses made most of the management agreements before 1918, but thereafter they ceased to grow and Parsi houses (like Tata) or Marwari houses (like Birla and Dalmia) expanded rapidly. The British houses usually financed the companies they managed. In 1948, 334 Indian companies were managed by foreign-controlled agencies that held only 14.6% of the total capital of the controlled companies.[6] A total of some 125 managing agencies controlled about 700 companies, most of them large.[7] Typically, they are paid a fee based on output, sales, or profits. The Company Law of 1936, however, forbade agency agreements for more than 20 years unless the terms of the agreements are renewed, required management fees to be based on profits (with a minimum fee) unless the stockholders approved another arrangement, and prohibited the agent from appointing more than a third of the directors. The largest industrial complex in India is the Tata concern, with a total investment of about $248 million. The top company, Tata Sons, Ltd. is a private company, 85% of whose stock is held by charitable trusts. This top company owns at least 51% of the stock in each of its operating enterprises. Tata Industries Ltd. (since 1945 a wholly owned subsidiary, of Tata Sons Ltd.) is the managing agency for all the

---

[6] Reserve Bank of India, *Report on the Census of India's Foreign Liabilities and Assets on June 30, 1948*.

[7] U.N., *Mobilization of Domestic Capital in Asia and the Far East*, 132.

firms in the group. Thus the top company controls all the subsidiaries, not only through managing agency arrangements, but also through its holding of a majority of their stock. Some of the larger merchant banks have in recent years absorbed other banks, not so much for their banking business but for their managing agency contracts and the control of industry which these contracts give.

All the more developed capitalist countries have modified their law in the past fifty years to permit companies to possess most of the advantages of the ordinary corporation without its responsibility for making public reports. Germany authorized the formation of private companies (*Geselleschaft mit Beschränkter Haftung*) in 1892 to meet the need of smaller enterprises for limited liability. Their securities are not freely marketable, there are typically fewer stockholders than in the corporation, there is less requirement of publicity, and no requirement of a board of directors or a general meeting. Operations are in the hands of the managers, who may not, however, be members of the corporation. The balance sheet is available only to members. This institution has been used not only for family businesses but also for holding patents, and even by a number of large enterprises (such as Siemens-Schuckert). By 1909 about 16,500 such companies existed. Similar arrangements were made in Britain in 1893 (for "private companies") although with much misgiving. Limitations were placed on their size, and their shares were not freely transferable. In 1929, the Companies Act gave wider scope for the formation of companies of this kind, and by 1943 about 200,000 such companies existed with an aggregate invested capital of about £2 billion.

Most countries have had arrangements for many centuries enabling individuals to entrust their property to one or a few others. Arrangements of this kind are usually made in writing (often in wills), and the trust document comprises the instructions of the owners to the trustees as to what they may do with the property. In the latter part of the 19th century the trust device was turned to business uses. In 1879, the Standard Oil interests used a trust to bring together previously competing business interests in the petroleum industry. A similar institution exists in German law (*Interessengemeinschaft*). The most famous example of the use of this instrument in Germany was the dye trust (I. G. Farbenindustrie). The trust is also used as a substitute for a mortgage or to concentrate the voting power of security holders. When the trust is used for purposes almost identical with those of the corporation, trust certificates may be issued which are in most respects equivalent to corporate stock certificates. The distribution of profits and losses is prescribed in the trust deed. Management is typically in the hands of the trustees, who resemble directors. The trust document provides how they shall be appointed. But in relations with non-members, the trustees have no legal personality and are thus differentiated from the corporation. One trustee may, however, be a corporation. In general, unless the trustees make it clear that they are acting as trustees, they are fully liable on all contracts they make. There is no statutory requirement to provide information to the trustors or the public.

The consumers' cooperative differs from the corporation in that the customers, rather than the contributors of property, possess the basic control and share profits. These differences involve others. Since anyone can join a consumers' cooperative at any time, the right to join has no saleable value. Capital is usually obtained by borrowing, and although interest is paid on such loans, no dividends are distributed in proportion to capital contributions. Capital can usually be reclaimed at any time. Most capital, however, has resulted from ploughing back past profits. The remaining profits on operations are distributed in the form of a patronage dividend, that is, among purchasers in the immediately past period in proportion to their purchases from the cooperative. Some societies have established separate profit pools for particular commodities like coal, bread, and milk. Most cooperatives, moreover, as a matter of policy, allocate a portion of profit to education. The management of cooperatives, like that of corporations, is in the hands of directors elected by the members each having one vote (irrespective of contributions of capital or purchases). Consumers' cooperatives resemble corporations in having a legal personality, limited liability, and reporting annually (at least) to meetings of members. The societies claim that they make no profit and that their dividends are a return of part of the members' purchase price not taxable as profit. Capitalist firms contend that failure to tax cooperatives like other enterprises discriminates in favor of cooperatives.

The first consumers' cooperative was established in Rochdale, England, in 1844, by workers, in order to reduce the cost of distribution. By 1946 there were some 70 million members of consumer cooperatives in the world. In Europe (except the U.S.S.R.) about 8% of the population were members. Ten million of the members and over 1000 of the societies were in Britain, and their major business was the wholesaling and retailing of food. They serve a quarter of the population and handle about 14% of all retail trade in foods and coal, and 10% of that in clothing and footwear.[8] Wholesaling is organized as a cooperative, with retail societies as members. The Cooperative Wholesale Society engages in some manufacturing and in importing, transport, insurance, banking, and newspaper publishing.

Outside Britain, cooperatives have been most successful in northwest Europe, Switzerland, Finland, and Poland.[9] In Germany, the Nazi government destroyed the cooperatives, along with the labor unions, but in most occupied countries in western Europe they were too important a part of the distributive system to be destroyed during the war of 1939-45. In

---

[8] Digby, *The World Cooperative Movement*, 30.
[9] *For. Agric.*, Sept. 1950.

Scandinavia cooperatives have been more successful than in Britain in serving the rural population. In Denmark about a third, and in Norway about a half of the members of consumers' cooperatives are farmers and small holders. In Sweden about a third of the population are members of cooperatives.[10] Manufacturing activities have been limited, and often initiated to defeat monopolies (e.g., in margarine, flour, electric lamps).[11] In Switzerland cooperatives for the purchase of agricultural production requisites also handle large amounts of consumption goods.

In all the Americas only 1% of the population belongs to such societies, but in parts of Canada and the U.S.A. settled by Scandinavians, 14% of the population are members. Elsewhere in the U.S.A. they have made very slow progress, except for rural electricity supply (where they have been fostered and financed by the government). In Asia, about 1% of the population are members but societies have recently grown on account of food shortages and government aid (in Burma, Ceylon, India, and the Philippines).[12] The Egyptian government offered loans and grants to consumers' cooperatives in 1950 if they would sell essentials at cost plus 5%.[13] The Russian government retained cooperatives as retail distributive agencies until the abandonment of the New Economic Policy in 1927, but urban distribution is now in the hands of state organizations, and consumers' cooperatives are restricted to the rural population. Cooperatives are controlled by the Polish government in the same way as government enterprises are, and have been used as a means of crowding out capitalist elements and socializing small business.

The consumer cooperative type of organization minimizes the inducement to charge prices in excess of costs. Such prices merely provide a larger amount to be returned to those who paid the high prices. Lower prices permit non-members trading at the cooperative to share its advantages. But even in western Europe they have been able to take over a relatively minor part of the distribution of consumer goods, and little manufacturing. They present complex problems of management and have often been unwilling to pay high salaries for skilled managers. In Britain management has been cautious and conservative, but it has been more skilled and vigorous in Sweden. But in a large part of the world the market for consumer goods is thin, and skilled (or even literate) local management is lacking.[14]

In a producers' cooperative the ultimate control rests with the workers, in contrast with the consumers' cooperative controlled by consumers and the corporation controlled by those providing the capital. This location of control gives these cooperatives other peculiarities. They cannot be

10 U.N., *Rural Progress through Cooperatives*, 1954, 60.

11 Robinson, E. A. G., *Monopoly*, 194.

12 U.N., *Rural Progress through Cooperatives*, 61.

13 I.L.O., *Ind. and Lab.*, Jan. 15, 1951, 70.

14 U.N., *Rural Progress through Cooperatives*, 63 ff.

opened to membership to all who wish to join. In fact, prosperous producers' cooperatives have sometimes prevented some workers in the cooperative from becoming members. Employing wage workers, they have abandoned the principle of producers' cooperation. Capital is usually borrowed and profits are distributed among workers, sometimes, but not necessarily, equally. Management rests with a board of directors elected by the workers. The relations of a producers' cooperative with non-members depend on the law, which sometimes provides that such associations have a legal personality, that the liability of members is limited, and typically provides for an accounting by the directors to the members.

Producers' cooperatives appeared in England in the 1820s among workers seeking to avoid the newly developing wage relationship and the wretched conditions of employment. Workers legally prohibited from forming labor unions to improve conditions, sought escape in self-employment. Later, these associations appealed to skilled workers deprived of their jobs by mechanization, depression, and strikes. Robert Owen visualized the producers' cooperative as the means to the ultimate socialization of industry. In France, Philip Buchez fostered similar ideas and began forming producers' cooperatives in the 1830s. These spread in the 1840s. At about this time the idea was taken up by Kingsley and others in the Christian Socialist Movement in England, and John Stuart Mill expected much of this type of organization (which preceded the development of the consumers' cooperative). Producers' cooperatives attracted renewed interest in the 1880s and after 1918 in England (in the Building Guild movement), but have achieved no success. The central association for such societies in England, the Cooperative Productive Federation, had forty-two member societies in 1931, employing 15,000 workers, with a total business of about £6 million. The producers' cooperative is equally old and unsuccessful in the U.S.A. The Philadelphia Carpenters set up a cooperative venture in 1791. Depression induced similar ventures in 1847, and additional ventures were set up after the Civil War. The Knights of Labor placed primary emphasis upon these cooperatives between 1883 and 1886, but most of them collapsed in the 90s.

In France, the earlier movement collapsed after 1848 and revived in the 1860s and again in the 1880s. In 1884 a central association was formed, and legislation authorized state subsidies and preference in the award of government contracts. The growth of producer's cooperatives was stimulated after 1918 by rehabilitation work in the devastated provinces and the nationwide housing program. By 1929, 603 societies were reported. In Italy, there have been two types of producers' cooperative. Cooperative labor societies (*Societa de lavoro*), virtually contracting societies of manual workers, undertake public works and construction projects that require relatively little capital. They were first organized in 1883, and by 1914 were undertaking a large part of all public construction in some parts of

Italy. In 1889 legislation provided for government credit and exemption from competitive bidding for government contracts. In 1921, a central federation was formed, which in 1950 suggested that investments of public funds, particularly in projects for the development of southern Italy, should be entrusted as far as possible to cooperative groups. In 1950, building cooperatives were responsible for building 37% of the new houses in Switzerland.[15] Cooperatives for industrial production in Italy are similar to those in other countries. They have typically developed under the auspices of labor unions as a result of struggles with employers (in the glass blowing, printing, baking, and tailoring industries). The Central Glass-blowing Cooperative formed in 1902 prospered until 1911, but later disintegrated. Producers' cooperatives were about as important in Italy in 1932 as consumers' cooperatives.

In Nationalist China the government supported the organization of producers' cooperatives after the country had lost about 80% of its modern industrial capacity in the early days of the Sino-Japanese war. The government provided most of the capital and a considerable part of the administrative expenses. By 1942 there were some 30,000 societies with a monthly output equal to $20 million (American). About one-third of them were engaged in textile manufacturing, one-third in light chemicals, and the remainder in tailoring, mining, metal work, machine making (including arms), food, carpentry, masonry, and other consumer goods. Most of the societies had a large number of members who subscribed for shares carrying a liability many times the amount paid in. The management was elected by the members and the meetings of members decided on wages, the duties of members, and the method of distributing profits (which on the average went about 20% to 30% for reserves, 10% for an emergency fund, 10% for bonuses to staff, 10% for a common welfare fund, and 40% to 50% for dividends to members).

Although workers in capitalist countries have made persistent efforts for over a century to organize production under their own control, they have generally failed in competition with capitalistic business without government assistance. Capital has been difficult to obtain, most associations having relied on personal savings or contributions from labor unions, consumers' cooperatives and the government. But the producers' cooperative is not constructed to maximize pressures to create efficiency in production. Improvements in efficiency may mean the destruction of the jobs of workers. Managers dependent on the workers, therefore, have difficulty in introducing labor-saving devices. Members interested in high wages, particularly for craft work, are unwilling to see craft activities replaced by machine operations. Finally, producers' cooperatives (unlike the consumers' cooperatives) are interested in high prices, although they have never been large enough to be able to achieve such prices.

---

[15] I.L.O., *Ind. and Lab.*, June 1, 1951.

Producers' cooperatives of artisans, handicraft workers, and handicapped workers have been organized in Russia[16] and by 1939 had some 1.5 million members. They produce a wide variety of consumer goods. The means of production are owned in common, the capital is provided by selling shares and charging dues. The cooperative is governed by a general meeting of all members and an executive committee. The members receive wages and may also receive a share of profits. But the cooperatives are completely controlled by the government.

Many countries, however, have experimented with compromises with the workers' desire for control (the extent of which desire is somewhat doubtful). In the U.S.A., there have been small efforts to induce employee stockholding. In Britain, Works Councils provide some control, and in Germany workers have obtained representation on boards of directors. There are workers' committees in nationalized industries in Britain. But in Russia and other socialist countries, the participation of workers' representatives in management has been tried and rejected.

2. STATE ORGANIZATIONS

State-operated primary production units differ little in organization from privately owned units. In Russia[17] the Director of a firm is an employee required to carry out instructions as to the quantity, quality, and assortment of output, the amount of materials and labor to be used, and similar matters. In some branches of industry, however, only total production in monetary terms is prescribed. Managers often make contracts with their ministries, specifying planned production and costs and prescribing penalties for breach of the contract. Within these limits, the Director is responsible for fulfilling the allotted program and setting tasks for the constituent units of the firm, which may operate a number of plants, each subdivided into shops under foremen, and brigades of workers under leaders. Before 1934, management was distributed among the director, the local representative of the labor union, and of the Communist Party. But this arrangement subdued mutual criticism and isolated the members of the "triangle" from the workers[18] and was abolished to pinpoint responsibility.

The enterprise, which may be a trust, a combine or an individual plant, has a charter and is a legal entity that may sue or be sued. It is also a financial entity with separate capital, a profit and loss statement, and balance sheet, an account with the state bank and legal responsibility for its debts. Within the framework of the plan laid down for it, it aims at maximum profit. It may make legally binding contracts to buy and sell, although purchases of industrial commodities, and also sales, are largely

---

[16] Schwartz, *op. cit.*, 197.
[17] Schwartz, *op. cit.*, Ch. 6.
[18] Granick, *Management of the Industrial Firm in the U.S.S.R.*, 216.

made by supply and selling subdivisions in each commissariat, and scarce commodities are distributed in accordance with allocation programs. Industry in eastern Europe has been reorganized on a similar plan. The first nationalized enterprises established in Czechoslovakia, for instance, were commercial entities subject to taxation and regarded as separate legal persons. The former managing committees, representing workers and the central authority, were abolished in 1948.[19] In Britain nationalization has caused little change at the operating level in transport, gas, electricity, steel, and most other nationalized industries, but the coal mines have been grouped into districts to eliminate uneconomically small operations.

There are usually administrative units in nationalized industries between the operating level and the national level. When a whole industry is operated by a single authority instead of by a number of firms, it is likely to be too large for the national authority to deal directly with each operating unit. In Britain, for instance, the National Coal Board and the Transport Commission each has some 800,000 employees.

This problem is especially serious in a country as big as Russia, and the government has experimented with various patterns of intermediary organization. Since 1934, there have been trusts and combines responsible for groups of enterprises, and chief subdivisions of Commissariats (*glavki*) above the trusts, responsible to the Commissariats. Combines usually consist of an integrated group of plants. The number of intermediaries varies, large enterprises being directly responsible to the *glavk* or even the commissariat, and smaller ones through trusts. Small local enterprises are responsible to commissariats of industry in the allied or autonomous republics. After 1936 the number of commissariats and *glavki* was considerably increased, and after 1938 the number of trusts was reduced, to bring the enterprises administratively nearer to the *glavki* and commissariats. After 1945 some of the ministries were again consolidated. Comparable arrangements are being made in eastern Europe.

The British government began with highly centralized administrations and increasingly decentralized control, but the patterns of administration have been influenced by the nature and problems of the industries taken over.[20] The Coal Industry Nationalization Act, 1946, left the establishment of intermediary authorities to the national board for the industry and the Minister. Nine divisional boards and, under them, 48 area managements have been set up. The Transport Act of 1947 provided for a single British Transport Commission, and a number of "executives" that have been set up for railroads, docks, inland waterways, road freight transport, road passenger transport, London transport, and hotels. For railway purposes the Commission has created six regional boards responsible to the execu-

---

[19] I.L.O., *Ind. and Lab.*, Oct. 1950.
[20] Chester, D. N., "The Organization of Nationalized Industries," *Pol. Quar.*, April, June 1950, 122.

tive, based on the existing bureaucracy, but the road transport executive was built anew because no national long-distance trucking business existed before. For road freight traffic the Road Haulage Executive established a corporation (British Road Services) with eight regional divisions and 31 districts to operate the trucking system. The chairman and members of each executive are appointed by the Minister and not by the Commission, which, however, must be consulted.

The Electricity Act of 1947 established a national board and 14 Area Boards. The central board is responsible for generation and transmission, and the Area Boards for the distribution of power. The Area Boards are subject to general control by the central authority, which must approve of programs of capital development prepared by the Boards. Only the central authority may borrow by issuing stock, but the Area Boards keep separate accounts, may decide how to use surpluses (with the approval of the central authority), and fix rates for selling electricity (subject to some central control). The chairman and the members of the Area Authorities are appointed by the Minister and not by the central authority. When the gas industry was nationalized in 1948, Parliament set up a central Gas Council and 12 Area Boards, but the latter are largely independent of the Gas Council, which is little more than an advisory coordinating body for the industry. It consists of the chairmen of each of the Area Boards and a Chairman and Vice-Chairman appointed by the Minister. The assets acquired are vested in the Area Boards, which alone have power to manufacture and sell gas. The Gas Council offers advice to the Minister, and he must consult it before approving any general plan for the development of the industry. The Gas Council alone has power to raise capital by issuing stock. The British Iron and Steel Corporation established under the Iron and Steel Act, 1949, acquired merely the securities of the iron and steel companies affected. The pre-existing companies remained with their Boards of Directors as the subsidiary organizations, the government holding company having the usual powers of a controlling stockholder over the appointment and removal of directors. The industry has since been de-nationalized.

The organization of socialized industries at the national level presents problems different from those of private industry. Ownership and control vest ultimately in the government, but legislative bodies have too wide a variety of responsibilities to control day-to-day industrial operations. They must, therefore, find a way of maintaining efficiency and ensuring operation in accord with national policy. In fact, they have built on precedents from two main sources, the government department and the business corporation. In general, the activities which fell under government control, at an early date, have been placed under the control of Government departments (the Army, Navy, Air Force, postal service, telegraphs, telephone and similar services). But the wholly socialized countries also rely considerably on the government-department type of organization, although with some variations.

In Russia, socialized industry is controlled at the national level by a series of ministries, each responsible for the enterprises in a branch of industry. There have been a number of multiplications and recombinations. Although multiplication of ministries brings each closer to its enterprises, it converts problems of coordination that can be handled within a larger Ministry into matters requiring coordination at the top, and increases the burden on the State Planning Committee and the Council of Ministers. In 1950 there were 27 ministers (including those for Foreign Trade, Labor Reserves, and Food and Material Reserves).[21] The chief instrument of coordination at the top is the Five-Year Plan. Each Ministry translates its section of the plan into plans for the combines, trusts, and plants under it, and endeavors to ensure compliance. The national organization in eastern Europe is being assimilated into the Russian. In Czechoslovakia, for instance, the large industries (representing 65% of the industrial capacity) were divided into 12 groups, such as energy-producing industries, chemicals, mining, textiles, glass and porcelain, steel and tools, paper and wood pulp, each having a Council of Managers and a General Manager appointed by the government.

In Socialist China the government, while aiming at complete socialization, is temporarily relying for production on private firms, mixed government and private enterprises, and government enterprises operated by the government or under concessions to private interests. But all are regulated by the government through taxation, control of credit, the allocation of the major raw materials, and control of the distribution of products. By 1950 the government was attempting some coordination at the top through the use of "control figures" and a five-year plan, since prepared, contemplates the gradual transformation of private firms into mixed government and private enterprises (Ch. 23).

Nationalized industries in societies where most industry remains private have been formally organized more along the lines of the business corporation. Government corporations, boards, or commissions generally possess substantial autonomy in day-to-day operation, the power to spend out of their own income (their expenditures being excluded from the national budget), considerable freedom in the appointment of employees. They are required to follow general policy instructions and periodically report results.

In Britain, the government took over an existing corporation when it nationalized the Bank of England merely by giving the Bank's stockholders government bonds in exchange for their Bank stock. It took over all the stock of nine foreign telegraph and radio companies in 1946. When it (temporarily) nationalized the iron and steel industry, it formed the

---

21 Schwartz, *op. cit.*, 174.

Iron and Steel Corporation of Great Britain to hold all the stock in pre-existing companies that was compulsorily sold by the holders. The directors of the corporation could require whatever over-all planning and rationalization by their subsidiaries they considered desirable in the national interest. In other industries, the government has established Boards or Commissions without the usual corporate financial structure. Some have been established to conduct new activities (the British Broadcasting Corporation and the Raw Cotton Commission), some to take over existing physical assets (the National Coal Board and the British Transport Commission insofar as road freight transport was concerned), and others to take over securities (the British Transport Commission for other than road freight transport, the Electricity Commission, and the Area Gas Boards).

The Directors of all British Boards are appointed by a Minister.[22] Their members are generally persons with wide experience in the specified field, or in industrial, financial, or commercial matters, or as organizers of labor, but they are not appointed as representatives of interested groups. The Trade Union Congress in 1944, and again in 1948, announced that trade unionists on public bodies must serve as individuals and not as trade union representatives. Generally their term of office is determined by the appointing Minister, who has power to dismiss any member who is in his opinion "unfit to continue in office or incapable of performing his duties," phrases which have not yet been interpreted. A number are part-time members. Their remuneration is generally much less than is paid to directors of private enterprises. The total remuneration of the members of the National Coal Board in 1948 was £48,339, compared with £313,730 paid to the directors of Imperial Chemical Industries, a considerably smaller organization. Of the 300 members of public boards, less than twelve received more than £5,000 a year.

In France, the government set up new corporations in some industries. When it completed the nationalization of railroads in France in 1937, it established the *Compagnie de Chemins de Fer de France* in which it took a 51% interest, the previous owners of private railroads receiving the remainder of the stock. The government operates the system, and there is provision for the government gradually to buy out private owners. The government corporation established to operate the coal mines (*Charbonnages de France*), has set up subsidiary companies in each field. It was intended that separate corporations should be established for electricity and gas (*Electricité de France* and *Gaz de France*), but the gas industry has been operated as a department of the corporation operating the electric power industry. These corporations are financially autonomous, costs

---

[22] Robson, "The Governing Board of the Public Corporation," *Pol. Quar.*, April-June 1950, 135. Formally, the directors of the British Broadcasting Corporation and the Bank of England are appointed by the Crown.

being met out of revenues, but in fact the government controls prices and wages, and has subsidized some of them. But the large deposit banks and insurance companies retained their former corporate organization when they were nationalized (Ch. 24). All the members of boards, except the chairman, are part-time, unpaid representatives of interests (typically of the state, consumers, and workers, in about equal numbers). The consumer and worker representatives are proposed by organizations of each and appointed by the cabinet or by a cabinet minister. A *Chambre de Comptes* examines the accounts, both national and regional, every year, and reports on the operations of each company. If the company operates at a loss, the directors are automatically removed, unless confirmed. Each industry has a director-general with full power of decision, usually a former industrialist or high government official.

In the U.S.A. government commercial operations have been organized in corporate form. A number of corporations were set up during the war of 1914-18 and during the inter-war period: the Federal Land Banks, Federal Intermediate Credit Banks, an Inland Waterways Corporation, the Reconstruction Finance Corporation, Commodity Credit Corporation, and the Export-Import Bank. Again, during the war of 1939-45, corporations were set up to deal with metals, rubber, petroleum, and general foreign commercial transactions, as subsidiaries of the Reconstruction Finance Corporation. The Tennessee Valley Authority has been established as a corporation, but a Commission is responsible for atomic energy operations. In India the new government plants have been organized as corporations, with some government officials and some persons of business experience on their boards of directors. Public corporations are also important in Uruguay.[23]

The distribution of authority over nationalized industry, among the legislature, the executive, and the board for the industry, has presented difficult problems in these countries. In Britain, the legislature has provided only vague definitions of policy (Ch. 13). It has usually empowered the appropriate ministers to appoint the members of the Boards within limits set in the legislation, and to dismiss them. Ministers may usually also direct the Boards to pursue policies believed to be in the national interest. The Minister of Supply, for instance, was all-powerful in matters of broad policy in the steel industry. He could issue directions on matters he believed of public interest, supervise the general program of development, compel the corporation to dispose of interests or activities, require information and reports, appoint committees to represent the interests of consumers, and define their powers. Parliament has sought to exercise some continuing control by questioning ministers in the House of Commons without great success. Ministers can be questioned only about matters for which they are responsible, which means any directions they give

---

[23] Hanson, S. G., *Utopia in Uruguay*, Ch. VIII.

to the boards. But they have mostly influenced boards informally, and for such influence they have not been held accountable to Parliament.[24]

The boards are also subject to pressure from consultative bodies. In the coal industry, for instance, consumer councils have been established respectively for industrial and domestic users. But the committee for industrial users has reported few complaints. That for consumers has reported a number of complaints, but it has met rarely and felt that it could do little about the complaints under existing conditions. A consumers' committee was set up in the steel industry to "protect the interest of users of steel, such as the automobile and ship building industries." Some of the national corporations are required by law to refer matters to their consumer bodies; others are not. In coal, there are no local bodies, and in gas and electricity there is no national consumer body. Consultative councils in electricity need publish no reports. Practically all members of consumer bodies are appointed by the minister concerned, and all the consumer bodies have defended the Corporations before the public.[25] In general, these bodies have not been effective because of their close association with the boards and of the difficulty of obtaining suitable personnel for the large number of such committees, and it has been suggested that local consumer councils be established to represent consumers in relation to all nationalized services.[26]

B. The Size of Production Units

The size of manufacturing units can be measured in a number of ways, such as the amount of capital controlled, the number of workers, or the value of output. Size in any of these terms depends not only on the scale upon which fairly homogeneous products are produced but also on the number of plants controlled (possibly in different countries), the variety of products, and the length of the series of production operations under a single control. Measurement by capital or employment is influenced by their relative importance in an industry.

1. Actual Size

Craft production units are typically small. Reliance on the skills, and often on the physical energy, of the worker generally precludes large-scale production. Numbers of craftsmen may, however, be assembled in large workshops as they were in ancient Greece and Rome (where they originated partly in the use of slave labor and the need for supervision), and in medieval Europe, and as they are in various parts of the East today.

Industrial methods involve larger units than craft methods do, but the

---

[24] Davies, "Ministerial Control and Parliamentary Responsibility of Nationalized Industries," *Pol. Quar.*, April-June 1950, 150; Acton Society Trust, *Accountability to Parliament*.

[25] de Neumann, *Consumers' Representation in the Public Sector of Industry*.

[26] Griffith, "The Voice of the Consumer," *Pol. Quar.*, April-June 1950, 171.

scale of production varies from industry to industry and place to place. Some activities are conducted on a large scale (if at all) in most countries, such as telegraphs, telephones, railroads, shipping, radio, heavy electrical goods manufacturing, heavy chemicals, and iron and steel. Some of these, particularly communication activities, may be conducted by one firm. Others may be in the hands of two or three firms, but not a great number. In Britain, 75% of all the establishments with 1000 or more employees (in 1947) were in the metal and allied trades and in chemical manufacturing. Of all employees in automobile and aircraft production, 60% were in firms of this size; and 55% in metal manufacturing and shipbuilding. In textiles, only 12% were in such large establishments, and in clothing 7%.[27] Industries operated on a relatively small scale in most countries are textiles, leather, pottery, and the like. The size of firms in the textile industry has, however, been steadily increasing, particularly in the U.S.A. and Britain, and there are pressures for larger-scale organization in the British pottery industry.

The scale of production also varies among countries. The largest firms in most industries are in the large capitalist countries. In smaller countries, some industries may not develop because a firm of economical size would produce more than the local market could absorb, and exports may be hampered. Where exports are not hampered, large concerns may develop, e.g., the Swedish Ball Bearing Company (SKF), the Phillips Electric Company in Holland, and the Nestlé Swiss Milk Company in Switzerland. These companies have, however, now extended their production activities beyond the countries of their origin. But industries may develop with a different technology from that in larger countries with the result that the optimal size of firm is smaller than elsewhere. In Japan 53% of all workers in industry in 1930 were in workshops with less than five workers, mostly producing light consumer goods, partly because of the low cost of labor compared with capital. But preparation for war expanded larger-scale activities. In São Paulo, Brazil, the average number of employees per enterprise was from 10 to 20, over 50% of enterprises consisted of one craftsman with no employees, and .9% of enterprises had more than 1000 employees.[28]

2. Influences Affecting Size

Within any production unit, costs per unit of output depend partly on the scale of production. At the optimal scale of production average, costs are at a minimum and would be higher above or below this scale. The optimal scale may not be a point, but a considerable range of output, over which costs vary little. Plants are expected to approximate the optimal size under competition.

---

[27] U.K., *Lab. and Ind. in Britain,* June 1948, 77.
[28] Spiegel, *The Brazilian Economy,* 227.

The optimal scale of production depends partly on technological influences. The scale of production of the largest indivisible unit of a factor of production tends to set the smallest output at which this unit of the factor can be fully and, therefore, most economically, utilized. This unit may be the single craftsman, as it frequently is in craft production. It may be a piece of industrial equipment with large capacity (like a blast furnace). Equipment is often available in various capacities, but usually one of these has a lower average cost at full utilization than others. Changes in methods of production often change the optimum. Increases in the size of equipment and the speed of machines have increased the optimum in many industries in the process of industrialization. But some changes have had little effect in this direction, and some reduce the optimum. Even the forces increasing the optimum must have operated within limits, otherwise there would have been a tendency for one plant to emerge in each industry for the whole world.

Differences in methods of production at different times are likely to be due in large part to the acquisition of new knowledge. But differences among countries are less likely to be so explainable, because much technical knowledge is fairly uniformly available throughout the world. But methods of production always depend on the knowledge it is economical to utilize, which depends on the relative cost of various raw materials, power, and of the factors of production. Generally, wages have risen in developing countries but the cost of capital has not, and the margin of substitution for labor and capital has moved. The substitution of capital for labor generally (although not invariably) raises the optimal scale of production, mainly because capital goods typically come in units with larger capacity than labor units. For instance, in the steel industry the continuous strip mill, one of the most highly capitalized forms of production, has an extremely large capacity.

Differences in the relative cost of factors of production in different countries have an especially marked effect on the scale of production through their effect on the optimum. In the less-developed countries wages are low and labor costs are often low, although output per worker is less than in the more developed countries. Capital, however, being relatively costly (Ch. 21), the best use of resources may be achieved by less capitalization in the same line of production than in the more developed countries. In eastern Europe, relative factor prices have been less favorable to mechanization than in western Europe, but they have been less favorable in western Europe than in the U.S.A., where wages are higher than elsewhere, production more highly capitalized, and plants larger. Socialist governments seek to plan their enterprise units on the most economical scale, but there, as elsewhere, the optimum is often difficult to discover, and does not necessarily remain constant.

The size of firms is influenced by factors in addition to those influencing the most economical size for plants. Economies external to the plant but internal to the firm may make the optimal size for a firm larger than for a plant, and place the firm under pressure to operate more than one plant. If the optimal-sized firm called for, say, one and one-half optimal-sized plants, it would be necessary to balance the effect on total costs on the one hand of carrying one function beyond the optimal scale, and on the other hand of performing other functions at less than the optimal scale. Multi-plant operation is sometimes due to economies of size in selling, because a widespread and well-organized selling force is costly, but its cost does not increase proportionately with increases in the volume of business. There may be economies of scale in advertising, where the media of advertising are costly and perhaps cover wide territory. This induces the firm also to distribute its goods over a wide territory, and, therefore, to have a large volume of production and possibly more than one plant. These costs vary in importance from industry to industry and country to country. They are highly important in many industries in the U.S.A. and (somewhat less so but increasing in importance) in western Europe, relatively unimportant in underdeveloped countries, and unimportant in socialist countries.

Economies in buying may also suggest large firm size. Although, theoretically, the cost of buying would be independent of size in a competitive world, in practice it is not. There are true economies in buying on a large scale, where the selling costs of the seller are reduced. Possibly his production costs will also be reduced, if he receives large orders for a long period ahead and can distribute his production more economically over time. But large buyers may receive lower prices than smaller buyers because the large firm is a quasi-monopolist in buying (an oligopsonist) and receives lower prices because of his larger bargaining power. Large firms may also obtain capital more cheaply than small firms. In the U.S.A. and the highly industrialized countries, the large firm typically has access to stock markets. If buyers of securities believe that those of large corporations are more attractive or safer, they buy them at a lower yield. Large firms are frequently able to obtain better terms from banks than smaller. The long standing complaint in the U.S.A., Britain, Canada, and many parts of western Europe that small firms are at a disadvantage in obtaining capital (Ch. 22) provides an inducement to firms to become large.

Large firms may also have advantages in research. In the earlier days of the 19th century, new methods of production and products were discovered by individual inventors working in attics and dreaming of profits from patents, by business managers, and sometimes by workers. Discovery and invention are, however, now organized. Research factories are not necessarily conducted by producing units. In a number of countries, much research is undertaken by the government or by universities and other such institutions. In the U.S.A. about 52% of all 1947 research and development expenses (including agricultural research) were incurred by government, 40% by industry, 4% by universities, and 4% by others. Research by production units is often economical only on a large scale and has given advantages to large firms, for example, in the chemical and electrical industries in the U.S.A., Britain, and Germany. In good business years before 1939 the German "dye trust" spent about 10% of its turnover on research. In 1944 it was reported in Britain that, although the cotton industry was in the hands of firms large enough to achieve technical efficiency, they needed to be larger to obtain advantages in research. In underdeveloped countries, however, the benefits of research are typically obtained from outside, and this influence has little effect on the size of firms.

The cost of management affects the size of firms because managerial efficiency in coordinating all the aspects of the firm declines beyond some size of firm. The optimal size for management varies widely not only from industry to industry but also from firm to firm, according to the capacity of the management. Since it is not possible for a firm to have more than one management unit, firms may economically grow beyond the size at which managerial costs are minimized if cost in other departments decrease with size sufficiently rapidly to offset the rise in management costs. Alternatively, the firm may obtain management of a higher grade, but it is likely to be more costly. The variation among industries in the optimum scale for management is due partly to variation in the complexity of their problems. Where an industry is highly complex, the scale of operations is apt to be smaller, although this tendency may be offset by others.

The most economical scale of management has changed over time. Pressures toward larger-scale production have pressed management to reduce its costs. They have been reduced by applying substantially the same principles that have been applied to production. Managerial work has been increasingly specialized, as the number of departments within the typical large business office and the size of the white-collar class in more industrialized countries indicate. Management has also been mechanized by communication through the telegraph and the telephone, the increasing use of control devices affecting bookkeeping, typewriting, filing, calculation, and the like. These devices, at their best, reduce the cost of large-scale management and, therefore, remove obstacles to large firms.

There are also wide local variations in managerial capacity. Underdeveloped areas lack experienced managers, and unless managerial staffs are imported, production is either at higher cost or on a smaller scale than elsewhere (possibly both). It is alleged that management in western Europe is less efficient than in the U.S.A. But it is not clear that over-all costs of production are higher than in the U.S.A. for the same operation, nor, where they are higher, that the ultimate reason is poorer management.

Influences external to the firm also affect its size. The cost of transport affects the cost of materials and the cost of reaching buyers. Where it is costly the economies of scale are partly, or perhaps wholly, offset by the high cost of localizing enough production in one place to achieve the economies of large plants. This influence affects plants more than firms, and may induce firms to establish a number of plants scattered within a country, or among countries. Transport costs vary in importance among industries, because the ratio of transport cost to total costs differs. In early times and in the Middle Ages when transport costs were very high (partly because of lack of safety), goods sent long distances were typically luxuries (including spices) or scarce minerals whose selling price was sufficiently high to cover not only the costs of production, but also the high cost of transport. But industrialization has generally been accompanied, if not preceded, by reduction in transport costs, first by road, later by canal, railroad, marine, and air transport. Both internal and foreign trade have been thereby stimulated. Contrariwise, industrialization is hampered and production tends to be widely scattered and small-scale in the underdeveloped countries where transport is poor and costly. In China, there is little other than river transport—and even roads are poor. India has about the fourth largest railroad network in the world, but most people depend on roads, which are poor: river transport is not dependable, canals are little developed and there is little coastwise transport. Mexico also suffers from poor transport.

High costs for power obstruct mechanization and keep firms small, although the ratio of power to total cost varies among industries. In the electrometallurgical industries, power is a dominant factor, but in others it is less important. The cost of power differs among areas with the availability of coal, oil, and hydroelectric power, and facilities for transporting them. Falling costs of equipment have also supplied economies external to the firm. Firms often produced their own machinery in the early stages of industrialization, but equipment manufacturing is now specialized, and as the scale of production has increased, costs have fallen and stimulated mechanization. The resulting benefits have generally accrued about equally to smaller and larger firms, except where semi-monopolistic influences favor the large firm. The differences among areas in this respect are much less than in others because capital goods can usually be imported, and the cost of transporting them is relatively unimportant in relation to the cost of the ultimate product.

The size of the market affects the size of firms in both capitalist and socialist countries if the optimal scale of production is larger than the aggregate national demand. Such a country might rely on imports, but they are not cheaper than home production if the cost of transport and handling offsets the higher production costs of a sub-optional-size plant in the importing country, e.g., in Australia, South Africa, and Brazil.[29] But where there is more than one enterprise of sub-optimal size, economies might be obtained by greater concentration. Even where imported goods would be cheaper than domestic, the government may be unwilling to become dependent on them, because supplies are uncertain in time of war, the prices of imports and exports are uncertain owing to depressions, or they believe that experimentation will reveal how production on a smaller scale can be made as economical as production on a larger scale.

The rate of expansion of the market affects the size of firms where competition is imperfect. Where the total demand for a product is fairly stable, a firm can expand only by capturing business from rivals. Where competition is imperfect, the cost of attracting this business may exceed the economies of larger scale production. But where the market for a product is expanding, the new business coming into the market, being unattached to any particular seller, can be obtained cheaply, perhaps without any cost. More economical methods involving larger-scale production are more likely, therefore, to be adopted. Britain benefited in this way during the 19th century, by capturing foreign markets (some of which have been lost again). But many American industries obtained this advantage by attracting population and as a result of a rising standard of living. Where markets are shrinking, it is especially difficult to adapt firms to an increasing optimum, or even to keep existing plants operating at the most economical rate. The slow improvement of methods of production in some of the older British industries (e.g., cotton, flour milling, and shoe manufacturing) is probably partly due to this. It has been suggested that plants and firms are larger in Germany and the U.S.A. than in Britain because those countries industrialized later than Britain and, therefore, set out on a bigger scale, using British experience. But these developments occurred seventy or eighty years ago and hardly explain why British firms have remained suboptimum in size for so long. Market imperfections provide a more likely explanation.

Desire to control prices and output may generate large firms in capitalist countries. Firms do not have to be large enough to serve the whole market if a few firms able to work in harmony (possibly because one is much larger than the remainder) can charge higher prices than would otherwise be possible. To achieve control by leadership (or otherwise) a firm may have to be larger than the optimum, but the gains of monopoly may exceed any increase in cost of production, and the firm is likely to try to minimize its costs. Between about 1890 and 1910, for instance, large firms were formed in the oil, tobacco, whiskey, steel, corn products, and other industries, and controlled a large part of the total market in the U.S.A., perhaps because of the legal obstacles to price agreements, although they were not particularly effective at that time. In Germany, the

[29] U.N., *Econ. Surv. of Latin America*, 1948, 37.

same objective was pursued through cartel agreements without the formation of such large firms. The same purpose was thwarted in British industries exposed to foreign competition, owing to the general free-trade policy. Those who manage industry may, however, desire size beyond that dictated by costs of production or even by profit. Size may be an index of personal success, and give a sense of power more important than monetary income. This objective is, however, more likely to be pursued where vast empires consisting of a variety of activites are brought together.

The forces impelling increases in the size of firms sometimes encounter obstacles. In France, a few large enterprises exist alongside many small family businesses with a strong precapitalist flavor. Small businesses closely associated with the family unit are more interested in conserving their assets than in vigorously expanding to increase them. They reject opportunities for expansion in order to avoid resort to outside capital, or because existing profits are adequate and higher profit could be obtained only with more effort than they wish to make. They prefer a live-and-let-live policy to vigorous competition, and some amortize their assets and build up large reserves.[30]

3. Consequences of Size

The size of firms affects the productivity of industry at any time, to the extent to which firms approach the most economical size. But increases in the size of firms reduce the number of firms in the market, sometimes to the point at which its effectiveness in allocating resources and facilitating increases in productivity is reduced.

Since the optimal size is not known, departures from the optimum cannot be appraised. Value of output per worker appears to be unrelated to average size of establishment in the same industry in different countries. If increasing returns exist, they are duly passed on to customers in lower prices. Nor is value of output per worker related to the size of the same industry in different countries. But in both the U.S.A. and Britain, increases in the size of both plants and industries have accompanied increasing returns per labor hour.[31] Actual size may diverge from the optimum because firms cannot speedily adjust to changes in the optimum.

The large size of firms involves few sellers in many markets in both developed and underdeveloped countries. But the resulting effect on the operation of the market is not at all clear. Numbers are likely to be small in underdeveloped countries where the market is small especially in industries in which the optimum is large. For example, only one firm produces steel in Australia, two in Brazil, two in India (of which one is predominant),

---

30 Landes, D. S., "French Entrepreneurship in the Nineteenth Century," IX, *Jour. of Econ. Hist.,* 1949, 45, 53.

31 Clark, *op. cit.* (2d), 288, 299.

one in South Africa, and one in Southern Rhodesia. In Brazil a number of industries have few firms.[32] Methods of production in the early stage of development may permit smaller-scale operations than in the same industries in more developed countries. They may use an admixture of craft and industrial methods, owing to shortage of capital, the lack of a labor force adapted to mechanical methods, and wage levels that discourage expensive labor saving devices. But some measure of monopoly is likely, and is said to have weakened incentives to improve the quality of products, for example, in Latin America.[33]

Large capitalist countries can afford optimal-size firms even when they are large, because their markets are large enough to permit more firms in each industry than in smaller countries. Nevertheless, the number of firms in many industries is relatively small. In the U.S.A. in about 1935 there was one firm producing virgin aluminum, four producing all the corn binders, six producing 91% of the corn planters, three producing 86% of the automobiles, three producing 90% of the cans, three producing 80% of the cigarettes, four producing 78% of the copper, two producing 90% of the safety glass, two producing 95% of the plate glass, and three producing 61% of the steel. At the other end of the scale, the industries with the most numerous firms were women's clothing, coal, baking products, flour, wood pulp and zinc.[34] In Britain, over 100 commodities (one-fifth of which were chemicals) were in effect the monopoly of one or two firms in 1935. The three largest firms produced 70% or more of the total output in 33 industries, including condensed milk, sewing machines, wallpaper, matches, nickel, bicycles, zinc, cast-iron pipe, tires, telephone and telegraph apparatus, distilling, margarine, soap, photographic apparatus, sugar, dyes, petroleum, explosives, phonographs, rayon, and stoves.[35] And similar conditions prevailed in Germany. Most industry was highly concentrated in Italy in 1947. Four interlocked companies produced most of the electric power. One firm produced most of the chemicals, one firm 74% of the rayon, two groups produced 80% of the cement, one firm most of the automobiles and one firm about 60% of automobile tires.[36]

A single firm in an industry is commonly expected (unless prevented) to restrict sales to the quantity yielding the maximum profit, charging prices higher than under competition. But where an industry is in the hands of a few firms, each knows that changes in its policy will affect the whole market through their effect upon its rivals, and the outcome is uncertain. One firm may become a price leader, all others selling as a

[32] Spiegel, *The Brazilian Economy*, 228.

[33] U.N., *Econ. Surv. of Latin America*, 1948, 36.

[34] U.S. Temporary National Economic Committee, *Competition and Monopoly in American Industry* (Monograph No. 21).

[35] U.K., *Lab. and Ind. in Britain*, June 1948, 77.

[36] Italy: Commission of Inquiry *Report to the Constituent Assembly*, cit., *New Statesmen and Nation*, Nov. 19, 1949.

matter of policy at the same price as the leader (which is likely to be the largest firm). They may do so to avoid price wars, but where firms differ greatly in size, the smaller may accept the judgments of the larger in their own interest. This policy has probably been important in the U.S.A. where price agreements are prohibited (although not in most other countries) (Ch. 13). A leader making the price for the whole group and certain that he will be followed is likely to approximate the monopoly price, except that the costs of production may be different from what they would be if there were one producer. But if the leader is uncertain as to the acquiescence of the followers (as he typically is), the leader's price decisions rest partly on guesses as to the point at which rivals will desert. A few firms may share the market without agreement, operating so as to avoid increasing or decreasing their share of the market. The market can be shared at any price level provided prices are uniform among sellers, and other forms of competition are adjusted to prevent changes in shares.[37]

Where there are relatively few firms in an industry, prices may be higher than if there were sufficient firms of optimum size to generate competition. But costs may also be higher, and profits not necessarily higher. Firms may have expanded beyond the optimum to achieve market control. A monopolist may be under less pressure to improve methods of production and reduce costs than firms in a more competitive environment. Oligopoly may make for competition not in prices, but in costs, particularly selling costs, but sometimes also in investments in plant. But the comparison is unreal if the market is inadequate to absorb all the output of a competitive number of optimal firms at a price covering costs and a normal profit.

C. Scope of Activities of Production Units

Firms influence production not only through the scale on which they produce each commodity or service, but also through the variety of goods and services they unify (or integrate) under a single control. The number of activities integrated and the relations among them both affect productivity. There is no satisfactory classification of these relations. Vertical integration involves the combination of processes, the output of one of which is the input of the next. Integration may also unify control of the production of competing products, complementary products (products used together in production or in final use), products involving the use of similar processes (such as milling and mechanical assembly) or similar materials. "Horizontal integration" involving the production of similar goods concerns, however, the scale of production, already discussed.

1. ACTUAL PATTERNS OF INTEGRATION

Craft production usually provides for considerable specialization.

---

[37] Burns, *The Decline of Competition*, Ch. III, IV.

Coordination of the sequence of processes, as when cloth passed through the stage of spinning, weaving, fulling, dyeing, and tailoring, caused considerable friction in Britain before industrialization. The bladesmiths became subservient to the cutlers, the tanners to the shoemakers, and the spinners to the weavers. But when the prosperous craftsmen in Britain developed craft guilds into exclusive livery companies, and most apprentices were limited to work as journeymen, the functions of buying materials, determining what to produce, and selling the product, sometimes became separated from physical production, and continued to be so separated under the "putting out" system.

The early industrial entrepreneurs were often compelled to make their own machinery, in the cotton industry, for instance. But as the production of machinery became complex and the demand for it expanded, specialized firms emerged to produce it. A similar disintegration occurred in other industries but it was followed by considerable reintegration in the larger capitalist countries.

Vertical integration of mining, smelting, and other processing of mineral products is common. In the U.S.A., the oil industry is vertically integrated in large part. Steel producers control the production of coal, iron ore, and limestone in the U.S.A. and Germany, and in Britain until coal mining was nationalized. Most producers of aluminum also produce bauxite, and copper processing is often integrated with copper production. The production of standardized manufactured materials is less integrated with their further fabrication. Steel and aluminum producers typically dispose of their semifabricated goods on the market, although the Krupp concern in Germany integrated "forward" much further than steel companies in other countries; it made pumps, turbines, office machinery, typewriters, elevators, and the like. Aluminum producers also fabricate some finished products in the U.S.A. Paper manufacturers may be under a single control with newspapers. There is little integration of cement and sugar production with subsequent use.

Transportation although usually organized independently is sometimes integrated with the production of the materials transported. In the U.S.A. pipe lines are owned by oil and natural gas producers. Railroads are occasionally owned by steel companies, where they transport ore. Aluminum and copper companies own short lines, and meat packers formerly owned fleets of refrigerator cars that operated on the railroads. Ore and oil companies own ships and many concerns operate truck transport. In Britain before nationalization, colliery companies often owned their own railroad cars.

Financing is usually organized independently of industry. But prior to 1939, and particularly prior to 1933, banks in Germany had a continuous interest in, and influence over, large industrial firms, although often not on the basis of stock ownership. But the power of the deposit banks over industry has declined in the U.S.A. Large manufacturing firms can exert pressure on banks rather than *vice versa*. But investment banks influence (to an unknown extent) a wide variety of activities through advice and representation on Boards of Directors. Some large manufacturing companies (producing agricultural machinery, automobiles and large electric-generating equipment) have financed the purchase of their equipment in the U.S.A. As corporations become larger in capitalist countries, they tend to finance themselves out of their own reserves, thus integrating the acquisition of capital with the management of the concern (Ch. 21).

Conglomerate concerns with access to capital may control a wide variety of subsidiary production units. Banks in some eastern European countries (for example, Hungary and Czechoslovakia) formerly exercised such control. Merchant bankers in India have similar control through ownership and managing agency contracts. The Tata concern controls corporations in steel production, utilities, textile mills, oil mills, hotels, and air transport. Similar concerns exist in Brazil,[38] New Zealand, and Australia.

In Japan, they took the peculiar form of *zaibatsu*. Prior to 1945 some seven or eight of these organizations consisting of family groups (such as the Mitsui, Mitsubishi, Sumitomo and others) controlled a wide variety of industries, banks and insurance companies. The family organization provided the foundation for industrial organization. The Mitsui, who were petty feudal lords in the 17th century, began their industrial operations by organizing a *saké* distillery in 1632. In the 18th century they formed a family pool binding all the members to act together under the guidance of the elders, and in 1900 wrote a formal constitution, most of which was secret. All important financial decisions were required to be taken collectively, no members or collateral families might take any action prejudicing the entire clan (and the family had eleven branches). The family used the holding company to exercise legal control. By 1940 its properties were worth about one billion dollars and included organizations in international trade, shipping, banking, lumbering, manufacturing, shipbuilding, and many others. The family compact was abrogated in 1946 after the holding company had been seized by the American occupation authorities. As a group, the *zaibatsu* controlled a large part of the Japanese industrial system (Ch. 22).

In the larger capitalist countries, manufacturing concerns often produce a variety of products involving similar materials, similar processes or occasionally goods which are competing or complementary. In socialist countries like Russia, integration within the plant is presumably dictated by considerations of cost. The coordination of the production of different goods and services, vertically or otherwise related, is a function of government, the national plans providing for over-all coordination. In mixed

---

[38] Spiegel, *The Brazilian Economy*, 229.

economies, nationalized industry is sometimes organized to provide for integration. The British Transport Commission controlled road, rail and canal transport and was expected to coordinate them (until road transport was de-nationalized). The preservation of pre-existing steel producing units under the government holding company preserved some vertical integration during the short life of the company. But railroads, gas and electric utilities, and steel producers were required to surrender their coal mines to the Coal Board. The nationalized gas and electric authorities in France, set out under a common control.

In less-developed countries manufacturing is sometimes more specialized. Industry may begin with a standardized output or onestage operations because less capital and skill are involved and managerial problems are simpler. Textile producers usually begin with the coarser fabrics (e.g., in Japan and Latin America) and take up the finer counts later, but steel plants are usually integrated. The Volta Redonda steel mill in Brazil is integrated from the production of pig iron to semifabricated shapes. The Tata Iron and Steel Company in India and the steel industries of Australia, South Africa, and Southern Rhodesia are all to some extent integrated.

2. INFLUENCES AFFECTING PATTERNS OF ACTIVITIES

Combinations of productive activities may be the result of efforts to minimize costs, although different combinations may be equally economical. Under competition, or in a socialist state seeking to minimize plant costs, the production technology may make it costly or impossible for every stage or process to be conducted by a specialized firm. A steel manufacturing plant can save heat by sending hot pig iron direct to open hearth furnaces. Many reactions in the chemical industry produce a variety of commodities, as the slaughtering of cattle does. The nature of demand may induce integration to reduce costs. Where demand has a regular time pattern of fluctuation (for example, seasonal demands), it may pay to undertake more than one line if these interlock in time and use some of the same facilities. Various products may be canned in a single plant, and the production of farm implements with different seasonal uses may be combined.

Influences internal to the firm, but external to the plant, may induce the firm to produce many products. The cost of selling may be reduced by handling a variety of products. Retailing is usually integrated in this way, and jobbers and wholesalers dealing with these retailers find it economical to handle a variety of products and spread the cost of a visit to each buyer over as large a volume of sales as possible. Manufacturers of consumer goods often spread the costs of advertising or large-scale physical distribution facilities over a variety of products. Where capital is more cheaply obtained by large firms, producing units may endeavor to become large by widening the variety of output, if there are obstacles to increasing their production of a single line. Some firms find it more economical or safer to conduct research, thus avoiding competition for patents obtained by others. Such firms enter lines of production in which the results of their research can be utilized. The integrated firm may be able to make a better appraisal of the profitability of its discoveries and may make more profit by exploiting than by selling the patent, especially if it has easy access to capital. Hence, the great size and variety of activities of companies like the German dye trust (I. G. Farben) which produced pharmaceuticals, explosives, rayon, photographic apparatus, petroleum, fertilizers, artificial precious stones, and coal. The pattern of activities of larger chemical and electrical engineering companies in the advanced countries have been thus influenced.

The proliferation of activities complicates management, and rising management costs or declining general efficiency place limits on integration. Automobile companies do not produce all their own components and materials. Steel producers are deterred from entering all the industries that use steel because of the great variety of problems involved. Those who produce containers are similarly deterred from further integration. Manufacturers are generally deterred from entering retailing where it is widely integrated. If a manufacturer of a few products undertakes to retail them, he must either make highly specialized retailing economical (which is usually difficult) or undertake to retail a great variety of things which he does not himself manufacture. Integration often stops at points at which there are great differences in the scale of production. The corn products, meat packing, textile, tobacco, and milk industries rarely produce much of their agricultural materials. But where the scale of agricultural production is fairly large, as in plantations, manufacturing and production may be integrated, as in sugar, paper, and to some extent rubber.

The desire for size may lead to wide-ranging integration, and seems to be almost the only explanation, apart from easy access to capital, of the unrelated industries brought under a single control by the former Stinnes concern in Germany and the *zaibatsu* in Japan. In Italy the *Instituto Finanziario Industriale* controls the Fiat automobile company and 135 other companies, producing commodities ranging from vermouth to cement. Firms may integrate back or forward to achieve monopolies at those stages and prevent rivals from obtaining supplies or outlets. Where two successive stages of production are conducted by few firms, a firm may seek to avoid the difficulty and indeterminacy of bargaining between the two stages by combining them. Firms whose monopoly is restricted by a competing good or service may integrate that good or service with their previous line. They may also bring under common control a number of products using a single material to obtain power in buying the material.

Firms may integrate to reduce risks. The ordinary enterpreneur is assumed to maximize his reward for taking risk and to minimize the risks he takes. But some firms pool risks, presumably because they prefer security to maximum profit. Vertical integration is not generally a good way of pooling risks, because all the processes are affected by the common risk of shortage of the means of production, or of changes in the demand for the final product. But non-vertical integration may more effectively pool risks. The International Harvester Company in the U.S.A., for instance, stated that the production of many implements, whose demand varied differently, reduced its risks. The combined control of plants in different regions also reduces risks where the different geographical sectors of the market behave differently.

Influences external to the firm also influence integration. Where supplying industries are competitive, there is little inducement for a firm to provide its own supplies. Usually it cannot produce more cheaply than it can purchase. By integrating it avoids paying prices, including the profits of its suppliers, but it would expect a profit from its own operations if it displaced its suppliers. The general failure of manufacturers to enter competitive branches of agriculture has already been referred to. A manufacturer buying from a monopolized industry may, however, decide to produce for himself to avoid monopoly prices or to share in monopoly profits unless technical difficulties and patents prevent him from doing so. These difficulties are especially great for firms in underdeveloped areas, who must generally buy their capital goods from other areas to obtain the advantages of specialization there. Similarly, monopoly among buyers may induce "forward" integration to avoid the power of the monopolist to beat down his purchase prices and restrict sales by raising selling prices. Where the buyers are competitive, this inducement is small, but competition among retailers has led to manufacturer control of the retail prices of their products in Britain and the U.S.A., such control being a partial "forward" integration (Ch. 13).

3. Consequences of Patterns of Activities

The patterns of integration that occur under full competition contribute to maximum productive efficiency. But competition is usually imperfect. Integration may then hamper the pursuit of efficiency by obscuring the cost of each activity. There are usually common costs (at least for management) that can be allocated only arbitrarily among different activities. The elimination of high-cost activities is often obstructed because, for instance, the profits of a vertically integrated firm are derived from all its operations, some of which may be efficient and others not. The market ceases to provide a check at each stage unless there is a number of unintegrated firms in each. Inefficiency may also appear because directors use integration to achieve power and prestige or to pool risks. The size of industries is also less readily adjusted through the capital market where firms are widely integrated. The investor is less able to decide which "industry" to invest in, and compelled rather to choose which management group to invest in. But these managing groups, because of their experience and information, may make better allocations of capital than the original investor of savings. Where competition is imperfect, integrated firms may be more effective than specialized ones would be. Competition might be better still, but it is not always compatible with the use of the most economical methods of production.

Chapter 12

Cooperation Among Production Units in Manufacturing

Cooperation among producing units is older and has been more pervasive in non-agricultural than in agricultural production.

A. Cooperation among Manufacturers in Particular Lines of Production

Manufacturers of similar products may cooperate to reduce costs or to regulate output and prices.

1. COOPERATION TO REDUCE COSTS

Manufacturers have cooperated less than agriculturalists to provide services for their members more cheaply than they can provide them for themselves. Manufacturing is usually organized on a larger scale than agricultural production, and firms are large enough to provide more services for themselves than in agriculture.

Cooperating groups may reduce costs to the firm by collecting information useful to all the members, such as information about prices, costs, freight, insurance, and methods of production. Cooperative selling might reduce the cost of distribution, but it is more likely to reduce competition by giving the group power over price and other forms of competition. It also separates the manufacturer from his customers and makes it difficult for him to leave the group if he wishes. Cooperating groups do not typically undertake research and improvement, although these might be more economically organized on a cooperative basis. The results of cooperative research must be made equally available to all members, which diminishes the opportunity for any one of them to get ahead of his rivals by introducing innovations, and may facilitate agreement not to take advantage of new methods.

2. Cooperation to Regulate Output and Prices

Cooperating groups alone can control output and prices unless there is only one firm in an industry or the government undertakes regulation. In fact, much cooperation has been aimed at such control.

a. The Prevalence of Cooperative Regulation of Prices and Output

The forms of cooperative organization have not changed greatly. Throughout history there have been temporary agreements among traders to "corner" markets (i.e., obtain a temporary monopoly).[1] Guilds of those following common productive activities existed prior to the Christian era in the Middle East and the Far East, and have been used by their members to promote their common interests, and sometimes by governments to control the behavior of the group. Guilds virtually took over the regulation of craft production in medieval Europe and they have survived until recently in continental Europe and the East. In India the urban (but not rural) handicrafts are organized in guilds based largely on caste lines, the most important being for textiles, but there are guilds for makers of weapons, enamelled jewelry, stone carving, gold and silver thread work, glass, and leather. Professional associations are modern descendants of the guilds.

Industrial employers began to form trade associations in Britain and the U.S.A. early in the 19th century, and they have since multiplied greatly in all industrialized countries. If the membership is large, these associations are typically directed by a committee, although major policies require submission to the members. Votes are allocated on a variety of bases, but it is usually difficult to enforce decisions opposed by any considerable minority. Specific contracts regulating output and prices are also ancient. The first of the modern era was made by British coal producers in the 17th century. These agreements, commonly referred to as "cartels" (from *carta*, contract), may be collateral to a trade association or be made without any association. To prevent evasion of the cartel agreement on prices or output, the members may establish a cooperative selling agency to market all the output of the members (known as a syndicate in Germany and a *comptoir* in France). Where products are not homogeneous enough to be dealt with by agreements covering prices or output, competition may be controlled by "conditions of sale" agreements, which have been particularly prevalent in Germany but occur elsewhere, sometimes as codes of business ethics or fair business practice.

The extent of price and output control has fluctuated in recent centuries. The expansion of craft production in medieval Europe induced a great multiplication of guilds closely associated with church and state. They typically obtained from the crown (for a consideration) charters giving

---

[1] Piotrowski, *Cartels and Trusts, passim.*

them legally enforceable powers, especially to prescribe qualifications for practicing the craft and standards of workmanship and, sometimes, to monopolize local markets. These powers, intended to protect both customers and members of the craft from pressures towards deterioration of work, were administered by a committee of members (often called Wardens). The power to determine the qualifications for practice, typically used to set minimum terms of apprenticeship to members, permitted regulation of the numbers in the craft. Later, high fees for full membership prevented many who complied with the apprenticeship requirement from becoming master craftsmen. The regulation of products and methods of production, held to be necessary to prevent unfair competition by substandard craftsmen, in fact led to control of prices, in earlier times under the influence of the religious principle of the "just price." In Britain the government began to regulate the guilds, but they disintegrated because their policies induced production outside the towns (in which alone their powers ran). The guilds in France were virtually destroyed by the Revolution, subsequent efforts to revive them being only temporarily successful. But in Germany they survived to retard industrialization in the first half of the nineteenth century. An anti-guild movement of German workers was unsuccessful in 1848, but many of the powers of the guilds were taken away in the 1860s although they remained in some professions and in navigation, and some were revived at the end of the century. The First International Congress of Craftsmen was held in Rome in 1930, fourteen European nations being represented.

Guilds controlled the crafts in Japan in much the same way as in Europe except that they played a smaller part in local political life and administration.[2] In many underdeveloped countries in the Middle and Far East where craft production remains important, guilds still exercise considerable control over prices and entry into production. But in Russia and eastern Europe the organizations of craftsmen now resemble agricultural cooperatives, purchasing materials and equipment for members and marketing their product under the control of the state. In Poland, for instance, all handicraftsmen must belong to guilds, which must belong to territorial unions of guilds, which belong to chambers of handicrafts, which belong to a union of such chambers, which is controlled by the relevant ministry.

The early stages of industrialization were relatively unfavorable to cooperation because of the rapid multiplication of new firms, desire for secrecy about methods of production, and willingness to take a chance of successful survival where a number of newcomers might fail. But employers began to join together in the U.S.A. and Britain early in the 19th century, often, at the outset, to deal collectively with labor. But by the middle of the century regulation of prices and output was increasing, although in different degrees in different countries.

---

[2] Allen, *op. cit.*, 13, 22.

In Britain, monopolistic regulation was probably fairly common prior to the industrial revolution. In the 17th century the tinners and smelters had a monopolistic organization, and the coal producers in the New-castle area made one of the earliest modern agreements regulating output and prices, one that continued until the middle of the 19th century, when railroads gave other coalfields access to the London market. (Ch. 9). But such agreements were uncommon during the period of most rapid in-dustrial growth in the 19th century when markets were expanding, and free trade restricted opportunities to raise prices by agreement. Re-strictive agreements have multiplied greatly during the 20th century, especially where foreign competition is weak. After 1918 industries with shrunken markets sought relief in cooperation to raise prices and some-times to reduce productive capacity.[3] The abandonment of free trade in 1933 further stimulated these restrictive policies, and by 1949, 1100 trade associations existed and largely controlled prices in building, food processing, and consumer goods trades. After 1932 steel prices were largely controlled through the British Iron and Steel Trades Federation. A new flexible tariff introduced in 1932 to enable British producers to make agreements with the international steel cartel was administered by an official Import Duties Advisory Committee. The Committee followed the advice of the Federation, which coordinated the activities of the more specialized trade associations in the industry. The prices of textile machin-ery, leather, agricultural machinery, and shoe machinery were also pri-vately controlled.

In the U.S.A. local group organizations of producers multiplied after the Civil War and began to control prices and output, but the Sherman Law of 1890 limited their power to restrain trade. While they are per-mitted to provide informational services (including information as to past prices) they are prohibited from agreements as to price, output, sharing of markets, and the like.

In Germany, private group controls have been more important than in Britain and the U.S.A. Controls appeared in the early stages of industrial-ization, accelerated after the end of the Franco-Prussian War (when heavy industry in particular was overexpanded), and increased still more rapidly between 1900 and 1914. Cartels were organized in the 1860s in the salt, tinplate, and iron rail industries (where there were few producers and homogeneous products). In the 1870s they appeared in the heavy in-dustries and chemicals. There were about 14 restrictive arrangements in 1879, 35 in 1885, and 385 in 1905. After 1918 German interests stimulated international cartels (Ch. 26), but turned more toward the outright consoli-dation of previously competing firms within the country after the "rationalization movement" had revealed the incapacity of cartel groups to regulate industry (p. 216). The National Socialist government used trade

[3] Lucas, A. F., *Industrial Reconstruction and the Control of Competition.*

associations as instruments of government control. The corporate state in Germany and Italy rested, in theory, on industrial government (including both workers and employers). After 1945 German industrialists generally opposed the decartelization proposals of the occupying powers.

In France, industrialization has been slower and less extensive than in Germany. But where large-scale corporate organization has developed, restrictive activities have also appeared, as in the iron and steel industry (regulated by the *Comité des Forges*), coal, cement, chemical, and textile industries. Industry syndicates have been characteristic in Poland, Italy and Spain, and common in Switzerland, Portugal and Latin American countries. *Sindicatos* in Spain regulate each industry, share markets among members, and allocate materials among members (sometimes corruptly). There was considerable cartelization in czarist Russia, where 80% of the output of steel and pig iron was subject to cartel control in 1902.[4]

Developing countries have generally borrowed the principles of trade associations and cartels from older industrial countries, often to achieve unity of action against foreign competition, especially by securing import controls from the government. Guilds and other cooperative organizations have characterized Japanese industry and were extended after 1931 when the laws governing manufacturers' and export guilds were revised to encourage cooperation. Cartel agreements have been common in Egypt.[5] In the more industrialized countries, cartels show considerable vitality, and mild liberalization of trade in Europe in 1949 and 1950 produced a new crop of cartels.

The occurrence of group controls of output and prices depends on the feasibility of control and the atttudes of producers. The feasibility of group organizaton depends on the number of firms. If they are numerous, cooperation is difficult because of the greater probability of non-joiners or violators of group policy. In the medieval crafts, and in agriculture and retailing in the U.S.A., control has been achieved only with the aid of the government. Differences in the products of firms impede price and output control (as, for instance, in the women's wear industry) and group policy is limited to regulation of methods of selling. Where there is only one producer, organization is unnecessary, and where the number is very small (as is especially likely in small countries or those in the early stages of industrialization) formal organization may be unnecessary because informal understandings are easy. In Germany, cartelization flourished perhaps partly because of a predisposition to organization. But industry, having been developed later than in Britain, was often on a larger scale (involving relatively few firms). The banks, interested in the flotation of industrial securities, and in granting intermediate and short term credit,

---

[4] Dobb, *Soviet Russia and the World*, 58.
[5] Issawi, *op. cit.*, 89.

were prepared to restrain their offspring from destructive competition and, being few in number, could take an industry-wide view. The government was sympathetic to group action and ready to protect new industry with tariffs against foreign competition. Legal prohibitions upon cartel agreements (as in the U.S.A.) tend, however, to force the desire for cooperative controls into channels beyond the reach of the law, such as community of policy regarding the sharing of the market or prices (Ch. 13).

The attitudes of manufacturers in general impel towards group control. If they wish to maximize profit, which is the assumed motivation of capitalist producers, they may, especially in the early years of a new industry, prefer to compete for business, anticipating that they can drive out others and be more prosperous in the longer run than if they submit to cooperative policy-making. If any considerable portion of the supply in a market is outside the association, the latter's controls are ineffective. But unanimity as to the desirability of restricting competition has been especially encouraged by the nature of industrial production. Overhead costs are a significant proportion of all costs, and in times of falling demand competition can (but does not necessarily) drive prices down to the point at which the proceeds from the sale of an additional unit of the product equal the additional cost of producing it. Prices then include no contribution toward overhead costs, which induces efforts to avoid short-term price-cutting by agreement (or convention). Cyclical shrinkages of demand in capitalist countries encourage group organization, especially if overhead costs are important and firms are few (as in steel, cement, aluminum, and chemicals).

b. Consequences of Cooperative Regulation of Output and Prices

Cooperative regulation of output and prices transfers the power to make vital decisions from the "entrepreneur" to the group, and thereby changes the kind of decision made.

Associations commonly embark on restrictive activities to obtain relief from distress through higher prices. They may begin with an agreed schedule of minimum prices and allowances, which usually persists after any short-period distress has been relieved. If they seek maximum profit and act in virtual certainty of loyalty to group policies, they presumably seek the price and output which maximize the profit of the group. The extent of their departure from competitive price and output depends on the price elasticity of demand (depending on the availability of substitutes, consisting either of imports of similar products or goods substitutable in use) and the relation of their costs to competitive costs. The group may arrive at a higher price even than a single monopolist, because their costs are different from his.

Since the price elasticity of demand differs among buyers, profits can be raised by grouping buyers according to the elasticity of their demand (all sellers using the same classification) and charging different prices for the same product sold to the different groups. A group which has a controlled market at home but sells on a competitive market abroad (where the elasticity of demand for its product is greater) may charge lower prices where it has to meet competition and higher prices where it does not. This discrimination may so increase demand that it permits larger scale production and lower prices at home than would result from a single price policy. But the discrimination may mean higher prices at home for the benefit of foreign buyers.[6] Such policies are frequently part of a transition to an international cartel (Ch. 26).

Guilds and cartels commonly claim that they do not aim at maximum group profit, but only at preventing unfairly low prices and product deterioration. The fairness of prices is determined by the industry group. If it avoids prices that may drive purchasers to substitutes or induce new competition, it merely avoids the maximization of profit in the short run in order to achieve it in the long run (which may, however, involve severe limits on prices). Groups are more likely, however, to aim at a profit that may in fact cover excessive costs. Their costs may be excessive either because of excess capacity in the industry, or because of inefficient management owing to the security resulting from the group control. Cartel agreements, made precisely because of excess capacity, which may otherwise stimulate price competition, are likely to seek a fair return on the actual investment, which may represent an undesirably large investment in relation to sales, although conditions of demand may frustrate their efforts. In any event, sustained profits for all producers are incompatible with competition in a dynamic economy, and industry groups are not impartial judges of the fair rate of profit or the costs that should be covered.

Agreements confined to prices often prove inadequate because they leave opportunities for members to increase their share of the market by non-price competition. The association is then under pressure to control such competition by agreements (a) prescribing total output and the production quota of each member, or (b) restricting competitive practices. It may concentrate all selling in a single syndicate in order to restrict non-price competition and ensure adherence to agreed prices. By 1905, at least half the German cartels included cooperative selling syndicates. Rivalry is then concentrated upon the terms of the agreement that establishes the relative positions of the members in the industry. But the determination of each firm's quota of output or sales is a delicate matter. The commonest bases for these quotas have been past sales, output, and production capacity, but there is usually considerable bargaining. Many agreements provide fines for production in excess of quotas, and premium payments for production falling short of quotas. Some firms may then

<hr>

[6] Robinson, *Economics of Imperfect Competition*, Ch. 15.

find it profitable to exceed quotas and pay fines, and others to restrict output below quotas and receive an income from premiums.

The combination of price and output control prevents attempts by any firm to improve its position. But it also increases the probability of competition from non-members sheltering behind the cartel price without carrying any part of the burden of output restriction. Members discouraged by small sales are also tempted to break away. These considerations may prevent even any profit under group control. Non-member producers may be former customers, attracted by high profits to enter the industry. Cartel controls of the prices of coal and iron ore induced German steel makers to purchase mines. Or the new producers may be suppliers of raw material to the cartellized industry, attracted by high profits there, or irked by the reduction of raw material sales due to the high prices charged for the products made from the material. Or the members of a cartel may undermine it by entering subsequent processes. Some German steel companies entered the fabrication of steel products on a large scale. Unintegrated fabricators had to buy steel at the cartel price, but steel makers were able to avoid output and price controls. In the shorter period, groups may seek to stabilize the price of their product, particularly to limit price competition during periods of depression. Sooner or later, however, changes in costs or demand require a more refined policy.[7]

The combination of price and output controls focusses all rivalry on the terms on which the quotas are determined at each expiration of the agreement. Members uncertain whether the agreement will be renewed at its termination may acquire sufficient productive capacity to take advantage of any reversion to competition in violation of the agreement, or when it lapses. They may also increase their capacity in order to strengthen their claim for a larger quota when renewal is negotiated. Some associations regulate productive capacity to cut off this line of escape.

The claim that cooperative groups are qualified to regulate industry was advanced in its most fanatical form in Germany, when inflation caused economic disintegration after the war of 1914 to 1918. Cooperating groups were to "rationalize" industry, which meant in part greater rationality in production processes. Many plants were redesigned (according to what was known as "Fordismus") to apply modern knowledge of mechanization, electrification, and chemicalization, which often meant more heavily capitalized, larger plants. Rationalization also meant the application of rationality to industries as a whole, the most important aspect of which was the adjustment of capacity and the distribution of production among firms. But rationality, from the point of view of the industry, conflicted with the property interests of individual firms. Private groups being unable to deal with the problem, firms turned to mergers

---

[7] Burns, *Decline of Competition*, Ch. V.

that, however, often proved difficult because, again, the terms of mergers were difficult to arrange. Rationalization also had all-industry aspects, particularly concerning scientific management, standardization, and research. Here again, the conflict between rationality on the one hand, and private property on the other, proved insoluble, largely because firms were unwilling to surrender their business secrets. The movement finally collapsed in criticism of "over-rationalization"[8] (an interesting concept).

The broader effects of group controls on the productive system lie in their effect on the allocation of resources, on progress, and on the distribution of incomes. Where groups are able to raise the price of their product above the competitive level, output falls short of the competitive output. If the group minimizes the cost of producing this output, a smaller proportion of total resources is allocated to the controlled activities and an excessive proportion to more competitive industries (where prices approach marginal cost). But cartels able to raise prices are often unable to hold down investment in the industry to the minimum cost level. They prevent resources from going into more competitive industries and keep them partially unemployed in the controlled industry. Monopoly prices may not then yield monopoly profits. Such misallocation may be due to high monopoly profits attracting resources into the industry, but it may also be due to the tendency of group controls to retard the reduction of resources when demand for the product falls. It is difficult to make agreements involving the failure of some members. Arrangements permitting firms to exceed their quota on payment of a penalty, or allowing the purchase and sale of quotas, permit concentration, but at a price which is a partial barrier to reorganization. The experience of Britain, Germany, and Japan indicates that industry groups are unsuitable instruments for reallocation.

Group policies, thus preventing prices from reflecting relative scarcities and relative demands, distort the use of resources. Purchasers of products at controlled prices use less of them than they would if prices were competitive. Group controls have also contributed little to industrial progress. Producers of products with controlled prices are likely to achieve less internal efficiency than under competition. Protection from competition may convert prospective losses into profits and reduce the stimulus to efficiency. Even if some firms reduce costs by increasing efficiency and raise their profits, there is little pressure on others to follow suit. If cooperation discourages the entry of new firms, it further reduces pressures to innovate, since new firms are likely to be equipped to use up-to-date methods. But group organization may in the longer run unintentionally stimulate reactions improving productive efficiency. Where it induces vertical integration, it may offer an opportunity to improve the coordination of successive processes under imperfect competition. It may, however,

---

[8] Brady, *The Rationalization Movement in German Industry*, *passim*.

stimulate group organization among purchasers of the product, or sellers of labor or materials to the organized industry, creating markets with bilateral monopolies, the outcome of which is difficult to calculate. It cannot be assumed that such monopolies have a countervailing effect.[9] The fear of such a response, however, may persuade the group to pursue moderate policies.

B. Cooperation among Manufacturers in General

Organizations of industrial producers in general (distinguished from those in each line of production) appeared in the later stages of development in capitalist countries (and later than organizations of workers in general). The first such organization was established in Germany in 1879, the National Association of Manufacturers in the U.S.A. in 1895, but the Federation of British Industries only in 1917 and the *Confederation Genérale de la Production Francaise* in 1919. In Japan the existence of a relatively small number of *zaibatsu,* or conglomerate concerns, made such an over-all organization less necessary.[10] The Federation of Industries in Egypt is subsidized by the government.[11]

These over-all industrial organizations have no direct production or price-making functions. They bring to a focus the common interest of industrial property owners and managers. They mobilize business interest in, and support of, a common program, seeking to use the state where it can be helpful, and to inhibit state activity where it may hinder their interests. They have urged protection against imports, government assistance to obtain foreign markets, minimal government control of business or, more positively, self-government in industry and the reduction of taxation and national debts.

These over-all industry organizations are of economic concern mostly in relation to the over-all integration of society. They centralize great economic power, which may overshadow the state. But in recent decades other organizations have appeared to concentrate the economic power of agriculturalists, retailers and workers; and these may somewhat offset the concentrated power of industrial organizations. But the outcome of these concentrations of power within industrial countries is not yet evident.

---

9 Galbraith, *American Capitalism, passim.*
10 Brady, *Business as a System of Power, passim.*
11 Issawi, *op. cit.,* 89.

Chapter 13

The State and Manufacturing

A. Influences Affecting State Policies

The attitudes of governments towards manufacturing vary with the importance of various groups in society and their political influence.

Those who receive manufacturing profits are generally interested in state action that will maintain or increase profits. But no such class exists in Russia and other socialist countries, and it hardly exists in the least-developed countries. Craft producers receive profit, but they are typically numerous and their incomes are too low to endow them with great political power.

Agricultural interests, particularly larger landowners, are interested in low prices for the manufactured goods they buy. Consequently, they have often opposed import duties on manufactured goods (e.g., in the U.S.A. and Australia), and monopolistic policies in industry. In agrarian societies contemplating industrialization, landowning groups have opposed the change because it provides alternative occupations for labor, may raise agricultural wages and threatens the political supremacy of the landed class. Such opposition was offered by the Junkers in eastern Germany. In underdeveloped countries in Latin America, the Middle East and the Far East, where development has been long delayed, present pressures for speedy development call for accelerated capital formation. This capital can be provided only by landed groups and merchants who fear taxation or expropriation, possibly through inflation.

Industrial workers are interested in the continuance and expansion of the demand for their labor and in increasing their share of the produce of industry. Agricultural workers are also interested in high wages in industry because they tend to lift agricultural wages, but such workers are also interested in low prices for industrial products. Both agricultural and industrial workers are interested in the policy of the state towards labor unions.

Many states, both capitalist and socialist, recognize a general social interest in manufacturing as a basis for military power. In preparation for war they encourage shipping, railroads and air transport, industrial expansion in general, and the heavy industries and the chemical industry in particular. The interest in industrialization in the under-developed countries also grows partly out of concern for their military power. Capitalist governments recognize the political implications of cyclical fluctuations in production and have intervened in industry, if not to modify fluctuations, to mitigate their effects. The socialist governments have taken over industrial operations, at least formally to ensure social justice.

State policies regarding manufacturing are the outcome of the push and pull exerted by these various interests and depend on the ability of each to exert political power. In Britain, the U.S.A., Belgium, and Germany power shifted from landed to industrial interests during the 19th century, as manufacturing grew. But during the 20th century the agricultural interests and organized labor have gained in political power at the expense of manufacturers. Nevertheless, industrialists remain politically powerful because their financial resources give them influence over political parties, and their control over production affects employment conditions and production for military purposes. The military authorities in Japan wished to take over industrial control from the *zaibatsu* from 1939 to 1945, but never quite succeeded. The *zaibatsu* were converted into national corporations with half control vested in the government, but all other property rights remained with the powerful industrial families. In the less industrialized countries, industrialists lack great power because they are so few, but their power is disproportionate to their numbers[1] where there is anxiety to foster industry.

The instrumentalities for state intervention in manufacturing are fundamentally similar to those for intervention in agriculture. They rest ultimately on the theoretical state monopoly of the use of force. The most important difference between industry and agriculture is that it is easier for the state to take over industrial than agricultural production.

B. The Scope of State Activities

1. ACCESS TO THE MEANS OF PRODUCTION

Access to labor is generally left to private arrangements in capitalist countries, although states prohibit slavery and may regulate wages and the activities of labor unions (Ch. 20). Access to land is typically not of primary importance, although states may compel the surrender of land (for example, to permit the construction of canals, railroads, or hydro-

---

[1] Spiegel, *The Brazilian Economy*, 228.

electric works) and they may make state lands available for industry, as they have in Turkey.[2]

Access to knowledge has generally been left to private initiative in capitalist countries, although patent legislation aimed at stimulating the acquisition of new knowledge temporarily limits access to it. In Russia the government rewards inventors but gives them no power to control the use of their invention. The British government, however, has attempted to improve knowledge and stimulate industrial progress by establishing Development Councils. After 1945 the government appointed working parties to survey a number of industries and recommend ways of strengthening and stabilizing them. The 17 reports made by 1948 suggested few sweeping changes in organization but many suggested an over-all policy body for their industry. Consequently, the Industrial Organization and Development Act of 1947 authorized the government to establish a Development Council in any industry, provided the Minister was satisfied that such a council was desired by a "substantial number" of persons in the industry. The councils were to consist of representatives of workers and employers and other disinterested persons, and were to have functions that would improve the industry's service to the community.

They were to provide more efficient production or distribution by better product design, better recruitment and training and better public relations. They could make a compulsory levy on the industry to meet their expenses, require firms to keep specified records and provide any information, and advise the Minister about the industry. Where no Development Council was desired, the Minister could make a levy to be administered by an existing or newly created industry organization with the same objectives prescribed for Development Councils. By 1951, however, it was clear that the program had failed. Councils had been set up only in the cotton, jewelry and silverware, furniture, and clothing industries. The Cotton Board was set up in 1940 to encourage exports, and by the time it was converted into a Development Council in 1948 it had acquired good-will in the industry, but the Jewelry and Silverware Council was rejected by one of the two chief trade associations and is inactive. The establishment of a council in the clothing industry was opposed by legal action, and it also is inactive. Attempts to set up a council for the pottery industry were unsuccessful after three years of negotiation.[3] Compulsory levies have been made without establishing Development Councils in only three industries, including lace and wool. This failure has been due to the opposition of employers, who fear that the Councils would undermine their trade associations, and that the government would control

---

[2] Weinryb, "The Industrialization of the Near East," LXI *Quar. Jour. of Econ.,* 1947, 474.

[3] *Economist,* June 25, July 16, 1949, April 28, 1951.

the Councils through its representatives and make them semi-government agencies.

In underdeveloped countries where the main task is to establish industries, some governments provide information about available resources, and the probable profitability of ventures, and a number have established government development corporations to facilitate new ventures (Ch. 22).

Access to capital was not a major problem for craft producers. Their tools are usually private property, but the amount of capital involved is small. Industrialization gave an entirely new magnitude to capital as a means of production. In capitalist countries governments generally permitted the provision and use of capital goods to become a private function. Craft production provided a small precedent, and the commercial revolution placed a new emphasis on trade for profit. State intervention under the Mercantile System was temporarily undermined by Adam Smith's argument in *The Wealth of Nations* that private property was the most appropriate device for maximizing efficiency in the use of economic resources. In Britain, western Europe in general, and the U.S.A., private property in the means of production provided the social framework within which manufacturing methods were revolutionized. Governments provided and maintained this framework, but played little part in providing capital. But in underdeveloped countries some governments help to obtain foreign capital, or provide part of the capital needed to get new enterprises started.

Private property in the means of production consists of a complex of rights to utilize and reap the fruits of use, but the body of rights has changed, most notably in the 20th century. The state usually has the right of eminent domain permitting it to take over property, although usually with compensation. It may reduce the profitability of existing property by legally prescribing minimum wages and working conditions, maximum prices, or rents. It may allocate materials, ration consumer goods, control the location of industry, allocate labor, or control the capital market. It may take over branches of production and exclude private competitors. It may reduce the benefits of ownership by taxation. In fact, policy regarding property is indistinguishable from general economic policy.

Property in the means of production has also been transformed to meet the needs of large-scale industrial production. Most producers' goods no longer "belong" directly to individuals. Since the development of the corporation (and even of the partnership), the individual property owner has a right to share in the control of an often large complex of physical means of production, organization, and knowledge. These changes have been guided by governments. They recognized the corporate enterprise as a fictitious legal person distinct from its members, in England since the early grants of incorporation by the crown, mostly in the 17th century, but in France for longer. The French commercial code of 1807 recognized pre-revolutionary practice. This recognition provides for concentrated continuous control over the enterprise.

The corporation can contract in its own name without signing the names of all its members, and sue and be sued in its own name. It can own stock in other corporations. Its existence is not affected by changes in its membership due to withdrawal, death, or lunacy of its members. The separate legal personality of the corporation commonly, but not necessarily, means that only the property of the enterprise is liable for its debts. If an individual entrepreneur is unable to meet his liabilities out of his business assets, his whole fortune is involved, but a corporation unable to do so may liquidate, and if its assets are not sufficient to meet its debts the burden falls upon the creditors and not on the private fortunes of the members beyond their ownership of securities of the corporation and any liability upon them. This privilege was slowly recognized. Limited liability was accepted in France as a corollary of the legal principle that the group property was separate from that of the members. But in Britain, although associations of more than 25 members were permitted to register as corporations in 1844, the liability of the members for the debts of the company was unlimited. Partial limited liability was granted in 1855, but it was not generally available in Britain until 1866. In the U.S.A., many of the early charters of incorporation limited liability, and general incorporation laws limiting liability were common by 1850, and were passed in Germany in 1870.

The formation of corporations is everywhere controlled by the state, which prescribes the conditions to be met before corporate privileges can be enjoyed. This control is based on various principles, namely that the right to permit incorporation is an attribute of sovereignty, that limitation of liability can be granted only by the state, or merely that fictional legal entities must be defined. In England, persons could at one time form a corporation without any legal grant but, in the course of the consolidation of the power of the Crown under James I, the King asserted that he created corporations, possibly because the Crown had power to grant monopolies and many corporations at that time were also monopolies. Most of the early merchant companies, such as the East India Company and the Levant Company, had monopolies of British trade with prescribed parts of the world. In the 18th century, the colonization company, used as a means of developing and administering colonies, was monopolistic. Later, railroads, because of their peculiar necessity, were often also granted monopoly. In the U.S.A., British common law was left intact after the Revolution and incorporation continued to be regarded as a franchise. But, with the appearance of corporations requiring no privileges of monopoly or eminent domain, the grant of incorporation came to rest mainly on the grant of limited liability (although some charters conveyed no such grant). Individuals in the U.S.A. still have a common-law privilege to join together in an association for business without a state grant. These "joint stock companies" are merely large partnerships; their capital may be divided into shares, but liability is limited only if specifically provided in every contract. This arrangement, not being very practical, has been very little used. The principle of the corporation as a franchise was never accepted in France.

The policies of states regarding the corporate form have passed through a number of phases. In Britain, corporations other than those associated with grants of monopoly were severely restricted for a long time. The South Sea Bubble in 1720 demonstrated how managers could over-reach owners, and the government prohibited the formation of corporations except by royal charter or act of Parliament. Corporations were in fact formed, but their legal status was dubious. The law was modified in 1825, but only in 1866 could corporations be formed with limited liability, on compliance with simple requirements. In the U.S.A. also, the corporation was made generally available only with reluctance because of fears of the consequences of limiting liability, and of the possibility of the use of the corporate form for monopolistic purposes. Business corporations were suspect during the colonial period, but some 18 existed prior to 1789. Hamilton proposed that the power of incorporation should be vested in the federal government, but the states rejected the proposal. For some time the procedure for obtaining a corporate charter in the New England states was the same as in England. Each company needed a special act of the legislature, which was cumbersome, expensive and often corrupt. The first general incorporation law was enacted in New York in 1811. It provided that organizers could write their own charter, with some limitations, and file it with an officer of state, after which incorporation followed automatically. For a time, however, there were limitations on the period of the charter and the maximum capital of the corporation. Only by the middle of the 19th century did most states have general laws permitting incorporation.

In Germany grants of incorporation were made by the sovereign (with a few local exceptions) until 1870 when the law was changed to permit incorporation on compliance with simple requirements, but subject to restrictions intended to protect stockholders and creditors. In France the Commercial Code of 1807 recognized pre-revolutionary legal principles regarding the various types of collective business organization. A *Société* (the general name for profit-seeking associations, from the partnership to the corporation) could be constituted merely by a contract between the parties, providing for the segregation of the common property, the establishment of a common enterprise, and a common administration. But the formation of a corporation (*société anonyme*) required government consent until 1867, when corporations could be freely formed by contract in writing before a notary, and registered. French law provides the basis for most continental European law (for example, in Belgium, Holland, Switzerland, Italy, and Spain), and most Latin American law. This general facilitation of incorporation in Europe, around 1870, resulted in greatly increased use of the corporate form. In the closing years of the 19th century the U.S.A. turned from cautious acquiescence to active encouragement. States competed for the taxes on corporations by offers of simplified procedures and increased liberties.

State policies regarding the corporation again changed during the 20th century. Old problems took on new importance with great increases in the size and prevalence of corporations. In the U.S.A. congressional hearings on stock market practices after 1929 (especially in relation to electrical utilities) revealed the dangers of excessive freedom of action by directors, particularly in regard to issues of securities. In Britain criticism focussed upon the relations between directors and the corporation on the one hand, and between the corporation and the general public on the other.

The internal relations of the corporation are regulated in the U.S.A. by the Securities Act of 1933, which requires revelation of the remuneration of directors, disclosure of dealings by directors in the stock of the corporation, and surrender to the corporation of profits on dealings in the stock of the corporation held by directors for less than six months. The directors were made responsible for statements in the prospectus. The Cohen Committee[4] reappraised corporate practice in Britain and some, but not all, of its recommendations were embodied in the Companies Act of 1947. The Committee recommended, and the Act required, that the remuneration of the directors as a group, but not individually, (including payments for loss of office) be made public. The law also requires disclosure to fellow directors of contracts between a director and the company, and permits the directors to vote on such contracts. The London Stock Exchange, however, requires that the articles of incorporation generally debar such voting. The Cohen Committee found difficulty in defining the size of the interest requiring disclosure, and recommended disclosure on contracts of any magnitude in which the director had a substantial interest. This disclosure was to be made to the stockholders. The Committee also condemned speculative profits from dealings in the shares of the company, and recommended that directors be obliged to notify fellow directors of holdings of company securities and *cesser* of such interest, the record to be open to all share or debenture holders. Loans to directors were to be prohibited unless it was the business of the company to make loans. The committee also recommended that the removal of directors be made easier and that provision be made for the compulsory retirement of aged directors. As to the responsibility of directors for statements in prospectuses, the directors should state all other

[4] Company Law Amendment Committee *Report,* 1945, (Cmd 6659).

facts known, or which on reasonable inquiry could have been known, omission of which from prospectuses would make them misleading. If they published the opinions of an expert, they should establish that they had reasonable ground for relying on the statements made by the expert.

In Germany abuses of flotation and company management in 1894 and 1897 led to revisions of company law imposing severe restrictions. The National Socialist government in 1937 established a minimum size for corporations, regulated methods of raising capital and the extent of publicity as to control and operation of corporations, and made some changes with regard to their internal administration.[5]

The large proportion of industrial resources controlled by corporations, the separation of ownership from control, and the concentration of control, have focused attention on the relations between corporations and the general public in capitalist countries. Information about corporate control and operation is necessary to enable potential investors to make rational investment decisions, and avoid being misled. Customers are often interested in profits as an indication of the justification for the prices charged, although profits are not in fact a good basis for appraising prices. Workers desire information to enable them to decide what wages the corporation is able to pay although, again, profitability is a very partial indication of the desirable level of wages. More important, the decisions of corporate managers influence the volume of employment. Company policies may restrict output or contribute to the instability of the economy. The way in which corporations, especially large ones, are using the resources under their control is, therefore, becoming a matter affecting national prosperity and sometimes foreign relations (particularly in countries where companies are of foreign ownership). Managements however have a general interest in secrecy based on fear of competition (sometimes foreign) and of the attitudes of customers, stockholders, and labor unions to high profits. But what appears to be secrecy is sometimes lack of knowledge on the part of the corporate management.

New legislation in the U.S.A. and Britain, requiring full disclosure in prospectuses and defining the responsibilities of directors for them, has yielded increased information of the type needed by investors. The Securities Act of 1933 in the U.S.A. established the Securities and Exchange Commission and required the filing of prospectuses. Publicity as to ownership has been partly avoided in Britain where, although the list of stockholders is annually filed with a government official and open to public inspection, owners may have their interest registered in the name of nominees. The Cohen Committee recommended, but the new act did not provide for, severe modification of this practice. Revelation of corporate operations may be largely avoided by using the private corporation,

---

[5] Kessler, W. C., "The German Corporation Law of 1937," *Am. Econ. Rev.*, XXVIII, 1938, 653.

but no change was made in the requirements of information from such corporations in Britain. The act of 1947 did, however, require a number of changes intended to make the reports of public companies more informative. The requirement of accounts including the transactions of all the subsidiaries made it necessary to reveal the profits of the group as a whole, and not only that part of the profits of subsidiaries which the directors had decided to transfer to the parent company. The Act also required more information regarding depreciation and other reserves. In less-developed countries there is frequently little control of corporate operations.

In the socialist countries the means of production may not be privately owned (except the tools and equipment of craftsmen). The state controls capital goods and accessory property, decides how they shall be used, and takes the reward in the sense in which a state can take any reward. Industrial operations in Russia and eastern Europe are organized in corporate form, and the government provides a model form of organization. But ownership vests in the state which also controls operations.

2. The Regulation of Manufacturing

a. Regulation Increasing the Rewards of Manufacturing

Manufacturing has been most widely encouraged by import duties, quotas, exchange controls and other devices prohibiting or impeding imports. Tariffs and quotas have the political advantage of concealing the cost of encouraging manufacturing, which appears not in the national budget, but in the budgets of individuals in the form of higher prices. Britain did not pursue this policy in the early stages of industrialization because it had few foreign competitors and, later, because, as an exporting country, it could help few of its manufacturers by keeping out imports. It was more interested in the duties imposed by countries importing from it. As the U.S.A. later became increasingly interested in export it also showed a new interest in low tariffs for other countries. But almost all countries attempting to follow the British example by industrializing have protected their industries from foreign competition. Alexander Hamilton[6] contended that infant industries needed protection from the competition of longer-established foreign producers, and industry generally in the U.S.A. has been so protected since 1820. By 1950, however, import duties were generally low. This infant industry argument was restated in Germany by Friedrich List,[7] and Germany and France imposed increasingly high tariffs after about 1880. Japan had a moderate tariff, partly protective, but partly aimed at keeping down consumption within the country.

Primary producing countries seeking to industrialize in recent years

---

[6] *Encouragement and Protection of Manufactures*, 1791.
[7] *Das Nationale System der Politischen Oekonomie*, 1841.

have followed the same course. Both world wars stimulated the establishment of industries which could not survive against foreign competition in peace time and, therefore, sought protection. In Australia the first commonwealth tariff in 1901 was for revenue but mildly protective duties were imposed in 1908. Higher duties were levied in 1920 to protect industries stimulated by the war of 1914 to 1918. The Tariff Board set up in 1921 has been a moderating influence, but rates were severely increased after November, 1929.[8] In the Union of South Africa, import duties were mainly for revenue until 1925, but thereafter were frankly protective. Most South African industry is now dependent on these duties. Most Latin American countries impose protective duties on manufactures, e.g., Brazil[9] and Mexico (which has greatly increased import duties since 1947). In Uruguay, taxes on imported manufactures go back to 1830 and were increased in 1875 and 1888. By the end of the century import duties were about 34% of the official value of imports (excluding those imported free of duty).[10] In Peru import duties provide most of the government revenue but are not levied on machinery, raw materials, or containers.[11] In India all duties were abolished in 1882, but subsequently reimposed until they yielded a considerable part of government revenues. Although based on the financial requirements of government, they also involve "discriminating protection."[12]

The British government, which imposed only a few revenue duties until 1913, was faced after 1918 with increasing obstacles to exports. It then attempted to use its power of importation to favor countries within the Commonwealth that were the most likely to continue to import from it. A few bilateral agreements culminated in the Ottawa agreement of 1933. Import duties (mostly not high) were imposed to enable Britain to give preference to countries within the Empire, and thus consolidate intra-imperial economic relations. The U.S.A. has achieved a similar result by free trade within the country, because most of its territory happens to be contiguous. Socialist governments have no need to use import duties, since they monopolize foreign trade and decide what to import.

The protection of infant industries implies only temporary protection. But industries in the U.S.A., for instance, find it difficult to acknowledge that they have grown up. They sometimes realize that an industry has grown beyond the size that would have been justified by comparative costs alone. The policy implies also that only industries likely to be able to operate efficiently when they reach maturity should be protected in

8 Wood, G. L. (ed.), *Australia, Its Resources and Development*, 223 ff.

9 Spiegel, *op. cit.*, 221.

10 Hanson, *op. cit.*, 11.

11 U.N., *Economic Development of Selected Countries*, 146.

12 U.K., Indian Statutory Commission *Report I*, 358.

their infancy. Because import duties on all manufactures may discourage rather than encourage industry, raw materials and machinery are typically exempt from duties, at least during the initial phase of industrialization. Protection beyond infancy dulls the stimulus to efficiency and re-organization. The new tariffs in Britain since 1933 may have protected the industrial system from changes in the outside world and be partly responsible for the inflexibility of British industry.

Domestic industry is sometimes protected by the perversion of health legislation, or the administration of ports and transportation. Some countries use "mixing laws" for the same purpose; for example, in Cuba and Brazil, automobile fuel must contain a certain percentage of locally produced alcohol and bread must contain local flour.

Governments do not typically purchase industrial goods (as they have purchased agricultural goods) to raise or maintain prices. Manufactured goods are typically less homogeneous and more difficult to store. The greater ease and speed with which supply can be adjusted to demand also reduces fluctuations in price. But governments in making their own pur-chases often prefer goods produced within the country, and they make purchases to maintain industries whose services are needed during war.

Subsidies may aid manufacturing where protection from foreign compe-tition is not sufficiently helpful. British industry developed without bene-fit of subsidy. In recent years, however, subsidies have been paid to in-duce shipping companies to purchase ships of a kind adaptable for use in war. In 1948 the government offered to subsidize the reequipment and modernization of the cotton spinning industry where it concentrated in groups with at least 400,000 spindles. About 60% of the spindles registered as thus concentrated. The government offered to subsidize up to 25% ap-proved expenditures for modernization. But in fact only about 25% of the capacity has been covered by approved modernization schemes, which is only about one-third of the original estimate. The high cost of machinery has discouraged modernization.[13] The government also subsidizes the steel industry and makes levies to equalize the position of firms importing ore and scrap, crude, and semi-finished steel with that of other firms using home-produced materials which are cheaper. These subsidies doubled between 1946-7 and 1948-9. In the U.S.A., some railroads have been subsidized both by state and federal governments, particularly by grants of land, and the federal government has paid considerable subsidies to shipping, air transport and the production of synthetic rubber. The German government has paid a great variety of subsidies at different times. The Italian steel industry, which relies heavily on imported scrap steel and has high costs, has been heavily subsidized since 1918. The Japanese government used subsidies freely to accelerate industrialization.

[13] *Economist*, April 19, 1949; April 15, 1950.

It subsidized shipbuilding, ocean transportation (providing at one time about 25% of the net income of the Nippon Yusen Kaisha line), steel, aluminum, and other industries.

Governments also stimulate industry by exempting new industries from taxation for a period, which is comparable to a subsidy. A Mexican decree of 1939 permits exemption of new enterprises, not only from import duties but also from a number of taxes, for five years where they will not compete with established firms. By the end of 1945 350 enterprises had benefitted from this provision. Similar arrangements were made in Argentina in 1944.[14] In Turkey the Five Year Plan of 1934 provided for similar exemptions (as well as the allotment of state lands and reduced freight rates).[15]

Governments have rarely (as in agriculture) directly restricted output to raise prices. But they have occasionally endowed private associations with controls over output and prices. The controls of the medieval craft guilds over prices, conditions of work, nature of product, and entry into the craft rested on government grants of power. The guilds in the Middle and Far East have exercised similar powers. Germany and Austria have, even in recent years, passed laws continuing or reviving the old guild system of craft controls. In Germany, a law of 1897 permitted guilds or craft organizations by majority vote to establish compulsory membership in accordance with a code enforceable by law. In the U.S.A., industry groups were empowered by the National Industrial Recovery Act of 1933 to agree on codes of fair competition. Industry groups in the petroleum and coal industries were empowered to control prices and the control of coal prices was continued in two subsequent laws.

In Spain the government controls industry according to fascist theory through compulsory syndicates for each industry. Each syndicate consists of representatives of management and workers, some five million workers being represented in the syndicates as a whole. The syndicates control production, often in considerable detail. In 1954, the government attempted to increase the voice of labor in measures to increase productivity. Until 1945, a similar system existed in Italy. In Japan guilds (*kabunakama*) were established very early by merchants to regulate prices and allocate materials. Under a new name (*kumiai*) they obtained legislative protection in the 1880s and were encouraged as a means to industrialization. The Major Industries Control Law of 1931 authorized the government to make private agreements among industrialists binding upon whole industries. These agreements could apportion orders among large firms, divide production by quotas or market areas, fix prices, and

---

[14] U.N., *Economic Development of Selected Countries*, 4, 20.
[15] Weinryb, "The Industrial Development of the Near East," LXI *Quar. Jour. of Econ.*, 1947, 474.

control distribution.[16] The appropriate ministry of the government designated the industries to which the law applied, and by 1937 it had been applied to over 100. In 1937 the law was amended to provide that the Minister of Commerce might require both members and non-members to comply on application from two-thirds of the parties to an agreement. By the end of 1937, 1,172 industrial associations were operating under this law. By 1943, about 15% of all the corporations in Japan, representing 38% of industrial assets, were organized under control associations. An Industrial Guilds law in 1931 provided for similar organizations for small-scale industry.

The British government endeavored to reduce capacity in the cotton textile industry after 1918, when it was suffering from excess capacity owing to the loss of foreign markets. The Spindles Control Act imposed a tax per spindle payable to a board appointed by the government, to be used to buy out and dispose of spinning equipment. The tax was to be paid for three years, and reduced the equipment in the industry. It slightly increased costs at a time when the need was for price reduction. It was not, however, quite a compulsory cartel. There was no direct government support for price agreements until 1939, when the industry was empowered to fix prices, set production quotas and agree upon reorganization schemes. Brazil has established compulsory cartels for salt and timber, with power to establish minimum prices and production quotas.[17]

Some governments regulate entry into industry to maintain the profitability of existing establishments and attract new industry. Such action is fairly common in Latin America, and the smaller countries of Central America and the Caribbean often grant monopolistic concessions for these purposes.[18] The government of Chile provided in 1932 that if a technical committee decided that an industry was in a state of overproduction, new firms might enter only with the consent of the government; since 1940 the government has been empowered to compel any plant to move to a specified new location, and to prescribe the sales zone, the remaining firms in the industry bearing the cost of the move.[19] In India the government has, since 1952, regulated the establishment of new undertakings and the substantial expansion of old ones in 37 of the most important industries. In Kenya, the Industrial Licensing Act of 1947 empowers the government to control by licensing the establishment of new firms in a rather short list of industries.[20] This law is intended to encourage new industries by giving the first-comer protection against later

---

[16] Allen, op. cit., 145.
[17] Spiegel, The Brazilian Economy, 220.
[18] U.N., Econ. Surv. of Latin America, 1948, 37.
[19] Ellsworth, op. cit., 80.
[20] Kenya Development Committee Report II, 185, 186.

comers unless the government is satisfied that additional firms would not result in over-capacity. Such control of entry requires the government, if it is to prevent inefficiency, to ensure that prices do not exceed necessary and efficient costs by more than a reasonable profit, but few states seriously seek such assurance.

Grants of monopoly are desirable in industries which cannot minimize their costs if there is more than one firm. In smaller countries many industries may satisfy this test although, even then, import might be cheaper. But in all countries the test is satisfied by many public utilities like electricity, gas, railways, telephones, and telegraphs. Monopoly is often granted for air transport, although the economic necessity is more doubtful there. It is sometimes granted for radio, although some countries have more than one private system, and some both private and public systems.

b. Regulation Stabilizing the Rewards of Manufacturing

Government countercyclical policies, involving expenditure on public works or relief while the government borrows or incurs a budget deficit in a depression, reduce the shrinkage of general spending and, therefore, of the market for industrial goods. But while such policies, if successful, tend to stabilize profits from industry, they are aimed mainly at maintaining employment for labor (Ch. 25).

c. Regulation Reducing the Rewards of Manufacturing

i. Taxation

Governments do not generally tax industry to restrict it, taxes on alcohol and, possibly, tobacco being the major exceptions. In the U.S.A., chain stores have been taxed to protect smaller retailers from the competition of a new, and presumably cheaper, method of distributing goods. Taxes on particular industrial products (for instance, tobacco, liquor, salt, automobiles), unless they fall ultimately on rents or monopoly profits, restrict the size of the industry to the extent that the demand for the product is elastic. In Japan, consumer goods were taxed during the period of development, partly to cut down consumption and enlarge the resources for development. In Russia, the turnover or sales tax cuts down demand to the planned output of consumer goods, not to discourage manufacturing in general, but to increase the diversion of resources toward the expansion of manufacturing.

ii. The Maintenance of Competition

Where a government seeks to maintain competition to eliminate monopoly profits, it reduces gains from monopolized industries. The latter, however, are probably a small part of national income. But it may endeavor to maintain competition as a means of minimizing costs and maximizing economic progress. Essentially, the government seeks to minimize detailed government planning and the determination of the correct prices for products by maintaining a self-regulating competitive system in which industrial firms have little alternative to selling at approximately competitive prices. This policy takes form in the control of market practices and of the structure of industry. The U.S.A. is the only country in which the government has made a long-sustained effort to maintain competition by law.

The types of competitive practice permitted determine the kind of firm that succeeds (for instance, the most deceptive or the most efficient). All countries have some law about fraud, deception, and similar matters. In more developed capitalist countries, this code has been expanded with the growth of markets for manufactured goods. In the U.S.A. the Sherman Anti-Monopoly Law of 1890 prohibits restraint of trade or monopoly. Firms charged with monopolizing or restraining trade (such as the former Standard Oil, and American Tobacco companies) were held to have engaged in practices aimed at monopolizing. The Federal Trade Commission Act of 1912 directly prohibited "unfair competition" in interstate commerce, leaving the definition of "unfair" (which is the essence of the law) to the Commission, but subject to review by the courts. Under this law firms have been ordered to cease and desist from mis-describing their goods, false advertising, false warranties, destroying the goods of rivals, and other similar practices, some generally accepted as immoral, and others of more dubious immorality. For some time, however, it was doubtful whether unfairness in competition was to be judged in terms of unfairness to competitors or to buyers. In fact, unfairness can be judged only in the light of the results desired from the system.

The Clayton Act and the Robinson Patman Act are more sharply focused on discrimination in price or service, which is in general prohibited within the federal jurisdiction. But the law does not require sellers to grant to large buyers prices reflecting all the economies of dealing with them, and discrimination is not prohibited where it is made in good faith to meet the equally low price of a competitor. By prohibiting sellers from "shading" their price to some buyers to get business, the law discourages one of the forms in which price competition survives in the more developed capitalist countries. The anti-discrimination laws, however, are aimed, not so much at the maintenance of the competitive system, as at the maintenance of one group of competitors, namely, the small distributors suffering from the competition of the larger.

The Miller-Tydings Act of 1937 permits resale price maintenance where it is permitted by state law. Manufacturers are thus permitted to set the minimum price at which the distributor (wholesale or retail) may resell the product. This law again shelters the small retailer from the competition of the larger retailer more than it maintains competition in general. So long as the business of retail distribution was small-scale, manufacturers were little interested in controlling it, and distributors were unable to control manufacturers. But large-scale distribution in more developed countries in department and chain stores caused small retailers to complain that large retailers were selling some products as "loss leaders" to attract business into the store, thus leading the public to think that these stores were in general cheap stores. Manufacturers were concerned because price competition at the retail level is reflected back on them. But the maintenance of resale prices greatly reduces price competition in retailing. A manufacturer, interested in having his goods available at a large number of stores, keeps the retailer's margin high, which maintains an excessive number of retailers, making the distributive system uneconomical, although not necessarily highly profitable. Manufacturers also control retailers in other ways through contracts requiring exclusive dealing, exclusive selling, tying clauses requiring that the retailer handle all the products of the manufacturer, and combination sales.

In Britain there is little specific law regarding competitive practices but there is common law with regard to contracts against public policy. Resale price maintenance, however, has attracted criticism. The Proprietary Articles Trade Association, consisting of producers and retailers of perfumery, toilet, medicinal, and similar preparations, has a "protected list" of commodities for which prices and margins at retail are fixed and actively enforced by black-listing non-cooperators. This activity has probably fostered the absorption of an unnecessary amount of resources in retail distribution. In 1949, a committee on retail price maintenance reported that about 30% of the expenditures of consumers were on products the prices of which were fixed or recommended by producers. It found that price maintenance by associations was undesirable and should be made illegal, but that nothing could or should be done to deprive individual manufacturers of the right to control the retail prices of their products. In 1951 the government announced that it would introduce legislation prohibiting both collective and individual price maintenance, but permitting manufacturers to prescribe maximum prices.[21] No legislation to this effect was introduced before the government resigned. In continental Europe there is also considerable legal regulation of competitive behavior. Competition in quality is often controlled: in the U.S.A., England, Germany, and most similarly developed countries, the sale of food and drugs is regulated in the interest of health.

The structure of industry may deny the fruits of competition even where market behavior complies with prescribed standards. Sellers may agree on prices and output, or may be so few that it would be irrational for them to behave as if they had no influence over market prices. Private group con-

---

[21] U.K., Committee on Resale Price Maintenance *Report,* 1949, (Cmd. 7696); Board of Trade *Statement on Resale Price Maintenance,* 1951, (Cmd. 8274).

trol of a product or line of production is an ancient problem.[22] In craft activities guilds often exercise such control (Ch. 12). During the medieval period, states attempted to induce competition in trade by insuring that goods passed through the periodic markets to protect the income from market tolls and to prevent the cornering of markets by forestalling, regrating, and engrossing. The prohibitions on these three offenses are still part of the law in Britain and the U.S.A. The British courts began to draw a line between permissible and undesirable restraints in 1711. In Mitchel v. Reynolds, 1 P. Wms. 181 (1711) the court upheld a sale of goodwill accompanied by a covenant by a seller not to compete with the buyer of a business, provided the covenant was a partial restraint and for good and adequate consideration.

This rule that restraint of trade may be permissible applied in the U.S.A., but in 1890 basic policy was laid down in the Sherman Act which prohibited restraint of trade and monopoly. In all the lines of activity to which this law applies, agreements regarding prices and output are illegal regardless of the reasonableness of their objectives or policies. But shipping, marine insurance, agricultural cooperation, and a few other activities have been exempted from the law. From 1933 to 1936, while the National Industrial Recovery Act was in operation, the government permitted the formulation of Codes of Fair Competition to eliminate "cut-throat" competition, thus accepting increased private control of industry, although subject to ultimate, and possibly nominal, government control. The thrust of this private control was fundamentally restrictive, but that of the accompanying pump-priming was expansionist. The Act was held to be unconstitutional in 1936.

Competition may be drastically modified without agreements among firms because sellers are few. This aspect of the structure of industry has posed a problem to which no satisfactory solution has been found where there is room in the market for too few firms (of the size that minimizes costs) to provide competition. To prevent this outcome is to prevent the minimization of cost (which is one of the major benefits of competition). To allow the outcome is to remove the prospect of benefits from competition in the future. In the U.S.A. a few large firms were partitioned under the Sherman Act, mostly around 1912 (e.g., the former Standard Oil Company, the American Tobacco Company, Du Pont de Nemours Company, and a few others) but generally not solely because of their size, but because of evidence of undesirable motives. Since that time, few firms have been broken up, and those have usually been compelled to shed allied activities rather than reduce the scale upon which they perform any one activity. Indeed, until 1945 the courts generally held that mere size was no offense. But in a decision relating to the Aluminum Company of America, the courts came near to deciding that size can be an offense, ir-

[22] Piotrowski, R., *Cartels and Trusts*, 1933, *passim*.

respective of the behavior of the large firm. Nevertheless, markets persist in which few large firms are in necessarily imperfect competition. Price leadership is beyond the reach of the law, for lack of any effective remedy.

Integration may also restrict the effectiveness of the market. Vertical integration not only circumvents the market, but also gives powerful firms at one stage opportunities to prevent unintegrated firms from entering later stages. Consequently, the meat packers, who were under prosecution, consented to separate their meat packing activities from their interests in stock yards and refrigerated transport; the Pullman Company was required to decide whether it would continue to manufacture cars or to operate them; and the moving picture companies have been required to dispose of some of their holdings in theatres. Common control of competing monopolized goods or services enlarges opportunities for monopoly profit, and Congress has prohibited the integration of some competing activities such as telephones and telegraphs in the U.S.A.

In Britain the line between permissible and undesirable restraints was somewhat sharpened towards the end of the 18th century when contracts to combine to raise prices or restrict supplies were held to be a public wrong, if not by statute, by common law. Contracts not falling within this rule but in restraint of trade were not enforced by the courts unless they could be shown to be in the public interest. This refusal to enforce was ineffective unless a dispute arose among the parties. In the 19th century, however, the courts began to approve of various pooling devices affecting stagecoaches and railways, and legal efforts to prevent monopoly waned. Free trade exposed British producers to foreign competition in some industries, although others were sheltered by economic considerations from foreign competition. A general tradition of individualism, however, tended more than in the U.S.A. to keep alive considerable numbers of firms in many industries. Although trade associations have resorted increasingly to price and output controls since 1918, and their activities have been investigated from time to time,[23] no government, including the labor government, elected in 1945, showed much interest in the problem.

The coalition government in Britain stated in its White Paper on Employment Policy (Ch. 23) that special measures were needed to give greater protection against practices harmful to the public interest. The Monopolies and Restrictive Practices Act of 1948 was the first statute on monopoly since 1624, and it reflects general scepticism about the danger of monopoly. The act provides for the establishment of a commission of from four to ten members to examine cases referred to it by the Board of Trade, which

---

[23] U.K., Committee on Trusts *Report*, 1918, (Cmd. 9236); Committee on Industry and Trade *Final Report*, 1929, (Cmd. 3282); Import Duties Advisory Committee *Report on the Present Position and Future Development of the Steel Industry*, 1937, (Cmd. 5507); Departmental Committee on the Patents and Designs Act *Second Interim Report*, 1946, (Cmd. 6789); Committee on Cement *Report*, 1947; Committee on Textile Machinery *Report*.

cases may relate only to industries (a) where one third or more of the goods of any description in the United Kingdom, or a substantial part of it, is supplied by one person or interconnected corporations, or by two or more persons who have a tacit or expressed arrangement to limit competition in any way; or (b) where by agreement or arrangement goods of a particular description are not supplied at all in the United Kingdom or in a substantial part of it; or (c) where an industry exports, and one-third of British production is in the hands of one firm, or subject to arrangements to limit competition. The law does not apply to arrangements set up under other statutes (e.g., the agricultural marketing boards or to nationalized industries). The Board must specify in each case whether the commission is to ascertain the facts or, in the event that monopolistic conditions are found to prevail, also to report whether these conditions are harmful to the public interest. Most reports on the facts and the effect on the public interest must be laid before Parliament, but reports on the facts alone are to be laid before Parliament only at the discretion of the minister. In its reports, the commission may suggest action, or report how far any remedial action it has suggested in the past is being carried out. It may report also on the general effect on the public interest of particular monopolistic and restrictive practices, provided the commission has dealt with them in specific inquiries.

The relevant ministers may prepare orders prohibiting the making or carrying out of agreements, boycotts, conditional sales, and preferential terms; but they may not interfere with patent rights. Such orders become operative, however, only after approval by both Houses of Parliament. The government relies primarily on publicity to remove undesirable practices, but civil action may be brought against persons contravening an order under the act. Finally, the law provides criteria of public interest; namely, efficiency of production, treatment and distribution in such volume and at such prices as will best meet the requirements of home and overseas markets; organization of industry and trade in such a way that efficiency is progessively increased and new enterprise encouraged; the fullest use and best distribution of the means of production; and the development of technical improvements, expansion of existing markets and opening new ones.[24] By 1951 the Commission had reported only on two small industries, and had found that practices in dental manufacturing had worked against the public interest, but that there had not been "any very great abuse."[25]

In Canada, governments have relied mainly on publicity regarding monopolistic conditions and practices to maintain competition. The Combines Investigation Act provided for a Commissioner to make investigations. The act was almost amended to nothing in the 1930s, but later

---

[24] Cohen, R., "The New British Law on Monopoly," 39 *Am. Econ. Rev.*, 1949, 485.
[25] Hansard, *Parliamentary Debates*, June 15, 1951.

strengthened until in 1946 the Commissioner was empowered to initiate investigations, compel testimony, and make reports which the government was bound to publish. Difficulties over the Commissioner's report on flour milling caused his resignation in 1949.[26] A clause in the Customs Act of 1897 provided for lowering duties on products in which a combine was proved to exist in Canada.

French law appears to be a mixture of theoretical concern and a practical unconcern for competition. Guilds and similar organizations were abolished under Turgot in 1746. The Chapelier Law of 1791 prohibited assemblies of workers or employers to consult about their common interests. The Criminal Code of 1810 applied to combinations only on proof that they have caused prices to be "above or below the price which the natural and free course of competition would determine." The amendment of 1926 required proof of profit "other than that which would result from the natural play of supply and demand." Thus proof of collusion to restrict competition or keep out new competitors is insufficient. Trade associations, although not illegal in themselves, and permitted to act in concert, even to agree on prices, are apparently subject to the Criminal Code.

In Germany governments made no attempt to prohibit monopolies until the Weimar Republic, under which cartel control was a confused mixture of attempts to protect purchasers by hampering cartels and to facilitate the reorganization of industry by helping cartels. At the end of the post-war inflation in 1923, cartels were blamed for having raised prices. A decree, Against the Abuse of Economic Power, provided that every agreement controlling production or prices must be in writing, and established a Cartel Court to which the Minister of Economics might refer any cartel agreement detrimental to the public interest. The court might declare the agreement void or permit the parties to withdraw from it. Parties to cartel agreements were also allowed to apply to the court for permission to breach cartel contracts. There were no important cases, but the law may have had some deterrent effect. During the Nazi period, the Minister of Economics had wide power over the price policy of cartels. He could form compulsory cartels, prevent entry of new competitors, and prevent increases in efficiency, or expansion of firms (to avoid undesirable demands for raw materials). As war approached, the cartels were increasingly used as an arm of government in each sector of the economy to ration materials in short supply, control prices, and often to control output and set quotas.

After the defeat of Germany in 1945 the victorious powers agreed at Potsdam in 1946 to break up all excessive industrial concentrations in Germany. An allied military government decartelization law provided for partitioning excessive concentrations of economic power, any undertaking employing more than 10,000 persons being *prima facie* of excessive size. I. G. Farben ("the dye trust") was divided in 1946 into thirty separate

---

26 *Economist*, Dec. 24, 1949.

parts. Most of the chemical business went to four successor companies, which have retained many common stockholders, and are expected to re-combine when the decartelization restrictions expire in 1956. The six major units in the steel industry were divided into 25 smaller ones. It was later decided to establish 23 coal companies separate from steel companies. The German government, however, refused to enter the Schuman plan under these conditions and the High Commission accepted a plan to set up 28 steel companies and to permit them, through ownership, to control about 75% of their coal requirements. The Commission also required the liquidation of the coal cartel by October, 1953.

The Japanese government had similarly not interfered with (if it had not fostered) the concentration of economic power. After its defeat the military government sought to destroy the major concentrations by taking over and partitioning the *zaibatsu*. The men at the top seem to have been squeezed out but often succeeded by their lieutenants, although there have been some eliminations from these and the middle ranks.[27]

In Norway the government was empowered to control cartel price and output policies before 1939, but no standards of control were established. In practice the government has generally aimed at reasonable profit, but with little attention to the reasonableness of costs, and has not generally prevented the pooling of profits. The federal government of Switzerland was empowered in 1947 to protect endangered industries and agriculture from the influence of cartels, and to regulate trade and industry.[28]

iii. Price Control

Governments commonly control prices in time of war because such governments divert resources to war more than they divert purchasing power through taxation and borrowing. The gap between purchasing power over consumer goods and the supply of such goods is inflationary, but rising prices would distribute goods in politically unacceptable ways, particularly because they would discourage war workers. Non-belligerent countries often control prices for similar reasons; the disruption of transport reduces imports, and high prices offered abroad sometimes induce exports which are not currently requited by imports, both of which create an inflationary gap.

Price control in peace time is usually restricted, in capitalist countries, to efforts to eliminate monopoly profit in industries where considerations of efficiency prevent the maintenance of sufficient firms to induce competition, or where the service would not be provided without a monopoly. Industries of this sort ("public utilities") have presented problems of control at least since the Middle Ages (when, for instance, bridge tolls were often controlled). In the early stages of industrialism the tolls to be charged on

---

[27] *The World Today*, July 1948, 293.
[28] *The World Today*, 1947, 501.

roads, canals, and, later, stagecoaches presented the same problem which grew to major dimensions with the development of railroads, telephones, telegraphs, gas and electric utilities, and air transport.

In the U.S.A. the principles of public utility control are more explicit than in most other countries. Controls are applicable under the constitution only where the property is held to be "affected with a public interest," which means when the courts decide that the industry ought to be controlled. The objective of control is to limit prices to those that will provide a fair return on a fair value of the property used to provide the service, which has given rise to endless controversy. The value of the property might include or exclude the capitalized value of anticipated monopoly profit. The value of the property depends, in fact, on the rates which its owners may charge. A "fair" return, being the same return as in other comparable activities, is impossible to discover because there are few if any comparable activities. Nevertheless, governments (state and federal) have made a long-sustained attempt to control such prices. The federal government regulates the interstate operations of railroads through the Interstate Commerce Commission, which must prevent unfair and discriminatory charges. It can, but in general does not, fix individual rates, but controls the general level of charges in order to insure that they provide no more than a "fair return." No such fair return, according to any standard, has been achieved for some time, because it is not within the economic opportunities of the industry, irrespective of government controls. The Commission also controls interstate trucks and busses. The Maritime Commission, set up in 1936, controls some coastal rates for shipping, and the Civil Aeronautics Board set up in 1938 controls charges for air transport. Electrical utilities are mostly subject to state control, although not all states choose to exercise their power, and the Federal Power Commission controls interstate rates. A great variety of activities of this general type are also controlled by municipal authorities.

In Britain, after 1918, the railroads of the country were consolidated into four systems to eliminate diseconomies, but a Rates Tribunal then set up achieved little control of rates. The government virtually took over the railroads between 1939 and 1945, and avoided the problem of deciding how much to pay for their wartime services when it nationalized them in 1947. It then acquired the power to fix rates through the Transport Board. Older systems of control applied to the gas industry, and some not very sweeping controls to the electric power industry, both of which, however, have also been nationalized. Since 1945, the British government has controlled the price of steel products through the Iron and Steel Board.

The French government after 1842 exercised power to control rates and safety on the railroads because it provided the roadbed and granted operating concessions. The earliest railroad companies in Britain and the U.S.A. were planned to provide the "way" but not vehicles or power. The

French government accepted responsibility for the roadbed. The concession companies provided the rails, the ballast, the stations, the rolling stock, and the working capital. When no company could be found to operate a road, a state company was established for the purpose. In the 1850s the government guaranteed the interest on the bonds of some of the operating companies, retaining a residual right to profit. In 1937, however, the problem of regulation was eliminated when the railroads were nationalized. In Germany the regulation of railroads was never a serious problem under the Empire because all railroads were operated by the Imperial Government, as were telegraphs and telephones. Attempts to control the prices of electricity, gas, and water through mixed government and private enterprises led finally to public operation.

Underdeveloped countries have often been more concerned to make public utilities attractive than to control them. In India the early contracts betwen the government and the railroad companies guaranteed a return of 5% on capital. Capital expenditure was to be supervised, but the supervision was inadequate. Half of profits in excess of 5% were to be used to repay past government payments under the guarantee, and the government could require the railroads to maintain rates yielding not more than 10% on their investment. After 99 years the whole property was to revert to the government with full compensation except for the land (which was given by the government), but provision was made for earlier nationalization. In the event of bad management, however, the government could take over after three-months' notice. The government had full power of control and could appoint a representative to sit with the directors with power to veto any decision except on legal matters. These arrangements operated virtually as burdensome cost-plus contracts, and the government began to build railroads in 1869, and took over existing railroads as opportunity offered under the various contracts. South American countries have also attracted railroads by guaranteeing profits.

The Indian Industries (Development and Regulation) Act of 1951 lists 37 important industries in which the government may investigate where it believes there is, or is likely to be, a substantial fall in production, deterioration of product, or an unjustified price rise. It may order corrective action where mismanagement is established and, in the event of noncompliance, take over management (but not ownership) for five years. Development councils are to be established in these industries to recommend production targets, coordinate production programs, and the like.[29]

3. State Operation of Manufacturing

Government operation of manufacturing has developed largely during the 20th century. In capitalist countries much nationalization has been due to the belief that competition does not keep itself alive, and that govern-

---

[29] U.S., *Foreign Commerce Weekly*, Dec. 10, 1951.

ment regulation of non-competitive industries is a failure. Partly monopolistic industry is criticized for inefficiency. But considerations of military effectiveness and development have played a part. Socialist governments operate their whole industrial system because they believe that private profit is based on the exploitation of workers.

Some countries have experimented with mixed private and public production units, but they have generally failed to achieve their purpose. In fact, they become predominantly public or private. They were important in Germany after 1900, chiefly as a device by which municipalities sought to control the electrical utilities, which were then growing rapidly in size and power. In 1930 one-third of the electricity supply of Germany was generated by mixed companies of this kind, which also existed in the supply of water and gas and the operation of tramways. But they were a step on the way to public ownership. In France large mixed companies were formed after the war of 1914-18 to meet the needs of reconstruction and to build hydroelectric works. When the French railways were nationalized in 1937 they were organized in a corporation, 51% of the stock in which was owned by the government, 49% by the stockholders of the previously privately owned railroads. In Austria the government could demand stock ownership up to half the total capital before permitting new incorporations or increases in capital. In 1928 the city of Vienna alone owned stock in 66 mixed companies, chiefly electrical and construction. Mixed companies have also existed in Italy and Holland. The British government has participated in mixed companies for military reasons. It owns 51% of the stock in the Anglo-Iranian Oil Company. Disraeli purchased for the British Government nearly half the capital stock in the Suez Canal Company (but thus acquired only ten votes in the elections to the general assembly of shareholders). The British Government also owns stock in Imperial Chemical Industries and it has made loans to the Cunard (later the Cunard-White Star) Shipping Company to build large ships on condition that the government might use the ships in time of war, and that it be represented on the board of directors.

Underdeveloped countries have used mixed companies to accelerate development. The Japanese government used companies in which it owned 51% of the stock as a vehicle for developing Manchuria. There were five mixed corporations in Brazil in 1947 for the production of iron and steel, alkali, electric power, and tractors. The government holds all or part of the common stock and controls the management, senior executives being appointed by the president of the republic.[30] The new National Steel Company operating the Volta Redonda plant has been financed partly by loans from the Export-Import Bank of the U.S.A. and partly by investments by the Brazilian government and private investors. The government-owned Chilean Development Corporation typically owns only sufficient stock in

30 Spiegel, op. cit., 218.

new enterprises to be entitled to representation on the board of directors, management and majority stock holding being private. Similar mixed companies are used in Argentina, Brazil, Chile, Iran[31] and South Africa (where the South African Iron and Steel Industrial Corporation is a mixed company.[32])

a. The Occurrence of Government Operation of Manufacturing

In countries where only part of the manufacturing system is socialized, there is a variety of patterns of division between private and public operations. In general, the socialization of industry spread after 1945.

The industries nationalized to obtain revenue are among the oldest socialized industries. They include tobacco, matches, alcohol, salt, and a variety of similar products. There are government tobacco monopolies, for example, in France, Austria, Italy, Portugal, Spain, and Sweden; match monopolies in France, Italy, Austria, Turkey, Iran, and Japan; and alcohol monopolies in France and Sweden. In Turkey in 1947 about 80% of the gross income of state monopolies went in relief of the budget. Such nationalization to obtain monopoly profits for the state is an alternative to the excise taxes levied on most of these products in most countries. A private industry may, however, be more enterprising, and provide a higher quality product than a public enterprise. Indeed, the history of tobacco monopolies in West European countries suggests that the consumer is often better served at the same price by private enterprise than by a government regie.

Transportation and communication industries are widely nationalized in many of their branches. Monopoly is often necessary for efficiency, and private monopoly has proved too difficult to control. But governments are frequently moved by military considerations to ensure service adequate for use in war. Railroads are operated by the government throughout western Europe. France built the roadbeds to ensure an adequate network, and the German government nationalized its railroads after 1870, partly to insure the construction and maintenance of strategic lines. Railroads are nationally operated in Australia, New Zealand, South Africa, and many other countries, but not in the U.S.A. and some Latin American countries. In India the government found private companies costly and difficult to control and began to take over private railroads, and build new public ones, in the 1870s. It managed some directly but made management contracts providing a guaranteed income with new or old companies to manage others. By 1922 about 70% of the mileage was government owned, of which about 30% was operated by the government. It has since taken over the private railroads as their contracts permit.

Air transport, particularly international air transport, does not call for a

[31] U.N., *Econ. Devel. in Selected Countries*, 1947, 20, 86, 107, 189.
[32] U.N., *Econ. Devel. of Selected Countries*, 1950, 250.

monopoly, but is monopolized by governments, for example in Britain, France, Sweden, Denmark, Switzerland, and Pakistan, but not the U.S.A., Australia, or India. Governments are involved in international shipping in France, Sweden, Germany, Poland, and the U.S.A. Telephone and telegraph systems, publicly operated in the majority of countries, are privately operated in the U.S.A., Spain, and parts of Latin America. Radio broadcasting does not require monopoly for efficiency, but there is a public monopoly in Britain, Canada, Germany, Sweden, and a number of other countries. Competing private systems exist in the U.S.A., France, and parts of Latin America. In Australia and New Zealand, public and private systems compete: the listener pays a tax to support the government stations, although he may listen entirely to private stations that obtain their revenue from advertising. The British government has decided to allow both private and public television systems.

Electric power systems are economical when integrated over wide areas. In the U.S.A. these economies are obtained by private systems, each with a large market territory integrated with others through wholesale exchanges of power. In smaller countries the generating system is public, but retail distribution may be in the hands of local organizations, often also public—for instance, in Britain and New Zealand, except in Southland. In Japan, Sweden, and the U.S.A., the government undertakes part but not all generation and transmission, leaving distribution to local bodies. Both public and private generation exist in Germany, Australia, and India.

Since 1945 Britain and France have nationalized industries on the ground that they are basic to the economy, which means that their efficiency and price policies affect much of the economy. In fact, basic industries are typically also large-scale industries like transport, energy sources (coal, gas, and electricity) and, possibly, steel, although other reasons are also given for nationalizing these industries. Industries may be nationalized because of their influence on the military potential such as railroads, air transport, shipping, steel and atomic energy (which is a government monopoly in the U.S.A., Britain, and France). Much of the industry taken over by the Japanese government between 1939 and 1945 was selected because of its military importance.

The different weight given to these various considerations in different countries results in a variety of patterns of public operation. In the U.S.A. there is little state manufacturing, but the government monopolizes atomic energy, operates the Tennessee Valley Authority, and leases ships to private operators. The federal, state, and municipal governments also engage in a number of smaller enterprises. In Belgium and Sweden, state operation is chiefly restricted to railways, telegraphs, and telephones, although the Swedish government is interested in iron mines.

In Britain, government operation was chiefly restricted before 1939 to posts, telegraphs, and telephones, with limited activities in electric power and transport. During the war of 1939 to 1945, the coalition government undertook many activities (mainly trading) to mobilize its economic resources. The Labor government elected in 1945 emphasized the necessity for expansion of national wealth and full employment with "Socialism in our Time" as the means. It continued into peacetime the government import of food and non-ferrous metals, and established on a permanent basis a government authority to import cotton (Ch. 26). It nationalized the Bank of England, coal mining, almost all ground and air transport, the generation of electricity, the gas and, finally, the steel industry. It announced a further list of industries to be nationalized (including water supply, ownership of minerals, meat wholesaling, sugar manufacturing and refining, industrial assurance, cement, and possibly shipbuilding and parts of the chemical industry). But the narrow margin by which it was returned to power in 1950 necessitated postponement of further nationalization. The nationalization of the steel industry, which had been postponed pending the results of the election, was effected in 1951, the power of the House of Lords to veto the bill being curtailed to ensure enactment of the measure.

The steel industry, however, marks, at least temporarily, the high tide of nationalization; it was again denationalized in 1954. The industry had been protected since 1932 and its prices had been made largely by a private monopoly (Ch. 12). The Minister of Supply in the Labor government, stating the arguments for nationalization, pointed out that the industry had been intensively supervised by the government through the Iron and Steel Board since 1945, but that the Board could prohibit, but not require, action by the industry. Although steel prices compared favorably with those of most other countries the industry depended on subsidies on imported ore and scrap and control of domestic prices for scrap. Steel was to be nationalized because (a) the industry necessarily involved monopoly, and since it was vital to the economy, the monopoly had to be public, not private, (b) there was a risk of inadequate supplies because the industry might not think it economical to expand capacity, and (c) requirements of defense made it necessary. Against nationalization it was argued that the steel industry was less of a public utility than railroads, electricity and gas, and less completely a failure in private hands than the coal industry. Because the steel industry would play an almost determining part in British recovery, it would be dangerous to interfere with its existing organization: it had operated for some years, relatively successfully, in terms of production and labor relations, although there was more question of its basic efficiency. The industry also presented peculiar difficulties in the way of nationalization. It was difficult to draw a satisfactory line between the steel and other industries, for actual firms in the industry were very widely integrated and in no uniform pattern. The Conservative government has also returned road freight transport to private hands.

In France the government had owned the potash mines of Alsace since they were transferred by Germany after the war of 1914-1918. It had owned an important part of the railroad system since 1908. In 1937 the railroads were partially nationalized when the state acquired a controlling interest in the principal railroads, which were merged into a single system primarily to relieve the national budget of large railroad deficits. The Bank of France was nationalized in 1936. The nationalization of armament and aviation had begun in 1936, but was not completed until after liberation in 1945. The Charter of the National Council of Resistance in 1944 called in general terms for nationalization. This became a major political issue after liberation. It was contended that nationalization of the key industries was essential for recovery; that reviving and modernizing industry would be a tremendous task that private enterprise probably lacked both the means and the will to undertake; that a financial oligarchy had in the past encroached on the sovereignty of the state; and finally that nationalization would stimulate the efforts of labor. The provisional government temporarily nationalized the coal industry, and took over the Renault automobile plant, and an aircraft engine plant; the two latter, however, largely in connection with the prosecution of collaborationists. The Constituent Assembly elected in October 1945 provided for the nationalization of coal, gas, and electricity, some insurance companies, and some banks, which has since been effected. By 1947 government-owned industries employed about 18% of the industrial working force of the country. There has been less concern in France to insure that the government controls the basic means of regulating the economy, than with monopoly and technical backwardness in the industries nationalized.

In Italy, the government controls industries employing about a quarter of all the workers in industry, transport and communication (including 74% of the transport industry, 72% of telephones, 100% of telegraphs, 72% of metallurgical industry, 68.4% of chemical industries, 46.4% of electrical power, and 31.6% of engineering). The government controls 80% of shipbuilding, 40% of rolling stock production, 60% of pig iron production, and 43% of steel production.[33]

Developing countries also face the problem of drawing a line between government and private operation, but where they are under pressure to develop at a revolutionary tempo, their governments may be compelled to be more active than those in capitalist countries during their initial stages of development. They may be compelled to establish industries that require unusually large amounts of capital, that mature over long periods, or have a broad influence on the general efficiency of the economy (such as railroads, electricity, and particularly hydroelectric plants). In Turkey economic development was mainly promoted through state enterprise from 1933 to 1950, but since that time emphasis on state enterprise has been

---

[33] U.N., *Econ. Surv. of Europe Since the War*, 1953, 76.

reduced and that on development of agriculture increased.[34] Nevertheless the government owns and operates the Sumer and Eti banks, which own and operate about 75% of all the country's industry and all transport. In Iran government enterprises are about 30% of all industry.[35] The five-year plan for industrial development is mainly concerned with those industries built up by the state in recent years. The Bank for Industries and Mines manages existing state enterprises and establishes new ones. In Egypt Mohammed Ali, seized with a determination to westernize the country in the early 19th century, established a number of monopolistic state enterprises (e.g., in textiles, glass, ironware, and munitions), most of which were abolished after 1838. Later in the century the Khedive Ismail made similar experiments but with little more success,[36] and there is now little nationalized industry.

The Indian government announced in 1948 that there would be exclusive state monopolies in the industries producing arms and munitions, atomic energy, and railway transport. Government, local or central, would also be responsible for all new undertakings in coal, iron and steel, aircraft manufacture, shipbuilding, telephone, telegraph, radio apparatus and receiving sets, and mineral oil production. Existing enterprises would be allowed to continue, although the state claimed the right to acquire them whenever the public interest required it. Existing enterprises will be allowed all facilities for efficient working and reasonable expansion for ten years, at the end of which the position will be reviewed. If the establishments are taken over, their owners will be compensated.[37] The government has already undertaken fertilizer manufacture. The government of Pakistan has announced its proposal to socialize hydroelectric power, arms and munitions production, locomotive and rolling stock production, and telecommunications equipment production. Otherwise, it will welcome private enterprise, although under somewhat restrictive conditions. The government of Southern Rhodesia operates a steel plant. Some Latin American governments have formed government enterprises, although mixed organizations are more common. The government established a meat packing plant (*Frigorifico Nacional*) in Uruguay in 1928, providing the initial capital, naming the first directors, and giving the company a monopoly of slaughter in Montevideo.[38]

Socialist governments have taken over all industrial production. Craft production involves so many small production units that it has not been

---

[34] U.N., *Econ. Surv. of Europe in 1953*, 83, 85.

[35] U.N., *Econ. Rev. of the Middle East*, 1949-50, 32.

[36] Bonné, *op. cit.*, 238; Weinryb, "The Industrialization of the Middle East," LXI *Quar. Jour. of Econ.*, 1947, 476.

[37] India, Advisory Planning Board *Report*, 16, 36, 45; U.N., *Econ. Devel. in Selected Countries*, 155, 169.

[38] Hanson, S. G., *Utopia in Uruguay*, Ch. VII.

nationalized. But producers have been organized in cooperatives controlled by the government (Ch. 12). Distribution facilities in Russia are owned either by the government or by cooperatives controlled by the government, private trading being restricted mostly to village markets. After the Revolution the government took over all industrial and trading enterprises above a prescribed capitalization, under a decree of July 28, 1918, and under a decree of November 20, 1920, all but the smallest. During the period of the New Economic Policy (1922-1927), some branches of smaller-scale activity temporarily reverted to private enterprise, but since the first five-year plan came into operation in 1928 all industry, and almost all trade, has been operated by the government or by cooperatives.

In eastern Europe the underground movement urged nationalization because it was dissatisfied with the operating policies of large-scale industry, its labor policies, and the political influence of those who controlled large manufacturing, especially where they were German. Socialization was facilitated by the fact that many owners had disappeared and many properties were owned by former enemy aliens whose property was somewhat easier to take over than that owned by citizens (e.g., in Czechoslovakia and Rumania).

Nationalization came in most of these countries in two waves. In Poland, however, government enterprises were extensive in 1938 when they included 100% of the enterprises in the production of potash salts, alcohol, tobacco, aircraft, automobiles, air transport, post, telegraph, radio and nearly 100% of maritime transport, dye stuffs, railroads and fire insurance. The government also owned 84% of the plants producing salt, 73% of the telephone industry, 70% of smelting, and 52% of insurance other than fire. In 1946, most of the remaining large-scale industry was socialized and by the end of 1948, 96% of the gross output of industry (excluding handicrafts) came from the socialized sector. In Czechoslovakia, much manufacturing prior to 1939 was owned by banks that were primarily holding companies, each controlling a wide variety of interests. About 100% of the porcelain industry had been in German ownership; 90% of the paper industry, and 70% of the chemical industry. In 1945 all basic industries, and all larger enterprises in other industries, were nationalized. By 1948 about 96% of all industrial workers were employed by nationalized enterprises, but a number of small private enterprises survived.

In Hungary the government first nationalized mining, and later, electric power, but the commercial banks were not taken over until 1947. All German assets were transferred to Russia under the agreement at Potsdam in 1945. Consequently, Russia achieved a powerful position in many industrial, agricultural, and transport undertakings. Russia established Hungarian-Russian companies to replace concerns which had been controlled by the government, and in 1945, the Hungarian-Russian trade agreement set up joint companies for oil, bauxite deposits, aluminum production, air communication, and river navigation. Railways belonging to the government were controlled by the Soviet government. By 1949, however, 81% of the value of gross output came from the socialised sector. In Bulgaria until 1947 only insurance, some mines, the transport, alcohol and tobacco industries were socialized, but by 1948 98% of industrial output by value was produced by socialized enterprises. In Rumania government enterprises had been important in the metal, engineering and tobacco industries before the war. There was no socialization law until 1948, although mixed Soviet-Rumanian enterprises were set up in various sectors of the economy. By 1948, 95% of the gross value of industrial output came from the socialized sector. In eastern Germany, where socialization was slower, about 70% of industry was socialized by 1950. Retail trade was usually not socialized in these countries, but merely frozen out by diverting supplies of goods to state stores and cooperatives. By 1952, 97% or more of the value of gross industrial output came from the socialized sector in all these countries except eastern Germany, where it was 77%.[39] In Jugoslavia socialization was rapid after 1945. By 1946, 80% of all industry, all banking, all transport and almost all wholesale trade were in the hands of the state. Retail trade was formally nationalized in 1948.

Socialist China is aiming at socialization, but has accepted an interim program of reliance on socialized enterprises, mixed government and private enterprises, and private enterprises. But they all operate within a framework of controls by taxation and credit and control of raw materials and finished products (Ch. 23). By 1950 some state enterprises were directly operated by it, and others were temporarily or permanently leased to provincial or military authorities. The five-year plan contemplates the transformation of most private firms into mixed government and private enterprises. Fifty percent of the consumer goods industries, however, was in private hands in 1953, but only 20% of the investment goods industries.[40] But the pace of socialization was accelerated in 1953 and the number of government enterprises increased. In Canton in 1953, of over 2,000 concerns under government regulation only seven (engaged primarily in foreign trade, communications, and transport) were mixed enterprises. The majority were regulated through the control of supplies, and, as retailers operating under strict state rules, about 20% were virtually purchasing agents for state companies and another 20% selling agents.[41]

b. The Policies of State Operated Industry

"The public interest" provides no rule for the guidance of public enterprises until it is interpreted, and it is differently interpreted by different individuals and in different countries. The basic problem is to decide how

---

[39] U.N., *Econ. Surv. of Europe in 1953*, 109.
[40] U.N., *World Economic Report*, 1952-53, 52.
[41] *N.Y. Times*, March 14, 1954.

the resources of the economy shall be used. Actual policies differ most notably in the consideration given to the choices of consumers as against the centralized decisions of government.

A government operating its industries with the object of following the choices of consumers would charge prices that would adjust demand to supply. It would increase the supply of each product or service until the value of additional output failed to exceed the value of the additional input of the factors of production, and would endeavor to minimize the cost of production. During short periods of time it would hold prices low enough to ensure the full use of capacity, except where such a price would not cover the marginal cost of production. Lower prices would attract mobile resources into the production of goods and services that the consumer values less highly than other goods that could be produced with these new resources. If prices so calculated do not, over the long run, cover all costs of production, the original investment has turned out poorly, but charging higher prices and selling less goods is not socially economical although it might have been privately profitable.

This policy is not easy to apply. The marginal cost which sets the lower limit to which price should be allowed to fall, is difficult to define. If the wearing out now of plant which might otherwise be used later is a marginal cost of production, there may be "unused capacity" in an engineering sense. When demand increases to a point at which it cannot be met by the optimal usage of existing resources, marginal costs and, consequently, prices rise. It is then necessary to decide whether to invest in additional productive capacity. Investment should be made if revenue from sales is expected to cover all costs in the long run. But where there are wide fluctuations in demand and long periods in which prices are below long-run average cost, it may be necessary to have periods of prices above long-run average cost if revenue is to cover the long-run cost of production. Policy should be aimed, however, not at the recovery of past costs, but at the most economical allocation of resources to meet such fluctuating demands.

No government, however, can operate solely in response to consumer choice expressed in the market. Individuals may be unwilling or unable, because of lack of income, to purchase goods and services that, if provided, would benefit society. Thus governments spend on education, public health, and defense, for which individuals make no payment when they benefit from the service. It may be contended that consumers would, if they were able, or should, choose these allocations of resources but, in any event, governments both capitalist and socialist make the choice. Most make heavy military allocations, but the less developed allocate little to health and education. But governments have become increasingly involved in industry also because of doubts whether the desirable rate of development is achieved if it is dependent on the volume of voluntary saving, and the guesses of investors as to the profit they can make by using savings in various ways. There is also room for doubt whether existing resources are always effectively used under private enterprise (especially where competition is imperfect). Nationalization offers the government an opportunity to regulate the speed and pattern of change in the economic structure and to ensure the efficient use of resources.

Some of the more developed countries have nationalized part of their economies because inefficiency or private monopoly in industries such as transportation, power, and communication is believed to have inhibited general development because of the resulting high costs. The government may seek to make these industries as efficient as they would have been if competition had been active and enterprisers had taken a long view. It may invest more in the expansion of these industries than private investors have been able or willing to do because private investors have been discouraged by taxation or increases in risk due to the uncertainities of international trade and war (for instance, in Britain and western Europe). As in Britain and France, the government may take over a few strategic industries to overcome the tardiness of their economies in adjusting to changing economic conditions and war damage. Governments in underdeveloped countries may also believe that many activities have never developed because entrepreneurs take too narrow and short a view, although such activities would cover costs and satisfy consumers choices in the long run, if established on an adequate scale. Unwilling to rely on voluntary internal and foreign investment,[42] these governments may establish enterprises to provide goods and services essential to development (as they have in Japan, India, Argentina, and Turkey), or take over all production (as in Russia and eastern Europe).

Mixed economies, being unable to follow any over-all plan, must define objectives for each enterprise. The British parliament required the Transport Commission to provide an efficient, economical, and properly integrated system of inland transport, and the Area Gas Boards are to develop and maintain "an efficient, coordinated and economical system of gas supply." The Raw Cotton Commission is required to buy and sell "at such prices as may seem to the Commission best calculated to further the public interest in all respects." The Board of the Iron and Steel Corporation of Great Britain was to see that the major products are available, in such quantities and of such quality, and at such prices "as seem to the corporation best calculated to further the public interest in all respects." These definitions leave the boards virtually free to make their own policy, but the relevant minister is usually empowered to give them directions. They are all, moreover, instructed to cover all their costs out

---

[42] Thakurdas *et. al.*, *A Plan of Economic Development for India* ("Bombay Plan"), Part II, para. 36.

of income, taking an average of good and bad years. The Transport Commission is also required to amortize its capital out of revenue, as well as provide for depreciation, which is an unnecessary, though small, burden. All the government enterprises must include in the costs to be covered the interest on the securities issued by the government in exchange for the properties or securities of the preexisting private enterprises or to provide funds to compensate them, as well as on any securities issued after nationalization.

Most of the British nationalized industries required considerable reorganization and reequipment, and there is a question whether the compensation was too high, in the sense that the boards may find it difficult for a long time both to achieve these improvements and balance their budgets. They were faced with problems of reorganization during a period of rising costs and shortage of capital goods. The government and its enterprises are influenced, moreover, by considerations which concern private business much less. For instance, the steel industry requires relocation and modernization of plants, which would involve considerable social cost. Unless the compensation paid took full account of these costs the state company could not compensate for them without incurring a loss, and the relocation might not be undertaken. The state may also, for military reasons, require greater expansion than private enterprise would have found profitable, and again incur losses.[43] Finally, out of consideration for the opinion of consumers or industries purchasing national services, the government enterprises may be too slow to raise prices, which causes shortages of supply and financial losses in the short run, and pressure for uneconomic expansion in the long run.

The British Transport Commission accumulated a deficit of £40 million in three years up to the end of 1950, but had reduced it to £35 million by the end of 1953. Wage increases in 1950 were estimated to cost £12 million a year, and coal price increases £3 million a year. The prices of gasoline, steel, and other materials were also rising. At the same time the administrative machinery delayed adjustments in the charges for freight and passengers that have been vigorously contested. The Commission estimated that delays in raising charges in 1950 caused losses about equal to its deficit for the year (£15 million). By 1951, however, freight charges averaged 190% of 1938 and passenger charges in London rose to 175%, and outside London to 190%. In fact, the Commission has despairingly stated that "measures to secure increasing efficiency and economy can only have a very limited offsetting effect" to rising costs.[44] But part of the difficulty lies in the fact that the units of management are excessively large, the hierarchy of management rigid, and attention to long-run adjustment insufficient.

---

[43] Langley, S. J., "The Iron and Steel Act 1949," LX *Ec. Jour.*, 1950, 311.
[44] *Economist*, April 21, 1951.

The Railway Executive is obligated to earn 3% interest on the sum paid by the government to the former owners at a time when the trades formerly providing heavy freight traffic are declining, and the road transport competes seriously with railroad transport, partly because the structure of charges for transport fails to reflect difference in the cost of rendering different types of service.[45] The Transport Act required the preparation of a new set of charges (both road and rail) by August 1949, but the Minister postponed this date for two years because of the difficulties of the task.

The Commission had an especially difficult task in nationalizing trucking, because there were 20,000 small trucking organizations, most of whom operated two or three trucks. The law required the Transport Commission to take over all undertakings more than half of whose business was "long distance," the definition of which in fact included relatively short hauls, but without which it might be difficult to operate nationalized trucking at a profit. Furthermore, the Executive, in taking over many undertakings, acquired facilities for short-haul traffic and preferred to utilize them, rather than concentrate on long-haul traffic and write off assets for which it was required to pay compensation. In 1949 the Road Haulage Executive earned about 2% on its investment (on which 3% interest and amortization had to be paid). But this result reflects the transition from private to public ownership. Numerous acquisitions during the year complicated management tasks, stricter compliance with the law increased operating costs, and wages were raised. By 1950 it had taken over 2,300 undertakings and had a fleet of 40,000 vehicles. But in 1952 the government announced its intention to resell the business to private enterprise (and impose a levy on trucking to recover some of the losses on resale).

The civil aviation companies are strongly tinged with a military interest, and by the end of 1950 had incurred a deficit of £35 million, but the deficit was only £2.3 million for the year 1952-3. The Electricity Commission made a profit of £28.2 million in the five years to 1952-3 while increasing output and charging rates in 1948-9 only 14.3% above 1938-9. The gas industry made a profit of about £4.45 million in the almost four years to 1952-3 in the face of a rise in the price of coal a month after the industry was taken over, and restrictions on capital investment. But charges for depreciation of a little over 4% of the original cost of plant, whose replacement cost is nearly three times as high as its original cost, appear to be inadequate. The Iron and Steel Corporation made a profit of £7.8 million in its first 7½ months (partly as a result of high export prices), and £16 million in the year 1951-2.

In France the results of nationalized enterprise are not clear. Their accounts are not very informative. The government controls price policy,

---

[45] Walker, G., "The Economics of British Transport," *Westminster Bank Review,* Aug. 1950.

and by the end of 1947 the price of coal had risen about as much as industrial prices in general. The coal industry was heavily subsidized in 1946 and 1947, and in 1948 amortization and depreciation were to be covered by loans. The coal authority does not pay most corporation taxes and little compensation was paid to the former owners. Gas and electricity prices had risen only about half as much as prices in general at the end of 1947. The Electricity Board incurred a loss of 7,363 million francs in 1947, realized a profit of 5,475 million francs in 1948, and incurred a loss of 5,546 million francs in 1949. Electricity rates are about twelve times as high as in 1939.[46]

Mixed economies face problems of coordination within their socialized sectors. Requiring nationalized enterprises to follow consumer choice, while covering and minimizing their costs, provides only a general framework for coordination. In fact they are almost all monopolistic enterprises and may charge prices covering uneconomically high costs taken over perhaps from private industry. Or their costs may be higher than those of private enterprises because socialized industries are expected to provide services in the national interest that private enterprises could not be expected to provide without special remuneration (e.g., provide steel making capacity sufficient to meet war needs). Prices covering these high costs place a greater burden on all users than they would carry if supplied by private enterprise. But other nationalized enterprises are among these users. The prices of coal and transport affect the prices of electricity, gas, and steel. The prices of coal, electricity and steel affect the cost of transport. In December 1949, for instance, the Transport Commission proposed an increase of 16.6% in freight rates. This was expected to cause considerable increases in the prices of coal and steel. But the Transport Commission contended that its deficit was partly attributable to the decision of the National Coal Board to raise the price of coal.

While the nationalized enterprises in general face little competition, the monopoly of the Transport Commission was achieved by giving it control of competing forms of transport, namely by road, rail, and canal. Before the commission was established there had been a long and inconclusive controversy as to the relative positions of road and rail transport in an efficient national system. The Commission was expected to resolve this controversy. The act establishing the Commission reserves to shippers the right to choose their own means of transport. Charges for truck transport that just cover its cost would take much business from the railroads and a Commission required to make the railroads cover all their costs might well be tempted to make trucking charges higher than would prevail under competition. In fact the Commission failed to adjust rail and road charges to induce the use of each for the types of transport for which it is most efficient (which would have involved the abandonment

---

[46] *Economist: Records and Statistics,* Dec. 30, 1950.

of unprofitable railroad lines and changes in the ways of handling traffic and in work practices). In 1952 the government abandoned hope that the Commission would solve the problem, and decided to return trucking to private hands. But trucking reverted to control of another kind, and was subjected to a levy to offset part of the loss to the railroads due to transfers of traffic to the roads. Electricity and gas which are in partial competition were set up under different authorities in Britain, and were intended to be under different authorities in France, but the French gas industry has been operated as part of the nationalized electric power industry.

In wholly socialized economies the state enterprise operates under instructions formulated by the government department to which it is responsible in accordance with the five-year plan and its annual and quarterly revisions. In general, but not invariably, the targets for the enterprise are stated in detail as to the quantity, quality, and types of goods to be produced, the labor productivity to be achieved, the size and average pay of the labor force, total payments for wages and salaries, the average cost of products, and the amount of capital investment. The enterprises make procurement and marketing agreements within the framework of these instructions. They pay turnover taxes that draw off from the enterprises profits they would otherwise make because production departs from consumers' choice and the prices that will hold demand down to the supply of some products exceed costs.

If the enterprise produces the planned output at planned costs, and sells at planned prices, it should show planned profits. In fact, the government places considerable emphasis on the relation between planned and actual profits as a test of compliance with the plan. But this relation is not used as the sole check. Plans for production have often not been very detailed and profits can be made by producing the most profitable items at the expense of others (an indication that prices do not always correspond to costs). Firms do not always make required repairs and provide adequately for maintenance and depreciation.[47] They may economize on experimental work aimed at cost reduction. Above all the quality of output may not comply with the plan. Payrolls and prices also cannot always be kept to the planned level. But precise compliance with the plan cannot be expected in an economy in rapid change. Indeed the propaganda to overfulfill the plan not only causes departures from the plan where it succeeds but may also prevent fulfillment in other sectors unless there is slack in the system (in the form of inventories or idle capacity) at points where it can prevent local breakdowns.

Although money results are important, the government also emphasizes production, materials consumed, and the trend of costs. It has attempted to keep the system flexible by giving only general orders from the higher authorities that set the tasks of the agencies immediately below them.

---

[47] Granick, op. cit., 127.

But the higher bodies can and do intervene. Because of the incompleteness of the production plan and the prospect of nonfulfillment, they attempt to ensure fulfillment of the most important parts of the plan by setting priorities upon some branches of activity (often changing them). But these priorities are also due to the inadequate definition of targets. Furthermore, because the intermediate agencies sometimes set unrealistic tasks for the units below them, technically illegal behavior by a manager is accepted where he is in general successful.[48] Enterprise performance is checked by the Commission on State Control attached to the Council of Commissars and the Commission of Party Control attached to the Central Committee of the Party at the same high level. The Prosecutor's Office and the courts deal with legal offenses, although (because the law is so drawn that violation is almost unavoidable) prosecution is not much used, and dismissals are not infrequent. The press also acts as a watchdog.

Russian authorities have themselves complained of the failure of enterprises to achieve their targets.[49] The losses of "unprofitable" enterprises amounted to 16 billion roubles in 1952, and were considerable in the first half of 1953 because the ministries, local party, and local government bodies were unsatisfactorily implementing the production plan. In particular, failure to achieve planned reductions in costs "undermines the foundations of cost accounting," retards capital accumulation, and reduces state revenues. Costs have remained particularly high in the timber and coal industries, in building, in many machine tractor stations, river transportation, and in trade. Insufficient emphasis is said to have been placed on the national organization of production, and the reduction of the proportion of workers not engaged directly in production. But planned profits are somewhat arbitrary, and the legally prescribed depreciation rates are probably too low.[50]

The official Russian index of output per man per year in large-scale industry increased from 100 in 1928 to 489 in 1951, the average annual increase being 10.3% from 1928 to 1940, and 12.6% from 1946 to 1951. But these figures are influenced by the upward bias in the measurement of production (Ch. 23). Indexes of physical output per worker show an annual average increase of 8.5% in coal mining from 1928 to 1938, 13% in iron mining from 1928 to 1937, 9.4% in steel mills from 1929 to 1939, 2% in cotton yarn from 1929 to 1939, and 1.7% in shoe manufacturing from 1928 to 1937.[51] These differences between the rate of increase in the productivity of producers' goods and consumers' goods respectively reflect the policy of increasing investment more rapidly in the producers' goods industries

---

[48] Granick, op. cit., 148.

[49] Malenkov: speech before the Supreme Soviet of the U.S.S.R., cit., N.Y. Times, Aug. 10, 1953.

[50] Bergson and Heymann, op. cit., 56.

[51] Galenson, in Bergson (Ed.), op. cit., 199.

and the basis on which new products are added into output (Ch. 23). Annual output per industrial wage-earner in Russia in 1937 appears to have been about 40% of that in the U.S.A. Between 1940 and 1950 productivity in industry generally rose 37%, according to official figures, but the increase in fact was probably between 5% and 10%, Russian productivity still remaining about 40% of that in the U.S.A.[52]

[52] Galenson, in Bergson (Ed.), *op. cit.*, 202, 207, 210.

Chapter 14

Relations Between Resources and Production

The productive resources of a society affect both production and consumption. Their effect on consumption is dealt with in Chapters 29 and 30. Their effect on production depends on the quantities available, the extent of their utilization, and their allocation among different uses.

A. The Quantity of Available Resources

1. THE MEASUREMENT OF RESOURCES

Economic measures of the quantity of resources must be based on their ability to increase the aggregate value of goods and services produced. Only then do greater quantities always increase the production potential. Quality is merged into measures of quantity. Measurement must take account of the fact that people or things can contribute to national income only with the collaboration of other resources. The contribution of any one resource should be calculated by deducting from the utilities produced in this collaboration those that could have been produced by the complementary resources in their most effective use, which is difficult in practice, but always being attempted.

Economic quantities of resources depend on physical quantities and on the nature of human wants and technical knowledge. Human wants determine what things and services, and how much of them, give satisfactions. Technical knowledge governs in part the things and services put into the productive process to yield those that give satisfactions. Human wants express themselves directly in desires for particular consumers' goods and services (e.g., food, clothing, housing, and light). But these desires can be translated into demands for a wide variety of other goods and for labor. Biological processes, mostly classified as agricultural, require land and water, solar radiation, and some minerals. Structural materials (of both mineral and agricultural origin) assist production by providing buildings for domestic, agricultural, industrial or transport use, or mechanical devices in any of these groups.

Energy is invariably required in order for production to achieve changes in the form and structure of matter (for instance, in the engineering and chemical industries) and also to guide biological processes. The chief energy sources are human beings, animals, minerals (including coal and oil), water power, and possibly in the future, atomic power. Transportation is necessary to enable matter to yield satisfactions, and it in turn requires energy and structural materials. The demand for these goods and services can be further translated into demands for broad categories of goods and services, conventionally known as resources, namely minerals, land, water, labor, and capital. Labor continues to be necessary in spite of the increasing use of machines and inanimate energy. Most physical and biological changes need direction, which must be human. Machinery is self-controlling only within limits, and its design requires human direction. Moreover, the tendency for changes in technique to reduce the need for labor has been partly offset by increases in aggregate production.

These translations of demands for satisfactions into demands for resources depend on the physical quantities of people and things (particularly their relative scarcities) and on technical knowledge. Minerals, land labor, and capital goods are resources only if we know how to make them yield utilities, and to the extent that they yield them. The productivity of resources is indicated in a competitive market economy by the value placed upon a unit of a resource (the rent of land, the royalty paid on minerals, or the profit paid on capital) because resources are purchased at a price dependent on the amount by which the price at which the ultimate product can be sold exceeds the price which has to be paid for all the complementary resources needed to provide the product. Since the only wants affecting this price are those backed by purchasing power, the productivity of resources depends partly on the distribution of incomes. In a socialist society no market measures are available, the state decides which wants shall be satisfied, and, therefore, the pattern of demand for resources and the extent to which things and people are resources in terms of its objectives.

2. The Influences Affecting Quantities of Resources

The economic quantity of the resources available to a society depends partly upon the structure and climate of the part of the earth upon which the group lives. Where a society obtains resources through trade with other societies, its available resources depend on the structure and climate of the earth occupied by groups with which it trades, and the terms upon which it is able to trade (Ch. 26). Resource supplies are also influenced by human action. Where resources are exhaustible, the supply at any time depends partly on the extent to which they have in fact been exhausted. Societies determine the time distribution of the resource. Most resources are, in fact, exhaustible. Mineral reserves can be used up, land and capital goods can be worn out, labor can be reduced in numbers and productive capacity, but water is periodically renewed by nature, although in limited quantities.

Some resources can be increased in supply (within limits), and the quantity available at any time depends partly on past additions to supply. Labor and capital can be increased, but not minerals, and land can at least be prevented from declining in productivity. These differences in the basic economic characteristics of the different resources, together with differences in the ways in which they contribute to production, necessitate separate discussion of each.

The measures of resources available in practice are rarely in economic terms and bear only indirectly upon productive capacity. Measurements in physical units, like acres of land, tons of mineral, numbers of people and the like are of little economic value, because these units are not economically uniform. Tons of mineral in the ground or acres of land differ in the amount of other resources they require to make available a product with economic value. Human individuals differ in the effectiveness with which they can use other resources in production. Some physical units of resources yield less than others of the final products which yield satisfaction. Some units contribute to the production of goods of greater economic value than others. But as economic measures are rarely available, discussion must rest on information in unsatisfactory physical measures corrected as well as possible for differences in economic quality.

B. The Utilization of Resources

Production is influenced by the utilization and not the mere availability of resources. This utilization is wholly a matter of human action. It depends upon the arrangements which permit and induce the use of resources. Most societies probably operate below their potential output, especially the most industrialized capitalist countries that have suffered from fluctuations in production.

Since most resources are capable of use in more than one way, they must be allocated among different uses. There is presumably some allocation which would yield the maximum addition to national income. Consequently, the best allocation is necessary to secure full utilization. Actual allocation within the limits set by the characteristics of the resources and technology is within human control. Decisions concerning utilization may be derived from the market, or from the decisions of socialist government.

Chapter 15

Mineral Resources

A. The Supply of Minerals

The fact that minerals are exhaustible makes it difficult to measure mineral resources in economic terms. The quantity of land or capital can be at least conceived of as the capitalized value of their contribution to production after allowing for the cost of the resources needed to complement them, and for any depreciation. But the contribution of minerals depends on the way their utilization is distributed over time, and allowance for depreciation is impossible because there is no way of offsetting the exhaustion of supplies.

Physical measurements of minerals in the ground (reserves) suggest that minerals are very differently distributed among countries. North America is richly endowed with 49% of the coal, 38% of the petroleum, 49% of the iron, 27% of the copper, 31% of the lead, and 40% of the zinc, but no tin. Europe has little petroleum, copper, or tin. The U.S.S.R. has little bauxite or tin. Countries outside these regions have 55% of the petroleum, 61% of the copper, 60% of the bauxite, 51% of the lead, 96% of the tin, and 37% of the zinc, but only 14% of the coal (Table 22). The more developed countries have about 75% of the reserves of coal and iron, 63% of those of zinc, and about half the lead, but less than half the petroleum, copper and bauxite, and very little tin. Reserves of coal in total, and especially per capita, are much higher in Canada and the USA,[1] the U.S.S.R. and Europe (Fig. 14). Estimates of the coal resources of the U.S.A. range from 1000 to 4000 times the current annual consumption. But figures regarding iron reserves are sharply conflicting, (Figs. 14 and 15 and Table 22) owing to

---

[1] Crichton, A. B., "How Much Coal Do We Really Have? The Need for an Up To Date Survey," American Institute of Mining and Metallurgical Engineers, *Tech. Pub.* 2428, Aug. 1948.

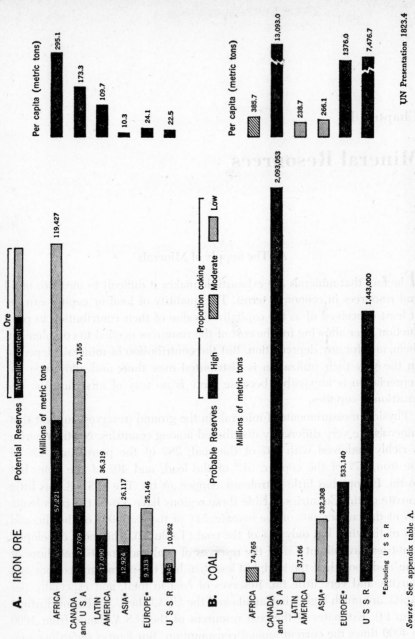

Fig. 14. Reserves of iron ore and coal by area. (From U.N. *World Iron Ore Resources and Their Utilization*, p. 18.)

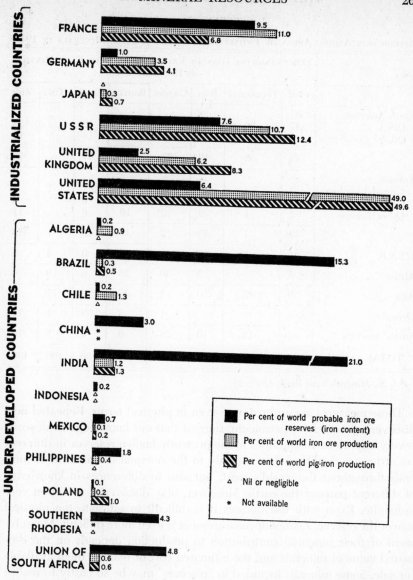

Fig. 15. Distribution of world production of iron ore and pig iron in 1948 and of iron content of probable ore reserves in selected countries. (From U.N. *World Iron Ore Resources and Their Utilization*, p. 10.)

differences in the grades of ore included.[2] Figures on petroleum reserves change too rapidly to be significant for any long period.

[2] The figures in Fig. 14 are of "potential" reserves, which are about five times as high as "probable" reserves, and include many less reliable estimates. U.N., *World Iron Ore Resources and Their Utilization*, 11.

TABLE 22

Distribution Among Areas of Estimated Reserves of Nine Minerals in 1948*

AREA	PERCENTAGE (BY TONS) OF KNOWN RESERVES OF EACH MINERAL IN EACH AREA							
	Coal	Petroleum	Iron	Copper	Bauxite	Lead	Tin	Zinc
North America								
U.S.A.	47	36	34	20	2	18	...	28
Other	2	2	15	7	20	13	...	12
	49	38	49	27	22	31	...	40
Europe								
United Kingdom	4	..	5	...	...	...	1	...
Germany	7	...	1	...	...	6	...	4
Other Europe ...	2	1	9	2	16	6	...	11
	13	1	15	2	16	12	1	15
U.S.S.R.	24	6	11	10	2	6	3	8
Africa	5	...	5	30	23	6	10	6
Asia	9	42	10	2	26	4	77	4
Oceania	...	...	...	1	2	32	1	17
South America	...	13	10	28	9	9	8	10
TOTAL	100	100	100	100	100	100	100	100

* U.S., *Minerals Year Book, 1949*, 28.

These measures are approximate even in physical terms. Repeated new discoveries, notably of petroleum, suggest that our knowledge of deposits is very imperfect. Inequalities in the presently known reserves in different countries are doubtless due not only to the unequal distribution of minerals throughout the world's crust, but also to differences in knowledge of different parts of the earth. Moreover, new discoveries are often very indefinite. Even with test borings it is difficult to estimate the physical size of the reserve. Economic measurement is even more difficult. Measurement of their potential contribution to production depends on the estimated value of minerals and the estimated cost of making them available for sale. Some minerals included in "reserves" may be so costly to realize that at present prices they do not represent economic assets at all. But changes in costs or prices move the boundary between reserves that are economic assets and those that are not. Finally, the present value of a deposit depends not only on future costs and prices, but also on the rate of discount, which requires estimates of future rates of interest as well as foreknowledge of the distribution of usage over time. Minerals in the ground are bought and sold in non-socialist countries, but these transactions provide little basis for the economic appraisal of deposits. Sales are usually not outright sales for cash, but rather for at least part payment in sums depending on output and sometimes on profits. Furthermore, the terms of one sale cannot be used to impute the value of other deposits of the same mineral because of great differences in their economic quality (as to costs of realization). Nor do sales occur frequently enough to provide a basis for imputing values. As a practical matter, therefore, mineral reserves can be discussed only in terms of estimates of physical quantities, subject to wide margins of error and frequent change due to new discoveries, and having a doubtful and complex relation to contemporary production and welfare.

B. The Utilization of Minerals

Minerals unused in the ground contribute little to national income. The right to utilize unmined minerals can be sold before they are utilized, and the resulting transfers of purchasing power (internal or foreign) may affect production. Sales to foreigners, for immediate payment of any part of the consideration, make foreign purchasing power available, and it can be used to increase other resources for production. But such transactions are not very important, and much of the payment for mineral reserves is in royalties payable as realization proceeds. For the most part, minerals affect incomes when they are produced. The system of mineral ownership and taxation, and the social structure, determine whether the benefits are distributed in lower prices, higher wages, more employment, profits, or ultimately in the support of a larger population with little increase in levels of living.

The speed of realization is important not only because it affects current incomes but also because it affects the minerals remaining to increase future incomes. But there is no criterion for appraising the distribution of mineral usage over time. The maximization of benefits to humanity would necessitate balancing the benefits to human beings at one time against benefits to different individuals at different times, and making allowance for future changes in population. It would also require foreknowledge of future discoveries of minerals that will doubtless provide greater supplies than are now known; of the reuse of minerals which economizes them; of new sources of energy (in the atom or of biological origin like alcohol) and of structural materials from less exhaustible sources (plastics with a vegetable base). Nevertheless, the growth of production during the past 200 years has been due partly to a great increase in the usage of exhaustible minerals, and may ultimately be slowed down unless technology can be changed.

The rate of utilization of minerals depends on the conditions of access to minerals and the conditions of realization.

1. MINERAL RIGHTS

Access to minerals is a matter of government policy. The ownership of mineral rights in some countries attaches to private rights over the surface of the land, because original land grants specifically included both surface and sub-surface rights, or because land grants were not specific but have been subsequently interpreted to include such rights. Even in these countries, however, mineral rights may have been sold separately from surface rights.

Surface owners were in control of minerals in Britain by 1688 (except for gold and silver) and in many British colonial areas until 1946. In the U.S.A. also most minerals were granted to surface owners, although considerable tracts of land (with their minerals) remain in the hands of federal government. An Ordinance of 1785 reserved one-third of all gold, silver, lead and copper on land deeded by the government, and in 1807, the lead mines of Missouri were reserved from sale to be leased for short terms. Since 1829, however, mineral lands have typically been sold. In areas of "permanent settlement" in India, the British government acquiesced in the disposition of mineral rights by landowners. The vesting of minerals in the surface owner gives the owner (or somebody to whom he sells mineral rights)[3] the power to decide whether, when, and how quickly deposits are to be worked. He may work them himself, or lease them to others. The lease may define the area to be worked and the minerals conveyed by the lease. It may control the speed of mining, and the amount of payment, either by royalty or for a capital sum.

Private ownership by "economic men" aiming at maximum profit might be expected to result in the most economical distribution of use over time (prices being accepted as a measure of utility). An owner might time his utilization to maximize the aggregate return reduced to a point in time by discounting. He would need to know the demand for, and competing supplies of, the mineral throughout all time, and the rate of interest to be applied. But he would also need to be sure of eternal life on earth to benefit from postponement of realization. Mortal men, lacking this assurance, might postpone usage to benefit their heirs, but they do not look far into the future. The right to buy and sell deposits enables individuals to hold reserves during their lifetime to benefit from expected increases in capital value, but the risks are great and the benefits are likely to accrue to heirs. Holding by perpetual corporations makes little difference because the stockholders are mortal. Consequently, private ownership induces fairly speedy realization because mineral owners usually prefer immediate benefits, and the heavy investment required for most mining creates pressure to recover minerals at a rate permitting economical use of the overhead. Uncertainty about the future price of the mineral, owing to the risk of changes in demand or in competing supplies, also contracts their time

---

[3] Where mineral rights have become separated from surface rights, the owner of the surface rights might obstruct realization of the mineral. The British Mines Act of 1923 permits coercion of the surface owner when this is necessary to permit working of minerals.

horizon. Since they use first the richer and more accessible supplies, leaving the leaner ores at greater depths for use when prices have risen, some of the more accessible minerals are approaching exhaustion in the more developed countries. But the tendency to fairly rapid usage can operate in respect only to the known supplies and techniques. In fact, discoveries of new deposits, new methods of mining and separating, improvements of transport, the development of substitutes, the reuse of metals, and other economies in use have hitherto more than offset any tendency to rising prices. The prices of minerals as a whole declined in relation to general commodity prices during the 19th century (the chief exception being bituminous coal in Britain and anthracite coal in the U.S.A.).

Where mineral rights are held in small pieces, moreover, the mineral may be wastefully exploited. Before 1938, many coal leases in Britain covered uneconomically small deposits and areas that prevented efficient mining, partly because owners granted many small leases to accelerate mining and the receipt of royalties.[4]

The principle of vesting minerals in the surface owner cannot be applied to liquid and gaseous minerals, because a well on one piece of land can draw the mineral from under other pieces. The U.S.A. courts therefore decided that title to such minerals was acquired by "capture" (which principle also applies to fish from international waters, some wild game, and war booty). This principle, naturally, caused competition to capture. An excessive number of wells was sunk to drain each pool where the surface rights were held in small lots. Haste to capture resulted in waste of gas, loss of pressure in the wells, and flooding. Wells were operated so long as the price of petroleum exceeded the usually small cost of pumping, where oil was pumped. Thus, except where the whole of a pool was under unified control, exploitation was vastly accelerated and some of the mineral was permanently lost, (e.g., in the U.S.A., Rumania, and Mexico, in the past).

State ownership of minerals is also common. Even where minerals belong to surface owners, the state controls those on public lands. This is important in the U.S.A., and British dominions and colonies. The state may, however, control all minerals where it can enforce a rule that minerals were not in mind when land was granted to individuals. In medieval Europe it was often held that the rights of the grantee penetrated no deeper than the plough, and that mining was not a normal use of the soil. Where minerals were known to be valuable when land was granted, the crown often specifically reserved mineral rights. Among the Greeks and Romans, the right to mine was apparently not separated from the right to cultivate, but in Britain the king claimed all minerals in 1066, although by 1688 he had lost all but gold and silver. In Germany, royal control existed in the 11th century and has persisted in most of continental

---

[4] U.K., Technical Advisory Committee on Coal Mining *Report,* 1945, 173.

Europe. For instance, coal rights belonged to the state in Germany and Poland prior to 1939.

The state may also obtain control of minerals by purchasing or confiscating private rights. Latin American governments began to assert claims to minerals at the end of the 19th century. Some claimed all minerals not already in private control, and some have since taken over these as well. Chile reserved to the state petroleum and nitrate reserves in which no private property rights had been established. Mexico expressly excluded the petroleum from the state prerogative as late as 1909, but in 1917 and 1925, it declared all oil reserves, if no positive acts of ownership had been asserted, the property of the state. This rule was somewhat modified in 1926 and 1927, but the government took over all private oil concessions in 1939. Brazil has taken over as public property all eventual deposits of petroleum.[5] Sub-surface minerals belong to the state in Colombia and Venezuela. The Bolivian government, by decrees in 1916 and 1920, took over all petroleum deposits, and thereafter granted concessions only on payments of royalties. In 1937 it ceased to grant concessions and nationalized virtually the whole petroleum industry,[6] and in 1952 nationalized tin production. The Russian government confiscated all private mineral rights soon after the 1917 revolution. The east European governments (including Jugoslavia) did so after 1945. The Japanese government declared all minerals the property of the state after the Meiji restoration in 1868[7] and the Chinese Communist government has taken over all mining properties. The British government took over coal deposits in 1938 (before it nationalized coal mining), and in 1949 a committee recommended the nationalization of all suitable minerals to secure planned and scientific exploration and to deal with technical and economic risks. Private mining might continue under government concessions. The British government also urged its colonial governments in 1946 to pass legislation (a) providing that mineral rights be retained when making land grants, and (b) setting out the methods of recovering mineral rights that had become private property. These colonial governments might, however, lease mining rights, but should ensure that mining be conducted in the interest of the whole community.

State ownership of minerals means that the state rather than individuals can regulate mining methods and the speed of exhaustion. Some governments have permitted "free mining," which means that any person discovering a mineral deposit may claim from the government permission to exploit it. This policy was adopted in parts of medieval Europe to increase mineral output when existing mines began to run out and land-

---

[5] Spiegel, *op. cit.*, 211.

[6] U.S. Tariff Commission, *Economic Controls and Commercial Policy in Bolivia,* 1946, 14 ff.

[7] Allen, *op. cit.*, 30.

owners failed to open new mines because mining was becoming deeper and they were unfamiliar with its problems. Free mining was also applied to gold, but not petroleum on the public domain in the western states of the U.S.A. A custom to this effect had developed among miners and was recognized by statute in 1866. A prospector making a strike reports to the authorities and obtains a possessory claim; after expenditure of a certain amount of labor, he obtains full ownership of the deposit. In parts of the British Commonwealth, free mining was allowed on Crown lands, in colonial territories until 1946. "Free mining" generally stimulates production as much or more than does the ownership of deposits by surface owners, especially where continued control of the deposit is conditional on attempts to work it.

Most governments have, sooner or later, imposed conditions on the exploitation of minerals under their control. "Free mining" then gives place to the mining concession, in which the government leases the right to exploit minerals under specified conditions. It may regulate conditions of production. It may charge a royalty on output or a capital sum in return for the concession, or both. It may specify the minimum rate of exploitation, and impose other conditions. This arrangement permits it to select the concessionaire and decide the size of the area conceded, as well as the rate of production. Such concessions may become property rights capable of sale or mortgage. France began to require royalty payments in the later middle ages, although it continued nominally free mining. But free mining had been abandoned before the Revolution, and the government was granting concessions to corporations and individuals. A law of 1791 provided for a degree of supervision and inspection that discouraged investments of the amounts necessary for deep mining. In 1810, therefore, the government provided for long enough concessions to justify the necessary investment, and limited state supervision to safety measures. In Germany also the states began to charge royalties in the later Middle Ages. The Prussian mining code of 1794 imposed controls that were modified in the middle of the 19th century to encourage mining (notably by lengthening concessions). Mining and petroleum production in the Middle East is under state concessions, which have also been granted by Latin American governments.

Governments can use their power of concession to control rates of utilization, but in fact they do not appear to have behaved very differently from individuals. They have generally encouraged exploitation and sought the highest price for the concession. In the past, however, some have doubtless been forcefully persuaded by powerful foreign governments whose citizens seek concessions. After Chile acquired complete control of the nitrate deposits in 1879 as a result of the war with Boliva and Peru, it endeavored to maintain the price of nitrate by regulating the rate at which it sold concessions by auction. British, German, and later

Chilean capital flowed into the industry more quickly than demand increased, and the government encouraged or participated in controls of output to maintain the price (Ch. 9), but apparently not with primary concern for conservation. In South Africa the government claims a 75% share of land discovered to bear gold, which it leases to mining companies in return for a share of net profits. This share is often about 25%, but it depends upon the estimated richness of the mine and the degree of certainty attaching to the estimate (which is partly dependent on the extent to which gold has been mined in the neighborhood). But "there are grave difficulties in the way of securing for the state an adequate return for its 75% share of mining rights."[8] In Malaya the government charges a royalty of about 13% of the value of tin output plus, sometimes, a capital sum for the right to mine. The Middle East governments have taken their share in the gains from petroleum in a variety of ways. The agreement between the Iranian government and the Anglo-Iranian Oil Company in 1933 provided for payment to the government of a royalty per ton of oil produced in Iran, a payment per ton in lieu of taxes, and a sum equal to 20% of additions to general reserve, the last to be paid at the end of the concession. A revised agreement negotiated in 1949 (but not ratified by the Iranian parliament) would have increased the government receipts about 30%. The government also obtained income from customs duties paid by the company, income taxes paid by company employees, and exchange sold to the company at a high rate. In 1950 the Arabian-American Oil Company agreed to pay increased taxes to the Saudi Arabian government, and the Iraq Petroleum Company agreed to increase the tonnage royalty 50% and to pay half its profits to the Iraq government.[9] A similar sharing of profits was agreed with Kuwait in 1951. In 1952 the Peruvian government required oil companies to pay it half their profits, and Venezuela takes nearly 50% of net earnings. In Germany and Poland, however, governments have designed coal concessions to permit mining on an economical scale and ensure conservation. But the transfer of British coal to the state under the Act of 1938 came too late to achieve this result, for many uneconomically small leaseholds were already in existence.[10]

Governments controlling mineral rights may themselves engage in mining. Such has been the policy since 1917 in Russia, since 1945 in eastern European countries, in Socialist China, in the coal industries of Britain and France, in tin mining in Bolivia, and in a number of Latin American countries for the production of petroleum. The rate of utilization is then directly decided by the state (Ch. 9).

---

[8] Union of South Africa: Committee on Gold Mining Taxation *Report*, 1946, 13.

[9] U.N., *Public Finance Information Papers: Iraq*, 27.

[10] U.K., Technical Advisory Committee on Coal Mining *Report*, 1945 (Cmd. 6610), 30.

2. The Conditions of Realization

The rate of utilization depends on the conditions under which mining is conducted, of which the terms of access to the mineral are only a part. Where mining is conducted by the state, the policy of utilization may be part of the general production plan (as in socialist countries) or it may be based on consumer choice and the minimization of production costs (as, in the main, in Britain). Where mining is a private enterprise, the rate of utilization depends largely on prices and costs (Ch. 9). State aid to restrict output retards utilization, and subsidies accelerate it. Taxes affect utilization in a variety of ways.

Taxes on mining are sometimes difficult to distinguish from royalty payments to governments. If they are imposed in the same amount and in the same way, they have the same effect on production. Governments that have allowed private property rights in minerals can recapture most of the value of such rights by taxation if they wish,[11] and with less serious effect than in regard to other types of property. Although high rewards in other lines of activity may be accepted because they attract resources and ultimately reduce profits, high profits to the owners of minerals cannot increase mineral reserves, although they do encourage prospecting for minerals.

Taxes do not always discourage mineral production. A tax imposed before the mineral has been leased may fall on the royalty payment and, if the payment is not reduced to zero, the mineral owner is still likely to lease. A tax falling on a lessee may also not prevent continued production if income from the mineral exceeds current costs, including taxes, and leaves something towards mining overhead.

The effect of taxes depends, however, on the type of tax. A tax on unused reserves (e.g., on petroleum in Venezuela) stimulates production. A uniform tax per physical unit of output sets a lower limit to the grade of mineral that can be worked even without a royalty, although the limit changes with the price of the mineral and the cost of mining. Mining is not undertaken if the anticipated cost of production, *plus* the tax, *plus* an attractive mining profit exceeds the anticipated value of the output. Taxes on physical output are fairly common. In Southern Rhodesia, for example, the sums payable to the government for minerals are prescribed by statute in terms of physical output, the rate charged to small mines being smaller than that to large mines. The different rates for different minerals are apparently calculated to induce production and open up the country.

Output by enterprises already committed to mining is influenced by the anticipated future rate of tax on output. If the tax is expected to rise, output may be accelerated, and if it is expected to fall, output may be re-

---

[11] Union of South Africa: Committee on Gold Mining Taxation *Report*, 1946, 12.

tarded. Taxes on the value of output affect output less when prices change than do fixed taxes per unit of output. In Tanganyika the government charges are based on the gross output of mines (e.g., 15% on the value of the output of diamonds). Taxes on the value of exports where most of the output is exported have a similar effect. In Chile from 1880 to 1930, the government imposed a tax on exports of nitrates equal to one-third to one-half of their export value. Bolivia has in the past taxed exports of tin. Peru imposes a tax of 22% on the value of petroleum exports, and Venezuela 16⅔%. Malaya taxes exports of tin ore and concentrates. Much the same result is achieved if the government requires the company to convert the foreign exchange proceeds of its mineral exports into local currency at less favorable rates than are used for other exports, or charges the company less favorable rates for foreign currency than are applied to other imports (e.g., in Venezuela, Chile, and Iran).

Where mineral enterprises are numerous and competitive, taxes on production or exports can sometimes be used to obtain monopoly profits for the state. The export tax may cause all sellers to raise their price (including the tax) above what they would charge under competition without the tax. Policies of this type were pursued by the Chilean government with regard to exports of nitrates until 1910, and by the Italian government regarding exports of sulphur until the American supplies were discovered. The amount of such profits depends on the elasticity of demand for the export, which depends on the availability of substitutes and competing sources of supply of the same mineral. Since 1945, a number of west European countries have held export prices for coal at about the landed cost of coal from the U.S.A. which has been 40% to 50% above the price in the producing countries. Such a differential indicates private or public controls. The domestic prices have been kept low (sometimes below cost) to combat inflation and assist general recovery.[12]

Simple taxes per physical unit of output, or even a percentage of the value of output, prevent the working of deposits below a certain grade while leaving high profits to the owners of high-grade deposits. Taxes on net profit avoid this disadvantage. The maximum yield from taxes on profits is obtained when the tax leaves mining enterprises profits just high enough to induce them to enter the industry if they pay no royalties. The government then takes the total value of minerals in the ground. Differences in the grade of deposit have been especially important in South Africa, where gold ores occur in a fairly continuous series from rich to very poor. Methods of taxation are important because gold has provided about 70% of foreign exchange, about 20% of the national income and a large part of government revenues.[13] But in 1940 it was estimated that,

---

[12] U.N., *Econ. Bull. for Europe*, third quarter 1949, 19.
[13] Union of South Africa: Witwatersrand, Mine Natives' Wage Commission *Report*, 1943, 47; Frankel, *op. cit.*, 83, 114.

under the then existing technical and economic conditions, the number of tons of ore likely to be mined would fall about 70% from 1940 to 1960, and 86% from 1940 to 1965. Deeper mining was so costly, and the margin of profit so small, that it would yield little state revenue.[14] Consequently, since 1936 taxation has been adjusted to take account of differences in grade of ore. The 1936 formula provided for no special mining tax where profit was 6% of the gross output of gold; as profits rose as a percentage of gross output, the tax rate rose towards 60% (though that figure was never quite reached). When profit on gross output was 10% the tax rate was 24%, and at 20%, 42%.[15]

In 1947 all taxes took about 72% of the net profits of gold mines. That they have been higher than in other countries[16] may be due either to the greater profitability of the deposits (after allowing for all royalties, costs of land, and other charges), or to the fact that the government has converted to public purposes a greater portion of the underlying value of an exhaustible resource than elsewhere. Since 1940 the financial prospects of the government have been greatly improved by the discovery of new gold deposits on the West Rand and in the Orange Free State (the latter expected to yield gold worth over £3.3 billion). The South African government also imposes special mining taxes on net profits from mining diamonds (22.5%) and base metals (25%).

[14] Union of South Africa: Industrial and Agricultural Requirements Commission *Third Interim Report*, 1941, 52.

[15] The formula for arriving at the rate of tax prior to 1951 was $60 - \dfrac{360}{x}$ where x is the percentage ratio of profit to value of output sold. In 1951 it was proposed to change the ratio to $63 - \dfrac{378}{x}$, to take account of the increased income (of about £2.185 million in 1950), due to sales of gold at a premium. Deductions are permitted for the lease payment and for the amortization of investment at 22½% per year, which latter allowance is a deferment of taxation where the mine continues to operate after all capital has been amortized.

[16] In 1935 taxation took about 42% of taxable profits on gold in the Union of South Africa, 23% in Rhodesia, 18% in Australia, 13 to 19% in Canada, 14 to 18% in the U.S.A., and 12% in West Africa (Evidence of Transvaal Chamber of Mines to Union of South Africa: Departmental Committee on Mining Taxation, 1935; *cit.* Frankel, *op. cit.*, 113). These taxes were not all at special rates applicable only to gold.

Chapter 16

Land Resources

Land differs from minerals in that its use in production does not necessarily cause exhaustion (although it may), and that partly exhausted land can sometimes be regenerated.

A. The Supply of Land

Quantity of land, in economic terms, should be measured by its capacity to contribute to production. Measurement by area is inappropriate because of diversity in the productivity of different acres (Ch. 5). Measurement by market value would be better, but it is far from universally available or perfect. Where land is nationalized (as in Russia), and where sales of land are not permitted (as in parts of Africa), no such measure is available. Even where land may be sold or rented, its value depends partly on taxes specifically on land or land rents. Market values do not separate the value of the land from that of improvements to the land (such as buildings and drainage) or improvements in the general area in which the land is located (such as transport, schools and the like). Such market values, moreover, are obtainable only when land is sold, which may be infrequently, and in imperfectly competitive markets. In the last analysis, the potential net contribution of land to the national product depends on the demand for land generated by the ultimate demand for goods and the means of producing them, the supply of land suitable for each purpose, and the supplies of the other means of production (which may be competitive with or complementary to land in production).

Information about the economic quantity of land in various countries is not available. The proportion of total land area that is cultivable is more useful than a crude area figure. In 1939, for instance, only 7 to 11% of the world's land area was estimated to be cultivable. But the definition of "cultivable" is vague and lacks uniformity among countries. Typically it does not refer to the land that could be economically used under present conditions. "Cultivable" land may include land that could be cultivated if more water were available, or if disease were controlled; for instance, malaria prevents the use of much of the cultivable waste in India, and the tsetse fly and rinderpest have kept out of use much land in central and east Africa. Furthermore, resources are usually necessary to clear the land for cultivation. In some areas this capital has not been invested, because the increase in production might be less than could be obtained by investing the same amount of capital in some other direction. Nor is account always taken of other costs of bringing land into cultivation; deforestation would make more land available in Java and Malaya, but would interfere with the water supply for land now cultivated (as it has in Italy and India). There is more information regarding the amount of cultivated land, but it relates to the utilization of land rather than the quantity that could be utilized.

Although the land potential of a country is difficult to measure, it is possible to identify some of the influences that affect it. Potential productivity per person being influenced by the economic quantity of land per person, the size of the population affects this ratio. Otherwise the quantity of land depends on the original endowment of the country, the extent to which that endowment has been depleted, the cost of utilizing the land, and the demand for its produce.

The original land endowment cannot be explained in economic terms. For agricultural use the structure of the soil (its chemical composition, rockiness, slope, humus, and the like) and climate (particularly moisture and temperature) influence productivity. In other uses, some of these and some additional qualities are important. But subsequent depletion has economic causes as well as consequences. Land has often been cropped so heavily as to exhaust its content of important chemicals or humus. Exhaustion was for long avoided in most parts of the world by moving cultivation when output declined. But it is now important in Mexico, North, Central and South Africa, the Middle East, Argentina, and Malaya.[1] This "mining" of the soil is more serious than before, because there is less land to which cultivation can be moved. Soil fertility, however, can be imported. The agricultural land of Denmark, Holland, and to some extent England has been built up by imports of feed for dairying, and within the U.S.A. milk sheds are being built up at the expense of feed producing areas.

Land productivity may also be reduced by erosion,[2] which differs from exhaustion, although both may be caused by overcropping. Some erosion is due to climatic and geological causes beyond human control, but some

[1] *Economist*, Oct. 21, 1944; *The World Today*, March 1949, 109; Keen, *The Agricultural Development of the Middle East*, 55; U.S. Tariff Commission, *Agricultural, Pastoral and Forest Industries in Argentina*, 194.

[2] Jacks, G. V., and White, *The Rape of the Earth: a World Survey of Soil Erosion*, 1939.

results from overgrazing and the removal of cover crops (such as grass and trees), permitting wind and water to carry away the top soil. Erosion also results from the cultivation of slopes in ways that fail to retard the run-off of water. Erosion may, however, convey soil to other places where it is used. The silt carried down by the Nile is used to fertilize lower parts of the basin. The rice-producing delta areas of the Mississippi, the Nile, and in Burma, India, and Malaya have been built up with eroded soil. But such soil is uneconomically used because it is deeper than is necessary; and much top soil is lost in the sea.

Soil erosion takes place in part of almost every country, although it has been taken seriously only in the last two or three decades. In the U.S.A. half of all the land in the country is said to have been damaged by erosion; the annual present loss equals about 500,000 acres of top soil a year (.014 per cent of total cultivable area), but one-third of the original fertile top soil has disappeared forever. There has been, and still is, much erosion in the Middle East, Java, India, Malaya, Australia, the Union of South Africa, Chile, and, to some extent, in New Zealand. In the distant past, North Africa, the valleys of the Tigris and Euphrates, and large areas in China and India produced enough food for the population, but have now ceased to do so, some having been turned into deserts.[3] In Israel and Jordan, centuries of excessive grazing, the destruction of forests, and cultivation of the hills have so deteriorated the land that grain yields are lower than in any Middle East country.[4] Half of the wheatlands of Australia have suffered from erosion, which is likely to lead to "national calamity" unless drastic action is taken within a decade.[5] In South Africa one-fourth of the original fertility of the soil has been lost owing to concentration on cereal culture and unwise farming practices (partly due to government aid to agriculture).[6] Native reserves in South and East Africa are being seriously exhausted and eroded as a result of population pressure.[7] In Chile about 20% of the arable land has been eroded. Acreage yields have also been declining in Canada, Argentina, and Venezuela. The Russian government announced in October, 1948, a fifteen-year development and reclamation project covering 300 million acres of land, aimed at the elimination of soil erosion and drought and the provision of irrigation and fertilizers.

Failure to maintain the supply of land has a variety of causes. Migratory agriculture, fallowing, and fertilizing have retarded exhaustion. Ero-

[3] *For. Agric.*, Feb. 1953, 28.

[4] Warriner, *Land and Poverty in the Middle East*, 52, 131; U.N., Econ. Surv. Mission for the Middle East *Final Report* II, 3.

[5] Australia: The Rural Reconstruction Commission *Third Report*, 46.

[6] Union of South Africa: Industrial and Agricultural Requirements Commission *Report*, 74.

[7] Kenya, *The Agrarian Problem in Kenya*, 14; Tothill, *Agriculture in Uganda*, 73. Witwatersrand Mine Natives' Wages Commission *Report on Remuneration and Conditions of Employment of Natives on Witwatersrand Gold Mines*, 1943, 9.

sion, being gradual, has often been accepted as unavoidable. But the owner-operator, whether a small farmer or a plantation company, is generally restrained from exhausting his land, if not interested in increasing its productivity. But it is not always in the interest of the owner to maintain his capital. In bad times he may be compelled to "live on his capital" in the land, just as a factory owner in a depressed industry may fail to maintain his plant for good economic reasons. Where land is so heavily populated as to cause poverty, the people may "mine" the land in the effort to keep alive (thereby making it more difficult for their descendents to survive).[8] A calculating owner who anticipates that the future price of the produce of the land will be lower than the present price, or one deciding that future prices are uncertain, may prefer to draw some of the capital from his land. But private property in land does not always induce land maintenance even when it is justifiable on economic grounds. Flood control works, wind breaks, and the like must often be built on a large scale in relation to the size of land holdings, and on land other than that protected. Government action may be necessary. But some governments have been responsible for erosion, as when they encouraged erosive crops in South Africa and Australia. Recently, however, the U.S.A. has discouraged the production of the most erosive crops.

The economic capacity of land depends also on the cost of putting it to use. If these costs exceed the value of the product, the national product would have been greater if these complementary resources had been used elsewhere. Until the latter part of the 19th century, there was unused land in the U.S.A. Taking account of the costs of clearing, cultivation, transport, and the price of crops, it would not have paid to use all this land. Much of the earth's surface was in this state at one time, and considerable parts of Canada, Australia, New Zealand, and South America until recently. The cost of using land varies widely with place, time and method of use. Low labor costs (with or without low wages) increase the productiveness of the land, although they may also reduce the demand for its produce. Cheap capital applied to the land may increase the value of its output by more than the cost of the capital, thus increasing the productivity of the land. The cost of utilization also depends on the location of the land in relation to supplies of materials and markets and on the cost of transport. The more accessible the land, the more productive it is because it requires less of other resources to make a given addition to the national product. Acres that are economically inaccessible may contribute less to well-being than physically poorer acres that are more accessible. But when people move, for instance, to the U.S.A., Canada, South Africa, Australia, New Zealand, and Latin America, they create newly located markets and new sources of supplies, and influence the productivity of previously occupied land.

[8] U.N., *Rural Progress through Cooperatives*, 21.

The economic potential of land depends also on the demand for its products. As land varies in its qualities, the quantity of land suitable for each product relative to the demand for such land affects its economic productivity. The value of the products of the land depends partly on total population (and world population is now increasing faster than in any period of recorded history). The values of particular products depend partly on the distribution of incomes in countries in which the produce may be sold. The rise in real wages in the North Atlantic countries since about the middle of the 19th century has increased the demand for tea, coffee, cocoa, tropical fruits (such as bananas and pineapples), sugar, tobacco, and other such products, and raised the productivity of land suitable for producing them. But the synthesis of substitutes for agricultural products, such as rubber, quinine and many flavorings, reduces the demand for the use of land and its economic productivity. The substitution of high for low buildings in urban areas also economizes the use of land.

Changes in ways of using land also affect its economic potential. Such knowledge has been increasing since the beginning of history at an accelerating pace, particularly since the latter part of the 19th century. Strains of plants and animals better adapted to particular local conditions (for instance, heat and drought resistant strains of cattle in the southern states of the U.S.A., India, and Central Africa), more prolific strains of rice, wheat and corn in various countries, oil yielding plants, and the use of fertilizers and pesticides all make particular types of land physically more productive. But the economic repercussions are complex. Some changes are equivalent to increases in the quantity of land and result in lower prices for products due to lower costs. But increases in population or levels of living may offset this effect.

B. The Utilization of Land

1. THE ACTUAL UTILIZATION OF LAND

The extent to which the full potential of the land is utilized is too complex to measure, partly because the potential is not measurable. Non-agricultural uses take relatively little land in most countries and, therefore, the rate of utilization is largely a matter of the proportion of cultivable land that is utilized for agriculture, and the efficiency of its use.

Over the long sweep of history man has been increasing the land under cultivation. Otherwise he could not have multiplied as he has. In Europe the area of cultivation steadily increased over many centuries; accelerating in the 18th century, when cultivation in the U.S.A. was also expanding. In the 19th century, cultivation was rapidly extended in North America, Australia, South Africa, New Zealand, and Latin America. Japan fed its rapidly increasing population by extending the acreage cultivated by over 40% between 1877 and 1939. Between 1913 and 1938, Russia increased its sown area 20 to 30% within the same boundaries. Nevertheless, among the countries which together have more than 75% of the world's cultivated land, the percentage of cultivated to total land ranges from 49.2% in Poland to 1.7% in Australia (Table 23). In other countries the pro-

TABLE 23

CULTIVATED LAND AS A PERCENTAGE OF TOTAL LAND AREA AND PER
HEAD OF POPULATION IN SELECTED COUNTRIES, ABOUT 1949[*]

	Cultivated Land Area as percentage of total land area	Cultivated Land Area per head of total population (acres)
Canada	2.9	5.29
Australia	1.7	4.71
Argentina	9.3	4.56
United States	22.8	3.13
Iran	10.2	2.47
Soviet Union	7.9	2.43
Spain	35.6	1.65
Poland	49.2	1.47
France	36.3	1.22
India	37.9	.98
Manchuria and Jehol	11.9	.89
Italy	47.9	.77
Germany	42.8	.72
China (excluding Sikang and Sinkiang)	13.8	.29

[*] "Cultivated land" includes land in field crops, gardens, tree and bush crops (excluding uncultivated growth), rotation meadows and fallow land. U.S. Department of Agriculture, *A Graphic Survey of World Agriculture*, 2.

portion is 6% in the Middle East, 12% in Mexico, 7.5% in Chile, 15% in the Union of South Africa, and 16% in Japan. Even when allowance is made for uncultivable land, there appears to be underutilization. In 1939, although 7 to 11% of the world's land area was classified as cultivable, only 4.6 to 7.3% was under cultivation.[9] As to particular areas, most of the cultivable land appears to be in use in Holland, Japan, and much of China, but only about 30% in the Middle East,[10] 60% in India and Pakistan (where 20% of the "cultivated" land was fallow),[11] 22% in Chile, 3.6% in Mexico and 65% in Cuba. In Russia, 80% of cultivable land is cultivated but 20% of the total is fallow.[12]

---

[9] Spengler, "The World's Hunger; Malthus 1948," *Proc. Ac. of Pol. Sci.*, 1949, 65.

[10] Bonné, "Land and Population in the Middle East," V, *Middle East Jour.*, 1951, 55. The lowest percentages are Iran, 20%, Israel, 20%, Turkey, 28%, and Iraq, 30%. Between 1938 and 1949 cultivated acreage increased about 75% in Syria, 20% in Iran, and 10% in Turkey. (U.N., *Rev. of Econ. Cond. in the Middle East*, 1951, 45).

[11] India Cooperative Planning Committee *Report*, 1946, 13; Wadia and Merchant, *op. cit.*, 13.

[12] U.N., *Ec. Bull. for Europe*, Nov. 1951, 25.

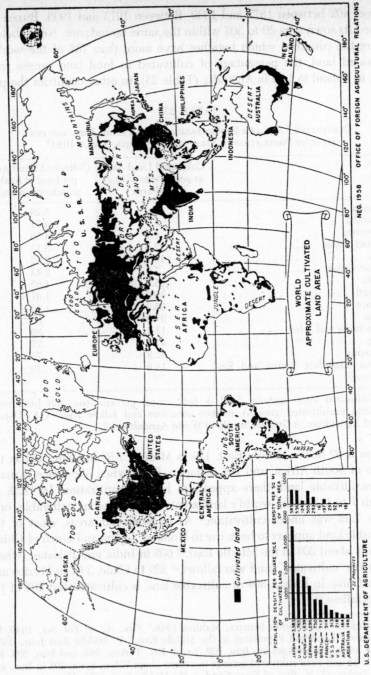

Fig.16. From *For. Agric.*, Feb. 1953, p. 44.

These figures, however, are questionable, largely because of the above-mentioned difficulty of defining "cultivable," and because even "cultivated" is not always clear. Some unused but "cultivable" land is not usable with existing methods of cultivation and resources. The migratory agriculture in many parts of Africa, the West Indies, and among Arab cultivators in North Africa utilizes a relatively small proportion of the total land each year, but it could not all be used simultaneously without more fertilizer. Similarly where land is used for migratory grazing, herds being moved over wide areas to follow rainfall and pasture, the land could not all be pastured all the time. Fallowing (a variation upon migratory agriculture) is necessary under some methods of cultivation. In parts of the Middle East and India only about one-third of the land is under cultivation at one time (in Iraq only 20%).[13] In some areas, however, the crop area (the cultivated area multiplied by the number of crops a year) exceeds the cultivated area because more than one crop is obtained each year from the same land. Such multiple cropping is possible only where there is a long growing season, with water available throughout a large part of the year. Much rice, for instance, is so produced in Java, Burma, India and Japan. The change from basin to canal irrigation in Egypt (Ch. 17) has raised the average number of crops from less than one to two a year in lower Egypt.[14]

The extent of the utilization of land depends not only on the amount of usable land in use but also on the effectiveness of its use. Physical output varies. It is twice as high in North and Central America as in Africa, and has been increasing faster in the former than in the latter. But elsewhere differences in yield per acre are not so great (see Table 15), partly, however, because regional figures average out wide local differences. The yield of wheat in a large number of countries in 1947 ranged from 250% of the average in New Zealand, 225% in Denmark and 222% in the Netherlands to 68% in Greece and 49% in India. The yield of rice ranged from 280% of the average in Australia to 90% in Burma. Yields fluctuate considerably from year to year with weather conditions, although much less where permanent irrigation is available. But departures from maximum attained yield are no measure of the extent to which the land use falls short of its potential. The potential is not known. Different pieces of land have different potentials. Economic conditions justify the application of varying quantities of other resources to land in both agricultural and other uses. In agriculture output per acre is high in China, Japan, and Egypt where labor is intensively used, often without much capital. But it is also high in New Zealand and Denmark where land is good but considerable capital is used. Output per acre is low in India in spite of the intensive use of labor. Output per acre has been greatly increased in the U.S.A.,

13 Warriner, op. cit., 101.

14 Bonné, op. cit., 200.

parts of western Europe, Egypt, and Japan by the intensive use of fertilizer. Japan fed its rapidly increasing population during the earlier stages of its development largely by irrigation and the more intensive use of chemical fertilizers that increased output per acre from 1878 to 1938 65% for rice, 50% for wheat, 50% for barley, although the area under cultivation also increased. Changes in the allocation of land to crops and in methods of cultivation, including the application of capital, have increased the output per acre of all the major crops in the U.S.A. about 50% between 1930 and 1950; previously such changes had been mainly offset by erosion and soil mining.[15] In Russia grain yields per acre have probably increased 25 to 33% during the past 40 years (mostly in the past 20 years).[16]

2. Influences Affecting Utilization

Although it is impossible to measure the extent to which the full potential of land is utilized, it is evident that it is overused when erosion and exhaustion reduce its future potential. But in some areas it is underutilized. This state of affairs is ultimately traceable to government policies, since all governments establish some arrangements affecting land use (except where land is not scarce).

a. Conditions of Land Tenure[17]

Primitive societies may hold their land in common, e.g., in Africa[18] and some Pacific islands. The group as a whole has more or less respected rights to a defined tract. Individual access depends on the organization of the group. There may be well-understood rules, or the chief or elders may decide which land each individual may cultivate.[19] Control by custom (or by the embryonic state) sometimes extends also to the total amount of land to be cultivated each year, and when and what to plant. The amount of land cultivated is often traditional, but if the crop is insufficient (possibly because the community is growing), the chief, medicine man or elders may decide that more land shall be cultivated, if it is available. Decisions as to when and what to plant and the date of harvesting are often also made by the chief or medicine man (who acquires skill in measuring the passage of the seasons and forecasting seasonal changes in weather). The allocation of work is typically determined by tradition, the women and girls usually being responsible for most agricultural labor. Hours of labor are set partly by custom, but sometimes by the medicine man. The woman who does not abide by these arrangements may be ostracized or sent back to her family. This, particularly in Africa, would often require

---

15 U.S. Dept. Agric., *Agricultural Statistics 1947, Crop Production 1948.*
16 U.N., *Econ. Bull. Europe* III, No. 2, 30.
17 U.N., *Rural Progress through Cooperatives,* Ch. 4.
18 Tothill, *Agriculture in Uganda,* 24 ff.
19 Franklin, *Economics in South Africa,* 1948, 130.

her family to return her "bride price."[20] These arrangements survive generally where methods of cultivation are primitive and stationary, and where population is not too dense. Changes in these conditions may lead to attempts to seize more land or control population, or to changes in the system. Increasing population pressure, coupled with rising economic expectations, can be met only by increasing production, particularly, but not only, in agriculture. In parts of West Africa an enclosure movement has occurred.[21] The introduction of commercial crops like cocoa, palm oil, and cotton has encouraged freehold possession (e.g., in the Gold Coast), or the conversion of family holdings into African estates worked by hired labor (e.g., in the Gold Coast, Nigeria and Uganda).[22] Individual ownership of land, although likely to facilitate the fuller use of land in agriculture, destroys the social structure (which makes little provision for non-agricultural production). Furthermore, in the conversion process the more astute members of the village may dispossess others.[23] In French Equatorial Africa *paysannat indigène* schemes aimed at improving agricultural methods are based partly on communal and partly on individual ownership of land.[24]

Communal ownership survives also in other societies. In the Middle East, as nomadic groups have turned to settled agriculture, collective grazing rights have been converted into collective cultivation rights (*Mushaa* or *Masha*). The individual owns no particular piece of land, but cultivates an area for a few years, then moves to another in accordance with a community system of rotation (e.g., in parts of Arab Palestine, Iran, Turkey, and Saudi-Arabia). Attempts to abolish the system since 1918 have not been very successful. Like the feudal system of land distribution it avoids discrimination among members of the village where they are unable to agree on any equation of good and bad land for purposes of permanent allotment.[25] In Morocco there are 12 million acres of collective tribal lands (about 20% are cultivable without loss of pasture, but only 10% are cultivated). The *Mahalwari* system of tenure prevalent in the United Provinces, Central Provinces, and Punjab in India, involves the joint ownership of a village area by a group of families, usually of common descent, and joint responsibility for land taxes. Cultivation rights are usually separate and secure.[26] In Java the Dutch colonial government recognized communal ownership in 1870, but subsequently sought (with

---

[20] Kenya, *The Kikuyu Lands*, 1946, 21, 56, 61.
[21] U.N., *Land Reform*, 28.
[22] U.N., *Rev. Econ. Cond. in Africa*, 1949-50, 14.
[23] Pim, A., *Colonial Agricultural Production*, 172, 173.
[24] U.N., *Land Reform*, 32.
[25] *For. Agric.*, Dec. 1950; Bonné, *op. cit.*, 107, 117, 197; Warriner, *op. cit.*, 66, 91.
[26] U.N., *Land Reform*, 52.

only partial success) to substitute private ownership.[27] Collective ownership also survives in some Caribbean countries.[28]

In Mexico such ownership came into existence as a result of inheritance,[29] but was abolished in 1857. But the redistribution of land since
1934 was aimed at restoring communal village ownership through the
ejido (which harks back to the pre-Spanish Indian land holding system and
the medieval commune of Spain). Redistributed lands of the former *lati-
fundia* were granted to the *ejido* or community rather than to individuals,
for cultivation by common agreement, and, as far as possible, by joint effort, although some land was also granted to individual members of the
ejido. But on some *ejidos* where cultivation was carried on in common
and the produce shared equally, the more energetic members objected
and individuals were allotted land. Now the majority of *ejidos* holding
unirrigated land permit individual cultivation, but in each *ejido* a committee decides the crops to be grown and investments to be made in
local improvements (e.g., schools and small irrigation projects), and
special banks for providing credit to *ejidos* exercise considerable control
over the crops grown and the use of credit.[30] In 1940, 47.4% of all crop
land, and 56.2% of all irrigated land, was in *ejidal* holdings.[31]

The land held under the older communal systems has often been progressively impoverished, although often because of population pressure.
Such systems hamper the initiative and enterprise of the individual because of his lack of continued interest in any piece of land and his
inability to raise capital by mortgage, and they obstruct large-scale cooperative operation. The new communal system in Mexico has been moderately successful, but it has also become less communal.

Feudal systems have originated mainly in the need to provide for
governmental functions in the absence of a developed money economy.
In western Europe the king or paramount chief was responsible for defense and internal order, but entitled to a share of the produce from the
area protected. Below the overlord one or more strata of intermediaries
contributed services and supplies for fighting, and received services and
produce from cultivators, either directly or indirectly. Land was allocated
among the serfs on the manor in return for a prescribed amount of labor
on the lord's land. The arable land was typically divided into three fields,
two of which were cultivated every year. Each year each field to be cultivated was divided into strips that were distributed by lot, a typical cultivator receiving more than one strip. The cultivator also had a right to
pasture cattle and cut wood on common lands. Where these were relatively
scarce, they were rationed or "stinted." The cultivator had some incentive

---

[27] Pim, *Colonial Agricultural Production*, 39.
[28] U.N., *Land Reform*, 52.
[29] MacBride, *The Land Systems of Mexico*, 103.
[30] U.N., *Land Reform*, 52, 60, 82.
[31] *For. Agric.*, Sept. 1951.

to maximize the output of the strips allotted to him. But the effort towards equity in distribution obstructed improvement. The cultivator, having no continuity of tenure, had no incentive to improve the land. Furthermore, labor was wasted going from strip to strip, and land was wasted because of the margins between the strips and the practice of fallowing. Even the arrangements for cooperative plowing involved control of the time of planting, and restricted individual initiative. But the more important reason for lack of progress was the lack of knowledge of better methods or the means for adopting them.

This system, possibly developed by the Germanic tribes, was common throughout Europe from the ninth or tenth century. It provided the security necessary to convert half-nomadic peoples into settled communities. But with the beginnings of the development of towns and a money economy, in the 13th century serfs began to press for the conversion of their labor rents into money rents.[32] The system was too rigid to be adapted to changing circumstances. In 1348 the Black Death killed about a third of the people in England, changed the land-labor ratio in favor of labor, and compelled manorial lords to accede to cash renting to retain a labor force. In 1381 the peasants revolted unsuccessfully against serfdom. But inflation in the 14th and 15th centuries reduced the real incomes of landlords who had rented farms for cash rents for long periods, and they, rather than the peasants, initiated the enclosure of a few of the open fields during the 16th century and until 1625. Commercial farming appeared during the 17th century. Sheep rearing was stimulated by a rise in wool prices, but landowners began to write on farm management and invest in drainage, soil improvement, and better live-stock. These developments resulted in the major enclosure of some seven million acres from 1760 to 1843, facilitated by a Parliament dominated by landowners, who were again being squeezed between rising prices and fixed rents. By 1850 few open fields were left.

The feudal system persisted longer in western Europe. An advanced horticulture was introduced during the 15th century around some of the flourishing cities in north Italy, the Rhineland, Flanders, and Brabant. But generally the open-field system continued until the middle of the 18th century, when the growth of urban industry and of population caused food prices to rise. Too inflexible to adjust to these new conditions, the system began to follow the same path as in Britain. In France, by the time of the Revolution much land was virtually owned by peasants or held on perpetual cash leases. The Revolutionary government abolished all remaining feudal tenures, and peasants holding land on such tenures acquired full ownership. The sale of the confiscated properties of the church and of emigrés, helped the landless peasantry very little. Some of the larger farmers of ecclesiastical lands bought the land they had previ-

---

[32] Clapham, *A Concise Economic History of Britain*, 99, 109 ff.

ously rented and some such land went to the wealthier peasantry, but the larger part went to the bourgeoisie, who first rented it out on a share-rental basis. In the Rhine country, manorial rights were converted into cash rents in the Middle Ages: scattered strips were consolidated and individual peasant farming emerged. In southern Sweden, Denmark, Schleswig-Holstein, and much of Germany enclosures began in the late 18th century and continued into the 19th century, usually under government control. Although in western Europe landowners typically rented their land for cash, those in southern Europe rented it for a share of the crop.[33]

In Russia, serfdom was legally abolishd in 1861, when the peasants obtained possession of the 50% of the land for which they had previously been required to pay a high compensation to the state over forty-nine years. The responsibility for these payments was on the community as a whole, and members could not leave without paying off their share. The community (or *mir*) had the right of periodic redistribution of land according to the number of "eaters" in each peasant household. Separate scattered plots continued to obstruct the intensification of production. About 80% of all land in Russia was thus collectively held during the later years of the 19th century, and little or no attempt was made to consolidate holdings. Households followed a common routine of seeding, harvesting, fallowing, and manuring. After widespread peasant insurrections between 1902 and 1905, the Stolypin Reform in 1906 replaced community ownership with private ownership, which helped mainly the stronger peasants.[34]

In Japan feudal tenures from the 16th century until 1869 were somewhat similar to those in Europe, except that the crop and not the land was shared, and the predominant rice cultivation precluded a threefold rotation of crops. The ruling Tokugawa family owned over 20% of the land, and local lords (*daimyos*) the remainder. The peasants cultivated the soil, often in strips scattered around the village, and delivered 40 to 50% of the rice to the lord, together with other payments in kind and service. They were forbidden to leave the land and go to the towns, and the type of crop, as well as types of clothing and housing, was controlled by the lord.[35]

In the Middle East, feudalism has existed intermittently and in various forms over many centuries. A money economy existed for some 600 years, with money taxes and money payments to soldiers and civil officials. But when this organization collapsed in the 13th century, military service was obtained by feudal grants to former tax farmers (or those who had usurped tax revenues).[36] The feudal landholders (perhaps because they were originally tax farmers) have regarded themselves as revenue (or rent) col-

---

[33] Turner, "Economic Discontent in Medieval Europe," *Tasks of Economic History*, 1948, 91.

[34] Florinsky, M. T., *Russia: a History and an Interpretation*, 888, 893, 1215.

[35] Allen, G. C., *A Short Economic History of Modern Japan*, 10.

[36] Bonné, *op. cit.*, 125, 137.

lectors with no concern for the use of the land. In 1839 the Ottoman Empire reestablished the state's right of ownership over former feudal properties, but with little result because influential individuals had much of the land registered in their names. The extreme moral and economic degradation of the *fellah* (peasant) has been attributed to this system, although the feudal relation of landowner and tenant does not everywhere result in such degradation. Even now semi-feudal relations are often established in areas where governments fail to protect cultivators and their crops from invasion by nomads. Villagers place themselves under the protection of a *sheikh*, agreeing to pay him a share of their produce (e.g., in Iraq).

Feudalism was never established in the countries newly settled from Europe in recent centuries, (e.g., the U.S.A., Canada, Australia, New Zealand, and South Africa). Experiments with feudal tenures in the U.S.A. (mostly in New York State) failed because the country vitally needed to attract labor, which feudalism could not do.

Private property in land, now widespread, has usually emerged as economies are monetized. Services to the state are replaced by taxes and labor services by wages or rents, according to the owner's choice either to operate the land himself or to allow others to do so. But economies can be monetized without private property in land (e.g., Russia). In fact, private property produces different results in different countries because of differences in the behavior of governments and owners.

In western Europe, private ownership emerged out of feudalism in the ways above described. In the U.S.A. and other newly settled areas, private ownership was dominant from the beginning of settlement. In most Latin American countries indigenous systems of land tenure were generally replaced by semi-feudal arrangements that gradually developed into individual holdings (Ch. 29). In India prior to the arrival of the British, land had generally been held by villages, subject to the payment of taxes to the king.[37] The East India Company took over the rights to taxes in the areas directly governed. But it recognized previous tax farmers and others as virtual owners of land (*zamindari*), subject to payment of taxes. The *zamindari* cultivate about 15% of their estates. Much of the remainder is held by individuals who have permanent leases (i.e., salable rights of occupation subject to fixed cash payments to the *zamindari*). Both the *zamindari* and these permanent lessees rent much of their land to sharecroppers, often through intermediaries (sometimes as many as 16). Outside the areas of *zamindari* estates, there are *ryotowari* and *mahalwari* systems. Under the *ryotowari* system, the actual occupants are liable for taxes but they also rent much of their land on sharecropping tenancies. Under the *mahalwari* system, a group of families is liable for the taxation on the village lands, but the members can cultivate or lease their land. The taxes

[37] Wrench, G. T., *Restoration of the Peasantries*, 56.

on the *zamindari* estates were fixed in cash in perpetuity, and on other lands they are periodically reassessed to yield in principle about 50% of the net produce of the land (Ch. 29). Thus, there is substantially private property in land.

In Japan the abolition of feudalism in 1869 gave the peasants absolute ownership of the lands previously held on feudal tenures. In 1872 the former compulsory deliveries of rice were replaced by money taxes which amounted to about 40% of net product.[38] Owners were free to choose their crops and methods of cultivation. But the new freedom to buy and sell land resulted in a 100% increase in the proportion of land cultivated by tenants between 1867 and 1887 (rents varying from 25 to 80% of the crop).[39] In China until the fall of the Nationalist government in 1949, most land was held as individual property,[40] although in the past private ownership appears to have alternated with government allocation of land (Ch. 29).

The essence of private ownership is the power of the owner to decide the use of the land, and his assurance that the results of his decisions will accrue to him. In parts of the Middle East, Bolivia, Colombia, Venezuela, and Haiti[41] there is more private property in principle than in practice because titles are insecure. Also, sometimes, in the Middle East[42] crops are seized by raiders.

Private ownership can achieve the maximum use of land in a market economy only if owners seek to maximize their income from land in the long run. An owner may use the land or allow others to use it, provided they pay a rent which absorbs the net produce of the land when used to its full capacity after payment for labor and other productive factors at their market rate.

Private ownership has operated generally in this way in western Europe and North America, Australia, New Zealand, and South Africa, although it is increasingly difficult to separate the effects of private property from the effects of government action (including taxation). But elsewhere there are many departures from ideal operation. Large landowners have often been unwilling to supply the energy necessary to maximize the produce of the land. They may receive enough income to meet their desires without such effort; they balance leisure against money income (a balancing assumed to be made also by workers). In Argentina and other parts of Latin America, land has been prized for its own sake and not fully used.[43] Small owners, however, may also be inefficient. Their holdings may be too small to permit use of the most efficient methods, including the use of draft

---

[38] Allen, G. C., *A Short Economic History of Modern Japan*, 27, 35.

[39] Allen, *op. cit.*, 59.

[40] Lee, S. C., "The Heart of China's Problem: The Land Tenure System," XXX *Jour. of Farm Econ.*, May, 1948; 259.

[41] U.N., *Land Reform*, 25; *For. Agric.*, Dec. 1950.

[42] Bonné, *op. cit.*, 131.

[43] U.N., *Land Reform*, 10.

animals or mechanical equipment. In much of India occupancy right-holders have from 4.4 to 11.7 acres, usually producing (owing to differences in fertility) around two tons of cereals.[44] In China in 1937, 67% of land holdings were less than 2.1 acres.[45] In Japan, holdings have been small but there and in China production per acre has been very high. But it has already been pointed out that lack of capital more than the size of holdings obstructs improvements in production, and, therefore, reduces the incentive to assemble larger land holdings. But social forces often tend to reduce the size of holdings. Inheritance, accompanied by the practice of dividing land among sons, has caused a progressive increase in the number of the smallest holdings in India in the past. Foreclosures upon the land of the smallest holders, who get into debt, has had an offsetting effect and tended to maintain the number of large holdings.[46] Japan has been saved from this progressive reduction in holdings by the custom of primogeniture. Redistributions of land by governments have also created uneconomically small holdings which, however, are in process of reconsolidation in eastern Europe.

Owners deciding to allow their land to be worked by tenants have in a general way charged rents sufficiently high to stimulate full utilization in developed capitalist countries. But in the agrarian countries rents are often customary and slow to change. They are also alleged to be excessive. Undoubtedly they are often too high to permit the tenant to obtain a decent living. But where all the available land is leased, rents are evidently not too high to prevent full utilization. The economic rent is high because the pressure of population causes intense competition for land. If the government bought the land in India and lowered rents or established maximum rents by law, it might subsidize the agricultural workers (Ch. 29), but it would have to allocate land on some other basis than ability to pay the rent and might not improve cultivation.[47]

The economic rent calculated within all the existing conditions (including the other terms of the lease) may, however, be less than that which could be paid if these other conditions were changed. The yield of the land (and its rent) might be increased if landowners would improve the land and train the workers. In fact, there is widespread criticism of landowners who make no such efforts and are mere inert rent collectors. In central and southern Italy large landowners have contributed nothing to cultivation. In the Middle East the gulf between town and village life is far wider than in Europe. "Islam is a civilization without a rural basis."

---

44 India: Famine Inquiry Commission *Final Report*, 254.

45 Lee, "The Heart of China's Problem: The Land Tenure System," XXX *Jour. of Farm Econ.*, May, 1948, 267. 33% of all holdings were less than 0.75 acres. In the fertile Red River Basin in 1942 4.1% of all holdings were less than 0.15 acres and 70% less than 1.5 acres.

46 India: Famine Inquiry Commission, *op. cit.*, 258, 264.

47 *Ibid.*, 272.

"Though the wealthy own land, there is no landed aristocracy and no sense of responsibility attaching to land ownership."[48] In India the *zamindari,* or large estate owners, have contributed so little to agriculture that they have been condemned by numerous provincial governments,[49] and recently steps have been taken to eliminate them (Ch. 29). The subrenting of land through a series of layers of intermediaries (subinfeudation) has seriously obstructed any desire on the part of Indian landowners to improve land. Where leases prevent the raising of rents for a long time, investment is not attractive. But the contention that rents are raised because so many layers of interests in the land have to be remunerated is less justified. More, probably, the rent is shared among more interests because of the wide margin between the taxes paid by the *zamindar* (which are his payment for control of the land) and the economic rent which can be charged to the peasant.[50] Similar subinfeudation exists in Malaya and in the Middle East under the *serkal* and *wakil* systems. But there remains the question whether private investments in land would be economical under present conditions.

The conditions of leases also affect the use of land. The size of rented holdings has not been notably uneconomical in North Atlantic countries, except perhaps in the sharecropping areas in the U.S.A. In Britain tenants are encouraged to improve their holdings by the legal liability (under the Agriculture Act of 1947) of landowners to compensate tenants at the end of their tenancy for the unexpired value of improvements made by tenants. A tenant who farms well and pays his rent cannot be ejected unless the owner intends to farm the land himself. In the Middle East, India, Malaya, and China, the smallness of holdings is doubtless due to the causes which also permit small-scale owner cultivation. Short leases also reduce the incentive to the cultivator to improve the land. The length of leases is not a serious problem in the North Atlantic countries, except in the sharecropping of the southern states of the U.S.A. But in the Middle East, India, Malaya, and parts of China leases are typically for one year or less with no security of renewal. In China in the past, though more than half all tenancies have been annual, some 10% have been permanent. The tenant has a permanent salable right to use the land, subject to payment of rent. In the Middle East, however, tenancies are often for one crop, which may be less than a season.[51] But again the poverty of the cultivator is the overriding reason for failure to improve the land.

Land and agricultural labor are often inefficiently used because of the fragmentation of ownership.[52] The cultivator-owner, but sometimes also

---

48 Warriner, *op. cit.,* 24, 120; *For. Agric.,* Dec. 1950.
49 India: Famine Inquiry Commission, *op. cit.,* 274.
50 *Ibid.,* 271, 282.
51 Warriner, *op. cit.,* 85.
52 U.N., *Rural Progress through Cooperatives,* 24.

the tenant, cultivates a number of widely separated plots.[53] Such fragmentation is not confined to underdeveloped countries. It occurs in Norway, Switzerland, Italy, France, the Netherlands and Germany. In the Netherlands legislation facilitating the consolidation of holdings was passed in 1910 and 1924, and in 1950 the government, in cooperation with farmers' organizations, was reallocating some 2.5 million acres.[54] In Heftrich in West Germany, one farmer owned 30 acres of land in 220 scattered pieces, requiring 300 miles of travel to reach all of them; 17 farm owners together owned 10,000 plots. These holdings were being consolidated in 1951.[55] In Norway a redistribution court assists in the consolidation of holdings.[56] After 1918, 47% of all farms in Poland had arable land in scattered plots.[57] Fragmentation is also common in the Middle East and India. In northeastern Syria some plots are only a few feet wide and a mile long. In some Arab villages in Palestine in 1944 only 6% of the holdings were in a single plot, the average having nine plots.[58] In India owners have typically one to five plots, although some have 40.[59]

Fragmentation often results from the subdivision of land (particularly when it is inherited) and the manner of subdivision. Inheritors often take a fraction of each plot to be sure that they get a fair share of the total in terms of productivity. Fragmentation is accentuated by the expansion of cultivation irregularly over waste lands, and in India by the break-up of the joint-family system, with its custom of cultivation in common. Both Hindu and Mohammedan laws of succession required succession to all heirs equally, and English judges showed a predilection for individual succession. Fragmentation also results sometimes when communal is converted into individual ownership (e.g., in the Middle East) and the members of the community are unable to agree on a fair distribution of land in consolidated plots. And even where holdings have been consolidated, with great effort, the laws of inheritance and the freedom of the owner to sell often lead to refragmentation.[60] Finally, even the redistribution of land in eastern Europe after 1945 resulted in fragmented holdings (e.g., in Hungary). Fragmentation may assist the cultivator to produce a variety of crops, although for this purpose, he need not have more plots than there are types of soil. But it involves waste of time, money, and effort, restrains improvement, enforces uniformity of crop, and restricts the growing of fodder crops because the animals are put out to graze after harvesting.

[53] U.N., *Land Reform*, 11.

[54] *For. Agric.*, June 1951.

[55] *Ibid.*, Jan. 1952.

[56] *Ibid.*, March 1952.

[57] Morgan (Ed.), *The Agricultural Systems of Middle Europe*, 263.

[58] Warriner, *op. cit.*, 64; *For. Agric.*, Dec. 1950.

[59] Wadia and Merchant, *op. cit.*, 170; India: Famine Inquiry Commission, *op. cit.*, 261.

[60] Keene, *op. cit.*, 14; India: Cooperative Planning Commission *Report*, 24.

Where land is placed in religious or family trusts, transfers have been complicated and improvement obstructed. In the Middle East such trust lands (*Wagf* or *Waqf*) cannot be sold or divided or their use changed. The system is less common in Turkey than in most Moslem countries, but a law of 1949 in Syria and 1952 in Egypt requires such family property to be distributed among the legal heirs.

Unrestricted private property also permits rights of different kinds over the same land (e.g., the right to utilize the land, to water, and even to the trees on the land) to pass into different hands. In the Middle East, "an individual may own one-fifth of a date tree which is on someone else's land, one-seventh of another which is on his own land, some of the part-owners may be local cultivators and the remainder residents in a distant town." Improvements in methods are almost impossible when, for instance, to replace an existing tree by a better one would first require agreement among all the part-owners.[61]

b. State Policies Affecting Utilization

State control of land use is comparable to communal ownership. Under communal systems, however, the public control is usually by smaller governmental units. The state may either restrict rights under private property systems or exercise full property rights itself.

States restrict private rights for a variety of reasons. Erosion and exhaustion of the soil reduce agricultural incomes and generate political pressures and yet are often beyond the power of landowners to remedy. Although this problem is most serious in the less developed, overpopulated countries they have so far taken the least action. In the more developed countries, and notably the U.S.A., the government has provided windbreaks and dams, reforested upland areas to retard water runoff, discouraged the cultivation of the most erosive crops, and reduced overgrazing on public lands. A few governments require efficient cultivation (which is not easy to define) as a condition of continued occupation of the land. The British government, under pressure to increase domestic food production, was empowered during the war of 1939-45 to dispossess inefficient farmers; this power was continued in the Agriculture Act of 1947. Efficiency is appraised by County Agriculture Committees consisting of representatives of farmers, unions of agricultural workers, and landowners, as well as public representatives, but a farmer may appeal to the Agricultural Land Tribunal. A dispossessed landowner is entitled to compensation and the government may purchase his land. The tenancy of an inefficient tenant may also be ended. Until late 1948 only 40 farmers had been dispossessed and they were not farmers in the proper sense.[62] In Greece, land redistributed by the government is

---

61 Keene, *op. cit.*, 15.
62 U.N., *Rural Progress through Cooperatives*, 21.

held subject to the recipient himself cultivating the land properly.[63] In Australia it has been recommended that, while private ownership of land should be the basis of land control, the government should be empowered to resume land if the owner refuses to develop it effectively or to accept required soil conservation, fire prevention, noxious weed, and insect control practices.[64] In some colonial areas where expanding populations press on the food supply (e.g., Southern Rhodesia and Fiji), governments have attempted to make good husbandry a condition of access to land. Such conditions have been established in parts of Southern Rhodesia available for native settlement, but not in the areas set aside in the constitution for the exclusive use of the indigenous population. But increasing pressure on these lands has led to discussion of the necessity for imposing similar conditions there.[65]

Some governments have attempted to force unused land into use by taxation or compulsion to rent. A Cuban law of 1948 provides that unless land is being farmed by the owners or by tenants, the owner must pay an increased tax, or rent the land in plots of not more than 167 acres each to the first farmer or collective group of farmers applying. The rent is fixed at 6% of the registered value of the land, and the lease may be from 3 to 10 years. The Act, however, excludes cane growing land and cattle land if enough cattle are being raised upon it. In Guatemala land left fallow is liable to seizure for distribution among landless peasants. Under this law the government expropriated 85% of one of the large estates of the United Fruit Company in 1953, although the Company claimed that 80% of all its holdings in the country were in use and that part of the remainder was needed as a reserve against natural wastage in banana growing. Finally, government action increasing the rewards of agriculture generally increases the utilization of land. But it does not increase the national income where it directs an uneconomically large proportion of all resources into agriculture, and possibly into branches of agriculture that are uneconomical and cause soil erosion and exhaustion (e.g., in the Union of South Africa).

The government may own considerable tracts in countries where private or local communal ownership prevails generally, more particularly in colonial areas where only part of the land was in use (or regarded as being in use) when the country was annexed. In general, governments do not impede, if they do not actively promote, the use of this land.

Complete state ownership of land (as in Russia) empowers the state to control all aspects of land utilization. The government in Russia has been under pressure to achieve the full use of land in order to provide surpluses of agricultural produce to feed a rapidly growing industrial

---

[63] *For. Agric.*, Aug. 1950.
[64] Australia: The Rural Reconstruction Commission *Ninth Report*, 60.
[65] Pendered Report, 53.

population. The arrangements affecting the use of land are different from those under private property but analogous (Ch. 6, 8). The cultivators, although they pay no rent, must (like a tenant on a share-rent) deliver a specified part of their crops to the state. The methods of specifying the part of crop to be handed over have been adjusted to make the compulsory deliveries dependent as nearly as possible on the potential of the land resources made available to them. The cultivators are, therefore, like tenants, dependent upon the balance of their crop for their own well-being. The stimulus to utilize the land fully is, therefore, comparable to that in capitalist countries. But in addition the state prescribes targets for the output of various crops and animals and enforces them, through the tractor stations as far as possible. Finally, it induces adherence to its general program by the offer of non-monetary honors and, in the last resort, by coercion.

C. Allocation of Land among Uses

The major uses of land are for agriculture (including forestry), dwellings, industrial use, mining (where some surface is needed for operation), transport, and recreation. The fullest utilization of land requires an allocation among these uses, such that the marginal value product in all is uniform. But no information is available for appraising allocation among crops or among agricultural and non-agricultural uses. Differences in allocation among uses partly explain, however, why the amount of land per head of the population is not closely correlated with national income per person. Land generally supports more people in industrial and urban uses than in agricultural uses. The Netherlands, Britain, and Belgium all have dense populations, but are industrialized and have high incomes. But Egypt, also with a high density, has little industry and low income. The U.S.A., however, has low density, high industrialization, and high income, whereas much of Africa south of the Sahara and Latin America have low density, little industry, and low income (Table 24).

Land is allocated by those who have power to dispose of it. Where there is private ownership and the owner uses or permits the use of land for the purposes which pay the highest profit or rent, the land is allocated according to its productiveness in each use, productiveness being defined in terms which accept the existing distribution of incomes and the pattern of prices for the products of land. But it has already appeared that there is considerable doubt whether owners in all countries actively seek the most remunerative uses of their land.

Where the state owns all land, it directly decides the uses to which various plots are to be put. In Russia these decisions are derived from the over-all plan of production. From this plan follow decisions where to build plants, railways, housing, where to establish mines, what land is to be used for agriculture, and the agricultural use to which it is to be

TABLE 24*

POPULATION DENSITY AND DEVELOPMENT

Country	Population p. sq. kilometre of total area (1950)	Urban Population as % of total	Culti-vated Land as % of total	Rural Popu-lation p. sq. kilometre of cultivated land
Highly industralized— urban concentration				
Netherlands	312	55 (1947)	68	182
England & Wales	291	81 (1951)	65	85
Belgium	283	63 (1947)	57	181
Germany (Fed. Rep.)	194	71 (1950)	58	97
Little industrialized— dense population in agricul-ture				
Egypt (settled area)	538	30 (1947)	2.5	542
Puerto Rico	249	41 (1950)	45	327
Ceylon	115	15 (1946)	22	451
India	113	17 (1951)	46	238
More developed but low gen-eral density—very low rural density				
United States	19	64 (1950)	39	18
Argentina	6	63 (1947)	11	20
Canada	1	58 (1951)	7	16
Australia	1	69 (1947)	2.4	13
Less developed—low general density—high density on agricultural land				
Mexico	13	35 (1940)	5	164
Union of S. Africa	10	42 (1951)	5	119
Honduras	10	31 (1951)	4	189
Brazil	6	37 (1951)	2.8	140

* U.N., *Prelim. Report on World Social Situation, 1952, 5.*

put. State-owned land in countries where most land is privately owned is not unimportant. In Britain there is considerable crown land, and government (central and local) holdings are important in most west European countries. Some is rented in the same way as private land. In Scandinavia, Germany and France and, more recently, in Britain, much is forest land. Some is waste. In Syria, Iran, and Iraq the government has much power to control the use of the land. In Syria much is state domain although controlled in fact in large blocks by absentees. In Iraq only .5% is privately owned, 36% is more or less permanently leased, and 58% leased annually. In Egypt about 30% of the land was state owned in 1949.[66]

When an outside power takes over a territory, it may take over some

[66] *For. Agric.*, Dec. 1950; Bonné *op. cit.*, 116; *La Revue d'Egypte Economique et Financière*, March 3, 1951.

or all of the land. In the U.S.A., Canada, Australia, New Zealand, and South Africa, the government claimed unoccupied land and subsequently transferred it to railroad corporations and individuals. In the U.S.A., a huge public domain was cut up and distributed among some 4.5 million relatively small farms between 1860 and 1930. Thus most of the more productive land became private property. But in colonial areas the governing power has typically taken control of all land (explicitly or implicitly acknowledging native occupation and custom), or taken control at least of unoccupied land. France and Belgium declared vacant and the property of the state all land not under cultivation in their colonial areas in Africa. In Tanganyika and northern Nigeria all land is subject to government disposition for the benefit of the native population, no title being valid without government consent, the government having announced that it is not intended to invalidate native rights. In Kenya all land is crown land except that already alienated (and definite areas have been set aside as native reserves). In part of the Gold Coast land rights are subject to no superior control by the state.[67] The Dutch government took control of all lands unoccupied by the native population when it entered Java.

Governments have used the lands thus acquired in various ways. In Java, Malaya, West and central Africa, some has been leased or granted outright to foreign individuals or plantations. When the Belgian government assumed control of the Congo in 1908, 11.5% of the total land area had been granted under concessions. This proportion was later reduced to 7.2% (most of which was in the most favored areas).[68] In French Equatorial Africa, about 66% of the land area was granted to about 40 corporations, but in 1926 it was provided that such concessions would be limited to 10,000 hectares each. The Dutch colonial government granted to foreign-holders private estates on "unoccupied" lands in Java, but by 1931 it had repurchased half of them. Subsequent criticism of plantations has caused most colonial governments in Africa to cease such grants. As present concessions (which are not all operated as plantations) expire, the government of the Belgian Congo intends to replace them with semi-cooperative forms of organization.[69] Colonial governments have made no experiments with state farms. The ill-fated ground-nut project of the British Overseas Food Corporation was a government project, but it was intended to be replaced by a cooperative if it succeeded.

The intrusion of colonial governments into local arrangements for controlling the use of land has had serious economic effects on indigenous populations. Some of the land classified as "unoccupied" was in fact necessary to the continuance of shifting agriculture that was the basis of

[67] Pim, *op. cit.*, 172.
[68] U.N., *Land Reform*, 32, 33.
[69] Pendered Report, 16.

subsistence (particularly in Africa). This problem was especially acute in Kenya. The Masai had been roaming with their cattle over enormous tracts of land from Abyssinia south. Although they had occupied the land thinly, they claimed the whole, but the government of Kenya allotted them some 14,000 square miles and later grazing rights over another 1,000 square miles. The total native reserves finally set aside are about 34,722 square miles.[70] In fact, native uses of land were often uneconomical and the new grantees were more productive. But as populations have increased, the native peoples can extend cultivation only if the government will release more land to them, which it has usually not done. In the Union of South Africa, for instance, the Native Land Act of 1913 prohibited Africans from buying or renting land outside areas scheduled as native land unless it was already in possession of a native. In 1936 provision was made for 11.5 million acres of land to be released to natives in addition to the 16 million acres scheduled in 1913. But much of this additional land was occupied by natives already, and much was poor, and after ten years less than half the additional land had actually been acquired for native use. In consequence, whereas 80% of the population is native, only 15% of the cultivable area of the country is reserved for native use. And of these reserved lands only 2% is arable compared with 15% for the whole country.[71] In Southern Rhodesia native reserves were provided in the constitution and were defined by a Commission in 1915, mainly by reference to the location of concentrations of native occupancy at the time. A further 8 million acres were set aside in Native Purchase Areas in which no non-native could buy land, but the native could buy on an installment plan. A further 8 million acres is reserved to natives, but is of undefined status. Insofar as land already in use by natives was reserved to them, the land was presumably adequate at the time. Furthermore, the indigenous populations often had the first choice as to the quality of land to use, but in Africa they were guided by the suitability of land for their traditional hoe cultivation, which resulted in a poor choice in terms of methods of cultivation subsequently introduced.

The reservation of land to natives means that others are legally prohibited from acquiring it, e.g., in Malaya, Java, and most parts of Africa. This provision, intended to prevent the dispossession of the native population, also restricts their ability to raise capital by mortgaging their land. The allocation of the reserved lands among individuals is typically according to native institutions and law. But in the Union of South Africa the trust lands are administered by the government. Native holdings are generally too small to maintain the family, and natives are compelled to offer their labor on the market. In the Transkei no native may have more

---

[70] Kenya, *The Agrarian Problem in Kenya*, 12.
[71] Franklin, *Economics in South Africa*, 126, 127.

than 10 acres.[72] But natives are frequently also prevented from buying non-reserve lands (e.g., in South Africa). In Kenya about 16,000 square miles of the highlands are reserved for white occupation. Thus native reserves perpetuate a dual economy, the indigenous subsistence society being segregated from modern economic development except insofar as the reserves are compelled to export labor.[73] In Fiji the native council requested in 1940 that all native land be placed under the administration of a government board for the benefit of the native population. Lands were set aside to meet the needs of the Fijian population, and these could be disposed of only to Fijians and could be mortgaged only with government consent. All other native lands are leased or licensed by the board, subject to restrictions as to length of lease, protection of the land from deterioration, and the expenditure of stipulated sums on improvement.[74] Thus the board acts as an official manager of the lands not needed for cultivation by Fijians, seeking to ensure full utilization to the benefit of the native population.

Government regulation of the use of privately owned land may be achieved by taxation. Major diversions can be achieved only by taxation differentiated according to use. But the higher the general tax on land the greater is the pressure to find the most remunerative use for it. In agricultural countries where political power is in the hands of landowners, land taxes are likely to be low, and this pressure to make the most economical use of land correspondingly light. Low taxation in Latin America may be one reason why wealthy families have often utilized their lands so poorly. They have been content to watch the value of their land grow as the result of the efforts of others, and of increases in population.

State regulation of the price of the produce of the land affects the allocation of land among uses. The support prices in the U.S.A. and Britain, for instance, direct land into certain uses and away from others. The British and French governments use price control to increase the output of meat and dairy products. The control of rents for housing also influences the use of land for that purpose. If the rents are below the cost of acquiring land and building new houses, little new private building is to be expected.

More direct control of land use results from state control of the output of specific agricultural products. A production quota must be broken down until it applies to individuals, and, in fact, often to pieces of land, as it has in the U.S.A. for some crops, in New Zealand for wheat, and in Australia and South Africa for sugar. This arrangement is unlikely to result in economical allocation because the most economical way to reduce output is to eliminate the marginal lands and not to reduce

---

[72] Franklin, *op. cit.*, 130.
[73] U.N., *Recent Econ. Devel. in Africa, 1949-50,* 11.
[74] Pim, *op. cit.*, 80.

production on all land in cultivation by a fixed percentage (as is usually done). In the U.S.A., for instance, cotton was not moved as much as was desirable out of the eastern sections of the cotton belt into the Mississippi delta area, and wheat production was maintained in areas with high climatic hazards.[75] As tastes and methods of cultivation change, moreover, the misallocation of land becomes increasingly uneconomical. Controls over the allocation of land among agricultural uses have also appeared in some of the colonial areas in Africa. In Uganda the government seeks to eliminate over-dependence on one crop; to prevent the congestion of population near the railhead with consequent soil exhaustion in such areas; to extend production to marginal areas; to encourage cash crops in areas with only subsistence crops; to discourage production in areas which, although most suitable, are already wealthy and would compete to the detriment of areas otherwise having only subsistence crops; and to encourage especially needed crops like soy beans for the army or fats for general consumption; and finally, to provide for famine relief. In the Belgian Congo the Governor-General can prescribe the areas in which cotton may be grown; it is, in fact, grown mainly in areas where large concession companies operate. In Kenya, commodity boards established by the government have at times sought to prevent native production of coffee, pyrethrum, and tea, in order to restrict competition and prevent a shrinkage in the supply of wage labor.[76]

Government control of the allocation of land among uses may result from control of the location of activities. The changing structure of British industry after 1918 caused depression in areas in which industries were declining and population was not adjusting sufficiently quickly to the relocation of jobs. Even if the labor force did move, there was a considerable loss of investment in housing and immovable social equipment. Consequently, the government made a series of attempts to assist the "depressed areas," (which were those unduly dependent on industries especially vulnerable to unemployment). The Distribution of Industries Act, 1945, empowered the Board of Trade to review employment conditions in these areas, and de-schedule some and re-schedule others. It also authorized the government to acquire land and erect buildings for new industries in "development" (formerly "depressed") areas, make loans to non-profit trading estate companies, and grants or loans for the improvement of basic services and assist individual undertakings, in such areas. But any firm proposing to erect industrial buildings or to extend buildings with a floor space of more than 1,000 square feet must obtain the consent of the Board of Trade, which "takes into account" the availability of surplus government war plants, whether the industry will add to the cyclical vulner-

---

[75] Schultz, *op. cit.*
[76] Pendered Report, 20, 29, 44.

ability of the area, the availability of housing, and the costs for civic services likely to be thrown on local public authorities.

The British government has also embarked on control of the allocation of land among all uses. Private control of land utilization had been limited by the legal rule that, though an owner may not use his land in ways which hinder others from enjoying their rights, its use could not otherwise be regulated without compensating owners for any losses they might suffer. Consequently, land had been poorly allocated among industry, agriculture, housing, recreation, and other uses. The health of workers had suffered and demands for transport had been excessive. The Housing and Town Planning Act of 1909 provided for the planned use of land, but by 1939 controls were negative rather than constructive, administered on too restricted a geographical basis, limited in enforcement, and especially restricted by the requirements of compensation. Developed land had to be purchased for public purposes at a price based on its most profitable use. If building (except agricultural) was prohibited in an area, all the owners of land there had to be compensated for the loss of potential building value, although building was unlikely except on a small part of it. Local authorities were empowered to annex part of increases in the value of land still in private hands, where the increase was due to public improvements, but usually failed to do so.[77]

The war damage inflicted on many cities necessitated redevelopment, and in 1943 the Ministry of Town and Country Planning was established with the duty of "ensuring consistency and continuity in the framing and execution of a national policy with respect to the land." The Town and Country Planning Act, 1947, provided a program of land-use control. Local Planning Authorities were required to submit to the Ministry (by 1951) "development plans" collectively covering the whole country. These authorities may purchase land and develop it, or make it available to private enterprise for approved uses. But private development may also continue within the framework of plans. To reduce the cost of development, the act provided that the owner of land to be developed may receive only the value of the land in its present use. All purchasers for development other than public authorities must pay to the Central Land Board (established under the act) part or all of the difference between the value of the land in its proposed and its current use (both of which must, therefore, be determined before the potential developer can decide whether development is worthwhile). The Board may also acquire land compulsorily where individual owners will not make arrangements for development, the owner receiving compensation based on the value of the land in its existing use. Wherever land is to be converted to a new use by its existing owner, for instance, farm land converted to factory or housing use, the Central Land Board may levy a charge upon the land,

---

[77] British Information Services, *Town and Country Planning in Britain*, 1949.

representing the whole or a part of the excess value in the new use, over the value of the land in its existing use. There is a story, probably apocryphal, that a man was charged one pound for introducing bee-keeping. The government did not, however, annex all increases in land values where there was no change in use. But increases in the value of land owing to a change in its use accrue to the benefit of local or central authorities. Furthermore, to avoid discriminating against owners whose land had increased in value for new uses, but who had not, at the time of the new law, captured this development value by selling the land, the government set aside an arbitrarily determined sum of £300 million to compensate for the loss of these accrued values. The compensation claims are in process of settlement, but may total less than the £300 million provided. The fund obtained by the government, by annexing development increments, is to be spent on developments not usually undertaken by private enterprise, such as parks and new highway systems, and for compensating owners of land whose value is reduced by the development of other land.

These increments in the value of land due to development were annexed partly because they were regarded as more than usually unearned. In fact they are the result of expenditures by public authorities or other individuals or merely of increases in population. But if the state takes all the difference between the value of the land in its former and its new use the landowner is left with little interest in development. The power of compulsory purchase, however, prevents an owner from obstructing development. As a matter of fact, the activities of the Central Land Board appear not to have retarded development. Building licenses being difficult to get, the cost of the site for development is a secondary consideration. Most transactions in land in 1949 took place at prices much higher than existing use value, and the board has tried to influence the market by occasionally using its powers of compulsory purchase.

Chapter 17

Water Resources

Water is limited in supply, but can be exported or imported to a limited extent. It can be a negative asset when floods destroy, and swamps prevent, productive use of land, cause ill health, or increase evaporation that reduces supplies elsewhere. The huge swamp in the Sudd in central and East Africa, for instance, causes a considerable loss of Nile water by evaporation. As a positive asset, water is beyond economic measurement, for without it there is no life and no production. In fact, water dominates the distribution of population. Its capacity to increase production must, however, be measured when it is necessary to estimate the benefits of bringing water to new areas and where water rights are sold. Water resources differ from minerals in that the supply consists of a revolving fund, and use is offset by inflows of new supplies.

Physical measurements of water supply are beginning to be made in order to discover the extent of unused resources. The Union of South Africa, which is extremely poor in water, has attempted to draw up a "water balance sheet." On the one side appears rainfall and on the other side the losses of water by usage in agriculture or for urban purposes, by evaporation, and by escape to the sea. But where all water is used, it may not be economically allocated among uses. And water unused is not necessarily an economic asset. To make it available at the places and times when it can be most productive may require resources (especially capital) that would add more to the national product if used in some other way. Only 6% of the water in rivers is used in India, largely because much of the remaining 94% falls in the monsoon period and storage works are costly.[1]

Water can contribute to national income through its use for human consumption, transportation, industry, agriculture, and power, each of

---

[1] U.N., *Econ. Surv. of Asia and the Far East*, 1949, 369.

which presents different problems of water management. The same water, moreover, may be used successively for a number of purposes.

A. Water for Human Consumption, Transport, and Industry

Urban concentrations of population require elaborate organization for the collection, storage, purification, transmission, and distribution of water. This service is increasingly provided by public authorities, but many cities in the less-developed countries lack adequate water, especially for sewage systems. In rural areas water is typically supplied from rivers, wells, and cisterns that, in some countries, are a serious source of disease. The use of standing water in irrigation ditches in Egypt for washing and drinking has caused a "truly appalling growth of debilitating diseases such as bilharzia and malaria."[2] Bilharzia afflicts 45% to 75% of the population in perennially irrigated areas in lower Egypt.[3]

Water has been used for transport from the earliest times and long provided one of the most important means of long distance transport. There is no measure, however, of the navigation potential of the water supplies of various countries, nor of their utilization. Water transport has been important in China, Europe, in South America on the Amazon, in the U.S.A. on the Mississippi, and on many smaller rivers. It is relatively unimportant in Africa and India. The supply of inland navigation facilities depends on the number of rivers, the constancy of their flow, depth, length, location, and the ease with which they are improved.

Navigation rights on rivers are rarely private property. Ships are private property, except in socialized economies. But navigation facilities are often increased by dredging and similar services, or by capital investments in levees, locks, and dams. Dams may be used to deepen rivers, stabilize their depth, or regulate their flow, but for this purpose alone they are typically not remunerative propositions. They are, however, becoming more important with the development of multiple-purpose projects. Such investments are typically made by public authorities.

Extensions of natural water ways (canals) were among the first types of transport to be improved in Europe, after the road system. The earlier canals were largely privately supplied, their cost being financed (or expected to be financed) out of tolls. Betwen 1770 and 1830 many canals were built in Europe and the U.S.A., but the railroad seriously curtailed their market. Canals are still an important means of internal navigation in France and Germany. They are now government property in Britain and parts of the U.S.A.

The availability of water often determines the location of industries requiring large quantities for cooling, cleaning, internal transport, chemical processes, and the like (which may pollute the supply and render it unusable for other purposes).

[2] U.N., Econ. Surv. Mission for the Middle East *Final Report* I, 37.
[3] Warriner, *op. cit.*, 42.

B. Water for Agriculture

1. Supply

The water potential of a country for agricultural production depends on the extent to which it contributes to crops, but since all agriculture requires some water, the whole agricultural output can be attributed to the water supply, which is not helpful. Even so, the same annual supply does not result in the same output everywhere. Temperature and soil composition are important. Too, the water potential does not necessarily depend on the effect of the water supply where and when it is provided by nature. It may be possible to increase the national product by investing capital to change the location of water in place or time. These works may either reduce the negative contribution to production of excessive water, or increase its positive contribution.

Excessive water reduces the productivity of a large part of the Mesopotamian plain in Iraq where former irrigation and drainage works have disintegrated. Subsoil salts sterilize the land unless irrigation is accompanied by drainage.[4] Capital has been invested in dykes, drainage ditches, and pumps in the fens in Britain and in Germany, France, Italy, and the U.S.A., and parts of Australia. In the Netherlands, large areas have been freed from seawater. The greatest single project, an enclosing dam on the Zuider Zee, was completed in 1932. When fully realized, it will make available 500,000 acres of fertile land. The works are undertaken at the cost of the government, and for the first few years the land is cultivated for government account, but thereafter it is leased to qualified farmers. In India and the Far East some 440,000 square miles are protected by 18,000 kilometres of main dykes.[5] But flooded land grows rice, and swamps may act like man-made reservoirs retarding the run-off from the land and reducing erosion.

Intermittent flooding endangers life and property. The Old Testament records a flood on the Euphates-Tigris in about 4000 B.C., and the floods on the Nile have caused great damage in the past.[6] Great floods have occurred in the U.S.A. (in the Mississippi valley, and on many other rivers) and still occur in China, India, Java, and north Vietnam. The average annual damage from floods in Asia and the Far East is estimated at over $200 million.[7] The Habbaniyeh flood control project on the Euphrates is now under construction.[8] But floods also deposit silt, a natural fertilizer in Egypt and in the rice growing areas in Vietnam and Thailand.

The water potential of a country, in its positive aspects, is important largely as a means of discovering the extent to which the potential is used.

---

[4] U.N., Econ. Surv. Mission for the Middle East *Final Report* II, 31.

[5] U.N., *Econ. Surv. of Asia and the Far East in 1949*, 362.

[6] Bonné, *op. cit.*, 173.

[7] U.N., *Econ. Surv. of Asia and the Far East in 1949*, 359.

[8] U.N., Econ. Surv. Mission for the Middle East *Report* I, 43; II, 31.

The water potential is not fully used if capital invested in irrigation works would increase national income more than if it were invested in some other direction. If capital in water works yields less than elsewhere, the works have to be subsidized because the highest income obtainable from water would not cover all costs. The water is then overutilized and the capital supply underutilized.

Measurements of water potential in terms of areas of land that could be brought under cultivation by irrigation are often unsatisfactory because of lack of information on the cost of irrigation and on the nature of the soil (especially in underdeveloped countries). In the Middle East, the percentage of irrigable land actually irrigated is said to be 70% in Egypt, 55% in Iraq, 30% in Iran, 20% in Lebanon, 13% in Turkey, and 10% in Israel. But the definition of "irrigable" is uncertain, and the cost of additional irrigation water would be high in Egypt and Israel, and the same investment might be more profitable in other parts of the Middle East.[9]

2. WATER UTILIZATION IN AGRICULTURE

Irrigated land supports about 10% of the human race,[10] but irrigation is very unevenly distributed among countries. Where rainfall is adequate and appropriately distributed over time there is little irrigation (as in western Europe, the eastern U.S.A., and New Zealand). It is important where there are long periods of dryness but occasional excessive flows of water. Where precipitation is low all the time within any economical distance, irrigation is impossible. The Sahara, and the Arabian and Australian deserts cannot be irrigated because there is not enough water to redirect. In South Africa, the Drought Commission of 1923 reported that less than 7% of the rain that fell in the Union was reaching the sea, but it was reported in 1948 that the desert was extending eastward and northward, grass giving place to karoo scrub. But where rain is unreliable and poorly distributed over time (as in India and Pakistan) irrigation can greatly increase agricultural output. It is estimated that 80% of the water in six rivers in northwest India and Pakistan (including the Indus) now flows unused into the sea.

In 1930 25% of all the irrigated acreage was in India, 25% in China, 10% in the U.S.A., about 4% each in Java and Asiatic Russia, and about 3% each in Japan and Egypt.[11] In Japan the area of irrigated land increased 42% between 1877 and 1939; some land was enabled to produce two crops a year, and about 50% of the land under the principal crops was irrigated in 1949. In Asia and the Far East generally the percentage was 33%.[12] In

---

[9] Bonné, "Land and Population in the Middle East," V *Middle East Jour.*, 1951, 43, 52, 55; Warriner, *op. cit.*, 3, 4, 29, 59.

[10] *For. Agric.*, Feb. 1953.

[11] *Ency. Soc. Sci.*, article on "Irrigation."

[12] U.N., *Econ. Surv. of Asia and the Far East in 1949*, 370.

the Punjab (Pakistan) 30 to 50% of the crops is attributed to irrigation, and in most of the Middle East 60%[13] (almost 100% in Egypt).

Many governments have sought to extend irrigation in recent years, and the largest increases in the produce of land in the near future are expected from this source. Between 1954 and 1957, areas under irrigation are planned to increase 20 to 30% in Latin America, Asia, and the Far East. India expects to increase its irrigated area 40% and Pakistan to contribute 30% of the planned increases in irrigated acreage by 1957. Indian provincial governments are sinking deep wells, but the chief extensions of irrigation will come from central government projects capable of adding 20 to 25 million acres to the irrigated area (although some of the land to be irrigated is presently under cultivation). The major projects in hand or under active consideration in 1947 would nearly double the irrigated acreage of India in ten years.[14] In Pakistan the Thal Development Authority created in 1951 is expected to bring 1.5 million acres of desert land into cultivation. Mexico, Thailand, and Egypt also plan large increases in irrigated acreage.

In the Middle East Egypt has the greatest irrigation system, upon which almost the whole country is dependent for survival. In 1940 it replaced the old delta barrage and thereby increased the area under perennial irrigation in lower Egypt, but one-fifth of the cultivated land is still under basin irrigation; it is planned to convert more of this to perennial irrigation. In Iraq the Kut barrage on the Tigris, completed in 1939, increased the irrigated area by 5 million acres, but another 15 million acres is suitable for irrigation, and, if irrigated, would permit the migratory Bedouin population to turn to settled agriculture and raise their present very low level of living. In Israel, 75,000 acres are irrigated, but the area could probably be doubled by full use of the waters of the Jordan and the Besian scheme. There are also projected schemes in Iran and Turkey.[15] In Mexico the projects of the Irrigation Commission from 1925 to 1946 served 2.36 million acres, but much land remains to be irrigated. In Peru there are plans for using the waters of the Santa River. In Bolivia it is estimated that irrigation would bring vast new areas under cultivation; an Irrigation Bureau was established in 1940 and one project has been completed.[16] In the U.S.A. the irrigated acreage increased from 14.4 million in 1910 to 21 million in 1940, and the total investment in irrigation from $321 million to $1,052 million.[17] Many of these new projects indicate past underutilization of water. Some, however, have become economical because of increasing

---

13 Bonné, *State and Economics in the Middle East*, 171.

14 India, Advisory Planning Board *Report*, 1947, 10, 72.

15 U.N., Econ. Surv. Mission for Middle East *Report* II, 19; *Econ. Devel. in Sel. Countries*, 1947, 187, 193.

16 U.N., *Econ. Devel. of Sel. Countries*, 14, 50, 125.

17 U.S.: Bureau of Census, *Sixteenth Census of the U.S., 1940, Irrigation of Agricultural Lands*, XXIX and Table 4.

pressure of population or reduction in the cost of capital, and some require subsidy.

The extent to which water is used depends on the arrangements controlling its use, knowledge of available methods, the cost of capital, and the intensity of concern for economic development.

Access to water is controlled in various, and often complex, ways. Water under privately owned land, when captured, is usually the property of the surface owner. But if water is withdrawn in amounts that lower the general subterranean water level, government controls may be imposed. In the Middle East, however, water rights are often separately owned. In Iraq, Palestine, Transjordan, Syria, and Lebanon, persons owning no land in an area may buy water rights and farm them out to the highest bidder or use them to force the sale of neighboring land. In Iraq, sheikhs and town notables who have installed pumps have claimed all the land served.[18] Surface water in streams and rivers may often be freely used by owners of the adjoining land, but the water rights may also be communally held. In Syria and Lebanon some water rights are vested in village communities whose authorities allocate the water (in ways which have been criticized as inequitable), and some are collectively owned (as *waqf*).[19] But river and lake waters are frequently controlled by the government in respect to the building of dams and the diversion of water to protect down-stream proprietors. In Australia the beds and banks of all streams and other natural sources of water supply have been vested in the crown since about 1905.[20] In the Sudan, pumps may be installed to take water from the Nile only with government permission, the number of pumps licensed being subject to an agreement between the Sudan and Egypt. Larger-scale irrigation works usually involve the transport of water from one location to another, access to the water source, and the construction of works. Access to the water where it is to be used depends, therefore, on the policies of those who operate the project, often, however, subject to government control.

Knowledge of water control devices goes back in Egypt, Mesopotamia, and Ceylon to the beginning of history. The chief advances in recent years have concerned methods of building water works on a large scale. Most important, however, have been experiments with the multiple use of water, mainly in the U.S.A. The oldest method of diverting surface waters is to raise water from rivers by waterwheels and pour it into ditches that carry it to the land. The most ancient device in Iran, Iraq, Egypt, and the Sudan consists of a series of jars or other containers on a wheel turned by an animal, or possibly a human being, and is still in use.[21] In recent years

[18] Warriner, *op. cit.*, 73, 79, 92, 115.

[19] *Ibid.*, 73, 92.

[20] Australia: The Rural Reconstruction Commission, *Irrigation, Water Conservation and Land Drainage*, 1943, 42.

[21] Bonné, *op. cit.*, 179.

some of these wheels have been replaced by electric or gasoline-driven pumps (e.g., along the Nile). Both devices depend upon a continuous flow of water in the river, but involve relatively little capital. Sloping land can be irrigated by terracing and enclosing each terrace so that the water can be held there and released to flow on to a series of successively lower terraces. This method of irrigation was introduced by the Moors, and carried during the eighth century A.D. to Africa, Spain, India, and the Far East, and is now also used in the South American Andes. Some terraces are kept continuously flooded for the production of wet rice.

River waters have also been used from ancient times for flooding the land. The Nile floods neighboring land, and the flood waters have for many centuries been controlled and retained on the land for a time by banks which divide the land into basins. The water was allowed to stay on the land for 30 days or so, during which time it deposited silt (which is eroded soil from Abyssinia) that fertilized the land, the water frequently being from four to six feet deep. There was one harvest a year and the seed depended on the one soaking of the soil for water throughout its period of growth.[22] The same device is used in India and Iraq.[23] Flooding can be induced by building barrages or low dams. The barrage constructed in the Nile delta in 1843 and allowed to fall into decay was repaired in 1890 and later reconstructed on a larger scale. Barrages near the mouths of the Tigris and the Euphrates provide for basin irrigation of relatively small areas and permit cultivation in the long scorching summer.[24] Basin-overflow irrigation was used in the deltas of the Ganges and Damodar Rivers over 3000 years ago.

Barrages and dikes are also used to raise the level of the river water, permitting it to flow through canals onto the land by gravity. These systems supply water, but not fertilizer, because the silt settles behind the barrages. This arrangement has made possible two crops a year in lower Egypt.[25] Irrigation canals in Iran are sometimes entirely underground to prevent their being washed away by flood waters. Some are as long as 40 miles and as deep as 120 to 200 feet, and, consequently, costly to maintain. The Min River Irrigation project in Szechuan, China, commanding some 400,000 acres, is one of the oldest. The elaborate system of dikes built in 250 and 200 B.C. to spread out the flood waters was repaired in the 13th century and is still in use.[26] Canal irrigation is also provided by taking water at an upstream point and allowing it to flow by gravity through canals onto downstream land. Canal irrigation provides summer water in the Po valley in Italy for rice and mulberry trees (for producing silk), in the Campagna for food and livestock, and in Spain for the production of

22 Hurst, H. E., *A Short Account of the Nile Basin;* Bonné, *op. cit.,* 174 ff.

23 Bonné, *op. cit.,* 172.

24 Warriner, *op. cit.,* 99; Bonné, *op. cit.,* 175.

25 Bonné, *op. cit.,* 180, 200 ff.

26 U.N., *Econ. Surv. of Asia and the Far East in 1949,* 368.

oranges, esparto grass, and cereals. In Asiatic Russia, irrigation is important, and the government is introducing such schemes in the Ukraine and the Caucasus for wheat and forage crops. In Mexico corn and food crops are irrigated, the water coming from mountain streams. The Mormons introduced into the United States the Mexican system of irrigating land from mountain streams, and showed that the land in the western states could be rendered fertile by this means.

Surface water may be stored for later use in the dry season by collection in tanks in the rainy season and subsequent release through canals and ditches. Such arrangements are very ancient, and some have been allowed to disintegrate. "In Syria, Jordan, Iraq and southern Palestine can still be seen ruins of one-time waterworks; great cisterns dug out of the rock below the earth to treasure the spring rains; stone headworks and channels to preserve the natural springs and dole their water out to the land; irrigation channels of mud and brick once filled from the perennial rivers by primitive but effective water wheels." "Old time wars destroyed these things. The land has dried up and the people have gone."[27] The Incas had a massive system of cisterns, dams, canals, and aqueducts. Such systems still exist in southern India and Ceylon. They require more investment than merely lifting water from rivers.

Water is also stored for later use by building dams to create reservoirs. These are also ancient, although the dams of early times were small compared with the largest built in recent years. Some are now large enough to provide not only for regularization of the flow within the seasons but also over a period of years. Large dams on the Nile now exist in Egypt and the Sudan. Mohammed Ali began strengthening the canals in Egypt early in the 19th century, and began raising the water level by barrages after 1820. Seasonal irrigation was then replaced in parts of lower Egypt by perennial irrigation. During the late 19th century, British engineers increased the effective supply of Nile water by building the dam at Assouan (the height of which was later raised), which permitted the irrigation of lands in upper Egypt, regularized the interseasonal flow in lower Egypt, and enlarged the area brought under perennial irrigation there, making two crops possible. In upper Egypt and the Sudan it has made cotton cultivation possible on a one-crop basis. Practically no Nile water now flows into the Mediterranean, because an earth dam has been built across the mouth of the Nile at Rosetta. Large dams have also been built in Pakistan and the U.S.A. (on the Tennessee, Columbia, Colorado, and other rivers).

Subsurface water has been used for irrigation since ancient times. For many centuries water was raised by human or animal power, but in recent years mechanical pumps have been installed, particularly in the U.S.A., Iraq and Israel. In Iraq, motor pumps (some riverside) increased from 166 in 1914 to over 3000 in 1948. Well pumps are used in Israel mostly for

27 U.N., Econ. Surv. Mission for the Middle East *Final Report* I, 2.

citrus culture. At some stage, however, well-pumping lowers the water table and calls for regulation.[28]

Access to capital plays a large part in determining the extent of water control. Some of the works in the ancient world (e.g., in Egypt, Mesopotamia, and among the Incas) were large and constructed by the state with slave labor, or under arrangements similar to the *corvée*. Small works are frequently undertaken by landholders. In the U.S.A., individuals and partnerships irrigated 45.7% of all irrigated land in 1910, and 34.8% in 1940. Where landholdings are large, works of considerable size can be undertaken by individual proprietors, but often are not because of lack of concern, or because the increase in revenues from the land is less than that from investments of other kinds in underdeveloped countries where rates of interest are high. In India water rights are often owned by *zamindari,* who have been criticized for not even maintaining water works.[29] Small owners have been deterred from sinking wells because they do not pay 25% (the rate of interest) in bad years. A few larger-scale investments have been made by private enterprise, but without marked success. The commercial water companies established in the western states of the U.S.A. after the Mormons had demonstrated the productiveness of irrigation have, in the main, been unsuccessful, because settlement was slower than was expected and some states prohibited water service charges exceeding the original cost of the proposition. Such companies were responsible for 12.5% of all irrigated acres in 1910 and 4.8% in 1940. Some of the irrigation projects in the Po Valley in Italy are privately organized but the fascist government acquired and enlarged a number of them. In India the British government endeavored to attract investment in water companies in much the same way as in railroads, but with no success. Only the smaller tanks and wells are private, but they supply about 55% of the irrigated area.

Cooperatives provide one of the most important methods of organizing small-scale irrigation in the U.S.A., and were responsible for about one-third of all of the irrigated land in the country in both 1910 and 1940. The capital is usually subscribed in cash or labor by the members. Cooperatives are also an important and efficient method of organization in older countries. In Italy associations or consortia of land owners are much used and were encouraged by the fascist government. In France, farmers' societies and cooperatives organize irrigation. In India, cooperative societies execute minor irrigation works (sinking wells, building small dams, and occasionally constructing and maintaining tube wells pumped by electricity) mainly in Bengal and the United Provinces.[30]

Large-scale water works are almost everywhere undertaken by govern-

---

[28] Bonné, *op. cit.,* 176, 202.
[29] Famine Inquiry Commission *Report,* 277.
[30] India, Cooperative Planning Committee *Report,* 1946, 17.

ments that have easier access to capital, better means of acquiring land, and are more exposed to political pressures generated by widespread poverty. For a long time in the 19th century, the U.S. Congress objected to the expenditure of public money on flood control works (particularly on the Mississippi River) because the benefits from these works would go to the owners of private property along the river, although these owners were individually unable to help themselves. Later in the 19th century, the federal government built and maintained levees, and in the 20th century the Tennessee Valley Authority, by retarding the runoff, somewhat reduced the height of the flood waters on the river. The government has also built a number of flood control dams in other parts of the country. But "floods cannot be controlled by building higher and higher levees or permanently by building dams if other things are neglected . . . water control inevitably leads us back to the proper conservation of forests and agricultural land."[31]

Irrigation works have been government enterprises in Egypt, Mesopotamia, and China for millenia. Recently most of the larger irrigation works in the U.S.A. have been semi-public or public. "Irrigation Districts" date back to the earlier part of the 19th century and often have power to issue bonds or levy assessments (which are virtually taxes) on the irrigated land. Such irrigation districts were responsible for 16.7% irrigated acreage in 1940. But the Bureau of Reclamation (in the Department of the Interior) has undertaken all the costlier projects in the 17 western states. The Bureau spent about $263 million on 34 projects between 1902 and 1930, and by 1940 about 10% of all the irrigated acreage was served by its dams. More recently Hoover Dam has been built at a cost of $165 million and irrigates about one million acres, and Grand Coulee Dam began to provide irrigation water in 1950. In Australia the large projects in Victoria and New South Wales have been constructed and maintained by the government. In India 45% of all acres irrigated are served by government canal systems,[32] and proposed multiple purpose projects will irrigate 20 to 25 million acres. In Pakistan all the large projects are public. In Mexico the government National Irrigation Commission is responsible for irrigation, but operated under the direction of a private enterprise from 1925 to 1934.[33] In the Sudan the government participated in the Gezira irrigation scheme by providing the Sennar Dam and the main canals and drains. It was to be repaid by a share of the proceeds of the main cotton crop. The Alternative Livelihood Schemes are organized in a manner very similar to the Gezira scheme, except that the government not only provides the dam

[31] President's Water Resources Policy Committee *Summary of Recommendations,* 1950, 2.

[32] Wadia and Merchant, *op. cit.,* 19; U.N. *Econ. Surv. of Asia and the Far East in 1949,* 370.

[33] U.N., *Econ. Devel. in Sel. Countries,* 14.

but also supervises cultivation. By 1944, 45,000 acres of irrigated land had been settled by 2000 families and a further 800 families had been settled on a temporary wheat growing scheme as a wartime measure.[34]

The amount of capital invested in irrigation depends on the tests of desirability applied by the investor. Private investments are likely to be made only when the price at which the water is sold is expected to cover the cost of the works and their maintenance and administration, plus an attractive profit. The price of the water cannot exceed the amount it adds to the value of the produce of the land. The main objections to this principle are that it involves private property in water rights, and that because water is a local monopoly, its price may yield profits greater than are needed to attract capital. Governments, however, should balance social benefits against social costs, which may involve wider considerations than should be expected of a private enterprise. Where the works are constructed by labor that would otherwise be unemployed (which is possible in a depression and at most times in underdeveloped countries), the social cost is less than the private cost. The government may also decide it is socially desirable to aid lower income groups or reduce dependence on foreign food supplies, considerations which a private enterprise would ignore. In India the government built irrigation projects only when they were expected to pay off all their costs including interest of 5% or more, and progress was slow. These "productive" works were financed by government borrowing. "Minor" works have been built out of current government revenues. But as a result of recommendations by the Indian Irrigation Commission of 1901-3, it undertook a third class of "protective" projects by taking into account the social cost of famines. These projects were not expected to be remunerative in terms of private bookkeeping, but were to be undertaken if their returns *plus* three times the cost of famine relief exceeded the capital cost of the project. These projects were financed out of a fund fed by Famine Insurance Grants of £1 million a year, which was the average cost of famines.

The financial outcome of public investments depends, partly, on the profit potential of the investment if it is operated as a private enterprise after it is established. Governments may deliberately, or because of poor estimating, provide a supply that cannot be sold at prices covering the cost of the works. The outcome depends also on the way in which the government in fact operates the project, particularly as to the price charged for water. The decision on this matter determines the incidence of the benefits from the original water source and from the government investment.

The proper allocation of the benefits of the water presents no problem where the owner of water uses it to irrigate his own land. But where

---

[34] Keene, *op. cit.*, 19, 20.

ownership of the water is separated from the ownership of the land to be irrigated, there is a problem which is solved through decisions on the level of charges for water and the plots to be served. If the water is privately owned, the owner may be expected to charge a price that will maximize his profit. All the benefits from the water accrue to its owner (who may have paid for it), the water may not be fully used, and the water used will be distributed among the pieces of land where it will be most productive. But when some of the early private companies in the western states of the U.S.A. pursued this policy, state governments intervened, and controlled the price of irrigation water. Private enterprise will not then appear unless expected income exceeds expected costs and an attractive profit. The state intervention may merely reduce the sums obtainable by private sellers of rights of access to water.

Public authorities providing irrigation pursue no uniform policy. They may act like a private owner, on the ground that a water resource is a national asset the benefits of which should go to the whole community, and not to the landowners in its vicinity. The important "productive" projects in India and Pakistan have generally paid a high profit, those in Sind and Punjab (now Pakistan) yielding, in 1938, a net return of 11.5% on investment.[35] Charges to cultivators are based on area irrigated, crop, and number of waterings. Some water is wasted because land is overwatered by cultivators not certain of future supply. The government may, however, charge for water only enough to pay off its capital investment with interest. If the resulting water charges are less than would be charged by private enterprise, the benefits go to the owners of water rights or the recipients of water rather than to the general taxpayer. The government may, however, seek the return of its capital without interest. The Bureau of Reclamation, which has built and operated most of the larger reclamation projects in 17 western states in the U.S.A., advances the total cost of the works, which is expected to be repaid by the water users (without interest) over 40 years, this period of repayment having been successively prolonged since 1902, when it was ten years. This arrangement increases the benefits distributed among owners of water rights and water users, and may make less economical projects acceptable to the government. Where the state buys the land at its unirrigated value and resells or rents it at its irrigated value, it recaptures the value of the water. But it sometimes places the resulting profits into the accounts from which it attempts ultimately to recover only the cost of its works. Consequently, those who get access to the irrigated land, ultimately obtain the benefits of the water resource.

Government projects may also charge for water too little to cover even the capital investment without interest, because the value of the water to

[35] Punjab Public Works Department, *Statistical Statement*, 1937-8.

users does not justify higher charges, an uneconomically high price has been paid for water rights, or because the state chooses to subsidize the agricultural producers in the neighborhood although it could charge a price which would eliminate the subsidy. The Loskop project in South Africa, for instance, recovers about 30% of its cost from the increase in the price of land as a result of the irrigation, and a further amount from water charges, but involves a considerable loss. As there has been a waiting list to settle on the scheme (and allegations of corruption in selecting settlers), it appears that higher charges could have been made for water. In fact, part of the value of the water or of the government investment is being distributed among the settlers. In France, the government makes grants up to one-third of the cost of works of farmers' societies and cooperatives. In Australia water charges planned to cover interest and capital have rarely done so. In Victoria the state has accepted responsibility for 80% of the capital cost. On the Murrambidgee scheme in New South Wales, the government bought the land at its unirrigated value and sells and rents it at the full irrigated value and charges for water, but it does not appear to be recovering the full cost of the works. The Rural Reconstruction Commission contended that the indirect effect of irrigation in increasing productivity and reducing unemployment justified the state in carrying part of the capital cost, but pointed out that low water rates encouraged the wasteful use of water and increased demands upon government finances, reducing the sums available for other social services.[36]

Finally, the government may make no charge for the water. The benefits from both the water and the public investment then accrue to the owners of land receiving water (who have no incentive to economical use). But taxation can be devised to recapture part of these benefits. In Java the General Water Works Service was set up as a government department in 1889 and provides an extensive irrigation system without water charges.[37] In Egypt the government has provided free irrigation since ancient times, but the chief source of government revenue was a land tax, and the ability of land owners to pay taxes depends on irrigation. In Iraq cultivators pay a tax of 12% of the value of the part of the crop which they sell, of which 2% is said to be for water. On the Gezira scheme in the Sudan, the method of charging for water has been assimilated to sharecropping, the government having received (until 1950) 40% of the cotton crop from the irrigated land. Wherever the price of water is less than the supply and demand price, the government must determine who may obtain water. In parts of India and in Syria groups of peasants or village communities allocate water. In Egypt the state makes the major allocations and local boards of magnates the local allocations.

---

[36] Australia: Rural Reconstruction Commission *Eighth Report,* 1945, 41.
[37] Pim, *op. cit.,* 28.

C. Water for Power

1. Supply

Estimates of the total energy in the falling water in a country merely set a ceiling on the power that could be obtained from water, irrespective of considerations of demand or cost. The economic water power potential depends on its capacity to make a net addition to national income. Unless the value of the power exceeds the cost of harnessing, transmitting, and distributing it, the power is not part of the economic potential of the country. The available estimates of water power potential fall far short of this test. The calculation of probable costs is elaborate and expensive, and estimates usually pay little or no attention to marketability. Estimates for 1937 show 41% of the world water power "potential" in Africa, 14% in Asia, and 13% in Latin America.[38] But much of this "potential" is of little present economic significance because of the cost of harnessing it in relation to the probable effective demand.

2. Utilization of Water for Power

The proportion of physically available water power actually used varies with the degree of economic development. In 1937 virtually none was used in Africa, about 1% in South America, 1.5% in Russia, and 4% in Asia. At the other extreme, 46% was used in Japan, 39% in Italy and 32% in Switzerland.[39] Much additional development has since occurred, but in 1949 47% of the world production of hydroelectric power was in North America, 30% in Europe, 15% in Asia, 2.9% in the U.S.S.R., 3.3% in Latin America, 1.4% in Oceania, and .4% in Africa; 73% was in developed countries and 27% in underdeveloped.[40] But only about 6% of the world supply of energy came from hydroelectric power, the percentage being about the same in all the major regions except the U.S.S.R. (1.4%) and Africa (.8%).[41] The total amount of energy, however, varied widely.

The further utilization of water power is in process in a number of countries. The White Nile, one of the largest potential sources of power in Africa (with a continuous capacity of 2.5 million kilowatts) is to be utilized at Owen Falls, where the river falls from Lake Victoria. The initial power plant will have a capacity of 121,500 kilowatts. A dam at Kariba on the Zambesi will make possible the generation of 750,000 kilowatts of electricity for Northern and Southern Rhodesia. In India plans under consideration will increase total generating capacity from 1.25 to 2.2 million kilowatts, although the potential is estimated to be 27 million kilowatts.[42]

---

[38] U.S. State Dept., *Energy Resources of the World*, 83.
[39] *Ibid.*, 83.
[40] U.N., *World Energy Supplies in Selected Years, 1929-50*, 17.
[41] *Ibid.*, 8.
[42] U.N., *Econ. Devel. in Sel. Countries*, 161; India, *Water Resources of India, Their Conservation and Utilization*, 1947; India, Advisory Planning Board *Report*, 1947, 73.

There are numerous projects in Latin America (especially Argentina) and in Portugal.

The extent of use of water power depends on the conditions of access to power sources, the availability of technical knowledge, the cost of capital, and the extent of the market.

As long as falling water was used to produce only mechanical power, plants were small and used small power sites, the rights to which were often attached to the ownership of the riverside land. But large power works, including dams, obstruct navigation and often affect the flow of water, and governments usually exercise considerable control. They may permit private ownership, as they do in the U.S.A., where a downstream owner whose works are adversely affected by an upstream dam is usually entitled to compensation. Lands to be flooded are purchased by the exercise, if necessary, of the right of eminent domain.

Knowledge of the means of harnessing water power is almost as ancient as knowledge of irrigation. Water wheels have been used for many centuries to provide small amounts of mechanical power. Larger wheels of the same sort provided one of the first sources of non-biological power in the early days of the Industrial Revolution, particularly in the textile and iron industries in Britain, western Europe, and the U.S.A. But even short-distance transmission of mechanical power involves great losses, and water power is often intermittent. Consequently, coal and steam superseded it in the 19th century in most industrialized countries, and permitted the location of industry away from water power sites. The invention of the electric generator in the latter part of the 19th century stimulated the redesigning of water wheels to drive electric generators, thus converting the energy in falling water into electricity, a flexible, transmissible form of energy. This knowledge is almost equally available everywhere as the services of construction firms, equipment, and maintenance personnel can all be imported if necessary.

Capital, however, is not equally available everywhere. The earliest hydroelectric plants were relatively small, and private investors supplied much of the capital in the U.S.A., western Europe, Japan, India, and many other countries. Many systems in western Europe and that in Japan have since become public, and the largest plants in the U.S.A. are public (e.g., in the Tennessee Valley and on the Columbia, Colorado, and other rivers). The new large projects in most countries are also public (e.g., the Damodar Valley project in India). Progress from the use of small to large projects requires investment beyond the capacity of private enterprise and involves natural resources on so large a scale that governments hesitate to place them in private hands. The cost of harnessing water depends on the volume and constancy of flow and the head of the fall. The more intermittent the flow the greater the time that plant investment is idle and, therefore, the higher the unit cost of the power. Reservoirs of water make possible a more continuous supply, but they add to the cost of the project. Their cost depends on the topography of the country and the alternative uses for the land which is flooded. Finally, the cost of using water power is influenced by the rate of interest.

The poorness of markets often explains the failure to use water power. The market may be poor because the power is located far from centers of population, although industries using much power usually go to the power site. Power cannot be transmitted more than 300 miles, and even then at considerable cost. But the market may be poor because the price of energy from other sources, such as coal and oil, keeps down the price of electricity. Finally, the market may be poor because industries using power have not developed (which may be partly because power has been costly).

The amount of capital invested depends, as with irrigation, on the tests of desirability applied by the investor. Uncontrolled private suppliers would seek to maximize their profit in the longer run, and they have done so, particularly in less-developed countries, e.g., India.[43] But in the more developed countries the price charged by private suppliers is regulated by the state, where the industry has not been nationalized. In the U.S.A. the price of electricity from all sources is generally restricted to yield only a fair return on a fair value of the investment (Ch. 23). Public authorities in general aim at a similar policy and are less inclined to subsidize hydroelectric power than irrigation. Insofar as only a normal return in fact goes to the operators of the project, they obtain no share in the value of the power source. But if the investment on which they are allowed a return includes the price paid for water rights, the owner of the power source annexes the capital value of the water power. If, however, the electrical rates are brought down to the cost of providing the power without payment for the resource, the benefits of the resource are distributed among the people who obtain power.

D. Multi-Purpose Use of Water

The most striking increase in knowledge of methods of using water resources lies in the development in the 20th century of water works serving more than one purpose, sometimes using the same water successively in several ways. The works of the Tennessee Valley Authority have provided a world pilot plant to demonstrate the possibilities of multi-purpose works.

The U.S. Congress recognized the relation between navigation and flood control in 1879, between irrigation and flood control in 1888, and between forest care, flood control, irrigation, and navigation in 1906. The General Dam Act recognized the relations among power, navigation, and fish, and an amendment to the Reclamation Act provided for disposal of surplus power at reclamation projects.[44] These principles were applied

---

[43] Wadia and Merchant, op. cit., 21.
[44] President's Water Resources Policy Committee, Summary of Recommendations, 1950, 5.

to large projects after 1918 but mainly after 1932. The dams of the Tennessee Valley Authority provide for flood control, navigation and power. The dams at Boulder on the Colorado River and Grand Coulee on the Columbia River provide irrigation and power. The plan for the Columbia contemplates 37.3 million kilowatts of power, and the addition of some millions of acres to the cultivated area. The President's Water Resources Policy Committee in 1950[45] recommended that in the future all proposals for water resources development should be submitted to Congress only in the form of programs for whole basins and that projects be evaluated only as constituent parts of such programs. The Tennessee Valley system also demonstrates the feasibility of utilizing a large part of the total fall of water in the river system by using a series of dams. The Damodar River project now under construction in India is designed to supply 350,000 kilowatts of power, irrigate 763,000 acres, and provide flood control. It will cost about $160 million and take about 10 years to complete. The river flows through one of the richest coal fields in India, into the Hooghlie west of Calcutta. The Nile project at Lake Victoria in Uganda is to generate power and contribute to irrigation. The Kariba project on the Zambezi between Northern and Southern Rhodesia is planned to generate 750,000 kilowatts and irrigate a large area.

The multiple use of water involves complex technical problems. Some uses conflict with others. Water may have to be released to leave room for flood control at times when it does not best serve power, navigation, or irrigation purposes. It may have to be released to provide for navigation when it is not most useful for power. These conflicts can often, but not always, be compromised. In order to use the waters of the Jordan for irrigation, it would be necessary to build a canal parallel to the river to keep the irrigation water high enough to flow onto the land, which would prevent the use of the fall in the river for power.[46] Erosion control is often needed in combination with other functions in a multi-purpose project. In the Far East, erosion would silt up reservoirs and limit their usefulness to one to 300 years.[47]

Multi-purpose projects are almost all provided by governments. They need large amounts of capital, cover a very wide area, and affect many private land owners. Their benefits cannot wholly be measured in cash and would be underrated by a private enterprise. The state may not wish to leave to private enterprise some of the services because of their monopoly aspect, and the difficulty of controlling monopoly prices. Some of the services may also be of a kind the cost of which is not easily recovered by charges to individual beneficiaries.

The most important consequence of multiple use of water is that it may

---

[45] *Ibid.*, 10.
[46] Warriner, *op. cit.*, 59.
[47] U.N., *Econ. Surv. of Asia and the Far East in 1949*, 378.

become economical to provide services that could not be economically provided by single-purpose projects. The generation of electric power makes possible irrigation and navigation projects that could not have been separately provided without subsidy. Even where the state properly decides to invest in a multi-purpose project only where the total benefits exceed the total costs (of construction, maintenance, and operation), the multi-purpose project offers more benefits than a single-purpose one, and the costs are usually not correspondingly increased. Furthermore, these projects often in fact develop a region, and the provision of each service (power, better navigation, irrigation) may build up the demand for others, although the development takes time. But a service that cannot be sold at a price covering the costs incurred solely to supply that service should be included only if the state desires to subsidize it, possibly because, as a practical matter, the service cannot be priced.

The pricing of the services of a multiple-purpose project presents essentially the same problems as a specialized project. Selling each service at a price which would in the long run equate demand with its available supply would determine who would receive service. If the resulting revenues exceeded all costs, including interest, the state would be annexing the value of the water resource and could use it for its general purposes. But wherever governments depart from this principle and seek to recover no more than their costs and possibly less, they must make some more or less arbitrary allocation among the various services of the costs incurred jointly to supply all (e.g., the cost of the dam and the inundated land) and these costs are usually a large part of total costs. The U.S. government has followed this policy and the President's Water Resources Policy Committee in 1950 failed to provide clear guidance as to the pricing of each service.[48] The formula selected determines the incidence of the distribution of the benefits of the water resource among the classes served.

---

[48] President's Water Resources Policy Committee, *Summary of Recommendations*, 12.

Chapter 18

Labor Supply

Labor resembles land, in that it can be exhausted by use in production, but exhaustion is not inevitable because human beings have powers of recuperation. It differs from minerals, in that the supply does not inevitably decline with use. It resembles capital, in that the supply can increase or decrease as forces constantly operating to reduce the supply are offset by forces increasing it. But labor differs from all other productive resources in being not only an agent of production but also its objective. The satisfaction of human needs is the end of production.

A. The Measurement of Supply

The supply of labor available to an economy might be measured by estimating future additions to output resulting from the use of all available labor power, discounted to a present value to allow for the distribution of the produce over time, after deducting the discounted cost of maintenance. Such calculations would determine the cost of a slave, but otherwise this approach is not helpful. But labor potential cannot be measured by population because population is measured in human beings, who vary widely in their capacities owing to age, health, training, and many other factors. The labor potential depends partly on the time period used as a base. In very short periods, children and pregnant women have a labor potential, but its utilization in one period reduces their potential in the future if children are not educated, or the health of children and women is impaired. The national potential, moreover, is not always the sum of individual potentials calculated separately. If mothers work to the neglect of their children, their potential may be used, but that of their children may be reduced, owing, however, partly to the exclusion of the rearing of children from "production."

Practical discussion of the labor supply must, therefore, begin with measures of total population and proceed to eliminate groups fairly obviously not part of the potential. But the resulting figure takes no account of differences in the capacities of the individuals included (which are important in international comparisons).

B. Total Population

1. NUMBERS IN FACT

The population of the world in 1950 was about 2.4 billion of which about 50% was in Asia, 25% in Europe, 8% in each of North America and Africa, and 5% in Central and South America (Table 25, Fig. 17). World population increased 30% from 1650 to 1750, 60% from 1750 to 1850, and 100% from 1850 to 1950. From 1850 to 1914 it was increasing at a rate of about 0.75% a year, but the rate accelerated after 1920 and by 1950 was about 1% a year, which is probably the highest rate in history. There was practically no change between 1914 and 1921, owing to the reduction of births (because of the absence of men at the war), military losses, the influenza epidemic (which killed about 10 million persons in India alone in 1918), and famine in Russia between 1917 and 1921 (which caused a loss of some 10 millions). But in the war years, 1939 to 1945, world population increased 7% in spite of war losses. The maximum probable rate of increase is 3.5% a year, corresponding to a birth rate of 45 per 1000 and a death rate of 10 per 1000.[1]

TABLE 25

WORLD POPULATION, 1650 TO 1950
(MILLIONS)*

Continent	1650	1750	1850	1900	1950
Europe	100	140	266	401	557
North America	1	1	26	81	190
Central and South America	12	11	33	63	137
Oceania	2	2	2	6	13
Africa	100	95	95	120	198
Asia	330	479	749	937	1,305
World total	545	728	1,171	1,608	2,400

* For. Agric., Feb. 1953.

Net increase varies widely among different parts of the world. Between 1750 and 1850, population increased 2500% in North America, 200% in Central and South America, 90% in Europe, 60% in Asia, and little in Africa and Oceania. Between 1850 and 1950, it increased 630% in North America, 550% in Oceania, 300% in Central and South America, 110% in Europe, 100% in Africa, and 75% in Asia (Table 25). The high percentages in North

[1] U.N., Measures for the Econ. Devel. of Underdeveloped Areas, 45.

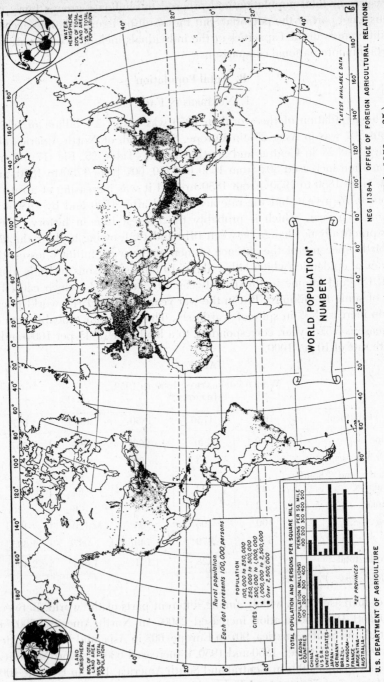

Fig. 17. Distribution of world population in about 1949. (Source: *For. Agric.*, Feb. 1953, p. 25.)

America and Oceania were due to heavy immigration into countries with small initial populations. In Europe the largest average annual rates of increase between 1800 and 1914 were in Poland, 1.28%; England and Wales, 1.25%; and Russia, 1.1%. The smallest increases were Ireland .17%, France, .35% and Spain, .47%. The population of Europe declined about 2.6% between 1914 and 1919. Population increased 150% in many Middle East countries (300% in Egypt) in the 19th century.[2] After 1920 the rate of increase slowed down in Europe, but accelerated in Asia and Africa, and especially in Latin America, where population is growing faster than in any other major region in the world, at a rate about twice that of the world as a whole (the population doubling about every forty years).[3] The annual rate of increase for Latin America as a whole increased from 1.8% between 1928 and 1938 to 2.3% between 1948 and 1951.[4] In Asia a rate of 2.11% a year was reached in the Philippines and 2.12% in Indonesia. In Japan population probably increased little between 1700 and early in the 19th century, when it began to increase slowly as the commercial and handicraft revolutions gained impetus. Between 1872 and 1950, however, population increased about 140%. After 1945 the rate of increase was for a few years the highest in Japanese history, but has since fallen.[5] There is no accurate information on the population of China. Estimates indicate 100 to 150 million people in 1650, 350 to 450 millions in 1850, and 450 millions in 1950. But before 1712 the population was probably under-enumerated because censuses were used for compulsory labor and tax purposes, and thereafter overenumerated to flatter the emperor.[6] In Africa the high rates are north of the Sahara and in parts of central Africa. The population of Russia is estimated to have increased nearly 50% (to 205 millions) between 1913 and 1950.[7] The lowest rates are in Europe (generally below 1%), Oceania (about 1%), and North America, where the slowest increase has been in the U.S.A. (0.7%). (Table 26.) The rate in the U.S.A. is, however, above that in Europe, and rising.

2. INFLUENCES AFFECTING THE SIZE OF POPULATIONS

The maximum population of a country obviously depends on the supply of consumption goods necessary for survival. But it does not follow that populations reach and stay at this maximum. Malthus at first contended[8] that populations in fact tended to reach this maximum because they propagated faster than they could expand their food supply, and were

---

[2] Bonné, *op. cit.*, 162.

[3] U.N., *Econ. Surv. of Latin America*, 1948, 146.

[4] F.A.O., *Prospects for Agricultural Development in Latin America*, 1953, 2.

[5] Taeuber, "Population Growth and Economic Development in Japan," XI *Jour. of Econ. Hist.*, 1951, 424.

[6] Ta Chen, *Population in Modern China*, 3.

[7] Bergson *et al.*, "Post War Reconstruction and Development in the U.S.S.R.," *Annals, Am. Acad. Pol. and Soc. Sci.*, May 1949, 56.

[8] Malthus, *Essay on the Principle of Population*, 1798.

limited only by vice and misery. But in later editions he accepted the possibility of restriction by self-restraint, and recommended measures to induce such restraint. Ricardo emphasized the tendency of populations to propagate until they reduced themselves to subsistence levels of living

TABLE 26

ANNUAL RATE OF POPULATION INCREASE IN SELECTED COUNTRIES
FOR LAST INTERCENSAL PERIOD*

	Date of previous census	Annual rate of increase (per cent)
Africa		
Egypt	1937	1.13
Union of South Africa	1946	1.74
Belgian Congo	1947	1.24
Algeria	1948	1.44
French Equatorial Africa	1936	1.38
French West Africa	1936	0.17
Madagascar	1939	2.23
Morocco	1947	2.54
Tunis	1948	2.16
Southern Rhodesia	1946	3.96
Uganda	1931	2.00
Northern Rhodesia	1946	1.32
North America		
Canada	1941	1.04
Cuba	1943	1.62
Guatemala	1940	2.67
Mexico	1940	1.77
United States	1940	0.70
Bermuda	1939	2.61
Jamaica	1943	1.70
Puerto Rico	1940	1.93
Virgin Islands	1940	1.24
South America		
Argentina	1947	2.19
Brazil	1940	1.50
Chile	1940	1.60
Venezuela	1941	2.77
Asia		
Ceylon	1946	1.55
India	1941	1.41
Japan	1940	1.09
Philippines	1939	2.11
Turkey	1945	1.06
Indonesia	1930	2.12
Malaya	1947	1.59
Hong Kong	1931	3.04
Europe		
Austria	1948	0.47
Belgium	1947	0.30
Czechoslovakia	1947	−0.85
Denmark	1945	0.11

	Date of Previous Census	Annual rate of increase (per cent)
Europe (continued)		
France	1936	−0.02
Germany	1939	1.36
Greece	1940	1.37
Hungary	1948	−0.16
Italy	1936	0.83
Netherlands		?
Norway	1946	0.65
Poland		?
Portugal	1940	1.24
Rumania	1948	−0.22
Spain	1940	0.94
Sweden	1945	0.93
Switzerland	1941	0.44
United Kingdom	1931	0.45
Oceania		
Australia	1947	0.96
New Zealand	1945	1.11
U.S.S.R.	1939	1.14

* U.N., *Demographic Year Book, 1948,* 86 ff.

but noted that people might change their standards regarding "subsistence." Marx embodied the essence of Ricardo's theory of wages in his own, contending that the value of labor, like the value of anything else, is determined by the working time necessary for its production. For labor, this is the cost of reproduction; that is, the value of the necessaries required to sustain its producer. But these necessaries must be adequate to maintain the worker in his normal condition of life, which depends on the degree of civilization attained by the country, especially customs and standards of life acquired by the worker class. "In the case of labor power a historical and moral element thus enters into the determination of its value, contrary to the case of all other commodities."[9] Thus all these writers came ultimately to the conclusion that population was regulated by social forces about which they had no specific theories.

Throughout most of human history, populations probably have approached the maximum number that can be supported near the biological minimum (except for a small wealthier class). Historically the maximum average number of children to all women surviving to the age of forty-five seems to be between six and seven. Births reached this level in much of the world over a considerable period of time among primitive peoples, in the western world in the not very distant past, and in the early 20th century in Japan and Russia. But death rates have often been high enough to keep populations about stable. As populations approach the maximum

[9] Marx, *Capital,* Modern Library Edition, 158.

that can be physiologically maintained, deaths exceed births, usually intermittently in famine years, as they have in North Africa, India, and
China. In China the census figures from the beginning of the Christian era
run in cycles, population being periodically reduced by pestilence, famine,
and war. In India up to 1600 there were similar cycles, apparently shorter
than in China.[10] The Indian population remained fairly stable for over

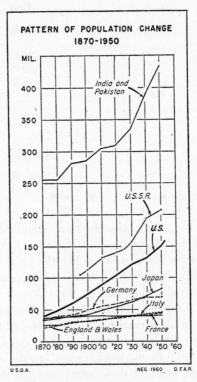

Fig. 18. Germany and France are the only countries shown on this chart that have
not had a steady growth in population since 1870. In nearly every decade, population
in the United States has grown more rapidly than it has in almost any other country.
The increase in our population from 1950 to 1952 greatly exceeded the relative rate of
increase of all countries during the period 1870-1952. (From *For. Agric.,* Feb. 1953,
p. 23.)

2000 years, up to 1650.[11] In Japan population rose less than 10% from
1650 to 1850. In China the population has probably been stationary for
the past century although it rose rapidly prior to that time. The populations of Africa and South America were stationary or declining over long
periods before the 19th century.

Populations most of whom live on the margin of survival are, however,

[10] Ta Chen, *op. cit.,* 3.
[11] Davis, *op. cit.,* 24.

not necessarily stable. For many centuries most of the human race was on this level yet it increased, although slowly.[12] Usually they were increasing the means of subsistence by bringing more land into use, or slowly improving their ways of using it. Abnormal peaks of mortality due to famine and disease were reduced, and births exceeded deaths. Death rates did fall in the 18th century in western Europe and North America, in the later 19th century in other areas, and in the 20th century in Asia, Africa, and Latin America. The later declines have been faster than the earlier ones in Europe, because the medical knowledge to be taken over has become increasingly effective. But increasing medical knowledge could not provide for the survival of more people if more food could not be obtained. Few underdeveloped countries now have populations that are stable at a subsistence level. Rapidly increasing populations in spite of high death rates (Table 27) must have been made possible by increases

TABLE 27

CRUDE BIRTH AND DEATH RATES AND RATES OF POPULATION
INCREASE IN SELECTED COUNTRIES*

	Crude birth rate	Crude death rate	Net annual rate of increase last inter-censal period
	(per 1000 population 1947)		
China	NA	NA	NA
Mexico	45.1	16.3	1.77
Malaya	43.2	19.5	1.59
Egypt (1945)	42.6	27.7	1.13
Puerto Rico	42.6	11.9	1.93
Ecuador	40.4	16.1	NA
Venezuela	39.5	13.9	2.77
Guatemala	36.8	17.4	2.67
Japan	34.8	14.8	1.09
Chile	33.8	16.7	1.60
Jamaica	32.6	14.1	1.70
Greece	29.1	14.6	1.37
India	26.6	19.7	1.41
New Zealand	26.4	9.4	1.11
U.S.A.	25.8	10.1	0.70
Australia	24.1	10.1	0.96
England and Wales	20.5	12.3	0.54

* U.N., *Demographic Year Book, 1948*, 86, 260, 312.

in the resources available, or increases in the efficiency of their use. Irrigation has increased the amount of usable land and crops per acre (e.g., in Egypt and India). More capital in other forms may have increased output. Improved transport may make food supplies more widely available. Access to foreign markets may enable countries to obtain by trade more

[12] Usher, "The Balance Sheet of Economic Development," *Jour. of Econ. Hist.*, Fall 1951, 334.

food than they could grow with given resources. But where they remain near the edge of subsistence, they must be propagating fully up to their means.

Populations may be growing towards the subsistence limit, and their means of living per head of population falling. For this to be possible the population must previously have been below the limit. War and pestilence have frequently reduced populations temporarily below the limit in the past in India, China, and most countries. Four successive outbreaks of the Black Death reduced the population of Britain sharply between 1348 and 1380 and it continued to decline slowly until about 1420. In India population increased over 300%, from about 100 millions in 1600 to 414 millions in 1946, despite famines and the influenza epidemic between 1911 and 1921.[13] Between 1871 and 1921 population increased 47%, but production 77%, but between 1921 and 1931 population increased a further 11% without any increase in production.[14] In Egypt population increased 100% between 1888 and 1937, but agricultural output increased less. Between 1924-8 and 1939 the population and volume of output of the main crops both increased about 19%, but the index of crop values, adjusted for price changes, fell 15% (largely because of a fall in the price of cotton, the bulk of which is exported). In Egypt, and possibly Iran, agricultural production has lagged behind population since 1939, but has been partly compensated by industrial production. In Israel population has increased (largely by immigration) at a rate well above the increase in production.[15] In Algeria the Arab population has been multiplying fast (owing to improvements in hygiene and security) while agricultural output per acre is almost stable. In Tunisia the population has increased 200% since 1881, and at an annual rate of 2.5% between 1937 and 1947 (almost the highest rate known), and it is increasingly difficult to maintain even the present low standard of living among the nomadic pastoral peoples. The Moroccan population doubled between 1915 and 1935; in 1948 the production of cereals (the basic diet of the people) was increasing only about 60% as fast as the population. Harvests fluctuate, and in 1945 famine was averted only by the importation of wheat. In Spain the population increased .94% a year between 1930 and 1940. In 1939 the country was almost self-sufficient in wheat, but by 1947 there was little prospect of self-sufficiency. The population of Java increased 200% between 1860 and 1930. Even by 1900 the supply of rice per head had fallen about 25%.[16]

Wherever populations respond to increases in total output by multiplying so as to remain on, or approach, a subsistence level, attempts at economic development end merely in enabling more people to live on a sub-

---

13 Famine Inquiry Commission *Final Report*, 73-4, 98, 431.
14 Clark, *Conditions of Economic Progress*, 2nd ed., 124.
15 Issawi, "Population and Wealth in Egypt," *Milbank Memorial Fund Quarterly*, Jan. 1949; U.N., *Rev. of Econ. Conditions in the Middle East*, 1951, 13.
16 *Econ. Rev. of Indonesia*, April-June 1949, 38.

sistence level. This frustration might be avoided if economic development could be achieved fast enough to bring about reductions in the birth rate like those of the more developed countries. But if the resources available for development do not reach a certain critical level, underdeveloped countries may not succeed in ever surmounting this "population hump,"[17] especially since their populations cannot migrate as easily as those of the developing countries could in the 19th century.

Populations on a subsistence level of living must decline when their means of living shrink. The population of Spain declined continuously from 1590 to about 1720 as a result of changes in the relative importance of northern Europe and the Mediterranean region.[18] When the potato blight in Ireland in 1846-7 reduced the economic potential of the land with existing techniques, population was reduced by deaths from starvation and epidemics, and by emigration, from 6.5 millions in 1841 to 4.4 millions in 1861. Population continued to fall steadily to 2.9 millions in 1926, and thereafter remained about stable.[19]

Populations do not always increase fast enough to absorb, through maintaining more people, all increases in production. Their failure to do so since early in the 19th century, when industrialization lifted the population ceiling, marks one of the greatest changes in the economic history of the world. The first response to industrialization was the age-old one of maintaining birth rates while increasing production facilitated survival and reduced death rates. Consequently, populations increased rapidly. In the Middle Ages the average age at death was probably about 30 but death rates began to fall in Europe and North America some time during the 18th century. In Britain, deaths exceeded births up to 1730, and death rates were rising (largely owing to excessive gin drinking, especially in London). But from 1730 to 1760 the death rate was falling; after 1780 it fell rapidly. Gin drinking was checked in 1751 by high taxation and regulation of sale. The decline in the death rate in the early 19th century was due in part to population changes in the late 18th century that had reduced the average age of the population.[20] But the decline was also due to improvements in food supply (assisted by better employment, rising wages, and increasing agricultural efficiency) and in medicine. Smallpox was a serious cause of death until Jenner discovered vaccination at the end of the 18th century. Privately endowed hospitals and improvements in the treatment of children (especially of orphans) also reduced deaths. The population increased from 5.5 millions in 1700 to 9 millions in 1800 and

[17] U.N., *Financing Econ. Devel. in Underdeveloped Countries*, 60; U.N., *Measures for the Econ. Devel. of Underdeveloped Countries*, Ch. VII.

[18] Usher, "The Balance Sheet of Economic Development," *Jour. of Econ. Hist.*, Fall 1951, 335.

[19] *Statist*, Feb. 3, 1951.

[20] Ashton, T. S., "The Standard of Life of the Workers in England, 1790 to 1830," *Tasks of Econ. Hist.*, IX, 22.

20.8 millions in 1850. Misery was not diminishing, and population increase was keeping up with the consumption goods available to the general population, which were increasing, including the resources devoted to health improvement. But because part of the increase in output went to the wealthier and into capital accumulation, population did not keep pace with increases in total output. The German population, which was probably about stable from 1600 to 1800, had increased 80% by 1870.[21] At a later time the Japanese population behaved similarly; death rates fell without much change in birth rate and population increased 136% between 1868 and 1940.[22] Population has also rapidly increased in Russia, from 130 millions in 1913 to 191 millions in 1945, despite war losses of about 20 millions.[23] Part of the rapidity of this increase is attributable to the youth of the population.

At a later stage of economic development birth rates were reduced in the developing countries. As the reduction in births exceeded the reduction in deaths, the rate of population increase fell. The crude birth rate began to fall in France in 1775 (when it was about 38.6 per thousand) and by 1850 it was 26.6. But elsewhere in western Europe, the decline began about 1880 (although later in Italy and Spain, where it was also faster). In eastern Europe it began in about 1914 and was faster still. It began to fall in Japan in 1910, when fertility was 5.34 and reached 4.3 by 1940 (mostly because of the reduction in the size of the families of those employed in western-type industries). Family size is probably also falling in the urban population of Russia, where the birth rate has fallen steadily from about 45 per thousand in 1913 to 30 per thousand in 1952.[24] Fertility began to decline in India in about 1910, and in Latin America in about the 1930s.[25]

The net outcome of changes in birth and death rates in Britain was that the population increase of 28% in the twenty years from 1861 to 1881 fell steadily in succeeding years to 9% in the 20 years from 1921 to 1941.[26] The decline in the rate of increase has been similar in most of western Europe, but in France the decelleration of population growth occurred earlier than elsewhere. Its population increased only 52% in the 135 years from 1801-1936, and was almost stationary from 1866 (38.2 millions) to 1936 (41.2 millions). Between 1936 and 1946 it declined 2%, but has since begun to increase. Nevertheless in 1951 it was only 11% more than in 1866. These figures include immigration, and France is the only European country with persistent immigration. In India and Japan the fall in birth rate has

21 Clapham, *Economic Development of France and Germany*, 33.

22 Mandlebaum, D. G., "Population Problems in India and Pakistan," *Far Eastern Survey*, Nov. 30, 1949; Thompson, *Population and Peace in the Pacific*, 93.

23 Bergson, *et al.*, "Post War Reconstruction and Development in Russia," *Annals, Am. Acad. of Pol. Sci.*, May 1949, 57.

24 *For. Agric.*, Oct. 1953.

25 Colin Clark, U.N., E/conf 7/plan/W 28, Aug. 8, 1949.

26 U.K., Royal Commission on Population *Report*, 8.

not overtaken the fall in the death rate and the effect of migrations, and population continues to grow rapidly.

Between 1930 and 1950, birth rates were probably about stable in the high-fertility, underdeveloped countries, and falling in south and southeast Europe. But birth rates rose again in the industrial low fertility countries in the 1930s and 1940s. In 1947 the rate was about 25 per thousand in North America, Europe, and Oceania, and 40 to 45 in Latin America, Africa, and Asia. The death rate fell dramatically in underdeveloped countries, from 30 to 50%, but more slowly in the more developed, where the rapid fall had occurred in the late 19th and early 20th centuries. But death rates are still 10 to 13 per thousand in North America, Oceania, and Europe, compared with 17 in Latin America and 25 to 32 in Africa and Asia.[27]

Changes in crude birth and death rates take a long time to have their full effect on the population. The prolongation of life may temporarily offset reductions in the size of families. It may be useful, therefore, to eliminate the effect of the changing age distributions of populations. "Net

TABLE 28

NET REPRODUCTION RATES IN SELECTED COUNTRIES IN 1939
(PER THOUSAND WOMEN)*

Czechoslovakia (1937)	755	U.S.A. (1940)	1023
Switzerland	785	Finland	1036
United Kingdom	808	New Zealand	1073
Sweden	830	Portugal (1942)	1090
Norway	849	Italy (1935-37)	1131
Belgium	859	Canada	1152
France	930	Netherlands	1168
Germany (1936)	934	Ireland (1940-42)	1192
Denmark	940	Chile	1195
Hungary	951	Iceland (1940-41)	1201
Palestine (Jews)	980	Greece	1250
Australia	995	Japan	1440
Spain (1940-41)	1010	Palestine (Moslems)	2460
Poland (1934)	1014		

* U.N., *Demographic Year Book, 1948,* 490 (except Japan).

Reproduction Rates" show approximately the average number of daughters that would be produced by women throughout their lifetime if they were exposed to current fertility and mortality rates at each age. They indicate the rate at which populations would eventually grow per "generation," after present birth and death rates have been stabilized long enough to stabilize the age distribution of the population, and if there were no migration. If the rate is 900, the population would ultimately fall 10% per "generation." In these terms most west European countries face absolute declines in population, and Japan and Palestine Moslems the most rapid increases (Table 28). But there is no reason to expect continuance

[27] U.N., *Prelim. Rep. on World Social Situation,* 1952, 6, 8, 11, 12.

of present fertility and mortality rates. In England the net reproduction rate was 1520 in 1880 and 805 in 1938-42. The population of the country can be stabilized only if the average family is about 6% larger than it has been among couples married in the decade 1927-38. In France the net reproduction rate was just about sufficient to maintain the population from 1841 to about 1900, but by 1936 to 1939 was only about .89. In 1946, however, it began to rise partly, because of the family-allowance system.[28] (Ch. 31). The recent increase in births in other countries, including the U.S.A., if they mean larger families, will raise "net reproduction rates." But even if populations stabilize in the developed countries, births and deaths are likely to be in balance at a level at which the standard of living is far above the subsistence level at which they have been in balance in the past and in less-developed countries.

The social forces regulating population behavior are not clear except where populations are on the margin of survival. Over most of human history, and still in a number of countries, marriage and childbearing habits varied little, the number of births being often the highest biologically possible. Methods of controlling birth were often not widely known. Religious influences have generally been on the side of multiplication (e.g., the Christian church for a long time, Islam, Hinduism, Judaism). The Roman Catholic Church opposes birth control, but most other churches are less explicit. But in many Catholic countries the birth rate is declining, although families are still much larger in the Catholic parts of Holland than in neighboring countries. Mahatma Ghandi in India regarded sexual union without desire for children as immoral for married people.[29] Total populations in these countries have been regulated by death rates (affected by the availability of food supplies, and social institutions such as infanticide, killing the aged, and medical knowledge and practice).

The decline in fertility rates which has slowed down population increase in some countries synchronized with the availability of knowledge and simple methods of controlling births, but these provided only the means. Intensive propaganda for birth control was carried on in England apparently without effect for 50 years. But in France at the same time the size of families was being reduced while there was relatively little public discussion of the subject.[30] The will to control family size has synchronized with fundamental alterations in conditions of living and in the values of the individual and society.[31] Industrialism opened up prospects of better living, people believed that these standards could be attained by

---

[28] Spengler, "Note on France's Response to her Declining Rate of Demographic Growth," XI *Jour. of Econ. Hist.*, 1951, 104.

[29] Wadia and Merchant, *op. cit.*, 107.

[30] Myrdal, A., "Population Trends in Densely Populated Areas," *Proc. Am. Phil. Soc.*, Vol. 95, No. 1, 1951.

[31] Taeuber, "Population Growth and Economic Development in Japan," XI *Jour. Econ. Hist.*, 1951, 426.

restricting the size of the family, and concomitantly acquired the means to restrict increase. These conditions have generally appeared where an increasing proportion of the people live under urban conditions, the status of women is improved, a large family ceases to give a man status, there is a desire for the better training of children, and where there are attractions for women other than childbearing. Family reduction is beginning in other countries, usually at first among the upper classes and in urban populations. A study in India showed a modal preference for 2 or 3 children.[32] But in Japan, and in most underdeveloped countries, any decline in birth rates is overwhelmed by reductions in death rates.

Governments have been ambivalent in their attitude toward population size. They act as if increases in population are desirable when they encourage multiplication and immigration and discourage emigration (often for military reasons). They act as if increases are undesirable when they discourage immigration, although partly for political reasons. But most have sought (except when they declare war) to maintain or increase births. Various governments have penalized failure to marry or have children, mainly through discriminatory taxation. The Nazi government in Germany provided medals for mothers of large families, and loans for those marrying; it taxed the unmarried and reduced the stigma attaching to extramarital motherhood. The increase in the number of children which followed was probably due, however, to parents making up arrears of births due to the depression, and would not have continued. Governments obstruct birth control in Roman Catholic countries. In Egypt birth control has been opposed by the ruling classes, who desire an abundant and cheap supply of labor, but not formally by any Islamic body. Peasant women endeavor by prolongation of lactation and abortion to restrict families.[33] Abortion is penalized in many countries.

In Russia, birth control clinics were operated by the government from 1917 to 1936, and abortion was legally performed in government clinics. In 1936 however, abortion was prohibited except for the preservation of the life of the mother, or on proof by a parent of heritable disease. Subsidies were provided for women with more than seven children, and lying-in homes, nurseries, and kindergartens were increased. There were penalties on divorced persons not paying allowances for the support of children, and a sharp increase in the fees for divorce, which were progressive with the number of divorces per person. During the war of 1939-45, the government imposed taxes on the unmarried and, later, on married persons with families of two or less, and gave medals to mothers of families of eight or more.

Governments have reduced the cost of rearing children through subsidized education, school medical services and meals and housing and,

[32] Davis, op. cit., 17.

[33] Issawi, op. cit., 196.

recently, children's allowances (Ch. 31). They have adjusted their military policies with demographic purpose. The German Nazi government aimed to increase the importance of the German population and diminish that of neighboring countries. It protected the population from bombing and endeavored to preserve the health of Germans (often at the expense of other populations). To maintain the birth rate during the war, it exempted German women and girls from compulsory war service and arranged periodic leave for men in military service. The short-fall of German births compared with anticipated peacetime rates for the four years 1914-1918 was three millions, but for the four years 1939-43, only .75 millions. The populations of neighboring countries were reduced by killing particular classes, starvation, excessive labor, and mass deportations to reduce birth (11-12 million married people were kept apart for some five years). Governments have effectively controlled migration. But, at least in the more developed countries, efforts to stimulate population growth are likely to be defeated if larger populations find their standard of living falling from previous relatively high levels[34] (which is not the effect of children's allowances).

Governments have begun, however, to endorse family limitation as a means of reducing the pressure of population on resources. The Japanese government has formally accepted family control, and birth control clinics have been established. The Indian Planning Commission[35] stated that, unless steps were taken to bring down the birth rate, continuously increasing effort would be used up in maintaining existing standards of consumption.

C. Potential Labor Force

To arrive at the part of the population that may be regarded as the potential labor force, it is necessary to take account of the age and sex distribution and the incidence of physical incapacity.

The proportion of a population at various ages varies widely among countries. If birth and death rates remained stable for a long time, the age distribution would be stable, but would differ among countries according to the level of birth and death rates. The lower the average age at death (the shorter the expectation of life), the smaller the proportion of aged and the higher the proportion in other age groups. But in many populations birth and death rates have not been stable for a long time. Where the birth rate is falling, the proportion of older people rises. Reduction of infant death rates first increases the proportion of young, but later of older, persons. Prolongation of life in later ages increases the proportion

---

[34] Davis, "Population and the Further Spread of Industrial Society," *Proc. Am. Phil. Soc.*, 1951, 18.

[35] *The First Five Year Plan*, 1951, 6.

of aged. Where population is emigrating, the emigrants being typically in the middle age groups, the countries losing the emigrants have an increased proportion both of aged and of young, whereas the countries receiving them have a high proportion in the middle age groups and a relatively low proportion of aged and young (e.g., in the U.S.A. until recent years).

In the world as a whole about 36% of the population was under fifteen years of age in 1947, but it was 25% in North America, 28% in Oceania, 30% in Europe, and 40% in Asia, Latin America, and Africa. The proportion 60 years of age and over was 7% in the world as a whole but 11% in North America, 10% in Oceania and Europe, and 5% in Asia, Latin America, and Africa. If the years between 15 and 60 years of age are arbitrarily regarded as the productive years, the proportion of the population of productive age is 57% for the world as a whole, but 64% in North America, 62% in Oceania, 60% in Europe, and 55% in Asia, Latin America, and Africa.[36] In Russia in 1939 36% of the population was under 15, but only 6.5% 60 or over, leaving 57.5% of productive age.[37] Generally the proportion of aged is high in the more developed countries, and the proportion of young is high in the less developed. Ultimately the produce of a worker is, on the average, shared with fewer non-workers in the developed countries than in the less developed, which contributes to the higher output per head of total population in the more developed countries. Productive individuals require an investment in consumer goods to enable them to reach maturity, and may consume after they have ceased to be productive. In each time period an economy is drawing benefits from past allocations of consumption to maturing human beings and making allocations to permit a new supply to mature. In India some 22% of the national income is used to rear persons who do not live long enough to make any real contribution to production.[38] Countries that have received large numbers of immigrants (e.g., the U.S.A., Canada, Australia, and New Zealand) have economized on the maintenance and education of children, which has been paid by the country of emigration,[39] and the immigrants have often been required to bring capital with them. It has been contended that the present capital of the U.S.A. is roughly equal to the amount it has saved by importing workers already nourished and trained to working age.

The productive proportion of populations is in process of change because of changes in birth and death rates. Where the proportion of aged is high because of declining birth rates, the proportion of aged will rise and proportion at productive ages fall, if birth rates remain stable. In the U.S.A. the proportion over 60 was about 10.4% in 1940 but is expected to be

---

[36] U.N., *Prelim. Report on World Social Situation*, 1952, 17.
[37] Schwartz, *op. cit.*, 28.
[38] F.A.O., *Agriculture in Asia and the Far East*, 1953, 8.
[39] U.N., *Econ. Surv. of Europe in 1953*, 194.

13.1% in 1960.[40] The population of Russia, now young, is aging. The age structure of the British population from 1841 to 1891 was similar to that now existing in Italy, the principal changes in northwest Europe having occurred since 1900. Changes in age composition in England and Wales increased potential productivity per male about 22% between 1875 and 1935.[41] In the underdeveloped countries, where the dependent population consists chiefly of the young, any fall in birth rates would reduce the proportion of young and increase that of older people. Substitution of the age composition of the U.S.A. for that of Africa, Asia and Latin America would increase their potential productivity per head about 15%.[42]

Differences in the proportions of males and females in populations are less than in the proportions of young and old. The largest excess of females occurs in France, Germany (1939), and England and Wales, and Russia,[43] although there is an excess in the U.S.A., Mexico, Brazil, Chile, Peru, Japan, Turkey, Austria, Belgium, Italy, Denmark, Norway, Poland, Portugal, Rumania, Spain, Sweden, Switzerland, Australia, and New Zealand. The largest excess of males over females occurs in India, but there is an excess in Canada, Cuba, and Argentina. In most countries, about 10% more males are born than females, but they have a higher death rate in infancy and over about fifty-five years of age. Consequently "older" populations are likely to have a larger proportion of females than others. Infanticide is more likely to reduce the number of females than of males, but it increases the chance that all women will marry and have children. Migration has affected males more than females, and for a time tends to reduce the proportion of males in the country of origin and increase it in the country of destination.

Sex distribution affects product per head of the population if the proportion of each sex working is different (Ch. 19), or if they differ in efficiency.

1. RELATION BETWEEN SIZE OF POTENTIAL LABOR FORCE AND PRODUCTION PER WORKER

The size of the labor force influences output per worker insofar as it influences the relative quantities of each of the resources that can be put into production, and the methods of production used. Countries with large populations (e.g., U.S.A.) may have high living standards, but countries with small populations (e.g., New Zealand and Australia) also do. Large populations may have low living standards (e.g., China and India).

---

40 Dewhurst et al., America's Needs and Resources, 50.

41 Spengler, "Economic Factors in the Development of Densely Populated Areas," Proc., Am. Phil. Soc., Vol. 95, No. 1, 21.

42 Spengler, op. cit., 24.

43 Lorimer, F., The Population of the Soviet Union: History and Prospects, 143, cit.; Schwartz, op. cit., 28.

There is a size of working force that permits greater average output than if the force were considerably larger or smaller while the quality of the labor force, knowledge of methods of production, and the supply of land and capital are fixed. Within a range, larger labor forces permit increasing returns to labor, because of greater specialization. Within any single production unit there is an optimal range of size for production which may be small (as frequently in agriculture) or large (as in the steel industry). A small country may not be able to maintain plants of the most economical size in some industries unless it has an export market, although if it has more than one suboptimal-sized plant in an industry, at least one could be more nearly the most economical size. Greater size for industries as a whole permits economies external to each industry because the production, possibly of its raw materials, and, more probably, of power and producers' goods, may be capable of organization on a more economical scale. Although the value of output per worker in similar industries in different countries does not appear to vary with the size of industry, "physical increasing returns are there, the whole benefit of which is passed on to the consumer in the form of lower prices."[44] Larger working forces on a given territory increase the volume of transportation without equivalent increases in cost, again providing economies external to most industries. Transportation is often costly in underdeveloped countries because it is underutilized.[45] Higher density of population may also permit production to be more widely scattered, and thus reduce the amount of transportation without sacrificing economies in production. Greater size in a sector may also permit reductions in cost through the greater specialization of firms. International trade offers only a partial escape from the disadvantages of a small labor force, because of the cost of transport and, in fact, because it is often neither free nor dependable.

If the foregoing factors causing increasing returns to labor with increasing size of labor force operated without limit, overcrowding would be inconceivable. But a population beyond some range of size in relation to resources suffers from decreasing returns to labor. The economies of specialization in the use of land and labor in agriculture eventually run out. Additional workers reduce average output in China, India, the Middle East and many underdeveloped areas. It has been estimated that under the agricultural conditions in pre-war Europe the marginal productivity of agricultural workers not only fell below the average but approached zero when the number of persons dependent on agriculture rose above 40 per acre.[46] If the supply of capital is fixed, a larger number of workers has a smaller amount of capital per head, which reduces output in agriculture

---

[44] Clark, *Conditions of Economic Progress*, 2nd ed., 295.

[45] Clark, *op. cit.*, 327.

[46] Spengler, "Aspects of the Economics of Population Growth," *South. Econ. Jour.*, 1948, 248.

and industry. Whenever the marginal product of labor is less than the average, the average output falls, and the marginal product may be zero or negative.

Historical information never provides evidence regarding the effect of different sizes of population while all other elements remain fixed. The supply of land changes when boundaries are changed, often as a result of war (e.g., Germany, Poland, Russia, Finland, and Japan). The supply of capital and knowledge, and the organization of production may change, as when open fields are enclosed or large estates are broken into smaller enterprises, but most notably in the process of industrialization. These changes also change the optimal population, although how, and to what extent, is not clear. A country whose population was previously above the optimum may, however, become underpopulated. And an underpopulated country may become overpopulated without a change in actual population.

Optimum and actual working forces often change at the same time and,

TABLE 29

RELATION BETWEEN INCREASE IN WORKING POPULATION AND
POTENTIAL° REAL INCOME PER HEAD†

	Percentage rate of increase in working population 1913-1930	Percentage change in potential real income per head 1913 to 1925-34
Bulgaria	41.2	−18
Germany	38.8	−22
Holland	38.2	−7
Canada	34.8	22
Greece	31.8	4
U.S.A.	24.5	16
Norway	24.1	13
Finland	23.9	−1
Australia	21.0	39
Sweden	18.8	23
Russia	17.1	−4
Denmark	16.8	9
Japan	14.5	105
Italy	14.1	−12
Hungary	11.4	31
Britain	10.0	13
Rumania	9.8	−20
Switzerland	8.6	38
Spain	8.2	39
Yugoslavia	6.7	23
Czechoslovakia	4.5	16
France	3.4	−8
Belgium	0.7	1
Austria	−9.0	1

° Assuming whole population in employment.
† Clark, *Conditions of Economic Progress*, 1st ed., 151.

as the optimum is never clearly known, the extent to which product per worker departs from what it would be with the ideal number of workers, is also not known. The industrial revolution was accompanied by great increases both in population and standards of living. But there is no means of telling whether these populations tended to the optimal size. They might have had a higher productivity per worker if they had been larger or smaller. Historically, some increasing populations have improved their standard of living (e.g., Britain in the 19th century, the U.S.A., Canada, Australia, Norway, Sweden and Denmark) while others have improved it little or suffered a decline (e.g., parts of the Middle East and North Africa). Populations may remain about stable with a low or a high standard, and possibly a rising one.

Increases in population and rising average income have more frequently accompanied each other in primarily industrial countries than in predominantly agrarian ones (Table 29). The rapid transfer of working force from agricultural to industrial activities somewhat offsets any tendency for increases in labor force to reduce agricultural productivity. But many factors are operating in addition to changes in the size of the labor force. Industrial countries are generally better able to add to their fund of capital than agricultural countries. Countries like Bulgaria, Germany, and Holland reduced hours of labor during the period covered in Table 29. The adjustment of average income to an assumed full employment of labor is somewhat arbitrary; in fact, there may be more unemployment as the importance of agricultural employment declines in relation to industrial.

TABLE 30

WORLD POPULATION ACCORDING TO DEGREE OF CONTROL OVER
BIRTH AND DEATH RATES[*]

	COUNTRIES IN WHICH BIRTH AND DEATH RATES ARE:		
	Largely under control	Passing under control	Not under control
Percentage of world population in			
1935	20.2	21.0	58.8
1970	15.6	20.2	64.2
2000	13.5	19.5-21.1	65.5-66.7
Per capita income per year			
(International Units) 1925-34	350	118	44
Percentage of world income	58.2	20.4	21.3
Percentage of occupied population in agriculture	22.0	56.6	74.7
Capital equipment per head (relatives)	100	39	11

[*] Spengler, "Aspects of the Economics of Population Growth," 26, *South. Econ. Jour.*, 1948, 248.

In general, the countries in which birth and death rates are about stationary have per capita income about seven times as high as in the poorest group; with 15% to 20% of the world's population they receive about 60% of world income, have a relatively small proportion of all workers in agriculture, and a relatively large amount of capital per head. Countries where birth and death rates seem to be stabilizing have about 20% of world population. The countries where birth and death rates are not under control have low incomes, mainly from agriculture; and little capital per head (Table 30).

Chapter 19

Labor: Utilization

A. The Amount of Potential Labor Time Utilized

Output per head of the population is affected by the extent to which the labor potential is used. Production may be lower than it could be because potential workers do not work all the hours they could (the subject of this chapter), or because hours used are not used to their full potential effectiveness (Ch. 20). There is no reason why societies should seek the maximum possible product, but it is well to know the extent to which they do not achieve it.

1. The Number of Potential Workers "Normally at Work"

Output may be reduced because some potential workers do not work at all, that is, are not "normally at work" or "economically active." The definition of "normally at work" is never precise and varies among countries (particularly with regard to agriculture and self-employment). It usually includes the unemployed as being "normally at work." Despite their low comparability, such figures give some indication of the proportion of the population contributing nothing to production, on the unreal assumption that the unpaid work of women in the home is unproductive.

The proportion of the whole population that has been "economically active" in recent years ranges from over 50% in Rumania, Russia, Bulgaria, Austria, and Denmark to less than 35% in Chile, Brazil, Guatemala, and Mexico, and is 49.2% in France, 47% in Britain, and 40% in the U.S.A. (Table 31). It is generally higher in Europe and lower in Latin America, Asia, and Africa. The proportion of wage earners to total population in Africa south of the Sahara ranges from 1.2% in Nigeria and 1.5% in French West Africa to 9% in the Gold Coast and 20.2% in Southern Rhodesia. But a large part of the remainder of the population is engaged in subsistence

341

TABLE 31

ECONOMICALLY ACTIVE POPULATION AS PERCENTAGE OF TOTAL
POPULATION IN SELECTED COUNTRIES

Country	Per Cent	Country	Per Cent
Africa *			
Egypt	38.3	Bulgaria	56.5
Tunis	42.0	Czechoslovakia	48.1
		Denmark	51.3
America *		France	49.2
		Germany	49.8
Canada	40.6	Greece	44.2
United States	40.0	Hungary	44.1
Argentina	42.9	Italy	43.2
Brazil	34.0	Netherlands	40.1
Chile	34.7	Norway	42.0
Guatemala	33.3	Poland	47.0
Mexico	32.3	Portugal	39.5
Peru	39.9	Rumania	57.9
		Spain	36.9
Asia †		Sweden	47.1
Philippines	52.9	Switzerland	46.7
Siam	47.2	Turkey	49.0
Japan	43.5	United Kingdom	47.0
India	42.2	Yugoslavia	46.5
Korea	40.9		
Malayan Union	40.8	**U.S.S.R.**	57.5
Indonesia	34.4		
		Oceania *	
Europe *		Australia	42.6
Austria	52.3	New Zealand	43.2
Belgium	46.3		

* I.L.O., *Year Book of Lab. Stat. 1947-48,* 7. Figures generally relate to last census.
† U.N., *Econ. Surv. of Asia and the Far East, 1948,* 109. Figures relate to years from 1930 to 1944 differing among countries.

agriculture or export agriculture that can be carried on on a small scale (palm oil and cocoa in Nigeria and French West Africa), or small-scale mining (in West Africa).[1] But the whole population is not even potentially productive, and it is necessary to eliminate some groups.

Older males decline in productivity after some age not clearly known. The older part of the population varies among countries in relative importance (Ch. 18), but the extent to which it produces also varies. The proportion of males over 65 years of age who are economically active appears to be higher in the less than in the more developed countries (Table 32) although information is obtainable only for a few countries and is not uniform. But failure to employ all adult males does not represent a waste of labor potential. Some are unable to produce for individual reasons. The age at which people in general cease to be productive is not

[1] U.N., *Rev. of Econ. Cond. in Africa,* 1951, 76.

TABLE 32

PROPORTION OF MALES IN OLDER AGE GROUPS ECONOMICALLY
ACTIVE IN SELECTED COUNTRIES*

Country	Proportion of males 65 years and over who are economically active
Egypt	89.7
Portugal	86.4
Peru	82.6
Hungary	76.1
Italy	72.6
Sweden	49.8
United Kingdom	47.9
Belgium	45.3
Netherlands	42.6
U.S.A.	41.7
New Zealand	40.0
Australia	34.3
Germany	29.7
Denmark	3.5

* I.L.O., *Year Book of Lab. Stat.*, 1947-8, 22.

known, but depends somewhat on techniques of production. Where techniques are primitive, people continue producing, although at a diminishing rate, to a great age (if they survive). Modern industry, on the other hand, places great emphasis on youth; the aged are not all permitted to produce because continuous capital extension creates unemployment, and employers choose younger workers. Social custom also influences the age to which people are employed. In the more developed countries older people increasingly expect to retire and the expectation is reflected in social security arrangements.

There is also a lower age limit below which individuals are not potentially productive. This part of the population also varies in importance among countries, but the extent to which it produces also varies. The proportion of males from 15 to 19 years of age at work has been markedly low in recent years in Canada and the U.S.A., but has been over 80% in most countries, although again the sample of countries is small (Table 32). In Latin America a relatively high proportion of the labor force in manufacturing is in the younger age groups: in Colombia in 1945-46 about 28% were 16 to 20 years of age.[2] Failure to employ all these young males is also no indication of waste of potential labor. The age at which it is in the long run efficient for males to enter production depends partly on techniques of production. In earlier times, and now in many underdeveloped countries, participation in production does not for the most part require literacy. But in the more developed countries prevailing types of production require considerable education and training, which prolongs the period in which individuals are too young to work. Social custom in

[2] U.N., *Econ. Surv. of Latin America, 1948*, 32.

TABLE 33

PROPORTION OF MALES IN YOUNGER AGE GROUPS ECONOMICALLY
ACTIVE IN SELECTED COUNTRIES*

Country	Percentage of males 15-19 years of age at work
Egypt	91.1
United Kingdom	88.3
Italy	88.2
New Zealand	87.9
Germany	86.1
Denmark	85.1
Hungary	84.4
Sweden	82.3
France	82.3
Czechoslovakia	82.2
Australia	80.9
Belgium	80.4
Canada	50.8
U.S.A.	36.5

* I.L.O., *Year Book of Lab. Stat.*, 1947-8, 22.

capitalist countries sets a minimum level of education and condemns exhausting work by children in their early years. Factory legislation and laws regarding compulsory education reflect these attitudes that rest not only on considerations of productivity, but also on concern for the general welfare of the population and its political stability.

The proportion of males between 20 and 64 years of age who are economically active ranges from about 93 to 99%—this range may well be accounted for by differences in measurement. The proportion was highest in the U.S.A. in 1940 with 98.7%, and among the lowest are Canada in 1941, 86.8%; Germany in 1933, 92.7%, and Portugal in 1940, 92.7%. But the proportion of "economically active" women in these age groups varies widely from about 17% in Egypt to about 50% in France and Japan (in a very incomplete list of countries). (Table 34.) The labor potential of women is also influenced by techniques of production. In agrarian societies women often work equally with men, but they are less likely to engage in skilled craft work. Women were also widely employed in the early stages of industrialization (partly because of the low wages of men) although again not very widely in craft work. But, as industrialization has evolved, the skill and strength required for many jobs has been reduced and women are able to do more jobs than formerly. Women have been less used in skilled work not because they cannot acquire skill in the same way as men, but because they provide a less satisfactory investment for training since so many of them subsequently leave their jobs to marry. The number of women employed in western Europe and the U.S.A. has recently increased considerably. In Britain between 1939 and 1948 the number of males in the civilian labor force declined by 400,000 while the number of females increased about 600,000. Female employment in industry has also increased in the Scandinavian countries. In the U.S.A. during the same period the number of males increased about 2 million and the number of females about 4.5 million.[3] Countries in the early stages of industrialization also employ large numbers of women. There were more female industrial workers than male workers in Japan until about 1930, but thereafter, as the heavy industries grew in importance, the number of male workers exceeded the number of female. In Latin America, women were 24.8% of the manufacturing labor force in Chile in 1945, 33.4% in Colombia in 1945, and nearly 33% in the state capitals in Brazil in 1944-48 (compared with 17.8% in the U.S.A. in 1940). In Russia the percentage of women in the labor force increased from 38% in 1940 to 53% in 1942.[4]

TABLE 34

PROPORTION OF WOMEN 20 TO 64 YEARS OF AGE ECONOMICALLY
ACTIVE IN SELECTED COUNTRIES*

Country	Date	Percentage
Japan	1930	49.9
France	1941	49.2
Peru	1940	44.9
Denmark	1940	44.1
Germany	1933	44.1
U.S.A.	1940	28.8
Hungary	1930	26.5
Netherlands	1930	24.5
Australia	1933	23.8
New Zealand	1936	23.5
Italy	1931	23.2
Portugal	1940	21.8
Canada	1931	20.0
Egypt	1937	16.9

* I.L.O., *Year Book of Lab. Stat.*, 1947-8, 22.

There is doubtless still a considerable amount of female labor that could be utilized in many countries, but the number of economically active women is low partly because many women are engaged in unpaid labor in agriculture and in maintaining homes, caring for and training the young, and caring for the sick. Paid labor of this sort is generally regarded as adding to the national product, but unpaid labor is not, hence the perversity that a man can reduce the national income by marrying his housekeeper. The utilization of the labor of women is influenced by social custom. In most societies the wealthier men prevent their wives from working, partly as a means of ostentation. In a number of Western societies workers have opposed the employment of married women to reduce competition in the

[3] U.N., *World Econ. Rep.*, 1948, 229.
[4] U.N., *Econ. Surv. of Latin America*, 1948, 32; Bergson, "Post War Reconstruction and Development in Russia," *Annals, Am. Acad. of Pol. Sci.*, May 1949, 58.

labor market. Nevertheless, in western Europe the proportion of women working has increased.

The number of potential workers who are in fact economically active depends on the incentive to work. Without economic incentives most people would be active, although not always as active or in the kinds of activity that they are under present conditions. For the mass of the population at all times, the chief incentive has been economic pressure. The alternative to work (usually starvation) is less pleasant than work with its rewards. But some individuals have always been able to live without work. They have received tithes, labor dues (under the feudal system), or money incomes from land. Landowners are criticized in a number of underdeveloped countries for their failure to contribute actively to production (Ch. 6). As private property in other types of productive resources has increased in importance during the last 200 years in capitalist countries, it has provided a means by which a relatively small number of individuals may live without working while the mass of the population has been under great pressure to work. This arrangement has been defended as an incentive to work and save. But it is usually operative only for a few people and in rapidly expanding economies. In the 20th century it has created social tension expressed in criticism of inequality of incomes. Most countries have made tax systems increasingly progressive, and the developed countries have begun to provide incomes without work to the unemployed, aged, parents of families, and the sick. To minimize the tendency of these incomes to reduce the incentive to work, governments usually require the unemployed to prove that they are "genuinely seeking work" (sometimes tested by the offer of work through a government employment office), the sick to obtain medical certificates that they are unable to work, and the aged to prove their age. In some countries, however, attempts have been made to induce the aged to continue to work (Ch. 29). Incentives vary considerably in detail and have become complex, but in their detail they are calculated to make people work more than they otherwise would, or at jobs which they would not choose, and, therefore, concern the productivity and allocation of labor (Ch. 20) more than the number of potential workers who do not work.

2. The Utilization of the Potential Labor Time of Persons "Normally at Work"

a. Definition of the Potential

The national product may be reduced by failure to utilize all the hours of labor that "persons normally at work" could perform. But it is difficult to define the labor potential. We do not know how many hours a day, days a week, or weeks a year of labor would maximize the output of goods and services. The maximum of net satisfactions is likely to be achieved where the supply of goods and services is less than the maximum because beyond some level of output further goods and services can be obtained only by incurring dissatisfactions in fatigue and loss of leisure in excess of the satisfactions yielded by the additional goods.

In the absence of a measure of this labor potential, it is necessary to consider various sources of reduction in labor time, leaving appraisal of the effect on net satisfactions to personal judgment (which must rest on unsure assumptions).

b. Actual Use of Labor Time

The chief sources of loss of labor time can be explored by considering hours of labor (per day or week) and the intermittence of work due to sickness, accidents, voluntary absence, industrial disputes and involuntary unemployment.

i. Hours of Labor

Information regarding hours of labor is available for few countries. It is least satisfactory for agricultural labor because of inadequate reporting and because hours vary widely with the seasons. In some underdeveloped countries, the number of hours worked is considerably less than in western industry, but in others the hours of agricultural labor are very long. Where they are relatively short (as in parts of Africa and in Malaya) workers are not necessarily working far below capacity, because climatic and health conditions may lower the number of potential hours. Some, however, work at less than capacity owing to the excess of workers in relation to land, and short hours of work represent concealed unemployment.

The hours of labor in industry (usually including mining and services) are generally higher in the less developed countries (e.g., Egypt, China, and Hungary) than in the more developed (e.g., the U.S.A. and Canada) (Table 35) but information is too sparse and lacking in uniformity for

TABLE 35

HOURS OF WORK PER WORKER OUTSIDE AGRICULTURE IN
SELECTED COUNTRIES IN 1947[*]

Country	Hours per week	Hours per day
Egypt	51	
Canada	43.5	
U.S.A.	41.2	
China		9.55
Czechoslovakia	47.76	
Finland	44.7[†]	
France	45	
Germany	37.5-40.3	
Hungary		8.7
Sweden	46.8	
Switzerland	47.8	
United Kingdom	46.2	

[*] I.L.O., *Year Book of Lab. Stat.*, 1947-8, 85. The statistics are not entirely on a uniform basis.

[†] Half the rate per fortnight.

generalization, and the figures are influenced by the relative importance of each industry in the different countries.

Reduction of working hours began in Britain in the first half of the 19th century, but after 1885 reductions were made in both wealthy and poor countries.[5] The movement accelerated after 1918, when the 48-hour week was widely adopted in Europe, and in some countries the work week was later reduced to 42 or 40 hours.[6] After 1945 hours of labor did not always return to the level of 1938. France and the U.S.A. are among the countries with somewhat longer hours of labor in 1946 than in 1938.[7] In general, the reductions have been later but larger in the less developed countries, and differences among countries are now small.

The influences affecting the hours of labor vary from country to country. Considerations of efficiency have not always been dominant. In the early stage of industrialization hours were very long (especially in Britain), largely on the ground that "the profit is made in the last hour."[8] So long as there was a large supply of new workers to be taken in when the older were exhausted, there may have been some economy to the employer (although not to society) in working at least fairly long hours. In some countries, such as Africa (with regard to mining labor) and India, workers frequently return from their jobs to agriculture, which may give them an opportunity for recuperation. But it is now known that output per day does not always increase as hours of work are lengthened. If hours are reduced, and sufficient time is permitted for benefits to appear, output per day increases down to a certain number of hours, below which it falls. But the optimal hours are not clearly known. Hours of labor have been influenced in practice by the bargaining power of workers, although this phrase has little meaning except in terms of what the workers succeed in getting. Nevertheless, the organization of workers into unions in the capitalist countries (often reinforced by middle-class humanitarianism) has forced employers to experiment with shorter hours of work, which have often turned out to be more productive. But in the more advanced countries, hours of work may have fallen below this efficiency level, which is unobjectionable provided workers prefer more leisure to more goods.

The state has regulated the hours of labor in many countries in recent years, setting maxima for minors, women, specified occupations, and occasionally wide sectors of industry. In socialist countries, governments decree hours of labor in general. In Russia the labor code of 1922 required an eight-hour day for adults, provided two weeks' holiday with pay, and prohibited child labor. The seven-hour day was introduced in April 1927. The continuous work week introduced in 1929 required five days work

---

[5] Clark, *op. cit.*, 44.

[6] U.N., *Econ. Surv. of Europe in 1949*, 205.

[7] U.N., *World Econ. Rep.*, 1948, 230.

[8] Marx, *Capital*, Vol. 1, Ch. 8.

with each sixth day a day of rest. This arrangement was found to reduce the responsibility of the worker for the machine or the work performed, especially in transportation, and the continuous work week was liquidated in 1931 when a six-day week with one day of rest common to all was provided. In 1939 the seven-hour day and five-day week were introduced, but since 1940 the government has required an eight-hour day and a six-day week. Similar government determinations have been introduced in eastern Europe since 1945.

There is no means of telling whether working hours have reached the point at which they maximize output per man year. They are, however, probably below the maximum output level in some countries and occupations. Other factors tending to increase output have usually more than counterbalanced any tendency for reductions in hours to reduce output. It has been calculated[9] that after 1885 only 10% of increases in productivity was taken in shorter hours, and an even smaller proportion in 1937 (when incomes were higher). In the U.S.A. from 1899 to 1937, output per man-hour in manufacturing rose 200%, but as weekly hours of work fell 33%, output per man-week (or year) increased only 100%,[10] and unemployment considerably reduced average output. But in Britain increases in output per hour approximately offset the reduction in hours of work between 1900 and 1924 and little was left for increases in standards of living in other forms. In general, after the reductions after 1918 "most countries just got back to their pre-1914 trend and continued climbing along it.[11]

ii. Sickness, Accidents, and Voluntary Absence

Intermittence of work due to sickness causes heavy losses of labor in many countries, especially the underdeveloped (Ch. 1), but there are no comparative statistical measurements of these losses. In the U.S.A. 500 million man-days were lost in 1942 by persons who would have been in the labor force but for permanent disability, and another 500 million man-days by persons who were normally at work. In industry about ten days per worker per year were lost owing to illness by males, and twelve by females (in 1942).[12] Labor time lost owing to accidents is also incompletely recorded. Fatal accidents alone have been relatively high in Luxembourg, Mexico, and Norway (in a very unrepresentative list of countries). The losses from non-fatal accidents and industrial diseases are far greater, but have not been measured in most countries. In the U.S.A. about 1.8 days of labor were lost in 1942 by men and 1.2 by women on account of industrial injuries, occupational diseases, and non-industrial accidents. Accident and occupational disease rates depend partly on the relative im-

9 Clark, op. cit., 44.
10 Fabricant, Employment and Manufacturing 1899-1939, 153.
11 Queensland: XV Economic News, April-June 1946, 2.
12 Dewhurst et al., op. cit., 249.

portance of the different industries. Coal mining, for instance, is one of the riskiest industries, although the fatality rate has notably declined since 1929.[13] Precautions against accidents and disease have increased in more developed countries, partly because the cost of accidents, which fell almost entirely on workers in the early stages of industrialization, has been shifted to employers (Ch. 31). Increased precautions are also due to the increase in the accompanying damage to equipment, realization of the psychological effect of accidents on workers, and the development of humanitarian attitudes.

Intermittence of work also occurs when workers voluntarily absent themselves for a time, although such absenteeism is not always distinguishable from unemployment during periods when workers are seeking new jobs. There are no comparative figures. When a working force is in process of divorce from agriculture, industrial workers sometimes return periodically to agriculture. In India textile workers return to their land and their families, particularly at the sowing and harvesting seasons. Workers and employers hardly regard these departures as absenteeism, but rather as a part of the regular method of working, although the resulting labor turnover is costly. But these arrangements may not reduce over-all efficiency, since they provide for meeting the peak demand for labor in agriculture. In Chile many industrial workers return seasonally to mining or agriculture. Migrant labor in Africa is also in transition from a subsistence to an exchange economy. But the intermittent absence of a large part of the population from agriculture in East and South Africa is causing loss of fertility and soil erosion, which further presses people to find work elsewhere. The intermittence of non-agricultural work also militates against the acquisition of skills (even where this acquisition permitted).[14] These returns to agriculture are often reduced when urban housing and conditions of industrial work improve sufficiently to overcome attachments to rural life. The strain upon the individual in transition to industrial conditions has often been excessively burdensome in both capitalist and socialist countries.

In the later stages of capitalist development, the unattractiveness of working conditions (especially in coal mining), increases in rates of pay that enable workers to afford more leisure, or lack of real rewards for labor when faith in the purchasing power of money is undermined, have all caused absenteeism. After the end of the war in 1945, the labor market failed to induce steady labor in many countries because of the lack of goods on which to spend money wages. In Germany from 1945-7, people worked irregularly because they took time off to look for food and fuel, time being better spent thus than in earning unspendable money. Higher rations for workers more effectively induced work than higher money

[13] I.L.O., *Year Book of Lab. Stats.*, 1947-8, 269.
[14] U.N., *Rev. of Econ. Conditions in Africa*, 1949-50, 13.

wages. In Britain in 1947 there was too little in the stores upon which to spend wages to maintain work incentives, and productivity was low. Conditions were similar in Italy, France, and many parts of the Far East and Africa. The import of incentive goods provided the greatest inducement to increased work and production.

iii. Disputes About Conditions of Work

Cessations of work to maintain or improve labor conditions go back to the beginning of recorded history. Slaves periodically revolted in early times. Peasants rose against landowners or their equivalent in Egypt long before the Christian era, in Britain from the 12th century, in Europe generally and Russia in the 19th century and in eastern Europe after 1918 and 1945. After craft production grew, and masters (liverymen) differentiated themselves from journeymen, the labor problem raised its head in modern dress. Riots of apprentices and journeymen foreshadowed modern strikes. When the guilds declined, the distribution between merchant profits and wages caused friction over the margin between the price of wool and the price of cloth, or, alternatively, over the piece-rate for making up yarn. The subsequent wide extension of wage employment, in addition to the organization of workers, has converted these disputes into strikes and lock-outs. And as workers have interested themselves in the effect of the general social framework on labor conditions, there have been general strikes in which large numbers of workers in many industries refuse to work, in order to apply pressure on the government (e.g., in Britain in 1926, repeatedly but briefly in France since 1945, and in Italy and Argentina).

Losses of labor through industrial disputes have been relatively high in recent years in Norway, Sweden, Poland, U.S.A., and Australia (Table 36). Between 1927 and 1947 these countries lost about .3% of available working time, which is about 50% above the average for the countries included, but far less than losses due to involuntary unemployment (which range from 3% to 10%). Losses from disputes were below average in Rumania, New Zealand, Japan, Hungary, Switzerland, and the Union of South Africa, and are, at least in principle, zero in Russia and other socialist countries. Losses vary widely from year to year, according to the size of industries in which disputes occur, and the disputes' duration. There was no trend in most countries, but a rising one in the U.S.A. and Canada. After 1945 losses rose almost everywhere where figures were available, and especially in Canada and the U.S.A. After the surrender of Japan in 1945, the military government notified the Japanese that it favored the development of labor unions. The Japanese proceeded rapidly and enthusiastically with labor organization which was somewhat disorderly and resulted in a number of strikes, some unconventional in form. The strength of labor unions, the temper and tradition of employers

TABLE 36

Days Lost Through Industrial Disputes in Mining, Manufacturing, Construction, and Transport in Selected Countries*

Days lost per 1000 persons employed (averages) 1927-1947†

Country	
Union of South Africa	58
Canada	416
United States	1103
India	532
Japan	193
Belgium	588
Czechoslovakia	332
Denmark	580
Finland	635
France	776
Hungary	153
Ireland	937
Netherlands	313
Norway	3351
Poland	1191
Rumania	218
Sweden	1460
Switzerland	91
United Kingdom	290
Yugoslavia	519
Australia	1061
New Zealand	202

* Woodbury, R. M., "The Incidence of Industrial Disputes: Rates of Time Loss 1927-47," Int. Lab. Rev., Nov. 1949, 451.

† Or so much of the period as available figures cover.

and workers, the speed and nature of economic change, and government policy are all influential, but their influence is not clear.

Higher labor organization in general accompanies greater loss of labor in disputes. The highest losses in past years have been in Norway, Sweden, the U.S.A., and Eire. But Britain, although highly organized, is an exception. In the three years 1919 to 1921 the average annual loss of labor in Britain due to disputes was 49.1 million working days; from 1922 to 1932 (omitting 1926, which was the year of the general strike) it was 7.6 million; but from 1945 to 1948, 2.3 million, and in 1949 1.9 millions.[15] But some strikes (e.g., in the U.S.A. and Germany) have been aimed at securing employer recognition of unions. Since 1945 a number of strikes have occurred in unionized industries without union support, particularly in Britain and the U.S.A. In France, where wages were controlled by the government until 1950, the restoration of collective bargaining was followed by a number of disputes. But there appears to be little general correlation between losses from disputes and national income per head in

---

[15] U.K., Ministry of Labor Gazette, May, 1950.

more developed countries. The loss was below the general average both in seven countries with the highest per capita income and in seven countries with the lowest national income per head.[16]

Predominantly agrarian countries have lost little labor on account of disputes in the past, because disputes are infrequent in agriculture and cause small losses. Each employer has few workers, who are often not very skilled, and have difficulty in coordinating their action. But where employers have a number of workers (as, for instance, on plantations), strikes have occurred, for instance in Mexico (on hennequin plantations), in Malaya (on rubber plantations), in France (in vineyards), and in similar situations. Unorganized strikes have, however, increased in agriculture (e.g., in Italy in 1954). Labor organization is impeded by the poverty of workers whose chances of raising wages are poor because there is a large pool of alternative labor on the land. Nevertheless, disputes have increased in these countries since 1945 (e.g., in India after 1945, Malaya, Uganda, on the railways in Southern Rhodesia, in Tanganyika, in Kenya, on the Sudan railways, in West Africa, and in the West Indies), mostly over the failure of wages to keep pace with the rising cost of living. Many have occurred in the absence of labor unions, but labor organizations are developing, and some labor disputes arise out of rivalry between unions.[17]

Disputes are likely when general economic conditions seem to offer an opportunity to change conditions of labor. Thus they may increase when production is either expanding or contracting, but the correlation of labor disputes with cycles in production is not very clear because of the operation of many other factors. Strikes are more likely when production is expanding, prices are rising, and real wages falling. They are less likely during recessions, when prices and the demand for labor are falling and there is unemployment; real wages are rising unless they have been adjusted to the fall in prices, but strikes are costly and difficult to win. Employers, however, are less resistant to change in periods of expansion and more insistent on change in periods of contraction. In fact, labor losses from disputes were relatively high in the periods of expansion from 1908 to 1912 and 1918 to 1922, and relatively low from 1933 to 1937. Between 1927 and 1947 they were higher during times of prosperity than during depression, in the U.S.A., India, Belgium, Czechoslovakia, Yugoslavia, Australia, Finland, France, Hungary, Poland, and Rumania; but lower in Union of South Africa, Canada, Denmark, Ireland, Norway, Netherlands, Sweden, Switzerland, United Kingdom, and New Zealand.[18] They were relatively high after 1945 in the U.S.A. because of the accumulation of

---

[16] Woodbury, "The Incidence of Labor Disputes: Rates of Time Loss 1927-47," *International Lab. Rev.*, Nov. 1949, 451.

[17] U.K., *The Colonial Empire 1939-47*, 1949 (Cmd. 7167), 75.

[18] Woodbury, "The Incidence of Industrial Disputes: Rates of Time Loss 1927-47," *Int. Lab. Rev.*, Nov. 1949, 451.

frictions during the war, when collective bargaining was muted, and because of increases in prices. In France, where the government control of wages until 1950 converted strikes for better labor conditions into more or less general strikes against the government, strikes increased for a time when collective bargaining was restored. In Britain, however, losses from labor disputes were low.

Governments endeavor to reduce these labor losses by policies ranging from the prohibition or obstruction of strikes to the facilitation of collective bargaining, conciliation, and compulsory arbitration. In socialist countries, failure to work when able is usually punishable under the labor code. It is contended that, since the government is the only employer, strikes would be against the state, and must be prohibited. Although these governments have eliminated most of the loss of labor from disputes, productivity losses owing to the dissatisfactions of workers compelled to accept the edicts of the state may exceed the losses from disputes if they were permitted.

In Western countries, the right to strike is regarded as the worker's basic freedom. Nevertheless, strikes have been prohibited in some countries in time of war. The British government prohibited strikes during the war of 1939-1945. Strikes by government workers are prohibited in Britain (where special arbitration machinery is provided for the settlement of such disputes), but the prohibition does not apply to nationalized industry. Strikes by government employees are not prohibited in France and Italy. In Chile the prohibition applies also to employees of municipalities; the formation of unions among government and municipal employees is also forbidden, but in fact unions exist (the railroad workers' union being one of the strongest). Strikes are sometimes prohibited in key industries. They may be illegal in certain public utilities in Britain under the Conspiracy Act of 1875. In colonial areas, strikes by native workers, if not prohibited, have been seriously obstructed. In Malaya the old Master and Servant Law inherited from 19th century England provided criminal penalties for breach of contract and for organizing a number of workers to stop work. Peaceful picketing is illegal, but this law is virtually inoperative. In the Union of South Africa, the African worker is not an "employee" under the Industrial Councils Act, and cannot participate directly in the work of the Industrial Councils. A strike is defined as a general cessation of work in order to enforce demands that have been refused by the employer, and native workers cannot argue that they all happen to be terminating their employment contract simultaneously. Strikes are also punishable under the Riotous Assemblies Act. In the mines, contracts (typically for periods of a few months to eighteen months) are subject to a master and servant law providing criminal penalties for breach of contract. Nevertheless, a strike occurred in 1945, but the criminal penalties could not be applied to fifty thousand strikers. The men were, however, forced to return to work and in the process nine were killed and 800 injured.

Governments have increasingly tried to reduce labor dispute losses by facilitating labor organization in the hope that it will provide machinery for continuing reduction of worker-employer frictions. In most of western Europe the elimination of legal obstacles to labor organization (Ch. 30) has been sufficient to induce employers to bargain with unions. Employers were, however, hostile to unions in Germany until 1945 and in the U.S.A., where unions were hampered by legislation and court decisions until 1935. The National Labor Relations Act of 1935 provided that it was an unfair labor practice for an employer to refuse to bargain with the freely chosen representatives of workers. This raised practical questions whether merely listening and refusing to accede to the requests of the workers' representatives constitutes bargaining. The act provided a procedure for determining who were the representatives of workers. Labor organization expanded thereafter, notably during the war of 1939 to 1945, after which disputes caused a great loss of labor power. In 1947 the "Taft-Hartley Act," amending the National Labor Relations Act, placed limitations on sympathetic strikes, secondary boycotts, and other types of union activity (Ch. 30).

Labor unions do not always achieve a satisfactory peaceful relation with employers. Strikes leave a legacy of antagonism. Workers often desire not only changes in working conditions and wages, but also a feeling that they are consulted and "know what is going on." Where the labor market is a bilateral monopoly with only one or a few bargainers on each side, the outcome of strikes and lockouts is indeterminate. Some governments, therefore, attempt to maintain continuous contact between workers and employers. During both world wars, governments in Britain, Canada, and the U.S.A. established works committees and joint industry committees, where representatives of workers and employers met to discuss their differences and attempted to settle them without cessations of work that would impede war production. The British Trades Union Congress resolved in 1944 in favor of the continuance of the Joint Production Committees after the war, but many employers opposed the proposal and many committees were terminated. Nevertheless, such joint organizations exist in many industries. The Whitley Committee recommended in 1917 that Joint Industrial Councils and Works Committees in each plant be established in industries in which labor was well organized. In 1944 Joint Industrial Councils were operating in the government service, local government, fishing, mining, engineering (some branches), building, textiles, docks, flour milling, public utilities, retail distribution, and a number of others. These councils are advisory only. The Works Committees have been less successful, have received little support from organized labor, and have dealt only with welfare in a narrow sense and not with terms of employment. There are Labor Advisory Committees in the nationalized industries and, although workers are not formally represented on the governing boards of these industries, at least one member typically has a labor union background. The position of British labor unions has also been strengthened by a legal provision that agreements between representatives of workers and employers can be made legally binding on all employers. Introduced as a wartime measure in 1940, the arrangement was extended for five years in the Wages Council Act, 1946. Disputes are referred to the Industrial Council for settlement. No inspection or government enforcement is provided, but workers have a right to civil action for recovery. These arrangements affect the wages of some ten million workers outside the less organized industries (where there are Wages Boards).

In France the government endeavored to enlist the support of workers in reactivating production after the war in 1945 by requiring the establishment of works committees in all factories of more than a hundred workers, and in 1946 the limit was reduced to fifty workers. In contrast with that of most other countries, the French law provides that the technical and supervisory workers as well as the hand workers shall elect representatives to the works committees (over which the employer presides). The committees have extensive power to deal with matters affecting production and the welfare of workers, including the right to information as to the profits of the firm. They are entitled to the help of an expert accountant in obtaining and analyzing this information. Two representatives sit on the board of directors, and the committee may report to the shareholders. But authority over production remains with the manager, and the committees are only consultative. They administer all the social institutions inside the factory, even those that are paid for by the employer. In December 1946 there were about 6,000 labor-management committees with, however, apparently little actual influence over management. Similar committees were set up in Norway in 1947 and in the Netherlands in 1950, where they must consider complaints and wishes expressed by workers, supervise conditions of work, and participate in managing the social institutions of the undertaking.[19]

In South Africa, under an act of 1937, Industrial Councils may be set up in any industry (except mining) in which both employers and workers desire it. Any agreement on conditions of work must be published by the Minister of Labor to become effective. In 1946 the government, anxious to prevent increases in the cost of living, did not publish all such agreements. If the council cannot agree there is no cessation of work, but the council must reconvene after seven days to discuss the matter again, and, if still unsuccessful, must reconvene again after 14 days. If the deadlock persists, the council is dissolved and the government takes over one-third of its funds in trust, to be used should a new council be set up in the

---

[19] I.L.O., *Ind. and Lab.*, Oct. 1950, 284.

industry at a later date. (Many councils have been repeatedly dissolved and reestablished.) The dispute then goes to compulsory arbitration. Most white workers and employers seem to approve the system, but it does little for African workers. The U.S.A. has made little legal provision for joint councils except in wartime.

If labor disputes threaten, despite these provisions (or if they are absent), the government may provide procedures to go into operation on a threatened cessation of work in an important industry. It may provide for a public investigation to expose the facts to public gaze without requiring either party to accept any findings. Such investigations are most likely to reduce labor losses when either side has taken a position difficult to maintain under public criticism, but the propriety and effectiveness of decisions reached under the pressure of public opinion is difficult to appraise. There were 20 such courts of inquiry in Britain between 1920 and 1938. A similar procedure exists in the Netherlands and in Canada (for utilities and key industries only). In Canada either side must give 30 days' notice of proposed changes in the terms of employment and, if a protest is made, no change in these terms, nor any strike or lockout may occur until a three-man board has reported on the subject (which usually has taken some two to three months). Between 1907 and 1935, 638 disputes were referred to such boards, and strikes occurred in only 49 of them. 657 strikes did, however, occur in violation of the act between 1907 and 1935, mostly in mining and shipping. Both workers and employers originally opposed the Act, but since about 1918 most of them have favored it. Five of the provinces have similar laws regarding intra-provincial disputes. In the U.S.A. after 1945, there was a number of presidential committees of inquiry regarding disputes. The Taft-Hartley Act provides for the President to appoint a fact-finding board, and for an injunction against a cessation of work for a period of 80 days in certain cases.

The pressure of public opinion may fail to prevent disputes, and the government may attempt to conciliate the parties to a dispute, making no settlement, but keeping the parties in contact, focusing discussion on the points of disagreement, and suggesting possible solutions. Such conciliation involves no incursion into the basic freedom of labor to bargain for the best terms it can get. The British Conciliation Act of 1896 authorized the Board of Trade to investigate disputes and promote amicable settlements by bringing the parties together under an impartial chairman or (at the request of the parties), by appointing an arbitrator. In 1919 these powers were extended in the Industrial Courts Act. The Ministry of Labor has a large staff for the purpose and a panel of citizens willing to act as voluntarily accepted arbitrators. Where both parties to a dispute agree (but not otherwise), the Minister can refer disputes to a permanent Industrial Court. Only if both parties previously so agree are the awards of the Court binding, but they have been generally accepted.

In France the act of 1950, which restored collective bargaining, provided that employers and workers unable to agree might present their dispute to a conciliation board on which the Minister of Labor is represented. In the Netherlands the government appoints mediators who discuss a threatened strike with employers and workers and generally negotiate a compromise. In Belgium, penalties are provided for causing a stoppage of work before any attempt has been made to settle the dispute under the prescribed procedure. Sweden provided for public mediation in 1916.[20]

In Australia the Commonwealth Arbitration Act of 1904 provided for conciliation (as well as arbitration), and in 1947 Conciliation Commissioners were appointed in an attempt to enlarge the scope of conciliation. Typically the union serves a "log of claims" on employers or their association (if the association will accept it). It requests a compulsory conference of those employers who do not accept. The Arbitration Court calls a conference, but the officials of the court attend only if invited. The U.S. Department of Labor has a conciliation service that has been increasingly active since 1945. Some states and cities also provide public conciliators.

The Indian Industrial Disputes Act of 1938 provides for a government conciliation service. Failing conciliation, if the government thinks the case important enough, it may appoint a court of inquiry to expose the facts and make recommendations, but without power to enforce its decisions. Bombay province (ahead of most provinces in these matters) passed its own Industrial Disputes Act in 1938, which is more detailed than that of the central government. Workers or employers may ask the government to declare illegal a proposed or requested change in work conditions. Where workers are poorly organized, labor officers are appointed by the government to act as union officials might have acted. In Chile cessations of work are illegal unless two-thirds of the workers support their claim in a meeting, their delegates wait on the employer, and he replies within five days in writing. If the dispute remains unresolved, it is referred to a conciliation board. In the absence of agreement, the parties must return on two successive occasions at intervals of one week. The Board then proposes a solution, and if it is not accepted, arbitration is recommended, but not compelled (and often not accepted). Disputes have resulted in some strikes. Conciliation services are now provided in some British colonial territories.[21]

Compulsory government arbitration is a long step beyond any of the foregoing devices to minimize disputes. The basic rights of workers are narrowed, and the government accepts responsibility for selecting the persons and procedures for settling labor's share in the national product. It must also enforce the settlement, which may be difficult since the government cannot fill the jails with workers who do not accept the

---

[20] Marquand, *Organized Labor in Four Continents*, 272.
[21] U.K., *The Colonial Empire, 1939-47*, 74.

award. The first and the most enduring arrangements for compulsory arbitration were initiated in New Zealand in the 1890s, and subsequently copied, and more continuously applied, in Australia. In Australia until 1947 the Arbitration Court had wide powers of arbitration (as well as conciliation). It determines the basic wage in interstate industry for unskilled work involving no unusual conditions. The first determination of the basic wage in 1907 was based on a family budget of a married couple and one child. The budget was later changed to adapt it to a study of family expenditures made in 1930. The basic wage changes automatically with changes in the cost of living. The Court also determines the basic work week. After 15 months of cogitation, it decided on a 40-hour week in 1947. In fact, very few workers receive only 100% of the basic wage, but unskilled women typically receive only 70% of the male rate. Awards for particular industries are stated for each job in terms of a percentage above the basic wage, based upon considerations of skill and special conditions such as unpleasantness of the work, inaccessibility of the job, and the like. They also prescribe the hours, and frequently other conditions of work, for particular classifications of job, and are made for three, six, or twelve months. Whenever the basic wage changes, the awards for all other jobs automatically change, since they are expressed in a percentage of the basic wage. The Commonwealth law applies only to interstate matters; these, however, include most industries. State compulsory arbitration courts set up in the 1890s to deal with intrastate disputes often enforce the awards of Commonwealth courts on recalcitrant employers. Consequently, changes in basic wages affect 80% of the male and 70% of the female workers in Australia.

Organizations of workers or employers who wish any protection under the law must register with the court. In the event that an award of the court is defied by either party, the court may fine that party, or deregister the organization, or both. Few fines have been imposed. One labor union of timber workers was fined and its property seized and sold to pay the fine. The court has never deregistered an employers' association, but has deregistered a few unions. Deregistration typically brings the union to an end. Employers are then able to bargain individually with workers, enforcing any conditions they can impose. The lead miners at the Broken Hill mines struck in 1915 against an award made by the court. The union was deregistered, but the miners are said to be receiving higher incomes than the court would have given them, partly owing to a bonus based upon the price of lead, which has risen greatly.

The effect of these arrangements on labor losses cannot be segregated. For many years they were generally regarded as beneficial, but it is impossible to prove that labor losses would have been greater without the court. Compulsory arbitration has been effective in sheep shearing (where the perishability of the product places pressure on both parties to accept some decision), but less so in mining, waterside work, and the metal trades. In 1946 and 1947, when the court accumulated arrears of cases (partly because of its protracted consideration of the basic work week), strikes increased. Coal miners and dock workers were both withdrawn from the jurisdiction of the court and placed under separate bodies. Apparently the Court was unwilling to pay the price of avoiding strikes, and the government could not afford them. In 1947 the Court was restricted to the determination of the basic wage, annual leave, the basic work week, minimum rates of pay for females, and appellate review on all legal questions under the Act. New Conciliation Commissioners then appointed were empowered to make compulsory orders if conciliation failed, and to intervene in disputes not voluntarily referred to them. Each Commissioner specializes on a group of industries, but there is no provision for coordinating their policies or reviewing their decisions (except on matters of law).

The Arbitration Court in New Zealand has in general resembled that in Australia. Until about 1930 the Court made awards of general basic wages and differentials for particular jobs. In the early 1930s it was almost suspended, until the Labor government returned to power and reinstated the Court to deal with all occupations paying £400 per annum or less. During the war of 1939-45, the Court virtually stabilized wages for a time at the 1942 level, but in 1946 and 1947 was allowing increases. In the Union of South Africa, a Wages Board established in 1937 may make decisions regarding industries with no Industrial Council, and its decisions are enforceable by criminal penalties. The Minister of Labor usually instructs the Wage Board to take a case, although his initiative is not necessary. The board is largely guided by the ability of industry to pay, and the existing structure of wages. It is prohibited from taking race into account, but the members know to which race each job is conventionally allocated. The margin between native and white wages has been reduced by about 20% in fifteen years. The Minister may exempt native areas from the provisions of the Wage Act.[22] The cost of living allowances have been set not by the Board but by the Minister of Labor.

Compulsory arbitration has been unusual in Europe. In the U.S.A. there is considerable question whether it would contravene the Constitution, except insofar as it is applied to public utilities. The Railway Labor Act of 1934 almost provides for compulsory arbitration. The chief opposition to compulsory arbitration in developed countries comes from organized workers. Nevertheless, it has been used in wartime in Britain, from 1914 to 1918. Again, in 1940 strikes and lockouts were prohibited unless 21 days' notice had been given to the Minister of Labor and he had failed to intervene. He could refer the dispute to the National Arbitration Tribunal, whose awards were binding, and enforceable by imprisonment and fine.

---

[22] Franklin, op. cit., 141, 197 ff.

But labor representatives, believing the Tribunal to be guided by the government's wage policy, and because its decisions were binding, often urged the Minister to refer disputes to a special court of enquiry. Strikes and lockouts were again legalized in 1951. Compulsory arbitration has occasionally been used in Scandinavian countries. In the Netherlands a statutory Umpires Board conducts compulsory arbitration proceedings and approves all collective bargains. Before fixing wages for an industry, it must consult with a joint organization of labor unions and employers associations. Since 1945 it has stabilized wages, and there have, in fact, been few strikes. In France prior to 1938, an arbitrator could make an award where two parties could not agree, the award being binding until the parties did agree, but enforceable only by the pressure of public opinion, or by damage suit on either side. In November 1938 penalties were imposed for failure to accept an award. The Weimar government in Germany appointed conciliators when unions and employers could not agree. The parties could request that the decision made with reference to one area should be extended to other areas, but the state could refuse to enforce the awards. In Poland wages were generally determined between 1920 and 1939 by bargaining between associations of workers and employers, but the government had final powers of decision.

Compulsory arbitration is thus least likely where labor organization is too weak to strike, or strong enough to oppose compulsion. But labor unions do not oppose the system in Australia, New Zealand or South Africa. Nevertheless, increasing interdependence within advanced societies has so magnified the losses due directly, and especially indirectly, to labor disputes in important industries that it is becoming increasingly urgent to find a method other than cessations of work for determining conditions of labor. But compulsory arbitration has not prevented all cessations of work, even though they are illegal, ultimately because of the impossibility of enforcement on large bodies of defiant workers.

iv. Involuntary Unemployment

Involuntary unemployment is difficult to separate in practice from voluntary unemployment. Many primitive peoples seem to do less work than is physically possible (e.g., in the South Pacific, Malaya, Africa, and among the Indian populations of South America). But some apparent unemployment is in fact not unemployment. What is physically possible is uncertain, and often diminished by climate and poor health (due to poor food and inadequate medical treatment). Some underemployment is voluntary and due to lack of the desire to work because of the relative values placed on material things and leisure. But the available variety of material things has been small. These peoples have often produced all the food, clothing, and housing they needed, and had time left, and did not know what else to produce. But (for good or ill) contact with the West is changing these attitudes, and native populations are becoming interested in bicycles, oil lamps, phonographs, and the like. Some unemployment is involuntary in these economies and due to the small amount of land per head. In some areas this shortage of land is focused on the native reserves, and insufficient food diminishes ability to work. Some unemployment is due to the slow adjustment of social structures. Where men have traditionally done only a few kinds of work in order to be left free for military activities, they tend to keep their old standards of "man's work" when the need for their warlike activities has declined.

Many agrarian countries also suffer from chronic though concealed unemployment owing to shortage of land and capital. Overcrowding of the land results in land holdings too small to provide full employment for cultivators, but measures of this concealed unemployment often include also unemployment due to seasonal fluctuations in the demand for agricultural labor. Agricultural laborers in India are generally without work for three to six months a year.[23] In Egypt about 2 million workers could be removed from agriculture without reducing its output, in China 20% of the rural population, in Poland in 1939 about 30%, in Bulgaria in 1939 37%, and in Russia in 1928 over 20%.[24] Some of this unemployment in agriculture is absorbed by craft work or seasonal migrations into urban labor markets (e.g., in India and parts of Africa). But cyclical fluctuations in the effective demand for labor are unimportant internally[25] but may be caused by fluctuations in the demand for exports.

Industrial countries provide more statistics of unemployment, although definitions of unemployment and methods of measurement vary. Measures of losses of employees in relation to the labor force often include losses by death and retirement, and voluntary separations to seek new jobs, as well as involuntary separations. In Britain such losses were only about 2.3% for men and 3.5% for women during four months in 1948. In the U.S.A. losses have been 4 to 5% a year since 1939.[26] Some unemployment is inevitable in a flexible labor market to permit individual employers to take more workers and workers to seek more acceptable jobs. But unemployment has far exceeded this limit in capitalist countries in a somewhat cyclical pattern since the beginning of the 19th century. Between 1900 and 1940 real output per person in work was growing steadily, but output per person normally at work grew far less in the U.S.A., Britain, Germany, Canada, Norway and probably France, owing to the increasing proportion of the labor force involuntarily unemployed. In fact, it has been stated that when

---

[23] Thakurdas et al., Bombay Plan, II, paragraphs 5, 18; India: Cooperative Planning Committee Report, 1946, 14.

[24] K. A. Murray, International Affairs, Jan., 1947; U.N. Econ. Surv. of Europe in 1949, 61; Fong, Weltwirtschaftliches Archiv, March 1937; Int. Lab. Rev., Vol. XXXIII, 356.

[25] U.N., Maintenance of Full Employment, 7, 27.

[26] U.N., World Econ. Rep., 1948, 230.

unemployment is allowed for, the standard of living in the U.S.A. was slightly lower in 1928-9 than in 1916; in 1937 it was about equal to 1900; and in 1932 as low as 1870; and markedly lower than 1921. But in Australia, New Zealand, and Sweden, real income appears to have increased with potential income. Actual output per person was only about 83% of calculated output with full employment in the U.S.A. in 1929, about 82% in Germany in 1937, and 85% in Britain in 1937.[27] More than 14% of the persons normally at work were unemployed in Belgium, Canada, Ireland, and the U.S.A. in 1939.

After the immediate post-war recovery after 1945, unemployment was much lower in capitalist countries than before the war (Table 37). Unemployment not of serious proportions existed in Denmark, Austria, Ireland and Finland in 1949, but it was of serious proportions in Belgium, Italy, and Western Germany. In Italy (which has suffered from both inflation and unemployment since 1945) the drafting of men into military service and the development of war industries reduced disguised unemployment in the rural population, but resulted in visible unemployment when these movements were reversed.[28] In Japan unemployment has often been concealed because employers habitually retained employees in times of depression out of a sense of enlarged family responsibility. In 1946, although output was 20% of normal, there was little overt unemployment. The occupation authorities, anxious to increase efficiency and reduce costs and prices, urged removal of redundant workers from payrolls.

The extent of involuntary unemployment in capitalist countries indicates the seriousness of the collision between the institutions impelling people to work and the organization of production providing them with jobs. The intermittent failure to use labor to its full capacity is a basic threat to the survival of the economic organization of these countries, in view of the increasing political power of workers who have borne the burden of unemployment.

This intermittent large-scale unemployment is due largely to the nature of industrial methods of production and the capitalist form of organization. The production system is bifurcated into the production of consumption goods and of producers' goods. As the producers' goods increase to the point at which they are capable of producing more goods than can be sold at prices covering all costs and an attractive profit, the inducement to invest falls away. Even replacements of existing capital goods are postponed, because they are durable. The producers' goods sector falls to a low level of activity. Outpayments by this sector for labor and materials fall, reducing the demand for consumer goods. In the past, continued wearing out of capital goods, the appearance of new

---

[27] Clark, op. cit., 1st, 6, 159.
[28] U.N., Econ. Surv. of Europe in 1949, 62; U.N., Inflationary and Deflationary Tendencies, 1946-1948, 20.

TABLE 37

UNEMPLOYMENT IN SELECTED COUNTRIES IN 1939 AND 1948

	Total unemployment as a % of labor force[1] (annual average)	
	1939	1948
Belgium	19.2	6.4
Canada	14.1	2.1
Denmark	8.0	4.7
Germany (UK-US zone)		4.7
Ireland	15.6	9.6
Japan	3.0[2]	0.7
Norway	2.7[3]	1.2
Puerto Rico	—	10.3
Sweden	9.2	2.8
Switzerland	6.5	0.6
United States	14.6[4]	3.4
Australia	9.7	0.9

	Non-agricultural unemployment as a % of non-agricultural wage and salary earners in 1948[5]
Norway	1
Sweden	1
United Kingdom	1-2
France	—
Netherlands	1-2
Switzerland	0-1
Austria	2-3
Denmark	4
Finland	
Ireland	6
Belgium	4
Italy	17
Germany (UK-US zone)	5

[1] U.N., *Stat. Year Book, 1948*, 84.
[2] 1938.
[3] 1941.
[4] 1940.
[5] U.N., *Econ. Surv. of Europe in 1949*, 62.

methods of production, or new goods have sooner or later revived investment, restoring effective demand and encouraging more investment. Thus economic growth has been spasmodic and wasted considerable potential labor, and monetary institutions have intensified the spasms (Ch. 23, 25). Furthermore, as levels of living rise, an increasing proportion of further increases tends to be saved and total purchases of consumers and producers goods can be maintained only by increasing investment faster than consumption.

Socialist economies also fail to use their full labor potential, but not because of the cyclical fluctuations in purchasing power characteristic of capitalist countries. Socialist governments plan for continuous full use of resources and have considerable means of maintaining purchasing power. The relative rates of growth in different parts of the economy (particularly consumers' and producers' goods industries) can be coordinated by plan, and lapses do not necessarily cause cumulative recession. The controls necessary for this purpose, however, involve costs in individual freedom, and in the absorption of resources in complicated control mechanisms. They divert resources away from what consumers might choose, and may reduce incentives to produce. Unemployment has occurred. It was considerable under the New Economic Policy (1921-7), largely because disorganization followed upon the Revolution and war, because communism resulted in shortages of raw materials and equipment, and because of poor supervision. In 1930 (soon after the beginning of the first five-year plan) the government announced that unemployment had been liquidated. Industry began to absorb people who had not worked before and, thereafter, the main complaint has been of a shortage of workers rather than of unemployment. But planning has not been perfectly and precisely enough coordinated to eliminate unemployment (which is not surprising in such a rapidly growing economy). The number of departures per month of wage earners from plants in large-scale industry in Russia rose as high as 152% of the average number of wage earners employed in 1930, after which date it fell steadily to 86% in 1935.[29] In 1930 much of the industrial labor force had recently left the farms (the number of wage and salary workers having increased from 11.6 million in 1928 to 19 million in 1931), and was pressed by hard times to seek the most attractive job. A decree of 1932 provided that no worker could be engaged without a certificate as to his reason for leaving his previous job, and one in 1934 that all penalties levied against workers were to be recorded in their labor books, but this latter practice was abandoned in 1938. This source of loss of labor has since been reduced, but rural labor is probably still not fully employed. Poor coordination of plans, or failure to implement them exactly, causes less than full labor utilization in industry. Production in some branches (especially those in process of expansion) may fall below capacity for lack of raw materials, power, or components from others. Workers sometimes produce much more towards the end of plan periods than at others. But the repercussions of economic fluctuations outside the economy can be absorbed more easily than in capitalist countries. When the rest of the world was depressed after 1929, the market for Russian exports of timber and skins was poor, but Russia probably obtained its imports cheaper, although not so much cheaper than the prices at which it had to sell its exports. But these economies deliberately plan to minimize their dependence on the non-socialist world.

---

[29] Bergson, *The Structure of Soviet Wages*, 148.

Chapter 20

Labor: Utilization (Continued)

3. Influences Affecting the Productiveness of the Labor Time Utilized

Differences in national income per person are dependent largely on differences in output per person at work. It has been shown (Ch. 3) that output per man-hour generally increased in Britain, France, and Germany throughout the 19th century, and that in the U.S.A., most northwest European countries and Australasia, it began to increase later in the century. Increases accelerated in some of these countries in the 20th century and began in Japan and Russia. But in the typical underdeveloped country in the Middle East, Asia, the Far East and Latin America, increases continue to be small.

These differences in productivity turn upon the proportion of the labor force in the different sectors of production, the economic quality of the labor force, the productive resources available for use with labor, and the conditions of work.

a. The Allocation of Labor

Average output per worker is maximized when the marginal value product of labor in all uses is equal. Any reallocation of labor then moves workers from more to less productive occupations. But since there are no satisfactory measures of marginal product in each use, we have no means of measuring the extent to which national products fall below their potential level because of less than ideal allocations of labor (Ch. 4). We can merely survey the broad outlines of labor allocation in different groups of countries and examine the major forces influencing it.

i. Actual Allocations of Labor

The allocation of labor among agriculture, forestry, and fishing, industry, and services is of major interest because it is closely correlated with differences in average income per worker.

366

The proportion of the working population engaged in agriculture is generally lowest in the wealthiest and highest in the poorest countries, ranging from 6% in Britain and 13% in the U.S.A. to 60 to 70% in Asia and the Far East (Ch. 4). Construction and manufacturing employ over 40% of the working population in Britain, Belgium, Switzerland, Germany, and Czechoslovakia, less than 30% in Canada and the U.S.A. (the most efficient industrial producers), but less than 15% in the typical underdeveloped country. The

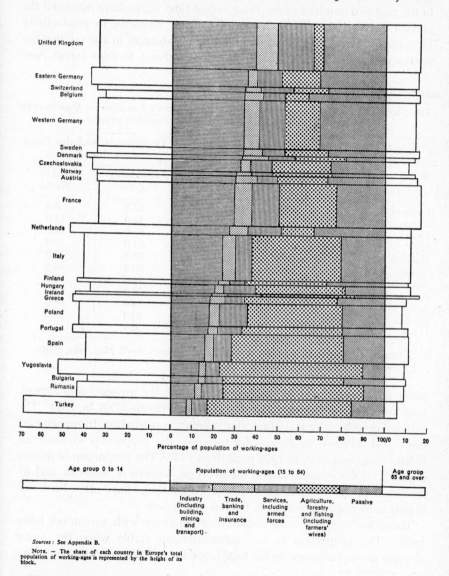

Fig. 19. Age structure and industrial distribution of the population of European countries in 1950. (From U.N., *Econ. Surv. of Europe Since the War*, 1953, p. 154.)

proportion in other activities is influenced by methods of classification, the occurrence of minerals, and standards of living. The proportion in mining is highest in Britain, Belgium and Chile. Where levels of living are high, the proportion employed in supplying services is high (Figure 19), the highest proportions occurring in the U.S.A. and Britain (both about 51%), Australia, and New Zealand.

These sharply contrasted patterns of labor utilization have been realized in the past two hundred years. Prior to that time, agriculture occupied the majority of the labor force in most countries. Increases in productivity have almost always been accompanied by a reduction in the relative importance of agriculture (Table 38). New Zealand and, to some extent, Aus-

TABLE 38*

THE REDUCTION OF THE PROPORTION OF THE LABOR FORCE ENGAGED IN AGRICULTURE IN THE COURSE OF DEVELOPMENT IN SELECTED COUNTRIES†

Country	Period	Proportion of the Labor Force in Agriculture (percent)	
		Beginning of Period	End of Period
England	1841-1946	22.8	5.3
Germany	1882-1933	42.0	15.0
France	1827-1936	63.0	24.0
Italy	1871-1931	51.0	42.0
Holland	1899-1948	28.5	15.0
Sweden	1870-1936	69.5	34.6
Australia	1871-1947	44.0	17.0
New Zealand	1861-1945	24.0	22.0
Japan	1872-1939	85.0	30.0
Canada	1901-1946	40.0	23.0
U.S.A.	1820-1940	70.0	18.0

* Queensland Bureau of Industry, *Rev. of Econ. Progress*, April, May, July, 1950.
† Forestry and fishing are included in some countries.

tralia, have been the chief exceptions. In Russia the proportion in agriculture, forestry and fishing fell from 77.6% in 1926 to 57.0% in 1939.[1] The expanding sectors are manufacturing, mining, construction, transportation, trade and services. In Russia, for instance, the proportion in these activities rose from 10.0% in 1926 to 24.0% in 1939.[2] The proportion in mining depends on the exhaustion and discovery of deposits of minerals, and increases in productivity in more developed countries have often been due in part to increases in mining in the less developed.

These reallocations have occurred in countries with expanding labor forces. The proportion in any sector remains stable when the sector changes at the same rate as the total labor force. The proportion increases

[1] Lorimer, *Population of the Soviet Union*, 106.
[2] *Ibid.*, 106.

when other sectors expand their employment more slowly than the total labor force. Thus the proportion in agriculture in Japan fell from 85% in 1872 to 50% in 1930,[3] with an almost unchanging number of workers in agriculture, the increase in population being almost wholly absorbed in other activities. In the U.S.A. until 1920, and in the Netherlands until the present day, agricultural workers have fallen as a percentage of all workers, but the total labor force has increased fast enough to permit increases in the numbers in agriculture. But the number in agricultural employment fell absolutely in Britain in the 19th century, and it fell about 17% in the U.S.A. between 1940 and 1948.

The numbers in agriculture in most western European countries have fallen since 1930 (in France and Germany by only 1% of the total population of working ages), but in Britain they increased from .9 million in 1939 to nearly 1.1 million in 1948 as a result of efforts to reduce agricultural imports.[4] In southern and eastern Europe agricultural populations have increased sufficiently to cause an increase in Europe as a whole of 5%. However, in Poland and Czechoslovakia, where the total population has declined, agricultural populations have fallen. In some countries with increasing populations, the proportion in agriculture has even increased, because non-agricultural employment has expanded slower than the population. In India the proportion of labor in the crafts declined between 1881 and 1911; that in industry also declined from 1881 to 1931[5] (Ch. 4). Consequently the proportion in agriculture rose from 60% to 70% between 1881 and 1911. In Yugoslavia the proportion in agriculture, fishing, and forestry rose from 71% to 80% between 1895 and 1931. In parts of eastern Europe planned industrialization will not in its early stages be fast enough to prevent increases in the proportion in agriculture.[6] In fact, labor withdrawals from agriculture have been small. The proportion of all labor in agriculture has also risen in Latin America.[7]

In western Europe generally industry has been expanding faster than population, and the proportion in agriculture has fallen as that in industry has increased (Ch. 4), although only in Denmark, Norway, and Sweden by 2% or more a year[8] (Figure 20). Increases in industrial employment in Britain since 1930 have been mainly at the expense of other urban occupations (including distribution services) or through drawing previously unemployed persons into work (notably women). In the Scandinavian countries also the industrial employment of women has increased but employment in service activities increased markedly between 1930 and 1950 in Denmark and Sweden. In most other European countries inade-

---

[3] Clark, *Conditions of Economic Progress*, (2d), 425.
[4] U.N., *World Econ. Rep.*, 1948, 229.
[5] Wadia and Merchant, *Our Economic Problem*, 105.
[6] U.N., *World Econ. Rep.*, 1948, 229.
[7] U.N., *Econ. Surv. of Latin America*, 1948, 32.
[8] U.N., *Econ. Surv. of Europe Since the War*, 1953, 150.

quate expansion of industry has caused overcrowding in agricultural and service employment. France is the only country in which employment in industry, construction, mining and transport was lower in 1950 than in 1930. Trade and services employment have expanded to the point where the marginal product of labor approaches zero. New entrants merely increase the numbers sharing a fairly stable output, and there is surplus man power in agriculture.[9] But generally in the developed countries in Europe, changes in the labor force in industry and in trade and service occupations are in opposite directions. In times of slow industrial expansion the trade and the service activities that require little capital attract people who can find nothing else to do but who are drawn off in periods of industrial expansion.[10]

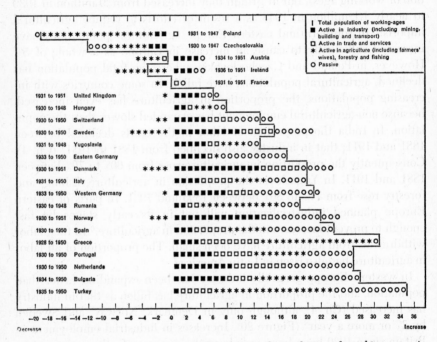

Fig. 20. Changes in the industrial distribution of population of working ages in European countries. (From U.N., *Econ. Surv. of Europe Since the War*, 1953, p. 152.)

Changes in the allocation of the labor force increase its total product wherever the number of workers in the more productive occupations increases at the expense of the less productive. In the U.S.A. 36% of increases in output between 1875 and 1925 have been attributed to increases in population. Of the remaining 64% attributed to increase in output per worker, 59% was attributable to increases within industries and 41% to

9 *Ibid.*, 79, 153.
10 *Ibid.*, 153.

shifts of labor from less to more productive activities. Where productivity increases at different rates in different sectors, maximization of product requires continuing reallocation. Differences among countries in the average productivity of labor as a whole may be due either to differences in their productivity with an ideal allocation of the labor force, or to differences in the degree to which they approach an ideal allocation, but in fact are probably due to both.

ii. Influences Affecting Labor Allocations

The allocation of labor depends, on the one hand, on the demand for labor generated by the demand for goods and services and, on the other hand, on the supply of labor of each type and at each location, and the extent to which these supplies respond to changes in demand.

(a) The Demand for Labor

The pattern of demand for goods and services depends on climate, social mores, and levels of income. This pattern can change little when populations are at a subsistence level, although it differs in detail from place to place because basic needs for food and shelter, and the available means of satisfying them vary. Industrialization has raised levels of living, but consumers have not proportionately increased their demand for all the goods previously consumed. The proportion of increases in income spent on food (or the income elasticity of demand for food) begins to fall at a fairly low level of income, in advanced countries. The income elasticity of demand for luxury foodstuffs such as meat, dairy products, fruits, and the like continues to be moderately high at higher levels of income, and that for clothing, furniture, etc., may remain fairly high at still higher levels of income. But there comes a level of income at which income elasticity is low for most products, in fact for everything except saving, which may be the position in the U.S.A. It has already been stated (Ch. 4) that the demand for farm products may tend to settle at 10% of national income, that for industrial goods at 20 to 25%, and that for tertiary activities at 70% or more (compared with the present 50% in the U.S.A., Britain, and New Zealand).[11]

The proportion of the labor force in manufacturing has in fact fallen from a maximum in Britain in 1861, New Zealand in 1886, Norway, France, and Denmark in 1900, Switzerland in 1910, and the U.S.A. and Sweden in 1920.[12] But the tertiary activities are a mixed bag, including not only consumer services, but also small proprietorships (which reflect the organization of production), and transport, banking and distribution (which reflect the complexity of the general economic organization). Primitive countries with self-contained villages require little transport. But in China,

---

[11] Clark, *op. cit.*, (1st), 182, 185.
[12] *Ibid.*, (2d), Ch. IX.

where roads are bad and goods have to be manhandled, the proportion of the working force in transport is as high as it is in complex communities, those with long internal journeys (Norway, Iceland, Australia, and New Zealand), and those doing a carrying trade for other countries (Britain, Norway, and the Netherlands). Banking and merchandising services also depend partly on the importance of foreign trade, and may be "invisible exports" (e.g., in Britain and the Netherlands).

The translation of demands for goods and services into demands for labor changes with changes in methods of production. After the middle of the 18th century, industrial methods reduced the demand for craft products, and industrial employment expanded at the expense, relatively, of craft employment and agriculture. The new methods also generated a demand for capital goods that are mostly produced by industry and construction. For a time withdrawal of labor from agriculture reduces concealed unemployment there and reduces the tendency for population growth to increase the pressure of population on the land. But if industry grows sufficiently fast, and for sufficiently long, agricultural wages rise.

In Britain agriculture is now too small to be a significant manpower pool for industry, and in northwest Europe generally the growth of industry has drawn relatively little labor from agriculture. But in all the countries where urban unemployment largely disappeared after 1945, agricultural wages increased much more than industrial wages, and some workers left agriculture. In Scandinavia the relative wage increase was especially large; the outflow from agriculture was also considerable. In Scandinavia, the Netherlands, and Britain agricultural wages by 1952 were little lower than industrial. But in western Germany, Belgium, and Italy, where there was considerable unemployment, agricultural wages increased little in relation to industrial wages.[13] The large relative rise in agricultural wages since 1945 has stimulated investment in agricultural machinery and increased production even as agricultural manpower shrinks (e.g., in Scandinavia and the Netherlands). Denmark and the Netherlands where wages in agriculture are nearly as high as in industry, are the cheapest producers in Europe.[14] Agriculture, therefore, generates in time a demand for industrial products, not only machinery but also fertilizers and insecticides. Increases in agricultural wages, or the availability of cheaper sources of agricultural products abroad, induce imports, which are usually paid for in exports of industrial products; this reinforces the tendency to expand the proportion of the labor force in industry. Britain began steady imports of food early in the 19th century, and most industrial countries have since become food importers partly because of population increases. But industrialization may increase the demand for raw

---

[13] U.N., *Econ. Surv. of Europe Since the War*, 1953, 157.
[14] *Ibid.*, 1953, 157.

materials produced by agriculture and, therefore, the demand for labor in agriculture; or it may reduce the demand for labor in agriculture by producing substitutes for agricultural products (e.g., rayon and nylon).

The demand for labor in agriculture has been increased by the import demands of rapidly growing industrial countries (in the 19th century in Russia and Hungary, for instance, and in the 20th century in Canada, Argentina, Australia, New Zealand, South Africa, and the U.S.A.). In Denmark, Australia, New Zealand, and Canada productivity and standards of living were high. But in Russia and Hungary they remained low in the 19th century and are still low in many countries exporting agricultural products to more developed countries.

Governments influence the pattern of demand for labor in many ways. Tax policy affects the distribution among individuals of disposable incomes and, therefore, savings and the demand for luxury goods. Government spending influences the allocation of labor to health, education, military, police, and other public services (Ch. 31). Regulation of imports is intended to, and usually does, divert labor from some uses to others. Some governments protect agriculture from foreign competition. Labor is further encouraged to stay in agriculture by government subsidies and price maintenance (e.g., in the U.S.A., Britain, and France). In virtually every west European country there are agriculturalists whose holdings are too small to give them full productive employment. Government price maintenance raises their incomes, and they persist without any opportunity to modernize their production. Labor is kept on the land when it could make even agriculture more productive if part of it were transferred to producing fertilizers, machinery, and the like.[15] Governments attract labor into industry by tariffs, in most developing countries (Ch. 26). These government policies may, but do not necessarily, reduce the productivity of the labor force as a whole. It is desirable in the long run to move labor from activities in which it is more to those in which it is less productive in the short run if the less productive sector will become the more productive when it grows to a sufficient size. And broader political considerations such as protection against military threats or interruptions of foreign trade due to war or depression may justify such action.

(b) The Supply of Labor

The occupational distribution of labor is influenced by the proportions in which individuals of each capacity are provided by nature, the arrangements for training, and individual, group, and governmental attitudes to labor allocation, particularly to changes in allocation.

The wage structure (or the relative pay available in different occupations) has been the chief instrument regulating labor allocation in both capitalist and socialist countries. In capitalist countries employers in each

15 *Ibid.*, 156.

activity employ as much labor as is profitable at the wages they must pay. Money income differentials among occupations persist where the needed supply cannot be maintained in some occupations without higher labor incomes than in others. Labor incomes tend to be relatively high in unpleasant and strenuous occupations and where skill is required (because incomes are usually low while individuals acquire skill) and, possibly, where nature supplies few individuals capable of certain kinds of work in relation to the demand for it. Changes in labor allocation can be made by changing the wage structure although it has already been noted that population increase or reduction of the demand for some kinds of labor may reallocate labor. But even the maintenance of the wage structure in these circumstances means that it is different from what it would have been without labor reallocation.

Workers often resist change in occupational distribution because it means a change in their way of life or their place of residence. Craft and home workers attempted to resist the pressures towards factory employment in Britain in the early 19th century, but their resistance was broken because factory goods took away the market for craft products. Agricultural workers are in a better position to resist if they can produce the necessities of life. But the rapid growth of population in Britain, and food imports, increased the difficulty of making a living in agriculture, and provided a pool of labor reserves for industry. But if industry continues to grow, wages increase in agriculture compared with industry, as they have done in Europe since 1930. Wages almost as high as for unskilled industrial work have proved insufficient to prevent some exodus from agriculture (which is often desirable where output per agricultural worker is increasing and the demand for agricultural produce is not).

The operation of the market in allocating labor is restricted by convention in some countries. In primitive societies the supply of labor for various kinds of work is often set by custom: jobs like gardening and child-rearing can be done only by women, and hunting, fishing, boat building, and house building only by men. The political insecurity of these communities necessitated the maintenance of a force of men for defense, and the maintenance of children somewhat immobilized the women. But convention disintegrates slowly even when the need for defense has passed. Conventions as to "women's work" exist in many countries. Men may thus protect their jobs, but where levels of living are very low, as in China and India, women bear a large part of the burden of production.

The market may also be restricted in operation because of the inheritance of status. The children of slaves are usually slaves, and almost always somewhat limited in the work they can do, although in the ancient world some undertook highly skilled work in the arts and business. Under feudal systems the children of serfs are often in fact bound to the soil in the same way as their parents. The Hindu caste system caused an unusually formalized and rigid distribution of work, since the castes were defined largely in terms of occupations. Thus the rate of multiplication in a particular caste determined the supply of labor for the occupations open to that caste, for mobility between castes (which is between jobs) was extremely difficult. Mobility is increasing with the appearance of new jobs and great changes in the relative demands for different kinds of work, but attempts have been made to establish castes for some of the new jobs (e.g., truck driving). The children of the well-off tend to follow occupations similar to their parents', and similarly well-paid. In aristocratic agricultural societies, princes, chiefs, and great landowners often pass on their status to their children. Even in individualistic capitalist societies the family to some extent determines the education and training of children and sets limits to the jobs they can take as adults. The "old school tie" has been more than a quip in Britain. Free state-provided education reduces this influence (Ch. 31). Labor unions and craft guilds often give preference to the children of members.

Labor unions may control entry into an occupation to restrict the number of workers below the desirable number, and may also keep out some workers who are more competent for the work than those who are allowed in. Some unions discriminate against women or non-white workers. The number of apprentices may be controlled to ensure proper training, but the imposition of considerable entrance fees by some unions indicates that the union enjoys a degree of monopoly power. Union rules may define the types of person eligible for apprenticeship. Racial discrimination has long existed in the U.S.A., but has an especially serious effect on labor allocation in South Africa. Labor unions do not accept African members, and command virtually all the skilled occupations.[16] Labor unions unwilling to accept the effect of wage policies or changes in technology that would reduce the demand for the labor of their members, may impose rules requiring the employment of unnecessary workers ("feather bedding"), which results in a misallocation of labor.

Labor unions often strive to maintain their position in the wage structure, thus tending to freeze the relative wages in different occupations and to obstruct reallocation. In Britain such policies are probably in part responsible for shortages of labor in some occupations, and for the "structural rigidity" of the economy in recent decades that has retarded Britain's adaptation to changes in its foreign markets. But in some industries unions have fought vigorously to raise their position in the wage structure. Such efforts by unions of miners have caused friction in coal mining in capitalist countries in recent decades, and have been successful. The position of coal miners in the wage structure has also improved in Russia.[17] The relative position of unskilled workers has improved during

---

[16] Franklin, *Economics in South Africa,* 196.
[17] U.N., *Econ. Bull. for Europe,* 1950, Vol. 2, No. 2, 55.

the 20th century in the U.S.A., Britain, and a number of other European countries, partly as a result of explicit programs of labor movements to improve the position of the lowest paid workers. The narrowing of the differential between the wages of skilled and unskilled labor in western Europe, especially since 1939, may, however, prevent the maintenance of the desired quantity of skilled labor[18] (Ch. 30).

Governments have operated labor exchanges in all the more developed capitalist countries. Established in connection with unemployment insurance to minimize unemployment and to ensure that insurance claimants are genuinely seeking work, the exchanges often also attempt to improve the allocation of labor by providing vocational guidance and investigating opportunities for work in various branches of industry. Some train the unemployed, especially the young. But no government (capitalist or socialist) has undertaken to tell every individual what job he must do. The task involves too many detailed decisions, is difficult to enforce, and, if enforced, incurs the disadvantages of slavery (discontent, low productivity, and high cost of supervision). Military organizations are highly authoritarian in their labor allocation, but even they have found it desirable to give opportunities for individuals to volunteer for particular arms of the service and to use judgment. The work of individuals in forced labor camps and prisons is, however, allocated by authority.

Even capitalist governments have influenced allocation. The British government attempted (abortively) to retard migration from agriculture to the cities in the 16th century, and forbade conversion of land from tillage to pasture. After 1939 it directed labor away from "non-essential industries" into war production. Because the market did not operate sufficiently quickly or effectively, the Ministry of Labor was authorized to direct workers to jobs and to control the quantity of labor in each type of work. Safeguards were provided to prevent employers thus assured a labor supply from taking advantage of it to pay low wages and provide poor conditions of work. These "Essential Work Orders" were withdrawn at the end of the war, but restored between 1947 and 1950 to channel labor into the production of goods for export at a time when additional exports were needed to fill the gap left by loss of income from foreign investments. The purchasing power in the hands of the public after taxation and loans to the government exceeded supplies at current prices. Purchases of essential goods were rationed and prices controlled, but the margin of income not spent on these rationed goods sought outlets in "non essential" occupations that then attracted labor. Criticism of the use of labor in football pools, dog racing, and of the number of "spivs" led to the Control of Engagement Order in 1947. It did not affect workers who were already in jobs, but only those who left jobs or appeared for the first time on the market. Those in prescribed employments and age groups

18 *Ibid.*, 1950, Vol. 2, No. 2, 54, 56.

were required to report to labor exchanges when unemployed. They were offered jobs in essential industries if the jobs were suited to their qualifications, but were not compelled to accept any job provided they were seeking one in essential work. Until January 1950 workers were not permitted to leave mining or agriculture in Britain (although permitted to move from one employer to another). But only 19 men and 10 women were "directed" to jobs throughout the operation of the Control of Engagement Order, although 9.5 million vacancies were filled. Between October 1947 and January 1950, 473 miners and 159 agricultural workers were refused permission to leave their industry.[19] The South African government helps to keep African workers out of the better-paid jobs through color-bar legislation for some occupations in the mines and by enforcing apprenticeship laws that effectively keep Africans out of skilled occupations because they have had little chance of acquiring the necessary educational qualifications.[20]

Government wage regulation affects labor allocation if it affects the wage structure. The French government tried to control the level but not the structure of wages from 1947 to 1950. Indeed, most west European countries have been primarily concerned to prevent excessive increases in the general level of wages, and have given the structure only secondary attention.[21] Compulsory arbitration of wage disputes in Australia and New Zealand (Ch. 19) has probably had little effect on wage differentials. The laws establishing the Arbitration Courts provided no criteria of economic policy, and the courts appear to have endeavored to set wage differentials that would adjust the supply of labor in each use to the demand for it, but they have never admitted to any such policy.

Only socialist governments have attempted to regulate the wage structure to achieve a particular allocation of labor, namely, that which will enable them to hit their production targets. Because they all aim at quick industrialization, they must rapidly change the existing allocation. Russia reduced its agricultural population about 16% between 1926 and 1938 in order to man the expanding industrial sector. During the war from 1939 to 1945, and immediately after, the agricultural population declined slightly, but it was planned to increase a little by 1955. The increase in non-agricultural employment between 1940 and 1955 is planned to be about equal to the increase in the population.[22] In the eastern European countries the labor force in urban activities increased 15 to 20% between 1947 and 1950, while agricultural populations shrank about 5%,[23] which was very little, under the circumstances. Labor for industry was obtained

---

[19] U.K., *Lab. and Ind. in Britain,* March 1950, 21.
[20] Franklin, *op. cit.,* 196.
[21] U.N., *Econ. Bull. for Europe,* 1950, Vol. 2, No. 2, 58.
[22] U.N., *Econ. Surv. of Europe Since the War,* 1953, 40.
[23] *Ibid.,* 36, 151.

mostly from the urban unemployed and underemployed in the handi-crafts, trade, personal services, and domestic activities. But when these reserves began to run out in 1952, socialist governments pressed unemployed married women and agricultural workers into industry.

The major shift from agriculture to industry, and the allocation among industries in socialist countries, are regulated through the wage structure and pressure on agriculture. The Communist Party stated in its program in 1919 that equality of remuneration was its ultimate objective, but could not be achieved in the transition period from capitalism to communism. Nevertheless, by about 1921 remuneration was approximately equal in most occupations.[24] Under the New Economic Policy, wages were fixed by collective bargaining, and inequalities appeared. In 1921-2, a fairly unified scale of wages appeared with about 17 grades, the seventeenth being about eight times as high as the first. Lenin stated that the objective was increased productivity, based partly on "personal interest." Until 1931 the Central Council of Trade Unions prescribed the series of scales of basic wages for various industries, the number of wage classes in each industry, and the wages in each, all being frequently revised. In 1931, Stalin attacked the equalitarian tendencies of trade union wage policy at a time when labor turnover was very high and wage differentials were apparently insufficient to attract workers into skilled jobs.[25] In that year the gap between the wages of the least and the most skilled was widened and bonuses were introduced in coal mining. Later the same principles were extended to many branches of production. In 1938-40 wage scales were revised to give the first preference to basic industries such as coal, oil, and heavy metallurgy, and the differentials for skill were further increased. The five-year plan for 1946-50 provided the highest remuneration for workers in coal, iron, steel, and oil (the industries most affected by war). In fact, the wage structure appears to have been governed by forces of supply and demand in much the same way as in capitalist countries, except that the demand in different uses is controlled by the production plan. Equality has not been achieved, and inequality among industrial wage earners increased after 1928, although in 1934 it was still less than in capitalist Russia in 1914.[26] Governments in eastern Europe have followed the Russian model. All workers are classified into standard groups, usually in six to eight categories in each industry. The basic rates in the highest category are about two and one-half times those in the lowest, and the inter-industry wage structure is prescribed.[27]

Inducing agricultural workers to go into industry has proved difficult in socialist countries. The well-being of agricultural workers has been

[24] Baykov, *op. cit.*, 43.
[25] Bergson, *The Structure of Soviet Wages*, 178.
[26] *Ibid.*, 153, 207, 208.
[27] U.N., *Econ. Bull. for Europe*, 1950, Vol. 2, 58.

regulated by the size of compulsory deliveries of produce and the price paid for all deliveries to the government. But these devices proved inadequate to adjust the relative well-being of workers on the land and in industry. Small holders often remain on the land although underemployed and living at a subsistence level. The excessive labor supply in agriculture expressed itself in inefficiently small-scale operations. Land reforms in eastern Germany and Hungary after 1945 increased the number of these small holdings. Apart from unwillingness to leave their land, agriculturalists found conditions in the towns unappealing. Housing was poor, and food supplies were less adequate and reliable than in the country. Consequently, Russia, early in the 1930s, and most east European governments in about 1950, pressed the collectivization of agriculture to increase output per worker on the land, facilitating transfers to industry, and to provide an administrative means of forcing transfers.[28]

The allocation of labor among enterprises has also been regulated in Russia. The relevant government department prescribes the number to be employed in each labor category. In 1934-5, plant managers agitated for greater freedom in matters of labor, but without success. In Czechoslovakia the sum to be spent on labor was prescribed for each undertaking in 1951 by reference to its production target, with notice that the permitted payroll would be reduced if the target were not achieved.[29]

Workers have generally been fairly free in Russia to choose their place of employment and occupation at established wages.[30] The Labor Code of 1918 provided for compulsory labor service and administrative transfers of workers, but that of 1922 declared that mobilization of citizens for compulsory work should be restricted to exceptional circumstances. In 1931 certain transport workers were compelled to return to their former jobs, and contracts between industrial enterprises and collective farms sometimes resulted in involuntary transfers of workers from agriculture to industry. But involuntary recruitment was officially condemned and was not general, and there are no labor union restrictions on entry into skilled occupations nor financial barriers to entry into the professions.[31] The government urged state enterprises to recruit from agriculture under contracts with collective farms, and to utilize the services of city councils and local communist parties, but enterprises have typically relied mainly on "hiring at the gate." Until rationing was abandoned in 1937, enterprises obtained supplies for their workers, sometimes operating farms for the purpose. They have also operated kindergartens and constructed houses. The plants in heavy industry operated 13,000 stores serving 4.65 million

[28] U.N., *Econ. Surv. of Europe Since the War*, 1953, 36, 156.

[29] I.L.O., *Ind. and Lab.*, May 15, 1951, 358.

[30] Bergson, "Soviet National Income and Product in 1937," *Quar. Jour. Econ.*, May 1950, 210.

[31] Bergson, *Structure of Soviet Wages*, 143-146, 152.

workers and employed about 200,000 workers on state farms at the end of 1934. In 1935 about 56% of the workers in heavy industry were housed by the enterprises.[32]

To reduce labor turnover the Russian government has often also restricted freedom to leave jobs, especially after 1930,[33] when labor turnover was very high. In 1938 all workers and employees were required to obtain labor books recording their trade, transfers of employment, the reasons for transfers, and any praise or distinction (although records of contraventions of the labor code are no longer included). Because these books are signed by plant managers when the worker receives a full discharge from his existing job, workers had considerable difficulty in leaving jobs and moving geographically. But people do leave jobs and are occasionally ordered back. In 1930, when unemployment was declared liquidated, the government decreed that the unemployed could be directed to any work, irrespective of their past experience and training. State enterprises were instructed to appoint officers responsible for the training and allocation of workers. The Commissariat of Labor, in agreement with the unions, could transfer skilled workers and specialists to more essential work, and move them from place to place. During the war of 1939-45, the labor force was mobilized and allocated to work, but labor registration broke down and many workers had no labor books. A relatively free labor market was restored after the war when the managers of state enterprises were told that the state could not supply them with labor and they must hire through agreements with individual workers and collective farms, attracting workers by offering better living and working conditions. But the Central Council of Trade Unions, concerned about the high labor turnover (largely due to bad housing conditions), restored controls later in 1946.

In eastern Europe labor controls have been severe during their initial period of transition. A Czechoslovak law of 1947 provided for the punishment of those who would not work at jobs assigned to them. Any worker could be ordered to leave his job because it had been suppressed as unnecessary by the government, or the worker had proficiency in some other job where the government believed he was more needed. When the worker was placed in a job and left it without government permission, he was liable to fines, jail, or labor camp sentences. In 1948 Works Councils were authorized to refuse employment to any person who could not prove that he left his last employment with the employer's consent, and compulsory labor camps were authorized.

Occupational allocation is influenced by freedom of geographical movement. As population growth in any area is unlikely to provide the numbers and kinds of workers from time to time required in occupations located

[32] Granick, *Management of the Industrial Firm in the U.S.S.R.*, 119.
[33] Bergson, *op. cit.*, 147.

there, continued maximum productivity requires movements of population. In very stable societies the need for movement may be small, but wherever countries are in process of development, the need may be great. Industrial development generally involves much migration from rural areas; this may continue for a long time because rural fertility rates are higher and death rates sometimes lower than in urban areas. The exodus is reinforced by increasing agricultural imports (e.g., in Britain in the 19th century) or by technical changes increasing output per worker in agriculture. During the 1920s agricultural workers failed to leave agriculture in the U.S.A. fast enough to compensate for rapid mechanization and the loss of foreign markets. Agricultural incomes fell, but workers left the towns and returned to agriculture in the depression of the 1930s, thereby deepening the agricultural depression and causing unemployment and underemployment. Between 1940 and 1945, however, 1.85 millions left the farms for the armed services and a further 5 millions (half of whom were dependents) moved to the towns. But industry has been moving into rural areas and small towns in the U.S.A. because of cheapening transport, cheaper distribution of electric power, the high cost of urban housing, the lower risk of loss of a small town labor supply in bad times, the ability of workers to use some land for part-time work, and the attempt to escape labor unions. But urban life still has a strong social appeal to workers.

Internal migration encounters more obstacles than movement among occupations in the same region. Family ties hinder movement, especially by married women. Unless industries are set up to take advantage of their labor, it may be wasted (particularly in coal mining areas). Information about distant jobs is less easily available than about nearby jobs. Movement is costly, especially in large countries in which economic change calls for movement over long distances. It is often retarded by failure to expand housing in pace with the expansion of job opportunities. Lack of housing retarded the relocation of British labor in the 1930s, and has held back the movement of labor from rural areas in Russia and, since 1945, in eastern Europe. When new mines, plantations and industries are established, it may be necessary for the employer to supply the housing and thus generate the difficulties associated with the industry or company town. Employers have endeavored to maintain supplies of cheap labor by preventing its migration to better jobs. Workers have been allowed to run into debt (in the southern states of the U.S.A. and in countries where plantation activities are important); the legal machinery for enforcing debt may then prevent workers from moving. Special and painful difficulties impede movement involving departure from a familiar social structure, as when native populations are taken out of their tribal organization and required to live in towns.

Government action often influences internal migration. Feudal systems in medieval Europe, the Middle East, and the Far East (e.g., Japan) almost prevented migration. In Britain in the 18th and early 19th centuries the local area in which a person had "legal settlement" was responsible for maintaining him when in need. As a result, people moving into a new area might be run out again to prevent them from living there long enough to obtain a "settlement." Most states and many local authorities have such arrangements in the U.S.A. In Britain, much of the unemployment after 1920 was concentrated in the "depressed areas" in the northeast and south Wales. The burden of relief raised local real estate taxes, and discouraged new industries from going there. As the movement of population into newly developing areas proved difficult, and would often result in obsolescence of social capital in the form of roads, railroads, sewers, schools, and the like, it was decided to bring the jobs to the people by redistributing on a national basis much of the cost of local relief, and in 1948 the relief system was completely nationalized. Mobility is also impeded by efforts such as those made in the depression of the 1930s in the U.S.A. to persuade employers to give preference in jobs to citizens and sometimes to people of the same state or city. Social security, on the other hand, is often provided on a national basis. Although unemployment insurance funds are state funds in the U.S.A., a person who has acquired rights in one state, can, if he has moved to another state, request the state in which he is resident to pay unemployment benefits as disbursing agent of the state from which he came. But mobility under such systems depends on decisions whether a worker must accept a job at a distance, or lose his right to unemployment compensation. Distant jobs may be temporary, housing is not always available, and movement may be costly, but payment of benefits despite opportunities for work elsewhere restricts mobility.

The government of South Africa severely restricts the mobility of the African population, allegedly to prevent an excessive number of Africans from entering the towns and, when they are unable to obtain work, resorting to other means of keeping alive. But the restrictions are also aimed at preventing workers from abandoning their indentured labor as miners or farmers and coming to town to look for jobs. Africans may not leave farms or any private property on which they are living without a pass issued by the owner or occupier of the property, and are restricted from living in urban areas or buying land outside the reserves.[34] Indians in Africa are prevented from moving from province to province or from buying land outside a few areas, and are confined largely to Natal and, in fact, almost to Durban. In Nazi Germany, Russia, and eastern Europe internal migration has been severely restricted to maintain political control of the population and to reduce labor turnover.

The British government, however, attempted to increase internal mobility before 1939. But its attempts to induce workers to move out of areas

34 Franklin, *op. cit.*, 146.

dependent on shrinking industries were, on the whole, ineffective largely because they were inadequate. It then attempted to attract potential employers to the available labor (which economizes on much civic equipment) through control of the location of new plants. During the war of 1939-45, however, the government was compelled to facilitate movement, and it paid for the cost of transportation of workers and arranged for their shelter. Russia, however, has moved labor to develop the eastern lands where local labor was scarce, the climate is unappealing, and there is little housing and few general living facilities. Industrial construction in the sub-arctic and tundra has largely been performed by the forced labor of deportees. In the early 1930s labor was obtained by deporting large numbers of *kulaks* from the Ukraine. In 1945 and 1946 some 1.5 million persons were deported to "other districts of the Soviet Union" for collaboration with the Nazi invaders. In 1947 the ministries were instructed to reallocate engineers and other technicians to meet shortages in the Urals, Siberia, and other eastern areas.

In general, the market has brought about great reallocations of labor that have facilitated increases in production. But there is no reason to think that it operates speedily enough to achieve the ideal allocation; also it operates erratically. It operates against a variety of resistances, and reallocations lag behind the optimum in times of rapid change. Exchange difficulties in western Europe, particularly Britain, after 1945 were partly due to failure to produce the "right" kind of goods. Even in the interwar period it was alleged that Britain, in the face of changing conditions of foreign trade, failed to make the "essential structural changes," that is, changes in the allocation of resources.

Shortages of industrial workers where there is concealed unemployment on the land in eastern Europe and in Russia[35] suggest poor allocation, but insufficiency of complementary resources (skills and capital) often prevents more rapid absorption in industry. Excessive numbers of workers in the distributive trades (notably in France) also suggest maldistribution owing, at least immediately, to the slowness of industrial expansion. In underdeveloped areas mobility is low because of unwillingness to move, the cost of movement, and (often) obstacles created by landowners. But lack of alternative work opportunities in industry has been the major cause. As already pointed out, industrial expansion is restricted by low incomes reducing the opportunity for capital accumulation. Movements out of agriculture are impeded, moreover, by rapid growth of population, which increases the demand for agricultural produce that most of these countries are in no position to import. Any additional saving, moreover, is likely to reduce the market for manufactured goods, and much of any increase in the presently low incomes is likely to increase the consump-

---

[35] U.N., *World Econ. Rep.*, 1948, 61.

tion of food by those previously unemployed or underemployed.[36] Finally, the increasing desire for economic self-sufficiency, in countries developed and underdeveloped, socialist and capitalist, results in allocations of labor that reduce productivity below what it could be in a world free from fear of war and depression.

b. The Economic Quality of the Labor Force

Output per hour worked depends partly upon the productive capacity of workers. This differs widely among countries, in the short run. Ill health, often due partly to poor nutrition, reduces the productive potential of well over half the workers in the world (in most of the Middle East, many parts of Latin America, in India, Java, Malaya, and Africa). In parts of Latin America labor efficiency is reduced by excessive heat or altitude.[37] Even in Britain in recent years, although the death rate has been falling, it has been falling faster for the better off than for the poorer classes. Lack of education and training goes with low productivity and income. Where literacy is low, productivity is usually also low. Less than 5% of the population was illiterate in 1939 in countries with average incomes of more than $200 a year, 20% in those with $100 to $200 a year and 78% in those with less than $100 a year.[38] In Latin America, "labor efficiency suffers from the fact that the general level of education is not satisfactory." Illiteracy ranged in 1939 from 82% in Honduras and 80% in Bolivia to 12% in Argentina, but the percentage of illiteracy is much lower among industrial workers.[39]

Neither the individual nor the family can typically do much to change these conditions, and *laisser faire* policies of government channel little resources into either public health or education. There is a vicious circular relation between income and expenditure on these services. In poor countries the productivity of labor is low because labor is poor in quality, because the country is poor and cannot afford expenditures on health and education. But lack of resources is not the whole explanation. Many societies with sick and illiterate populations have unemployed labor that could (often indirectly by displacement) be diverted into health and education. The necessary buildings and equipment are not costly in the early stages, but the young must be withdrawn from work for some years, and parents object to this withdrawal. The major problem is that of distributing the cost and the only feasible way is through taxation. Individuals do not commonly lend on a commercial basis for education because the security is too uncertain. Where the cost of education falls largely on parents, education is restricted to persons whose parents can pay for it,

[36] U.N., *Econ. Surv. of Europe Since the War*, 1953, 153.

[37] U.N., *Econ. Surv. of Latin America in 1948*, 36.

[38] Spengler, "Economic Factors in the Development of Densely Populated Areas," 95 *Proc. Am. Phil. Soc.*, 1951, 50.

[39] U.N., *Econ. Surv. of Latin America in 1948*, 32.

and these are only a few in the poorer countries. Churches have at various times and places paid for some education, but employers and labor unions, both of whom might gain from education, have in fact rarely thought investment in it worthwhile, although the early New England cotton mills provided education to their workers, as the Japanese cotton mills did much later.

In the typical underdeveloped country governments have been unwilling to tax for these purposes (Ch. 31) partly because the governing classes are none too hospitable toward general education. Mass education in the more developed countries has come largely as a response to pressure from workers who have been unable to exert similarly effective pressure in underdeveloped countries. But the desire for education is growing rapidly. Education widens the variety of jobs that persons can do and facilitates organization by improving communication with the worker. But it is also a form of consumption, increasing individual satisfactions often not economic. Health services raise potential output per worker but may, at least for a time, merely result in accelerated population increase and a fall in the standard of living. Increasing the labor potential in these ways does not always raise actual output. It may merely widen the margin between potential and actual output until production is reorganized (by reallocating labor and obtaining access to more of the other factors of production). Public health and education services raising physical output per head in industry reduce the demand for industrial workers per unit of output, but wherever wages rise or cost reductions lead to price reductions, demand increases may prevent any decline in industrial employment.

The technical training of workers also affects productivity. For workers in general, training in craft production was transmitted from generation to generation through apprenticeship or its equivalent, which still exists in industrial countries in such occupations as carpentry, electrical installation, and the like. In the non-industrial countries it is the main channel for the transmission of skills. Industrial employment in general makes relatively small demands for skills acquired by long training, but calls for acceptance of factory discipline. The adaptation of rural people, accustomed to control their own ways of working, to this discipline is invariably difficult, and productivity is usually held down during periods of adaptation. Early in the 19th century British factory workers objected to long hours, monotonous work, continuous application, and lack of self-determination. Employers complained of drunkenness (attributable to the strain of work and the cheapness of gin) and the poor response of workers to pecuniary inducements. Higher pay resulted in intermittent work. These problems slowly disappeared during the 19th century due to the influence of the church, social movements in general, and labor unions. Similar difficulties appeared in Japan. During the depression of 1929-32 great pressure was exerted to increase the efficiency of organization, technical skill, and the size of the labor force. Marked improvements occurred in engineering, metallurgy, chemicals, and mining, and by 1937, the workers rivalled in skill those in much older industrialized countries. Starting with the skills of a few crafts, Japan quickly built a massive new industrial system on the basis of a nucleus of organizing ability and craftsmanship, and of a mass of docile unskilled workers.[40] Russia could build its industrial system only by converting peasants into industrial workers, and encountered the same difficulties as other countries. But it organized an intense educational campaign to eliminate illiteracy, provided secondary and higher education for selected students, grants for the entire period of education, and for the selection of students for various types of professional work.

The historical record shows that the problem can be solved, although not always as quickly as is desired. It is yet, however, far from solved in Africa, India, and other areas where industry is being set up, and there is widespread criticism of the inefficiency of industrial workers. In West Africa, for instance, industrial wages are low, but output is also low. It takes about four years for the native population to become accustomed to even unskilled repetitive work, and there is yet no native managerial class. The stamina of the people's bodies and the concentration of their minds has been undermined by bad diet, low wages, and disease. Laborers work hard only under supervision, and have little initiative. There is no evidence, however, that some peoples are biologically incapable of adjusting to industrial methods, though there is plenty of evidence of social factors limiting the speed of adjustment. The ways of the fathers are passed on to the children, and can only slowly be modified.

The availability of skilled management dominates economic progress. But now that experience has been gained in some countries, others can import it. Germany, France, and the U.S.A. all imported skilled workers and managers in the 19th century. Russia made its start by importing foreign experience (mostly from the U.S.A.), but the rapid rate of industrialization has caused a continuing shortage of technically skilled workers. Eastern European countries are receiving technical aid from Russia. Latin American and other underdeveloped countries and India have employed foreign technicians and managers, but they are increasingly resented if they remain and keep the best jobs. Consequently, they are frequently required to train members of the native population and withdraw. A country may attempt to develop by training its own managers, perhaps by sending them abroad, but development is likely to be retarded. In the later 19th-century Germany led the world in organizing technical education, which provided the basis for the rapid advance of its chemical and electri-

---

[40] Allen, *A Short Economic History of Modern Japan*, Ch. X, 144.

cal industries. The Russian five-year plans allocate resources for training technicians. Britain has increased emphasis on such training since 1945. The more highly developed countries have shown increasing concern for the supply of the scientific workers who are the source of new technical knowledge. The German *Technische Hochschule* produced a great volume of research and research workers, institutes of technology have performed the same function in the U.S.A., and Britain is now conscious that it has allocated too little of its labor force to this work.

c. The Availability of Complementary Resources

The availability of other productive resources fundamentally affects production per worker (Ch. 15, 16, 17, 21). In the U.S.A., where productivity is higher than anywhere else, the large supply of natural resources in relation to population (particularly minerals and land) is probably the ultimate basis of high productivity. The large capital fund that greatly increases productivity is due partly to the existence of ample opportunities for profitable investment. Britain preferred to export capital during the 19th century rather than invest it at home, while the U.S.A. imported capital because it could be productively invested. The vigor of the labor force, which also contributes to productivity in the U.S.A., is also partly the result of high productivity and income. Many of the workers came from European countries where their labor was far less productive. The large internal market area of the U.S.A. permits more effective division of labor than in a small country, and therefore higher productivity. But New Zealand has prospered with a small domestic market by selling most of its produce in Britain, which imposed no duties upon New Zealand products and was, therefore, part of the same economic system. Lack of restriction in trade is evidently important, but transport costs are fairly high among some parts of the U.S.A., and unavoidably restrict division of labor.

The lack of other resources for use with labor holds down productivity in underdeveloped countries. Where land is scarce in relation to labor, agricultural productivity is low. The withdrawal of workers from agriculture depends on the availability of non-labor resources for industrial expansion. In general, these complementary resources are most available in countries well industrialized. For instance, industry has expanded in northwest Europe since 1930 and absorbed workers from agriculture. Levels of productivity there have been high enough to permit capital accumulation. But in the less developed countries in Europe agricultural populations have increased and remained relatively unproductive.[41] But it does not follow that underdeveloped countries cannot increase labor productivity. Most of the now developed countries were once primarily agricultural and relatively poor.

---

[41] U.N., *Econ. Surv. of Europe Since the War*, 1953, 153.

d. Conditions of Work

Conditions of work affect productivity by providing incentives to produce and work conditions facilitating production.

i. Incentives to Production

Incentives to produce rest ultimately in all societies on the unpleasant results of failure to produce. But they operate through a variety of devices in different countries and at different times. In some primitive societies, those who do not work may nevertheless eat and find shelter because private property in consumer goods is restricted. But there are always social pressures preventing the able bodied from continuing to refuse to work. The pressures range from critical comment, to ostracism, and finally to expulsion from the group (which may mean a hard life or starvation). A large part of the indigenous population in colonial areas in Africa lives on reserves organized on a tribal basis, which, not being adaptable to the use of modern methods of production even in agriculture, has prevented material progress. In Southern Rhodesia, for instance, the native population will work prodigiously when it sees fit but lacks incentive because the standard of "necessities" is low and the individual can remain on the reserve, where his family may maintain him if he does not work. But the communal organization of labor is breaking down, and even on the reserves economic life is often organized on an individualist basis.

Slavery permits the use of physical force to compel work selected by the owner, who receives the proceeds of the work. Slaves may be well treated and entitled to protection, but their ultimate status is that of work animals. Much productive work was done by slaves in the Asiatic empires, Egypt, Greece, and Rome. The low status of labor at that time was probably due to association with slavery, although citizens and slaves frequently worked side by side. The aristocratic ideal was based largely on military values, work (except that of killing enemies) being looked upon with disdain. Skilled slaves emerged and took over much of the artistic work of the time, and it became necessary to give them an interest in their work, better living conditions, and increasing independence, which frequently meant the opportunity to buy their freedom.

Slavery was common in eastern Europe in the Middle Ages, but not in western Europe, and was undermined by Christianity. There were a few slaves in England until the 18th century. But in 1772 the courts decided that no person in England could be a slave and slaves brought to the country automatically became free. The slave trade was abolished in all British territories in 1807, and slavery in 1832. Between 1820 and 1830 a great many European countries also abandoned slavery. The plantations in the southern states of the U.S.A. were originally operated by free (often indentured) white labor. But African slaves were imported into Virginia in 1619 and used mainly on the plantations, whose survival became dependent on slave labor. The importation of slaves ceased in 1807. After the slaves were emancipated by decree in 1863 many plantations disappeared, but others continued to operate with Negro tenants, cash renters, share-croppers, some with wage labor (wages being somewhat nominal), and some with a virtual peonage system.

In many colonial areas the indigenous labor force was originally en-slaved, and the abolition of slavery did not for a considerable time greatly change labor conditions. Workers were economically and politically servile, with nominal wages, criminal penalties for leaving work, and little power to migrate. In parts of India agricultural laborers still mortgage their personal liberty in bad times. For a small sum they agree to serve the lender until the loan is repaid and often thus become a lifelong bond slave.[42] Slavery was illegal, however, in all countries by the end of the 19th century partly for humanitarian reasons, but partly because of its general inefficiency, especially in industrial production. But the line be-tween slavery and work under labor contracts made under coercion and enforced by coercion is a fine one.

Governments have contributed to the coercion of labor by enforcing debts by almost forced labor. Such debts may arise out of long-term con-tracts for labor with a payment on the signing of the contract, and sub-sequent severe penalties for failure to fulfill it. Workers have also been allowed to get into debt through company stores, and the state has per-mitted the enforcement of debts in ways which make work better than imprisonment for debt. This is especially prevalent in countries, both de-veloped and underdeveloped, where company towns are established by mining companies, plantations and others whose location of activity is far from any urban center. The combination of employer and employee, plus landlord and tenant, plus controller of the local group life as well as employment, has often been inimical to free social institutions.[43] Quasi-compulsory labor is exacted in parts of Iraq. Workers receive advances and are not permitted to leave their place of work without permission; the government brings them back if they do leave.[44]

Taxes payable in cash have forced colonial populations into the labor market intermittently to obtain the money necessary to pay their taxes and avoid imprisonment. They could have maintained themselves, at least on a subsistence basis, on the reserves, without entering the labor market, except for the necessity of paying taxes in cash.[45] In recent years, how-ever, some native populations having some agricultural surplus, and being able to sell it at rising prices, have been able to meet their tax bills out of the proceeds of the sale of their produce, particularly where general

---

[42] Wadia and Merchant, op. cit., 260.

[43] Frankel, Capital Investment in Africa, 11.

[44] Bonné, State and Economics in the Middle East, 132.

[45] Franklin, op. cit., 143; Union of South Africa: Witwatersrand Mine Natives' Wages Commission Report, 1943, 15.

criticism of this tax policy has deterred colonial powers from raising head or hut taxes when the general price level has increased. In the Belgian Congo a decree of 1933 and an ordinance of 1935 required every native not in employment to do sixty days compulsory work a year within his native area. The work is agricultural, carried out in accordance with pre-scribed methods, and aims at raising productivity and increasing wealth. It is unpaid, but the produce is the grower's, and he may consume or sell it.

Compulsory labor has been exacted in western countries in time of emergency. The National Service Act required labor from all men and women between prescribed ages in Britain from 1939 to 1945 and was enforced by prison sentence in a very few cases. Compulsion has also been applied in socialist countries where national plans call for rapid development, although the main incentive to work is that failure to work means lack of access to food and other satisfactions. Failure to work is regarded as sabotage and punished. In Russia there was a brief period of early communism in which it was assumed that each would receive ac-cording to his need (which provides no direct economic compulsion to work). But the labor code of 1918 instituted obligatory work for all citizens between 16 and 50 years of age. Free to choose their occupation, they were obligated to accept any work offered when they were unemployed. In January 1920 a new law introduced conscription for all labor, and "labor deserters" were liable to prosecution. Under the New Economic Policy (1921 to 1927) jobs rather than workers were scarce, and compulsory labor was abolished. But after unemployment was declared liquidated in 1930 unemployed members of workers' families who were not members of labor unions, children who had not yet entered employment, and unem-ployed wives and widows of workers who were not members of labor unions were registered, and could be directed to work, refusal to accept direction involving loss of the right to employment for a specified period. During the war of 1939-45 the labor force was virtually militarized and compelled to work. In Czechoslovakia, compulsory labor was first intro-duced as a temporary measure to accelerate postwar reconstruction, and the constitution of 1948 declared the obligation to work in the interests of the community to be one of the basic principles of the right to work.[46] In Bulgaria in 1948, those not employed in a way useful to the community could be denied all rations. In Poland a decree of 1945 imposed a universal obligation to work upon men from 18 to 55 years and women from 18 to 45 years of age. There is also an unknown number of criminals, officials who have violated Soviet economic laws, and political prisoners (including prisoners of war) engaged at forced labor in mining, building roads, fac-tories and canals, and other productive installations, and working in the forests, often in regions so harsh that recruitment by reward would be

---

[46] I.L.O., *Ind. and Lab.*, April 1949, 264.

costly. This forced labor is an important element in labor relations in Russia both directly and indirectly (as a threat to all workers).[47]

Incentives to work in feudal Europe consisted mainly of access to land without which the cultivator could not live. In return for access to land he worked on the lord's land. But those who refused to work were fined, sometimes physically punished, and ultimately expelled (which meant a meagre livelihood, no personal protection, and often early death). The serfs were not slaves, and they gradually acquired rights to an allotment of land in return for only the traditional services. This, or a comparable system, was important over a good part of Europe and in the Middle East, but attempts to introduce the system in the U.S.A. were unsuccessful. Evidently the system did not appeal to workers and they rejected it when a scarcity of labor and plenty of land enabled them to do so.

The sharecropping arrangements common in agriculture in the Middle and Far East, parts of Latin America, and the southern states of the U.S.A. provide a share of the crop as the incentive to produce. But the outcome of any added effort by the worker must be shared with the landowner. The feudal serf paid a labor rent, the sharecropper pays a produce rent, and the labor of both has been relatively unproductive partly because the incentive was weak.

Wage employment now provides the main incentive to work outside agriculture in both capitalist and socialist countries. Marx emphasized that the development of a labor market was necessary to capitalism. The market facilitated the freeing of methods of production from guild controls, but it required the detachment of workers from the soil to which they had access. So long as they had the alternative of working on land they were not a wholly reliable source of labor, more particularly at prices which employers would prefer to pay. When the worker's alternative to wage employment in the form of work on the land was removed, the mass of the population came to be converted into employers and employees. Where most of the population has little or no income from property, it must work, demand and supply being mutually adjusted through the level of wages.

Wage employment in agriculture varies greatly in importance. The enclosures in Britain in the 16th and 17th centuries converted much of the farm population affected into wage laborers. The labor force of the former large estates of eastern Germany, Hungary, and much of eastern Europe was on a wage basis. But landless wageworkers have been relatively unimportant in French agriculture except on the great estates in the Bordeaux and other wine districts, on the big farms north of Paris, and in the forests. Sons of peasants have sometimes worked for wages, but they usually had some land and acquired more by inheritance or purchase. In the U.S.A. there is wage labor, but much agriculture is in the hands of small enterprisers remunerated by profits rather than wages. In less developed areas share-

---

[47] Schwartz, *Russia's Soviet Economy*, 484.

cropping retards the development of wage labor which requires active supervision by the employer. Wage labor has developed, however, on plantations and other organizations for large-scale agriculture (e.g., in most tropical areas, India and Mexico). The work on the large agricultural estates in the Nile delta is largely performed by wage laborers organized in gangs. This system is abused, particularly the employment of children and exploitation by gang leaders. There is no government supervision of labor, and it is reported to be not uncommon to see girls five years old picking cotton, followed by a gang leader with a whip. In Palestine in 1931, about 22% of the Arab agricultural families relied on wage labor and the numbers are believed to have increased since that time.[48] The market for wage labor for agriculture has probably developed least in Africa. South of the Sahara the proportion of the population in wage labor is generally considerably less than 10%.[49] But as tribal organization breaks up, an indigenous proletariat is appearing.

Wage labor appeared in non-agricultural work earlier than in agriculture. In the later years of the craft guilds in Europe, the journeyman appeared. He was a day laborer for wages. The home work which undermined the guilds often developed a wage relationship. Some weavers and others were small entrepreneurs, buying materials and selling finished products, but in the course of time some were supplied with their material by merchants and paid a piece rate for working it up. This arrangement provided a subsidiary income to the peasant, and sometimes helped him to remain on the land. But when factory products (at first textiles) came on the market, these auxiliary incomes of workers from home work disappeared. In the textile industry they had gone by 1830, and home workers were forced into the factories. A similar process was going on in the textile industry of Germany between about 1840 and 1870, but home work of this type was important in Japan until the 1930s. Industrial production is almost wholly dependent on wage labor.

Labor markets in general provide the means by which the capitalist entrepreneur can calculate labor costs and adjust his labor force. When calculations of profit suggest a restriction of output, he can expel workers into the market, and when these calculations suggest an increase in output, he can obtain more workers in the market at a price he knows in advance. General increases in demand necessitate offers of higher wages. But even in capitalist countries labor markets do not work like markets for goods. Low wages do not reduce the supply of labor offered (except in the long run through adjustments of population), and may increase it. Low wages for men in the early stages of industrialization increased the labor supply by compelling women and children to work. Thus they further reduced the wages of men, and perpetuated a supply of labor of low quality where

---

48 Warriner, *Land and Poverty in the Middle East*, 38, 63.
49 U.N., *Rev. of Econ. Conditions in Africa*, 1951, 73.

low and the cost of rearing and educating children
mily. For similar reasons, higher wages do not al-
e labor. In recent years workers in most of the
vith relatively high incomes have increasingly bar-
s, thus reducing the labor time offered. Such reduc-
labor offered in response to higher pay were wide-
tries in the early days of industrialism. They are
y criticized by employers with Western capitalist
nize labor forces in the Middle East, Africa, and
ers" seek a given money income and respond to
shorter hours or more intermittently. Where
potential labor force extend little beyond mere
targets is the major obstacle to recruiting wage
ds of time, and particularly with the increasing
ds and services, workers raise their sights as
he labor supply becomes positively elastic
of labor is also influenced by factors other
ant death rates increases the proportion of
reduction of death rates in older age groups
tion of workers or of dependent aged.
contracts depends on their form. During
contracts are sometimes of long duration to
y. In the transition from feudal to capitalist
a icultural labor was often employed on annual
contracts. Many workers were hired in Britain by the year at annual
"hirings," and the practice was similar on the continent of Europe. Before
1939 some 100,000 workers were employed on annual contracts on large
agricultural estates in Hungary. They were paid in produce, lived in
miserable barracks on the estates, and worked under the supervision of
bailiffs for almost unlimited hours. During the early stages of the industrial revolution in England, the old institution of apprenticeship was
adapted to establish indentured labor in the early textile mills. Orphans
were shipped to mills; the children of the poor were compulsorily indentured to work in these mills, their parents being refused relief if they did
not agree; children were whipped if they did not work. Bad conditions in
factories frequently created a supply of orphans to be swallowed up by
this system, which disappeared, however, early in the 19th century.

Indentured workers provided an important source of labor in the
northern states in the U.S.A. in earlier periods of settlement, due to labor
shortage, the necessity for obtaining labor from a distance, and the high
cost of transportation. Indentured labor has also been used on a large scale
by the cotton spinning mills in Japan. Factory agents make contracts with

[50] Bonné, *op. cit.*, 154.

the heads of peasant families by which girls work for a few years in the mills. The employer houses and feeds the workers and provides them with entertainment. Obligations of a paternal kind were accepted by employers and later came to be regarded by workers as a right—for instance, the payment of dismissal allowances on discharge, and the payment of semi-annual bonuses.[51] In some ways this system is comparable to that used in New England to attract female labor to the mills in the earlier part of the 19th century. African labor is now obtained on contract for the mines in central and South Africa. Typically, the labor is recruited at a considerable distance from the mines. The average length of service by natives has increased from 10.88 months in 1931 to 13.6 months in 1942.[52] The workers are required to stay within the mine compound during the period of work unless they obtain the permission of the employer to leave. Contracts must now usually be signed in the presence of a Native Affairs Officer responsible for minimizing coercion and misunderstanding of the contract.

There is nothing inherently undesirable in long-term contracts. Indeed, in recent years a minimum work-year has been advocated in capitalist countries to reduce the burden of unemployment (but with an option to the worker to leave whenever he wishes). Long-term contracts have facilitated migration by workers by providing a means of meeting its costs. But employers who meet these costs expect power to enforce fulfillment of the contract in which they have made an advance investment. These contracts are also assumed to be voluntary, although in Japan parents contract for the labor of their children in return for an advance payment. But, as workers generally prefer not to be bound for long periods, such contracts can be made only if the worker is in a poor bargaining position, or if force or deception is used.

Methods of calculating remuneration have been refined to intensify the incentive to work. Payment by the week or other period of time provides an incentive to get and keep the job. In small enterprises, efficiency may be encouraged by paying higher time rates to the workers who are deemed most efficient. But larger organizations increasingly pay a uniform rate to all workers in each class, and labor unions reinforce this tendency. The maintenance of output then depends on supervision, except where machine speeds determine the rate of output. Payment by volume of output stimulates production and reduces costs. Incentive may be further sharpened by paying progressively higher piece-rates beyond a prescribed basic output. Within limits, overhead costs do not increase with output, and progressive rates can be profitable.

Piece-rates are important in western Europe, but are not spreading

---

51 Allen, *op. cit.*, 72.
52 Union of South Africa: Witwatersrand Mine Natives' Wages Commission *Report*, 1943, 15.

much, for they are already applied to most of the kinds of work to which they are applicable; 40% of hours worked in industry were paid at piece-rates in 1938 in Norway and Denmark, 34% in Britain, and 48% in Sweden. These proportions had changed little by 1946, but later increased to 57% in Norway, though little in Denmark, Sweden, and Britain.[53]

The socialist countries have increasingly used piece-rates, and especially progressive rates, to stimulate production, thus emphasizing the pecuniary motive in workers. The labor-day basis of distributions in cash and in kind among the members of agricultural cooperatives in Russia involves payment by results, since jobs are rated in labor days that may differ from the actual days taken to perform the work. In industry the General Law of Wages in 1920 authorized piece-work and premium systems. After 1927, various funds were set up for the payment of premiums, and in 1931 they were made mandatory by the Supreme Economic Council. In December, 1935, the Communist Party decided that progressive piece-rates were to be the chief method of remuneration in industry, and the proportion of working hours in large scale industry so paid rose from 57.5% in 1928 to 70.7% in 1935 and 75% in 1940.[54] The proportion was to be increased further in the plan period 1946 to 1950. Bonus systems apply to management as well as to the mass of workers. In 1940 premiums were about 11% of the total earnings of all engineering and managerial personnel of industry.[55] The governments in eastern Europe all follow the same policy as Russia. The proportion of hours worked at piece-rates increased from 38% in 1946 to 55% in 1948 in Czechoslovakia and from 36% in 1946 to 70% in 1949 in Hungary.[56] The Central Council of Czechoslovakian Trade Unions resolved in 1951 that trade union groups must put aside all equalitarian methods of remuneration and ensure that the principle of payment by results is applied with all its consequences.[57]

If piece-rates stimulate production, they yield increased earnings; if employers then reduce piece-rates, workers may conclude that it is impossible for long to increase their money wage by increased effort, and the incentive effect of the rates is lost. This problem has been especially serious in the socialist countries, where the government has been stimulating output by rationalizing work. In 1935 Stakhanov hewed a record amount of coal in a single shift, as a result of an analysis of the job, a new division of labor, and the improved use of tools. By working more efficiently, but not harder or longer hours than others, he attracted attention to the possibilities of motion study and scientific management (although these terms were not used) and stimulated a number of experiments. The government has also introduced more and improved equipment. Failure to lower piece-

53 U.N., *Econ. Bull. for Europe*, 1950, Vol. 2, No. 2, 59.
54 Baykov, *op. cit.*, 250.
55 Granick, *op. cit.*, 193.
56 U.N., *Econ. Bull. for Europe*, 1950, Vol. 2, No. 2, 59.
57 I.L.O., *Ind. and Lab.*, May 15, 1951, 356.

rates when such improvements permit higher output, even without increased effort, channels the benefits of the improvements to the workers in the industries concerned. But the socialist governments contend that these benefits should go to consumers as a whole in reduced prices, and into further investment. They attempt, therefore, to make differences in the earnings of workers performing similar tasks reflect differences in their productivity, but to prevent increases in average productivity from increasing earnings except in the very short run.[58]

Rising earnings in the industries increasing efficiency fastest aggravate the problem of adjusting wage differentials in different industries to achieve the allocation of labor called for by the production plan,[59] especially in the early stages after the introduction of such rates. The wide use of piece-rates also increases the difficulty of stabilizing the general level of wages and prices. Holding piece-rates constant increases payrolls as output per man increases, and causes overexpenditure of the wage funds allotted to enterprises. Even if increases in money earnings are matched by increases in output, inflation may follow if the increase in output is concentrated in the capital rather than consumer goods industries[60] where the workers seek to spend their increased incomes. Plant managers in Russia, anxious to retain a stable labor force, have been reluctant to hold down earnings (presumably because workers believed they were not being held down everywhere). Consequently, the standing rule that norms (for both time- and piece-workers) are to be changed when jobs are rationalized or mechanized has been difficult to enforce. Revisions (as well as extended applications of piece-rates) have been made as a result of periodic "drives" by the state and then inefficiently because so speedily.[61] But the accumulation of slack since the previous "drive" often permitted sharp increases. In eastern European countries piece-rates have been repeatedly reduced (or output norms raised) as average productivity has risen. In Hungary, for instance, wage norms were reset in terms of current performance in 1949, 1950, and 1952. Industries in which output norms were easier to surpass attracted labor from other industries.[62]

Incentives to work may also be provided by giving workers a share in profits. Scattered experiments of this sort have been successful in Britain and the U.S.A. The managers of many corporations in Europe also receive a share of profits. In Chile a law of 1950 requires firms to distribute 25% of their profits among workers. In 1946, the Brazilian constitution recognized the right of workers to share in profits, but the method of sharing has not been determined. Profit-sharing has also been extensive in socialist coun-

---

58 U.N., *Econ. Surv. of Europe Since the War*, 1953, 32.
59 U.N., *Econ. Bull. for Europe*, 1950, Vol. 2, No. 2, 60.
60 U.N., *Econ. Bull. for Europe*, 1950, Vol. 2, No. 2, 60.
61 Granick, *op. cit.*, 84.
62 U.N., *Econ. Surv. of Europe Since the War*, 1953, 32; *Econ. Bull. for Europe*, 1950, 60.

tries. In Russia a "directors' fund" was set up in each enterprise in 1936. It is fed by contributions of 4% of planned profit and 50% of profit in excess of that planned. It is used (subject to the approval of the plant labor union committee and the commissariat) for housing, social services, premiums for workers, and capital construction and rationalization beyond the plan. Similar funds have been established in each nationalized undertaking in Czechoslovakia, to be used by the director to stimulate output. In Hungary 2% of the profits of state undertakings is available for profit-sharing, 40% of which is spent on purposes of general interest to workers. The total share to be distributed is raised where actual profits exceed planned profits.[63] In Yugoslavia, workers' committees in each enterprise were allowed to dispose of undistributed profits after taxes by reinvestment in the enterprise, housing and amenities, or bonuses on wages. They generally chose bonuses on wages, which were about 30% of total worker income in 1950. But in 1954 the share of profits to be used to supplement wages was restricted, the proportion falling sharply as profits increase. For example, profits (after taxes) of 15% of the wage bill may all be used for wage bonuses, but of profits eight times the wage bill only 3% may be used for bonuses.[64]

The effect of profit-sharing depends on the definition of profit and the satisfactoriness of the basis of sharing. The looseness of the relation between added individual effort and share of profit (which is affected by general business conditions, efficiency of management, competitive conditions, taxation, and other conditions beyond control by workers) dulls their incentive effect. In socialist countries government control of the cost of materials and the prices of products make profits reflect productivity more than in capitalist countries, but taxation operates severely in the opposite direction.

ii. Facilitation of Production

Incentives spur the worker, but his response depends partly on the extent to which the conditions of work permit high output. Capitalist employers might be expected to arrange optimal conditions, taking account of the effect on costs and profits. Small employers vary widely in their efficiency in this respect and are generally limited in their knowledge and facilities to increase it (e.g., in crafts and small-scale agriculture). Where labor is cheap the incentive for employers to use it effectively is reduced. The harsh conditions of work on plantations have been partly due to the low remuneration of labor in the country because of the scarcity of land and capital in relation to workers, but they have sometimes involved the inefficient use of labor, even under prevailing conditions. Hard labor conditions in industry have often not resulted in the most efficient use of labor.

---

[63] I.L.O., *Ind. and Lab.*, April 1949, 283, Aug. 1949, 191.
[64] U.N., *Econ. Surv. of Europe in 1953*, 115.

Sometimes they have been in the short-run interest of the employer, although not in the long run interest of society, because the marginal private net product of labor diverges from its marginal social net product. The employment of children may involve "mining" the labor force, which may, nevertheless, pay each employer. The prevention of accidents may involve costs to employers but be beneficial to society. But sometimes harsh labor conditions have not even been in the short-run interest of the employer: they have not always minimized costs. Employers operate within the limits of their knowledge, and until the 20th century they put less effort into acquiring knowledge of the conditions most likely to maximize labor productivity under a given technology than into improving technology. Employers imposed hours of labor that were excessive even in terms of costs. Conditions of lighting, heating, and sanitation were often inefficient. The general atmosphere in which these conditions prevailed suggested unconcern for the human needs of workers. This created hostility rather than active cooperation. Fear of loss of work remained the overwhelming incentive.

Exploration of conditions of work most favorable to production has been systematized and intensified in the more developed countries in the 20th century. In the U.S.A. high wages stimulated the economization of labor, and "buying off" labor opposition became more costly than redesigning labor relations. Studies of physical conditions of labor (motion study and the like) have been followed by psychological research, and personnel managers and labor advisers have become a recognized part of the large corporation. In Britain labor unions achieved improvements. Where desired improvements do not result in immediate reductions in cost, the individual employer may be hampered by competitors unwilling to make similar changes, although in the long run, and if widely adopted, the improvement might raise general productivity (e.g., reduction in hours of labor or the elimination of temporarily cheap child labor). Improvement in physical conditions of work has led to efforts to improve psychological conditions, although information in this area is still inadequate. Where employers fail to show an interest in removing obstacles to production, not only is production directly reduced, but also workers are frustrated, which indirectly reduces output. Encouraging workers to make suggestions about methods of improving conditions of work has sometimes had a psychological as well as a direct effect upon output. But increasing division of labor and monotony of work sap the interest of workers. The more interesting parts of the production process are specialized out into the hands of a few workers who represent management. Mass production has undermined the mental and moral vigor of workers partly because of the loss of a sense of responsibility. Shorter hours and leisure time activities are only a partial compensation, and the enlistment of the emotional cooperation of workers remains a serious problem in industrial societies.

Copartnership is a device for enlisting the cooperation of workers by giving them a share in management, but it has never achieved widespread success. In the early years of industrial development in Russia, "triangles" consisting of the plant manager, the plant's communist party chief, and the plant's trade union head supervised operations. But they were abolished in 1928 to give the enterprise director complete control and responsibility.[65] In Czechoslovakia workers' committees frequently took over plants after the liberation of the country in 1945, and subsequently works councils were established in all larger plants, with full access to all records, but without power to interfere with the decisions of management. They are used to effectuate government policies in increasing production.[66] In Yugoslavia, however, there is generally a management council for an enterprise or group of enterprises, of whom three-quarters represent the workers. The council plans for the undertaking, controls its operations, and appoints the director (who is an *ex officio* member of the council).[67]

British unions (unlike French) have refused to share managerial responsibility in nationalized industry in the belief that the competing interests of worker and employer are best dealt with by organizations specializing in the advocacy of each. Labor union leaders appointed members of the boards of nationalized industries are required to resign their union offices. Provision was made in France in 1917 for the issue of labor shares not freely transferable, but little advantage has been taken of the provision. A similar provision was made in New Zealand. The government of Argentina has announced its intention to increase labor's share in management and profits by issuing shares to workers. Economic advantages are to be offered to corporations voluntarily granting labor shares carrying participation in both profits and management, but few such shares have been issued. The labor unions in West Germany, long tinged with a syndicalist philosophy, demanded a share in control because of the part played by employers in two wars and their opposition to social legislation under the Weimar republic. The workers also feared nationalization and state socialism. In 1951 (under threat of a strike) they obtained the statutory right to appoint five of the eleven members of the Boards of Directors and one of the three members of the Board of Management of all the larger coal, iron, and steel producers. In 1952 enterprises in nearly all other industries, except public enterprises, were required to provide for worker participation in control, but on terms less liberal than in the iron and steel industries. Divided responsibility has, however, usually reduced efficiency, and few workers can, as a practical matter, have a sense of participation.

Workers influence the conditions of work only where they have an

---

[65] Schwarz, *op. cit.*, 182.
[66] I.L.O., *Ind. and Lab.*, May 15, 1951, 357.
[67] *Ibid.*, Oct. 15, 1950.

alternative source of livelihood (such as migrating to the land in the U.S.A. in the past), or where they are effectively organized. Labor unions, however, represent sections of the labor force and seek to increase each section's share in the national product. "Business union" policies (aimed at using the unified power of workers to employ skilled agents to bargain for improved conditions of work) (Ch. 30) have probably improved the use of labor by raising its cost. Increased wages threaten the employer with a loss of profit, the fear of which may be a greater inducement to improve methods of production than was the prospect of a higher profit from better use of labor before the increased wages were demanded. But higher wages reduce the demand for labor in the occupations affected. The outcome depends partly on the effect of higher wages on costs and on prices, and partly on the elasticity of demand for the product. Some unions may accept the prospect of reduced sales and employment, virtually sharing a semi-monopoly profit obtained by employers. Some labor unions have actively suggested ways of increasing productivity, to remove the employer's objection that he cannot pay more wages, and are more likely to do so where the union is large and the typical employer small (e.g., the Amalgamated Clothing Workers in the U.S.A.). But unions have also obstructed changes in technology by maintaining a demand for their labor beyond what is necessary with known methods of production. Such "featherbedding" rules raise prices and reduce the goods and services available to the community in general, although they may raise the proportion of the reduced national output going to workers as a group or to the section indulging in the practice.

When labor unions in general acquire predominant power over the government (as they did for instance in Britain from 1945 to 1950), they may increase the workers' share of the national income by redistributing existing incomes (by progressive taxation and the distribution of progressive incomes in goods and services, for example, social security). But when the limits to this policy are reached, any one group of workers can improve its position only at the expense of other workers, and workers in general can improve their incomes only by increasing the national output. Profits become a relatively less significant source of increases in labor incomes. Thus, after the British Labor Party took over full responsibility for government after 1945, it accepted the fact that inefficiency in production was mainly at the expense of workers. In 1948, the labor unions, realizing that, far from getting favors from the Labor Government, they would have to make sacrifices to enable it to surmount the grave economic crisis, agreed to campaign for increases in efficiency and to give up prewar restrictive practices based on the fear of unemployment. In Holland, also, since about 1946 the unions have realized that they cannot return to the pre-war standard of living without increases in efficiency, although they argue that management and plant efficiency must be improved as well as labor practices.

In socialist countries, labor unions operate as the personnel department of the government regulating the utilization of labor in accordance with the national plan. They are required not to protect the worker from exploitation (which is held to have been eliminated), but to remedy inefficiencies pointed out by workers, and protect them from unreasonable or inefficient managers. The Communist Party Congress in 1920 resolved that, "under the dictatorship of the proletariat the trade unions are transformed from organs of the struggle of sellers of labor power against the ruling class into an apparatus of the ruling workers' class. The tasks of the trade unions lie mainly in the sphere of the organization of economic life and of education." (The Nazi government in Germany used the *Arbeitsfront* in somewhat the same way after 1933.) When private entrepreneurship was permitted under the New Economic Policy, the trade unions resumed the protection of workers against exploitation. In 1927 the All Union Central Council of Trade Unions was given a "consultative voice" in the Supreme Economic Council. But the unions found it difficult both to protect workers' interests and to participate in the socialist organization of production, and they were reorganized in 1929. As the socialized sector ousted the private sector after the beginning of the first five-year plan, emphasis on labor discipline and labor productivity increased, and emphasis on participation in planning and the protection of the worker from exploitation decreased. The labor union organization was finally merged with the Commissariat of Labor in 1933. Until 1940, employing establishments contributed most of the funds of labor unions.[68]

In 1939 about 80% of all workers in Russia were members of unions whose approval was required for all changes in piece-rates and work norms, and for all overtime work. With plant commissions and management representatives, they settle labor disputes and are responsible for all safety precautions. They supervise the fulfillment of enterprise plans for housing and nurseries, and operate dining rooms and commercial stores. But they have failed to attract effective leaders and their accomplishments have not been impressive. [69]

In eastern Europe the position of labor unions is similar to that in Russia. In Czechoslovakia a single confederation of all labor unions was formed in 1945, consisting largely of the wartime underground movement and members of works councils. It decided in 1946 that wage increases should not be requested or granted except for increases in productivity or reductions in cost of production, and supported the introduction of piece-rates. In 1948 it reintroduced the six-day week because the five-day week had had a disastrous effect on production. In 1951 it resolved in

---

[68] Bergson, *op. cit., Quar. Jour. of Econ.*, May 1950, 228.
[69] Granick, *op. cit.*, 259.

favor of the extension of piece-work, the use of shock workers and a variety of measures to increase output.[70] Labor unions have no power to bargain collectively or strike. In Bulgaria collective bargains may (since 1949) contain no clauses concerning wage rates or cash earnings and (since 1951) none regarding benefits in kind. These latter were held to have contravened the principle of payment by results and hindered efforts to increase output. Earnings in cash or kind are determined by the national legislature.[71]

Government regulation of the use of labor in the long-run social interest developed early under industrialism, often under the immediate stimulus of humanitarian sentiments rather than efficiency. Working conditions adverse to the efficient use of labor often cannot be remedied either by individual employers or labor unions. The state alone has power wide enough to control all employers, and as the suffrage widened, the state was compelled to deal with labor conditions. In general the regulation of hours of labor has begun with children and been later extended to women, and subsequently in some countries to men, at least in some occupations. In Britain (commonly believed to have been dominated by *laissez-faire* during the 19th century), the state began to regulate employment conditions in the opening years of the 19th century. The Health and Morals of Apprentices Act in 1802 somewhat limited the employment of children. In 1833 factory regulation was delegated to Home Office inspectors and in 1844 restriction of working hours and conditions began to be systematized. A Prussian royal decree of 1839 restricted the employment of women and children in factories and mines, and similar restrictions were imposed in Bavaria and Baden in 1840. In 1845 a formal industrial code regulating hours and conditions of labor was introduced in Prussia; and in 1871, on the establishment of the Reich, the code was applied to the whole of the new empire.

Most advanced countries now set minimum standards of safety. First the more dangerous occupations such as mining were controlled, and later general controls were applied to factories. Pressure towards increased safety conditions at work has been increased by the shift of the cost of accidents from the worker to the employer (Ch. 31).

In the less developed countries, legislation of this type has developed slowly. Wage employment has developed slowly, the worker is in a poor bargaining position, and labor unions are weak. Moreover, much of the legislation has not been enforced.[72] In India legal prohibitions on child labor in factories, women in night work or underground work, and legal maximum hours of 11 per day, and 60 a week for seasonal factories are

---

[70] I.L.O., *Ind. and Lab.*, May 15, 1951, 356.

[71] I.L.O., *Ind. and Lab.*, May 15, 1951, 363.

[72] Issawi, *op. cit.*, 97; Spiegel, *The Brazilian Economy*, 100 ff.; Hanson, *Utopia in Uruguay*, Ch. IX.

imperfectly enforced. In Japan virtually all legislation protecting workers had been suspended by 1945. The Labor Standards Act, passed under pressure by the occupying authorities, dealt with physical conditions of employment, liability for accidents and occupational diseases, hours of work, labor contracts, personal rights of workers, minimum wages, and apprenticeship, but enforcement has been slow.[73] The social security legislation of the past three or four decades in more developed capitalist countries may increase productivity by removing fear and uncertainty, but it may reduce incentives to work and considerable effort has been made to reduce this risk (which has probably been overrated).

Where the state is the employer, it determines conditions of work for some or all of the labor in the country. Where only some productive activities are nationalized, workers are likely to expect the state to be a "model employer"—this may mean operating industries more in the interest of the workers than a private employer would do. Most nationalized industries in these countries are relatively new, and there is yet no evidence that governments have been more or less liberal to their employees than private employers dealing with powerful unions. In Britain, advisory committees of workers have been set up in all the nationalized industries,[74] and workers may legally strike, but have rarely done so. In 1946, the London Passenger Transport Board required all its employees to be members of a prescribed union and gave notices of dismissal to members of minority unions to avoid a strike by the majority unions. The difficulties of the Coal Board with the labor union are primarily a legacy from the period in which the industry was under private control, and miners were almost forced to form fighting unions and follow aggressive leaders. Workers do not quickly surrender the idea that the only possibility of gain comes from "fighting the boss." But workers in other industries in Britain realize that when the coal miners fight the boss other members of the union movement pay in terms of cold homes and unemployment. The government sought peace and increased output in the industry by introducing the five-day week, but a consequent reduction in output compelled • return to a longer work week. But attempts to raise labor productivity have encountered opposition. Efforts by the Coal Board to increase productivity, sometimes by closing inefficient pits and moving miners to other villages, have caused local strikes, and the Transport Board is similarly hampered in improving the efficiency of the railroads. There is a danger that reorganization and labor-saving will be opposed by workers out of fear of unemployment, and slowed down to the pace permitted by the normal wastage of labor through death and retirement. In Italy since 1946 there has been one over-all organization of government workers. It

---

[73] Reubens, Beatrice G., "Social Legislation in Japan," *Far Eastern Quarterly*, 1949, 269, 272.

[74] Clegg, *Labor in Nationalized Industry*, 1950 (Fabian Society).

reserves the right to strike, and includes about 6% of all the workers in Italy (in railroads, telegraphs, telephones, and the like). In Mexico, excessive concessions to a powerful union made the nationalized petroleum industry economically unsuccessful. In 1947, the manager of Pemex was removed and fifty leaders of the oil workers' union were expelled for illegal work stoppages and violence; the company has since been more successful.

In socialist countries, the state is almost the sole employer, and labor policy is a major factor in the fulfillment of its production plan. Policy is therefore aimed at intensifying labor effort. Wages are the chief incentive, but their effect is reduced whenever there is a shortage of goods on which to spend money wages. Shortages occur when the government fails to achieve the output of consumer goods which is demanded at the prices set by the government when payrolls are spent. Rationing, until 1936 and from 1941 to 1947, was evidence of such shortages and was designed to stimulate output. But since 1947 the government has relied on money payments as the chief incentive to effective work. It abolished rationing (which in fact meant a minimum real income for workers when rationed goods were available) and extended the payment of wages based on output. Repeated reductions in prices represent general increases in labor incomes. Improvements in equipment and industrial organization increase the worker's opportunity to increase output.

Socialist governments rely more than others on non-monetary incentives. Since Stakhanov hewed a record amount of coal in a day by the better organization of work, the government has widely and vigorously publicized notable contributions to production. Stakhanovites are now merely those who produce a specified percentage above a normal output, and shock workers are those producing a lower percentage above the norm. In July 1939 about 33% of all union members in industry were Stakhanovites and nearly 20% shock workers.[75] "Shock brigades" are used to exemplify standards of productivity. The first shock brigade appears to have been used in a Leningrad textile mill in 1928. Other workers are expected to emulate the shock workers once the possibility of increases in output is demonstrated. Competitions to stimulate production are regulated by a decree issued in 1929. Exemplary workers were given advantages in rations, permits to get manufactured goods in short supply, and places in rest homes. The production plans of Czechoslovakia, Hungary, and Poland, based on annual increases in industrial output of 5 to 7%, attach special importance to the extension of piece-work, the Stakhanovite movement, and work competition.[76]

In 1938 the Russian government introduced distinctions for outstanding industrial workers, the highest being "Hero of Socialist Toil." It also offered medals for "Prowess in Labor" and "Distinguished Labor." The

---

[75] Granick, op. cit., 249.
[76] U.N., Econ. Surv. of Europe in 1949, 216.

idea was extended to agriculture in 1948 when managers of state farms, directors of mechanical tractor stations, and collective farmers became eligible for the Order of Hero of Socialist Labor, the Order of Lenin, and the Order of Red Banner on achieving norms of output per acre prescribed separately for each region. In 1949, when the government intensified its effort to increase the output of livestock, it offered as distinctions to "zoo-technicians" the titles of "Honorary Livestock Specialist of the Republic," "Honorary Livestock Worker of the Republic," and "Honorary Veterinary Worker of the Republic." But in the last resort potential workers are coerced to work if necessary.

There has been continuous official criticism of the low productivity of labor in socialist countries. The Russian government has criticized wide-spread failure to introduce new engineering methods, failure to make full use of new high-capacity machinery, and poor organization of flow pro-duction. Labor turnover is often high and labor efficiency is reduced by "storming" (the wasteful use of labor in the closing days of the month in order to reach quotas); producing 60 to 70% of monthly output during the last third of the month involves idleness at the beginning and overtime at the end. But inefficiency is not surprising in view of the revolutionary tempo of economic change and the magnitude of the problems of control under these conditions in so large an economy.

Chapter 21

Capital: Supply

Capital, like minerals (and, to a lesser degree, land) is generally exhausted by use. But, unlike minerals, it can be replaced and increased. If the capital supply increases at the same rate as the labor force, the amount of capital per worker is unchanged, and any change in output per head depends on the effect of increases in the size of the labor force on productivity (Ch. 18). But an increase in capital supply per worker increases output per worker; societies with a larger fund of capital per worker always have a higher output per worker than others. The amount of the increase in output, resulting from a given increase in the capital fund, falls with successive increases unless changes in technology require increased capital per unit of output (which they have required in the past). Although the rate of increase in investment is one of the major determinants of the rate of increase in income, there is no economic optimal rate of increase. The loss from present diversions of resources from consumption must be balanced against the anticipated future benefits in increases in production. Different societies may differ in their appraisal.

A. Measurement of Supply

The capital supply of an economy consists of man-made improvements in environment—buildings (including transportation facilities), tools and equipment (agricultural and industrial), and working capital. Investments in the education and training of people and the acquisition of knowledge might be included, but they are difficult to measure and are usually excluded from available figures. It is not easy, however, to define an "improvement" to environment. An improvement must increase capacity to produce. Some man-made changes in environment, like the pyramids, were never intended to increase production (which is no objection to them). Some changes were intended to increase material welfare, but have lost their capacity to do so because of shifts in population or technology.

Most countries have abandoned towns, houses, canals, roads, factories, and mines. Some changes intended to aid production were too poorly designed to achieve their purpose or to achieve it fully.

The capacity of improvements to add to production should be measured by the discounted present value of all future additions to production that they are expected to make possible. The use of a rate of interest or discount places a lower value on long-postponed benefits than on more immediate ones. But no accurate measurements of the total capital of countries on this basis are available. Anticipations of contributions to future production are liable to error, part of which, however, can be allowed for in the rate of discount. Much capital is never valued, for example, tools and public improvements like bridges, roads, and parks. Shares in corporations may be traded on stock exchanges, but some of their capital may be invested abroad and much capital is not owned by private corporations. The best available estimates rest on the book value of assets after deduction of depreciation, but depreciation allowances are estimates and do not always reflect actual reductions in productivity. Obsolete or excessive plant equipment should be valued in terms of its contribution to production after allowing for direct costs of production, but its depreciated book value may be very different. Changes in prices are difficult to allow for. When prices change, the book values of assets are usually not adjusted until they are replaced.

B. Actual Supply

The amount of capital per worker or per person in the population (rather than the total) affects product per worker (or per head of the population). If the population increases and capital does not, capital per head declines and usually also output per head. In Israel and the underdeveloped parts of Latin America, the Middle and Far East, large annual additions to capital are now needed to prevent capital per worker from falling. Available information varies as to the basis of valuing capital (market value, original cost, or replacement cost) and as to the completeness of coverage. Not even crude measures are available for most countries. The estimated market value of capital (excluding land) per person in work in about 1939 was about 5,820 international units in the U.S.A., compared with 6,600 in Britain (in 1932-4). The figures generally fall as one proceeds to western Europe, southern and eastern Europe, Latin America, the Middle East and the Far East.[1] But they include foreign investments and are erratic because of differences in methods of calculation. In 1939 real capital per worker in Asia and the Far East outside Japan was about 10% of that in the U.S.A., and in Japan about 50%.[2] In China the amount of manufacturing capital per head of the total

[1] Clark, *Conditions of Economic Progress*, (2d), 486, 510.
[2] U.N., *Econ. Surv. of Asia and the Far East in 1949*, 296.

population in 1930 was about .6% of that in the U.S.A.[3] Investment per worker is still increasing in the more developed countries. In Europe net investment during 1949 in fixed capital alone per head of the population ranged from $59 (of 1938 purchasing power) in Norway, $41 in Britain and $36 in Sweden, to $9 in Italy and Poland and $8 in Czechoslovakia.[4] But investment per head is lower and increasing more slowly in the less-developed countries because of their poverty and their population increases.

Inequalities in capital must have been small until some four centuries ago, even where there were differences in levels of living. Few forms of capital were available beyond tools and houses. Much construction activity was not directly intended for productive purposes (irrigation projects and roads being the chief exception). Elaborate means of production like factories, machines, and means of transport and communication have appeared in the last two centuries, but they are important only in some countries. There are still primitive societies in which the capital is small and fairly stable. In Middle and Far Eastern regions it is small but slowly rising. In Russia it was relatively small in 1917 but has risen rapidly. In the more developed countries it is large and rising. Consequently, inequalities are still increasing.

C. Influences Affecting Supply

The stock of capital at any time is the result of the operation of opposing forces, namely past additions to and past subtractions from the stock.

1. Past Additions to Supply

a. Actual Savings and Investment

The fund of capital is increased when resources are used to acquire capital goods. But if the capital is invested abroad, it does not directly affect productivity at home, although it does increase the disposable income of the home country if the foreign investments yield income. Investments out of the home income stream represent diversions from consumption except in economies not fully employed where investments can be made out of the fuller employment of resources. Consumption everywhere absorbs by far the largest part of the national income. Even in more developed countries, 85 to 95% of national income is consumed over the long run.

Gross capital formation includes both net additions to capital and expenditures necessary to maintain the capital fund against erosion by wear and obsolescence. Net capital formation, which consists only of the net additions to the fund, varies widely as a proportion of net national income. In Europe it ranged in 1938 from 2% in France, 5% in Turkey and

---

3 Staley, *World Economic Development*, 70.
4 U.N., *Econ. Surv. of Europe in 1949*, 39.

Austria, 6% in Belgium, 7% in Italy, and 8% in Britain and the Netherlands, to 12% in Sweden and 15% in Norway. Net capital formation increased nearly 35% in north, northwest, west and central Europe between 1938 and 1948,[5] in spite of increased allocations of national income to arms and to government consumption expenditures on health, education, and similar social services. It was notably high in 1949 in Norway and Finland (Table 39), and rates have subsequently increased in some countries.[6] But in other countries (e.g., Austria, the Netherlands, and Norway), large excesses of imports over exports permitted high investment without great reduction in consumption. In the U.S.A. *gross* capital formation was only 2.3% of of gross national product in 1933 but rose to 10.8% by 1939 and 17.3% by 1950.[7]

In Russia, 4.2% of the national income was invested from 1900 to 1913, 5.6% in 1928, and 12.3% in 1938. But after various adjustments to make the figures more comparable with those elsewhere, the percentage is estimated to have been 25.2% in 1937, when national income per head was between $175 and $250. In 1937 Russia was investing about 6% more of its income than was the U.S.A. from 1869 to 1878, when U.S.A. income per head was about the same as in Russia in 1937.[8] A different method of calculation suggests that in 1940 about 32% of the national product was for defense and investment.[9] Less detailed estimates for 1948 indicate that net investment was about 21% (or 27% if the rebuilding of stocks is included) of national income in Russia compared with 12% in Britain and 17.6% in the U.S.A.[10] (gross capital formation). In Poland, investment (probably gross) rose from 8.2% of national income in 1947 to 19.4% in 1951, in Czechoslovakia from 17.3% to 24.7% and in Hungary from 10.6% in 1947-8 to 24.5% in 1951 (compared with 13.8% in 1938).[11]

Information for other countries is scattered, and sometimes for gross and sometimes for net investment. Gross private investment has been high in New Zealand, but not increasing from 1938 to 1948. In South Africa net investment was about 25% of national income in 1947-8, and in Southern Rhodesia it was 29.2% of gross national expenditure in 1948, but investment was aided in these countries by heavy inflow of foreign capital.[12] In India gross capital formation was 4.5% of gross national income in 1950-1. In Brazil net capital formation in recent years has been about 10%

[5] U.N., *Econ. Surv. of Europe in 1949*, 212.

[6] U.N., *Econ. Surv. of Europe since the War*, 1953, 69.

[7] U.S. Dept. Commerce, *National Income and Product of the U.S. 1929-1950*, 151.

[8] Bergson, "Soviet National Income and Product in 1937," *Quar. Jour. Econ.*, 1950, 35, 220, 440.

[9] Baran, "National Income and Product of the U.S.S.R. in 1940," *Rev. of Econ. Stat.*, Nov. 1947, 226 ff.

[10] *Economist*, Dec. 18, 1948.

[11] U.N., *Econ. Surv. of Europe Since the War*, 1953, 24.

[12] U.N., *National Income Statistics 1938-48*, 222.

TABLE 39*

DOMESTIC CAPITAL FORMATION AND BALANCE OF PAYMENTS AS PERCENTAGE OF NET NATIONAL INCOME (AT FACTOR COST) IN SELECTED EUROPEAN COUNTRIES IN 1938 AND 1949

COUNTRY	1938				1949			
	DOMESTIC CAPITAL FORMATION		Balance of Payments	Consumption†	DOMESTIC CAPITAL FORMATION		Balance of Payments	Consumption†
	Net	Depreciation, etc.			Net	Depreciation, etc.		
Austria (1937)	5	8	...	95	17	9	−20	103
Belgium	6	7	3	91	7	8	2	91
Denmark	9	13	1	90	12	15	−2	90
Finland (1948)	17	10	1	82	26	13	2	72
France	2	14	...	98	11	13	−1	90
Germany (western zones) (1936 and 1948-9)	17	9	...	83	19	12	−4	85
Italy	7	11	−1	94	11	13	−3	92
The Netherlands	8	13	2	90	19	14	−7	88
Norway	15	22	...	85	26	21	−14	88
Sweden (1938-9)	12	19	...	88	10	22	2	88
Turkey (1936 and 1948)	5	...	3	92	5	...	−3	98
United Kingdom	8	9	−2	94	11	11	...	89

* U.N., *Econ. Surv. of Europe in 1949*, 23.
† Personal and government consumption.

of the national income and in Chile 5%.[13] The few estimates of investment in Asia and the Far East indicate that it has been very low[14] outside Japan. Additions to capital from internal sources are generally low or zero among the native peoples of Africa and the Pacific.

The proportion of national income invested falls to very low levels in depression in capitalist countries (e.g. in the U.S.A. it fell to 2% from 1929-1938) and is high in times of high production. Some countries have also achieved a very high rate of investment for short periods. Net investment reached 16.6% of national income in Britain from 1860 to 1869, 19.3% in the U.S.A. from 1904 to 1913, 19.1% in Germany from 1901 to 1910, and 37% in Japan from 1919 to 1924, 33.5% from 1925 to 1930 and 28.5% in 1939.[15] But in the long run the proportion of income saved does not continuously increase as the national income increases. In the U.S.A. the percentage ranged from 12 to 14% from 1869 to 1918, but was 10.9% from 1919 to 1928, after which it fell drastically during the depression after 1929, reducing the average from 1929 to 1938 to 2%. Nevertheless, there is yet no evidence of any great long-term decline.[16] In Britain the rate was 18% in the 1860s, but only about 7% between 1924 and 1937. It also fell in Germany, France, Holland, Switzerland, and Norway after about 1911 until 1939. In the U.S.A., net additions to capital (as a percentage of real income in 1880 prices) were between 8 and 9% in 1880-1890 and 1900-11, but between 6 and 7% in the period 1911-29.[17] But the rate was increasing before 1939 in Canada, Spain, Italy, Sweden, and Russia. It has increased since 1945 in the U.S.A. and most west and east European countries. But in France the rate in 1949 and 1950 was only half as high as in 1939.[18] In India and Pakistan the percentage rose from 1939 to 1942, but fell thereafter to zero or a negative quantity in 1946-7 and 1947-8.[19] But generally absolute investment increases in developing countries because any decline in the percentage invested is more than offset by increases in income.

b. The Influences Affecting the Amount of Investment

Relatively primitive societies often invest little in agriculture, their chief productive activity, and have few institutions for the purpose (e.g., in most parts of Africa).[20] As native agriculture begins to produce for the market, however, capital has been made available by holding back part

---

[13] U.N., *Econ. Surv. of Latin America in 1948*, 38.
[14] U.N., *Econ. Surv. of Asia and the Far East in 1949*, 190.
[15] Clark, *Conditions of Economic Progress*, (2d), 406.
[16] Kuznets, *National Income: A Summary of Findings*, 52.
[17] Clark, *op. cit.*, 92.
[18] France: National Council of Credit *Fifth Annual Report* 1951; ILO, *Ind. and Lab.* 1951, 166.
[19] *Eastern Economist, Annual Supplement*, 1948.
[20] Pendered Report, 61.

of the proceeds of sale and placing them in "betterment funds" used for such investment (Ch. 8).

But even where there is saving, productive investment does not necessarily follow. Individuals may merely hoard precious metals and jewelry during periods of relative prosperity. In India, China, Mexico, and the Middle East, the poorer classes buy jewelry to obtain a reserve of precious metals in a form easily carried by women. A similar practice prevailed in Japan before its active development. Such purchases provide social security to the individual but do not add to the productive capital of the economy. Holdings of silver and gold coins in Mexico in 1948 amounted to about 800 million pesos,[21] and there are considerable holdings in the Middle East. The amount of new investment otherwise depends on the incentives to invest and on attitudes to saving.

In a capitalist economy, the incentive to invest is the anticipation of profits. A new investment is made if the anticipated value of the resulting products after deducting all other costs (including depreciation) is sufficient to induce the investor to give up present purchasing power in return for the right to receive the anticipated net return. This value of output depends partly on conditions of demand. Consequently, in countries where most of the population receives a very low income, the only investments likely to be attractive are those which provide the few goods bought by the poor at lower prices than previously, or the goods bought by higher income groups. But if enough new investments were made, they would perceptibly increase national income. Their effect on the inducement to invest depends, however, on the disposition of the increments in income. If these all go to the higher income groups, they increase the demand for the goods bought by such groups or for investment goods if they invest. If all increments are channelled into investment, possibly by taxation, the effect on demand is concentrated on investment goods or the export goods with which to pay for them. If most of the increments are distributed among the population at large in wages or social services, demand for consumer goods is likely to rise and attract investment.

The profitability of investment is also influenced by the organization and technology of production. The commercial revolution in western Europe in the 17th century increased the profits from investments in commerce, especially in Holland and Britain. The industrial revolution provided far wider opportunities for investment in production. Such changes increase the profit incentive to invest and the demand for capital. Over most of the past 200 years, much of the new knowledge of production methods has induced increases in average investment per unit of output throughout developing economies. Such is the meaning of "capitalism." The demand for capital has, of course, also increased with the expansion of total output. But in recent years some new knowledge of

---

[21] U.N., *Econ. Surv. of Latin America in 1948*, 70.

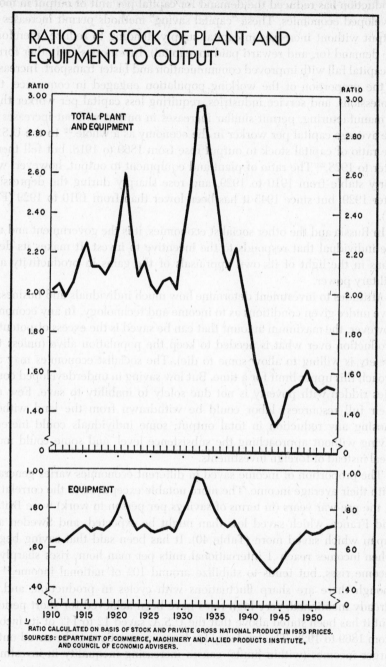

Fig. 21. Ratio of plant and equipment to output in the U.S.A. from 1910 to 1951. (From U.S.A. Economic Report of the President, Jan. 1954, p. 62.)

production has reduced the demand for capital per unit of output in more developed economies. These "capital saving" methods permit increases in output without increases in capital supply (tending to reduce, therefore, the demand for, and reward paid to, capital). Inventories and other forms of capital fall with improved communication and faster transport. Increases in the proportion of the working population engaged in commerce, the professions, and service industries, requiring less capital per worker than in manufacturing, permit similar increases in output without increases in the average capital per worker in the economy as a whole.[22] In the U.S.A. the ratio of capital stock to output rose from 1869 to 1918, but fell thereafter to 1928.[23] The ratio of plant and equipment to output, however, was fairly stable from 1910 to 1929, and rose sharply during the depression after 1929, but since 1945 it has been lower than from 1910 to 1929 (Fig. 21).

In Russia and the other socialist economies, it is the government and not the individual that responds to the incentive to invest. It makes its decisions in the light of its own appraisals of the gains in productivity and military power.

Attitudes to investment determine how much individuals and businesses save under given conditions as to income and technology. In any economy, however, the maximum amount that can be saved is the excess of potential production over what is needed to keep the population alive (unless the society is willing to allow some to die). The socialist economies may approach this upper limit for a time. But low saving in underdeveloped countries ridden with poverty is not due solely to inability to save. Few use their full resources: labor could be withdrawn from the land without causing any reduction in total output; some individuals could increase saving without approaching the subsistence level, and some could make local instead of foreign investments.

The proportion of income saved in different economies varies generally with their average income. The more notable exceptions to the correlation in the pre-war years (in terms of savings per person in work) were Britain and France, which saved less than might be expected, and Sweden and Japan which saved more (Table 40). It has been said that saving begins when incomes reach .1 international units per man hour, rises sharply as income rises, but tends to stabilize around 10% of national income,[24] although there are sharp fluctuations with cycles in production, and, as already mentioned, very high rates have been achieved for short periods. But it has been stated above that the U.S.A. saved 12 to 14% of its income from 1869 to 1928. The tendency for larger proportions to be saved out of larger incomes (within limits) causes increasing inequality in investment

22 Clark, *op. cit.* (2d), 503.
23 Fellner, *Monetary Policies and Full Employment*, 80.
24 Clark, *op. cit.*, (2d), 504.

TABLE 40

NET SAVINGS PER WORKER IN WORK AND REAL INCOME PER MAN-HOUR
IN SELECTED COUNTRIES*

Country	Date	Real income per man-hour (I.U.)	Net savings per person in work (I.U.)
U.S.A.	1941	.999	386
Canada	1938	.747	163
Britain	1937	.536	98
The Netherlands	1938	.445	140
Germany	1938	.434	116
Spain	1930	.419	113
Norway	1939	.410	123
Belgium	1939	.358	67
Switzerland	1925-30	.339	73
France	1938	.338	14
Sweden	1925-30	.305	103
Eire	1926	.295	64
Palestine Jews	1936	.272	—3
Austria	1927-8	.231	35
Italy	1939	.213	52
Japan	1938	.192	155
Chile	1936-40	.19	50
Palestine Arabs	1936	.189	2
South Africa	1934-8	.177	46
Russia	1938	.159	65

* Clark, *Conditions of Economic Progress* (2d), 506.

per head between the poorer and the richer countries especially as populations are growing faster in the poorer.

The amount of saving depends upon who makes the decision to save, and under what circumstances. Investment from domestic sources in capitalist economies may come from saving out of personal income, business saving, or investment by public authorities. The relation of each of these items to total gross capital formation varied widely among west European countries in 1949. The proportion of private saving was notably high in 1949 in Belgium (which was remitting funds abroad) and notably low in Norway (Table 41). In Russia in 1937 the total savings of households were about 2.8% of their income (compared with 5.3% in the U.S.A.), but government investment was more than ten times private savings.[25]

Private savings have provided most of the capital for industrialization in non-socialist countries. Individual saving is a larger proportion of larger than of smaller incomes. Consequently the savings potential of a given average national income is greatest where inequality of distribution is greatest. Social systems that concentrate in a few hands all income above the subsistence level, therefore, maximize their savings potential (although

[25] Bergson, "Soviet National Income and Product in 1937," *Quar. Jour. Econ.*, 1950, 235.

TABLE 41

FINANCING OF GROSS CAPITAL FORMATION IN SELECTED
EUROPEAN COUNTRIES IN 1949*

COUNTRY	PERCENT OF GROSS CAPITAL FORMATION			
	Borrowings & gifts from abroad	Depreciation and Maintenance	Surpluses of public authorities and enterprises	Private savings
Austria	78	35	....	—13
Belgium	—14	56	—22	80
Denmark	7	56	15	22
France	6	50	4	40
Germany (western zones 1948-9)	13	40	26	21
Italy	13	55	—7	39
The Netherlands	19	43	6	32
Norway	28	46	16	10
Sweden	—6	70	12	24
Switzerland (1948)	12	41	24	23
United Kingdom	0	47	13	40

* U.N., *Econ. Surv. of Europe in 1949*, 49.

The figure for depreciation and maintenance is an estimate based on replacement cost. Economic Cooperation Administration funds do not appear in government balances but in "Borrowings and Gifts from Abroad." "Private savings" are a residual and subject to a wide margin of error.

it need not be high). In predominantly agrarian countries considerable concentration results from concentration of land holding and competition for land that reduces labor incomes to subsistence levels and correspondingly raises rents (as formerly in Europe and now in the Middle East, particularly Egypt, Japan, India, and much of Latin America). Merchant activities operate in the same direction. The large trading profits of Holland and Britain in the 17th century provided considerable investment, and increasing trading profits in Japan before 1869 provided some of the early investments in industry thereafter. Large-scale merchant activities in India have similarly provided investment funds.

In capitalist industrial countries inequality in the ownership of industrial property and high profits therefrom caused a similar concentration of incomes, especially during the 19th century. High savings early in the century facilitated development and subsequent further saving, but they placed heavy burdens on the mass of the population. The extraordinarily high savings during the earlier development of Japan were also made possible largely by low incomes in agriculture that kept down industrial labor incomes. The rate of multiplication of the population automatically kept down wages in both sectors. But in western Europe subsequent improvements in standards of living somewhat reduced inequality and tended to reduce saving, although the tendency was offset by other factors.

Underdeveloped countries now carry a heavy burden of poverty, but without much development. They face an unpleasant choice. They may divert part of the increments in national income to the relief of widespread poverty and lightening the burdens of production on the mass of the population (by reducing hours of labor and by more comprehensive labor legislation). The mere knowledge on the part of the population of higher levels of living elsewhere urges these countries in this direction, which is doubtless one of the reasons for the "iron curtain" around Russia and eastern Europe.[26] But by following this course, developing countries reduce the proportion of increments in income available for saving. Land reforms redistributing income more widely similarly reduce the saving potential. Morever, immediate improvements in levels of living may also accelerate population increase and prevent development from attaining the minimum speed necessary for continued progress.[27] Alternatively, concentration of increments in the hands of a small class with a high propensity to save (which however is often absent), or the state, could accelerate the accumulation of the capital necessary for the adoption of more efficient production methods, but this would permit little alleviation of present poverty.

Differences in saving in different countries are due to differences in the propensity of individuals to save as well as to differences in average income and in income distribution. In medieval Europe the wealthy spent considerable sums on retainers (to maintain their political position, which was the source of their incomes) and to provide the core of a military force. They also spent on luxury consumer goods, including the precious metals. The Spanish nobility used the loot from Central and South America mainly for luxury spending. Their attitudes were due to their political environment and to the sparsity of investment opportunities. In many underdeveloped countries now the wealthy enjoy much personal service and buy jewelry and precious metals (e.g., Indian princes, Middle-Eastern potentates, Chinese war lords, and Latin-American landowners). A tradition that the upper classes should not engage in trade has evolved into unwillingness to engage in the active development of resources (even when the prospective profits are high).[28] But lack of confidence in monetary stability has encouraged hoarding (e.g., of gold coins in Syria,[29] Greece, and the Middle-Eastern countries). Some have saved but invested abroad for the same reason.

The wealthier classes in the capitalist countries have shown a greater propensity to invest than those in agrarian countries, partly because of their active participation in production. The Puritan revolution in western Europe, emphasizing both frugality of personal living and the careful

---

[26] Nurkse, "Some International Aspects of the Problem of Economic Development," *Proc. Am. Econ. Assoc.*, 1952, 578, 583; U.N., *Econ. Surv. of Latin America*, 1949, 72.

[27] U.N., *Methods of Financing Econ. Devel. in Underdeveloped Countries*, 7.

[28] *Ibid.*, 13; Bonné, *op. cit.*, 162.

[29] U.N., *Econ. Surv. Mission for the Middle East*, I, 35.

use of resources, provided a justification for saving and for taking advantage of new and profitable opportunities for investment. This attitude has persisted and become deeply rooted. But France (often regarded as populated by inveterate savers) has not in fact a high rate of saving. It has saved less than Britain and Germany because income per head has been lower, income has been more equally distributed, and slow population growth has checked pressure on the land and the growth of urban areas that tend to inequality. The slow growth of population (and its political implications) may explain relatively heavy exports of capital that tend to retard internal development.[30]

An increasing amount of saving in capitalist countries results from business decisions. In Britain much of the early development (when manufacturing required relatively small capital) was financed by plowing back profits. Small businesses and farming are still in part financed in this way (notably in France). But in the more highly capitalized economies where business has passed into the hands of corporations, they continue to behave like the former entrepreneurs, plowing back part of their profits. They now supply a large part of all net savings in the more developed countries,[31] and in the most developed, most of the capital needed for purely industrial purposes. In the U.S.A. from 1919 to 1928 business saving was about 10% of all net saving, but only 5% from 1919 to 1938 (which included the great depression).[32] The ability of corporations to save depends, like that of individuals, on their income, but their actual savings depend on the attitudes and power of directors and stockholders, and whether they desire to provide against future risks or to expand.

The rate of return on investment affects both the demand for and the supply of investment funds. When the returns from investment rise, the demand for investment funds rises. But increasing returns from investment do not necessarily increase the proportion of a given income saved. Saving to provide against future needs due to the education or marriage of children, unemployment, or sickness may be little affected by rates of return, and some would occur without any return. Premiums for life insurance in western countries include interest, but it is doubtful whether insurance would completely disappear if interest were eliminated. State provision for security of the individual and his family may weaken the incentive to save for security, but it may also cause lower income groups to "raise their sights." When the risks eventuate, dissavings occur. The capital fund of the economy, however, is affected only by changes in the total revolving fund of savings against these risks. As the younger members of the population save for these purposes and the older members dissave, the age distribution of the population influences aggregate saving. The

30 Spengler, XI *Jour. of Econ. History*, 1951, 409.
31 U.N., *Econ. Surv. of Europe in 1949*, 50.
32 Kuznets, *National Income: A Summary of Findings*, 21.

increase in the proportion of aged in the population in western Europe and North America in the past 50 to 75 years may therefore have somewhat offset the factors making for accumulation.[33]

The rate of return does, however, affect saving by increasing the incomes of people who have a relatively high propensity to save. It also increases the opportunity for business saving. But in underdeveloped economies the supply of saving offered for internal investment is often insufficient to reduce interest and profit rates to the levels prevailing in developed countries. Interest rates of 20% or more prevail in Syria and Iran,[34] and 8 to 18% in Mexico. Some well-known Mexican corporations have paid dividends of 40% on capital.[35]

Religious prohibitions on the taking of interest survive in some countries. Most religions have condemned interest, but largely because loans were typically for consumption purposes. Since the loan did not increase the productive capacity of the borrower, it was held to be unfair to charge him interest. The ancient Jews proscribed usury, and in their early period provided for the periodic cancellation of debts. In medieval Europe it was held to be wrong to charge interest if no risk was taken, but the ethical problem faded in the 16th century as the idea that money was barren gave way to the idea that a loan might be turned to good account. The discussion then shifted to the determination of a legal maximum rate. Usury laws continued in England from the 16th to the 19th century, by which time interest had become respectable enough to be a key part of the thinking of economists. Mahomet forbade usury, but interest has, in fact, been charged in Mohammedan countries typically by recording the debt at a sum often greatly in excess of the amount of money actually handed over. But the Mohammedan objection to taking interest on loans is said to have hindered the growth of banking in Pakistan, and other Mohammedan countries. In India the village custom of *damdupat* formerly prohibited the moneylender from receiving twice the amount lent, but has now lapsed.[36] But both prohibition of interest and the setting of maximum rates have usually been ineffective. If effective, they are likely to discourage risky ventures and, possibly, most investment where the free market rate of return would be high.

Over long periods of development, high profits permitting high saving have set limits on increases in profit. On the other hand, it has been feared that continued accumulation would steadily reduce the rate of return on capital as investors must resort to decreasingly profitable uses. In fact, new uses for capital have, so far, appeared in sufficient quantity to prevent any such decline. But some of these have involved exports of capital

[33] Queensland, *Rev. of Econ. Prog.*, Feb.-March, 1950.
[34] U.N., *Econ. Surv. Mission for the Middle East*, I, 35.
[35] U.N., *Econ. Surv. of Latin America in 1948*, 38.
[36] Wadia and Merchant, *op. cit.*, 190.

that have presumably tended to maintain rates of return in capital exporting countries. Nevertheless, there remains a serious question whether
the rate of return, or any other mechanism, ensures investment equal to
saving. Saving in excess of investment reduces total spending and causes
unemployment. Investment in excess of saving stimulates production
until there is full employment, when it causes an increase in the general
level of prices. But increases in production increase profits and investment, and accelerate the process. Consistency between saving and investment is, however, not enough to prevent unemployment or price
increases. Consistency is also necessary between investment and consumption. Anticipated returns from investment will be realized only if aggregate incomes increase sufficiently to provide a market for the increment
of output owing to increases in investment.[37] If incomes do not increase
sufficiently, investment is discouraged and production recedes. If a society
continues to increase its capacity to produce goods while preventing the
consumption of these goods, the productive mechanism is not fully employed and levels of living are restricted. In capitalist economies the rate
of profit has achieved some consistency, but has done so through spasmodic expansions and contractions of investment that have increasingly
threatened the survival of the system. These fluctuations are far less in
countries where there is little saving, although they often suffer from the
secondary repercussions of fluctuations in countries more highly capitalized. Nor do such fluctuations occur in the completely socialized economies.

Investment in a country is facilitated if foreign resources are made
available. Foreign loans and gifts permit either greater investment or
greater consumption in receiving countries, and restrict domestic investment in capital exporting countries. But it is not possible to trace the use of
resources from any single source, foreign or domestic. Contemporaneous
changes in foreign loans and capital formation are not necessarily causally
related. The importance of such foreign resources differs among countries,
and has changed over time.

The Netherlands exported capital in the 18th century, and Britain began
to do so early in the 19th century. France, Germany, and other west European countries followed as they developed, mostly towards the end of the
century. But the U.S.A. became a net exporter only after 1918 because of
the continuance of opportunities for internal investment.

Imports of capital contributed somewhat to early development in Britain
and later to development in the U.S.A., France, Germany, western Europe,
and many primary producing countries. Japan, however, obtained only
modest amounts of capital from abroad between 1869 and 1895, most of
which had been repaid by 1919, but it imported capital again after 1920.
After the setback of the war from 1914 to 1918, foreign investment revived
for a time until 1929. After 1945, in many countries "net foreign invest-

---

[37] Harrod, *Towards a Dynamic Economics, passim.*

ments" increased in importance in relation to total internal expenditures because of international grants and loans and the drawing down of foreign exchange balances (which were the result of previous favorable balances with foreign countries). By 1948 these net foreign investments, both positive and negative, had begun to decline, but were still considerable. As a percentage of net national income, net imports remained high in 1949 in Austria (20%) and Norway (14%), but there were net exports from Belgium (2%) and Sweden (2%) (Table 38). But investment was assisted by capital imports much less in eastern Europe and most underdeveloped areas, until the International Bank for Reconstruction and Development and the U.S. Government Export Import Bank began to lend to underdeveloped countries[38] (Ch. 26). Export surpluses due to reparations also inhibit domestic capital formation (e.g., in Finland). But some underdeveloped countries in the Middle East and Latin America at least in part offset the effect of capital imports by exporting capital to more developed countries.[39] In Mexico and Brazil, for instance, the wealthier classes and private businesses have accumulated capital abroad, especially in the U.S.A., because of fear of political unrest, currency instability, postwar foreign competition with domestic industry, and labor disputes. Thus international movements of capital are influenced not only by profit opportunities but also by the desire to find a safe haven for funds, and by political influences determining government transfers.

Governments influence accumulation by directing resources into investment goods, or by their monetary policy. A government may use part of the proceeds of taxes and loans for investment (e.g., in nationalized enterprises). In 1949 public savings were 10% of public and private savings in France, 27% in Britain, and 66% in Norway (Table 42). In Asia and the Far

TABLE 42

PUBLIC SAVINGS AS A PERCENTAGE OF PUBLIC AND PRIVATE SAVINGS
IN WESTERN EUROPE IN 1949*

Denmark	40
France	10
Netherlands	16
Norway	66
Sweden	42
United Kingdom	27

* U.N., *Econ. Surv. of Europe in 1949*, 50.

East, government investment ranges from 5 to 25% of all government expenditures (Table 43), but the proportion of national income thus saved depends on the proportion of the national income passing through the

[38] U.N., *Econ. Surv. of Europe in 1949*, 50.
[39] U.N., *Econ. Surv. of Latin America in 1948*, 70.

TABLE 43

INVESTMENT AS A PERCENTAGE OF ALL GOVERNMENT EXPENDITURES IN
SELECTED COUNTRIES IN ASIA AND THE FAR EAST*

Country	Period	Investment by government as a percentage of all government expenditures
Ceylon	1949-50	28
China	1950	24
Thailand	1950	24
India	1950-51	17
Burma	1949-50	11
Pakistan	1949-50	11
Indonesia	1950	5

* U.N., *Econ. Surv. of Asia and the Far East in 1949,* 154.

state budget (which varies widely). In socialist countries virtually all saving is controlled by the state.

Government investment has usually not been large in the past because the available forms of investment were few. Water control works were among the largest for many centuries. Where money is not in general use and labor is the principal resource other than land, capital improvements have been made by compulsory levies of labor, and such levies (often known as *corvées*) have persisted until recent times in some countries, although often used for maintenance rather than for net addition to capital. In primitive societies the members of the community can frequently be called upon to supply labor for capital projects that, however, are usually small. In European feudal societies compulsory work was required not only for the maintenance of roads but also for the construction of capital goods. The *corvée* was also important in 19th-century Egypt; under Mohammed Ali (1805-1850) considerable governmental capital works were constructed with labor supplied by the *corvée,* which continued to provide for the construction as well as the maintenance of dams and canals up to the time of the British occupation. But when economies are monetized, taxes in money usually replace taxes in labor.[40]

Although taxation transfers to the government purchasing power, part of which can be invested in capital goods (roads, bridges, public buildings and the like), net additions to capital exceed those that would have been made without the taxation only if the taxation does not cause an equivalent reduction in voluntary saving and investment. Regressive taxation (such as taxes on salt in China and India) may compel low income groups to reduce their standard of living and transfer to the state funds which they would not have saved. Peter the Great (1682-1725) financed new enterprises in Russia through increased taxation of the already heavily

[40] Tirana, "Government Financing of Economic Development Abroad," X, *Tasks Econ. Hist.,* 1950, 192.

burdened peasantry, through imposing excise taxes (for instance, on beards, chimneys, water, baths, and cucumbers), and through monopoly profits (equivalent to taxes) from salt, tobacco, fish, oil, oak coffins, and similar products. In 1701 he confiscated the incomes from the large monastery estates. The considerable economic expansion of Russia in the last half century of czarist rule was also financed by the government directly, and aided through the state bank, the funds again being obtained by heavy taxation of the peasantry.[41] Progressive taxes in most underdeveloped countries would not greatly deter investment within the country, because higher income receivers, although lightly taxed, have not invested. But where higher income groups have invested, progressive taxation may well reduce voluntary saving.[42] In India taxation amounting to 20% of the national income retards development, partly because about 50% of the state budget in 1949 was for military purposes.

But the countries most in need of development have been least inclined to tax to obtain funds for investment. The wealthier groups are politically dominant and resist such tax legislation and its enforcement. The Middle East governments, which have obtained considerable incomes from petroleum (e.g., Iraq), have in the past used much of the income to meet current government expenses, thus indirectly transferring purchasing power (in lowered taxes) to the wealthier who have had a low propensity to invest. But in Egypt, Mohammed Ali (1805-1850) bought the major agricultural products at prices that were fixed before each season and were usually well below the market price (sometimes as low as 33% of it), using the resulting profits for investment in public projects. The Argentine government after 1945 bought the principal export goods (except meat) inside the country at relatively low prices and sold them at higher world prices for export, thus in effect taxing exports. It indirectly taxed meat exports through its foreign exchange control. But its attempts to initiate development were largely frustrated by the decline in export profits, internal policies of raising wages, increasing social security benefits, increased food subsidies (which encouraged consumption), and heavy military expenditures (Ch. 8). Some of the "betterment" schemes in parts of Africa hold back from the cultivator part of the market price of his produce, to be used at least partly for reinvestment in agriculture. These devices for skimming off part of the national income to the government are easiest to administer where there are valuable exports of relatively few products (as in Argentina, Brazil, Chile, West Africa, or Malaya) and are more difficult in countries like India.

In the more developed countries, where tax systems as a whole have become increasingly progressive, taxes fall on those otherwise most likely to save. Increasing social security benefits may possibly diminish the stimu-

---

[41] Schwartz, *Russia's Soviet Economy*, 54, 62.
[42] U.N., *Methods of Financing Econ. Devel. in Underdeveloped Countries*, 7.

lus to voluntary saving by lower income groups, but the funds accumulated by the government (especially for the payment of old age benefits) may in fact exceed the aggregate voluntary savings that would otherwise have been made by the same group. And in some Latin American countries (e.g. Brazil and Chile), the government has invested part of these funds in new industries.[43] In Austria social security funds could be invested in "safe domestic securities" in 1948; in Belgium in industrial projects, "in special circumstances"; in Italy in public utilities; in Czechoslovakia investment was unrestricted. Otherwise funds are typically invested in mortgages and state-guaranteed loans, but the accumulation of large social security reserves is declining.

Governments can also obtain investment funds by borrowing. Voluntary loans to the government are less likely to increase investment than to change its form and direction. When governments borrow to meet their current purposes, they are likely to reduce total investment, but taxation to meet current expenses might also have reduced saving. Governments may increase net investment if they borrow and invest when private investment falls short of saving (e.g., during a depression). Budget deficits financed by borrowing may permit the state to put to work resources that would otherwise be wasted, and increase investment without reducing consumption, possibly increasing it.

Changes in the supply of money may affect saving. In capitalist industrial economies an increase in money supply without any corresponding increase in goods and services or fall in velocity of circulation (increase in money holdings), increases spending and stimulates production. As the economy approaches full employment of its resources, prices rise, and the distribution of real income changes. Those whose money incomes do not rise as fast as prices lose real income. Receivers of fixed interest and rents save less, dissave, or consume less. Insofar as salaries and money wages lag behind price increases, their recipients must also adjust to lower real incomes, largely, however, by reducing consumption. The chief beneficiaries of such changes are profit receivers and the government. Real business profits are often less than apparent profits because of the increased working capital needed and the necessity for increased provision for depreciation. But this class (including those who ultimately receive profits from these activities) has provided much of the past savings in the capitalist countries, and transfers of income to them from rentiers and wage earners are likely to increase investment. The government shares in gains from inflation where it taxes profits or finances budget deficits by borrowing from state banks and issuing currency.

Monetary policy has probably contributed perceptibly to the rate of investment during recent centuries. The influx of American treasure into

---

[43] *Ibid.*, 12; *Econ. Surv. of Latin America in 1948*, 40.

Europe in the 16th and 17th centuries caused prices to rise more than wages and the resulting profits, together with those from the East India trade, were employed to build up capital. Again in the second half of the 18th century the lag of wages behind prices stimulated economic development at a revolutionary rather than an evolutionary pace.[44] During the 19th century the volume of purchasing power increased greatly in all developing countries (through increases in the quantity of paper money and bank loans). The tendency to rising prices was partly offset by increases in the volume of transactions due partly to increases in population (Ch. 30). But in most of these developing countries pressure to invest in excess of current savings stimulated production until it caused inflation. The failure of real wages to rise much until the middle of the century,[45] although productivity was increasing, facilitated investment. These pressures were notably insistent in the U.S.A. during the 19th century. Banking expanded rapidly and often disastrously after about 1830, but it achieved investment out of involuntary saving. The struggles between the hard money and the soft money groups later in the century arose out of pressure to accelerate development by investment beyond current voluntary saving. But as productive capacity repeatedly ran ahead of increases in income necessary to purchase the output resulting from increased investment, adjustments came with intermittent depressions and severe reductions of investment. Over the long run the rate of development in capitalist countries was influenced by the policies of banks with regard to their reserve ratios, and the reserve policies of the currency issuing authorities, rather than by conscious control by governments (Ch. 30).

During the 20th century inflation has been due also to attempts to finance wars without corresponding increases in taxation and borrowing, but much of the increase in profits has been taxed away. After 1945 investment was needed in these countries merely to restore pre-war levels of production. But there were also arrears of consumption, and in many countries accumulations of purchasing power that could not be exercised in war time. Some of these accumulations were withdrawn by governments (Ch. 30). But investors lacked confidence in the political and economic stability of governments. Government efforts to provide capital to fill the gap without increasing taxation or borrowing by a corresponding amount (without balancing their revenue budget) caused general inflation. Capital was thus involuntarily provided, often by workers whose real wages were reduced by increases in prices or hours of labor (e.g., in France).

Inflationary price increases do not have the same effects in underdeveloped as in developed capitalist countries. These effects depend partly on

---

[44] Hamilton, E. J., "American Treasure and the Rise of Capitalism (1500-1700);" *Economica*, 1929, 338; "Profit Inflation and the Industrial Revolution," LVI *Quar. Jour. Econ.*, 1942, 256.

[45] Kuczinski, *A Short History of the Working Classes*.

the extent to which money is used. In Iraq, for instance, money is used by only a small proportion of the population.[46] The effects depend also on the social structure and on economic attitudes. Fixed interest receivers are relatively unimportant in underdeveloped countries. Landowners taking a share of the crop as rent are protected against price increases. Salary and money incomes are less important than in developed countries. The transfers to profit receivers are therefore a smaller proportion of all incomes. These profit receivers moreover are also less disposed to invest. Farmers are often too poor to save; business enterprises are few and merchants are more likely to speculate in commodities. By increasing their holdings of commodities instead of money, they accelerate the price increase. Or they buy precious metals and jewelry (e.g., in Mexico[47]). It has been suggested, however, that inflation may have increased the share of the national income going to agriculturalists and, possibly, wage earners, in countries like India, thus somewhat reducing saving.[48]

Nevertheless, governments in Latin American countries have obtained from their banks money for development expenditures, which, together with their revenue expenditures, exceed the purchasing power obtained from taxes and ordinary loans. Thus they increase aggregate spending and, as there has been a high level of employment since 1940, prices have risen. In Turkey prices rose after 1937 for this reason. The activities of the Chilean Development Corporation contributed to a 250% increase in prices from 1939 to 1947. In Mexico prices have risen for the same reason, but inflation has been somewhat reduced by limiting the expansion of credit by commercial banks and by selective control of credit.[49] Inflation in Argentina has already been mentioned. In India, however, heavy public investments appear to have been offset by a decline in private investment[50] (i.e., the government changed the direction but not the total amount of investment). This general resort to forced saving has been due to the low level of voluntary saving and a general unwillingness to invest in development or even in government bonds. Lack of faith in the government expressed in this way at a time of increasing internal pressures for higher levels of development further undermines the government.[51] Furthermore, forced saving by some classes has sometimes been offset by increased consumption by others. In Chile while prices were rising, the proportion of gross national income spent on consumption goods rose from 59% in 1940 to 64% in 1942.

[46] U.N., Econ. Surv. Mission for the Middle East II, 36.

[47] U.N., Econ. Surv. of Latin America in 1948, 70.

[48] U.N., Mobilization of Domestic Capital in Certain Countries of Asia and the Far East, 1951, 8.

[49] U.N., Econ. Surv. of Latin America, 1948; International Bank for Reconstruction and Development Annual Report, 1948-9.

[50] U.N., Econ. Surv. of Asia and the Far East in 1949, 190.

[51] U.N., Econ. Surv. of Latin America, 1948, 41; U.N., Economic Surv. Mission for the Middle East, I, 35.

Socialist governments controlling production and the allocation of income might be expected to have no need to resort to inflation. In fact, however, there has been considerable inflation in Russia. From 1917 to 1924, production was low and government income was small because many sources of income had been eliminated by the Revolution. In 1919 the government was authorized to issue as much currency as was needed, and it thus financed its huge deficits and almost completely destroyed the value of the ruble, and in 1924 a new and more stable currency was issued. During the five-year-plan period, the state has planned its currency issues and its volume of credit to provide the quantities necessary to implement the planned production. But in fact currency and credit have been used to cushion failures to implement the plan. If the planned level of costs is not achieved, the disbursements of the productive system are higher than was planned for a given output, and there is upward pressure on prices. Failures to achieve output targets (which were especially important in agriculture in the 1930s) or failure of private savings to reach planned amounts have a similar effect. The imposition of rationing in the early 1930s indicated severe upward pressures on prices. In fact the prices of many basic foods rose tenfold between 1928 and 1940. During the war of 1939-45, the government diverted resources not only by direct planning and loans but also by the offer of heavy monetary inducements, although consumers' goods and services on which to spend the inducement funds were not available. In this respect their policy was similar to that in all the other belligerent countries. Prices on legal markets for extra-ration goods rose sometimes to 100 times the legal price for rationed goods. But in 1947 the government withdrew a great deal of this accumulated purchasing power.[52]

In Russia, investment is directly controlled by the government. Consumption is restricted to the consumer goods and services the state decides to produce, and investment is determined by the capital goods it decides to produce. The ultimate ceiling on saving (the whole surplus of production above what is needed to keep the population alive) is the same as in any other society. But the decision how near to approach this limit is governmental, although it must be influenced by the resistance expected from the population. It has already been shown that high levels of saving have been set by the Russian and east European governments. Prices are set by the government at levels expected to take off the market the quantities of goods it expects to produce, keeping in mind the wage and other disbursements it expects to make. There is provision for individual saving. In 1922 the government opened savings banks and issued its first loan, but since all the funds of the savings banks are invested in government loans, almost the entire personal savings of the U.S.S.R. are government bonds,

[52] Schwartz, *op. cit.*, 397 ff.

which have been a continuous but subsidiary means of attracting the resources of the population into the industrialization program.

Government borrowing was about 4% of the budget in 1938, and 8% in 1945, but in 1939 25% of all government bonds were taken by banks, production enterprises (which invest all their liquid assets and reserves in bonds), and the state insurance fund. During the war of 1939-45 the government set obligatory quotas of government bonds to be taken by enterprises (on the basis of their profits), and applied "moral pressure" to the public to purchase bonds through collective farms and other places of employment.[53] But loans to the government do not much influence investment. The government plans disbursements to the population somewhat larger than the charges to be made for consumer goods and services, assuming some savings. If savings are less than are estimated, individuals are endeavoring to spend more than was anticipated, which will tend to force up prices. Insofar as prices are controlled, they find that some of the money which they do not wish to save they cannot spend, and are thus compelled to save.[54] In fact, government investment is ten times as large as private saving, the funds being provided by excise (or turnover) taxes, and by deliveries of agricultural products at lower prices than those at which they are resold. Investment is not allocated by reference to consumer choice; thus there is a wide gap between the cost of producing some goods and the price which will equate demand with the restricted planned supply. The turnover tax fills this gap. This administrative machinery has been used to attain rates of investment so high that it causes food shortages at times. Food exports to pay for industrial equipment have so reduced reserves as to threaten famine in poor crop years (e.g., in Russia in the 1920s and 1930s, Bulgaria in 1949, and Yugoslavia in 1950).

2. Subtractions from the Supply

Individuals can reduce their capital by spending more than their current income on consumption and selling investments. But these sales merely transfer rights to income without reducing the capital fund of the economy. Such sales are possible, however, only if some people are currently saving enough to be able to pay for the old investments. Current savings then result in less new investment than could be made if none of the new savings were being offset by disinvestment. Disinvestment cannot absolutely reduce the capital fund invested in the country, although sales to foreigners may absolutely reduce the investments held there.

Disinvestment by individuals occurs in all countries owing to bad luck, lack of skill, the cost of educating children, old age, sickness, and the

---

[53] *Ibid.*, 422.
[54] *Ibid.*, 422, 434.

prodigality of sons. It happens intermittently to some people in low standard agrarian economies in the Middle East, China, and India.[55] It may increase as the proportion of the aged in the population increases,[56] and as interest rates fall. People in the middle and upper classes who have saved in the hope of living during their old age on income from investments, bequeathing the capital to their descendants, may be forced by falling rates of return to purchase annuities or otherwise "live on their capital." But the amount and causes of disinvestment are not known.

The capital fund may be reduced by war or by earthquakes, tornadoes, and other disasters of nature. War has become increasingly destructive, especially during the 20th century. Physical means of production are destroyed, but resources are also diverted away from the maintenance of equipment. Even though corporations accumulate funds to pay for deferred maintenance, the productivity of capital is likely to fall. The British government estimated its losses from the war of 1939-45 at £7.25 billion, which included physical destruction on land, losses of shipping and cargoes, deferred maintenance of assets and inventories, and losses of foreign investments (the last reduced investments owned in Britain, but not those directly affecting production there). The losses in western Europe, excluding Germany and Norway, have been estimated at 90 billion international units, and there were further heavy losses in Japan, Java, Malaya, China, and other Far Eastern theaters of war where also assets were destroyed and factories, railroads, houses, plantations, and irrigation systems deteriorated.[57] Consequently, considerable new saving was needed after 1945 merely to restore the capital supply of these countries to its former level.

Wear, deterioration, and obsolescence continuously tend to reduce the capital fund. The individual firm calculates its net profit after deducting the estimated annual reduction in its capital supply from these causes. If its estimates are too low, its profits are overstated. But, even if the provision is correct, the accumulation of depreciation funds results in considerable saving (even in Russia), wherever total depreciation fund balances are increasing (as they have been in all developing economies).

In an economy as a whole, the amount of resources that must be diverted from consumption to offset this erosion of the capital fund depends on the total amount of invested capital and the average economic life of its assets (which depends on the proportion in economically more durable and less durable forms respectively). As a percentage of net national income in 1948, depreciation ranged from about 10 to 20% in European countries (Table 39). In Russia in 1937 it was about 2%, compared with 7.6% in the

---

[55] Mukerjee, K. M., "The Problems of Agricultural Indebtedness in Bengal," *Indian Jour. of Econ.*, April 1949, 375.

[56] Clark, *op. cit.* 2d, 505; Harrod, *Towards a Dynamic Economic Theory*, 440 ff.

[57] Queensland: *Rev. Econ. Prog.*, Feb.-March, 1950.

U.S.A., where the capital fund is larger in relation to income.[58] The proportion of gross capital formation each year absorbed in maintaining the capital fund varies widely, owing to differences in net capital formation. It averaged 40% in the U.S.A. between 1919 and 1938,[59] 50% between 1920 and 1929 and 90% between 1929 and 1938. Before 1939 the proportion (including repairs and maintenance) was about 50% in France and Denmark.

It is impossible to discover whether these allowances have been adequate, and they probably have not been adequate in some countries. Obsolescence is especially difficult to measure. It may occur because consumers shift their preferences or because new sources of supply appear. Some investments in Britain have declined in production potential because of the loss of foreign markets, and the persistence of out-of-date equipment may be partly due to continuing uncertainty as to markets.[60] Improved methods of production also render existing investments obsolete. But the value of obsolete assets may not be sufficiently reduced, especially where monopoly conditions permit their continued use. Depreciation is likely to be underestimated in times of rising prices, especially where it is calculated as a percentage of the original cost of assets. When the asset is economically finished, the sums set aside to replace it will be insufficient. Enterprises obtaining high profits during such periods may establish supplementary reserves for depreciation, but inadequate provision for depreciation increases profits and, therefore, taxes on profits. Adequate financial provision for depreciation does not however maintain productivity in particular industries unless obsolete equipment is in fact replaced. The high average age of equipment in some west European industries in which obsolescence has been rapid suggests that capital had not been maintained in 1945. In Britain deep mining of coal was little mechanized, and 20% was cut by pick and shovel; 66 to 75% of cotton textile equipment was more than 20 years old; only 5% of looms were automatic and over 60% of floor space was built before 1900; some wool carding machinery was 80 years old, 25% of the spindles dated from the 19th century, and many looms had been in use for more than 50 years. In France most coal equipment was more than 30 years old; engineering equipment averaged 25 years; the iron and steel plants in east and central France were all over 30 years old; 56% of the spindles and 58% of the looms in the textile industry were installed before 1919. Conditions in Belgium were similar[61]. In general, because new equipment is more efficient than the equipment replaced, a reduction in the average age of equipment increases output per worker.

[58] Bergson, "Soviet National Income and Product in 1937," *Quar. Jour. Econ.*, 1950, 220.

[59] U.N., *Econ. Surv. of Europe in 1949*, 203.

[60] See reports of British "Working Parties" and of the Anglo-American Productivity Council established by the Economic Cooperation Administration.

[61] U.N., *Econ. Surv. of Europe in 1949*, 203.

But considerable investments have been made since 1945, especially in agriculture, electricity, steel, and coal, and it is estimated that continuance of this rate of investment will increase European output 50% in ten years because of reduced obsolescence and the expansion of industries using high capital per worker. Countries of more recent development, however, enjoy an advantage in the low average age of their equipment.[62]

---

[62] *Ibid.*, 204.

Chapter 22

Capital: Utilization

The contribution of capital to the national income depends on its allocation among sectors and the intensi... of its use in each.

A. The Allocation of Capital Among Uses

The allocation of capital among different sectors of an economy has a direct and important effect on its over-all productivity. The striking changes in the relative importance of different sectors as development has proceeded (Ch. 4) have been made possible by the allocation of capital to the more productive sectors. In underdeveloped countries, stagnation in agriculture at low levels of productivity is often attributed to the lack of capital.

1. THE ACTUAL ALLOCATION OF CAPITAL

The allocation of the existing capital fund among different sectors is not known for most economies. But there are obviously great differences among countries. Everywhere there is some capital in agriculture, if only working capital to keep the cultivator alive during the production cycle, and in stocks of animals. In primitive societies, there is little other capital. Implements consist often of one or more hand tools, and in the poorest societies the stock of draft animals is small. Some rely upon the energy of women rather than animals for transport and cultivation. There was considerable agricultural capital in the ancient world. Greece and Rome invested in the improvement of land and the development of long-cycle crops like grapes and olives, and Egypt, Mesopotamia, and China in irrigation. Agricultural investment is also small in most underdeveloped areas, except in the production of export crops, and in irrigation, especially in wet rice areas. But as countries develop, agricultural wages rise and capital is invested in buildings and implements. Population increases are likely to induce investment in clearing, draining or irrigating land. Agri-

432

culture is now highly capitalized in the U.S.A. and western Europe. The decline of agriculture in Britain in the later 19th century discouraged investment there, but it was greatly increased after 1939 (Ch. 6), and it has greatly increased in Russia since the Revolution.

Trade has also attracted capital since ancient times to finance inventories of goods in hand and in transit. Trade depends on, and expands with, increased specialization of labor indicated by the rise of, first, craft and, later, industrial production and increased local specialization. In Europe international trade grew after the ninth century, and was conducted mainly at periodic fairs. As long as the high cost of transport restricted exchange to goods of high value in relation to the cost of transport, trade was dependent mainly on the growth of wealthy classes and institutions (mainly the Church). But the availability of some minerals and agricultural products (e.g., spices) in only some parts of the world also generated trade. More local markets developed later in western Europe to conduct trade between the rural areas and the growing towns, and as subsidiaries to international trade, which expanded after the geographical discoveries of the 16th and 17th centuries. Reduction of the cost of transportation further stimulated domestic and international trade in the late 18th and 19th centuries. Larger-scale methods of production generated more local concentration of production and, therefore, more trade in raw materials, capital goods, and manufactured products. The uneven adoption of these methods throughout the world magnified this increase in trade and its capital requirements.

Investments in transport facilities are small in primitive societies. But in the ancient world there was considerable investment in shipping and the Romans invested heavily in roads, bridges, and aqueducts. Shipping and caravan transport increased in the 17th century, when investments in roads also increased (notably in Britain). Subsequent investments in canals in the late 18th century, railroads after 1830, and steamships a little later called for the first large-scale investments in modern times. In the 20th century, capital has been invested in automobiles, trucks, the redevelopment of roads, and in air transport. The investments in transportation, however, are lower in the underdeveloped countries than in the developed. In Africa, India, China, and the Middle East, there is a serious lack of road transportation, and railroad facilities are more sparse than in more populated countries. But they are more extensive than they would otherwise be where they facilitate the export of agricultural products and minerals. Poor transport nevertheless holds down productivity by restricting opportunities for specialization.

Manufacturing capital is small where craft methods prevail. Even industrial production required small capital in its early stages, but increases in capital per unit of output in many industries, and in the volume of production by industrial methods, has greatly increased capital in this form in western Europe and North America, and more recently in Japan, Russia, Brazil, and other countries. Capital in mining has also greatly increased owing to increases in capital requirements per unit of output, and to increases in output.

Housing has always required investment in durable consumers' goods, although the amount of capital involved varies widely with climate and level of income. In the U.S.A. of $12 billion gross expenditure in the 20 years from 1920 to 1939 for capital goods, some $3.23 billion were for consumer construction, residential and other.[1] In Britain in 1938, of a total net investment at home and abroad of about £250 million, about one-half was for housing. But in recent years other durable consumers' goods, such as automobiles and domestic machinery, have greatly increased investments in this form in the highest income countries.

Public buildings, one of the earliest forms of investment, date back at least 5000 years. The remnants of these buildings in Iraq, Crete, Egypt, Syria, Central and South America, India, and the Far East are impressive in their scale. Many, however, were not for strictly productive purposes. Some were monuments and temples and others palaces (in part, government offices). These investments also continue and increase in importance in the highest-income countries.

2. The Influences Affecting Capital Allocation

Considerations of maximum productivity from the whole capital stock suggest that it should be allocated among different uses so that its marginal value product in all uses is equal. Changes in consumer demand and in methods of production change this optimal allocation, but it is not easy to change the actual allocation of capital at all quickly. The economic quantity of capital in any use falls when its productivity falls owing to depreciation and obsolescence (due, for instance, to shifts in demand or changes in methods of production). The physical goods may, however, remain in use for some time, earning less than full depreciation allowances and normal profit. The quantity of capital in any use may also rise because of increases in demand for the services it can perform, but in capitalist economies such increases are likely to attract new capital, which tends to reduce again the value of older competing capital goods. Thus the principal influences changing the allocation of the capital stock are shrinkages due to wear and obsolescence, and allocations of new investments.

The allocation of new investments is known for only a few countries. During 1951 gross investments in agriculture were less than 10% of all investment in most west European countries, except Greece and Norway. Investments in manufacturing and mining were over 40% of the total in West Germany, Italy, and Britain. The proportion of investments in

---

[1] Dewhurst, et al., op. cit., 374.

transport were highest in Belgium and Norway; in housing it was highest in Greece, Belgium, Sweden, and West Germany. Available information for East European countries indicates about 10% in agriculture, 40 to 50% in manufacturing and mining, and 10 to 15% in housing (Table 44). In Russia the five-year plan for 1950-55 provides for continuing

TABLE 44

COMPOSITION OF GROSS INVESTMENT IN FIXED CAPITAL IN VARIOUS TYPES OF INVESTMENT IN SELECTED EUROPEAN COUNTRIES IN 1951

COUNTRY	PERCENTAGE OF TOTAL GROSS INVESTMENT IN FIXED CAPITAL IN				
	Agriculture Foresting & Fishery	Mfg. and Mining	Transport and Communication	Govt. and Other Sectors	Dwellings
Western Europe°					
Belgium	5	26	28	17	24
Denmark	9	18	11	45	17
France	9	na	10	8	22
Western Germany	8	42	13	14	23
Greece	13	33	15	9	30
Italy	9	41	16	na	na
Netherlands	6	35	22	22	15
Norway	13	26	28	17	16
Sweden	7	35	19	15	24
United Kingdom	5	47	13	17	18
Eastern Europe†					
Poland	8.6	42.6	15.8	22.0	11.0
Eastern Germany	11.1	46.0	11.1	15.9	15.9
Hungary	10.3	51.6	na	na	na

° U.N., *Econ. Surv. of Europe since the War*, 1953, 61.
† *Ibid.*, 24.

emphasis on investment in heavy industry and building as against agriculture and light industry.[2] These allocations of capital are the result of individual, business, and government decisions.

a. *Private Organization*

In non-socialist countries individuals and businesses make the decisions in the light of the anticipated gains from different investments, after allowing for the risks and the cost administering investments. Savers may themselves select their investments, but, especially in the more developed countries, advisors and intermediaries of various sorts influence allocation.

Savers select their own investments in primitive societies when individuals sacrifice leisure or consumption to produce capital goods such as boats, houses, or chipped flints. To make larger investments they sometimes call upon other villagers to cooperate (as the New England farmers

[2] U.N., *Econ. Surv. of Europe since the War*, 1953, 47.

did for their "raisings"). In monetized societies, savers may themselves select investments in small businesses, small- and medium-sized agriculture and some housing. They are influenced by the anticipated money returns or satisfactions (e.g., from owning their own house). They can somewhat influence the returns from the investment by participating in management, and the amount of investment of this sort may be determined by the savings of people willing to be active managers.

In predominantly agrarian societies, most investments are selected by individuals (except in foreign trade and plantations). Landowners have invested comparatively large amounts in Latin America in the production of export crops (sugar in Cuba, coffee in Central America, Colombia and Brazil, cotton in Peru, bananas in the Caribbean, meats and wool in the River Plate region, and wheat in Argentina). But those with larger incomes have invested little in agriculture for the domestic market because of the poorness of the market and their unwillingness to undertake active management. Other factors, such as the place of middlemen in marketing, the absence of cooperatives, unclear land titles, poor transport (hindering marketing and inspection of properties offered as security), and the low educational level of farmers who do not always know what facilities are available for supplying capital nor how to use it effectively,[3] have, however, been important contributories to this situation. In consequence, working capital for small-scale agriculture (and for craft production), where it is not owned by the producer, is often provided by moneylenders who select their own investments. These lenders may be landowners, but more frequently are merchants purchasing agricultural produce and selling farm requisites and household supplies.[4] Local lenders operate speedily, flexibly, and informally on the basis of detailed local and personal knowledge. But in India, China, southeast Asia,[5] and the Middle East, rates of interest are ruinously high, and the combination of lending with merchant activities often compels the borrower to sell his produce at less than market prices and buy supplies at more than market prices. In the Middle East, interest rates of 30% have been common, and some have reached 200% a year. In India large borrowers pay 9 to 12% for secured loans, but small borrowers pay 12 to 50% on secured and up to 300% on unsecured loans.[6] In Indochina rates range from 50 to 100%. Even in Mexico, where there is an extensive system of agricultural credit institutions, 75% of agricultural credit is supplied by merchants and processors; short term interest rates have been as high as 5% a month, and average 3%

---

[3] U.N., *Econ. Surv. of Latin America in 1948*, 130 ff.

[4] U.N., *Land Reform*, 37; U.N., *Rural Progress through Cooperatives*, 1954, 6, 37.

[5] U.N., *Mobilization of Domestic Capital in Asia and the Far East*, 1951, 39.

[6] Warriner, *Land and Poverty in the Middle East*, 136; U.N., *Land Reform*, 38; Mukerjee, K.M., "The Problem of Rural Indebtedness in Bengal," *Indian Jour. of Econ.*, 1949, 375.

a month.[7] In Africa, there has been little money lending outside West Africa, but in Nigeria and the Gold Coast, the farmer may borrow a maintenance loan from a middleman on a crop before the season opens. The rates on these loans are fantastic and the contract not uncommonly provides that the borrower's son shall serve the lender without reward until the loan is repaid.[8]

These high rates reflect the general shortage of capital, but indicate also the high risks on unsecured loans. Laws preventing foreclosures increase the difficulty of borrowing; in Egypt, foreclosures on land holdings of five acres or less are prohibited (except by the quasi-government agricultural bank), and native populations in colonial areas are frequently prohibited from alienating their land to non-natives.

The net return to the money lender is below the interest charge because of bad debts and the high cost of administering small loans. The rates also reflect the fact that banks rarely operate outside large cities or make small personal loans. Moneylenders enjoy local monopolies not only of lending but also of dealings in produce and supplies, owing to poor transportation and communication. This combination of circumstances frequently compels small owners to sell their land, or enables lenders to foreclose on mortgages. In the Middle East a large proportion of cultivators have been forced to sell their land to wealthy town merchants and become share tenants, particularly in Syria and Iraq. In Iraq crops are often sold as soon as the green appears, at prices which are ruinous to the cultivator (sometimes about one-fourth of the current price of grain).[9] In India, non-professional money lenders often aim at eventual possession of the land.[10] Nevertheless agriculture does get financed. The volume of debt is, however, criticized as excessive. In the Middle East, the break up of collective types of ownership and semi-nomadic forms of social organization, and their replacement by settled cultivation and a market economy, has resulted in rural indebtedness of extraordinary proportions (in spite of the prohibition on usury). In India rural debt has been great, although it has probably fallen since 1939 owing to rising prices. The ultimate problem, however, is not the volume of debt but the poverty of agriculturalists that drives them into debt as poor risks, and the general shortage of capital.

In the less developed countries, savers have made few long-termed investments in industry in their own country. Such investments as have been made have been by foreign investors (except in Japan). In many such countries (e.g., Egypt[11] and in Latin America), savers have often pre-

---

[7] U.N., *Econ. Surv. of Latin America in 1948*, 131.
[8] *Pendered Report*, 5.
[9] Warriner, *op. cit.*, 22, 114.
[10] India: Famine Inquiry Commission *Final Report*, 294.
[11] Nazmy, "The Land As a Bottomless Sink for Egyptian Capital," *L' Egypt Contemporaine* XXXV, 239.

ferred to buy land less for income than for prestige reasons, long-term capital gains, and as a hedge against inflation. Such purchases add nothing to the productivity of the economy unless the sellers invest the proceeds in productive form. In fact, however, many of the sellers are in process of dissaving; they sell to repay debts for consumption purposes or to maintain consumption. But this preference for buying land has given place to some extent to investment in urban building, mainly in Latin America. In Chile in 1940-44, 23 to 38% of gross investment was in building (excluding public works, direct investments by the government development corporation, and railways). In Brazil, 65 to 70% of net savings was invested in building construction in 1947 (of which 66% was in office and residential buildings for the upper-income groups in the main cities), and in Mexico also investment has been concentrated somewhat on industries supplying goods to the wealthier classes (including building).[12] Thus investment has shifted only to a type of durable consumers' goods and not much to productive investment. Furthermore, investments in commerce are preferred to investments in industry, and business firms keep a large proportion of liquid assets. These preferences are in part traditional and in part the consequence of local spending and saving habits. But, in countries with a long history of rising prices, commercial profits are generally higher than industrial. In 1946 commercial operations in São Paulo and Rio de Janeiro yielded about 32% profit on investment; manufacturing yielded about 17%. In Mexico also inflation has induced investment in inventories and in lines expected to be highly profitable in a short time.[13]

In more developed capitalist countries, savers allocate investments to agriculture and small business, but they have also invested in large-scale industry, mainly in western Europe and North America because of the greater supply of savings and corporate securities. More individuals invest in industry in the U.S.A. than elsewhere, but a considerable number do in Britain (where public issues of industrial corporation securities were important only after about 1875). In France, the general public has made direct investment in bonds, but used intermediaries for other types of investment. In Germany there has been considerable individual investment, largely guided by intermediaries, especially banks. But in Japan, since few enterprises have issued public securities and the public has been little acquainted with them, savings have been channelled into investment almost solely through intermediaries.

Investment in large-scale industry is facilitated by the existence of brokers and stock markets, which reduce the risks by enabling a holder to sell his security easily. Stock markets now exist in most large cities outside socialist countries. All deal in local securities, but they vary in the international securities bought and sold and in the facilities for

---

12 U.N., *Econ. Surv. of Latin America in 1948*, 38, 70.
13 U.N., *Econ. Surv. of Latin America in 1948*, 39.

speculation. The first specialized stock exchange was established in London early in the 18th century. The Paris bourse, which is less specialized, was established in 1723. The *bourses* in both Paris and Berlin have been regulated by the government. In the U.S.A. there are stock exchanges in New York and the major cities throughout the country. In 1934, the Securities Exchange Act brought these exchanges under federal control, with minor exceptions, and the Federal Reserve Board may specify the maximum credit to be allowed on security transactions. But although these arrangements greatly encourage the holding of corporate securities, they enable investors mainly to choose among management groups rather than among sectors of industry. The more widely integrated the corporation, the less the investor can influence the allocation of capital among uses.

The enterprise saving that has become important in developed capitalist countries is allocated among uses by the managers of the enterprise, who are presumably guided by probable rates of return. They are better informed than most individual savers about investment prospects, and have more opportunity to oversee the investments made. But they may be motivated by the desire to see their corporation grow, and may favor it in allocating funds, which might be more difficult if they had to expose their projects to the test of the market by offering securities. But they also save the cost of going to the market. Corporations able to save must have been profitable in the past, but it does not follow that they will continue to be so, nor that the retained profits will be invested in the same lines of business as those from which they were derived. Large corporations often use such funds to widen the scope of their activities; this facilitates the growth of industrial empires.

The allocation of investment may be determined by the preferences of investors in a lending country. These preferences have in general been based on profit prospects. British investments in the U.S.A. after 1800 were used partly to finance the first Bank of the United States, and after 1812 for land schemes, banks, and canals. Later investments went into railways and insurance. British investments in Europe from about 1840 to 1890 were predominantly in railroads, gas, coal mining, metal mining, iron works, engineering, textiles, and plantations. The German foreign investments that began toward the end of the 19th century were primarily in railroads, utilities, and banks, with very little in mining. Considerable investments were made in Argentina (mainly through Argentine firms) in a variety of industries. Capital exports from the U.S.A., which did not begin until after 1918, have been in mines, particularly petroleum, plantations, and in branches of United States manufacturing firms (copper and nitrates in Chile, bananas in Central America, sugar in Cuba and Puerto Rico, and telephones in Latin America).

In some countries this allocation set off a cumulative development, but in others there has been no such sequel. In China and India, much British investment was in foreign trade and ancillary transport, which did not greatly stimulate internal development. Banking in Egypt was long mainly in foreign hands, and concerned with financing foreign trade (especially cotton exports). Investments in mining and plantations have similarly had little repercussion on the domestic economy. But it has already been pointed out that where the local market is thin, investments to supply that market are unattractive. Thus the allocation of capital resulting from the attitudes of foreign investors has not necessarily been at fault in terms of the circumstances of the time. National incomes have often increased in the capital importing countries, but the increments have not been used for development—many of these countries have continued as exporters of primary goods and importers of manufactures. In Japan, for instance, increments of income were mostly plowed back into development whereas in China, which received much more foreign capital, there was little investment in development. Profits on foreign capital have often been taken out of the country, but lenders expect to be paid, and they have usually reinvested where the profit prospects were attractive.

Institutions for channelling savings into investment develop as savings increase and investment opportunities multiply. These institutions exert considerable influence on the allocation of investment, but are in turn influenced by rates of return in different sectors. Some of these institutions are temporary intermediaries, and others administer a continuing capital fund. Some administer investment in particular sectors (agriculture, industry, or consumer durable goods) and others are varied in their activities.

Temporary intermediaries introduce savers to investment opportunities and retire from the transaction. Stockbrokers, in so far as they advise investors, affect capital allocation, their advice being guided by profit maximization. Investment banks act mainly as middlemen, organizing long-term investment propositions and arranging for their sale. They appear where saving has attained a considerable volume and savers can be induced to buy securities. They generally provide opportunity for investment only in government loans and large enterprises. In varying degree they appraise the profitability of projects, eliminating those least likely to be profitable and, therefore, likely to undermine their reputation. In Europe investment banks developed out of the merchant bankers of the medieval period. They were relatively few in Britain at the beginning of the 19th century, but railroad building required tremendous amounts of capital and brought forward a group of contracting and financing houses in the middle of the century. Subsequently, some of the business of the investment banker was taken over by commercial banks, and finance and investment companies. In Germany, commercial banks were also investment banks and played a large part in organizing corporate business after 1850, and especially after 1870. They sometimes formed subsidiaries to hold long-term investments and thus became continuing intermediaries, but they were mainly concerned with advancing capital until the project seemed to be ripe for flotation on the market, when they arranged the issue and repaid their loan. Investment banking in the U.S.A. developed more slowly than commercial banking. British investment bankers had branches in the U.S.A. in the early 19th century. American houses developed when local accumulations of capital appeared, and were stimulated by the disappearance of the Second Bank of the United States in 1841 (which cut off foreign capital for a time). The growth of railroad financing and the Civil War also stimulated American investment houses. In 1910 some deposit banks formed subsidiaries to issue stocks, and competed with the investment bankers, but commercial and investment banking were separated by law in 1935.

Commercial banks allocate capital when they relend funds lent to them by depositors. In the U.S.A., Britain, and the British dominions, they have made fairly short-term loans and influenced chiefly the allocation of working capital. During the 19th century the British banks financed much of the rapidly expanding foreign trade through direct and indirect holdings of bills of exchange, the German banks entering the field towards the end of the century. They also provided working capital for internal trade, but such financing has probably declined because an increasing proportion of business is in the hands of large corporations with (a) direct access to the capital market, (b) increasing amounts of undistributed profits, and (c) increasing distrust of the policies of banks in time of emergency. Allowing for price changes, advances to business by British banks fell about 35% between the 1930s and 1949 partly because much commodity trade was being financed by the government and advances to non-essential activities were restricted. Large advances were being made by the government to nationalized undertakings in the coal, transport, electricity, gas, and air transport businesses. But in the U.S.A., Canada, and Britain, the commercial banks supply most of the working capital for agriculture.[14]

In continental Europe, commercial banks developed more slowly than in Britain and the U.S.A. and have also acted partly as investment companies, obtaining more of their funds by the issue of their own securities and lending more on long-term projects. The first of such institutions, the *Société Générale (pour Favoriser l'Industrie Nationale)*, formed in 1822 in Belgium, granted loans, discounted commercial paper, accepted drafts and undertook long-term financing. A large part of its capital was obtained from the issue of its own stock and bonds. The *Crédit Mobilier*, established in France in 1852, partly to offset the power of the Rothschilds, furnished long-term credits for large-scale business obtaining funds by the sale of its own bonds and shares to numerous small investors, and from en-

---

[14] U.N., *Progress in Land Reform*, 1954, 213, 214.

gaging in industrial promotions. After getting into difficulties, it was reorganized as a bank of deposit and discount, but it shaped the development of banking in continental Europe and Japan. After 1860 a number of large banks in France used savings accounts for commercial loans, for permanent investments, and for the underwriting of a small part of a number of long term issues of capital. In Germany, deposit banking developed mostly after 1848, but by 1870 there were a number of banks operating largely with their own capital, but with some time deposits at low rates of interest. After the formation of the *Deutsche Bank* in 1870, banks began actively to collect deposits and lend to industry. The long term investment function of banks was still more important in eastern Europe, where there were fewer potential depositors. In 1939 the Hungarian banks owned all heavy industry, and the Czechoslovakian banks were diversified investment companies. In Japan the large commercial banks obtained much of their funds from fixed deposits and used them to buy industrial securities and make long period loans to industry, and advances on real estate and personal property. This illiquid policy caused difficulties in 1927; depositors lost faith in the banks, and turned to trust companies, which had previously been unimportant.

Commercial banks have played little part in mobilizing and investing funds in underdeveloped countries. Banks exist only in the large cities and invest mainly in foreign trade and large-scale merchant activities. Of the advances made in India, however, in 1948 about 30% were for industry.[15] In Japan nearly 70% of bank advances were to industry and in both countries only 2 to 3% of their loans were to agriculture.[16] In many parts of Asia and the Far East, the high proportion of bank funds from demand deposits discourages long-term investment. In Burma and Ceylon some banks have discouraged deposits because of the lack of profitable uses for funds, and outside Japan, India, and Pakistan a large proportion of all bank assets is in cash and deposits at central banks.[17] In Latin America, commercial banks lend more on real estate than to industry. In Argentina, however, 42% of all bank loans were to industry in 1947[18] and the Bank Misr in Egypt (founded by local capitalists in 1920) is an ordinary commercial bank that has actively financed industry.[19]

Savings banks, mobilizing the savings of lower income groups, come into existence when these groups achieve incomes that permit saving, and if they have confidence in banks. Originating in Scotland in 1810, they spread in Britain after the Napoleonic War, partly with encouragement and sponsorship from the Church. They appeared in the U.S.A. in 1816 (in Philadelphia), in France in 1818, and a little later in Germany. In

---

15 U.N., *Progress in Land Reform*, 213.
16 U.N., *Econ. Surv. of Asia and the Far East*, 1951, 223.
17 U.N., *Mobilization of Domestic Capital . . . in Asia and the Far East*, 34.
18 U.N., *Econ. Surv. of Latin America in 1948*, 40.
19 Issawi, *Egypt: An Economic and Social Analysis*, 90, 121, 130.

small measure they met the needs of the new permanent wage-earning class in fluctuating and rapidly changing economies without provision for social security. They channelled savings mainly into real estate and bonds but usually not directly into industry. Savings banks gathered funds on a considerable scale for ultimate investment in industry in Japan after 1868 and now exist in a number of less developed countries (e.g. Egypt and Latin American countries). In Mexico they had invested about 19.8% of their funds in industry in 1948 (mostly in the stocks of government corporations).[20]

Trust companies, mainly an American invention, act as trustee for the funds of middle- and upper-income groups in more developed countries. They allocate considerable amounts of capital in the U.S.A., Australia, New Zealand, and South Africa, but not in Britain. The first trust company of the modern type was established in the U.S.A. in 1818. They rapidly expanded between 1875 and 1900, with the growth of large fortunes and of corporate trusteeship, and began to invade the banking field. But in Britain, trusteeship is in the hands of a government official (the Public Trustee), the large commercial banks, and the legal profession. In Germany most trust companies were controlled by the commercial banks. The allocation of investments by trustees is often restricted by the trust document or the laws limiting the risks that may be taken.

Investment companies and investment trusts play a large part in channelling investment, in the more wealthy capitalist countries. They use the corporate or trust device to organize the assemblage of funds and their management. In Britain such organizations were mainly concerned with foreign investment from 1875 to 1890, but a number of failures after 1890 undermined their repute until 1900. The British investment trusts differ from those of other countries in that they usually issue bonds and preferred stocks and hold mainly senior securities. The financial land and investment companies are often small investment companies finding capital for dealings in Australian real estate, tin mines in Malaya, or rubber and tea plantations. Investment companies became important in the U.S.A. after 1914, when they invested abroad until 1921, and thereafter largely in internal industrial securities. Many were in serious difficulties in 1929; they are now subject to federal regulation.

In France and Belgium the *banques d'affaires* are both investment companies and promoters of investments. They obtain most of their capital from the sale of their own securities, and originate and distribute as well as hold long-term securities. Since 1945, the larger of them have been controlled by the government in France. Somewhat similar institutions have recently developed in other countries. In Egypt finance companies for industry and trade often also actively engage in trade. In Mexico, industrial

[20] U.N., *Econ. Surv. of Latin America in 1948*, 40.

credit banks (*sociedades financieras*), authorized in 1932, and mostly subsidiaries of commercial banks, have obtained capital by selling their own bonds (often to the Bank of Mexico), and have bought and held industrial securities. But they have not stimulated industry as much as was hoped. They have aided established commercial and industrial firms rather than small infant industries; they are also alleged to have financed objectionable consumption industries to the detriment of capital-formation industries.[21] The trust banks (*fiduciarias*) in Mexico, which are largely investment trusts, are a small but important part of the financial structure. In the more developed countries these companies enable investors to spread risks and profit from specialized knowledge of existing securities. They can also invest in lesser-known projects with good profit prospects, but do so to only a limited extent.

Insurance, and particularly life assurance, companies collect considerable amounts of funds in more developed countries where they administer very large amounts of capital. In the U.S.A., life assurance companies held about $64 billion worth of assets in 1950. In 1945 they held about 20% of all farm-mortgage debt, but they have increasingly invested in industrial securities. Life assurance companies appeared in Britain in the 18th century, in France and Germany in about 1830, and in the U.S.A. in 1843. But they cannot exist on any large scale where most of the population is on a low economic level. In less developed countries, insurance was therefore in the hands of branches or agencies of foreign companies until recently. But, as the business has grown, local companies have been set up often to take over the business of foreign companies (e.g., in Egypt and Latin America). Local companies are also appearing in Asia and the Far East, although they handle small funds except in Ceylon, India, and possibly Singapore and Hong Kong.[22] The government usually restricts their choice of investments. In Egypt, they invest mainly in government and public utility securities, Egyptian and foreign. In Mexico (where they are mostly subsidiaries of the larger commercial banks) they had invested about 50% of their reserves in buildings in 1948. In Chile (where life insurance is not very popular because of a long history of inflation), the companies invest primarily in real estate, especially apartment houses. In India and Pakistan they are required to invest a considerable part of their funds in government bonds.

Japan developed an unusually efficient system of institutions for mobilizing savings, small and large, and channelling them into development. By 1913 small industrial and commercial enterprises were financed by many small local banks with few branches. The large business concerns owned by the *zaibatsu* owned most of the large city banks, savings banks, trust companies, and fire and life insurance companies, which

21 U.N., *Econ. Surv. of Latin America in 1948*, 40.
22 U.N., *Mobilization of Domestic Capital in* . . . *Asia and the Far East*, 56.

mobilized funds for investment in the industrial and commercial enterprises of the *zaibatsu*. Fifteen *zaibatsu*-owned concerns in 1945 together controlled ordinary banks holding 57% of all bank assets, savings banks with 99% of all savings bank assets, trust companies with 69% of all trust company assets, fire insurance companies with 74% of all fire insurance assets, and life assurance companies with 38% of all life assurance assets. The public never became accustomed to buying industrial securities, few of which were offered on the market. The public did, however, buy the debentures of the specialized agricultural and industrial banks which were supported by the government.

The foregoing institutions, though they guide investment, are not organized to invest in particular sectors. Specialized agencies are, however, important and increasing in number.

Agencies for channelling capital into agriculture are many and varied. Mortgage banks (banks of hypothecation) obtain capital by selling their own securities, and lend for long periods against mortgages on land. The *Crédit Foncier* in France was the first such modern bank, but they are common in western Europe (not however in Britain) and in Japan. In Egypt, the *Crédit Foncier Egyptien* and the Land Bank of Egypt (both foreign owned) have lent on mortgage to large landowners. Loans to small landowners have been discouraged by the law prohibiting foreclosures on land holdings of five acres or less, and by the cost of dealing with small borrowers. In 1936, mortgage debt was about 5% of the value of all land.[23] Such banks are common in Latin America. In Mexico, however, only 5% of all mortgage credit has been for rural development, most of it having been for building construction. In Chile, the mortgage banks make loans by handing the borrower Mortgage Bank bonds carrying about 6% interest which the borrower typically has to sell at a discount to obtain cash. Nevertheless, their activities have helped to diversify agriculture, provide some major irrigation works and finance construction.

In continental Europe agriculturists dissatisfied with the arrangements for providing capital, and with its cost, have developed Agricultural Credit Cooperatives[24] which mobilize the savings of their members for investment in agriculture and facilitate borrowing by joint guarantee. These cooperatives developed first in Germany where Raffeisen in 1854 introduced the small society of members with unlimited liability. From 1873 Raffeisen rural banks became general. They had no regular capital, but a loan fund into which peasants put their savings and from which loans were made, largely on personal security, but with the security of the land in the background. A central cooperative bank was formed in 1876, the shares of which were mostly held by the village banks, and in the next year a union of all Raffeisen banks was formed. In 1953 there were more

---

[23] Issawi, *op. cit.*, 129.
[24] U.N., *Rural Progress through Cooperatives*, 1954, Ch. 6.

than 12,000 rural credit cooperatives in West Germany. In France, the comparable organizations, the *Caisses Durands,* were financially aided by the government. In Denmark, Luxemburg, the Netherlands, and Switzerland, almost all long-term and much short-term credit is provided by such associations, and in Sweden and Finland the government has provided them with capital.[25] In Russia half the peasant households belonged to such cooperatives in 1917.

In Asia and the Far East credit cooperatives have not been very successful outside Ceylon and Korea. In Japan[26] an ancient institution (*mujin*) was a peculiar sort of mutual loan society. The members subscribed capital in fixed installments at regular intervals, and credit was allocated by lottery.[27] But they were partly reorganized after 1899, and the credit cooperatives reestablished after 1948 have taken over much of the provision of short-term credit to agriculture. Nevertheless, farmers are still partly dependent on usurers, although inflation has reduced the burden of past debts.[28] There were some 41,500 specialized credit societies in China in 1948. In India, although cooperative credit societies have existed for nearly 50 years, they supplied only .5% of rural credit in 1941, and members' deposits supply only 12% of their working capital. Nevertheless they supplied twice as much capital to agriculture as the commercial banks.[29] The societies rarely meet all the needs of the members but are only an additional source of credit. Many of the societies have but a short life, and even in Bombay and Sind only 30% of all the societies are regarded as sound: elsewhere the proportion is very much less and falls as low as 1.6% in the United Provinces.[30] In 1940 about 45% of all their loans were overdue.[31] Such cooperatives are growing in the Caribbean area and in parts of the Middle East. In Egypt one-fifth of the rural population are members, and in Turkey they have about half a million members in about a quarter of all the villages.[32] They have also prospered in Cyprus. But deep poverty and insecurity deny agriculturalists in many underdeveloped countries the means of helping each other and nip any budding spirit of mutual help. In Britain, Australia, and the U.S.A. the commercial banks have supplied most agricultural credit. But credit cooperatives have developed in Canada and the U.S.A. (where they provide credit to about 100,000 farmers).

In Australia, New Zealand, and South Africa, stock and station agents

[25] U.N., *Progress in Land Reform,* 1954, 216.

[26] Japan, *Financial and Economic Annual,* 1915, 138.

[27] U.N., *Mobilization of Domestic Capital in . . . Asia and the Far East,* 43.

[28] U.N., *Mobilization of Domestic Capital in . . . Asia and the Far East,* 224; Feary, R. A., *The Occupation of Japan, Second Phase, 1948-50,* 90.

[29] Wadia and Merchant, *Our Economic Problem,* 209; *Indian News Digest,* Oct. 1, 1951.

[30] Famine Inquiry Commission *Report,* 293.

[31] Wadia and Merchant, *op. cit.,* 209; India, Cooperative Planning Committee *Report,* 1946, 4, 11, 19, 22, 35, 70 ff.

[32] U.N., *Land Reform,* 40.

provide working and medium-term capital, buy and sell livestock, sell implements and supplies to farmers, and provide auction service and stockyards. They are typically incorporated concerns obtaining capital from abroad and sometimes from public issues of securities, but supplementing their own capital with bank borrowing. In the U.S.A. large agricultural implement manufacturers have provided capital to enable farmers to buy implements. And capital has been invested in agriculture in less developed areas by plantation companies, many of which have sold securities in the more developed countries (for the production of rubber, tea, edible oils, and the like).

Specialized agencies to direct capital into consumers' durable goods exist only when the standard of living is high enough to permit the purchase of such goods. The first institution of this type appears to have been the building and loan association, which is a cooperative for financing the building or purchase of houses through mortgage credit. Such associations developed in Scotland in the early 19th century, but encountered difficulties in England until the Benefit Building Societies Act was passed in 1836. They appeared in the U.S.A. in 1831 (in Philadelphia). Formerly they obtained their funds mainly from the issue of stock, but now, at least in Britain, they obtain most of their capital on time deposits, which are large. They exist also in the British dominions, but little outside English-speaking countries.

More recently in these countries capital has been invested in financing purchases of other durable consumer goods. The "hire purchase system," developed to facilitate the purchase of furniture in England in the early part of the 20th century, has been expanded in the U.S.A. under the name of installment-selling to finance purchases of automobiles and household equipment. The funds for this form of capital have been obtained from the manufacturing companies concerned, commercial banks (which discount the notes signed by purchasers), and from specialized corporations floating long-term securities to obtain capital to relend in this way.

Few private agencies have specialized in providing industrial capital. The managing agents for industrial firms have, however, channelled capital into industry, notably in India. These agencies were formerly partnerships and private companies, but are now often public companies. They have had considerable capital of their own and have promoted companies and provided both long- and short-term capital. "The system provides to some extent the industrial leadership which is needed so acutely for economic development,"[33] but it has deteriorated in recent years.

The allocation of capital resulting from individual and business decisions, and the operations of the network of intermediaries between saving and investment, is difficult to appraise. "Shortages" of capital in agriculture in underdeveloped countries are due in part to the shortage of

---

[33] *Mobilization of Domestic Capital in . . . Asia and the Far East,* 132.

capital in general. But the shortage is often attributed to the absence of institutions to channel capital into agriculture. The institutions are often absent, however, because investments in agriculture are relatively unproductive because of the general organization of agriculture, its riskiness, the cost of administering small loans, and poor security for loans. Capital would doubtless increase agricultural productivity, but it might increase productivity in other forms of production even more. Shortages of capital in industry in the same countries reflect the over-all shortage of capital and the thinness of the market for industrial products (attributable to the lowness of most incomes and the spending habits of those with higher incomes). In more developed countries the supply of capital to industry is mainly criticized because it flows excessively into large enterprises to the detriment of the small and especially of the new. But investors often prefer to invest in large, well-known rather than small, unknown concerns. The cost of investigating a small loan is larger per dollar of loan than that of investigating a large one. Large firms are sometimes more profitable because they are more efficient than smaller ones and, therefore, the direction of capital toward them is desirable on grounds of efficiency of production, although it may reduce competitive pressures for increased efficiency.

b. Government Influences

Governments influence capital allocation by direct investment or by influencing the flow of private investment funds.

Direct government investment is an ancient practice. It has always been necessary to direct investment into buildings and other capital goods needed to provide government services, because there is no profit incentive to make such investments. In primitive societies when levies are made to provide buildings or settings for public ceremonies and, occasionally, to clear land, the chief or other authority decides the form of investment. The impressive investments in water works in ancient times testify to public allocations of capital. But in recent years the scope of government provided services has expanded. In monetized economies taxes have been imposed to provide roads, although the heavy expenditures needed in many countries in the 18th century were privately financed by turnpike trusts, which were repaid out of charges for the use of the roads. More recently the heavy expenditures for reconstructing the road system in the U.S.A. to meet the needs of automobiles and trucks have been financed by public borrowing to be repaid out of similar tolls. Industrialization brought urbanization, and governments, central and local, have taxed and borrowed to direct capital into sewers, water systems, schools, and so on.

The Japanese government made direct investments in industry to stimulate development, but sold most of its pilot plants to private interests in the 1880s. A number of governments helped to provide capital for railroad building (including some state governments and the federal government in the U.S.A.). In recent decades governments have nationalized industries (Ch. 13) and established new ones. Most governments are now responsible for railroad transport, and many for other utilities. Governments undertake most multi-purpose water projects, and also atomic energy operations. The government then decides the amount of investment in these industries. In Norway the government provides about 25% of the capital needed to bring more land on existing farms into cultivation, and subsidizes the establishment of farms on previously uncultivated land.[34]

In underdeveloped countries governments find it difficult to raise sufficient funds to make large investments, especially in recent years because of increased expenditures on defense and maintenance of order (which account for 30 to 50% of government expenditure in Asia and the Far East). In Burma, Indochina, and Ceylon, government capital expenditures are small, but in a number of other countries in Asia and the Far East such expenditures are 20 to 30% of all government expenditures.[35] Such expenditures have also been low in the Middle East. But the Egyptian government has financed considerable investments in irrigation, drainage, and transport the funds for which are obtained by taxation and borrowing.

National debts have rapidly increased in all developed countries (but largely on account of wars). Postal savings banks provide a minor amount of funds for government use. These banks developed in Italy and France and were adopted in England in 1860, and later in Germany, but only in 1910 in the U.S.A. They have been important also in Japan and have now spread to many countries including Asia and the Far East.[36] They encourage small savers but have often been opposed by commercial banks. Many now handle considerable amounts of savings, and some provide checking facilities. In Ceylon, Pakistan, and Thailand postal savings are larger than commercial savings accounts.

In Russia the government allocates all investment according to its general production plan. Savings are assembled from the socialized sectors of industry and distribution, mainly through the turnover tax and shares of profit due to the state. From agriculture they are obtained through the compulsory deliveries at prices below resale prices, and from individuals through taxation, savings banks and sales of government bonds. These funds are administered by a series of institutions, all part of the Ministry of Finance.[37] The State Bank (*Gosbank*), with some 5500 offices, has administered all short-term capital since 1930, granting short-term loans to enterprises, usually for specific purposes for fixed periods and at interest. Because the amount of working capital allowed to enterprises free of in-

---

[34] *For. Agric.*, March 1952.
[35] U.N., *Mobilization of Domestic Capital in . . . Asia and the Far East*, 75.
[36] *Ibid.*, 53, 54.
[37] Schwartz, *Russia's Soviet Economy*, 430-438.

terest is kept low, the Gosbank has considerable control over operations. A credit plan covering the whole economy provides the framework within which the bank operates.

Long-term capital is administered in Russia by specialized banks that obtain their funds mainly from the government but also from the obligatory amortization allowances of enterprises, profits taxes, and the capital funds of collective farms. The *Prombank* (Bank for Financing Industrial and Electrical Capital Construction) makes unrepayable grants to industrial, transport, communications, and road building organizations, and local and provincial industries. The *Selkhozbank* grants long-term repayable credits to collective farms for construction, repair of buildings, purchase of equipment and cattle, irrigation works, and the like, and finances state farms. The *Tsekombank* (the All-Union Bank for Financing Municipal and Housing Construction) provides municipalities with credits or non-repayable grants for housing, public utility, and related construction, in cooperation with local municipal banks (which also obtain grants from the social insurance fund and the trade union central committee). The *Torgbank* (Bank for Financing Capital Construction of Trade and Cooperatives) provides capital to cooperatives and domestic and foreign trading enterprises of the Ministry of Requisitions. Grants to cooperatives are repayable, unlike those to government organizations. These banks may finance only projects specifically authorized, and are directed to control in detail the execution, progress, quality, and cost of construction. The State Bank and the specialized banks can inspect the activities of the productive organizations, and can stop credits or even execute the forced sale of securities where clients are not operating in accordance with the plan.

Thus the production plan in Russia determines the allocation of capital. The Communist Party regards interest as a bourgeois idea, and consequently apparently does not include it in costs. Major fixed investments and also basic working capital carry no interest, but additional working capital does. The inclusion of interest in costs in capitalist countries introduces into comparisons of the relative profitability of projects an allowance for the varying periods of delay between investment and returns from production. If interest were completely ignored in planning, investment would be allocated in uneconomically large amounts to longer-term investments. If a hydro- and thermoelectric generating plant with equal capacity could produce power at equal unit costs, including depreciation but excluding interest, they would appear to be equally desirable if no account is taken of interest. But the hydro plant would involve higher capital investment and higher interest charges in a capitalist economy and would be rejected. At the time of construction it requires a greater diversion of resources than a steam plant, without any advantage in over-all cost of production. But, in fact, Russian administrators allow informally for the postponement of benefits when they decide on the priorities which underlie the production plant itself.[38] Their allocations have in fact given high priority to early investment in basic industries to reduce the dependence of the country on foreign supplies and to increase the country's military power as quickly as possible. But the decision may also have been efficient in long-run terms, in that the basic external economy industries are being provided although at the cost of serious sacrifice of consumption during the earlier stages of development. The organization of east European countries within the Russian orbit is becoming similar to that in Russia. In Czechoslovakia, when the banks were nationalized in 1945-6 they were reorganized to specialize in particular fields of industry, each enterprise being allowed to deal with only one bank. In 1947, all banks were nationalized in Hungary.

Governments influence the flow of private funds through controls or by establishing institutions for channelling private savings to meet criticisms of the inadequacy of existing private institutions.[39]

Governments sometimes regulate the purposes for which bank credit may be used. The National banks in the U.S.A. have been thus controlled (Ch. 25), and the Federal Reserve authorities can regulate instalment credit and borrowing on securities. Government ownership or control of central banks may be used to control the purposes for which bank credit is used. In Argentina the government can control all bank loans except those made out of the bank's own capital. In Mexico, loans by the Bank of Mexico to the government have in part offset private hoarding. The Bank has taken up about 90% of the government bonds issued to finance the public works program, and has provided funds, directly or indirectly, to all government lending agencies. To reduce the inflationary effect of these operations, the government has sought to restrict bank loans to the more desired activities.[40] In Norway the government has sought to channel private funds into projects that will increase exports, expand manufacturing, or increase agricultural efficiency. The Ministry of Finance requested the private banks in 1951 to allocate credits in accord with a priority list of uses.[41] In France the government attaches a *commissaire* to each *banque d'affaires* with a capital over 40 million francs, with power to attend all meetings and to veto any decision held to be contrary to the public interest. But in addition the government took over the largest insurance companies

[38] Hunter, "Planning of Investment in the Soviet Union," *Rev. of Econ. Stat.*, Feb. 1949; Zauberman, "Economic Law and the Theory of Value," XV *Rev. of Econ. Stud.*, 1948-9, 1; Miller, "Some Recent Developments in Soviet Economic Thought," I *Soviet Studies*, 2d issue 1949-50, 119.

[39] Tirana, "Government Financing of Economic Development Abroad," X *Tasks of Econ. Hist.*, 1950, 92; Rostow, "Government and Private Enterprise in European Recovery," *ibid.*, 105.

[40] U.N., *Econ. Surv. of Latin Amer. in 1949*, 492, 499.

[41] Klein, L. R., "Planned Economy in Norway," *Am. Ec. Rev.*, Dec. 1948; Harris, *Economic Planning*, 347.

in 1946, holding about 66% of all insurance assets, and thus obtained control over another large volume of investment funds. It has also taken over four of the large deposit banks with national business. Since it also controls the central bank, it controls a considerable part of all loanable capital.

In Britain, the Chancellor of the Exchequer announced the control of new security issues in 1936 without any statutory authority. A Capital Issues Committee, which had operated before 1945, was continued for five years by the Borrowing (Control and Guarantee) Act of 1946, with power to regulate issues of securities for cash, to capitalize reserves or in mergers, the circulation of prospectuses, and the selling of new units by investment trusts. But as long as the corporations had large liquid resources in undistributed profits and depreciation reserves, much investment could go on without any appeal to the market and, therefore, without control by the committee. The Treasury has been chiefly concerned to reduce competition with government borrowing to keep interest rates low, control the export of capital (which influences the balance of payments), and regulate cyclical fluctuations in investment (so far with little success). But, as the Capital Issues Committee considered no applications not supported by building licenses and allocations of the necessary materials, the departments administering these controls regulated internal investment in fact. The Treasury regulated foreign investments because the Committee followed its advice. The Labor Government also set up the National Investment Council in 1946 to plan the national investment program as a whole. The Council was, however, only advisory, and was to collect information about the flow of investment, and suggest means of stimulating it to promote full employment. The Act of 1946, however, also authorized the Treasury to guarantee loans for industrial development. The direction of investment has similarly been controlled in a number of west European countries, since 1945, through building licenses and allocations of scarce materials. In India control of security issues has been used to direct investment into essential channels.

Governments indirectly influence the allocation of capital when import duties, excises, subsidies, support prices in agriculture, and the like influence the relative profits in different sectors of the economy (Ch. 8, 9, 13). Similarly, tax privileges have been used to stimulate investment in agriculture, e.g., exemptions from taxation on land being reclaimed (in Belgium, Portugal, Formosa and India). In Britain, New Zealand, and Australia some development expenditures are allowed as current costs for tax purposes, and high rates of depreciation are allowed on farm machinery.[42] Maximum legal rates of interest on loans to farmers (e.g., in Chile, Haiti, Portugal, Cuba, India, and Norway) have generally been

---

[42] U.N., *Mobilization of Domestic Capital in . . . Asia and the Far East*, 266.

ineffectual,[43] and if effective could not be expected to stimulate investment in agriculture.

Governments have established an increasing number of institutions for channelling capital into particular sectors of production. Many countries have sought to channel capital into agriculture, sometimes subsidizing institutions for the purpose. In the U.S.A. the Farm Credit Administration has fostered a combination of government-sponsored cooperative credit agencies, the government providing much of the capital. Twelve banks, financed largely by the government, lend to cooperatives. The Federal Land Banks, originally government-financed but since 1952 owned by national farm loan associations and local cooperative associations, make long term loans. The Farmers Home Administration has lent to low-income farmers for development and operation.[44] The British government encouraged the commercial banks to form the Agricultural Mortgage Corporation in 1928. The government guaranteed a minimum dividend of 5%, and was in fact called on to provide a subsidy which, in 1944, it agreed to extend for 15 years. The governments of New South Wales and West Australia operate rural banks, and the Commonwealth government runs the Commonwealth Mortgage Bank as a department of the Commonwealth Bank of Australia. There are also government land banks in the Union of South Africa and in Southern Rhodesia that are of no assistance, however, to the native population. The Japanese government established a Bank of Hypothecation in 1895 as part of its comprehensive organization for managing the nation's capital supply. This bank (which was patterned on the French *Crédit Foncier*) issued government guaranteed debentures and accepted deposits. It could make loans repayable in installments over 50 years on agricultural land, salt fields, forests, and fishing rights. Agricultural and Industrial Banks in each prefecture acted as local advisory bodies.

In the Middle East, government-owned or subsidized agricultural banks have so far taken over little of the rural debt. In Egypt the *Crédit Agricole Egyptien* (established in 1931) lends to small farmers and landowners directly or through cooperative societies, for short, medium and long terms. Half of its capital was supplied by the government, and the remainder by banks and finance companies (whose dividends are guaranteed by the government up to 5%). The government has also made loans to the bank and controls its operations. It is exempt from the general legal prohibition of foreclosure on land holdings of five acres or less. In 1932 the government also established the *Crédit Hypothecaire Agricole,* a mortgage bank to assist small farmers. Special government credits for cooperatives have yielded little to the peasantry.[45] Similar banks have been established in

---

[43] *Ibid.,* 230.
[44] U.N., *Progress in Land Reform,* 214.
[45] Issawi, *op. cit.,* 79, 129.

Syria and Iraq.[46] In Turkey the government set up a bank to make loans to agricultural producers as part of its general development organization. In partnership with other government banks, it also operates cotton spinning and weaving mills.

In India there were five central mortgage banks in 1947-8, 80% of whose capital was borrowed on debentures (usually guaranteed by the provincial governments), most of the rest being obtained from deposits. The central banks financed 260 local land banks, whose total loans amounted to only 40 million rupees.[47] In Ceylon both the State Mortgage Bank and State Credit Corporation borrow from the government and lend on long term, but their operations have been restricted by lack of clear land titles.[48] In Java rice (or paddy) banks developed early in the 20th century out of the traditional village granary. They obtained their resources from voluntary contributions by the community, which in part replaced a tax paid in rice by Moslems for charitable purposes. These banks made loans in rice repayable in rice at 25 to 30% interest for cultivation expenses and consumption. They prospered until 1917 and thereafter declined as the economy became monetized, but there were still some 1680 in 1949. In 1949 there were also 1200 village banks (*desa* banks), operated in money by village administrations, which obtained funds from contributions from rice banks and from the government bank. The Peoples' Credit Bank, partly financed by the government, lent about 10% of all its loans to small cultivators. Government pawnshops have also successfully made very small loans since 1900, and by 1950 there were about 260 pawnshops which have also in part displaced moneylenders in Indo China.[49]

Many Latin American governments have established agricultural credit institutions.[50] In Argentina the *Banco Hipotecario Nacional,* a government mortgage bank, operates under the direction of the Central Bank. In Mexico the National Bank of Agricultural Credit, established in 1926, now lends only through cooperative farming societies whose processing and marketing activities it controls. An Ejidal Bank provides credit to *ejidatarios* (Ch. 16). The Agricultural Bank charges 9% interest on loans to credit societies, and the Ejidal Bank 8%, but the two banks together supply only 10% of the agricultural credit in the country.[51] In Chile the Agricultural Credit Institute grants medium- and short-term credits to agriculture at an average interest of 5% (with commissions 6%). Many large landowners are said to have obtained credit which has been used to build apartment houses or to finance travel abroad, while small agricultural cooperatives complain of their inability to obtain credit. The Agricultural Bank of

[46] Warriner, *op. cit.,* 223.
[47] U.N., *Mobilization of Domestic Capital in . . . Asia and the Far East,* 60.
[48] *Ibid.,* 59.
[49] *Ibid.,* 42, 152.
[50] *For. Agric.,* March 1952; Hanson, S. G., *Utopia in Uruguay,* 73.
[51] U.N., *Econ. Surv. of Latin America,* 133.

Bolivia, created in 1942, provides financial assistance to agricultural producers, and is also charged with planning and executing a broad policy for agricultural mechanization and development.[52] There are similar organizations in Peru, Salvador, Nicaragua, Ecuador, and the Dominican Republic, mostly with small resources.

Government banks to supply capital for industry are also increasing in number. In western Europe and Canada, they are designed to fill the gaps left by the private institutions supplying capital to small businesses, and providing medium- and long-term finance. The Special Areas Reconstruction Association, Limited, was established in Britain in 1936 to provide funds to enable small firms to establish themselves in "depressed areas." In 1945 the commercial banks were encouraged to form the Industrial and Commercial Finance Corporation to borrow from the banks up to £30 million and to lend on medium and long term to small- and medium-sized businesses. But it has lent less than was authorized, and largely for working capital. In 1945, the British government also announced the formation of the Finance Corporation for Industry (not a government corporation and without government guarantee), the stock in which is held 40% by insurance companies, 30% by investment and trust companies, and 30% by the Bank of England (which is government owned). It was authorized to borrow £100 million, mostly from commercial banks and make short- or long-term loans to industry to permit quick rehabilitation and development. It was anticipated that the corporation would be most concerned with the iron and steel, cotton, railroad, and coal industries. The last two were soon nationalized and the cotton industry apparently sought no aid. Consequently, the corporation provided capital mostly for the steel industry while under the threat of nationalization. But during 1948, when the accumulated liquid reserves of many companies became inadequate to their needs, the company began to increase its loans. In 1944 the Canadian government established the Industrial Development Bank as a subsidiary of the Bank of Canada, with a capital of $25 million to assist small industries to reestablish themselves after the war. The Netherlands government established a Netherlands Industrial Bank in 1945. The government controls the bank and provided about half its capital, the remainder being provided by banks and insurance companies (who are guaranteed 3% interest by the government). State banks in Norway finance investment in certain industries and in housing.

In Japan the specialized financial institutions planned in 1882 were partly financed and controlled by the government or the Bank of Japan. The Yokohama Specie Bank (formed in 1880) provided capital for foreign trade, and the Industrial Bank of Japan (formed in 1900 on the model of the *Crédit Mobilier*) provided long-term loans on the security of movable property, including bonds and shares. The Industrial Bank sold its deben-

---

[52] U.N., *Econ. Devel. in Selected Countries,* 60.

tures abroad and guided the capital so obtained, at first mostly into new large-scale industries, particularly public utilities, ship-building, iron and steel, and chemicals. In 1951 the Development Bank of Japan was established to be financed out of counterpart funds from the U.S.A.

Many underdeveloped countries have recently formed specialized organizations to provide capital for industry. Most Latin American countries established development corporations (fomento) in the late 1930s and 1940s. Largely financed by the government, as well as controlled by it, they invest in new enterprises and act as investment bankers, maturing and selling securities to the public. In Chile (where government agencies invest about 12% of all savings), the government established a Credit Institute to plan development, but in 1939 transferred these functions to a new Chilean Development Corporation (Corporacion de Fomento de la Produccion). The Minister of Economy is President, and representatives of the executive and legislative branches of government, the government credit institutes, private agricultural, industrial, mineral, and commercial associations, and professional and workers associations are members.[53] The Corporation obtains its funds from earmarked taxes (a sur-charge on taxes on inheritances and gifts), loans from the (U.S.A.) Export-Import Bank guaranteed by the Chilean government, credits from local institutions, and a small amount from its own operations.[54] It develops economic activities into which private initiative moves slowly, such as public works, hydroelectric power, steel and petroleum production, forest industries, and similar activities. It acts as engineering consultant, purchasing agent, and banker for private concerns desiring to expand or improve their production facilities. It also develops new industries, usually establishing a corporation capitalized in part by the Development Corporation and in part by the sale of securities by the new corporation. Generally the Development Corporation has only a minority representation on the new company's board of directors, even where it has supplied more than half the capital. The steel mill at Concepcion (of the Compania de Acera del Pacifico) is one of its most important projects.

The Mexican government established the Nacional Financiera in 1934, and reorganized it in 1941 as an investment bank to promote industrial development. Of its capital 51% was provided by the government and the balance by government and private banking institutions, but it may obtain further funds by selling bonds, rediscounting with the Bank of Mexico, and selling participation certificates (backed by designated securities in its portfolio, carrying fixed interest and repayable on demand). By 1947, a large percentage of its funds was obtained from the sale of participation certificates, and considerably less from rediscounts with the Bank of Mexico: 35% of the certificates were held by private investors,

---

53 Ibid., 98 ff.
54 Ellsworth, Chile: An Economy in Transition, 85.

26% by private credit institutions, and 41% by the Social Security Institute. The *Financiera* has purchased industrial securities and made loans to industry, but in 1947 only about 40% of its loans were in private investments. Nevertheless, it has invested in practically all the large industrial corporations in Mexico, including those in the steel, hydroelectric, cement, rayon, sugar, motion picture, electrical products, fertilizer, paper, glass, and copper industries. It has purchased both stocks and bonds, although more bonds, and often has a controlling interest. But much of its total lending has been for short periods.[55]

In Argentina the new central bank, established in 1946, administers all government economic policy. The Industrial Credit Bank, set up in 1944, obtained all its capital from the government and is authorized to lend to industrial enterprises, market issues of industrial securities, form and participate in industrial enterprises, and finance technical development. It has made possible considerable advances in a variety of industries.[56] The Venezuelan Development Corporation, established in 1946 to provide a General Production Plan and to give technical and financial aid to government and private interests, establish new enterprises and improve existing ones, obtained all its capital from the government. There is also an Industrial Bank of Venezuela, of whose capital 60% was provided by the government, but which has operated only on a small scale. The Bolivian Development Corporation is largely a Bolivian government agency through which the U.S. Export-Import Bank is effectuating a development plan recommended by an American mission. The Export-Import Bank appoints half the members of the board (with the approval of the Bolivian government). The Industrial Bank of Peru, controlled by the government, has limited capital, and industry is largely financed by other banking institutions. In Colombia the government holds the major interest in an autonomous development bank (*Caja Credito Agrario Industrial y Mineral*).[57] The Cuban government established a Bank of Agricultural and Industrial Development in 1950 providing all its capital, empowering it to borrow from the National Bank and to issue its own bonds. It has already financed a variety of industrial activities, mainly mining and food processing. The Puerto Rican Industrial Development Company, established by the U.S. government, has provided facilitating services for new industries, acquired land, and provided capital for pilot plants. Industry has expanded rapidly, but mainly because of low taxes and tax exemptions for industrial concerns.

In Spain, the National Institute of Industry (I.N.I.) intended to foster enterprises essential to the national welfare but not suitable for private backing, is used as an instrument of government control. When the Turkish

---

[55] U.N., *Econ. Devel. in Selected Countries*, 8.
[56] *Ibid.*, 44, 47.
[57] *Ibid.*, 49, 91, 118, 134.

government turned in 1933 from its policy of encouraging private investment to one of active government investment, it established or took over three banks to provide capital to three (somewhat overlapping) sectors of the economy. Since 1945, however, the government has reverted to greater reliance on private initiative, and in 1950 established (with the aid of the International Bank for Reconstruction and Development) the Turkish Industrial Development Bank to provide technical and financial aid to private enterprises. The bank's stock, amounting to 25% of the total capital involved, has been subscribed by private businesses and banks (who intend to resell it on the market). The government guarantees these holders 6% interest for five years. The Bank is wholly under private management and is to aid only private industry. The Industrial and Mining Bank of Iran was set up in 1945 to manage government industrial establishments and mines, to apply the general industrial policy of the government to eight new industries and supply the necessary facilities for existing ones, and to found companies for mineral exploration and exploitation. In Egypt the government authorized a privately owned bank (*Bank Misr*) to lend government funds to small businesses. In 1939 the government assisted the bank when it was in difficulties, but it has financed a number of industries.[58] In 1948 the government established the Industrial Bank to participate in industrial concerns, make advances to them, purchase their debentures, and guarantee advances to them by banks. The government subscribed 51% of the capital, banks 30%, and the public 19%. The government guarantees the private stockholders 3½% dividend, and may guarantee debentures sold by the bank. The Agricultural and Commercial Bank of Ethiopia was merged into a new Development Bank of Ethiopia in 1951 to foster industrial and agricultural production and encourage foreign capital.

A few countries in Asia and the Far East have recently established similar institutions, financed wholly or in part by the government, to channel capital into industry. In India the Industrial Finance Corporation was established in 1948 with capital from the government, the Reserve Bank, the commercial banks, insurance companies, cooperative banks, and investment trusts. Two provincial governments have since established similar institutions. The corporation has provided capital to corporations and cooperative societies (mostly cotton textiles, rayon, engineering, and aluminum industries), partly by issuing its own bonds. In Pakistan the government established the Industrial Finance Corporation in 1949. It obtained capital by the sale of its own securities and is to provide medium- and long-term finance. The government also established the Pakistan Industrial Development Corporation to channel capital into large-scale industrial enterprises, ultimately passing them over to private enterprise. In the Philippines the Rehabilitation Finance Corporation, a government

---

[58] Issawi, *op. cit.*, 132.

agency set up in 1947, was provided with capital by the government and authorized to issue its own securities to finance agriculture, commerce and industry; in 1950 38% of all its loans were to industry. In Malaya the government financed the rehabilitation of tin mining after 1945, and established the Industrial Rehabilitation Finance Board to guarantee bank loans to plantations and industries.[59] In China the Industrial Development Corporation was established in Peking in 1950, and the South China Enterprises Co., Limited, in Canton in 1951. The capital of the latter came 30% from government funds and 70% from private investors. A Tientsin Investment and Trust Company was also projected in 1951.

In Africa the government of the Union of South Africa owns and operates the Industrial Development Corporation that finances industry. It has invested its own funds, but aims at transferring investments to private hands when they have matured. The government also established the National Finance Corporation in 1949 to provide short-term funds.[60] The Industrial Development Commission in Southern Rhodesia provides information and general aid to new enterprises, makes loans, and occasionally invests in their equity securities.[61]

B. The Intensity of Utilization of Capital

There is no general statistical information measuring the contribution of capital to national outputs in relation to its potential contribution (that is, no measure of the waste or unemployment of capital). "Unused capacity" in engineering terms does not indicate economic waste because plants may be obsolete or excessive in relation to demand, and the use of labor and materials to keep plants in full use might divert such current resources away from lines of activity where they would be more productive.

In capitalist countries private property in capital goods generally provides owners with an incentive to maximize their income from ownership and, therefore, to use capital goods economically, but monopoly and cyclical fluctuations in production have caused waste even in these economies. An owner of capital goods may increase his income by monopolistic restriction of their use. A secure monopolist would presumably use no more capital than is necessary to produce the monopoly output, which would result in an uneconomical allocation among uses. Where the members of a monopolistic group are uncertain about the future of their monopoly, they may not hold prices as high as a secure monopolist, or reduce output so low, thus reducing the misallocation of resources. But they may invest capital beyond the amount necessary for the monopoly output with the result that there is "excess capacity" which is not utilized. Such excess

[59] U.N., *Mobilization of Domestic Capital in Certain Countries of Asia and the Far East*, 1951, 63, 134, 172, 198.
[60] U.N., *Econ. Devel. in Selected Countries*, 1950, 249, 270.
[61] *Ibid.*, 226.

capacity may be due to competition in the past, the desire for a bargaining weapon against other members of the group, shifts in demand, new sources of supply, or changes in technology. It is desirable to use capital goods if the value of the resulting product exceeds the cost of resources that must currently be attracted away from other uses to put the capital goods to use (that is, if prices exceed the marginal cost of production). But if owners achieve a common policy and find that higher prices and smaller output involve less loss or more profit, their capital goods contribute less to production than they could. Waste of capital assets in this way has probably occurred in a number of the more advanced capitalist economies.

Cyclical fluctuations in demand in capitalist countries involve considerable losses from the intermittent use of equipment, especially in the producers' goods industries because expenditures on capital goods fluctuate more than those on consumption. It is estimated that during the decade 1929-38 Europe lost the equivalent of 2.5 years of capacity production of steel, 1.5 years capacity production of producers' capital goods, and one year's capacity production of cement.[62] The failure to use capital goods may prolong their life, but insofar as they deteriorate with time, owing to the weather, or become obsolete, the prolongation of their life has no economic significance.

The productivity of capital goods also depends on the hours of plant operation. Where workers object to night work, or where the cost of operation at night is higher than in the daytime, capital goods may not be in continuous use. The length of shifts may sometimes cause a period of idleness for capital equipment during the day; labor disputes also cause intermittent use of capital goods.

Where production is monopolized by the state, price policies are not necessarily those of private monopolies. The tendency to expect nationalized industries to make a reasonable profit, however, may lead to policies similar to those of private industry. The more comprehensive the power of the state over production, the more likely is it to seek to minimize waste. But there is yet little basis for judging state policies, except that complete control greatly reduces the extent of cyclical fluctuations in use of the productive factors, although it may achieve a less satisfactory integration of the economy and, in the long run, be less progressive than capitalist systems. But appraisal of some west European economies since 1920 suggests that a capitalist framework of production does not ensure progressiveness (Ch. 21).

---

[62] U.N., *Econ. Surv. of Europe in 1949*, 203.

Chapter 23

Integration of Production—Intra-National

The effectiveness of the organization for production and for regulating the supply and utilization of resources depends on the extent to which the various parts of an economy are integrated—that is, that economic behavior is coherent with reference to the objectives of the society. Conflicting decisions involve waste. But achievement of the maximum output of goods and services is not the ultimate test of integration because it may conflict with the attitudes of the society regarding the relative values of leisure, on the one hand and spiritual and material satisfactions on the other hand.

The degree of integration in a society cannot be measured against its objectives because they are usually vague. Nevertheless, it is probable that few societies could meet any strict test of integration. An individual living in isolation would be most satisfied when his efforts were most successful in terms of his criterion of success. Integration becomes more complex for a family unit, within which there is division of labor. It has become vastly more complex within whole societies as specialization has increased in recent centuries, and economic systems have grown in numbers of people.

A. Instruments of Integration

Productive systems are integrated by authority, by reliance on the market, but usually by a blend of both.

1. AUTHORITY

Authoritarian integration occurs when relatively few people make the basic decisions that harmonize productive activities in accord with the social objectives. In fact, however, authority carries considerable power to define social objectives. Authority of varying scope is usually distributed throughout society. Within families, intrafamilial authority regulates the allocation of production activities among the members. If families were economically self-sufficient, no further economic integration would be necessary. But even among indigenous populations in Africa, Latin America, and the Middle and Far East, most households are parts of villages, clans, tribes, or nations, and chiefs, village councils, and the like coordinate interfamilial activities. These authorities may be restricted in their action by custom and tradition, but tradition never remains unchanged over long periods and there is always some arrangement for dealing with new situations.

As economies become larger and more differentiated, subconcentrations of coordinating power appear in economic enterprises, and in industrial, agricultural and labor organizations. But ultimate power rests in the state, which becomes more highly organized because of the broadening scope of its problems and the need for increased flexibility of control. Chiefs and elders give place to legislatures, executives, and judiciaries. Legislatures capable of changing policy can provide an element of flexibility. They may be restricted by constitutions, but these are subject to amendment or re-interpretation. Where there is no provision for flexibility, or legislatures refuse to provide it when the attitudes of the members of the society, or economic conditions alter, change may be brought about by violence (e.g., the change from peasant to industrial economies in some countries). The change from feudal to enclosed agriculture was achieved by law in England and a number of other European countries. Large estates are being broken up by law in eastern Europe, and in India, but where widely demanded land reform is not conceded, land may be seized, as in Italy, or the government overthrown. The industrial revolution was facilitated by changes in law, more particularly with regard to banking, the organization of business units, and the relief of the unemployed.

The outcome of authoritarian control depends on the limits within which it operates and policy chosen within these limits. The ultimate limit is set by available economic resources. A secondary, and more uncertain, limit is set by the attitudes of the population and the power of the state to modify these attitudes or suppress opposition to their frustration. Policy may be aimed at maintaining an existing economic and social structure or at making structural changes (as in Russia).

2. The Market

A market providing opportunities for the continuous exchange of goods and services facilitates the division of labor by enabling specialized producers to enjoy wider variety of goods than they produce. It is not the only method of making specialization work. The feudal societies and the Incas enjoyed some specialization based upon an authoritarian redistribution of goods, but all highly organized economies, including the socialist, rely heavily on the market.

The outcome of market operation varies with the way people behave. In the more developed capitalist economies, market behavior is dominated by individual effort to maximize satisfactions. Consequently, in the short run, supplies are allocated to those who will pay most for them. When individual demands change, the prices of products change, and with them the profits of producers in different lines. In the longer run resources move to the lines of production that seem most profitable, thus reallocating resources to maximize satisfactions within the limitations set by the distribution of incomes. Each resource, including managerial ability, is attracted into the use where it is most productive. The owner of the resource aims at a maximum return from its use, and the employer of the resource aims at a maximum contribution to production over the price paid for the resource. Finally, no resources will be unemployed; if they are capable of adding to production someone will pay something to put them to use.

These results are generally desirable, but the market can achieve them only in a favorable environment. Individuals must diligently and effectively pursue their material interest. This condition is fairly well satisfied in the western world, but less so in the underdeveloped countries. Individuals need facilities for effecting exchanges, comparing values and recording debts; this need can be satisfied by money. The economies of western Europe have been increasingly permeated by money over the past five centuries, but it plays a smaller role in many less developed areas (Ch. 24, 25). Individuals must be well informed about available market opportunities. Industrialization has increased the variety of products so greatly that it is difficult for consumers to be well informed. At the same time sellers increasingly influence the attitudes of buyers by means other than the type of product offered and the price. Insofar as prices tend to cover costs, they cover this selling cost, and the consumer contributes to the cost of having his mind changed, which can be to his advantage or his disadvantage.

Business enterprises have been assumed to minimize costs and produce those things that would yield the maximum of profit, because the least successful would be squeezed out. But as the corporation has gained in importance in capitalist countries, the management of resources has been separated from risk-taking, and it can no longer be argued that the market operates effectively because decisions are made by those who directly bear any resulting losses and receive any resulting profits (Ch. 11). Industrial methods of production have also modified the simple picture of a market. The instruments of production consist in increasing proportions of durable facilities, which complicates the calculation of profit. Entrepreneurs cannot postpone the calculation of profit until all their durable equipment is worn out (which is usually never, because different components have lives of different length). To calculate profits for annual periods, they include in the cost of production for the period an amount for the depreciation of their overhead investments, thus distributing these long-run costs over time to allow for wear and obsolescence. But since these depreciation allowances must be guesses, the resulting allocation of capital must be based in part upon a guess. Overhead investments, however, are made not only for the production of a stream of goods over time, but frequently also for the production of a variety of goods at a given time. Cost accounting may be used to allocate costs to various units or lots of the product, but costs, and therefore profits, then depend on the formula used. Many corporations accumulate reserves because they realize that costs may not be covered in some short periods, and more than covered in other periods, and because they doubt the validity of their cost figures. Consequently the profits influencing resource allocation are necessarily a matter of estimation.

Competitive markets may destroy themselves. Where the most economical firm happens to be large in relation to the market, the surviving firms may be too few to maintain the competition that is expected to ensure continued efficiency. Price and output agreements, or tacit modifications of competitive behavior, introduce elements of monopoly that usually mean a poor allocation of resources and higher prices than otherwise (Ch. 14).

The theory of competitive individualism was elaborated in the 19th century, a time of rapid economic change. Yet economic theory contributed remarkably little by way of explanation of changes in the available quantities of productive resources that dominated changes in production in capitalist countries. In its strict form, it was concerned with the most economical use of a given set of resources. The rapid increases in the supply of capital in developing capitalist countries can be explained only partly by the operation of the market. The great inequality of incomes was equally important. Similarly, the relatively large supply of labor was due to the rate of multiplication of the population, its survival rate, and its class structure.

Economics has also been little concerned until recently with the way in which, and the speed at which, market dominated economies adapt to changes in demand or technology. The recurrent business cycles or crises throughout the 19th century were regarded as aberrations from the normal operation of the system. But they revealed that development was spasmodic and wasteful partly because new techniques of production involving the increasing use of durable production goods and increasing "length" of the production process caused the "laws of supply and demand" to work slowly. And periodic depressions developed into a major threat to the survival of capitalist systems.

B. Policies Regarding the Integration of Production and Their Results

1. PRIMITIVE SOCIETIES

In primitive societies most integrative functions are in the hands of the state, represented by the chief or the elders. These frequently decide who may be a member of the society (often important in controlling marriage), allocate land and work obligations, decide the timing of the major productive operations, and control output. Decisions are effective because those who do not obey may be physically punished, excluded from the community, ostracized, or merely ridiculed. As these societies consist of fairly small slowly changing populations with a stable technology, the machinery for dealing with change is embryonic. But unprecedented events occur and societies make their own arrangements for dealing with them. If markets exist, their scope depends on the extent of private property and of specialization creating a need for exchange. Their operation depends on the mores of the society. Exchange oriented towards the acquisition of prestige by giving more than is received may provide an incentive to acquire valuable goods to exchange in such markets, but it is difficult to see how it can operate throughout a society over long periods. Exchanges of surplus produce in small village markets (where they exist), motivated by the desire to treat other members of the society as if they were members of a single family, depend for their operation on the interpretation of the objective. Exchange governed by individual self-interest has been relatively uncommon. Rarely applied to the means of production (especially land) it more frequently appears in foreign trade where standards of conduct applicable within the group do not usually apply.

The outcome of this pattern of coordinating devices must vary widely. Such societies have provided for defense in varying degrees, obtained a supply of food, achieved some specialization taking advantage of the qualities of different pieces of land, and some have developed specialized crafts. They have often not achieved maximum output or increasing productivity, partly because such conduct is out of harmony with their general spirit. Increases in population have been dealt with by using more land or by preventive devices.

2. Predominantly Agrarian Societies

In larger, predominantly agrarian societies, authority was for centuries a more effective coordinating force than the market. In the ancient world markets probably appeared relatively late and were limited in scope. In the Greek world they first provided a means of distributing imported goods and war booty (including slaves). The development of cities required the concentration of food from the country and its distribution. Local city markets existed (notably in Athens) but only a small proportion of all produce passed through them. The state often controlled market prices (with reference to some concept of a just price). Hammurabi issued price control regulations in Assyria in the second millennium B.C. and similar regulations were issued in Rome. Governments and religious institutions made levies in kind (in grain and occasionally animals) that may have influenced the amount of production. Governments in Egypt, Mesopotamia, and China invested in public works, notably roads and irrigation. They usually also allocated land resources, often by way of a feudal system, which provided an interested hierarchy for land management.

Most of western Europe was regulated by a feudal system in the Middle Ages. The king or overlord allocated rights over land and the labor supply. He determined the general status of labor and engagement in war, and delegated to sub-rulers or lords power to determine the amount of land which workers might occupy. The lords controlled the movements of people and general methods of cultivation. But the economic position of serfs, the timing of work and the type of crops to be grown became customary matters. The system provided for some specialization. There were estate managers, shepherds, swineherds, and the like, but their numbers and incomes were typically controlled by the lord. Markets were probably restricted to foreign goods and exchanges with other parts of the country; these exchanges were small in volume. The system rested on the authority of the king, who could deprive the lords of their access to economic resources (so long as the king retained sufficient power), and of the lords. They implemented decisions regarding the workers on the manors who could be fined, physically coerced, or driven from the manor if they did not comply. If they were driven off the manor, they had little means of making a living, and little protection. They could become tinkers and charcoal burners, regarded as the lowest in the social order.

These feudal systems appear to have developed in Europe and the Far East out of the need for defense on a larger scale than primitive and village communities could provide, and the absence of any developed bureaucracy. The low level of development of monetary institutions necessitated taxation in kind, which was paid by the workers in labor and levies in kind, and by the lords partly in goods (to maintain the king and his court) and partly in military service and supplies. The system provided sufficient defense to permit a considerable development of settled agriculture and thus facilitated greater production. But the open field system and the labor dues hampered production, especially the improvement of methods of cultivation and the introduction of new crops. In the Middle East, however, feudalism seems to have developed because of the breakdown of a pre-existing monetary and market system.[1]

Craft production developed in the ancient world in association mainly with courts and temples, at first within a framework of slavery, and later by free workers who often formed guilds. These developments never seriously disrupted the general economic organization of ancient society (and persist in many contemporary underdeveloped countries). But in many cities in western Europe craft production developed first for international

---

[1] Bonné, *State and Economics in the Middle East*, 125, 137.

markets supplying courts and, later, feudal lords who had previously consumed their incomes in "rustic hospitality."[2] The crusades provided the crafts with their first "war market."[3] The growing market for craft goods (mostly luxuries) engendered the development of more towns to supply the new demand and reduce transport. The burghers accumulated capital and bought their freedom from feudal dues and restrictions. Some townsmen continued to grow their own food, but many concentrated on their craft and created a market for agricultural produce and a supply of goods with which to pay for it. The towns undermined the existing feudal organization by providing the rural population with a competing source of livelihood and by awakening in the feudal lords an urge to increase their incomes to buy urban products. But the market in craft products was not free. The attempt to ensure "just" prices resembled the efforts of primitive societies and ancient states to ensure exchange on a brotherly basis. But private controls of prices also appeared when craftsmen formed guilds from about the 12th century in western Europe and regulated entry into occupations, price, quality, and conditions of work. The crown at first eyed them suspiciously, until they offered to pay for charters freeing them from feudal obligations and labor controls, and enabling them to buy and sell, go and come, hold and bequeath property, and change occupations. But they were brought under state regulation in the 16th and 17th centuries.

This organization with islands of half-free individualism facilitated increases in production through the spread of new methods and the introduction of new products. But it aroused material interests, and strained, and finally broke, the rigid frame of rural organization. It facilitated accumulation and developed class divisions in the towns that were reinforced by the expansion of foreign trade following the era of exploration.

In contemporary predominantly agrarian countries the state has, until recently, been relatively inactive although it provides irrigation service in Egypt, China, and India. It has also supported a variety of rights to land (Ch. 16) often referred to as feudal, but not so in fact. In general property incomes have been in the form of share rents rather than the labor rents characteristic of the European feudal system. But the family is usually the important influence in production. Markets handle landowners' shares of produce, primary goods for export, and imports, often of luxuries but sometimes of goods of wide consumption. But these, however, are often a relatively small proportion of all produce. Many of these economies are highly decentralized because of lack of transport, communication, and money and credit systems.

The relatively narrow scope of government control and wide scope for individual action has not, however, inspired much improvement in

[2] Smith, *Wealth of Nations*, Book III.
[3] Turner, "Economic Discontent in Medieval Europe," *Tasks Econ. Hist.*, 1948, 88.

methods of production in these countries, although most of them have succeeded in maintaining expanding populations. Their relative economic stagnation in a world in which many countries have developed rapidly (some for more than two centuries) is not easy to explain except in terms of social attitudes. The system has provided incomes from land without labor, and a supply of imported luxuries, thereby favoring the persistence of ancient aristocratic traditions hostile to productive activity and, therefore, to entrepreneurship. Most of these countries fail to make use of all their resources but the mass of the population has been unable or unwilling to overthrow the system.

3. Capitalist Societies

Capitalism rests on the pursuit of individual interest, which requires predominant reliance on private property and the market. But societies commonly called capitalist have always relied on some state action even beyond that necessary to preserve property. Property, consisting of rights to buy, sell or use, provides the opportunity to allocate resources in the interest of the owner. A free market permits acquisition of the means of production, the disposal of produce and calculation of the profitability of various lines of production. At the outset, the establishment of free markets required the elimination of internal barriers to trade, particularly restrictions established by the guilds upon entry into various occupations, the methods of production pursued there, and the prices to be charged. Property and the market can facilitate business based on the careful calculation of profit and loss only if supported by a calculable legal system free from the "whim of the king" or his courtiers, and from bribery. Rational organization for the enforcement of contract was provided by modern western types of courts of law. When western traders went abroad, they frequently found these institutions so necessary that, where possible, they obtained extraterritorial rights (to operate under the law of the country from which they came). Finally, capitalism required a supply of labor free from a servile status.

The major components of a capitalist organization of production had existed for many centuries. Foreign trade had been permeated with individualist attitudes, supported usually, but not always, by private property. Double entry bookkeeping systematizing the calculation of profit and loss was in use in Genoa and Florence at least by the 14th century. Capitalist institutions had begun to crystallize and permeate internal economic life in Britain by the 16th century. The growth of towns implied an expanding internal market. Landowners were attracted by the prospect of profit in the export of wool and enclosures establishing private property in land opened the way for capitalist farming.

The authoritarian influences that had supplied the coordinating element in the feudal period were transformed, but not eliminated. Larger, more centralized states were establishing themselves; they reorganized the provision of military services. Taxation to pay for armies provided a solution to the problem of organizing for war, if the expanding bourgeoisie or merchant class provided tax revenues, and the king came to terms with them. Lacking belief that the pursuit of private interest would best serve the public good, governments regulated industry and commerce with a view to national rather than consumer interests, and the merchant class played a large part in interpreting the national interest. The resulting "mercantilist system" was aimed at the enhancement of national power through economic self-sufficiency and the exploitation of trade with other countries. Foreign trade was regulated through elaborate discriminatory duties, the protection of national shipping by Navigation Laws, and the grant of regional foreign trading monopolies to newly formed corporations. Internally the government displaced the control of the guilds, thus liberating economic activity. It also regulated apprenticeship and provision for the poor, and in Britain encouraged tillage (discouraging sheep farming and migration from rural areas). This embryonic economic planning developed during the 15th century in Britain but had disintegrated by the end of the 17th. Policy followed a somewhat parallel course in France (under Richelieu in the 16th century and Colbert in the 17th century) and in Germany, Holland, and Sweden, although French government attempts to control the guilds were frustrated in the 16th century and succeeded in both France and Prussia only in the 17th century. Nor was the abandonment of mercantilism anywhere so clear and complete as in Britain.

Under this mixed system, with expanding markets and nationalistic economic planning, division of labor was extended both internationally and intranationally, and trade grew. But attempts to discourage movement from the land and the development of sheep farming, in Britain, impeded structural change. Policy was realistic in seeking to provide security, but mistaken in some of its interpretations of national interest (especially concerning the desirability of the import of bullion). But policy was beyond the currently available techniques of social control, and became rigid and corrupt. Above all, by furnishing a target for Adam Smith's discussion of the national interest and the proper scope of state action, it provided a foundation for the economics of the 19th century.

The market reached the zenith of its influence as a coordinating instrument in industrial societies in western Europe and the U.S.A. in the 19th century. Adam Smith's *Wealth of Nations*, a polemic in favor of economic organization involving a minimum of government control and predominant reliance upon the "invisible hand" coordinating economic activity through the market, ushered in accelerated industrial development. Much preexisting state regulation was eliminated. In Britain, import duties were reduced from 1823 to 1827, and more comprehensively in 1842. The Corn Laws were finally repealed in 1846, and the Navigation Laws in 1849. The guilds had largely disappeared by the 18th century, mainly because their restrictive policies had stimulated competing and cheaper methods of production (especially home work outside the towns). The statutes controlling them were mostly in abeyance, but were not finally repealed until 1835. In France the freedom of industry was proclaimed in 1791 and the guilds were abolished. In Germany legislation withdrawing the privileges of guilds was not repealed in all states until 1865.

But while some government controls were being removed others were being imposed, almost in step with the removals. *Laissez faire* was a powerful myth in Holland, Belgium, and the U.S.A., and even in Britain. New enterprises desired new freedoms and new services—they obtained them from the state. Old enterprises and workers lost their old protections and sought new ones. In 1799 the British government placed the first slender restrictions on the freedom of employers to bargain with workers. The first effective Factory Act was passed in 1833, the Miners Act in 1842, and the important Ten Hours Act in 1847. The government was influencing the types of persons who could be employed, the conditions of their work, and their liberty to form labor unions. In the 1840s the government began to protect public health, and later to regulate and require education. It established a few controls over monopolies (particularly gas and railroads). The movement was cumulative after 1832. The landed classes, sceptical of the identity of national and private interests, committed the state to intervention in nearly every economic activity, usually on humanitarian and anti-industrial grounds.[4]

In the U.S.A. slavery was maintained until the Civil War, industry was protected against foreign competition, labor union activities were controlled, banking was controlled, and from about the 1860s there were various controls over monopolies. France and Germany, more cautious about reliance on the market, never altogether abandoned mercantilism, and the state has always been an integrating force. For a few years Germany seemed likely to embrace *laissez faire*, but an ambitious new business class arguing for the protection of infant industries against well established British ones[5] brought about a reaction in the 1870s. Germany turned to an economy regulated by the state along nationalist lines (involving tariffs, the planning of railroads with strategic considerations in mind, taxation for heavy armaments, and the like), with a hierarchical social organization based on the army, the bureaucracy, big business and the proletariat.

The market performed one outstanding economic function in the developing societies of western Europe and the U.S.A. in the 18th and 19th centuries. It served to bring about the structural changes that converted

---

[4] Brebner, "Laisser Faire in Nineteenth Century Britain," *Tasks of Economic History,* 1948, 65, 66, 69.

[5] List, Friedrich, *The National System of Political Economy,* 1841.

their manufacturing from a craft to an industrial base. People were up-rooted and resources redeployed through an impersonal market agency that, unlike a government achieving the same results, could not be blamed (although there was bitter complaint). The possibility that development might be too rapid was never effectively articulated, and periodic unemployment (which averaged 25% in about three-quarters of the years between 1856 and 1913 in Britain)[6] was attributed to the rigidity of wage rates and the immobility of the labor force. But it now appears that authority was only temporarily eclipsed by the market as a regulator of economic life.

The war of 1914-18 accelerated the movement towards increasing reliance on governments for the control of economies. Wars undermine confidence in the identity of individual and national interests, which had weakened in the preceding few decades. The rational attitudes upon which scientific and industrial progress had been built were increasingly applied to social organization[7] and to questioning whether societies were organized so that they could adapt means to ends. Interest shifted from the question whether there was a natural right to property, to how, and how well, the institution worked. Was the prevailing inequality of incomes desirable? Unemployment, poverty, poor housing, and the like suggested defects in means or ends or both. The instability of production, evidenced by periodic depressions, caused general uneasiness. The development of monopolies caused more concern in the U.S.A. than elsewhere.

The pre-war trend towards the expansion of government controls of the economy was resumed after the war. Wartime controls of economic resources in developed countries (by price control, rationing, and the allocation of labor and materials) were eliminated, but international markets never fully regained even their pre-war freedom. The gold standard, suspended in most belligerent countries in time of war, was only slowly reestablished. Recurrent unemployment was recognized as a serious threat to the survival of capitalist systems. Governments attempted to meet the threat with a minimum of incursion into the scope of the market as a coordinator of their economies. They sought to limit control to the monetary system, thus improving the operation of the price system.

The depression that began in 1929 frustrated these efforts. The discount rate and open-market operations proved to be weak instruments of control and the government in the U.S.A. adopted a countercyclical fiscal policy, increasing public spending in 1933 to offset the shrinkage of private spending. Increased public relief payments placed added purchasing power where it would revive the consumers' goods industries, and investment in public works increased employment generally by increasing demand for producers' goods. As increased taxation to finance these opera-

---

[6] Beveridge, *Full Employment and a Free Society*, 43.
[7] Veblen, *Industrial Germany*.

tions would have neutralized them, the government operated with a budget deficit. But this policy stimulated questioning as to the extent to which the market was being undercut. Investments in parks, highways, schools, and other capital goods commonly regarded as the proper province of government, cannot be selected by applying any market test because they provide no financial income. But investments that promise income usually compete with private enterprise and narrow the scope of private enterprise. In fact, however, the only government investments in the U.S.A. in the 1930s that competed at all seriously with private production were in the electric power industry, where the private corporations had underestimated the elasticity of demand for electricity; the industry had lost public sympathy because of the financial reorganizations of the 1920s; and the public projects were so large that they were often beyond the reach of private investment. The policy could be truly countercyclical, however, only if government debts expanded during depressions were reduced during periods of business expansion by increased taxation. The political feasibility of this second half of the program remains in doubt.

The government in the U.S.A. did not in fact assume that this type of intervention made more specific controls unnecessary. After 1933 the New Deal program included further interventions in banking; control over the flotation of securities, stock and produce exchanges, and public utilities; provision for social security, and assistance to agriculture. Nevertheless, the experiment in countercyclical fiscal policy has dominated all subsequent full-employment policies.

In 1933 Sweden, for instance, adopted the principle that public works expenditure should be increased in periods of unemployment, but did not put the program into practice because of increases in exports and strikes in the building trades. In 1937, the Riksdag (parliament) divided the national budget into a revenue budget to be balanced annually and a capital budget whose items were to be transferred to the former by specified annual percentages. This policy was not effectuated because of the outbreak of war and large government deficits due to armaments. In 1945, a number of new stabilization devices were introduced, including government subsidies for the purchase of durable goods by families receiving family endowment grants in time of depression. But cyclical adjustment of unemployment benefits was rejected. The categories of expenditure to be placed in the capital budget were widened. Corporations are permitted to make tax-free allocations of profits to reserve, provided these reserves are spent in years designated by the government.[8] But the depression for which the government prepared in 1945 did not materialize and, faced with overemployment, the government did not put into operation the half of the plan intended for periods of inflation but, on the contrary, adopted the inflationary policy of abolishing the turnover tax, and relied on direct

---

[8] U.N., *Maintenance of Full Employment*, 1949, 17.

controls of building. In December, 1948, however, the president of the Riksbank resigned, protesting that government measures against inflation had been inadequate and that the Bank of Sweden had become a passive instrument for carrying out the policies of the party in power. By 1949, however, the government had set aside a fund of about $41 million out of surpluses on the annual budget to be used to finance a public works program if unemployment appeared, and which would be supplemented with further funds if necessary.

The war of 1939-45 further magnified the element of authority in the capitalist economies. During the war, all the principal belligerents again controlled production. They allocated all important materials and often labor, rationed consumer goods, controlled prices and the use of capital and credit, and used taxes, subsidies, and government operations in foreign trade to channel resources into war. In fact, their economies moved considerably closer to the Russian methods of organization and control. In the U.S.A. most controls were removed soon after the end of the war. But in most other countries controls continued because it was doubted that an unaided market system could solve their economic problems.

Full employment has been accepted as an objective of state policy in most countries. New Zealand, Britain, Norway, Sweden, and Switzerland decided to finance increased expenditures in time of depression by increased budget deficits rather than by taxation.[9] The coalition government in Britain announced in 1944, before the war ended, that one of its primary aims would be the "maintenance of a high and stable level of employment."[10] Prices and wages must be reasonably stable and there must be mobility of workers among occupations and localities. To maintain total expenditure, the government was "prepared to take responsibility for taking action to arrest . . . a threatened slump"; it was no longer willing to wait for a depression to correct itself, and recognized that control through the interest rate and monetary policy was not sufficient. To regulate capital expenditure the government would encourage private enterprises to plan their expenditure in accordance with the stabilization policy, possibly providing deferred tax credits; it would influence public capital expenditures, as far as possible, to offset fluctuations in private expenditure, setting a target for public works expenditure each year. If these measures did not stabilize employment, consumption expenditures would have to be adjusted, by raising the weekly contributions of employers and employed under the new social insurance system in times of full employment, and lowering them in times of unemployment. If this device was not enough, the general tax system would be adjusted, although the budget must be balanced over long periods of time. The National Insurance Act in 1948 provided some stabilizing machinery; the receipts and payments there-

---

[9] *Ibid.*, 18.

[10] U.K., *White Paper on Employment Policy*, 1944, Cmd. 6527.

under are expected to balance with an unemployment rate of about 8.5%. When unemployment is below this level the system operates in a deflationary direction, and when unemployment is above it, unemployment benefits in excess of receipts are expected to offset about one-tenth of the decline in purchasing power.[11]

In the U.S.A. Congress refused to include in the Full Employment Act of 1946 a commitment to maintain "full employment," but did place on the national government responsibility "to use all practical means consistent with its needs and other essential considerations of national policy . . . to coordinate and utilize all its plans, functions, and resources" to "maintain maximum production, employment, and purchasing power." The law provided, however, only that the President must send an economic report to Congress at the beginning of each session, which report would set out levels of employment, production, and purchasing power necessary to achieve the objectives of the Act, prescribe a program, and recommend legislation.

Postwar reconstruction, rather than the maintenance of full employment, in fact dominated the policies of most of the developed countries other than the U.S.A. in the immediate postwar years. There was, however, considerable unemployment in Belgium after 1949, and in Italy in most postwar years. Industrial plant, agricultural investments, transport systems and housing had been in varying degrees destroyed or under-maintained, and inventories of materials had been run down. Much capital was needed for redevelopment but national incomes had fallen, and foreign markets and foreign investments had been lost. Propensities to save and invest had been reduced in some countries by uncertainty about their political and economic future. Even more disturbing, private entrepreneurs had failed to maintain and improve the productive system in the older west European industrial countries even in pre-war years. Yet wartime governments had promised workers a better postwar world. This combination of difficulties was too serious to be solved by the market system alone. In the U.S.A., which did revert to the market, prices rose because of the efforts of domestic consumers, and many foreign buyers, to exercise purchasing power accumulated in wartime or subsequently borrowed. Belgium followed a similar policy.

In other countries the wartime controls were only gradually relaxed, and were used in the meantime to convert their economies from war to recovery from war and modernization. These objectives were converted into more or less specific national plans in all European countries except Finland, Switzerland, and Spain.[12] Belgium, the Netherlands, and New Zealand have all emphasized that, because employment in those countries is greatly affected by conditions of foreign trade, their efforts to maintain

11 U.N., *Maintenance of Full Employment*, 1949, 13.

12 Harris, *Economic Planning, passim*.

full employment may be frustrated by deflationary elements abroad.[13] The New Zealand government, however, plans to insulate the economy "at least for a few years from the worst of the fluctuations of the more highly industrialized overseas countries." In Australia there is no single authority charged with responsibility for national economic planning, but a number of bodies plan in specific fields. In New Zealand "economic development . . . has long been considered a normal part of government activity" and no single body has been made responsible for it. In the Union of South Africa, an advisory Social and Economic Planning Council was established in 1942 to formulate an integrated economic policy. This planning was facilitated by knowledge of the Russian five-year plans, and the methods of securing consistency in the various parts of the plan. Belligerent governments had faced these problems when allocating materials in war time. But economists also contributed by their analyses of the flow of purchasing power and its influence upon production in capitalist countries. The British, Netherlands, and Norwegian governments, for instance, have published national accounts summarizing the operations of their economies as a whole.[14]

Economic planning by government violates the basic premise of a capitalist society that resource allocation should depend on private decisions expressed through the price and market system. The British government drew a sharp distinction between totalitarian and economic planning, and insisted that "a democratic government must conduct its economic planning in a manner which preserves the maximum possible freedom of choice to the individual citizen. . . . The government must lay down the economic tasks for the nation; it must say which things are the most important and what the objectives of policy should be and should give as much information as possible to guide the nation's economic activity; it must use its powers of economic control to influence the course of development in the desired direction. When the working pattern has thus been set, it is only by the combined effort of the whole people that the nation can move towards its objective of carrying out the first things first and so make the best use of its resources." "The execution of the plan must be much more a matter for cooperation between the government, industry, and the people than of rigid application by the state of controls and compulsions."[15]

West European countries in general have sought a division of coordinating functions between authority and the market that will preserve as much of the market system as possible, although government controls are enlarged. The tripartite committee (representing business, labor unions, and the government) appointed in Britain in 1947 to draft a four-

[13] U.N., *Maintenance of Full Employment*, 1949, 10.
[14] Harris, *op. cit.*, 158, 347, 361.
[15] U.K., *Economic Survey for 1947*, Cmd. 7046.

year plan was advisory only. France rejected a proposal to set up a Ministry of National Planning in 1944 to control the economic policy of the country, and set up an advisory planning council. The Dutch National Welfare Plan of 1946 was advisory. In Sweden a *Conjunctur Institute,* a semi-independent agency within the treasury, makes estimates of employment, investment and the like, and submits proposals to the government, which, however, makes its own decisions. Thus plans are not complete programs to be enforced by the state, but a set of considered and mutually consistent objectives for guidance of governments in the exercise of specific controls and of business concerns. Most of them focus on estimates of the amount of investment needed to make up for wartime devastation and lagging structural change and modernization in pre-war years.

Partial nationalization necessitates the integration of the nationalized and private sectors which may be achieved through the prices charged by the nationalized undertakings and competition between nationalized and private enterprises. The nationalized industries in Britain and France are mostly monopolies providing goods and services that enter into the costs of most other industry. Generally Britain more than France has restricted losses on nationalized operations (Ch. 13). Competition between nationalized and private industry could limit the policies of nationalized industry, but is not very common because in the partly socialized economies the nationalized industries are typically those needing large size for minimum cost. In Britain, however, the government railroad and truck services competed, until 1952, with private firms transporting goods in their own trucks, although the latter were hampered because they could not obtain return loads. The nationalized steel industry also competed somewhat with private producers until 1952 through its fabricating subsidiaries. Privately owned fabricators producing 33% of the tubes, 40% of the wire, and 25% of the cold rolled strip had to obtain their raw materials from the nationalized industry. The Indian government is establishing a steel mill, and has announced that all new firms in certain industries shall be operated by the state. If such firms are established, they will compete with existing private firms. Even where nationalized industries do not meet domestic competition, if they export they will still be limited, at least in their export trade, by competition. In the export market for coal, there may be competition among nationalized industries in France, Britain, and Poland.

Authoritarian control, therefore, expanded at the expense of market coordination during the first half of the 20th century. The market revealed little capacity to guide steady economic progress, and recurrent depressions showed no sign of diminution. Nor did the market achieve necessary adjustments in the allocation of resources in a changing world. In some directions it generated monopolies; this undermined its effectiveness and induced regulation in the U.S.A. and nationalization in western Europe.

The increasing organization of workers and increasing power of their organizations sometimes impede changes in the technique of production that might reduce the demand for labor. They may insist on the employment of unnecessary workers and obstruct mobility among industries and locations. Centralized control of labor also increases bilateral monopolies in labor markets, leading to indeterminate bargaining and periodic cessations of production. In highly differentiated societies much of the whole system can be crippled by a conflict in one sector.

Two wars causing high taxation and diversions of resources to military purposes have further undermined the market, but it may have lost vitality because interest in risk-taking has waned among both workers and businessmen while interest in security has waxed. Such a change in the general spirit of society raises questions that go beyond the sphere of economics. A highly competitive society is flexible and may achieve rapid development but also stomach ulcers and neuroses. There may be a limit to the tension and upset that populations will accept. It has been said[16] that capital and labor in Britain agree in desiring a non-competitive social order. Neither desires change at a pace that involves loss of investment or jobs. "The whole climate of a mature civilization militates against the crudities and disturbances of a turbulent economic system. . . . All the fruits of success in England give a man the strongest possible interest in a quiet life," which makes him unadventurous.

The outcome of the shifts in the relative importance of control and the market as integrating principles is obscure because the deficiencies of the market system have been overlaid by problems created by war and internal shifts in political power that increase the emphasis on income redistribution. In Britain, social revolution was superimposed on pre-war difficulties. The Labor Party elected to office in 1945 on a program of "socialism in our time" raised hopes in the minds of the workers of a better world. In 1946 Britain was planning national health and education services, the extension of social insurance, the expansion of building activity, the repair of war damage, and making good arrears of maintenance due to war. Efforts to re-equip various industries and at the same time export 75% more by volume than in 1938, to pursue a policy of colonial development, maintain armed forces about twice the pre-war level, and to shoulder part of the responsibility for western Germany were beyond the resources of the country. In France, resistance to political change produced uncertainty and unwillingness to invest when foreign assets had been lost, and much capital was needed to modernize the industrial system, and replace the destruction of war.

Production increased in western Europe between 1945 and 1951 less than was hoped, but more than after 1918 or 1929. The industrial output of western Germany in 1951 was 20% above 1938, and industrial output in the

---

[16] *Economist* July 2, 1949.

rest of Europe about 50% above 1938. Increases of 60% to 80% occurred in eight smaller industrial countries, including former neutrals. Agricultural output increased less, except in Britain, and there was no increase in output per head of the population in Italy, France, and Germany. The output of services increased less than that of commodities. The total national product in Germany and Italy was about 12% higher in 1951 than in 1938, of France 20%, of Switzerland, the Netherlands, Finland, Denmark, Belgium, and Britain 30%, and that of Sweden 50% above 1938. But, after allowing for international transactions, real incomes increased less. Losses of income from foreign investments were especially heavy in the Netherlands, Britain, and France, but nowhere more than 3% of national product. Deterioration in the terms of trade was equivalent to about 3% of the output of western Europe, but up to 6% in Britain, the Netherlands, and Denmark.

Real national income per head of population (which was affected by population increases) was lower in 1951 than in 1938 in western Germany, about the same in Italy, about 10% higher in the Netherlands, 10 to 15% higher in Britain, France, and Denmark, 20% higher in Switzerland, 25% higher in Belgium, and over 30% higher in Sweden. Consumption, however, increased less because of expenditures on defense and investment. The proportion of the national income devoted to military purposes in 1951 was about the same as in 1938 in France and slightly higher in Britain, but it almost doubled in some other countries. Expenditure on capital goods between 1947 and 1952 was higher than in any corresponding period between the wars. In all except Britain it was also a higher proportion of national income. In Britain productive investment increased but there was a sharp drop in investment in housing.[17]

The contribution of governments to this outcome is difficult to appraise. Outside events, such as loans and grants from the U.S.A., later the European Recovery Program and the Mutual Security program, contributed considerably. The application of integrated public policies ran into obstacles because of the difficulty of implementing central plans in capitalist economies. Governments could not directly determine the structure of wages and prices to induce production, or control the distribution of incomes. Wages were a matter of political bargaining. Being part of a world economy, the western European countries were influenced by events in the outside world that affected their foreign trade.

Most of west European countries found it impossible to control their economies through general monetary and fiscal policies. The aggregate demand for consumption and investment goods was not held down by budget surpluses because of the difficulty of increasing already high levels of taxation (which absorbed 20% to 25% of gross national product in the

---

[17] U.N., *Econ. Surv. of Europe Since the War*, 1953, 53 ff.

Scandinavian countries and 33% in Britain). In the presence of full employment, prices rose and governments in varying degrees controlled inflation by direct regulation of prices and demand. Denmark, the Netherlands, Norway, Sweden, and Britain maintained full employment with lower price increases than in other parts of Europe through considerably more direct control than before the war. In addition to rationing and price controls they regulated investment, except in Denmark and the Netherlands (through building licenses, allocations of materials, licensing imports of machinery, or informal controls).

France maintained full employment but suffered a price increase of 400% between 1945 and 1952. Under the Monnet Plan the government invested on a larger scale than elsewhere in western Europe to steer capital into providing a foundation for the future growth of the economy. The plan lagged behind schedule, and was spread over two additional years in 1949, but investment under it never exceeded 20% of all fixed investment. Nevertheless, investment and consumption demand was high, and after 1947 there were few restrictions on the spending of incomes, and few allocations of resources. Apparently inflation was the only politically acceptable means of checking consumption and achieving the investment of a higher share of all resources than before the war. Government control of wages for much of the period in fact threw much of the burden of investment on wage earners, mostly in the form of longer hours. Belgium, Italy, and West Germany maintained relative price stability, but suffered unemployment. In many countries low rates of interest inherited from the war, and further lowered immediately after the war, stimulated inflation. Rising wages and prices encouraged imports and discouraged exports, thus increasing the difficulty of settling international balances and necessitating resort to controls of foreign trade (Ch. 26).

Reform of the distribution of incomes, superimposed on the effort to stimulate production, often reduced the profit incentive to production and raised the wage incentive to consumption. Norway went farthest in preventing high profits, and Britain in taxing them away. In the Netherlands and France much of the postwar adjustment was made by reducing working class consumption. In western Germany the influx of refugees weakened the bargaining power of workers, who suffered while profit recipients gained. In fact, governments increasingly abandoned efforts at wide economic planning in the effort to suppress inflation, and it remains to be discovered whether private enterprise economies can reach a full employment level of private capital formation without inflation or, more fundamentally, whether a system based on self interest can command the kind and degree of loyalty necessary to economic growth.[18]

---

[18] Clark, J. M., in National Bureau of Economic Research, *Problems in the Study of Economic Growth*, 35.

4. SOCIALIST SOCIETIES

The socialist societies have adopted industrial methods of production within a social framework relying less on the market and more upon authority than in the countries that developed in the 19th century. Authority is highly centralized. Private property is restricted in the main to consumption goods (excluding housing). The land and all means of production are vested in the state which thereby acquires direct control over production. The government plans the allocation of resources among consumption, military purposes, and economic development by defining production targets for all branches of production. It plans the distribution of incomes through its control of wage scales. It plans the rate of economic progress by basing the inputs of resources on planned increases in productivity, as well as on planned output. Detailed controls all operate within this framework. Five-year plans are modified in annual and sometimes quarterly plans embodying minor amendments of the annual plan.

Five-year plans[19] have covered the periods from 1927-32, 1932-37, 1937-42; 1946-50 and 1951-5. The outbreak of war prevented the completion of the third plan. The plans also cover differing territory and population. Russia took over Polish, Finnish, and Rumanian provinces, and Lithuania, Latvia, and Estonia in 1939 and 1940, increasing its population some 13%. The various changes in 1944 and 1945 involved a net population increase of only one million.[20] The plans have become increasingly comprehensive. The General Planning Commission, established in 1921, was empowered to work out a plan for the reconstruction of the national economy. In 1925, it drew up an annual plan in the form of "Control Figures of the National Economy" for 1925-26. Some years later Gosplan's Control Figures became a plan for the national economy.[21] In the course of subsequent administrative reorganizations, planning institutions were set up in every republic and in every administrative and economic district. In 1935, the State Planning Committee was reorganized, the powers of the chairman being enlarged and a committee of seventy members being appointed.

Before the end of each year the estimated figures for that year are compiled and the Council of Ministers defines the broad objectives of the plan for the succeeding year. The State Planning Committee and the commissariats simultaneously compile specific plans. The commissariats consult their enterprises, which compile tables of their requirements to fulfill the plan, and may suggest changes. The State Planning Committee compares its plans with those of the commissariats and compiles a compromise plan for submission to the Council of Ministers, which prescribes the final plan. This procedure is so time-consuming that plans are often not approved before the beginning of the plan period. The plan for 1951 to

---

19 Schwartz, *op. cit.*, Ch. V.
20 Bergson and Heymann, *Soviet National Income and Product 1940-1948*, 6.
21 Baykov, *The Development of the Soviet Economic System*, 426.

1955 was approved only after one-third of the plan period had elapsed. Counter-planning by workers has been encouraged, but in practice has had only a peripheral effect on the over-all plan.

One part of the staff of Gosplan consists of a series of sections, each responsible for a sector of production. A second part is concerned with the coordination of the various parts of the plan[22] by the use of "balanced estimates." Some hundreds of these estimates are in physical terms to ensure that the demands for a raw material, type of equipment, or other intermediate goods implicit in the general plan are consistent with the planned output of the material or product. Other "synthetic" balances check the consistency of the plan in financial or labor terms. The money and credit supply is coordinated with the anticipated demand for it and the demand for and supply of labor are similarly checked. Balances are also made on a territorial basis. In 1940 Gosplan worked out its first plan for improving techniques of production. The plans become increasingly specific as they pass down through the Ministries to the enterprises.

Markets, although minor, are not unimportant. Consumer goods are distributed through the market in that they are sold for money and purchasers are free to allocate their expenditures (except when goods were rationed, from 1928-35 and from 1939-47). Nevertheless, Stalin regarded the market as a transitional device for use on the way to real communism.[23] But the prices of consumer goods are determined by the government to equate demand and supply. The mechanism in capitalist countries for adjusting supply in order to move prices towards costs does not exist in Russia. Resources flow in accordance with the plan, although the government does investigate consumer preferences.[24] Prices may also diverge from supply-demand prices because the actual supply diverges from the anticipated demand.

Prices and money are also used as a method of controlling the use of resources. Costs are measured in money, and there is constant pressure to reduce them by reducing the intake of resources for a given output, or changing the kind and proportions of resources used (taking their relative prices into account). From the adoption of full-scale planning in 1927-49, "1926-7 prices" were used to measure output, labor productivity, and industrial costs.[25] New products were included at "assimilated prices" fixed in a variety of ways at the time of introduction. By 1948 a considerable number of the "constant 1926-7 prices" were in fact "assimilated prices."

The prices of goods purchased by production enterprises have sometimes been held above the costs of production to ensure their use only for

---

[22] Baykov, *op. cit.*, 448; Schwartz, *op. cit.*, 148, 161.
[23] Stalin, in *Bolshevik*, *cit. N.Y. Times*, Oct. 4, 1952.
[24] Chossudowsky, E. M., "Derationing in the U.S.S.R." *Rev. of Econ. Stud.*, 1941, 22.
[25] Kaser, "Soviet Planning and the Price Mechanism," LX *Ec. Jour.*, 1950, 81.

the most important purposes. But from 1927 to 1936 many products, especially those of heavy industry, were transferred at prices below their cost of production (the difference being covered by state subsidies). These subsidies were restricted after 1936, some transfer prices being raised to cover costs but some costs being reduced. After 1939 subsidies were restored and rose from 2.7% of gross national product in 1937 to 6.5% in 1948, after which date they were again restricted when plans were for the first time expressed in current rubles. The proportion of all subsidies paid for producers goods increased from 32% to 54% between 1937 and 1948, and in the latter year they represented 22.7% of the prices of fixed capital goods.[26] In planning investment the prices used were generally equal to the above transfer prices after adding back subsidies (i.e., investment plans were based more nearly on actual costs). Unless the prices of the means of production are proportionate (not necessarily equal) to the real costs of producing each, the minimization of money costs of production will not ensure the most economical fulfillment of planned objectives. It has in fact proved difficult to set prices to achieve economical fulfillment, and most important intermediate products are allocated among enterprises, not through the monetary demand, but directly from Moscow (more than 1600 being allocated in 1952).[27]

Capital enters into the current costs of enterprises through charges for depreciation as in capitalist economies. But interest is charged only to cooperative, and not to government enterprises (except on working capital in excess of that allotted). But capital is allocated among sectors not on the basis of the profit prospects of each but in accord with the production plan. The government grants credits to enterprises which it plans to expand unless the enterprise can finance the expansion out of its own resources. Wages enter into costs and wage rates, and methods of calculation are determined by the government to stimulate output and to bring about the allocation of labor required by the plan in a relatively free market for labor until 1940. But since 1940 labor has been severely controlled.[28] Finally, enterprises pay taxes and receive subsidies. Excise or turnover taxes approximately bridge the gap between planned cost of production and the selling prices necessary to reduce demand to supply. They indicate to some extent the disparity between the production plan and that which would result from following consumer choice. Enterprises also pay to the government a fixed share of their profits. The accounts of the enterprises indicate in a general way the extent to which they have achieved their targets of output, prices, and costs, but the government also emphasizes production in excess of the plan (which may be attained at the expense of under-

---

[26] Bergson and Heymann, *op. cit.*, 54, 66, 91.

[27] *N.Y. Times*, June 16, 1952.

[28] Bergson, *The Structure of Soviet Wages*, 153, 208, Ch. 20; Bergson and Heymann, *op. cit.*, 14.

achievement in other sectors) materials consumed, and the trend of costs (Ch. 13).

The outcome of this regulation of the economy has been a remarkable increase in output. Net national income as officially calculated increased at an annual average rate of 16% between 1928 and 1937, about 11% between 1937 and 1940, 19% between 1948 and 1950, and 12% between 1950 and 1951,[29] but in 1950 it was only about 40% above 1940. The fifth Five-Year Plan (for 1951-5)[30] contemplates an increase of 60% in national income (70% in industrial output and 40 to 50% in agricultural output). By 1952 national income had already increased 24%, and gross industrial production 70%. But measurement of the national product is extremely difficult during periods when its composition and relative costs and prices change rapidly. Any measurement leans heavily on the pattern of prices used (for example, at the beginning or the end of the period). As physical output rises in the process of industrialization, costs fall, and the use of costs at the end of the period as the basis for measuring changes throughout the period gives a lower, and often a strikingly lower, rate of growth than if costs at the beginning of the period are used.[31] The government has expressed the total value of industrial production in ruble values of the fiscal year 1926 to 1927. New products have been included at their prices during the first year of their production, which are likely to be high, and exaggerate increases in production. Inflation beginning in 1930 further exaggerated the official measures. Removal of the inflationary bias and the use of 1926-7 prices suggests an average annual increase in national income of about 8% from 1928 to 1937, but if 1937 costs and prices were used the average annual increase was only about 5%.[32] Russia recovered from the war of 1939-45 faster than many western commentators had expected, but while Russian official statistics (in "1926-7 rubles") suggest a national income in 1948 16% above that of 1940, physical output may have been no larger than in 1940, if not smaller, despite the annexations of territory, mostly in 1939 and 1940.

These increases have been achieved partly by increases in population, from 147 millions in 1926 to about 200 millions in 1950, but chiefly by expanding the industrial sector. In 1914, industry was relatively small but growing, and agriculture was technologically backward. Agricultural technology has been improved, but mechanization, the use of fertilizers, seed selection, irrigation, and agricultural reorganization have in the main reduced the toil of agricultural labor rather than increased output. The introduction of tractors was partly offset by the decline in draft animals.[33]

---

[29] Grossman, in Bergson (ed.), *Soviet Economic Growth*, 9.
[30] U.N., *Econ. Surv. of Europe Since the War*, 1953, 38 ff.
[31] Grossman, in Bergson, *op. cit.*, 3.
[32] *Ibid.*, 5.
[33] U.N., *Econ. Surv. of Europe Since the War*, 1953, 46.

But about 16% of the agricultural population was pushed, or attracted, into urban life between 1926 and 1938, and made much of the expansion of industry possible. In spite of heavy loss of life during the war, the agricultural population has fallen little since 1939, and the present plan implies a slight increase. By 1955 non-agricultural employment will have increased by about the same amount as the working population, and increases in industrial output are expected to come from 50% increases in product per worker rather than from increased employment. The increase in agricultural output will come from increases in yield per acre, since the sown area is to increase only 16%.

The expansion of industry has been made possible by a high rate of investment, maintained by holding down consumption. "The party has firmly and unswervingly implemented its line in the struggle against the Trotskyist and right wing capitulators and traitors who opposed the construction of heavy industry and demanded the transfer of funds from heavy to light industry. Acceptance of these proposals would have meant the doom of our revolution . . . we would have found ourselves disarmed in the face of capitalist encirclement."[34] Net investment adjusted to take full account of depreciation has been estimated to have been 12% to 15% of gross national product in non-war years (compared with 6% to 11% in the U.S.A. in non-war and non-depression years).[35] Investment both in industry and in agriculture has been a much larger proportion of all investment than in the U.S.A., and investment in trade much less. Between 1913 and 1940, the output of coal increased nearly 470%, steel 335%, petroleum 240%, and electric power nearly 5000% (from previously low levels). In these fields, Russian achievements brought the economy to about the position of the U.S.A. from 1905-15, and took about as long. But they were attained in spite of revolution and severe devastation in war (neither of which impeded development in the U.S.A.), and they were financed almost wholly from internal sources. But Russia had a larger population than the U.S.A. and could take over a more advanced technology from abroad.

The war of 1939-45 retarded this process by eight or nine years, but industrial output probably increased as much in the ten-year period 1940-50 as under pre-war or present five-year plans. The absorption into industry of more than the manpower planned, together with war damage, prevented the fulfillment of the plans for consumer goods or agriculture. But, allowing for enlargement of territory and population, agricultural output was about the same in 1950 as in 1937. National income was above 1939, but the bulk of the increase had been devoted to defense and investment and consumption was about on the pre-war level. The increases in physical output in some of the major industries between 1937 and 1950

---

34 Premier Malenkov: speech before Supreme Soviet, cit. N.Y. Times, Aug. 10, 1953.
35 Kaplan, in Bergson (ed.), op. cit., 46.

were coal and lignite 100%, crude petroleum 30%, electric power 150%, steel ingots 60%, rolled metal 50%, cement 100%, mineral fertilizer 100%, tractors 90%, automobiles and trucks 100%. But grain production was about the same. Cotton cloth production increased 10%, woolen cloth 60%, and leather shoes 45%.[36] In 1951, Russia, with a population of 207 million (which is about the same as that of western Europe), produced about half as much coal, electricity, and steel as western Europe. But output is increasing faster than can be expected in western Europe, and by 1960 Russian production of the major industrial raw materials may be about equal to that of the seven most industrialized countries of western Europe.

The five-year plan targets for industry for 1951-55 appear likely to be reached, (that for manpower in three years). But the planned increase in average yield per acre in agriculture of 40% in five years is less likely to be attained, although the plan provides for an increase of 50% in the number of tractors and 88% in the supply of fertilizer in the five years. In 1950 yields were 25 to 33% higher than in Czarist Russia, but grain yields did not increase during 1951 and 1952. Investment during the 1951 to 1955 period is planned to be 90% above that during the five years 1946 to 1950, investment in industry being doubled and in agriculture more than doubled while the investment in transport, communication and housing will increase less. The chief industrial investment will continue to be in heavy industry and the generation of electricity.[37] But in 1953 after the death of Stalin the new premier, Malenkov, recognized that the Russian population was ill-fed, ill-clothed, and ill-housed. The government decided to increase the production of consumption goods and, even more important to enforce plan fulfillment in this sector more vigorously. It proposed to increase its productive efficiency by reducing the substandard proportion of output and adjusting wage scales. The government also ordered an increase in the number of retail stores and an improvement in their service.[38] Rapid industrialization has been achieved, however, at a great cost in personal freedom. This loss may, moreover, inhibit research and innovation, although there is yet no evidence of such an effect.

The eastern European countries under the influence of Russia have all been assimilating their economic organization to that of Russia, with central planning, nationalized industry, and collectivized agriculture. Governments have sought to achieve industrial revolutions more drastic than anything attempted in western Europe,[39] with high rates of capital accumulation and limited concessions to consumers. In general, until about 1949, they were primarily concerned with recovery from war and conversion of the social framework to the Russian pattern. All the countries

[36] Bergson and Heymann, op. cit., 9.
[37] U.N., Econ. Surv. of Europe Since the War, 1953, 48.
[38] U.N., Econ. Surv. of Europe in 1953, 48.
[39] U.N., Econ. Surv. of Europe Since the War, 1953, Ch. 3.

nationalized foreign trade. In Poland and Czechoslovakia, all large-scale industry was nationalized soon after the war, many of the former owners having died, fled, or been expelled. Small firms, however, remained in private hands. Nationalization was more gradual in Hungary, Bulgaria, and Rumania. Land reform measures varied according to the importance of large holdings. Tax changes were small.

All the countries of eastern Europe published two- or three-year reconstruction plans for large-scale industry between 1946 and 1949 aimed at reconstruction, the full utilization of manpower, and the increase of investment, although in all except Poland considerable private industry survived. Outside industry the government set targets, but was in no position to enforce them. Planned industrial output was achieved, and, in Poland and Hungary, surpassed. But the industrial output figures relate to gross output and involved double-counting where the products of one industry are incorporated in the product of another, and this double-counting probably increased. Furthermore, the output of the more imperfectly recorded handicraft sector fell. But bad weather in southern Europe kept agricultural output below target levels in Bulgaria and Rumania in 1948 and 1949.

National income, which is somewhat less open to statistical criticism, was at about the 1937 level in Czechoslovakia in 1948. In Hungary it was 8%, and in Bulgaria 5% above pre-war. In Rumania it was 33% below. But changes in population affected these figures. In Czechoslovakia national income per person was 20% above pre-war. The Hungarian and Bulgarian populations had changed little and were better off than before the war. The Polish population was considerably smaller, and probably slightly better off than before the war. In Rumania and eastern Germany populations were higher and living standards lower than before the war.

Long-term planning began in 1949 and 1950. A second wave of nationalization eliminated most private enterprise except in retailing, where it was starved out by the diversion of supplies to state stores and cooperatives. Tax systems were remodelled to increase the importance of the turnover tax. This, with contributions from profits and depreciation allowances, became the chief source of both investment and government finance. With their economies under more complete control and in better working order, governments began to plan production and the allocation of future increments in production in more detail. All made five-year plans (except Poland, which made a six-year plan) emphasizing investment to achieve rapid industrialization. Poland and Czechoslovakia planned to invest 20 to 25% of the national product, Hungary 25%, Bulgaria 19%, and Rumania 27% by the end of the plan period. All these rates were as high as any in western Europe, where income levels are much higher, and higher than in southern Europe, where incomes are low and there is little central planning. All, like Russia, emphasize the heavy industries, and therefore expect no early increases in the production of consumer goods, and all neglect agriculture. Planned increases in the gross output of producers' goods were 130% in Czechoslovakia (already fairly well industrialized), 154% in Poland, and 226% to 286% in Hungary, Bulgaria, and Albania. Increases in the gross output of consumer goods ranged from 70% in Czechoslovakia to 224% in Albania, and increases in agricultural output from 11% in Albania, 37% in Bulgaria, about 50% in Poland, Czechoslovakia and Hungary, to 88% in Rumania. But after the deterioration of relations with the West they increased emphasis on defense and heavy industry.

Without government intervention increases in income accruing from industrialization would have gone to very low income groups with a high propensity to consume. During the reconstruction period inflation had facilitated investment out of forced savings, but after governments had achieved tight control, inflation was unnecessary for this purpose. They controlled wages (the major source of money incomes), but inflation occurred in most because of miscalculations of the supplies of consumer goods (especially agricultural). But it seems unlikely that inflation will seriously interfere with plans for industrialization. In general, these countries have achieved their targets of industrial output, which means that they are laying the foundation for future economic growth. They have encountered difficulties in particular industries, and notably in agriculture, where weather conditions may cause agricultural incomes to outrun the plan. Control of agriculture will also facilitate transfers of labor to industry as the urban labor reserve runs out. In Poland, Czechoslovakia, Bulgaria, and Hungary, however, industry is expected to absorb an additional 1 or 2% of the population, which is expected to increase 5%. Industrialization will not, therefore, immediately alleviate pressure on the land.[40] Nevertheless, all these countries began in about 1950 to press the collectivization of agriculture for political reasons as in Russia (Ch. 8) and to raise productivity in agriculture. These eastern European socialist countries have been preoccupied with postwar reconstruction and revolutionary changes in political organization to enable them to follow the Russian example, but they have made remarkable economic progress. There is little doubt that development (judged mainly by investment) is considerably faster than it would have been without such active control by the state, but at the expense of political liberty and consumption. They suffer from inefficient coordination, which is not surprising in view of the magnitude of the task and lack of experience in dealing with it.

Yugoslavia adopted the Soviet pattern of economic organization after 1945, and launched a five-year plan in 1946. But it was beyond the resources of the country, and political difficulties eliminated trade with eastern Europe and Russia. After Yugoslavia was expelled from the Communist Information Bureau in 1948 it quietly dropped comprehensive

[40] U.N., *Econ. Surv. of Europe in 1948*, 206.

economic planning. In 1950 the government began to decentralize production decisions to regional councils. At the factory level the factory director was required to report on matters of welfare to a workers' council. In agriculture, compulsory deliveries and consumer rationing were abandoned in 1951. In 1952 all production decisions were made the responsibility of individual enterprises, the control of which was formally vested in the workers. But although the turnover tax was modified, a tax on payrolls took its place and varied among industries. It also varied among enterprises in the same industry and was used to tax efficient and subsidize inefficient enterprises. Enterprises could dispose of their profits (after paying taxes) as they wished—including bonuses on wages (for which in fact a preference was shown). But in 1953 a steeply progressive tax was imposed on profits. In 1954 a tax was imposed on fixed capital, the rate being low for capital-intensive industries like electricity and transport, but otherwise non-discriminatory. Many other changes in taxes were made and the distribution of profits as bonuses on wages was restricted. In general the changes are aimed at reducing the number of decisions to be made by government authorities concerning resource allocation and at correlating efficiency and reward. Government production targets are vague statements of wishes or expectations rather than objectives to be enforced.[41] The most interesting aspect of the program is the attempt to use taxation to guide the economy.

Socialist China is still on the path towards nationalized industry, but the path is different from that of Russia and eastern Europe. The Political Consultative Conference in 1949 proclaimed the power of the state to "coordinate and regulate" the various parts of the economy. The party proposed to control industrial production through private firms producing for state enterprises, mixed government and private enterprises, and government enterprises operated by private interest under concessions.[42] Like Russia it has promoted cooperatives in agriculture and government control of cottage type production. By 1950 it operated under "control figures" and was allocating industrial labor, animals, and vehicles. A series of specialized state trading organizations under the Ministry of Trade had centralized the distribution of many raw materials and finished goods and is intended ultimately to handle most goods and eliminate private trade. The Ministry of Trade controls the production plans of state enterprises, regulates private enterprises and determines prices in the major markets. All state agencies keep accounts with the People's Bank, which operates as a financial clearing house. A five-year plan has been adopted, but socialization has been slow and regulation only limited in

[41] U.N., *Econ. Surv. of Europe in 1953*, 114, 115, 119.

[42] Paauw, D. S., "Economic Principles and State Organization," *Annals Ac. Pol. and Soc. Sci.*, Sept. 1951, 106; Eckstein, A., "Conditions and Prospects for Economic Growth in Communist China," VI *World Politics*, 1954, 21.

effect. The chief emphasis on reconstruction is in Manchuria where all large-scale industry is state-operated.

5. UNDERDEVELOPED COUNTRIES IN PROCESS OF DEVELOPMENT

Failure to develop in the past suggests the necessity for change if a country is now to develop. Insofar as economic stagnation is due to a low level of interest in material things, a change in attitudes may be the primary need if they wish to develop. In most underdeveloped countries there are no more legal obstacles to new activities than there were in European countries when their development accelerated. But mere postponement of development has changed the size and nature of the problem. The methods of production now available in the more developed countries provide an example, but they require more capital than was needed in the early stages of development in the west. The underdeveloped countries are also under pressure to develop more rapidly than western Europe in the 19th century; this also requires much capital and speedy reallocation of resources. Political forces press for improvements in living standards that were achieved in the west only a considerable time after productivity increased. Whether market mechanisms can solve all these problems is doubtful. Faith in the "invisible hand" has waned in the west during the past 40 years, and Russia has demonstrated that rapid economic development can be achieved mainly through centralized authority with only minor reliance on the market.

Agrarian countries seeking development face problems of structural change similar to those in eastern Europe and not very different from western European countries needing reconstruction after 1945. Productivity in agriculture can be improved in some by the utilization of knowledge already available elsewhere, but not within the existing framework of agricultural organization involving poverty and systems of land tenure inhospitable to change. Reorganization of land tenures is a function of the state. Other improvements in agriculture require capital for irrigation, mechanical equipment, and the like. But as the ratio of labor to land is high and increasing, many of these countries have pronounced in favor of industrialization as a means of raising general productivity and relieving population pressure on the land. But neither the capital nor the willingness to invest it in local industry has hitherto been present. Thus the government suggests itself as a source of capital and entrepreneurial leadership. But government in these countries is often in the hands of people with no keen desire for development, which may raise the cost of agricultural labor and reduce incomes from agricultural surpluses. In many, government and administration are neither honest nor competent enough to initiate and effectively control rapid structural change. Many lack the skilled personnel and resources even to draft effective plans— as the International Bank for Reconstruction and Development has repeatedly remarked (Ch. 26). The irresistible argument for state action meets the (at least temporarily) immovable objects of government inertia and inefficiency.

Plans have nevertheless been made for a number of less-developed countries. Most do not plan the disposition of all the resources of the economy (as in socialist countries), but schedule desirable new activities in varying detail, and with varying provisions for effectuation. Some schedule projects by economic sectors and for annual periods projected some time into the future. Some provide for government encouragement and some for government financing.

In the Middle East, economic development was left mainly to private enterprise after 1918, and there was little enterprise. But the governments of Turkey and Iran adopted a variety of measures, ranging from technical and financial assistance to private enterprise to the establishment of public enterprises. In Turkey, a law of 1913 offered privileges to certain enterprises.[43] Soon after Turkey was declared a republic in 1923, the government made plans for economic modernization, including industrialization. In 1933 a policy of state encouragement by offers of free land and tax privileges was abandoned for one of direct state action. But until 1947 there were only uncoordinated sectional plans. Various agencies such as the state banks, the monopoly administration, the postal and telegraph administration, and the railway administration produced plans covering different periods of time. The coordinating agency was the Council of Ministers, but it seems not to have been effective. Iran attempted a comprehensive plan in 1937, mostly concerned with agriculture.

After 1945 planning was resumed in both Iran and Turkey. In Iran a government commission prepared a plan in 1946 and, after a survey of the country's resources by American and British private consulting firms, a seven-year plan was enacted in 1949. The government already operated some of the textile plants and sugar and tobacco plants. Petroleum royalties received by the government had been paid into a special account to be used only for capital expenditures. But they had not always been so used. The new program, based largely on the expenditure of oil royalties, involves an expenditure of $650 million emphasizing first, health, agriculture and education; second, industrialization; third, roads, communications, social reform, and town planning.[44] But little progress has been made in effectuating the plan because of political opposition, organizational difficulties, and the stoppage of oil production due to the nationalization of the Anglo-Iranian Oil Company. The five-year plan in Turkey for 1947-51 was mainly concerned with industrialization, and supplemented earlier plans.[45] In Egypt a five-year plan prepared in 1945 con-

---

43 Bonné, op. cit., 274.
44 I.L.O., Ind. and Lab., July 1949, 29.
45 U.N., Econ. Devel. in Sel. Countries, 1947, 189.

sisted mainly of a list of projects that government departments expected to increase the national income speedily.[46]

In India, planning has been retarded by the disorganization following the achievement of political independence and the consequent refugee and military problems. A number of prominent industrialists published the "Bombay Plan" in 1944, and the Indian Federation of Labor published the "People's Plan." The central government established a Department of Planning and Development that was succeeded by an Advisory Planning Board and, in 1950, by a Planning Commission to assess the country's resources, plan their effective use, and review progress from time to time.[47] In 1952 the government adopted a five-year plan contemplating an expenditure of 20 billion rupees, of which about 60% was to come from domestic and 40% from other sources. About 17.4% is to be invested in agriculture, 24% in transport and communication, 27% in irrigation and power, 8.4% in industry and mining, and 16.4% in the development of "social capital." The plan is expected to increase gross national product some 10%, but to increase real income per head little (because of the rate of population increase). In 1952-53, the government of Pakistan allocated 594 million Pakistan rupees (35% of government revenue) to projects for increasing production.

In Asia and the Far East generally, national plans have been concentrated mainly on agricultural improvement (e.g., the "Colombo Plan" Ch. 22). They anticipate a level of agricultural production in 1956-7 about 19% above the 1934-8 average—this means, however, about 90% of the pre-war average per person.[48] In the Philippines a program for economic development was promulgated in 1935 almost simultaneously with the establishment of the independent commonwealth. The National Economic Council then established was hampered by lack of capital and trained personnel, and the plan was set aside in 1945 because of more immediate problems. But the National Economic Council, reconstituted in 1947, recommended the Five-Year Program adopted by the government for 1949 to 1953. The government encourages new industries by tax exemption, but can engage in production.[49] Planning has been directed chiefly to adjusting the economy to the decline in U.S. payments after 1951 and the progressive imposition of U.S. tariffs after 1954.

Latin American countries have prepared many plans for economic development,[50] but have had difficulty in financing them. They all consist of lists of desirable projects, and none involve government control of all resources. At the outset many emphasized industrialization, but a population increasing about 2.3% a year poses increasing problems of food

[46] *Ibid.*, 190.
[47] *Ibid.*, 151 ff.
[48] F.A.O., *Agriculture in Asia and the Far East,* 1953, 49.
[49] U.N., *Econ. Devel. in Sel. Countries,* 1950, 145 ff.
[50] *Ibid.*, 1947, 1, 18, 49, 62, 77, 84, 93, 117, 132.

supply. A few have already imported food, but such imports cut into the foreign purchasing power available to pay for imports of the capital goods needed for industrialization. Consequently, a number of the five- and six-year plans were amended to include programs for agriculture.

In Mexico the first six-year plan, formulated in 1933, and the second, for 1941-6, were both directed primarily towards industrialization. The Federal Industrial Development Commission was established in 1944 to plan, finance, and establish industries important for the industrialization of the country that have not been established by private interests, and to coordinate public and private investment in industry. But in 1953 the government announced a six-year agricultural plan, to cost almost $2 billion, to expand cultivated areas, improve livestock breeding, and provide more farm equipment and fertilizers. About 30% of the cost was to be met from public sources. In Argentina a five-year plan of national reconstruction and development, aimed at greater economic self-sufficiency, came into operation in 1947. One-third of the expenditure was for the provision of power (including petroleum, gas, and electricity) and much of the remainder for roads, sanitation, schools, railways, a river fleet, and town building, although a number of industries were listed for expansion. The plan was estimated to provide increases in wages of 52%, employment 44%, and motive power 50%. The National Economic Council established in 1947 coordinates public policy regarding economic activity. The government relied on profits from foreign trade, tax privileges, control of exchange rates, subsidies, and mixed public and private corporations to implement the plan, although the executive is empowered to set the production of the establishments under its control. No explicit provision is made for modernizing or diversifying agriculture. But when the price of Argentine exports fell, development was seriously slowed down (Ch. 21).

In Chile, the Ministry of Economics and Commerce was established in 1942 to coordinate all economic agencies of the government, and a National Economic Council in 1946 (with representatives of the various economic interests) was to study and plan the national economy. The Chilean Development Corporation (Ch. 22) executes economic plans prepared by the Council. The Brazilian constitution of 1946 provided for a National Economic Council to study the economic life of the nation and make recommendations. A five-year economic plan was published in 1947, but Brazil has followed no general program of development. It has sought to remedy only the most serious deficiencies in domestic production, partly by organizing mixed public and private corporations, the most important of which is the National Steel Company. Venezuela has also operated on a short-term basis, although the Development Corporation established in 1946 was expected to provide a long-run plan. Colombia adopted in 1940 a general five-year plan that depended on private initiative, but postponed it in 1948. Peru and Bolivia have no general plans, but have programs in particular fields.

The government of Puerto Rico embarked on an industrialization program in 1940 to absorb unemployed labor. It was financed mainly by taxes on rum refunded to the Puerto Rican government by the U.S.A. A Planning Board prepares one- and six-year plans, and in 1945 an Agricultural Development Company and an Industrial Development Company were established. The government relies mainly on encouraging private enterprise, but it has undertaken some projects. A Development Bank, organized in 1942, lent government funds to private interests and government enterprises and was given wider powers in 1948.

In Africa[51] there is a ten-year plan for the Belgian Congo, primarily to increase agricultural output (mainly coffee, rubber, bananas, and vegetable oils) by resettling on family farms and by establishing village communities with controlled crop rotation and cooperative organization of preparation for the market, transport, and processing. The other major expenditure will be on communications and electricity. Part of the capital is expected to be private and part public (from Belgium). The Sudan government initiated a Five-Year Post War Development program in 1945 for railroad development, agriculture, irrigation, and public works, to be partly financed by the British government. The Liberian government prepared a plan in 1946. An advisory Coordinating Commission appointed in 1947 in Southern Rhodesia prepared a plan for agriculture.[52] A development plan for Fiji, like a number of British Colonial programs emphasized welfare rather than development and was criticized because it would lead to heavy increases in current expenditures but not in the means of meeting them. A new plan in 1950 allocated 36% of its cost to production and the development of natural resources (compared with 12% in the earlier plan) and 25% for social services (compared with 59% under the first plan).

The outcome of these arrangements for coordinating production in underdeveloped countries cannot be appraised because little progress has yet been made in effectuating their plans, and in none (except perhaps Turkey) has sufficient time passed for results to show. Outside eastern Europe and China they have not chosen the socialist framework of state control of all resources. But governments do not restrict themselves (as did those of western countries) to the removal of obstacles to enterprise. Generally, they have decided that they must provide more active entrepreneurial services by positively encouraging innovation and often partly financing it. Public utilities are often owned by the government, largely because private capital is not attracted to investments faced with a long profitless period before other activities develop to provide them with a

[51] *Ibid.*, 237, 283.
[52] *Ibid.*, 1950, 221.

market. Steel industries are often partly or wholly public because of the amount of capital needed and because of anticipated difficulties in their infancy. Most rely, however, on a considerable measure of private enterprise. Turkey has experimented with both the encouragement and the displacement of private enterprise. Between 1923 and 1933 it offered inducements to private business in the form of tariff protection, tax advantage, duty-free entry of plant, and free land for factories. Development occurred, but it was felt to be too slow and the government increased the scope of state enterprise, but after about 1950 it returned to the encouragement of private enterprise. The Finance Minister of India stated in 1948 that "the general pattern of our economy must be a mixed economy in which there is scope both for private enterprise and for state enterprise.[53] The Planning Commission announced that the expansion of industrial production under the five-year plan (1952-6) will be "largely the responsibility of private enterprise." Public expenditures are to be confined chiefly to projects under way. The government seeks to encourage private industry by liberal depreciation allowances for tax purposes, exemptions from income tax for new undertakings for a specified period, and the reduction of import duties on machinery and raw materials. But one-third of the expenditure (of $210 million) under the plan is to be spent on loans and grants to private industry. Argentina has endeavored to secure development partly by attracting private enterprise. Tariffs permit home-produced goods to sell at 25% above the cost of imported goods for at least 50% of the total national demand; the government favors domestic sellers in making its own purchases. Subsidies have been paid for forestry, mining, and fishing. Public operation is proposed for electric power (the core of the program) and all transport and social services.

The scope of public enterprise is dictated partly by the shortage of private venture capital. Capital being the scarce factor of production, governments are impelled to increase the supply and to program its use. In the main the supply of domestic saving has not been greatly increased outside the socialist countries. Incomes are generally low in both groups of countries. But the socialized can, and the non-socialized underdeveloped countries cannot, directly determine the proportion of the national income to go to capital formation.

Most of the non-socialist governments can borrow little internally, and they look, as the socialist countries do not in so great a degree, to foreign capital to finance the initial upsurge of development. But, in fact, their efforts to increase domestic investment have usually increased internal purchasing power without a contemporaneous increase in the supply of goods and services, and caused inflation. Some have accentuated their difficulties by attempting simultaneously to increase investment and consumption when increases in productivity were not sufficient for both, and

[53] *Ibid.*, 1947, 159.

foreign loans were not large enough to bridge the gap. Prices have risen, exportable surpluses of food fallen, and the foreign exchange position has deteriorated.

In Turkey, private internal investment was small and some capital was obtained for development from Russia, Britain, and Germany before 1939, but the government amended the statutes of the central bank in 1938 to require the bank "to ensure the monetary requirements of the state agricultural and commercial enterprises of an economic character . . . by the discounting of bonds guaranteed by the treasury and issued by these establishments." It was also authorized to issue paper money for the operations envisaged, up to a limit to be fixed by the banking committee. After 1945, loans and aid were provided by the U.S.A., but the conditions laid down by the Turkish government discouraged private foreign investment, and defense expenditures competed with development. Taxation and the profits of government monopolies were not high enough to prevent government deficits and inflation.

In Argentina agriculture is the major internal source of funds for development, and the government endeavored to use its foreign trade monopoly (I.A.P.I.) (Ch. 21) to obtain and allocate funds under the National Economic Council. But Argentina used part of its wartime accumulated balance of sterling to buy back its railroad system, thus in effect exporting capital, and used its dollars partly for military purposes and partly for others, sometimes ineptly and corruptly. Development has not been fully financed by private saving and taxation. Costly social security programs tended to increase consumption, and the budget has been in deficit although government contributions to social security funds and defense expenditures have been charged to a special budget (intended to be covered by assets). The government has borrowed from banks, and the means of payment increased about 175% between 1939 and 1945, although production increased about 16%. In Brazil over 70% of the cost of development was to be met by the government (out of its ordinary budget and domestic and foreign loans). But part of the cost of internal financing came from the Bank of Brazil.

Government attempts to allocate capital[54] have also been restricted by the basically private enterprise character of the economies. They can select lines of production for privileged treatment in the taxation of imports, exemptions from internal taxes, favorable credit terms, and the like. But, as these devices are not always effective, they often resort to partial or complete government financing. When Turkey turned to state enterprise, it used three government banks to administer government investments. Even the limited government programming of development calls for decisions on the general pattern of future production, the more

---

[54] Adler, J. H., *The Underdeveloped Areas: Their Industrialization.*

desirable investment sequences, and the disposal of the resulting increases in productivity. Many countries are handicapped by lack of knowledge of their resources and of skills to plan their use. Most have elected to emphasize industrialization. But, although industry has been the source of most of the increase in production in the western world, agriculture offers considerable scope for increased productivity in many of the underdeveloped countries, especially since growing populations are pressing for better nourishment and cannot follow the British example of relying partly on imports of food. To make the most economical plans for using the capital at their disposal, they must estimate their future place in the pattern of international division of labor. They often seek to minimize foreign trade because they believe that the terms of trade have become increasingly adverse to them, or because the commercial policies of other countries, cycles of economic activity in the larger countries, and war have made trade undependable. Brazil began to organize a steel industry in 1942, and Argentina, Chile, and Peru have all sought to follow this lead. But they must, at least for a time, import most capital goods and, unless the whole cost can be borrowed abroad, they must export. Even if the whole cost is provided out of foreign loans, servicing the loans requires exports that must be increased unless domestic production displaces imports.

The effect of a given amount of investment may be reduced by poor coordination. It has been reported that in Turkey a coal field was developed without a port to provide an outlet for its products, and a steel works without direct rail connection with its ore supply. Too many projects were started, with the result that few were completed. Similar difficulties have appeared in Iran. In Spain the productivity of investments in industry has been greatly reduced because of failure to provide the power supply necessary to activate them. Plants have repeatedly worked short hours or closed because drought has curtailed the supply of hydroelectric power.

The selection of the most desirable investment sequences is especially difficult because the model of a developed society is naturally obtained from western Europe and North America, where economic organization has reached a high degree of complexity (which partly accounts for high productivity). Ultimate high productivity can best be achieved by building "external economy" industries such as transport and power. But they take long to come to fruition, and even longer to work out their full repercussions on the remainder of the economy. During this long barren period a suffering and demanding population may conclude that planning is getting nowhere. Because these activities require unusually large amounts of capital, there is a temptation to start other smaller projects that, however, may fail to attain full productivity for lack of the external economies.[55] Nevertheless, shortage of internal savings and difficulties of obtaining foreign funds may compel small-scale development, although larger-scale development yields greater returns because one project provides a market for the output of others. Again, the results of development may be disappointing.[56]

Cumulative development requires that part of increments of productivity be plowed back into development. Capital should not, in the early stages, be introduced widely into consumer goods industries (except for export). Efforts to ameliorate poverty by immediately increasing standards of living slow development (which may be swamped by population increase). Both in the western countries in their early development, and in present socialist countries, development has been accelerated by the slowness of improvements in standards of living. But governments in chiefly private-enterprise economies may not be as politically able to postpone the alleviation of poverty as they have been in socialist countries and rates of population increase are likely to hold down the general level of living without freeing resources for development.

[55] Singer, "Economic Progress in Underdeveloped Countries," 16 Social Research, 1949, 6.

[56] Ibid., Rosenstein-Rodan, "The Problems of Industrialization of Southern and South Eastern Europe," LIII Ec. Jour., 1943, 203.

Chapter 24

Monetary Organization: Forms and Location of Control

Where people live in organized groups, they need some means of regulating their economic relations. For many centuries most people produced most of their consumption goods, but provision for defense and internal order as well as religion usually required economic transfers from immediate producers. Obligations for such purposes can be defined in labor (for instance under the feudal system and among the Incas) or as a share of the crop (as in feudal Japan). But money provides a more flexible means of definition. For more than 2000 years, therefore, the use of money has been spreading, until most economies use money although many individuals still do not use it much. Monetary institutions have not only spread, but they have developed to great complexity.

Monetary units probably arose out of the need for defining obligations that in early times arose out of status (e.g., obligations to the ruler). Where exchange develops, these units simplify the calculation of the value of one commodity in terms of others. Where monetary units are represented by a medium in circulation, money facilitates the settlement of obligations, including those arising out of exchange, and avoids the difficulties of barter. In highly organized societies concerned with the rational use of resources, monetary units are used also to measure costs, output, and profit. They also simplify the economic relations among the individuals participating in production and, therefore, facilitate specialization and the division of labor and the assembly and allocation of resources.

A. Forms of Money

In the ancient world, the economic relations among the king, the temples, and the people were often defined in metals, grain, olive oil, and other products, but obligations were not necessarily settled in the com-

498

modity in which they were recorded. Exchange was probably unimportant within communities, but important in international trade, which has existed at least from the third millennium B.C. Cattle, gold, silver, and cowrie shells were used as units of value. Metals, always important in international trade (because of their uneven distribution in nature) have been widely used (by weight) as a means of payment. From the beginning of the bronze age (in which silver was also available) the metals were traded in over wide areas (largely for weapons or for luxury goods). Having a considerable value in use, they were used for the payment of tribute, temple dues, and the like. The wall paintings in the Egyptian tombs portray metal being weighed out in payment of obligations.

Circulating currencies defined in the unit of account have existed for at least 2500 years. Metal coinage developed in the Middle East, probably in the sixth century B.C. in Lydia.[1] The earliest coins were pieces of metal imprinted with a seal probably certifying the fineness of the metal, but not its weight, because the early coins were so imperfectly made that it was easy to clip off pieces without marring the seal. When precious metal coins were introduced into the local city markets of the Greek world, those needed to settle lesser transactions were inconveniently small. To avoid this difficulty, cities issued smaller value coins of cheaper metal. But if they contained metal worth their nominal value, difficulty arose when the relative values of the two metals changed. Consequently, smaller coins were made as tokens which were worth less as metal than as coins, and whose value depended upon the quantity in circulation. In the ancient Middle East and China there were also various forms of paper money and bank credit. But money in any form played little part in the life of the mass of the rural population, except in the payment of tribute and taxes.

The monetary arrangements of primitive societies often resemble those of the ancient world. Obligations to the state are often stated and settled in goods or labor. Although internal trade is usually small, various commodities such as seashells are freely accepted in exchange, often at conventional values in terms of each other, thus virtually providing money of a series of "denominations." External trade is typically restricted to articles of considerable value that may also become a medium of internal exchange. Primitive societies have used salt, iron, copper, axeheads, knives, tobacco, blocks of tea, and the like. Although the commodity may not be durable or particularly portable, the fact that it can be consumed sets a floor under its value. But some societies provide an elaborate variety of monetary media, each for a separate type of settlement. In the native kingdom of Dahomey in the 17th and 18th centuries, one unit was used for foreign trade, another for wholesale trade, and another for retail

---

[1] There is some evidence that coins were used earlier in India and China. (Burns, A. R., *Money and Monetary Policy in Early Times*, 14, 37).

trade. The rate of exchange between the units was sometimes controlled to yield profits to the state or to those to whom it granted monopolies in the various types of trade. Coins and paper money exist in primitive societies only where they are introduced from outside, and are chiefly used in transactions with the non-primitive world.

In western Europe, coins were in use by 150 B.C. when gold imitations of the *stater* (originally issued by Philip of Macedon) were made in Britain. In the 4th century A.D. and thereafter, gold *byzants* of the eastern Roman empire provided an international currency. Money remained in continuous use although for few transactions. Some gold coins were used in northern Italy, France, and Flanders towards the end of the 13th century.[2] Silver increased in internal use with the growth of cities but gold was for a long time mainly used in foreign trade. Both gold and silver were coined in Britain in the 8th century A.D., but silver was the principal internal currency until the 18th century.

Paper currency came into use in 13th century Italy, to enable full value coins to be kept in a safe place. The safe custody receipts for stored coins could be exchanged without risky movements of precious metal and came to be accepted as currency. During the 17th century, foreign and domestic trade expanded, and the monetary supply was increased beyond the available quantity of precious metals, mainly in the Netherlands and Britain. The London goldsmiths took over the practice of accepting precious metals for safe custody, but issued receipts, often in round sums, that circulated as notes. But, realizing that, in spite of withdrawals, they usually held a considerable residue of coins, they began to make loans, thus ceasing to keep 100% currency reserve against their obligations. They also began to accept written orders from depositors to pay out cash, and thus developed the bank check. European cities formed municipal banks. The Bank of Amsterdam, established in 1609, issued notes partly to facilitate exchange when there was a great variety of coins in circulation. Coins paid in were appraised in bank units, in which terms credit was given. It was intended that the bank should keep 100% reserve against its liabilities; but it failed to do so, and finally closed.[3] The Bank of England was formed in 1694 with a monopoly of joint stock banking (which was assumed to mean the issue of paper currency) within 65 miles of London, but it also accepted deposits. There were also many unincorporated banks issuing notes and accepting deposits. The American colonies found it difficult to acquire a metallic currency because they produced little currency metal and could not supply sufficient exports to pay for imports of both goods and metal for coin. The few coins that did circulate were dollars from the West Indies, mostly of Spanish and Portuguese origin.

[2] Kemmerer, *Gold and the Gold Standard*, Ch. II.
[3] Adam Smith, *Wealth of Nations*, Book IV, Ch. III.

The development of industry and the growth of population vastly increased the volume of exchange and payments, and the volume of money was greatly increased, chiefly by adapting the existing monetary devices. The volume of metallic currency increased greatly. Full-value coins circulated generally until 1914, and token coinage was improved and increased in volume, but coins were supplemented by greatly increased quantities of paper currency. From 1844 to 1914, however, the volume of paper currency increased little in Britain and bank debt (transferred by checks) supplied the rapidly increasing demand for means of payment. Clearing houses greatly facilitated these transfers. Bank debt and checks subsequently increased in use in the U.S.A., Germany, Belgium, Holland, and the British Commonwealth.

In contemporary agrarian societies the majority of the population makes little use of money because relatively few goods are exchanged. Rents, and sometimes taxes, are often paid in kind. But full weight coins have circulated in most of these societies and have often been used to store savings. Paper currency has been less attractive, but has nevertheless increased in circulation, especially after each of the World Wars. It is now used in China, India, the Middle East and Latin America.

Commercial banking entered most of these countries in the form of foreign banks, often British, German, and American (in India, China and Latin America) and French (in Indo-China and parts of the Middle East). More recently Indian banks have been active in Burma, Pakistan, and Ceylon, and Chinese banks in Malaya, Hong Kong, and Indo-China. In India, the liabilities of the foreign banks were 15% of all bank liabilities in 1947, and in Pakistan foreign, including Indian, banks held 62% of the deposits of all scheduled banks in 1950. They limit themselves mainly to foreign trade, and still play little part in internal trade and have offices only in the largest cities. Checks, therefore, are not an important means of payment.

Socialists have often hoped to abolish money. The Congress of the Russian Communist Party resolved in 1919 that although it was impossible to abolish money in the transition from capitalism to communism, the Party nevertheless aimed "to widen the sphere of moneyless settlements and . . . pave the way for the abolition of money."[4] In fact, modern socialist societies make great use of money. They seek to increase production by increasing the division of labor and economic incentives to work. Consequently, they need a means of paying wages, and workers must be able to translate wages into real income. Paper notes are the chief means of payment by individuals, but the government provides token coins for settling small transactions. Government organizations pay for labor and other resources used in production and receive payment for their products. Payments other than those in cash are settled through a

[4] Arnold, A. Z., *Banks, Credit and Money in Russia*, 106.

clearing system comparable to that in capitalist countries and operated by the state bank (Gosbank).[5]

B. The Means of Controlling Money

The functioning of monetary arrangements depends on how they are controlled—this depends partly on who controls them. Most monetary instruments appear to have begun under private control, but to have drifted under public control.

In primitive societies the size of the unit of value depends on the commodity and the quantity of it chosen for the purpose. In the long run, the cost of producing and importing the commodity and the demand for it determine its value. Where the commodity has a non-monetary use (e.g., salt or axeheads) the non-monetary demand, as well as the monetary demand, affects its value. But where the commodity is not scarce, some authoritarian arrangements exist for regulating the currency supply. Where shells are used, for instance, "money" may be differentiated from the general supply of shells by requiring that only shells threaded in a particular way shall be acceptable as money. The threading is typically done by the medicine man under conditions of solitude, low diet, sexual abstinence, and other conditions which keep down the quantity of money.

In the ancient world, the state and the temple authorities (typically a part of the state) presumably selected the units in which tribute or tax obligations were prescribed, and defined the conversion rates at which other commodities would be accepted. Governments did not at first enjoy a monopoly of coinage. Merchants and temples as well as governments imprinted their seal on pieces of metal. But by the 4th century B.C. the issues of the Greek city-states had driven out the private issues,[6] and the Empire and Republic of Rome monopolized coining. In medieval Europe coinage was a royal monopoly, but it was occasionally granted to more powerful feudal lords.[7] In Japan many local lords issued coins until the 1870s. In modern times most governments monopolize coining, although some allow the circulation of foreign coins. But the circulation of standard coins declined after 1914, and was not resumed in Britain after 1918; it ceased in the U.S.A. in 1933, and is now largely restricted to the Middle East.

Paper currency also began under private control and is now mostly under public control. The paper notes of the London goldsmiths in the 17th century were private and unregulated, but issues by corporations in both continental Europe and Britain were controlled, largely because the right to form a corporation was a government prerogative. Thus in 1694

---

5 Schwartz, *Russia's Soviet Economy*, 433.

6 Burns, *op. cit.*, 78 ff.

7 The difference between the cost of the metal content in standard coins and the circulating value of the coins is still referred to as "seignieurage."

the Bank of England was given a legal monopoly of joint stock note issues within sixty-five miles of London. In the U.S.A., colonial legislatures faced with a shortage of metallic currency issued notes. The Continental Congress issued $240 million in bills between 1775 and 1779, and the state governments issued another $200 million. The Constitution of 1789 specifically forbade state issues of paper currency, and paper money was issued by banks chartered by the federal and state governments with little or no control (and widespread losses) until 1836. Thereafter, state banks alone issued paper currency until the national banks were established in 1863.

State control of note issues developed mainly during the 19th century. In Britain no additional notes could be issued after 1844, except by the Bank of England, and by 1921 all non-government paper currency in England (not Scotland) was issued by the Bank of England against reserves prescribed in the Bank Charter Act of 1844. When gold coins were withdrawn in 1914 they were replaced by notes issued by the government. The two issues were consolidated under the Bank of England in 1928, and the nationalization of the Bank in 1946 converted all paper currency into government issues. In France paper currency was issued by the Bank of France, set up in 1800, and occasionally by other banks until 1848 when the Bank of France became the only issuing bank. In Germany the note-issue prerogative of the states was taken over by the imperial government when it was established. In 1875 the Reichsbank and 33 other banks were issuing, but by 1914 the Reichsbank was the sole issuing authority. In the U.S.A. the federal government in 1863 authorized the establishment of "national banks" with power to issue notes, and in 1865 imposed a prohibitive tax on notes issued by banks chartered by the states. By 1939 the paper currency consisted only of federal reserve notes and silver certificates, the former issued by 12 closely regulated federally chartered banks and the latter by the Treasury.

Commercial credit banking, which provided so much of the increased means of payment in developing countries, also began as uncontrolled private enterprise. Government control began in the U.S.A. After 1837 state governments began to require minimum reserves, and the National Bank Act of 1863 applied this control to federally chartered banks. Virtually all banks have been so regulated since 1863 (Ch. 25). The Japanese government prescribed the minimum capital for a joint stock bank in 1901. But it was only after 1914 that governments generally controlled bank credit by prescribing the proportion of deposits that must be covered by defined reserves that are usually required to be deposited in a central bank. In Britain, however, the reserves of commercial banks remain virtually uncontrolled, although when the Bank of England was nationalized in 1946, it was authorized to request information from commercial banks and make recommendations to them. If so authorized by the Treasury, it directs them to give effect to its recommendations and policies. In the U.S.A. the state and federal governments restrict the number of branches a bank may have (and, therefore, the region in which it may operate) and also restrict the concentration of private banking. After 1945 the U.S.A. used its influence to reduce financial concentration in Germany and Japan. But in most other developed countries (e.g., Britain, France, and Canada) there are few banks, each with many branches.

Some governments now own rather than control commercial banks. The four largest deposit banks in France (all those with a national network of branches) were nationalized in 1946, because they are "in the nature of a public service." The stockholders exchanged their shares for treasury certificates carrying an annual return of 3%, and have no control. Each bank is run separately by 12 government appointees, three representing each of commerce, industry, and agriculture; labor unions; the Bank of France; and persons with banking experience.[8] But an attempt to nationalize the banks in Australia was held unconstitutional.[9]

Central banks appeared as banking systems developed, as an instrument of monetary control. They usually issue the paper currency, keep the government accounts, provide the basis of the clearing system, and hold the ultimate reserves of the country, by virtue of holding the reserves of the commercial banks. The first and most famous central bank, the Bank of England, was established as a privately owned bank in 1694. It was relatively unimportant until the 19th century, when it worked out the techniques of central banking, although it was slow to recognize itself as a central bank. Central banks now exist in most countries. In the U.S.A. the First or Second Banks of the United States might have developed into a central bank early in the 19th century, but did not. In 1913 twelve Federal Reserve Banks were established and are now coordinated by a Board of Governors. This unusual arrangement is attributable to the size of the country, limitations on the size of banks and the consequent large number of banks, and a fear of financial centralization.

Governments have almost everywhere increased their control of central banks. The Bank of England was indirectly influenced by the government from its beginning because its charter of incorporation was granted only for relatively short periods and renewals of the charter in the first half of the 19th century were often preceded by investigation of the policies of the Bank. Furthermore, any inflationary pressures resulting in demands for gold for export or internal hoarding concentrated on the Bank. If it was unable to meet them or wished to avoid losing its gold reserves, it could only refuse payment or obtain parliamentary authority to refuse

---

8 Myers, M. G., "The Nationalization of Banks in France," LXIV *Pol. Sci. Quar.*, 1949, 189.

9 Wilson, V. S. G., "The Future of Banking in Australia," LIX *Econ. Jour.*, 1949, 208.

to pay out gold. After the government prescribed the minimum reserves to be kept by the Bank against note issues (but not against deposits) the Bank could not meet demands for paper currency beyond the legal limit without breaching the law (which was done from time to time, but with an understanding that the government would pass exonerating legislation). Although there was no legal regulation of the Bank's reserves against its deposit liabilities, the government through the treasury exercised increasing control over the Bank until it was nationalized in 1946. The Bank of France also regarded itself as a private institution that had undertaken a few obligations and received a few privileges. Its maximum note issue was prescribed from time to time by parliament, but its reserves were uncontrolled until 1928. The German Reichsbank was owned by private stockholders, but the government shared in its profits and controlled its reserves against note but not against its banking liabilities.

The 12 Federal Reserve Banks in the U.S.A. are cooperatively owned by their member banks, but both their currency and banking reserves are regulated by statute and the Board of Governors coordinating these banks is appointed by the President subject to confirmation by the Senate. The Bank of Japan, established in 1882, was modelled partly on the Bank of England and partly on European central banks. The government supervised the Bank, and its minimum reserves against notes were prescribed. But it never established itself as a bankers' bank. It held only the clearing balances and not the reserves of the commercial banks, and was never able to control the volume of bank deposits. In fact, instead of being able to impose terms on the commercial banks in times of emergency, it was often compelled by the government to make heavy loans to them. In 1921, the private banks successfully opposed the Bank of Japan's proposed policy of deflation.[10]

The collapse of the gold standard in Europe during the war of 1914-18 produced a reaction against increasing government control of central banks. Efforts to restore the gold standard were accompanied by recommendations that central banks should be made sufficiently independent of governments to enable them to resist the government demands for loans that had led to inflation between 1914 and 1920. These proposals were rejected. No government could subject its war or depression policies to an independent board of bank directors. Central bank directors could not, moreover, have maintained independence in making painful political decisions in times of emergency. In fact, governments have since taken over many central banks. The Bank of England was nationalized in 1946. The Bank of France had been intermittently criticized during the last half of the 19th century because the senior officials of the Bank, although appointed by the government, were dominated by business interests. After 1926 it refused loans to cover budget deficits, and the government in-

---

[10] Allen, *op. cit.*, 45, 52, 54.

creased its control. But the Bank was popularly regarded as the means by which the "two hundred families" dominated the French economy. In 1936 the government abolished the Board of Regents of the Bank (which had been elected by the 200 largest stockholders) and substituted a Council of 23 members, 21 of whom were appointed by the government and 2 by the 40,000 stockholders. In 1946 the Bank was finally nationalized.

Central banks in Argentina, India, The Netherlands, New Zealand, and all the east European countries have been nationalized since 1945. By 1947, 36 out of 57 central banks were owned by governments, nine were owned partly by governments and partly by private owners, and 12 were private. Among those not publicly owned are the Bank of Italy (whose shares are held by banks and financial institutions), the National Bank of Switzerland (which is largely owned by the Swiss Cantonal Banks, which in turn are owned by the Swiss cantonal governments) and the Federal Reserve Banks of the U.S.A.[11] After the military collapse of Germany in 1945, a two-tier system of central banking somewhat resembling that in the U.S.A. was established in West Germany.

In the less-developed countries, coins and paper currency are typically issued by the government or a bank controlled by it. In Argentina since 1946 the central bank has had power to control all lending of deposits by commercial banks (which are, therefore, merely lending agents for the central bank, except insofar as they lend their own capital). Most Latin-American governments now own or control their central banks (e.g., Argentina, Mexico, and Chile), and there are numerous government-owned central banks in the Middle East. The Bank Melli, the central bank in Iran, is owned by the government. In 1940 the charter of the National Bank of Egypt was renewed for 40 years, after parliament had been assured that it would be converted into a central bank (which had not been done by 1950). But the bank has often accepted the responsibilities of a central bank, making advances to the government and to other banks under pressure, and assisting in the establishment of a clearing system. Bankers' balances with the National Bank increased after 1939, but other banks are not legally required to keep such balances.[12]

Many of the central banks in Asia and the Far East were established after 1945, but those in Korea (1909), China (1928), India (1935) are older, and there is no central bank in Indo-China, Hong Kong, or Malaya. All are state owned except Pakistan's (51% of the capital of which is government owned) and the Java Bank which is owned by shareholders. The Reserve Bank of India was nationalized in 1949. All except the Union Bank of Burma have a monopoly of note issue, the minimum reserves against which are prescribed by law.[13] In colonial territories the currency is often

---

11 Kriz, M. A., "Central Banks and the State Today," 38, *Am. Ec. Rev.*, 1948, 565.
12 Issawi, *Egypt: An Economic and Social Analysis*, 31, 120, 135.
13 U.N., *Mobilization of Domestic Capital in . . . Asia and the Far East*, Ch. II.

pegged to that of the colonial power, but government control of commercial banking is uncommon. In the British territories in East Africa and in Southern Rhodesia and Malaya, for instance, notes are convertible into sterling and the reserve consists of sterling balances and securities.

In Russia the Bolsheviks attempted to make some arrangement with the banks at the time of the Revolution. For a month they controlled the transactions of the private banks to prevent political loans, the sabotage of government policy, and the concealment of capital. They occupied the head office of the State Bank only when it refused to pay over funds at the request of the revolutionary government. Lenin explained that the government had wanted to collaborate with the banks, but it had not proved possible.[14] Banking was declared a state monopoly, and all banks were merged in the state bank in December 1917. Since that time all coins and notes have been issued by the state bank on behalf of the treasury, and all deposit banking is operated through a series of state-owned specialized banks. All banking has been similarly nationalized in the east European countries and almost all in communist China.[15]

---

[14] Baykov, *The Development of the Soviet Economic System*, 34.

[15] Eckstein, "Conditions and Prospects for Economic Growth in Communist China," VI *World Politics*, 1954, 21.

Chapter 25

Monetary Organization (Cont'd)

C. Policies of Monetary Control

Power over monetary arrangements can be used mainly to define the monetary unit and control the relative quantities of the different forms of money. We are here concerned with decisions about money in their effect on the size of the unit of value or account. Changes in the unit cause gains and losses to holders of monetary instruments that fluctuate in value, and to debtors and creditors (except where changes have been correctly anticipated and allowed for), and influence buying and selling and plans for production.

Units of account have often been legally defined as a physical quantity of precious metal. But in economic terms their "size" is measured by their purchasing power over goods and services. When prices in general rise, the purchasing power of the unit shrinks, and when prices fall, its purchasing power increases. The legal definition, however, is important when it influences the quantity of money (and, therefore, its purchasing power). But the size of the unit is also influenced by the demand for money, which depends on the customary ways of organizing individual, family, and business financial operations, the size of the population, the volume of transactions, opportunities for spending, and anticipated changes in the value of money. An increase in the supply of money without a corresponding increase in demand reduces its purchasing power (or raises the price level).

1. PRE-INDUSTRIAL SOCIETIES

In primitive societies, monetary controls have little effect on production because obligations and production plans are rarely expressed in money. The devices used to control the quantity of money (Ch. 25) probably avoid sharp changes in its value, but there is little general information on the subject.

In the ancient Mediterranean world, when the unit was a physical quantity of a commodity, it must have fluctuated with changes in the value of the commodity. But it was also changed by changing the conversion rates at which other commodities were accepted in settlement of obligations defined in the standard commodity, and by changing the physical measures of weight or bulk in which the standard commodity was measured. Insofar as these changes were made to adjust to changes in the relative scarcity of the standard commodity, they stabilized the unit of account. But some changes may have been intended to increase real obligations (usually to the state) and were, therefore, comparable to modern deflations.

The invention of coinage necessitated definition of the unit of account as a prescribed quantity of prescribed metals (usually gold or silver). So long as the amount of metal in the unit was stable, and full weight coins were the only monetary instrument, the size of the unit was affected only by changes in the value of the selected metal in relation to other goods and services. This value is unlikely to have been stable because of changes in populations and their use of money as well as changes in the supply of the metal. Nevertheless the introduction of coins facilitated exchange and the collection of taxes and probably stimulated production for city markets. But the size of units of account did not long remain stable even in terms of monetary metal. The Greek city states soon discovered that they could obtain revenue by reducing the amount of monetary metal in the unit. Existing coins were called in and replaced by coins of the same metal but smaller content, or, occasionally, of metal of lower fineness. The state thus had left over a supply of monetary metal which it could sell, but more often used to increase the number of coins in circulation. Such debasement of the currency[1] caused an inflationary rise in prices, except where it was offset by increasing demands for money or a falling supply of monetary metal. The gain to the state was at the expense of holders of currency and creditors at the time, but inflation may have stimulated economic activity in the ancient world. After Alexander the Great dispersed the metal reserves of Persia, there was an outburst of progress in the Mediterranean and deflation may have contributed to the destruction of the Roman Empire.[2]

Medieval Europe in general used silver coins for internal circulation, but Britain and other countries from time to time issued gold coins which were used mainly in international trade. Prices were influenced by changes in the supply of monetary metals, additions to the money supply resulting from issues of paper money not fully covered by monetary metal, changes in the demand for money due to changes in population and in the proportion of goods and services exchanged for money and, finally, changes in

[1] Burns, *Money and Monetary Policy in Early Times*, Ch. XIV-XVI.
[2] Keynes, *Treatise on Money* II, Ch. 30.

the metal content of the standard coins.[3] The use of coins was somewhat impeded because they varied in weight and quality in consequence of periodic debasements without complete withdrawal of previous issues, the clipping and sweating of coins, and shortages of domestic coins. In trading centers like Amsterdam and London in the 17th century, money changers sorted, assayed, and weighed the various foreign coins in circulation. International movements of coin and precious metals increased because of rapid changes in the volume and pattern of trade and of efforts to define units of value in both gold and silver. The two metals could remain in circulation only if their relative value in coins was about the same as their value as metal. Merchants began to discuss these international movements of "bullion" and argue in favor of controls of trade that would insure net imports to increase the treasure of the country (Ch. 23).

Prices rose for 30 years after the Black Death in 1348. Populations fell at a time when the money supply was increased by an inflow of gold into western Europe from Silesia, Hungary, the Crimea, and northwest Africa, and by a revival of the coinage of gold in Britain, Flanders, Germany, and parts of Spain. But, because the shortage of workers forced up wages more rapidly than prices, economic development was retarded. From about 1380 to 1500 prices were fairly stable over longer periods. The demand for money increased because of rising populations and the increasing use of money at a time when the monetary metals were steadily flowing to the Orient to pay for imports of spices. Spices were needed to make meat palatable in countries where many cattle were slaughtered at the beginning of winter because pastures were poor and fodder supplies low. These forces making for falling prices were, however, in the main offset by debasing the coinage or reducing the metallic equivalent of the monetary unit.[4] Prices rose moderately from 1500 to 1550, and more slowly from 1600 to 1650. Gold began to flow into Europe from America through Spain in the beginning of the 16th century. Silver flowed in after 1519, rising to a flood from 1560 to 1600, after which imports declined. Increases in population and the use of money in the 17th century reduced the inflationary effects of the increasing supply of monetary metal, and the discovery of the all-water route around Africa to the East Indies stimulated imports of spices and exports of metal in payment. Thus part of the new metal supplies passed through the European monetary systems to the Orient, in a trade profitable enough to provide a considerable basis for European commercial expansion. But, in addition, wages rose much more slowly than prices in Britain and France in the 16th and 17th centuries. Profits were, therefore, high and probably increased inequality of income and savings, and stimulated development. But in Spain, where wages rose

---

[3] Hamilton, Earl J., "Prices and Progress," XII *Jour. Econ. Hist.*, 1952, 325.
[4] Hamilton, E. J., "Prices and Progress," XII, *Jour. Econ. Hist.*, 1952, 330.

more than prices after 1570 without any gain in labor efficiency, the leading industrial cities began to decay in the 17th century. Prices generally
fell somewhat in Europe from 1700 to 1735, but increased imports of
silver from Mexico and gold from Brazil arrested the decline and caused
a marked increase during the remainder of the century, aided by the
Napoleonic wars at the end of the century. Again wages lagged behind
prices, and savings greatly increased the capital supply in Britain in the
critical early stages of the industrial revolution; they did the same in
France.

2. INDUSTRIAL CAPITALIST SOCIETIES

a. Nineteenth Century

Increasing specialization and growing dependence on the market during the 19th century greatly increased the demand for money. Money
wages increased in importance and, therefore, production for sale in
markets in which wages were spent (notably in the developing towns).
This increasing demand was met by increases in the supply of monetary
metals and of substitutes for full-value coins (at first paper currency and
later bank debt). But changes in the value of the monetary unit increasingly affected production, cyclical fluctuations in which characterized
capitalist industrial economies. Changes in the value of monetary units
also affected foreign trade through their effect on rates of exchange.

The definition of money units in both gold and silver was abandoned
in practice in Britain in 1720. When gold began to flow out to be replaced
by silver (because gold was overvalued in coins), the government raised
the value of the gold coin in terms of the unit of account (or reduced the
gold equivalent of the unit of account). Thus it protected the gold supply
and laid the foundation for the gold standard (in fact, although not in
law, since silver could still be offered for coinage). But in other developing countries, bimetallism lingered on until about 1870. It was argued
that the value of a gold unit would vary with fluctuations in the value of
gold, whereas, if both gold and silver were used, at least some of their
changes in value might offset each other and the elimination of silver as a
monetary metal would reduce the supply of money, cause a fall in prices,
and discourage development. Silver producers had an obvious interest in
opposing the elimination of one of the major demands for their product.
But bimetallism failed to stabilize foreign exchange rates. This was important because international trade was expanding rapidly. This failure
was due to the failure of governments to use the same ratio between the
value of gold and silver in their coins, and to changes in the relative
market values of the two metals. Silver left countries in which it had become "undervalued," and went to those where it was "overvalued." Thus,
in fact, some countries had silver standards and others gold standards, and
exchange rates moved with changes in the relative value of the two metals.

Britain became increasingly interested in foreign trade early in the 19th century and in 1816 legalized the *de facto* adoption of the gold standard in 1720 (although the legislation in 1816 still left room for the resumption of issues of full-weight silver coins, which would have restored bimetallism). The pound sterling grew rapidly in importance as an international monetary unit. But other countries struggled to maintain bimetallic systems. France re-established a bimetallic system in 1803, after the collapse of its revolutionary paper currencies. The German states had a similar system. The Constitution of the United States mentioned both gold and silver coin. Hamilton preferred a gold standard, but since gold and silver were both scarce, he believed that gold alone would not be in adequate supply. Consequently the legislation of 1792 provided for full-weight coins of both gold and silver. The discoveries of gold in Australia and California in the middle of the century upset the former relative values of the metals and increased the difficulties of bimetallic countries. The Netherlands adopted a single silver standard in 1847, and the chief German states in 1857 made a convention with Austria, contemplating a silver standard.

In 1865 France led an effort to revitalize bimetallism by establishing a common unit of account and uniform monetary ratios between gold and silver, but without success. Germany, which was beginning to develop, was interested in a stable exchange rate with Britain to facilitate competition with Britain in foreign markets, and adopted a gold standard in 1873. The U.S.A. followed in the same year. The monetary demand for silver was thus reduced at a time when the output of gold was falling, that of silver was increasing, and Germany was selling the silver from its now obsolete coinage. The resulting fall in the relative value of silver caused it to flow into bimetallic countries. Had they continued to accept silver in exchange for gold, they would have found themselves on a silver standard. In fact, the Netherlands in 1872 and France in 1873 restricted the coinage of silver. In the same year the Currency Act in the U.S.A. omitted provision for the coinage of full-weight silver coins. Such was the "crime of '73," although few such coins had been made since 1834, because the monetary ratio favored gold. The Gold Standard Act of 1900 declared the gold dollar to be the standard unit of value, and provided for all forms of money to be maintained at par with it. But since 1878 the government has made a series of arrangements to buy silver.[5] The Latin Monetary Union was dissolved, although abortive efforts to restore bimetallism continued until 1896. Japan (which had had a bimetallic standard since 1878) decided to adopt the gold standard in 1893, and did so in 1897[6] By the end of the 19th century, most industrial countries were using a gold standard or a standard which tied their unit to gold.

---

[5] Seavers, *Silver Money.*
[6] Allen, *op. cit.*, 34, 40, 47.

The definition of monetary units in precious metals was intended to regulate the supply of money. But the proportion of the monetary supply consisting of full-weight standard coins diminished rapidly during the 19th century. Consequently, governments turned to the regulation of the supply of monetary substitutes for metal, namely notes and bank credit.

French experience during the Revolution showed that paper money could drive metal reserves out of a country. Governments sought to prevent excessive issues of paper money by making them convertible on demand and by segregating reserves to provide for conversion. The French revolutionary government issued paper *assignats* against real property between 1789 and 1794, but they lost almost all value. In fact, they had not been convertible into the real property against which they were nominally issued. In the U.S.A. some state governments attempted to prevent the suspension of payment of bank notes (and their circulation at a discount) by requiring the state-chartered banks to post government bonds against all notes issued. The National Bank Act of 1863 followed this principle, thus making notes as safe as government bonds, but leaving the quantity of notes that could be issued dependent on the supply of eligible bonds, and the profitability of note issues, rather than on the need for additions to the means of payment. Japan made a similar experiment in 1872 and abandoned it in the 1880s.[7]

Effective arrangements to convert notes into monetary metal on demand prevent the value of paper money from diverging far from the value of the monetary metal. This requirement was the sole means of controlling private note issues in Britain until 1844. But considerations of profit tempted banks to expand note issues, and the convertibility check operated spasmodically. Loss of confidence in bank notes, or a general decline in business, caused notes to be presented for payment. Note expansions causing prices to rise more than in other countries with a similar monetary standard caused a demand for gold for export. If the banks could not meet these needs, a financial crisis occurred and sometimes banks failed.

The devices for controlling the quantity of notes were elaborated during the second half of the 19th century. No country required 100% reserve of monetary metal against notes (which would have prevented note issues from increasing the monetary supply beyond what it would have been if metal only had been used). The gold certificates circulating in the U.S.A. until 1933 required such a 100% reserve, but were only part of the note issue. The British Bank Charter Act of 1844 set the maximum amount of notes the Bank of England could issue against securities (the "fiduciary issue"), and required that every additional note be covered 100% by metal. It was assumed that a certain amount of notes would be needed, even in times of lowest business activity, and would not be presented for payment

[7] Allen, *op. cit.*, 39, 46.

unless faith in the note issue were seriously undermined. The amount of the fiduciary issue was increased when issues by private banks lapsed, and when the note issues of the Bank and the Treasury were amalgamated in 1928. It has also been subsequently increased. Japan adopted a modified version of this device in 1881.

The alternative principle of a "proportionate reserve," introduced in the German monetary legislation of 1875, has since become the most common. The German law established a fiduciary issue, but also provided that a minimum proportion of the total issues be covered by reserves of gold and legal tender, the balance being covered by good short-term securities. Many countries other than Britain now provide that a stated percentage of all paper notes be issued against monetary metal.[8] In 1913 the Federal Reserve Act in the U.S.A. required a 40% gold reserve against Federal Reserve notes, but in 1946 the proportion of gold certificates to be held against notes was reduced to 25%.[9] Germany introduced a proportional reserve in 1924 and France in 1928. France, however, had imposed specific parliamentary limits on note issues since 1848. But the device had little effect, since the limit was usually raised when it was likely to become operative, and convertibility had to be suspended in 1848, 1870, and 1914. The proportional reserve requirement causes greater fluctuations in the note issue limit than the fiduciary-issue system. If the gold reserve increases, note issues can be increased by a greater amount, but if gold reserves fall, the limit on note issue falls more.

These controls over note issues, permitting more currency than if full value metallic money alone had been permitted, somewhat offset tendencies to falling prices as economies expanded and became increasingly monetized. But none of the controls could be expected to stabilize prices, and note issues responded very crudely to short-term changes in monetary demand. By the 20th century, however, the control of note issues had become unimportant. Notes had become relatively small change in Britain, the U.S.A., and Germany, where an increasing proportion of all payments was made by transfers of bank debts.

Attempts to control deposit banking ran parallel to those to control note issues. It was again argued that bank loans could not give rise to an excessive amount of purchasing power if the loans were sound. When the British government borrowed from the Bank of England during the Napoleonic wars, the price level rose, the legal requirement on the Bank of England to meet its notes was suspended (between 1797 and 1816), and its notes were at a discount in gold. Nevertheless, the directors of the Bank insisted that there could be no inflation because all their loans were backed by good security. When modern commercial banking developed, it was assumed that the requirement of convertibility would regulate bank

---

[8] League of Nations, *International Currency Experience*, 96.
[9] Hart, A. G., *Money, Debt, and Economic Activity*, 97.

debts. If the banks were required to convert deposits into legal-tender money on demand, they would control the demands upon them by controlling their loans (and their reserves of legal-tender money and quickly convertible securities). But (as with note issues) considerations of profit encourage banks to lend. Considerations of convertibility impel banks to limit their loans sufficiently to enable them to keep what they regard as a safe reserve. In fact, the requirement of convertibility caused periodic difficulty. More liberal lending by banks stimulates buying and, when demand presses against capacity to produce, prices rise. If prices rise in only a few countries, these countries are good places to sell in but less attractive to buy in. Notes and bank deposits are converted into gold for export to pay the balance on international account. Reserves decline and if the banks call in loans or sell securities or apply higher standards in granting new loans, they depress business. Business men may restrict credit and reduce production to make their assets more liquid. Should doubts arise about the ability of banks to convert deposits into legal-tender money, the banks may be unable to meet all demands for conversion during the "run," and suspend payment. If some suspend, the pressure on others increases. Deposit banking rests on the assumption that few bank creditors will demand repayment at any one time, although all are entitled by law to do so.

The expansion of bank lending caused the greatest difficulties in the U.S.A. because of the severe pressure on banks to finance economic development beyond the limits set by internal accumulation, the relative smallness of individual banks, and the absence of a central bank. Consequently, controls on bank lending were first imposed there. Between 1837 and 1863 some state governments regulated banks, mainly however, to protect bank notes. In 1863 the federal government prescribed the amount and kind of reserve to be kept by national banks, and also the kind of loans they could make. At first most incorporated banks became national banks, but later many reverted to being state incorporated banks (which involved the surrender of their note issues).[10] The Federal Reserve Act of 1913 required banks in the system (including all National Banks and some state banks) to keep as a reserve a deposit at a Federal Reserve Bank of a prescribed percentage of their deposit liabilities, the percentage varying as to time and demand deposits and the size of the city in which they are located. In 1935 the Board of Governors of the system was empowered to vary requirements between their existing level and double that level (this authority has been used). But these arrangements have failed to prevent large numbers of bank failures. The Federal Deposit Insurance Corporation established in 1935 provides a government guarantee of deposits in the subscribing banks up to a maximum per depositor. All member banks in the Federal Reserve system must, and others

[10] Hart, *op. cit.*, 27.

may, join the Insurance Corporation, paying a premium based on their deposit liabilities to provide the fund out of which losses are paid.

In most other industrial countries, deposit banks were subject to no legal control during the 19th century (e.g., Britain, France, and Germany). But there was some actual control, because the commercial banks turned in time of stress to the central bank. The Bank of England developed a management policy to help maintain the gold standard. It kept reserves against its note issues well beyond those required by law and varied the actual reserve from time to time. It indirectly controlled the reserves of commercial banks by advice and pressure and by regulating its rate of interest on loans. But, in times of real difficulty, the Bank turned to the government for authority to suspend payments or reduce its reserve below the legal minimum; thus the government could also somewhat control the Bank of England. The German Reichsbank was closely controlled by the government. The Bank of France was actually, though not legally, more independent of the government than the central banks of Britain or Germany. It was, however, authorized to suspend payments on several occasions. The concentration of banking in these three countries almost compelled the government to avert the failure of a large bank, irrespective of the legal requirement of convertibility.

Governments progressed, therefore, from the definition of the standard to control of notes and bank debt. Concern with the safety of notes and bank debts through convertibility could stabilize the value of the various forms of money only in terms of each other. The value of monetary units in terms of goods and services changed in response to changes in total monetary supply and the demand for money. Demand increased greatly because of increases in population and the volume of trade. In the U.S.A. the monetary supply was about 10% of the national income in 1840 and 95% in 1945. The supply was increased beyond the amount that would have been available if it had consisted only of full value metallic money, by the increases in paper money and later of bank debts. In fact total supply progressively increased in relation to the supply of monetary metals. The monetary base changed in most countries, but the value of gold was unstable because supply did not change with changes in demand for monetary and nonmonetary purposes. From 1815 to 1848 the output of gold was falling. Any resulting tendency for prices to fall in Britain (then the only gold standard country) was reinforced by an increasing demand for money, but partly offset by a decline in the proportion of the money supply backed by gold. Between 1848 and 1870 the output of gold increased, notably in California and Australia, and gold prices rose. There followed the golden age of capitalism, characterized by tremendous railroad building, the Second Empire in France, and the rise of Bismarck in Germany. Between 1870 and 1895 the output of gold was falling, and the demand for it increased when Germany and many other countries adopted the gold standard. From 1895 to 1914 a steady supply of gold from South Africa joined with prevailing monetary policies to induce a general upward movement of prices and marked increases in production.

Prices fell markedly in Britain and the U.S.A. from 1815 to 1850, but money wages fell a little in Britain and rose a little in the U.S.A. Real wages of fully employed workers rose, but chronic and cyclical unemployment largely offset the increase, and costs of production were falling because of the new technology, improved transport facilities, and the exploitation of natural resources in new areas. Profits were high and progress was rapid, but at the expense of a degrading exploitation of labor.[11] Changes in the supply of and demand for money combined with changes in technology to generate an industrial revolution that might otherwise have been an industrial evolution.[12] But this stimulus failed to diffuse purchasing power and thereby provide an internal market for expanding production. In fact, the gold standard failed to achieve continued steady growth of production. In the past century, the gold standard has operated simultaneously in Britain, France, Germany, and the U.S.A. for only 40 years, but during this period there occurred the depression of the 1890s, the creeping inflation of 1899 to 1913, and the financial crises of 1883, 1904 and 1907. From 1925 to 1931, when attempts were being made to restore the gold standard, there was serious unemployment in Britain and Germany, the stock market boom in the U.S.A., and the depression beginning in 1929.[13] These recurrent fluctuations in production were not caused by monetary policy, but they were exaggerated by it. After 1870, however, international trade was facilitated by the stability of exchange rates among gold-using countries.

b. 1914 to 1950

The gold standard that evolved during the 19th century fell victim to the wars and depression of the first half of the 20th century. By 1950 governments had abandoned the search for automatic monetary controls and accepted responsibility for overt monetary management.

Governments are rarely able to maintain an unimpaired metallic standard during major wars. They increase their expenditures beyond the amounts taken over from the population in taxes and loans. The resulting increase in total spending raises prices and would cause monetary reserves to be exported unless preventive action were taken. Britain suspended payments during the Napoleonic wars, and inconvertible paper currency was issued in the U.S.A. during the Revolutionary and Civil

---

[11] Clark, J. M., in National Bureau of Econ. Res. *Problems in Economic Growth* (mimeo), 42.

[12] Hamilton, E. J., "Profit, Inflation and the Industrial Revolution," LVI *Quar. Jour. Econ.*, 1942, 256; "Prices and Progress," XII *Jour. Econ. Hist.*, 1952, 325, 344; Keynes, *Treatise on Money*, II, Ch. 30.

[13] Hart, *op. cit.*, 373.

Wars. All belligerent governments abandoned the gold standard during the war of 1914-18, resorted to inflation to pay part of the cost of the war, and suffered from severe price increases. In Germany the mark had lost almost all value by 1924. Monetary history repeated itself during the war of 1939-45, but the cost of the war and its financial repercussions were larger. The British and U.S. governments covered a much greater proportion of the cost of the war by taxation than in 1914. In the U.S.A. about 40% of the cost of the war was paid out of taxes and in Britain a considerably higher proportion. But expansions of bank debt increased the supply of purchasing power beyond what was needed to exchange the available goods and services at stable prices and prices rose (Table 45).

TABLE 45

INCREASES IN PRICES IN SELECTED COUNTRIES BETWEEN 1936 AND 1946*

	Index
Argentina	216.4
Australia	144.8
Belgium	336.7†
Brazil	273.3†
Canada	135.6
Chile	264.5
Colombia	212.8†
Costa Rica	211.5
Cuba	235.8†
Czechoslovakia	302.0
Denmark	192.7
Egypt	296.7
France	808.3
Greece	15,834.2
India	335.0
Iran	512.3
Italy	5,884.5
Mexico	284.8
Netherlands	250.2
New Zealand	156.2
Norway	176.4
Peru	262.5
Poland	11,900.0†
Sweden	167.3
Switzerland	199.0
Turkey	392.9
Union of South Africa	165.5
United Kingdom	171.2
U.S.A.	163.1
Uruguay	157.9†
Venezuela	155.6

---

* Source: Metzler, L. A., "Exchange Rates and the International Monetary Fund," in *International Monetary Policies*, Federal Reserve System Post-War Economic Studies No. 7, 1947. The base period is generally October 1936 to June 1937, and the period to which the index relates is generally November 1946. Prices are wholesale prices except where otherwise indicated.

† Cost of living.

Governments sought to minimize the effect of the "inflationary gap" by price control and rationing (to reduce demand). In France and the U.S.A. these controls were only partly effective because black markets appeared, in which commodities could be bought either in excess of the legal ration or above legal maximum prices (or both). Insofar as price control was effective, some purchasing power was immobilized, but remained ready to be spent on postwar purchases. Occupying powers typically diverted goods and services to themselves during hostilities by increases in currency and loans from banks.

Faith in the gold standard survived the experiences of 1914-18. The U.S.A. returned to free dealings in gold in 1919, Germany in 1924, Britain in 1925, and France in 1926. The French franc had a gold content of 20% of the pre-war franc, but in the other countries the gold content of the unit was the same as in 1914. But the relative gold content of the units was not the same as their value in international trade. French exports, for instance, were encouraged and British exports hampered,[14] and the system was unstable. Furthermore, it was by then evident that while the gold standard stabilized exchange rates, it did not assure stable prices. In fact, widespread attempts to establish or increase monetary gold reserves would raise the value of gold and depress prices.

An international monetary conference at Genoa in 1922 recommended the general return to a gold base but extensive use of gold exchange standards (using foreign exchange as a reserve) and explicit cooperation among central banks to regulate the value of gold.[15] Central banks, including those of France and Germany, were authorized to hold part of their reserves in foreign exchange between 1922 and 1931.[16] But the U.S.A., which was attracting gold from other countries (Ch. 26), sought to avoid rising prices, and became concerned with the type of price behavior most likely to induce stable production. Price stability was advocated on the ground that it would be equitable, would eliminate long swings in the value of money, and possibly reduce business cycles. But not enough was known about the speed and extent of responses to monetary controls to make stabilization possible, and it was doubtful whether the available instruments of control were adequate. Furthermore, stable prices alone would not prevent depression. Prices falling in general harmony with falling costs transmit the benefits of improvements in production to purchasers in general, and enable them to buy the increasing output. Stable prices with rising wages transmit the benefits to workers and again provide an

---

[14] Hart, op. cit., 371; Keynes, J. M., Economic Consequences of Sterling Parity; League of Nations, International Currency Experience: Lessons of the Inter-War Period, 1944, Ch. 1.

[15] Hawtrey, Monetary Reconstruction; League of Nations, International Currency Experience, Ch. II.

[16] League of Nations, International Currency Experience, 30. The foreign exchange reserves of central banks amounted to $350 million in 1913 but $2000 million in 1920.

outlet for increased production. But in the U.S.A. during the 1920s both wages and prices were fairly stable while costs of production were falling. Credit was expanded sufficiently to offset the effect of these falling costs on prices. Profits increased, heavy speculation ensued and the now-famous crash of the stock market occurred in 1929. Prices fell and the gold-standard countries faced falling wages and capital values; declining tax yields increased the difficulty of balancing government budgets. There was no purely monetary device for stimulating business again. Britain abandoned the gold standard again in 1931, and Norway, Sweden, Egypt, Denmark, Finland, Canada, and Portugal, followed. The U.S.A. followed in 1933,[17] France, Switzerland and the Netherlands by 1936, and Japan in 1937. Germany remained on the gold standard in law, but nullified it by a series of manipulations.

When governments shift from a gold to a managed standard, they must choose their objectives. Except in time of war, the maintenance of reasonably full use of resources (Ch. 23) has been the primary objective, and general government fiscal policy one of the principal instruments for achieving it. The U.S.A. initiated its first "New Deal" program in 1933, providing increased government loans, programs for raising industrial wages and farm incomes, and expenditures on relief and public works;[18] other countries adopted similar programs.

After the war of 1939-45 monetary policies were influenced by war-time increases in purchasing power and by the necessity for diverting resources to rehabilitation and reconstruction. In the U.S.A. price controls were abandoned in 1946. Consumers spent an abnormally high proportion of their disposable income in 1946-7 because of their reserves of purchasing power. Business men, for the same reason, embarked on plant expansions, and wholesale prices increased about 50% in 1946 and 1947. Although inflationary pressures were released in the U.S.A., they continued to be partly suppressed in Britain by postwar price control and rationing. But purchasing power was thus diverted into uncontrolled activities (like travel and dog racing) that attracted resources from needed production. Inability to exercise purchasing power also reduced the incentive to work. In Belgium, Holland, and Austria the government withdrew much of the wartime additions to the currency. A large part of all holdings of currency and bank accounts was placed in blocked accounts later liquidated out of capital levies, taxes on war profits, and the like.[19] The German mark lost virtually all value after 1945, and a new mark was issued in 1948. In France some large denomination notes were withdrawn at the liberation, but no other steps were taken to reduce the volume of money. Extraordinary measures to reduce the volume of currency were also taken in Nor-

---

[17] Hart, *op. cit.*, 382 ff.

[18] *Ibid.*, 321.

[19] Dupriez, *Monetary Reconstruction in Belgium*, Ch. III.

way, Denmark, Greece, and Japan. By 1948 the total currency in circulation in a number of European countries ranged from 220% to 12,925% of that in 1938. But as prices did not rise proportionately (partly owing to price controls and subsidies), the real value of the currency in circulation in 1948 was only 45% of its 1938 value in France but 287% in Norway (Table 46).

TABLE 46

CURRENCY CIRCULATION IN EUROPEAN COUNTRIES IN 1948
COMPARED WITH 1938*

	Fourth quarter 1948 as percentage of 1938	
	Total currency circulation†	Real value‡
Norway	451	287
Czechoslovakia	908	281
Denmark	336	199
Sweden	293	187
Portugal	365	171
United Kingdom	304	167
Austria	576	158
Ireland	279	153
Finland	1,217	150
Switzerland	238	145
Netherlands	295	142
Spain	465	101
Belgium	366	97
Poland§	12,440	94
Italy	4,468	92
Hungary	220	68
Greece	12,925	51
France	847	45

* U.N., *Econ. Surv. of Europe for 1948*, 32.

† Includes notes and, usually, coins (except in the United Kingdom where the figure includes notes and demand deposits).

‡ Total volume deflated by change in cost of living.

§ Adjusted for change in population.

The need for postwar reconstruction, and the inadequacy of private investment, dominated the monetary policies of countries in western Europe between 1948 and 1950. Unbalanced budgets led to inflation and forced saving, notably in France, where the value of the franc has depended partly on the willingness of the French to pay taxes, which have, in fact, fallen short of government expenditures. In Italy, however, inflation was accompanied by large-scale unemployment, partly because industry was expanded in wartime by drawing upon disguised rural unemployment that reappeared as visible unemployment in towns at the end of the war.[20] Britain maintained low interest rates after 1945 to encourage investment while, for the most part, it balanced its budgets.[21]

[20] U.N., *Inflationary and Deflationary Tendencies 1946-8*, 10.

[21] Rowan, D., "Banking and Credit under the Labor Government, 1945-1949," 12 *Jour. of Pol.*, 290 ff.

This policy would tend to cause inflation, which was, however, partly suppressed. In Germany, the minimum reserves of the central and commercial banks were regulated to control inflation. The outbreak of the Korean War in June 1950 increased the burden of armament expenditures on national budgets. Most countries then sought to avoid direct controls on wages, consumption, and the allocation of materials by raising rates of interest, restricting bank lending, and increasing taxation.[22]

Between 1914 and 1950, therefore, the gold standard was displaced by managed standards used to divert resources to facilitate military activities or postwar reconstruction.[23] But the need to stabilize employment and production has increased in urgency while the inadequacy of purely monetary devices to achieve this object has become evident. Differences in the impact of war, and in national attitudes, have resulted in differences in the rate of shrinkage of units of account and necessitated new rates of exchange. Many governments have accepted responsibility for stabilizing output but they still have to show that, though they are willing to unbalance their budgets and go into debt to stimulate production, they are equally willing to raise taxes in excess of expenditures and pay off debt when signs of inflation appear. And even if they succeed, their success may undermine the capitalist character of their economies. Such exchange stability as has been achieved has been largely at the expense of controls over foreign trade. Exchange within the typical capitalist economies has also been considerably interfered with because controls have cut into the operation of the free market economy.

c. The British Dominions

The British dominions except India defined their monetary unit in gold until 1914, all except Canada and India using the pound as a unit of account. Typically they had no central bank, the commercial banks keeping reserves in London in bank accounts or securities. They maintained a stable rate of exchange with the pound and were in fact on a gold exchange standard. Notes were typically issued by the commercial banks with little government control beyond the requirement of convertibility, except in South Africa (where a 40% gold reserve was required[24]). Bank loans were generally uncontrolled, except in Canada, which followed the general policy of the U.S.A.

After 1914 most of these countries began to control note issues. In Australia the treasury began such control in 1910, and the power was transferred to the Commonwealth Bank of Australia in 1924.[25] In South Africa the Reserve Bank took over all note issues in 1922. In Canada the

---

22 Federal Reserve Bank of N.Y., *Monthly Review of Credit and Business Conditions*, March 1951, 35.
23 Brown, W. A., "Gold as a Monetary Standard," IX *Tasks Econ. Hist.*, 1949, 39.
24 le Cheminant, *Colonial and Foreign Banking Systems, passim.*
25 Giblin, *Growth of a Central Bank,* 13.

central bank established in 1935 took over the Dominion note issue and the reserves held by the Finance Ministry against the issue. These countries also began to establish central banks, South Africa in 1920, Canada in 1935, and New Zealand in 1936. The Commonwealth Bank of Australia, established in 1911 as a government owned trading and savings bank, became increasingly influential as a central bank after 1930, but commercial banks were not required to keep minimum reserves at the Commonwealth Bank until 1945. The other central banks all held the required minimum reserves of the commercial banks, and their own minimum reserves were prescribed.[26]

The monetary units of these countries were linked with the pound sterling, and fluctuated in purchasing power with it. But during the depression beginning in 1929, the sterling reserves of Australia and New Zealand fell and both countries reduced the value of their currency in sterling. But South Africa, having a special interest in gold, remained on the gold standard until the end of 1932.[27] After 1939 these countries (except Canada) remained part of the sterling area with, therefore, a stable exchange with Britain, which required severe controls over foreign trade and domestic prices exercised partly through monetary controls.

After 1939 they sought to minimize price increases. The commercial banks in Australia transferred to the Commonwealth Bank practically all increases in their investible funds throughout the war, thus sacrificing any potential gains from wartime inflation.[28] Price controls, wage controls by the arbitration court, import and exchange controls, rationing, government fiscal policy and monetary policy, achieved a relatively stable price level. New Zealand followed a similar policy, but in South Africa wartime controls failed to prevent wholesale prices from rising over 80% between 1939 and 1948, and in Canada wholesale prices rose about 50% between 1939 and 1946.

After 1945 Australia and New Zealand endeavored to insulate themselves from rising world prices. In Australia the government restricted exports of goods consumed in the country, thus maintaining supplies there. It restricted imports to the foreign exchange available to pay for them (especially dollars). But by 1951 wages and prices had risen, and the government reduced inflationary pressures by increasing taxation, reducing development expenditures, and further restricting imports. In New Zealand also, wages and prices rose and the National Party government elected in 1950 to replace the Labor Party government was committed to reduce inflation. In 1951 one-third of the proceeds of wool exports were "frozen" in the bank accounts of the growers, where it was guaranteed by the government. South Africa, dominated by its interest as

---

[26] Giblin, *op. cit.*, 73, 218; League of Nations, *International Currency Experience*, 51.
[27] De Kiewiet, *A History of South Africa*, 174.
[28] Giblin, *op. cit.*, 286, 357.

a gold producer, left the sterling area in 1947 and in 1949 began to sell gold at $38.20 an ounce when the American price was $35.00, thus devaluing the South African pound to the advantage of gold mining. Canada chose, however, to subsidize gold production rather than to sell at premium prices (Ch. 26).

3. PREDOMINANTLY AGRARIAN COUNTRIES

The predominantly agrarian countries have been influenced by the nature of their economic relations with industrial countries and by monetary developments in those countries. Most had metallic standards and full-value metallic currency in circulation during the 19th century, although the importance of currency as a means of exchange and a store of value varied. Some used full-value coins issued by other countries. The Maria Theresa silver dollar (issued by the Austrian mint long after the death of Maria Theresa) circulated in Eastern Europe, the Middle East, North Africa and Abyssinia. Foreign coins remained the principal circulation in Egypt until 1914; the British gold sovereign is still used in the Middle East, and Egyptian coins (and notes) now circulate in the Sudan. The Mexican silver dollar circulated in the Far East.

A number of these countries (e.g., Mexico, China, India, and Iran) had silver standards in the 19th century. Their price levels depended on the value of silver, and when gold became the monetary base in all the major industrial countries in the 1870s, exchange rates between gold- and silver-using countries fluctuated with changes in the relative values of gold and silver. As gold rose rapidly in value relatively to silver after 1870, the value of silver monetary units fell in gold, and silver prices rose. Imports became more expensive in silver money, and exports yielded a diminishing amount of foreign exchange. India abandoned the silver standard in 1893 and tied its currency to the pound, but China retained the silver standard until the 1930s (when it was forced on to a paper standard), and Mexico and Iran retained it until 1930.

The typical underdeveloped country did not adopt a gold standard. Many adopted gold-exchange standards, under which the government accepted an obligation to convert its currency at a fixed rate into a selected foreign currency based on gold, and to sell its currency in return for the foreign currency at almost the same rate. To meet these obligations the government kept a reserve in the country into whose monetary unit their own was convertible. Most exchange standards before 1914 were based on the British pound. The Austro-Hungarian government linked its money to the pound in 1894, and the government of India in 1898. Most British dominions except Canada, most British colonial areas, and Egypt and Turkey followed the same policy before 1914. But the Russian currency was pegged to the German mark from 1892 to 1894. The currencies of the French colonial territories (and of Syria under the French mandate after 1918) were linked to the franc. Other colonial governments typically linked their colonial currencies to their own and the Philippine currency was linked to the dollar after 1903.[29] The Japanese currency was on a gold exchange standard before 1914.[30]

Exchange standards were cheap to operate. Instead of non-interest-bearing gold, reserves consisted largely of interest-bearing bank deposits and securities. The system economized the monetary use of gold, but it did so by enlarging the pyramid of money built on the world's gold stock. It required only a minor degree of management. When the foreign exchange reserve fell, the government had to decide whether it was a temporary, possibly seasonal movement, or due to a decrease in the purchasing power of the currency in relation to that of gold. In the latter event, it normally raised the interest rate. The basic management, however, was by the country into whose money the exchange standard country converted its currency, since the purchasing power of the two currencies were bound together through the virtually fixed exchange rate that, however, facilitated foreign trade.

When Britain left the gold standard in 1914, all countries with currency reserves in Britain were automatically converted from gold exchange to sterling exchange standards. Most of them followed Britain back to gold in 1925 and off again in 1931. Additional countries joined the system (including most of the Scandinavian countries, Argentina, Japan, and, for a time, France). The group of countries using a sterling exchange standard was known as the "sterling area."[31] The members were free to leave the system and to change their exchange rates without reference to London. Pounds sterling were freely convertible into any other currency, although not at a fixed rate. In fact, after 1930 prices in sterling remained fairly stable though prices in gold fell. But after 1939, most non-Commonwealth members (especially would-be neutral countries) left the system and the freedom of its members was restricted. Payments among them were uncontrolled, and exchange rates among them and with the U.S.A. were stable, but the non-sterling exchange resources of the members were pooled. Although each controlled its own import policy, the central pool of dollars and non-sterling exchange was controlled by the British government.

After 1945 the sterling area countries continued for a time with fixed exchange rates maintained by controls over foreign trade. Their dollar purchases were regulated mostly by over-all financial allocations. But by 1945 the sterling assets of member countries, other than Britain, were £2,700 million compared with £200 million in 1939. Britain was unable to meet these liabilities in goods and services because such unrequited

---

[29] Kemmerer, *Money*, 155.
[30] League of Nations, *International Monetary Experience*, 30.
[31] League of Nations, *International Currency Experience*, Ch. III.

exports would have reduced the exports needed to pay for badly needed imports. But the U.S.A. was fearful that the sterling area would operate to favor British exports to member countries, although it recognized that Britain could not immediately liquidate the accumulated wartime balances in London. Consequently, in agreeing to lend to Britain in 1945, it required that any balances liberated must be expendible anywhere (i.e. convertible into dollars) and that the current earnings of foreign exchange by sterling area countries should be available to them for current payments in any part of the world. In accordance with this agreement, sterling was made convertible in 1947, and as a result Britain lost much of its reserves of dollars and gold. Most sterling area countries agreed to restrict imports from dollar countries more severely, and to stop leaks of capital, but convertibility of sterling had to be suspended. The system was strained during 1949 because the appeal for dollar abstinence cut into its voluntary character. Members felt that they did not share equally in the formulation of policies affecting them all, and some disagreed with the devaluation of the pound (concerning which they were not consulted in advance). By the end of 1949, about £700 million of the accumulated sterling balances had been released, requiring British exports to sterling area countries at the expense of dollar exports, and contributing to the dollar shortage of the sterling area. A number of non-Commonwealth countries left the system, but in 1952 it still contained countries with a quarter of the world's population (Australia, Ceylon, India, New Zealand, Pakistan, South Africa, Southern Rhodesia, and the United Kingdom (all part of the British Commonwealth); and Burma, Iceland, Iraq, the Irish Republic, Jordan, Libya, and all British dependent territories.)

In the Middle East, Turkey, and Egypt had gold-exchange standards before 1914 when they became sterling exchange standards, and Iran a silver standard until 1930. Syria under the French mandate had a franc exchange standard after 1918, and Palestine under the British mandate was part of the sterling area. Paper currency increased in most of these countries in the 20th century, but commercial banking is little developed outside Egypt. During the war of 1939-45 there was severe inflationary pressure in the region (Table 47). Outside Turkey the presence of allied troops buying labor and supplies, and troops spending money, forced up prices. In Turkey, although there were no allied troops, the governments of countries on both sides in the war raised prices by competing for minerals and vegetable oils. Shortages of imports reinforced these pressures. Generally budgets were balanced but price controls were ineffective. Most of these countries possessed considerable sterling balances at the end of the war which were then partly immobilized although the British government has made a number of releases to Egypt. Nevertheless in postwar years most of them imported greatly in excess of their exports. After 1945 the level of prices followed no uniform pattern throughout the

TABLE 47

PRICE LEVEL CHANGES IN SELECTED COUNTRIES IN THE MIDDLE EAST,
1939, 1945, AND 1950[*]

	1945	*Wholesale prices* *(1939 = 100)* 1950 *(second half)*
Egypt	318	334
Iran	468	425
Iraq	503	488
Israel/Palestine	319	373
Lebanon	1038	118[†]
Turkey	439	437

[*] U.N., *Rev. of Econ. Cond. in the Middle East*, 1951, 84.
[†] 1950 = 100.

region (Table 47) because of differences in population pressure, government policy, rates of investment, the repercussions of the Arab-Israeli war, and monetary devaluations.[32]

These countries are now adopting a number of the monetary institutions of industrial countries. No reserves other than government securities are required against note issues in Egypt. Iran requires reserves of 100% against token coins, 30% against note issues, and 100% against deposits, the reserves consisting of gold, silver, the crown jewels, and dollar and sterling balances. No reserve requirements are imposed on commercial banks in Egypt and Syria, but in Iraq banks must keep minimum deposits at the central bank equal to 15% of their current and fixed deposits. But some parts of the Middle East use little currency and banking hardly exists outside the large cities. The banks, having invested little in local enterprises, have invested much of their funds abroad until recently (the Bank Misr in Egypt being a notable exception). And the ends to which monetary institutions can be used are limited by political and economic relations with other countries.

India had a silver currency, at least in the 17th century, but when the major industrial countries adopted a gold standard in the 1870s India stood between the gold-using west and the silver-using east with a considerable debt in pounds, which were becoming increasingly costly in rupees. Consequently, the Indian government stopped the free coinage of silver in 1893 and adjusted the supply of rupees by buying and selling sterling. After 1898 it stabilized the rupee at one-fifteenth of a pound sterling.[33] Since that time India has remained virtually on a sterling exchange standard. It formally declared a dollar value for the rupee in 1945, but the value was the equivalent of the previous sterling value, and when sterling

[32] U.N., *Rev. of Econ. Cond. in the Middle East*, 1951, 17 ff.
[33] Keynes, J. M., *Indian Currency and Finance*.

was revalued in dollars in October 1949, the rupee was devalued by the same amount. During the period 1939-45 India made heavy unrequited exports to Britain, not only paying off its debt but also accumulating heavy balances there. But Pakistan did not devalue its rupee when Britain devalued in 1949. Paper currency was issued by the Indian government mainly against gold, silver, and foreign exchange reserves.[34]

Money lending has a long history in India, and it is estimated that some 300,000 persons lend money but do not receive deposits.[35] Commercial banks under British, French, Japanese, and American control became active during the present century, mostly in financing foreign trade, and held 18% of all bank deposits in 1949.[36] The Indian-owned banks, however, had a checkered career during the first few decades of the century. They mainly finance trade rather than industry, and have offices only in the larger towns. They cover 12 to 15% of their deposit liabilities with deposits at the central banks in India and Pakistan (this is considerably less than in other parts of Asia and the Far East). But in 1949, 40% of the deposits of scheduled banks were invested in government securities. Bank deposits are increasing, but accounted in 1950 for only 35 to 37% of all the money supply in India and Pakistan.[37]

Central banking appeared in attenuated form in 1920 when the three Presidency banks in Calcutta, Bombay, and Madras were consolidated into the Imperial Bank of India. This bank held the deposits of other banks but could deal in bills of exchange only if they were payable in India, and might not borrow or accept deposits outside India. These restrictions prevented it from invading the sphere of the exchange banks.[38] Furthermore, it had no legal power to regulate private banking. The Reserve Bank of India, established in 1935, was required to keep reserves of gold or securities equal to 40% of all its liabilities, and in fact kept little gold. All the scheduled banks were required to keep balances at the Reserve Bank equal to 5% of their demand deposits and 2% of their time deposits, but in fact keep higher reserves. These scheduled banks were about 15% of all banks by number in 1950, but held about 85% of all deposits. The proportion of cash to deposits of these banks was 14% (compared with 15% for nonscheduled banks).[39] The Reserve bank has been partitioned to provide separate central banks in India, Pakistan, Ceylon, and Burma. In 1950 the Reserve Bank of India held gold and foreign securities equal to 55% of the notes it had issued, and 39% of all the credit it had granted was to the government (40% in Pakistan).[40] The Bank is subject to directions from

---

34 U.N., *Econ. Surv. of Asia and the Far East, 1950,* 459.
35 U.N., *Mobilization of Domestic Capital in . . . Asia and the Far East,* 1951, 39.
36 U.N., *Econ. Surv. of Asia and the Far East, 1951,* 465.
37 *Ibid.,* 462.
38 le Cheminant, *op. cit.,* 80 ff.
39 Reserve Bank of India, *Indian News Digest,* Aug. 17, 1951.
40 U.N., *Econ. Surv. of Asia and Far East, 1951,* 479.

the government after the Bank's governor has been consulted. During the war period 1939-45 deposits increased 65% in India, but in subsequent years the money supply has decreased somewhat. Prices in 1946 were about 150% above 1939 in India and Pakistan, and were relatively stable from 1946 to 1949. Inflationary pressures reappeared, however, especially in 1950, under the stimulus of heavy armament expenditures. After a period of decontrol in 1948 price control and rationing were reintroduced in India.

In the Far East outside India, Pakistan, Japan, and China prior to 1939, monetary systems were generally exchange standards.[41] Those in Burma, Ceylon, Hong Kong, Malaya, British Borneo, and Thailand were linked to sterling; in Indo-China to the franc; in Indonesia to the guilder; and in the Philippines to the dollar. Burma, Ceylon, Hong Kong, Malaya, British Borneo, the Philippines, and Thailand kept a foreign exchange reserve of 100% against their currency, and Indo-China and Indonesia kept 40%. Banking was relatively unimportant except in Ceylon, and there were no central banks. Since 1945 rigid exchange standards have been relaxed,[42] and most countries have established central banks. Managed currencies have been established in the Philippines, Ceylon, and Korea, but Burma has been on a foreign exchange standard since 1946. As in India, foreign banks (mostly British, Dutch, American, Indian, and Chinese) finance foreign trade but accept few local deposits and make few local loans. The locally owned banks hold mainly demand deposits (which are 80% of all deposits except in India and the Philippines). They finance local trade and little industry, and are restricted to the large cities. Partly for lack of other acceptable outlets for their funds, they covered 30% to 40% of their liabilities with deposits at the central bank in 1950 and some held considerable amounts of government securities. Bank deposits are increasing, but only in Ceylon do they constitute more than 40% of the money supply. Private money lending is important in Burma and Indo-China.

Central banks are now generally responsible for note issues, and are required to keep prescribed reserves. The Java Bank, which is also a commercial bank, must keep reserves equal to 40% of its note and other demand liabilities. But in the Philippines, Ceylon, and Korea there is no prescribed reserve, and the banks have flexibility as to note issues. But, regardless of legal requirements, the central banks keep relatively high reserves, usually 40% or more of the total money supply. Central banks in Ceylon, Korea, and the Philippines have wide powers to control credit, but those in Burma, Indonesia, and Thailand are more restricted. In practice, however, the power to control the interest on loans by the bank has been

[41] *Ibid.*, Ch. XV, XVI.
[42] U.N., *Mobilization of Domestic Capital . . . in Asia and the Far East,* 1951, Ch. II, III.

of limited effect because commercial banks have borrowed little from the central bank. Most central banks now set minimum reserves for commercial banks, and in Ceylon, Korea, and the Philippines, the central bank can vary the requirements from time to time. In times of inflation they may require 100% reserve against increases in the deposits of commercial banks. Generally the required reserves must be in deposits at the central bank. But in Burma and Indonesia, commercial banks are not required to keep a minimum reserve at the central bank. In Ceylon, Formosa, India, Japan, South Korea, Pakistan, and the Philippines, central banks use selective credit controls, but moral suasion and supervision of banks are important instruments of control.[43] Most banking laws restrict loans by the central bank to the government in order to prevent inflation due to government compulsion on the central bank to lend, and the provision has generally been observed. But in most countries except those on a foreign exchange standard, the government can raise funds by selling securities to the central bank, and these securities can usually be used as part of the note issue reserve.

The statutes for the central banks in Asia and the Far East generally do not define the policies to be followed except in the Philippines, Korea, and Ceylon. Philippine legislation lists the "maintenance of a high level of production, employment and real income," "maintenance of the stability of the economy," and maintenance of the international stability of the monetary unit. But most of the central banks are recent. Inflation was general in the region after 1939. In 1946 prices were about 200% above 1939 in Malaya, 300% in Burma, 500% in the Philippines, 700% in Indo-China, 1000% in Thailand, 2300% in Indonesia and 5000% in Korea. But the movement decelerated after 1946, and prices fell between 1946 and 1949 in the Philippines, Indo-China, and Malaya.

Most of the Latin American countries had bimetallic currencies while under Spanish colonial rule. The *peso* was the most general unit, but it varied in weight from place to place and was of both gold and silver.[44] There was neither paper money nor banks. After gaining independence, most countries endeavored to maintain their bimetallic systems, retaining pre-existing coins with new emblems. But paper money appeared early in the 19th century in Argentina. Bimetallic standards were abandoned under local inflationary pressures, or as a result of their collapse in Europe in the 1870s, and most countries used managed standards based largely on inconvertible notes which persistently depreciated. In some countries (e.g., Peru) accounts were kept both in the local inconvertible and in a foreign metallic unit, although abortive efforts were made to establish gold standards. In Brazil persistent inflation has been only occasionally interrupted by brief periods of deflation; between 1840 and 1945 wholesale

---

[43] U.N., *Econ. Surv. of Asia and the Far East, 1951*, 211.
[44] Subercaseaux, *Monetary and Banking Policy of Chile*, 9, 34.

prices increased 2700%.[45] In Chile the peso has depreciated almost continuously for fifty years. Argentina, however, was virtually on a sterling exchange standard before 1914. Paper currency was issued in some countries by the government and in others by commercial banks, no country having a central bank. Commercial banking developed mostly after 1850 largely in the hands of foreign banks interested in the export trade and at the outset mainly British. They were subject to little control.

After 1929 many countries established gold exchange standards. When the Central Bank of Peru was established in 1931, it was required to maintain a fixed rate of exchange between its notes and gold and similar arrangements were made in Chile, Colombia, Ecuador and Bolivia.[46] Where the central bank became a mere exchange office, the money supply fluctuated widely in countries dependent on exports of a few commodities, the demand for which fluctuated. During the depression after 1929 the proceeds of exports fell drastically, and although imports were paid for (for a time) out of reserves of gold and foreign exchange, most countries were finally driven off gold again. A number of them devalued their currency and thus reduced the decline in the proceeds of their exports in local currency, relieving the planters and reducing downward pressure on wages.

Note issues were made by the government, a government commission, or the central bank. Central banks have been established in many Latin American countries, all under government control and with legally required reserves, e.g., in Chile in 1925 (with a monopoly of note issue) and in Mexico in 1931. The Bank of Brazil performs many of the functions of a central bank, but a separate organization was set up in 1932 to hold bank reserves and assist banks in difficulty. Commercial banks are often required to keep deposits at the central bank equal to a minimum proportion of their deposits, e.g., Chile, Mexico, Brazil. In Mexico banks must have a prescribed minimum capital, and current liabilities may not exceed ten times their capital and surplus. The proportion of loans of each type is also regulated. In Chile commercial banks are restricted in the proportion of their resources lent to a single borrower or another bank. They may not own real estate, livestock or farm produce or invest in ordinary corporate securities. Some central banks are restricted in their power to lend to the government.

During the war of 1939-45 exports from Latin American countries typically increased in both volume and price, while imports were severely restricted. Foreign balances consequently increased, but increased receipts for export goods and increased wages raised the demand for the short supply of consumer goods and, therefore, their prices (Table 48), price

---

[45] Spiegel, *The Brazilian Economy*, 43.
[46] Kemmerer, *op. cit.*, 162; *Gold and the Gold Standard*, 169.

TABLE 48

INCREASES IN MONEY SUPPLY AND WHOLESALE PRICES IN
LATIN AMERICAN COUNTRIES, 1938-48

	Money Supply (1937 = 100)*	Wholesale Prices (1937 = 100)†
Argentina	503	533
Bolivia		347
Brazil	472	335
Chile	699	
Colombia	555	
Cuba	659	
Ecuador	481	
Guatemala	359	
Mexico	544	218
Paraguay	602	416
Peru	760	396
Uruguay	340	180
Venezuela	482	174

* U.N., *Econ. Surv. of Latin America*, 1948, 243.
† U.N., *Monthly Bull. of Stat.;* Dec. 1950, 185.

controls being generally ineffective.[47] Military expenditures by the U.S.A., government development expenditures (e.g., in Mexico and Chile), and budget deficits (especially in Argentina and Brazil) reinforced these inflationary tendencies. While rising prices stimulated attempts to increase domestic production, these efforts were limited and caused further increases in incomes.[48] For a time after 1945 they paid for part of their increased imports out of their holdings of gold and foreign currency (which had increased over 100% since 1938).[49] But as the reserves ran down, internal monetary controls were tightened.

The economies of most Latin American countries are dependent on exports of a few mineral or agricultural products for the means of paying for imports. As the demand for their exports has fluctuated, they have been intermittently under pressure that has been intensified where exchange rates with more developed countries have been stabilized. Depressions and, more recently, wars have intensified the desire for internal development. But, because the propensity to save and invest in these countries was low, governments have supplied funds in excess of local saving, thus increasing the money supply and inducing inflationary price increases. Central banks have often financed part of development expenditures as well as government deficits. Central banks endeavoring to minimize inflation have been frustrated. In Chile the original restrictions on loans to the government by the central bank have been relaxed to permit it to finance budget deficits and the development institutes. On a num-

---

[47] U.N., *Survey of Current Inflationary and Deflationary Tendencies*, 1947, 80.
[48] *Ibid.*, 76 ff.
[49] U.N., *Econ. Surv. Latin America 1948*, 238.

ber of occasions the reserves required to be kept by the central bank and the commercial banks have been eased, and the banks have borrowed heavily from the central bank. In Mexico the commercial banks were required to become members of the Bank of Mexico and to keep minimum deposits in the central bank; the minimum was raised in 1941. The commercial banks have been kept highly liquid since 1940, but the central bank has been less liquid because it has become the principal holder of government securities issued to finance development and cover budget deficits. These holdings represent nearly half the increase in money supply since 1941. In Brazil commercial banks must keep reserves on deposit with the *Banco do Brasil* equal to 4 to 8% of their own deposits, the percentage being fixed by the Superintendent of Banks. But in 1946 they were allowed to substitute federal bonds for 50% of these reserves. In Argentina efforts to finance development without inflation, by means of state export monopolies and special exchange rates for meat exports, have been offset by inflationary wage, social security, and subsidy policies (Ch. 23).

After 1948 inflationary pressures were somewhat reduced. Central banks, finding quantitative control difficult, sought to direct new credit into productive rather than trade and speculative activities (notably in Mexico).[50] In Chile, exchange controls have been used to facilitate the import of capital goods and raw materials, and in Argentina imports and exports have been controlled through a variety of exchange rates. But in 1951 Chile sharply raised the reserve requirements on existing deposits in commercial banks, and imposed high requirements on increases in deposits. Peru also imposed high reserve requirements on increases in deposits before 1952, and again in 1953, and Mexico required a 100% reserve against increases in deposits in 1951. But the underlying forces making for a decline in the purchasing power of the monetary unit remain, and efforts at development intensify. Rising prices bring rising profits but often a fall in real wages.[51]

In Africa money affects the indigenous population far less than the European. Currency is little used where the population is engaged in subsistence agriculture, although the two wars of the 20th century have increased the circulation of paper money. Banks are relatively few, of foreign origin, and concerned almost wholly with the European population and the export trade. In the typical colonial area the currency is linked to that of the imperial country, paper money issues (but not banking) are controlled, and there are no central banks. Since 1939 attempts have been made in British colonial areas to prevent rising prices for exports from generating inflation within the area (often by holding back from agricultural producers part of the proceeds of exports) (Ch. 8), but in

---

[50] U.N., *Econ. Surv. of Latin America, 1949*, 492, 499.
[51] U.N., *Inflationary and Deflationary Tendencies, 1946-8*, 26.

postwar years these policies have met with increasing resistance. In British West Africa, the sterling exchange standard caused the volume of currency to vary with the export surplus, which depended mainly on the size of the cocoa crop and its price. The Marketing Board was intended to cushion these fluctuations by holding back from the farmer a part of the proceeds of his crop, but in fact it has held back only as much as is politically feasible rather than as much as is desirable for economic stability. Some governments have increased their acquisitions of dollars by allowing gold producers to sell their output in the premium market (e.g., West Africa and Southern Rhodesia).

In general, agrarian countries have suffered changes in the value of their monetary units in step with those of industrialized countries. But there have been changes in the value of their units in relation to those of industrial countries and they have mitigated the local effect of fluctuations in the proceeds of export sales. More recently monetary units in some underdeveloped countries have fallen in value as a result of attempts to industrialize and diversify their economies more rapidly than real capital formation, foreign loans, and the availability of exports permit. But inflation is often less effective in increasing real savings than in more industrial societies, because agrarian societies are less dependent on the use of money, and the mass of the population lives so near to subsistence that it can contribute little even in forced saving. As fixed money incomes are relatively unimportant, inflation has little effect in redistributing income. Inflation is likely to accelerate and delay the transition to a monetary economy necessary to the development of specialization because confidence in money is undermined and its use diminished.[52]

Although many of the instruments of monetary control are being introduced from more industrialized countries, they are confronted by special difficulties. Raising the cost of bank credit at best affects the volume of bank deposits, which are a relatively unimportant part of the money supply. Currency, the more important part, can be reduced only by balance of payments deficits or increased taxation. Even the short-term loans of banks are in fact difficult to control where commercial banks do not borrow from the central bank (and often keep reserves considerably in excess of legal and normal requirements) and where open market operations are hampered by the lack of an organized securities market. Central bank control is also weakened where foreign banks can obtain cash either by borrowing from their head offices or in foreign money markets (where there is no exchange or capital import control). Restrictive credit policies may also merely force transactions into the large non-monetized sector, leaving prices in the monetized sector as high as before.[53]

---

[52] Singer, "Economic Progress in Underdeveloped Countries," XVI *Social Research*, 8.
[53] U.N., *Econ. Surv. of Asia and the Far East, 1951*, 203.

4. Socialist Societies

The notion that money would die out in a socialist economy has long since been repudiated by the rulers of Russia. Personal incomes are paid in money, and goods and services are paid for in money by both individuals and state enterprises. Money units are used for calculating costs, profits, and taxes. The supply of currency and bank debts is controlled by the state, which uses its controls to achieve its economic aims. Russian monetary policy has had much in common with that of capitalist countries, notably in its use of inflation and its later attempts to use the monetary system to stimulate production and appraise productive operations.

Soviet Russia has never had a true metallic standard. The czarist budget had been in deficit since 1914, and by 1917 the deficit was over four times the state revenue. Between 1917 and 1924 the former monetary system was destroyed. In May 1919 the revolutionary government was authorized to issue as much money as was needed to acquire purchasing power. Few taxes were collected, and by March 1924 the currency circulation was 497 times greater than in July 1914, and the price level 62 billion times higher than in 1913.[54] But as early as 1921, the Congress of Soviets recognized the need for a gradual transition to a stable monetary unit to facilitate trade and provide a unit of account. In 1922 the state bank was empowered to establish a new currency unit, the *chervonetz,* equal to 10 czarist gold rubles, against reserves 25% in gold and stable foreign exchange and 75% in short-term bills and easily marketable commodities. By the end of 1923 this currency provided 75% of the total, the remainder consisting of old issues of rubles that had lost practically all value. It provided a bridge back to a more stable currency, but did not place the country on a gold standard. In 1924 the government authorized a new paper currency defined in gold rubles and legal tender, but inconvertible and without specific reserve. Previous government issues were redeemed (at 50,000 1923 rubles and 50 billion 1922 rubles for one new gold ruble). Silver and copper small change were issued, and in 1924 the issue of paper money to cover budget deficits was ordered discontinued.[55] The convertibility of the *chervonetz* was abrogated in 1926, when also its export and the export of treasury notes and coin was forbidden. In 1928 imports of coin and notes were also forbidden. An official exchange rate in U.S. dollars was established by a commission at the state bank. The government holds reserves of gold and platinum, but not specifically as reserves against the paper currency, and does not publish the amount of its holdings of metals. The currency was, therefore, based on a managed standard, where it has since remained in spite of the definition of the ruble in gold.

The monetary system is managed to effectuate the production plan. The government aims at supplying the amount of currency and bank debt

[54] Arnold, *Banks Credit and Money in Soviet Russia, loc. cit.;* Schwartz, *op. cit.,* 398.
[55] Schwartz, *op. cit.,* 400.

necessary to effect the transactions under the plan. Currency needs are estimated by reference to the planned payments to individuals and the planned provision of consumer goods. The needed supply of credit is estimated from the working balances of enterprises and individuals required by the plans for investment, trade, and the state budget. The government has avoided the runaway inflation of the early revolutionary years, but has not stabilized the purchasing power of the ruble. Between January 1928 and April 1935 the total currency in circulation increased nearly 400%, but the need for money also increased. The industrialization program greatly increased the volume of monetary transactions, especially since increasing numbers of workers were paid in money. Increased purchasing power was also needed after 1927 because of increases in wages to encourage output and allocate labor. Reductions of some wages could have been used to reallocate labor, but were found to be difficult. Payments exceeded the amount planned because the cost of capital construction exceeded the planned cost, labor productivity fell short of planned productivity, accumulation fell short of planned accumulation, and because socialization was faster than was planned. At the same time, supplies of agricultural goods were reduced by the collectivization program in the early 1930s, and supplies of consumer goods were reduced generally by the planned diversion of a high proportion of national resources into investment. The cost of living rose 400% to 600% between 1928 and 1937,[56] although during the early 1930s stringent rationing in urban areas ensured minimal supplies to workers, but reduced reliance on money as a distributive device.

During the war of 1939-45, supplies of consumer goods were greatly reduced and the government returned to the issue of paper money to cover its budget deficit (especially in 1942). In three years the supply of currency increased 2.4 times although taxes were raised and bonds were issued in large quantities. As in other belligerent countries, financial inducements to increase output, both in industry and agriculture, were not wholly offset by the fiscal policy of the government. The government offered premium prices for goods vital to war, for production in excess of planned output, and for quality above a prescribed level (e.g., the octane rating of gasoline). Payroll disbursements increased because of increased hours of work, payment of overtime rates, bonus payment systems, and subsidies to workers who followed plants as they were moved eastward. The effect of inflation upon prices was partly suppressed by the reimposition of rationing and the sale of rationed goods for some years at pre-war prices. But farmers were allowed to sell their surplus produce in free markets, and inflation expressed itself there. In 1943 the price of black bread was one ruble per kilo within the ration, and 130 rubles per kilo outside the ration. The free market was probably maintained to provide an

---

[56] Chapman, Janet, "Real Wages in the Soviet Union," *Rev. Econ. and Stats.*, May 1954.

outlet for the free rubles and give some reality to incentive payments in rubles. After 1944, when the supply of food and consumer goods began to increase again, the government opened chains of stores and restaurants selling unrationed goods. At first, they charged about the free market prices, but gradually their prices were reduced, and in 1946 the price of rationed goods was tripled. Thus the two sets of prices were brought together in preparation for the abolition of rationing. By 1948 the cost of living was about three times as high as in 1937.[57]

After 1945 the Russian government decided to restore and emphasize pecuniary incentives to produce by abolishing rationing and restoring to the holders of money the right to dispose of it as they wished (at the prices the government decided to charge). But (as in most other countries where inflation had been partly suppressed), the population held abnormally large amounts of purchasing power that, if spent freely, would force up prices and wages, as happened under similar circumstances in the U.S.A. In 1947 the government announced that, as a result of war, the quantity of money (some of which, it said, had been issued by the enemy and was false) had greatly increased. In consequence of this increase, and the decline in the supply of goods, prices had increased ten or fifteen times over the pre-war level. The government, therefore, decided to provide for "the circulation of new money at full value and the withdrawal from circulation of false money as well as money not of full value," to prevent the "speculative elements who enriched themselves during the war and accumulated considerable sums of money" from buying up goods when rationing was abolished. It abolished rationing and the two-price system and exchanged all currency (except coins) at one new ruble for 10 old ones. This 90% tax on holdings of notes fell most heavily on the farmers who had hoarded cash out of lack of faith in banks and bonds, and on speculators who held cash for fear of revealing their profits. Accounts at government banks and government bonds were revalued in the new currency at more favorable rates. Bank accounts were converted: on the first 3000 rubles, one new for one old ruble; amounts between 3000 and 10,000 rubles, two new for three old rubles; and amounts in excess of 10,000 rubles, one new for two old rubles. The bank accounts of cooperatives and collective farms were converted at four new for five old rubles. All previous government loans (except those of 1938 and 1947) were revalued at three rubles of the old loans for one ruble of a new 2% loan. All taxes, obligations to the state, wages and other fixed obligations were payable at the same rate in the new ruble as in the old.

As the supply of consumer goods was increasing, many prices were reduced. Staple foods were priced at or just below the previous prices for rationed goods. Manufactured goods were priced higher than the previous rate for rationed supplies, but much lower than the previous free

---

[57] Chapman, loc. cit.

prices. The average price for consumption goods in the first quarter of 1948 was about 30% below their price in the first quarter of 1947.[58] The distribution of incomes changed, mainly at the expense of the agricultural sector, which bore much of the burden of the 90% tax on holdings of cash. But even agriculturalists were probably better off than when they hoarded cash. The fall in the price of agricultural produce in the farm bazaars was roughly compensated by the fall in the price of manufactured consumer goods, and the price for produce delivered to the state remained unchanged.[59] The urban population (especially skilled workers and higher paid officials who had previously spent a considerable part of their money incomes on unrationed goods) received increased real incomes as a result of the elimination of high prices for unrationed goods. And the difference between the real incomes of skilled and unskilled workers increased. But no large group suffered a reduction in real incomes, for aggregate production was rising. The abolition of rationing increased incentives to production, which increased remarkably in 1948. A little later, when prices in basic industries and transit charges were raised to conform to higher costs and obviate the need for state subsidies, it was stated that "money and prices have again become essential regulating factors in economic life."[60] The prices of a number of important consumer goods were reduced a further 8% to 49% in 1950 when Russia redefined the ruble in gold, and similar reductions have been made in each subsequent spring (those in 1953 being considerable) (Ch. 31). In 1952 the cost of living was 900% to 1400% above 1928, but about 30% below 1948.[61]

A socialist country might be expected to guide its economy by direct control of the allocation of resources, backed by control of prices and taxation. But in fact inflationary devices were used to achieve both development in time of peace and defense in time of war; on both occasions its policies resembled those of non-socialist countries. In wartime the high prices of consumers' goods in free markets diluted the ruble rewards offered to induce increased industrial production, although the resulting benefits to the peasants who sold in these markets were but temporary. Thus while the Russian monetary system has been regarded as a mere appendage of the productive system, it has in fact been used to fill gaps when the basic plan is not fulfilled as to costs, productivity of labor, savings, and the like.

The monetary arrangements of eastern European countries have been assimilated, at various speeds, to those of Russia since 1945. These countries came under Russian influence with currencies greatly inflated compared with 1939, for the same reason as in Russia and other belligerent

---

58 U.N., *Inflationary and Deflationary Tendencies,* 47.
59 U.N., *Econ. Surv. of Europe in 1948,* 27.
60 U.N., *Econ. Surv. of Europe in 1948,* 28.
61 Chapman, *loc. cit.*

countries. In many, military occupation authorities had also issued currency to finance their activities. In Czechoslovakia, for instance, the currency was about fifteen times as large in 1945 as in 1938, and in Hungary it had lost all value by 1946. Most of these countries eliminated much of these currency expansions. In Czechoslovakia the government reduced the currency about 80% in 1945 and announced that prices would be stabilized at about three times their level in 1939, while wages were raised above their 1939 level less than prices. In Rumania the volume of currency was reduced in 1947 and in Hungary a new currency was issued after 1946.[62] The new units have all been managed units, and in Czechoslovakia and Rumania inflation began again. Rumania raised the exchange value of its currency for a second time in 1952 and reduced prices and wages 80%. Poland established a new *zloty* unit in 1950 equal to the Russian gold ruble. Banking systems in all these countries have also been taken over by their governments, and operate in much the same way as the government banks in Russia. In Czechoslovakia, for instance, the banks were bankrupt in 1945 largely because the German authorities had filled them with worthless currency and debts due from Germany.

China has for some years suffered from runaway currency inflation. The central government was almost limited to customs duties as a source of revenue. Other taxes were controlled by local lords, who remitted little to the central government, which, therefore, issued inconvertible paper currency in large quantities to meet war expenditures prior to 1945. During the war of 1939-45 Japanese issues of occupation currency caused further inflation. This occupation currency was repudiated after 1945, leaving a vacuum later filled by additional issues of Chinese national currency. In 1946 Shanghai prices were about 400,000 times as high as in 1937. The communist government at first accepted the abandonment of money as a unit of account. Victory bonds, for instance, were issued in *Fen* units defined in prescribed quantities of rice, flour, white shirting and coal. Using a weighted average of the wholesale prices of these commodities in six cities, the government announced the money value of the *fen* every ten days. Somewhat comparable units were established for wages and bank deposits. Manufacturers and producers of materials were encouraged to barter, and taxes (especially agricultural taxes) were paid in kind. By 1952 the government controlled 90% of all loans and deposits through the People's Bank, which was the central clearing house for all transactions, and the repository of all capital (including the working capital of the state enterprises).[63]

---

[62] Nogaro, "Hungary's Recent Monetary Crisis and its Theoretical Meaning," XXXVIII *Am. Econ. Rev.*, 526.

[63] Eckstein, A., "Conditions and Prospects for Economic Growth in Communist China," VI *World Politics*, 1954, 21, 23.

Chapter 26

International Coordination of Production

The national incomes of most economies are influenced by the position they occupy in the international scheme of production. The extent and effectiveness of international specialization depends on the arrangements affecting the exchange of goods and services and the movements of capital and labor. These arrangements consist partly of international markets and partly of authoritarian influences, national and international. How far these arrangements result in the maximization of world satisfactions from production is a proper but unanswerable question. But it is possible to indicate some of the ways in which these arrangements react upon economies of different types.

A. Market Influences

1. The Market for Goods

International exchanges of goods began some thousands of years ago. Indeed, trade between political units is probably older than internal trade based on gain. Egypt, Minoan Crete, Greece, and Rome were all dependent on supplies from abroad, partly of minerals, partly of food (e.g., wheat). India, Egypt, and later Britain exported wheat under the Roman Empire. Such exchange indicates international specialization. But the high cost of transport (owing partly to lack of security), and the small differences in economic potentialities in a world in which most economies were on a subsistence basis, held trade to a small volume. Primitive societies often prohibit profit-seeking trade among their members, but permit such trade with "foreigners." The trade of most northwest European countries during the early centuries of the Christian era was also chiefly limited to minerals not available everywhere (gold, silver, iron, copper, tin), vegetable products such as could be grown only in a few places and transported fairly easily (spices and tropical products such as sugar

540

and olive oil), and fabricated articles based on local skills (silks, cotton cloth from India, woollen cloth, and steel from Toledo and Damascus).

International markets began to expand in the western world in the ninth and tenth centuries and again in the 16th century. But the great expansion came after 1800, especially between 1870 and 1913. During this period the foreign trade of Britain, Germany, France, and the U.S.A. increased about 155%—that of the U.S.A. and Germany 300 or 400%. The market never recovered after 1918 the broad integrating functions it had exercised during the 19th century. Controls of foreign trade were greater than before and subsequently greatly increased. The collapse of the gold standard removed one of the principal instruments that facilitated the operation of the international market in goods.

Methods of organizing trade have changed with increases in its volume and in business organization in general. In the ancient world a merchant frequently fitted out a ship, acquired a cargo of exports and went with it to buy imports which he brought back and sold to resident merchants. Sometimes part of the capital was obtained by mortgaging the ship and the cargo, thus separating ownership and control. In the ninth and tenth centuries much trade in the west was conducted at international fairs, where goods were assembled for sale from over wide areas at intervals of six months to two years. Merchants travelled to the fairs in caravans for safety. These fairs survived to be used by early capitalist merchants. Later, merchants resided abroad at key trading posts, usually settling in groups (like the Hanse merchants in London or the British Merchant Adventurers in Calais).

In the 17th century some of the forms of organization later important in the domestic organization of production appeared in foreign trade. Joint-stock companies appeared in the 17th century (the East India Company being the most famous of the early ones). In the 19th century, the machinery for foreign trade was elaborated. Extraterritoriality was slowly abandoned (most recently in China and Turkey). Commercial agencies or brokerage organizations (in which Greeks, Armenians, and Chinese were long prominent, and still are in some areas) increased, notably in Britain, Holland, and Germany. Import and export firms began to specialize in the class of products or the countries dealt with. Commodity exchanges (organized markets for particular classes of goods) developed to facilitate foreign trade, more particularly, imports into Europe through markets at the major points of entry. Such less homogeneous products as tea, wool, furs, and hides were, and continue to be, sold at periodic auctions. Still more recently, large corporate units for production have established branches in foreign countries to distribute their products or purchase materials. Some manufacturing firms have begun to undertake assembling and partial manufacturing abroad (such as the American automobile, electrical goods, and other manufacturing companies).

International trade creates problems of payment more complex than those of domestic trade. In the ancient world there was some banking for this purpose, although exporters often brought back goods in payment for exports. Merchant bankers appeared in Europe during the period of merchant capitalism. As merchants with correspondents in foreign countries, they could easily add to their trade in goods a financial business involving money-changing and dealing in bills of exchange, thus facilitating payment and financing goods in transit. But after about 1850 large incorporated banks in the major countries began to take over much of the short-term financing of foreign trade from the merchant bankers. After 1870 the larger German banks formed foreign subsidiaries, the British banks followed, and later those in France, Holland (for the East Indies), Belgium (for the Congo), and Japan. By the end of the 19th century much foreign trade was paid for directly or indirectly through London. The bill of exchange drawn on London was not only the primary instrument of settlement but also the means of financing goods in transit and until sale. Merchants in most countries trusted the stability of the British pound and the willingness of the London banks to permit the free withdrawal of funds whenever they were needed. Free trade and foreign investment provided an economic and psychological basis for broadly international attitudes. During the 20th century, however, London has declined relatively as New York has grown.

The international market for goods has in general been competitive within limits set by government regulation, private monopolies, and imperfections of knowledge. Prior to the industrial revolution the international location of production changed primarily because of changes in sources of supply owing to the opening up of new countries, the dissemination of improved methods of production (indicated by the growth of cities based on craft production in western Europe), increases in the purchasing power of the wealthier classes, reductions in the cost of transport, and improvements in the organization of trade. First the trade in rich fabrics and costly weapons increased, and later that in metals from South and Central America, and sugar, coffee, tea, cocoa, tobacco, and naval supplies.

The industrial revolution created new demands and changed the pattern of international specialization and the volume of trade. Because industrialization was confined for a century and a half chiefly to western Europe and the U.S.A., production in other countries changed mainly in the direction of meeting new demands for minerals and raw materials. British supplies of most minerals have given out, and those of France and Germany were never great except for coal. Consequently there has been a rapid expansion in international trade in coal and most minerals (particularly copper, aluminum, silver, and gold) and in biological raw materials. Cotton was imported into Britain from the middle of the 18th century, first entirely from the U.S.A., but recently from Egypt, and Brazil. Japan built up a cotton industry like that of Britain on the basis of the wholly imported raw material. Jute, wool, rubber, and hides all remain important in international trade. The reduction in transport costs also changed production patterns through the operation of the market. Railroads providing cheap mass transport permitted production for export in areas without access to water, facilitating agriculture, mining, and manufacturing in new areas and opening up new markets for manufactured goods. Shipping accelerated transport and developed specialized facilities for carrying perishable products.

Industrialization (partly because it developed so unevenly throughout the world) also attracted labor from agriculture in the more developed countries until many of them became importers of food. The last year in which Britain had a surplus of wheat for export was 1792. Less than one-eighth of the grain supply of the country was imported up to 1850; by 1914, four-fifths was being imported. Industrializing countries in northwest Europe imported food from other parts of Europe until new countries offered it more cheaply. Increases in population increased the demand for food, and rising standards of living after about 1850 generated a demand for higher quality and more varied food, particularly tropical and semi-tropical (such as oranges, lemons, early vegetables, and bananas) all of which added to the food imports of the country. By 1880 Germany was spending about $250 million a year on imported food, and by 1912 about $800 million. France was spending about $350 million in 1910. In the U.S.A. imports of food began to exceed exports about 1924, the net import accelerating thereafter; in 1935 food imports were nearly three times food exports. These imports, however, are mostly of coffee and sugar. Exports of farm products from the U.S.A. were about 7% of farm production in 1898, *minus* .8% in 1913, and *minus* 5% from 1916 to 1937. These changes in demand, operating mainly through the market, resulted in a world fairly well divided by 1914 into exporters of industrial goods, on the one side, and producers of subsistence goods and primary goods for export on the other. By 1929 about 23% of world trade was in food and 33% in industrial raw materials. Even so, however, the proportion of the world food supply entering foreign trade is small. The chief exporters of food in the last half of the 19th century, particularly grain, were the U.S.A., Canada, Argentina, Russia, the Balkan countries, and Hungary. Cattle were obtained from South America and Australia, and dairy products from Denmark, Holland, and New Zealand. In recent years the U.S.A. has been exporting the produce of about one-third of its wheat area.

Foreign trade figures are influenced by the location of international boundaries (which determine which trade shall count as domestic and which as foreign). The more countries there are the more of the trade of the world counts as "international," because of the smaller variety of resources in small countries, the greater importance of transit trade, and the difficulty in small countries of reaping economies of scale in many industries. The volume of world trade also depends partly on the nature of the activities of countries. The wider the variety of resources within political boundaries, the less is likely to be the foreign trade per head. The per capita foreign trade of the U.S.A. is relatively low because specialization can be pressed far within the boundaries of the country. But New Zealand and Iceland have the highest imports per capita because they are dependent on foreign supplies of most raw materials and manufactured goods.

In the second half of the 19th century, capital exports facilitated the spread of industrialization and generated exports of producers' goods. In due course these exports displaced some exports of consumer goods as the importing countries made some of their own finished products. Nevertheless, the trade of the industrial countries continued to grow, especially their trade with each other. The full effect, however, of the export of producers' goods has not yet been felt. Often industrialization in new countries created a market for still other consumer goods that also were imported for a time. Some of the capital exports, however, facilitated the production and export of primary goods from non-industrial countries.

2. The Markets for Resources

If resources (except natural resources) were completely mobile, markets in resources would bring about general equality in the marginal return to each resource in each country, provided no non-economic considerations outweigh in the minds of individuals the attraction of moving themselves or their capital to places where they will obtain greater rewards. Markets in resources, although they have existed for a long time, have not been free enough to achieve this result. But they have been free enough to bring about great changes in the distribution of production and population.

a. The Market for Capital

International movements of capital were relatively small before the 17th century. Capital was of no great importance in production and facilities for international movement were few. Such capital as did exist was mostly merchant capital, and it moved internationally with the development of trade. During the medieval period, Jewish and Italian houses dealt in foreign exchange, the Italian houses basing their activities partly on the remittances of "Peter's Pence" to Rome. Some loans were negotiated at the international fairs. During the 16th century, the Fuggers of Augsburg, an international investment house, financed copper mining in north and central Germany, silver mining in Hungary, and the military activities of the Hapsburgs throughout Europe. In the 17th century the foreign trading corporations invested trading capital abroad. But most capital movements during the 17th and 18th centuries were due to the war needs of newly established rulers. International financial dealings of a more modern type developed with increasing accumulation in some countries, and expansion of trade. Dutch merchant bankers undertook most of the international banking until the end of the 18th century, Amsterdam and Antwerp being the capital markets of the world. The importance of Holland was due partly to its geographical position at the mouth of the Rhine on important land and sea routes, and partly to its financial organization. The dislocation of economic life on the continent during the Napoleonic wars shifted the money market to London. By 1932 world international long-term debt was about $49 billion which, however, was only a small part of world gross capital formation.[1]

The organization for international capital movement developed as an addition to the business of international merchants who were necessarily involved in exchange operations. Early in the 19th century some developed into investment bankers and arranged foreign loans. During the latter part of the century, the British joint stock banks took over from the merchant bankers much of the arrangements for exporting longer-term capital, and German and French banks followed. International banking relations also provide facilities for individuals and large business enterprises to move funds from country to country to invest through stock markets or directly in enterprises.

The international capital market has operated to export capital from countries with considerable internal accumulation, first the Netherlands, then Britain from early in the 19th century, France and Germany towards the end of the century, and the U.S.A. after 1914. After the Napoleonic wars, when the British became accustomed to investment in bonds, British capital exports were considerable for a time, and increased rapidly again between 1870 and 1904, and more rapidly until 1914, when about half Britain's savings were being invested abroad; 10% of its national income came from foreign investments, which were about 25% of its national capital. France began to export capital in the middle of the 19th century, and achieved considerable volume in the 1860s. After a recession during the period of payment of the war indemnity, there was a further considerable increase of exports between 1894 and 1914. In 1850 and 1869 about one-third of savings were being invested abroad, by 1899 two-fifths, and by 1911 over one-half. In 1914 France was the second largest exporter of capital, about 15% of its national wealth being in foreign investments. The industry and thrift of the French caused rapid accumulation, and industrialization was slower than elsewhere. The U.S.A. began to export capital in the decade 1909-18.

The gross foreign holdings of the four chief exporters of capital, with 75% of all foreign holdings, rose between 1874 and 1914 from £1.2 billion to about £7.75 billion (of which over 50% were British, about 22% French,

---

[1] Kuznets, *International Differences in Capital Formation* (mimeo).

TABLE 49[*]

THE GROSS LONG-TERM FOREIGN INVESTMENTS HELD BY THE PRINCIPAL
CAPITAL EXPORTING COUNTRIES, 1855 TO 1929

(millions of pounds)

	Britain	France	Germany	U.S.A.
1855	472	205		
1870	1006	513		
1885	1602	678	390	
1900	2485	1068	986	103
1914	4004	1766	1376	513
1929	3737	719	226	3018

[*] Staley, *cit.* Clark, *Conditions of Economic Progress* (2nd), 514.

less than 20% German, and less than 10% from the U.S.A.). (Table 49.) Over the whole period these countries invested abroad an amount about equal to their income from foreign investments.[2] Between 1914 and 1918, Britain, France, and Germany lost foreign investments valued at $4 to $5 billion but the U.S.A. appeared as an exporter. Britain returned to the export of capital soon after the war, and France more slowly. Germany was an importer, but the U.S.A. exported capital for a short period from 1924 to 1929, when it almost ceased. In the mid 1920s about $2 billion of capital were annually exported. But capital exports were small from 1929 to 1939, although Sweden, Switzerland, and Holland exported capital to repatriate much of their foreign debts, and Denmark exported some capital.[3]

The war of 1939-45 caused further heavy losses of foreign investments owing to sales to provide foreign exchange to pay for imports of war goods, and destruction and seizure of properties. British income from foreign holdings declined over 50% between 1938 and 1946. French foreign investments were reduced about 66%, those of Germany were mostly lost or repatriated, and some U.S. foreign investments were lost. The U.S.A. made heavy unrequited exports (mostly under the Lend Lease arrangements) that, however, were for war and not for productive purposes. A number of peripheral countries became involuntary exporters of capital on short term. When the belligerent countries bought export goods but were not able to supply import goods in payment, these countries obtained balances in sterling and dollars (Ch. 25).

After 1945, the U.S.A. was almost the only country able to export much capital, but its private exports amounted to only 2% of its domestic saving. The former European capital exporters were suffering from war losses calling for increased domestic investment while their income from foreign investments was reduced; in 1948 Britain, France, and the Netherlands were importers rather than exporters (Table 50). But much of this flow was intergovernmental. During the seven years from 1946 to 1952 there

---

[2] U.N., *International Capital Movements During the Inter-War Period*, 1.
[3] Clark, *Conditions of Econ. Prog.* (2d), 496.

TABLE 50

NET FOREIGN INVESTMENT IN SELECTED COUNTRIES AS A PERCENTAGE OF
GROSS NATIONAL EXPENDITURE IN 1948*

	Percentage
Australia	3.6
Canada	2.7
Czechoslovakia	—0.8
Denmark	—1.4
Finland	1.3
France (1947)	—3.3
Netherlands	—0.1
New Zealand	1.3
Norway	—7.7
Peru (1947)	—1.8
Southern Rhodesia	—26.5
Sweden	—1.7
Turkey	—2.8
United Kingdom	—1.0
United States	0.7

*U.N., *National Income Statistics 1938-48*, 221.

was a net outflow of private long-term capital from the industrialized countries of about $11 billion and probably more, of which $7.9 million was from the U.S.A. and the remainder from Britain, Belgium, Switzerland, and France. Some net capital importing countries nevertheless exported capital, (e.g., Canada, Germany, and Italy to Latin America, Argentina to other Latin American countries, and Denmark to Central Africa). Private pre-war loans to foreign governments have been reduced by repayment or repatriation, and investments in foreign railroads and other utilities have been reduced, partly out of credits obtained in wartime. Private investments were heaviest in extractive industries, but not unimportant in industry. But about 75% of the additions to private business investments represented the reinvestment of undistributed profits.[4]

In the postwar years the flotation of government bonds and corporate securities in foreign countries was relatively unimportant, and direct investment by business enterprises in foreign utilities was reduced, most foreign direct investment being in the petroleum industry. Such investment as was made in industry was mainly in economically advanced countries, although the U.S.A. has made considerable manufacturing investments in the larger countries in Latin America. But movements of private capital probably totalled 25 to 30% of all capital movements, the remainder consisting of intergovernment loans and grants. The private capital market was a shrunken version of its 19th-century self.

Some of the countries that have received foreign capital have promoted their economic development and finally became capital exporters, whereas others have remained chiefly exporters of food and raw materials to the

[4] U N., *The International Flow of Private Capital*, 1954, 5, 6.

more developed countries. Before 1815 Britain borrowed from the Netherlands. Between 1815 and 1840 British capital exports went to the continent of Europe (France, Spain, Prussia, Greece, Portugal), Latin America, and the U.S.A., largely in mining and plantations. Between 1840 and 1870 a good deal was invested in railroads in a variety of countries. After 1890 more than 40% of the loans from Britain went to its own dominions and colonies to finance new sources of supply within the Empire. In 1913 nearly half British foreign investments were within the Empire. French exports were first directed mainly to Latin American countries, the Latin countries of Europe, Russia, the Balkans, and Turkey. In 1914 half of its foreign investments were in countries expected to be allied with it in time of war, and less than 10% was within its own empire, in spite of efforts to encourage such investment by government guarantees and the exclusion of foreign capital. About half the capital exports from Germany went to European countries (Austria, Hungary, Russia, Balkan countries, Turkey, France, Spain, Portugal). During the period in which the U.S.A. exported capital about half went to Europe, during the years from 1925 to 1928. In 1929, however, only about one-fourth went to Europe. By 1931 about one-third of American investments were in Europe, about a quarter in Canada, and the remainder in Latin American countries. Japan imported a small amount of capital between 1869 and 1895, but virtually paid off its foreign debt between 1895 and 1919 (without retarding its development), but imported capital again between 1920 and 1929.

By 1914 nearly 30% of the outstanding foreign investments was in Europe, about 25% in the U.S.A. and Canada, about 20% in Latin America, 15% in Asia, 10% in Africa, and a small amount in Oceania.[5] More detailed figures for 1928 (Table 51) show wide variations in the total foreign capital per worker then invested in various countries. The more developed countries do not appear because they are exporters and not importers. Importing countries have high foreign investments where they are relatively developed but still dependent on foreign capital. They have low foreign investments where little developed, or where they are developed largely out of domestic saving (possibly because they have been paying back past foreign investments).

Between 1918 and 1929 much of the international capital flow went to Europe (especially Germany). The underdeveloped countries received less foreign capital absolutely, and in proportion to population, than the more developed.[6] There was a notable inflow into Palestine by 1940, but not on a commercial basis.[7] During the 1930s the principal capital exporting

[5] U.N., *International Capital Movements During the Inter-War Period*, 2, 5.

[6] *Ibid.*, 14, 16, 17.

[7] Clark, *op. cit.* (2d), 497; Warriner, *Land and Poverty in the Middle East*, 71; U.N., Econ. Surv. Mission for the Middle East *Final Report*, 1949, I, 38.

TABLE 51

ESTIMATED FOREIGN CAPITAL PER OCCUPIED WORKER INVESTED
IN SELECTED COUNTRIES IN 1928*

	International Units
New Zealand	1800
Canada	1700-1785
Australia	1660-1715
Malaya	1055
Cuba	955-1040
Chile	900
Argentina	605-700
Norway	420-630
South Africa	410-730
Belgium	465
Mexico	410
Denmark	380
Venezuela	352
Germany	281
Austria	253
Manchuria	253
Greece	190-253
Peru	239
Brazil	183-187
Rumania	155
Hungary	155
Poland	99
Czechoslovakia	84
Russia (1913)	83
Indonesia	70
Yugoslavia	24-70
Africa (excluding South Africa and Egypt)	45-70
Japan	55-56
India	23-28
China	21
Bulgaria	14

* Clark, *Conditions of Economic Progress* (2nd), 512.

countries were liquidating their external assets, and few underdeveloped
areas received any foreign capital.

During the seven years 1946-52 a large share of foreign capital flowed
to countries already fairly well developed. Canada received Can. $1.129
billion, in addition to reinvestment of the profits of foreign enterprises in
Canada of about the same amount. South Africa received $1.6 billion in
long and short term capital, in addition to reinvested profits, and Australia
was also a net recipient. Underdeveloped countries generally attracted
private capital only where they were rich in natural resources (e.g., Brazil,
Chile, Colombia, Mexico, Peru, and parts of Africa) and especially those
with petroleum (such as Venezuela, Saudi Arabia, and Iraq). In fact, a
number of underdeveloped countries better supplied with manpower than
with natural resources exported private capital on balance (e.g., Ceylon,
India, Indonesia, and Egypt) through the repatriation of bonds and the

liquidation of equity investments (facilitated in some by the withdrawal of sterling balances).[8]

The international capital market has been steered by differential changes in the supply of and demand for capital in different parts of the world. Such changes cause differences in anticipated returns from investment, which tend to be eliminated again by capital movements, unless prevented by political influences (p. 571). In the 17th century high commercial profits in the Netherlands and Britain supplied both a source of capital and an attractive outlet for it, and some of the outlets were outside these countries. The exhaustion of mining in some places and the opening of mines in others also caused some capital movements.

The industrial revolution provided new outlets for capital that came at first largely from commercial and mining profits in the industrializing countries, although the profits of the East India Company in Bengal after 1753 contributed to the development of Britain at a critical point.[9] So long as industrialization was restricted to a few countries, it created increasing demands for raw materials and food outside these countries. Mining, some branches of agriculture, and the internal and external transport necessary to facilitate the export of these products, attracted capital that was supplied out of rising industrial profits in the developing countries. In many of the countries of destination, foreign investment did not generate cumulative development. But in other countries development did follow. These countries appeared as profitable fields for further investment and attracted capital from their predecessors in industrialization. The prior developing countries could for a time invest all their accelerating accumulation internally but any tendency for profits to fall with continued increases in the capital fund increased the appeal of foreign investment and the resulting capital exports tended to maintain investment returns at home. In the longer run, the spread of industrialization generated increases in accumulation in the new industrialized countries. They began to export capital to repay previous imports when a higher rate of return could be obtained in this way than by further internal development. When they are free from foreign debt they may continue to export capital for the same reason the pioneers in industrialization did. But accumulation may decelerate because of a decline in return within the country (due to technological changes slowing up or taking the form of capital saving), a decline in population increase, or redistributions of incomes in the direction of greater equality (through the mechanism of taxation, social security payments, and the like). An increase in the return on domestic investment may then slow up exports.

The spread of industrialization tends to reduce the profitability in the earlier industrial countries of the industries facing increasing competition

---

[8] U.N., *The International Flow of Private Capital*, 1946-52, 7.

[9] Wadia and Merchant, *Our Economic Problem*, 288.

from abroad (as happened in the British textile industry). But it increases the demand for exports of capital goods and reduces the cost of producing them, thus providing external economies to industries using their products[10] both at home and abroad. By raising the profits of these industries it helps to maintain the capital supply available at home to finance exports of capital goods. But the followers in industrialization in time turn to producing capital goods, increasing the competition faced by the leaders. The leaders need not, however, suffer absolutely so long as industrialization spreads at an accelerating pace, which requires continued capital export. In general the international capital market assisted the spread of industrialization from Britain to western Europe, the U.S.A., and Japan during the 19th century (when the market was for the most part free). But elsewhere, capital imports generally financed activities subsidiary to those in the capitalist countries. During the 20th century, however, political pressures for a wider dissemination of industrial production have increased at a time when the international market in private capital has progressively declined.

The international capital market has not operated perfectly. Anticipated rates of return on foreign investments are subject to wide margins of error because of risk due to (a) imperfections of knowledge regarding profit opportunities, and (b) the difficulty of anticipating the policies of governments concerning the protection of property in general, monetary policy, taxation, and controls of exchange. To minimize these risks some private loans to foreign governments have been secured by mortgages on taxes (in China and Turkey in the past), or by the appointment of financial advisers who have been accused of cutting into the sovereignty of the states in which the investment is made. For the same reason there has been an increasing tendency during the 20th century for exports of capital to go to countries under the same political control as the exporting country. Between 1918 and 1939, an increasing proportion of British exports went to commonwealth countries. In fact many anticipations have been shown by subsequent events to have been optimistic. After allowing for all repudiation and refunding of British foreign investments, such loans have yielded less than domestic investments while they have reduced productivity at home, and set up foreign firms to compete in foreign markets with domestic firms. At the end of 1947 nearly half of the capital invested through the London Stock Exchange in Latin American countries was receiving no interest, and on a total of £910 million nominally invested, the interest payments were about 2.3%. If a few of the more successful investments, particularly oil in Venezuela, are excluded, the rate of interest was extremely low. On £438 million invested in railroads, the interest payments were about .7%.

---

[10] Singer, "The Distribution of Gains between Investing and Borrowing Countries," *Proc. Am. Econ. Assoc.*, 1949, 474.

Some foreign investment has been influenced by the fees obtainable from issuing securities when investors are optimistic (e.g., in Britain during the early 19th century and later during the early history of the investment trust, and in the U.S.A. during the 1920s). Finally, some international capital movements are impelled more by fear of loss of capital at home due to inflation or taxation, than by opportunities for more productive use abroad. After 1930, the U.S.A. (and to some extent France) was used as a haven for "hot money," not only from European countries, but also from Latin America and China. This money is likely to move around from place to place in response to short-term changes in estimates of safety in different parts of the world. Capital would not have flowed into the U.S.A. during this period in a world in which investment was uniformly safe.

b. The Market for Labor

International movements of people can adjust population-resource ratios in different countries and, therefore, production and productivity in each. Such movements have been woven throughout human history by cataclysms of nature, wars, and the desire to exploit new opportunities. The earlier migrations were largely in groups, probably originating in central Asia. Later there were many group movements by Greeks and Arabs, but they hardly represent the operation of an international labor market, although basically they were motivated by forces operating in such a market. The slave trade forced the migration of some 20 million persons between 1538 and 1888, chiefly from Africa to tropical and subtropical countries. These movements also were influenced by the relative supply and demand for labor, but not in a free international labor market.

Migrations of skilled craftsmen and Jewish merchants occurred in the Middle Ages. Small numbers of Spanish and Portuguese migrated to Latin America in the 16th and 17th centuries. But individual and family migrations are chiefly a matter of the past two centuries. They could begin only after the free wage earner had emerged. Early in the 18th century Germans and German-Swiss migrated. Later in the century the enclosure movement and agricultural crises and the harsh conditions in industry caused emigration from Britain. This movement increased fairly continuously from 1820 until about 1850 (especially from Scotland and Ireland). Thereafter emigration fluctuated without any notable trend from 1871 to 1941.[11] After 1850, workers began to leave Germany. But from about 1860 accelerating industrialization in northwest Europe reduced the pressure to emigrate, and an increasing proportion of European emigrants came from southeast Europe. Until 1870 the extension of settlement in the U.S.A. beyond the Appalachians attracted the depressed populations from Europe, largely from Britain, but between 1870 and 1890 free or

[11] U.K., Royal Commission on Population *Report*, 9.

cheap land attracted farm emigrants. Seventy per cent of the immigrants were from southeastern Europe. Italy was the most important source of emigrants between 1896 and 1900, Austria-Hungary from 1900 to 1910, and thereafter Italy again. During the whole period from 1846 to 1924 some 40% of the European emigrants came from Britain (Table 52). Between 1700 and 1930 the population of Europe rose from 180 to 480 millions while the number of persons of European stock in overseas countries rose to 160 millions. In recent years emigrants from Italy have been equal

TABLE 52

SOURCES OF EMIGRANTS FROM EUROPE, 1846 TO 1924*

Country of Origin	Number (millions)
United Kingdom	16.974
Italy	9.474
Austria-Hungary	4.878
Germany	4.533
Spain	4.314
Russia	2.253
Portugal	1.633
Sweden	1.145

* Encyclopedia of the Social Sciences, article on "Migration."

to about 65% of the additions to its population at the working ages. The slowness of the increase in the Irish population is due partly to emigration.

The destinations of the emigrants depended on anticipated opportunities for economic well-being, climate, and social conditions. Latin America attracted rather small numbers of immigrants for two centuries after 1500. North America, a huge and sparsely occupied territory, attracted about 500,000 from Britain in the 17th century, and 1,500,000 in the 18th century. A widening circle of countries supplied increasing numbers in the 19th century. About one million emigrants arrived between 1776 and 1840, and about 9.5 million between 1840 and 1880 (of which 90% came from Europe). In fact about 60% of the 60 million intercontinental migrants between 1800 and 1924 went to the U.S.A. (Table 53). There were also considerable migrations from Britain to Canada, New

TABLE 53

THE CHIEF COUNTRIES OF DESTINATION OF IMMIGRANTS
FROM 1800 TO 1924*

Country	Period	Number (millions)
U.S.A.	1821-1924	33.188
Argentina	1857-1924	5.486
Canada	1821-1924	4.520
Brazil	1821-1924	3.855
British West Indies	1836-1924	1.477
Cuba	1901-1924	0.766

* Encyclopedia of Social Sciences, article on "Migration."

Zealand and Australia, South Africa, and the West Indies. After the abolition of slavery in the British colonies, labor was obtained in tropical and subtropical areas by contracting Indian and Chinese coolies. The migration of Indian workers on three- to five-year contracts reached its peak of about 46,000 per year in 1850, but by 1916 it was prohibited in all British possessions. The recruiting of indentured Chinese laborers began in the 1850s.

International migration has been influenced by differences in the attractiveness of living in different countries that have been dominated by differences in rates of economic progress, and the extent to which benefits have been passed on to the mass of the population. The early stages of industrialism in Britain and Germany induced emigration that slowed after the condition of workers in those countries improved and population increase decelerated. The U.S.A. was unique in providing tremendous opportunities for immigrants, first from the developing countries, but later from the periphery of the capitalist world where standards of living were low. Before the industrial period, the immigrants into the U.S.A. were often fleeing from distasteful religious or political environments, but after industrialization they mainly sought a higher standard of living than was offered by the less industrialized countries of central and eastern Europe. Latin America and the British dominions have exerted a similar but far less powerful attractive force.

Migrations have not, however, achieved anything approaching uniform standards of living throughout the world. Average incomes ten times as high in the U.S.A. as in China are unlikely to be offset by other advantages of living in China compared with the U.S.A. and similar countries. If they were, present legislation seriously obstructing migration would be unnecessary. In fact, influences other than the immediately material ones affect the way the market operates. Individuals are often unwilling to leave their families and friends, but enough of the poorest members of the world population would overcome these obstacles if they were permitted to. Knowledge of probable standards of living in different parts of the world is admittedly poor, but not poor enough to explain the present distribution of population. The cost of movement also deters migration, but the greatest deterrent is the action of national states.

B. Authoritarian Influences

The chief authoritarian forces bearing upon the distribution of production among countries are private international agencies, national states, and public international agencies.

1. PRIVATE INTERNATIONAL AUTHORITIES

Private international authorities are chiefly concerned with particular commodities. They seek to raise or maintain profits by controlling prices and output and sharing markets. They sometimes obstruct production in new areas by dumping or other devices. They may override national tariffs by restricting imports into a country below the amounts that would be competitively imported.

International cartels came into existence mainly after 1918, and by 1950 nearly 50% of world trade was subject to some form of cartel control. National groups of producers had found themselves limited in their price policies by foreign competition (Ch. 7, 12) and by surplus capacity called into being by the war of 1914-18.[12] International monopolies, like intranational ones, being most easily operated where only one or a few producers are involved, are most likely to appear where minerals can be obtained from only a few sources, where agricultural production or manufacturing is highly concentrated, or where national cartels provide a foundation upon which an international cartel can be built. But cooperation has been difficult among groups in more than a few countries.

Private international controls of agricultural production have been relatively few, and restricted to commodities produced on a plantation or on a similar basis. Beginning as agreements to reduce output to raise prices, they have generally failed for lack of general compliance. Such was the outcome of an agreement among British and Chinese rubber planters in Malaya, and Dutch planters in the Dutch Indies. When the price of tea fell in 1920 because previous high prices had stimulated planting and demand had fallen, planters' associations in India, Ceylon, and the Netherlands Indies agreed to restrict output. Until 1927 prices rose, but the acreage under tea was increased, prices fell, and the planters turned to their governments for help in 1932. But producers of quebracho (which yields a tanning product) in Argentina and Paraguay successfully controlled output to maintain prices after 1916, and from 1918 to 1939 there were international controls of kapok, cocoa, coffee, quinine, sugar, and lumber.[13]

International controls of minerals and fairly standardized products like semi-finished steel and aluminum have been somewhat more successful. Of 46 international cartels in 1930, 16 were concerned with mineral products and seven others with various forms of rolled steel. Various attempts have been made to control the price of copper since 1890. In 1918 the Copper Export Association was formed to control exports and maintain or raise the price of copper, and in 1926 Copper Exporters Incorporated, was formed for the same purpose. It included most of the major producers in the world. It endeavored to control prices by setting export quotas and export prices from the U.S.A. The price of copper remained stable in the U.S.A. during 1929 and 1930, but the output of the African mines was stimulated and the organization came to an end. Another organization,

[12] Mason, *Controlling World Trade*, 11, 26, 33.
[13] *Ibid.*, 15.

formed in 1930 to reduce output, also collapsed. In 1935 the producers in the western hemisphere (including the U.S.A., Chile, and Mexico) agreed to curtail output between 30 and 40%.

A world aluminum cartel was formed in 1929 after unsuccessful attempts in 1918 and 1926. A cartel including producers in Germany, France, Switzerland, Britain, Austria, but not the U.S.A., sought to fix prices and allocate markets, but came into conflict with the Aluminum Corporation of America, especially in colonial markets, until the depression in 1929 produced an understanding between the European and the American groups; the Alliance Aluminum Company was established in 1931 with practically a world monopoly. The price of diamonds has been controlled since 1893, recently through the Diamond Producers' Association, which includes producers of about 90% of the world output, including the government of the Union of South Africa. The cartel has sought to stabilize prices, and sets output quotas for its members,[14] but has had considerable difficulty in dealing with the Mwadui mine in Tanganyika. A tin cartel was formed in 1921, and there have been cartels controlling platinum, asbestos, mercury, sulphur, potash phosphates, soda ash, petroleum, nitrates,[15] and various other chemicals and steel products. In 1952 the U.S. Federal Trade Commission reported that three major companies out of five controlling the production, refining, and distribution of most of the petroleum in international markets agreed in 1928 about output and allocation of markets, and in 1934 also on prices, restrictions on numbers and kinds of distributors, elimination of competitive expenditures for market facilities, and sales promotion. These arrangements became virtually a custom of the trade, and were supplemented in the U.S.A. by the interstate oil compact (Ch. 9). Competition between European synthetic and Chilean natural nitrate was regulated by a world cartel before 1939 that virtually allocated the U.S. market to Chile and the European to European producers.[16] But there have been no international controls of coal. It has been produced by a number of countries, the producers have been numerous and uncartellized in some of them, and some countries developing their coal have aimed at an increased share of the world markets (e.g., Poland).

Private controls over manufactures have affected production and trade in cement, steel rails, and other steel products, tin plate, cables, dyes, paper, linoleum, plate glass, various chemicals, electrical products (including electric lamps), pharmaceuticals, optical glass, matches, tungsten, carbide, and magnesium.[17] The pooling of patents that may result in the

14 Frankel, *Capital Investment in Africa*, 68.
15 Mason, *op. cit.*, 76, 206, 213.
16 *Ibid.*, 35, 209.
17 *Ibid.*, 15, 102, 105.

wider use of new knowledge, has also been used to restrict and control the distribution of production among countries.[18]

These agreements although not aimed at improving international specialization, often stimulate production in new areas by raising prices above a competitive level and enabling new areas to overcome the initial difficulties of entering the market. But during their periods of monopoly profit, cartels distort the production pattern. They protect the national markets of members and often share other markets among them. They typically adjust supply to consumption by reducing supply rather than by stimulating consumption.

The international capital market is not susceptible of private international controls because of the variety of sources of capital. Commercial and investment bankers in the monetary centers do not agree on capital allocations among countries.

International labor organization appeared before there was much international organization of employers. The International Working Men's Association (the "First International") was formed in 1864, with the assistance of Karl Marx, in the belief that workers in all capitalist countries had common problems. But workers have not everywhere sought a common solution. The First International collapsed in 1872 and a second, formed in 1889 with a gradualist socialist policy, collapsed during the war of 1914-18 when European social democratic parties cooperated in the war programs of their governments or became inactive. The Third International was aimed at protecting the Russian revolution by using Russia as the territorial base from which to organize the "decisive battle of the European Proletariat" with trained revolutionaries and a rigid party discipline. But it failed to generate revolution, and was kept alive only as an instrument of Russian foreign policy until its executive committee decided to dissolve it in 1943 because it had become a "drag in the further strengthening of the national working class parties." The Communist Information Bureau (Cominform) was formed in 1947, and in 1949 the non-communist labor movement withdrew from the World Federation of Trade Unions and formed the International Confederation of Free Trade Unions.[19] Since that time international labor organization has been bifurcated along lines of policy like the internal labor organizations of many countries. These international organizations have been concerned, however, not with the international labor market, but with propaganda aimed at common policies in national labor markets.

2. The Policies of National States

National states have intervened in international economic relations to benefit their national economies (and polities) more often by restricting

[18] *Ibid.*, 99 ff.
[19] I.L.O., *Ind. and Lab.*, Oct. 15, 1950.

than by facilitating the operation of international markets. They often compete among themselves, and there is no reason why their policies should add up to an economical international pattern of production. Nations often seek gains involving greater losses to others, and they have often taken a short and narrow view of the consequences of their actions even upon themselves.

a. National Commercial Policies

i. Control of Imports and Exports

National policies regarding the trade in goods and services are expressed in import and export taxes, subsidies, quantitative controls, foreign exchange controls, sanitary and port regulations, transport subsidies, and the like.

In medieval Europe some states attempted to control exports to ensure domestic supplies of food. But the commercial revolution of the 16th and 17th centuries stimulated mercantilist controls that, in their international aspects, restricted imports to stimulate domestic production, and encouraged exports to produce a "favorable" balance of trade. It was hoped thus to enhance the economic and military power of each state at a time when the distribution of political power among recently established national units was unstable. The policy rested on the assumption that power could be increased only at the expense of that of other countries. The controls were not always well devised for their purpose, but the most fundamental difficulty was that all countries could not possibly achieve their object in the long run. Some might succeed at the expense of others (that might be annexed). In fact this policy led to the commercial wars of the later 17th and 18th centuries, culminating in Napoleon's Continental System and the British Order in Council of 1807 establishing economic warfare.

Adam Smith's attack on these mercantilist policies in *The Wealth of Nations* provided a philosophical basis for substantial freedom of international commerce. Assuming international mobility of resources, national intervention could only reduce national welfare. Britain began to reduce import duties after 1823, repealed the Corn Laws in 1846, and the Navigation Laws in 1849. Foreign trade was virtually free by 1860, and so remained almost until 1932. The Netherlands freed its trade in about 1840 and most countries reduced import duties (the U.S.A. in 1846, Germany between 1843 and 1853, and France in the 1860s). But intervention increased again after 1870, 1914, 1918, and 1929. Germany began its modern period of protection in 1879, and France in 1881. The U.S.A. imposed high tariffs during the American Civil War, partly as compensation for high internal taxes, and these high tariffs existed until recently. The high U.S. tariff of 1890 strengthened the general movement for protection in northwest Europe. Duties were also imposed on imports of manufactures in other countries, but for other reasons (Ch. 31). In Brazil, tariffs have been increasingly protective since 1889.

It was argued that the development of industry and the protection of agriculture were necessary for nationalist reasons, military and sociological.[20] But it was also argued that completely free international markets would not in the longer run bring about the best international distribution of production. British priority in industrialization, its adoption of free trade, and a continued fall in the prices of its exports in relation to those of its imports (Ch. 28) resulted in the rapid expansion of manufacturing in Britain, but not elsewhere, until the middle of the 19th century. The widening gap between productive efficiency in Britain and in other countries was likely to persist in the absence of state intervention, although it was not due to the relative long-run productive advantages of different countries. These beliefs expressed themselves in the arguments for protecting "infant industries" that appeared early in the U.S.A. and later in Germany (Ch. 23) and have been used by most countries, other than Britain and the Netherlands, at the outset of industrialization. In the 1920s all the southern European countries changed over from revenue type to protective tariffs—often protecting agriculture as well as industry. Although sound within limits, the argument has been used by interested groups to secure protection for industries that never could grow up, and to continue protection long after industries have, or should have, grown up. Governments yield to such pressures partly because the ultimate costs of protection are concealed.[21]

During the 20th century, other considerations have influenced state intervention. Threats of war loomed darkly after 1890, and after 1918 controls imposed under pressure of actual war were not easily removed. After the 1929 depression had revealed the influence of the U.S.A. in the world system of production, and the tendency of the relatively free market to transmit abroad on a magnified scale fluctuations in American production, most governments endeavored to use foreign trade controls to divert the burden of depression from themselves to other countries. This effort could not be universally successful and further deteriorated international specialization. Increased interest in controlling trade begot new devices for the purpose. After 1918 import quotas became more common. They were set by products, and by country of origin, or by rationing foreign exchange by product and by country of origin. Such quotas fix the maximum imports of each commodity. Britain, the foremost practitioner of free trade during the 19th century, reestablished import duties under the Ottawa agreement in 1932 to enable it to give preference to members of the Commonwealth. Germany intensified controls over trade, partly in preparation for war. It subsidized exports by controlling foreign

[20] List, *The National System of Political Economy passim.*
[21] U.N., *Econ. Surv. of Europe in 1953,* 177.

exchange, special currencies being made available to foreigners buying German goods. The Nazi government also made bilateral agreements, using its buying power as an importer of raw materials to secure outlets for manufactures. It paid for imports in "compensation marks" available for the purchase of only some German export goods, and some foreign countries were never paid; they provided long-term credits for Germany that were cancelled as a result of the war.

Some underdeveloped countries sought to stimulate development by preventing the import of luxury goods. But the richer may then hoard, induce the domestic production of luxury goods, or absorb labor in additional personal services.[22] When war came, most countries controlled imports, exports, and dealings in exchange by licensing. Shipping space was allocated, and a number of governments entered the importing and exporting business (including Britain, France, the U.S.A., and Germany) owing to the disorganization of private trading arrangements and the need to increase the effectiveness of conversion to war (especially of shipping) and to annex any monopoly profit that might arise out of price controls.

After 1945 a number of countries, including the U.S.A., Belgium, India, and South Africa, removed many controls over international trade, thus creating a tremendous demand for goods from the U.S.A., whose productive system had suffered least from the war. Prices increased in the U.S.A. to the disadvantage of both American and foreign purchasers; the dollar resources of many of these countries largely disappeared and many of them later reimposed controls. But other countries maintained their controls (e.g., Britain).

The U.S.A. appeared in a new role when it attempted to reduce barriers to international trade in the belief that national commercial policies had contributed to war, and because of its growing interest in the export trade. The Lend-Lease agreements made during the war required the recipients to cooperate in the policy of greater freedom for postwar international trade. Toward the end of the war, the U.S.A. urged the abandonment of state trading when the war was ended, and in 1945 it announced a program for a general reduction in trade barriers. Loans by the U.S.A. to the governments of Britain, France, and Poland also required acceptance in principle of a policy of reducing barriers to trade. The U.S.A. also promoted the International Trade Organization, and signed multilateral agreements in 1947 and 1949 providing for the reduction of import duties. But domestic legislation to implement the policy has met with increasing resistance. In 1953 the 17 member nations in the Organization for European Economic Cooperation decided to remove quantitative restrictions (as distinct from tariffs) on at least 75% of the trade of each, and all but France complied. High costs and prices in France hampered its exports

[22] Nurkse, "Some International Aspects of the Problem of Economic Development," *Proc. Am. Econ. Assoc.*, 1951, 571.

and compelled it to ration its foreign exchange proceeds unless it was prepared for internal deflation or a reduction in the exchange value of the franc.

Belgium, the Netherlands, and Luxembourg sought in 1944 to establish free trade among themselves without political union and with tariffs against other countries. In 1947 they agreed on a common tariff regarding other countries and on free exchange within the union. But quotas, licensing arrangements, and minimum prices have severely restricted internal trade. Agricultural imports from Holland have paid a Belgian license tax, preventing them from being sold in Belgium at prices below those fixed by the Belgian government for comparable products produced in Belgium. The Dutch were similarly slow to facilitate imports from Belgium into Holland. The chief obstacle to the creation of a common market is the substantial disparity between the general level of wages and prices in Belgium and the Netherlands. Dutch labor costs in industry are, on the average, 20-25% below Belgian, and Dutch products tend to flood Belgian markets. An agreement in 1953 established criteria for imposing import quotas within the union to meet "hardship cases."[23]

In the war-damaged countries, especially those which had lost income from foreign investments (e.g., Britain and the Netherlands), trade controls have been aimed at concentrating imports upon basic consumption goods or goods necessary to rehabilitate and modernize the productive organization. In Germany and Japan, foreign trade has been controlled by occupying powers, partly to ensure the use of foreign exchange to minimize demands on the occupying powers for the supplies necessary to prevent disease and unrest. Reparation for war required the export of German productive equipment as well as current output. To determine the equipment that could be exported, the permissible level of production was fixed in 1947 at about the 1936 level of production for the British and American zones. Actual exports of current output went mainly (but not wholly) from the eastern zone to Russia, and there have been considerable exports of equipment, again largely to Russia. Disarmament policy required the destruction or export of equipment for producing war material, and control of German production of a number of materials, the most important of which were coal, aluminum, many chemicals and machine tools; these controls were removed in 1951.

State operation of foreign trade operations permits more precise control than regulation of private trade. But it is difficult to discover how far imports and exports by the state differ from those that would be made by private interests and, therefore, to apply to state trading countries policies aimed at increased freedom of international trade. After 1945 the U.S.A. urged the governments that had engaged in foreign trade to revert to private enterprise. The British government, however, continued

---

[23] U.N., *Econ. Surv. of Europe in 1953*, 14.

for some years government importation of raw materials and food, and established a Raw Cotton Commission to import and distribute raw cotton. But it reopened the market in rubber in 1946, tin in 1949, cocoa in 1951, and lead in 1952, when it also allowed cotton importers to choose whether to buy cotton through the commission or directly. The Argentine government established an institution (IAPI) to conduct most foreign trade, and the government in Turkey took over some exports.

Governments may conduct foreign trade to subsidize or to tax (as in Argentina). They may seek to hold down the cost of living in a world of rising prices by importing food and reselling it at a loss, as in Britain. But the British government trade in raw materials has shown both profits and losses (Ch. 9, 31). Governments may seek to trade more advantageously by reducing the administrative costs of trading, which was one of the reasons for establishing the British Cotton Commission. They may seek to use buying or supplying power to drive better bargains, in which case their success depends on the extent to which they can control the world market. In general, Britain has had little such control. Its purchase of food under term contracts providing for an annual review of the price seem to have been made at less than world prices until 1949. But in 1950 the Netherlands, Australia, New Zealand, and Denmark, dissatisfied with the prices offered, reduced their exports. Raw materials (except cotton) have generally been purchased at world prices and sold later at prices based on cost. Consequently, resale prices have been higher than foreign prices on a falling market (when British manufacturers need most help) and lower on a rising market. The government may also use its trading organization to restrict imports to those most necessary to effect its domestic and foreign policies. But state trading focuses criticism of prices on the government. Trade bargains become involved with concessions on other aspects of government policy: but commercial treaties also may involve such "package deals." Obdurate situations arise when a centralized buyer faces centralized seller. British negotiations for the purchase of Argentine meat were deadlocked for nearly a year, until April 1951, and settled in combination with agreements to export petroleum, coal, tinplate, and other scarce commodities, and with various financial transactions.

Socialist countries cannot, consistently with their political principles, permit private foreign trade. Imports and exports are planned in Russia as part of the general production plan. Goods needed for export are planned by the Ministry of Foreign Trade, which markets them abroad, obtaining foreign funds with which to pay for the planned imports. During the inter-war period the chief Russian exports were oil and timber. Reliance on these primary products exposed it to great pressure during depression, but toward the end of the inter-war period it began to export small quantities of manufactured goods (agricultural equipment, automobiles, tractors, textiles, sewing machines, coal and coke, cement, fertilizers, and leather). Its principal imports have been of capital goods, technical services, and some raw materials (especially wool). Its foreign trade policy has been similar in kind, though more vigorous, than those of other developing countries, namely to use foreign trade to obtain capital goods. But it has minimized its dependence on foreign trade, used foreign operations for political purposes, and sought all the advantages of centralized buying and selling. It was a party to a number of international cartels during the inter-war period.[24] Since 1945 its trade with its eastern European satellites has been regulated by trade treaties periodically negotiated, joint trading and banking institutions, and Russian or jointly-owned corporations for production within the satellite countries.

ii. International Commodity Agreements

National governments have also injected themselves into international economic relations by assisting their nationals to operate international cartels. After the failure of private agreements, and of a single-handed effort by the British government to restrict exports of rubber to raise prices, the British and Dutch governments (whose territories produced 97% of rubber exports) agreed in 1934 to restrict exports in accordance with the decisions of a committee of Dutch and British government officials. In Malaya the aggregate quota was suballocated among plantations and individual producers, but in the Netherlands Indies restriction was effected by export taxes (which in 1935 were about 13 times the net yield to producers).[25] Thus the major gains from restriction went to the government in the Netherlands Indies but to producers in Malaya. In 1938 exports were restricted to 45% of 1929 to 1934 productive capacity. Extensions of acreage were prohibited, but the replanting of existing plantations to higher yielding stock was permitted until 1940, but thereafter prohibited. The restrictions lapsed because of the Japanese invasion. Regulation was finally terminated in December, 1946, when a free market was restored, partly because synthetic rubber production had been established in the U.S.A. during the war of 1939-45 and it had been decided to maintain such production in peacetime as a war-preparedness measure. By 1945 U.S.A. capacity for synthetic rubber production was about 170% of its total rubber consumption in 1939, and the war had also greatly stimulated the reuse of rubber and synthetic production in Canada. Until 1952 the U.S.A. government maintained the market for 220,000 tons of synthetic rubber by prescribing the minimum amounts to be mixed with natural rubber in a variety of products, including automobile tires.

---

[24] Mason, *Controlling World Trade*, 14.

[25] Bauer, *The Rubber Industry*; MacFadyean, A. (ed.), *The History of Rubber Regulation*; Knorr, K. E., *World Rubber and Its Regulation*.

The governments of India, Ceylon, and the Netherlands Indies agreed in 1933 to regulate exports (but not production) of tea. Private controls had previously broken down, as they had for rubber. The forms of control were similar to those for rubber (quotas stated as a percentage of output in a base period and changed from year to year). Between 1933 and 1939 quotas varied between 82.5 and 92.5% of base period production. The cessation of Chinese exports helped the producers, and price policy was moderate.[26] Although the export of seeds and cuttings was restricted, tea production expanded in Kenya, Tanganyika, Nyasaland, and Uganda, who joined the control only after being allocated quotas based on their potential production.[27] The agreement was renewed in 1938, 1945, and 1948 (for two years), but export quotas have been too high to have much restrictive effect.

International coffee control has been sought without great success. Brazil failed to achieve international control at an international conference in 1931 because its competitors believed (correctly) that it would act alone if they did not cooperate. Brazil called the first Pan American Coffee Congress in 1936 and a second in 1937 after its share of the world market had fallen as a result of its singlehanded efforts to maintain prices by restricting exports. Neither congress acted, but a third conference in 1940 resulted in agreement with the U.S.A. (the principal importer) to establish quotas of imports into the U.S.A. from each of the 14 chief Latin American producers. The exporting countries each set minimum prices, that were successively raised and that collided with domestic price controls in the U.S.A. in 1941. The agreement terminated in 1948, but export quotas and price provisions had terminated earlier. A special commission on coffee was set up under the Inter-American Social and Economic Council of the Organization of American States in 1948 to continue cooperation.

Intergovernmental agreements to control mineral prices and output have been rare, partly because of conflicts of interest among producing nations. In 1929, however, the governments of Bolivia, the Federated Malay States, the Dutch Indies, Nigeria, and Siam agreed to control the output of tin. The demand for tin was inelastic, competition among producers might reduce the price considerably, and they depended heavily on tin for their foreign income. Consuming countries (predominantly the U.S.A.) opposed the arrangement, without success. Quotas were at first reduced from 120% of 1929 tonnage to 80%, but war demands resulted in increases in base tonnages in the middle of 1940, and soon thereafter Japan occupied the tin producing area of Malaya. The pre-war cartel agreement was not renewed in 1941, but a new agreement was made in 1942. The cartel probably held prices high enough between 1931 and 1939 to keep

---

26 Mason, *op. cit.*, 226.
27 Wickizer, V. D., *Tea under International Regulation.*

in production many Bolivian producers who otherwise would have ceased to produce. But in the long run it would have stimulated the use of substitutes.[28] From 1945 to 1949 a Tin Committee in London fixed the price and sought to reduce fluctuations by adjusting stocks, but these stocks were too small to be effective.[29] An agreement was drafted in 1948 to continue this policy, but it was not signed. Spain and Italy, the chief exporters of mercury, have for long agreed on the price of that metal, but proposals for intergovernmental control of petroleum have proved abortive. An Anglo-American Oil Agreement in 1945, emphasizing the need to conduct the international petroleum business in "an orderly manner" and to provide equality of access to supplies by consumers on a competitive, non-discriminatory basis, was intended as a prelude to general international agreement. In 1946 a world petroleum authority under the Economic and Social Council of the United Nations was proposed to hear complaints by firms or countries that had been unfairly treated or discriminated against.

After 1945 international commodity agreements of a new type appeared, of which the International Wheat agreement of 1949 was the first example. A previous agreement in 1933 had broken down when Argentina exceeded its quota because of a large harvest and inadequate storage.[30] The 1949 agreement between five exporting countries (excluding Argentina and Russia) and 37 importing countries, was aimed at setting upper and lower limits to the price of wheat, and distributing the resulting benefits and burdens among countries. It provided a maximum price of $1.80 per bushel and a minimum price of $1.50 for the year 1949-50, the minimum falling by ten cents a year to $1.20 a bushel in 1952-53. Whenever the price reached the maximum, each of the exporting countries was required to export, at the fixed price, the quotas provided in the agreement, and the importers were entitled to receive the import quota set for each country at the maximum price. When the price reached the minimum, each of the importing countries was required to accept at the minimum price its full quota as stated in the agreement, these imports being shared among the exporting countries according to their quotas. When the price ranged between the maximum and minimum, trade in wheat was uncontrolled. The total quotas in the original agreement covered about half the world trade in wheat. But accessions of new importers and increases in guaranteed quantities raised its coverage to about two-thirds of world trade in wheat and flour. Rising prices for wheat outside the agreement, and a desire to ensure supplies, resulted in 94% of quotas being delivered in the second year of the agreement, and in requests for increased import

---

[28] U.S. Tariff Commission, *Economic Controls and Commercial Policy in Bolivia*, 1946, 21, 29.

[29] Mason, *op. cit.*, 213, 217.

[30] *Ibid.*, 225.

quotas (which could be granted only when exporting countries offered larger quotas). The agreement in fact favored importers, and the exporters lived up to the agreement, although they could have sold much of their quota wheat at higher prices. The U.S.A., being required to maintain the internal price of wheat at about 50 cents a bushel above the ceiling price under the agreement, subsidized exports during the first year of the agreement to the extent of about $80 million. When the floor prices in the agreement become operative, importing countries pay more than they could have obtained their wheat for on the open market. But when the agreement was renewed, the British government withdrew, which involved a 20% reduction in the U.S. quota.[31]

Sugar has long been the subject of efforts at international control. Cuba unilaterally controlled output from 1926 to 1928, and agreed to reimpose control under an international agreement if one could be concluded. In 1931 a five-year agreement (the Chadbourne plan) among eight of the principal exporting countries sought to maintain a price of two cents a pound f.o.b. Cuba, but this price was not maintained. In fact, prices rose little and by the time the agreement lapsed in 1935 the signatories' share of the world market had fallen drastically. In 1937, 21 nations controlling 85 to 90% of world production again agreed on export quotas for the "free market" (markets free from bilateral or other preferential agreements) which was about 13% of world consumption. But during the war a number of countries dropped out. Quota control lapsed in 1944, and the agreement thereafter provided only for international discussion of sugar problems. It may have reduced stocks, but it stimulated production in non-signatory countries. In 1953, after the price of sugar had fallen 60% in two years, 50 nations signed an agreement to maintain prices between 3.25 and 4.35 cents per pound in Cuban ports by increasing or decreasing, within limits, the quotas of exporters to the "free market." The new agreement did not, however, require importers to take any specific quantities, and it permitted the price range to be changed if conditions required it.[32] There have been international study groups for rubber, tin and wool, some of which have proposed controls, but conflicts of interest between producing and consuming countries have prevented agreement.[33]

International fishing agreements have also restricted output (e.g., of fur seals and Pacific halibut) but mainly to prevent overfishing (owing to the absence of private property in fish in international waters).[34] Agreements regarding whaling have been signed by a number of nations, but not by all those interested.

[31] *For. Agri.*, Oct. 1951, Jan. 1954; U.N., *Review of International Commodity Problems*, 1951, 5.

[32] U.S. Tariff Comm., *Economic Controls and Commercial Policy in Cuba*, 1946, 20; *For. Agri.*, Jan. 1954; Mason, *op. cit.*, 203.

[33] U.N., *Review of International Commodity Problems*, 1951.

[34] Mason, *op. cit.*, 163.

International commodity agreements, aimed at assisting producing countries faced by an increase in supply or a fall in demand, have generally sought a remedy in reducing supply rather than increasing demand. Producing countries have sometimes gained in the short run, but have encouraged competing production in the long run. Multilateral arrangements aimed at limiting price fluctuations yield benefits and involve costs to both buying and selling countries, and they may prevent excessive fluctuations in supply and prices, but experience is too short to provide the evidence necessary for an appraisal.

iii. Monetary Policy

Monetary policy increasingly influenced foreign trade after 1918. Between 1870 and 1914 the gold standard had virtually stabilized exchange rates among the more developed countries, and between them and their dependent economies and a number of smaller countries (although still others, notably in Latin America, continued to suffer from exchange fluctuations). But the international gold standard broke down under the shock of war and depression during the 20th century. In the war of 1914-18 governments abandoned gold and controlled rates of exchange (Ch. 25). By 1926 the major countries had returned to gold standards, but under conditions very different from those of the 19th century. The international distribution of industry and pattern of international trade had changed (partly as a result of war). The older economies of Europe were slow to adjust partly because of rigidities in prices and wages. They suffered from unemployment, and Britain endeavored to maintain the pound at a foreign exchange value at which, in view of its level of wages and prices (and, therefore, costs of production), it could not find sufficient foreign markets for its goods. It had to pay for part of its imports in gold, which, if continued, would have compelled it to abandon the gold standard. Many countries were unwilling to forego imports from the U.S.A. and thereby caused gold to flow to the U.S.A. At the same time, the U.S.A. sought repayment of foreign debts (many of which were incurred in the period 1914-18) while accepting imports only of the goods on the free list, or those that could pay high import duties. It lent abroad spasmodically and often on short term, and France lent mainly on short term at a time when Britain was less able to export capital than previously. Thus the most flexible means of balancing international payments largely failed to operate at a time when it was most needed. Moreover, lack of confidence in political security and fear of inflation in countries failing to balance their budgets caused capital to move in search of security, often to the U.S.A. This intensified the problem of balancing international payments. The flow of gold to the U.S.A. was not permitted to operate, as it had in the 19th century, to bring about its own termination (through price increases in the receiving country and price reductions in the gold-exporting countries).

Britain, for instance, preferred to expand credit rather than face reductions in prices and wages. The U.S.A., now a great economic power, was less concerned with the mechanism of international dealings than Britain had been in the 19th century, and more concerned with internal economic conditions. It attempted both to maintain and to manage an international gold standard, that is, to preserve its gold standard and also stabilize its prices. In a single-handed effort to manage the world value of gold, the Federal Reserve Banks bought gold and sold earning assets. Consequently, American exports were encouraged, gold continued to flow in, and the international gold standard was doomed.

The collapse of the productive mechanism in 1929 brought a sharp realization that the stabilization of production with reasonably full employment was a prerequisite to political stability and the survival of capitalism, which the gold standard with its implicit internal controls was unable to assure (Ch. 25). In 1931 Britain and a number of other countries abandoned the gold standard, and were followed by the U.S.A. in 1933; by 1936 the international gold standard was gone.[35]

Emancipation from the restraints of the gold standard enabled governments to pursue their separate national interests as they saw them. As their policies did not have parallel effects on the purchasing power of their currencies, exchange rates began to fluctuate. Some changed the international value of their money to assist their nationals in the export trades. Exchange controls increased after 1931, when the German government restricted the purchase of foreign exchange to pay outstanding German debts abroad.[36] This economic warfare revealed, however, that national sovereignty over monetary policy must be adapted to the reality of membership in a world monetary system, and the major countries sought to modify exchange fluctuations.[37] In 1931, after abandoning the gold standard, the British government established an "Exchange Equalization Account" that was used to buy and sell foreign currencies in order to reduce (but not eliminate) exchange fluctuations. In 1932 the pound dropped to $3.21, but from the devaluation of the U.S. dollar in 1933 until 1938 the pound was about $5. The U.S.A. established an exchange stabilization fund of $2 billion in 1934, but only $.2 billion were used (the remaining $1.8 billion being ultimately used to finance the U.S. contribution to the International Monetary Fund). Canada established a similar fund in 1935. In January 1934 an amendment to the Agricultural Adjustment Act in the U.S.A. empowered the President to reduce the gold content of the dollar as much as 50%, and the power was amended in the Gold Reserve Act of 1934 to provide that the new dollar should not be equivalent to

---

[35] Brown, W. A., "Gold as a Monetary Standard," IX *Tasks of Econ. Hist.*, 1949, 39.
[36] Hart, *op. cit.*, 369; League of Nations, *International Currency Experience*, Ch. VII.
[37] *Ibid.*, 143 and Ch. VI.

more than 60% of the gold in the old dollar. In fact the gold content of the dollar was reduced by proclamation a little over 40% (the price of gold being raised to $35 an ounce). Thus the U.S.A. protected itself against both the rising value of gold and falling prices.

The average gold value of 45 currencies fell nearly 50% between 1929 and 1937 (mostly after 1931). Between 1934 and 1936 the exchange value of U.S., British, French, Belgian, Netherlands, and Swiss currencies was stabilized. But in 1936 the continental currencies (except the Belgian) fell in dollars and in pounds.[38] Britain, France, and the U.S.A. agreed to consult in advance of future devaluations, and avoid competitive devaluation, but not to fix exchange rates. The Netherlands, Belgium, Switzerland, Italy, and Brazil adhered to the agreement until 1939, although the British, French and other currencies began to fall in value in dollars in 1937.[39] A large number of countries stabilized their currencies with that of Britain, but many primary producing countries arrested the internal deflation that would have resulted from sharp reductions in the prices of their exports by reducing the exchange value of their monetary units (Ch. 25).[40]

By 1945 the purchasing power of currencies had fallen unequally in different countries, and controlled exchange rates could be maintained only by controls of trade, often accompanied by the rationing of foreign exchange, or the use of different rates for different types of imports and exports to control capital movements and ensure the imports regarded as most essential. In 1945 the British government agreed with a number of west European countries (except Norway, Portugal, and Spain), to set an agreed exchange value for their currencies in sterling to facilitate foreign trade in the area. Each central bank made its currency available against that of the others, if necessary by granting loans, although beyond a stated limit gold was to be supplied. But the general problem of restoring freedom of the exchanges and preventing a renewal of economic warfare through exchange rates was dealt with by the Bretton Woods International Conference, which drew up the charter for the International Monetary Fund. The Russian government, although it participated in the conference, has not joined the Fund.

The Russian government announces an official foreign exchange value for the ruble, but the rate has little bearing on Russian foreign trade, which is conducted by a government monopoly mainly in foreign currencies. The rate greatly overvalues the ruble in terms of purchasing power. Until 1950 it followed the rates for currencies based on gold (e.g., the dollar). In 1950, however, the government redefined the ruble in gold, saying that gold was more stable than the dollar. Pointing out that there had been

[38] Hart, *op. cit.*, 366.
[39] *Ibid.*, 385.
[40] League of Nations, *International Currency Experience*, 134.

three general reductions of prices in Russia between 1945 and 1950 while the currencies of the U.S.A. and other western countries had been falling in purchasing power, it raised the gold equivalent of the ruble nearly 20% (declaring the dollar worth 4 rubles). The principal consequence of the change was to increase the cost of visits to Russia and the maintenance of foreign establishments (mainly diplomatic) there. Since the ruble was defined in gold, the eastern European currencies have been fixed in value in rubles. The Polish *zloty* was pegged at par with the ruble in 1950, the Rumanian *leu* at 2.80 to the ruble in 1952; the intention appears to be to establish a "ruble area."

Confidence in the free operation of international markets for goods has never been widespread. Most nations turning to development have protected their new industries. Such protection can facilitate the better location of production in the long run. But many countries maintain protection after industries cease to be new (notably the U.S.A.) and may thus obstruct the best location of resources for a peaceful world in which production is fairly stable. But war, threats of war, and fluctuations in production in the capitalist countries push governments to seek a larger measure of economic self-sufficiency through control. Even so, strong forces make for the continuation of international trade relations. Small countries having few advantages of scale, and a small variety of resources, are likely in the long run to gain more from international division of labor than from the protection of infant industries to increase their independence from foreign trade. Developing countries need imports of producers' goods, and even large developed countries usually rely on imports of some strategically important materials. Planned economies, finding it difficult to plan for foreign trade because of its dependence on the national policies of other countries, have tended to develop industries producing substitutes for imports rather than exports. But complete economic independence can be bought only at the price of a subsistence level of living, and even then all of the present population cannot always be supported.

b. National Policies Regarding Resources

i. Water

Where rivers cross international boundaries, the construction of waterworks on one side may influence the water supply on the other. The major works for increasing the Nile water supply in Egypt now lie outside the country, since the Blue Nile rises in Ethiopia and the White Nile in Lake Victoria in Uganda, the two joining at Khartoum in the Sudan. The Nile Waters Agreement of 1929 regulates the sharing of water between Egypt and the Sudan by prescribing the amount and timing of water releases at the Sennar dam. A further agreement providing for increasing the use of Nile water by building dams at Lake Victoria and at Lake Tana in

Ethiopia will (after completion in some 25 years) add between 1.5 and 2.5 million acres of irrigated land to the Sudan and about seven million acres to Egypt, provide power, and improve health conditions by draining the Sudd marshes in the Sudan. It will regulate the water supply interannually, as well as interseasonally, and increase the supply by reducing evaporation in the Sudd. Egypt is to contribute $11.2 million and Uganda (which will lose land but gain electricity) is to pay $22.4 million.

The lack of international agreement has prevented the full use of the waters of the Jordan river, which flows partly through Israel and partly through the Hashemite kingdom of Jordan; the Yarmuk, its most important tributary, is partly in Jordan and partly in Syria.[41] The use of the Colorado and Niagara waters has required agreement between Canada and the U.S.A., and there are many similar situations. The partitioning of India in 1947 drew boundaries between sources and areas of utilization of water that have caused acute problems.

ii. Capital

Exports of capital were controlled by national governments only on a minor scale before the 20th century. In the late 16th and 17th century some west European governments attracted capital into foreign trade by granting regional monopolies. But from the beginning of the industrial revolution until 1914 they interfered relatively little with capital movements, although foreign loans were rarely floated in the closing decades of the 19th century without consultation with the Foreign Office in the country of issue. Such interventions as did occur were to preserve capital for home development, withhold aid from competitors, protect investors from excessively speculative or unwise loans, and support political objectives like colonial expansion and the promotion of political alliances.

In Britain, interventions were limited to informal pressure from time to time. The German government intervened on some ten occasions between 1870 and 1914. In France, however, the Finance Minister could exclude an issue from dealings on the Bourse, and practically every large issue between 1900 and 1914 involved some government action, largely to promote political alliances.

Governments more often protect past investments by their nationals, which doubtless affects willingness to lend abroad and the willingness of other countries to accept loans. Virtual state bankruptcy combined with internal disorder led to first Anglo-French, and later British, occupation of Egypt from 1882 to 1922. Imperial powers generally administered colonial and dependent areas for the benefit of the mother country, restricting investments to the production, transportation and export of primary products. But a similar trade relation often developed with countries that were not politically dependent. The Japanese government participated di-

[41] U.N., *Econ. Surv. Mission for the Middle East*, I, 4.

rectly in the export of capital to develop Formosa, Korea, and Manchuria. The Bank of Taiwan, formed in 1899, had close connections with the Bank of Japan and the Bank of Chosen (Korea) was formed to set as a central and mortgage bank for the development of that country. The Oriental Development Company was established in 1908 to finance industrial enterprises in Korea and Manchuria. All of these banks were capitalized in part by the government and the Imperial Household, but they also had close connection with the *zaibatsu*.

During the 20th century, governments intervened more frequently, sometimes to open the way for investment, or to secure monopoly (e.g., the China Consortium, the Anglo-Russian conflict over spheres of influence in Iran, and the U.S. policy in the Caribbean). Some protected past investments by their nationals, Britain mostly by diplomatic pressure, France by naval demonstrations and military occupations in the Ottoman Empire and Santo Domingo, and the U.S.A. by intervention in Haiti and Nicaragua. Attempts to influence new loans were increasingly aimed at reducing later pressure to protect investors. The U.S.A. government arranged in 1922 for issuing houses to consult the State Department before granting foreign loans, and in 1925 vetoed proposed loans to the German potash syndicate, the Coffee Institute of São Paulo, and some rubber companies, in order to protect American buyers from the monopolistic price policies of foreign concerns. But official control was discontinued in the early 1930s[42]

The British government speedily relaxed controls over capital movements after 1918 and removed them in 1921. The market was free for ten years, except for unofficial control by the Bank of England in 1924 and 1925. After the government abandoned the gold standard, it controlled foreign loans to protect foreign exchange from excessive strain by strengthening relations with sterling area countries and promoting exports, and to keep down the rate of interest to domestic borrowers (both government and industry). The Capital Issues Committee was instructed to favor British-owned enterprises abroad against foreign governments and municipalities; take account of the treatment of British enterprises by foreign governments; and to favor loans to sterling area countries to stabilize exchange rates. The Russian government after the revolution prevented private exports of capital, and the German Nazi government virtually prohibited all capital exports to prevent a general flight of capital to escape its domestic policies.

In time of war, capital movements are typically controlled to assist political allies and prevent assistance to enemies. During the war of 1939-45, however, the U.S.A., having realized the heritage of misunderstanding and friction left by the loans made during the war of 1914-18, largely replaced intergovernment loans for war purposes with Lend-Lease aid.

---

[42] U.N., *International Capital Movements during the Inter-War Period*, 55.

After the end of hostilities in 1945 there was virtually no private international capital market, even though capital movements were greatly needed to restore productive capacity in all the belligerent countries (except the U.S.A.) and to meet demands for development in others. Consequently, most capital movements have been managed by governments or by international authorities. The U.S.A., the chief exporter, realized that, without the support of friendly powers, friction with Russia would have serious consequences. Efforts by European countries to rehabilitate their economies out of internal resources would have involved reductions in the standard of living that would have overthrown existing governments and encouraged revolution. After loans to Britain, France, Poland, and a few other countries, the European Aid Program (Marshall Plan) was established to systematize foreign aid by loans and grants. Between April 1948 and December 1950 about $13.3 billion was lent and granted under this plan, of which $12.3 billion was in grants. Because the program created serious political problems concerning the amount of aid and its distribution among countries, the U.S. government suggested the establishment of the Organization for European Economic Cooperation, consisting of representatives of the west European governments, to consider and comment upon the various national economic programs.

The European countries became dependent on the U.S.A. for the maintenance of their standard of living, and the U.S.A. was concerned with the national policies of the recipient countries, particularly with the speed at which they were likely to restore the countries to economic independence. Because economic cooperation among west European countries was seriously impeded by trade barriers, the U.S.A. pressed for European economic integration. But sweeping away national controls of trade to create a wider free market, whatever its long-run economies, would involve a relocation of industry requiring enormous investment and losses in previously protected activities (as the Benelux countries discovered). To stimulate intra-European trade, the U.S.A. permitted recipients of aid to finance deficits in trade with other recipients. But, as the dollar tended to become the principal working currency in Europe, the U.S.A. established the Intra-European Payments Plan in 1948 to stimulate intra-European trade as a first step toward economic integration. Under this plan, part of the aid given to some European countries was to be used to grant stated amounts of credit in their own currency to other European countries. Intra-European trade was thereby encouraged, but its channels were controlled by decisions made in the U.S.A. as to the countries to be thus assisted to lend to others, and the choice of the ultimate beneficiaries. These beneficiaries, moreover, were pushed into trade with the countries enabled to grant them credits, even when those countries were not the cheapest sources of supply. This last restriction was modified in 1949, when it was provided that 25% of the credit passed on by recipients of U.S.A. aid was to be convertible into the currency of any other participating country. In 1950 the U.S.A. promoted a further freeing of intra-European trade by suggesting the establishment of the European Payments Union to provide for a single settlement by each member country of its balances with all other members. The U.S.A. provided a sum of $600 million to finance, within limits, countries in debt on balance to other members. In total the U.S.A. government lent $8.9 billion and granted $26.9 million to other countries during the seven years from 1946 to 1952.

The Russian government set up the Council of Mutual Economic Assistance, including representatives of the Soviet Union and its satellite governments, to organize economic aid in Eastern Europe. There is no published plan for the coordination of the economies of these countries. Following a trade treaty between Czechoslovakia and Poland in 1947, a series of joint committees was appointed to promote economic cooperation and pave the way for the integration of the two economies. But it appears to have produced little coordination except in a few industries, and there has been no capital investment by either country in the other. The move was designed partly to provide substitute markets for those to the west lost as a result of the changed political orientation of these countries. Trade treaties originally for one year have now been replaced by treaties for a period of years to facilitate long-term planning. Mixed industrial enterprises operated jointly by more than one government, and agreements for the joint construction of industrial enterprises and transportation and communication facilities are used to promote coordinated development in the Soviet orbit. The U.S.S.R. is said to have agreed to provide industrial equipment and specialists, but there remains considerable doubt whether Russia will accelerate the development of Eastern Europe by exporting Russian capital, and it is possible that countries like Czechoslovakia have in fact exported capital to Russia.

Exports of capital to underdeveloped countries changed in form during the 20th century because of changes in national policies. Rising political unrest in colonial areas induced imperial powers to plan the economic development of their dependencies, both to assist the recovery of the mother country and to improve living conditions in the colonies. The British Colonial Development Act in 1929 authorized the provision of £8.8 million over eleven years, and an act of 1940 provided a further £10.4 million over five years, and approved a further £19.6 million.[43] The Colonial Development and Welfare Act of 1945 provided £120 million more over ten years.[44] The total resources available for colonial development in 1948 were estimated at £625 million of which £120 million was from the above mentioned colonial development fund, £240 million from local

[43] U.N., *Econ. Devel. of Selected Countries*, 1947, 240.
[44] British Information Service, *The British Development and Welfare Acts*, 1949.

taxes and loans from colonial areas, and £100 million from local interests. The Colonial Development Corporation was established after 1945, with power to invest an additional £110 million, and the Overseas Food Corporation with power to invest up to £55 million.

In France a law of 1946 required the Minister of Overseas France to establish ten-year development plans for the economic and social development of the territories, and to set up an investment fund to be supplied by metropolitan France, the governments of the territories, and the Central Bank of Overseas France.[45] The government included plans for its colonial areas in the "Monnet" plans, the second of which provided for considerably accelerated development of the colonial areas to reduce their net demand for dollars and increase their supply of products for consumption, both local and in France, to reduce the French demand for dollars. The Belgian government announced a plan for the industrial and agricultural development of the Congo in 1949, the capital to come mostly from Belgian private sources. The plan provided for the gradual elimination of the parallel economies of white and native populations, but progress has been seriously behind schedule partly owing to a shortage of labor. The Dutch government has been limited in planning for its colonial areas because of the war in Indonesia, finally concluded in 1949 by the Declaration of Independence of the Indonesian Republic within the general limits of the Dutch Empire.

In 1950 the Ministers of seven British Commonwealth countries began the preparation of a comprehensive plan for the economic development of India, Pakistan, Ceylon, Malaya, Singapore, and North Borneo (including Sarawak and Brunei), Burma, Thailand, Indo-China, and Indonesia, all in southeast Asia and including a quarter of the world's population. The initial plan consisted of six-year agricultural development plans for India, Pakistan, Ceylon, Malaya, Singapore, and North Borneo, costing £1,868 million of which £1,084 million was to come from outside these countries, £246 million from sterling balances, and the remainder from private foreign investment, private foreign investment in government loans, the International Bank for Reconstruction and Development, and gifts and loans from other (largely Commonwealth) governments. During 1951 Australia, Canada, New Zealand, Britain, and the U.S.A. made funds available to the countries concerned. In 1952 the Japanese Economic Stabilization Board announced that the Japanese government was prepared to underwrite foreign investments in southeast Asia of $91 million by Japanese firms over five years.

During the three years 1946-48, of $136 billion of net investment in the world, $100 billion was invested in the country of origin, (70% in the U.S.A., Canada, and Britain) and only $36 billion abroad. No more than $13 bil-

---

[45] U.N., *Econ. Devel. in Selected Countries*, 1947, 267.

lion went to underdeveloped areas.[46] Yet $19 billion a year has been estimated to be needed from both internal and external sources to increase national income by transferring one per cent of the population out of agriculture into non-farm occupations each year, and to increase agricultural yields (of which 70% is needed for Asia). This amount is 20% of the incomes of these countries in 1949, and might increase their national incomes 2.5% per year; or, after allowing for increases in population, per capita incomes might increase 2%.[47]

Imports of capital have not always been welcomed by governments, and property acquired by foreigners through capital imports has not always been protected. Diplomatic pressure and an occasional show of force restricted government attacks on property before 1914 (although they did not prevent heavy losses on investments). Russia seized virtually all foreign (as well as domestically owned) property after the 1917 revolution without compensation. In consequence, Russia has been able to finance little of its subsequent development with foreign capital, although it floated some small loans in New York between the wars. It also received considerable capital equipment from the U.S.A. under Lend-Lease, and some from Britain under parallel arrangements during the war of 1939-45. Subsequent nationalizations of foreign-owned properties (e.g., in Mexico, Iran, and Bolivia), and fears that the state may inflate the currency or impose heavy taxes, have discouraged foreign investors, although in some countries governments would not have survived without doing some of these things.

Since 1918, and more intensely since 1945, governments, although anxious for development that could be accelerated by capital imports, have feared the foreign political or economic domination arising from such investments, and the effect of withdrawals of capital on their ability to meet their balance of payments. Some have discouraged imports of capital by regulations restricting subsequent withdrawals of income or capital, or regulating the number of foreign personnel that may be employed. In the past few years, however, governments have lightened restrictions of this sort to attract capital. In Brazil not more than 8% profit can be withdrawn or 20% of capital, but Argentina permits the export of profits up to 8% on investment from abroad and the removal of such investments in installments after ten years. In the Middle East, foreign exchange controls have restricted remittances of profits. In Egypt the minimum percentage of the capital in corporations that must be held by Egyptians was 51%, but a flexible limit was established in 1950. Iran guaranteed repatriation of profits and capital to foreign investors in 1951, and

---

[46] U.N., *Methods of Financing Economic Development in Underdeveloped Countries*, 63.

[47] U.N., *Measures for the Economic Development of Underdeveloped Countries*, 1951, Ch. XI.

provided guarantees against loss of capital due to "untoward events." In 1949 India promised reasonable facilities for remitting profits or repatriating capital consistently with the exchange policy, and fair compensation for property nationalized. Pakistan has promised opportunities for full remittance of profits, but in a number of essential industries, 51% of all capital must be held by Pakistan nationals. Colombia withdrew all restrictions on foreign capital in 1952. But there remains the overriding political uncertainty in the world as a whole, and a great excess of demands for capital over the supply of it.

After 1945 foreign aid went chiefly to the war-damaged non-enemy countries, directly or indirectly from the U.S.A. Western Eurpoe needed aid to restore its productive system to enable it to assist in the development of other parts of the world, and it was better prepared to make immediate use of foreign funds. A number of the underdeveloped countries were neither psychologically nor politically ready for development funds, nor did they have plans for their economical use.

iii. Labor

National policies regarding the international movements of persons, like those regarding capital, have moved in the direction of increasing restriction in recent years. In earlier times the dangers of travel, and the difficulties of settlement, so restricted migration that governments did little to restrict (or encourage) it. In the 18th century the British government encouraged emigration when the crown granted tracts of land along the Atlantic Coast of North America and in the West Indies to titled landowners and chartered companies, although the signers of the Declaration of Independence contended that the British Crown had interfered with immigration and settlement in the North American colonies. Between 1787 and 1867 Britain, Germany, Switzerland, and Sweden transported paupers, vagrants, and convicts to colonies. Towards the end of the 19th century the British government again encouraged emigration to empty spaces within the empire that might tempt foreign aggression or induce demands for the entry of immigrants from other countries. But the British population was somewhat immobile, the dominion governments feared the costs of transporting and equipping immigrants who were short of capital, and the empty spaces were often empty because they were not very productive. Until 1840, however, workers with special skills and knowledge were prohibited from migrating (even though they went). But generally workers were free to migrate in the 19th century, and still are in Britain, France, and the U.S.A. But the German Nazi government severely controlled emigration, and it is virtually prohibited from Russia and the eastern European countries. Prohibitions of emigration are usually aimed at preventing mass emigrations that would reduce the labor and military forces and imply opposition to internal policies generating internal discontent. Some of the countries in Europe suffering most from population pressure (e.g., Italy and Greece) encourage emigration.

National attitudes to immigration have ranged from encouragement to selective control to virtual prohibition. It is often difficult for a "foreigner" to become a member of a primitive society, and in the ancient world the activities and privileges of persons from abroad were often restricted. With the development of craft production in the Middle Ages many states (notably Britain) encouraged immigrants possessing skills, thus widening the distribution of craft production. In the 17th century German rulers attracted immigrants to remedy population losses from the Thirty Years' War. In the 18th century the British government sought to accelerate the expansion of population in the American colonies by liberalizing the conditions of entry from continental Europe, and occasionally subsidizing immigrants. In the 19th century there were few obstacles to entering the U.S.A. During the war of 1939-45 the German Nazi government brought numbers of persons to Germany for forced labor in both industry and agriculture. But during the present century, governments have increasingly restricted immigration.

Countries of recent settlement, although needing additional population, have increasingly limited entry to persons expected to enter parts of the market where labor is scarce (often agriculture or domestic service), or to persons coming from selected countries. Countries of European settlement have generally excluded Asiatic immigrants. American ships were prohibited from transporting Chinese coolies to the U.S.A. as early as 1862, and Chinese coolies were wholly excluded in 1882. Increasingly, persons have been excluded for reasons of health, education, or political opinion. Between 1880 and 1900 provision was made for exclusion from the U.S.A. of prostitutes, persons suffering from various diseases, contract laborers and polygamists. In 1903 anarchists were excluded, and in 1917 a literacy test was added. In 1921 the U.S.A. began to select immigrants according to their country of origin, the quota for each country being based on the number of people in the U.S.A. of each origin in the year 1910, (which discriminated against southern and eastern Europe). In 1927 the annual quota of immigrants from all countries was limited to 150,000. This system continued to provide the general basis of control in legislation in 1952. Britain almost totally prohibited immigration after 1914, largely due to the burden of unemployment. But France and Germany had both become dependent on immigrant workers, partly seasonal but partly permanent, for agricultural work between 1918 and 1939. Immigration into Russia and eastern European countries is highly restricted on a political basis.

These restrictive policies are partly attempts to avoid excessive heterogeneity of population or the strengthening of dissident groups. Heterogeneity creates political difficulties when sub-groups have special interests and partial allegiance to the countries of origin. There may be friction between sub-groups within the country. These difficulties are usually serious, however, only where immigration is rapid. But economic considerations have also been important. Fear that immigrants will take jobs from residents may be justified in the short run in times of underemployment, but in the longer run new workers add to the demand for goods, (and, therefore, workers) as well as to the labor supply. Large numbers of immigrants accustomed to low wages may depress wages in the short run, and even in the long run, if the ratio of workers to other productive resources rises. From the international point of view immigration controls seriously obstruct any tendency of the international market for labor to reduce present inequalities among nations in labor incomes. Free migration would, however, probably encourage continued high rates of multiplication in many low income countries, and frustrate the desire of peoples in others to improve living standards by restricting increase. Whether it would reduce saving in general is more difficult to say. Morever just as inequality of income within a country facilitates saving or luxury consumption, inequality among countries has facilitated saving, higher general living standards, and luxury consumption. But the higher-income countries controlling immigration must choose whether to lend part of their savings to countries which might industrialize, to allow foreigners to come and use the capital in the country which it accumulates, or to refuse both and enjoy their own resources including their savings and face any consequences of being relatively well off.

3. Public International Authorities

By the 20th century it was evident that the operation of international markets controlled by national states often in competition with each other, was unsatisfactory. War and the fear of war extended intervention by national states at the expense of the market organization, and international economic frictions were increasingly translated into frictions among governments. War is no solution; it creates more economic problems than it solves. Bilateral negotiation has become increasingly burdensome and inappropriate for all countries. The countries with little coercive or bargaining power had special problems. They became increasingly dissatisfied with the operation of the world economic system because of their increasing consciousness of their inferior economic position. Experience of unilateral aid by the more developed created a preference for aid through multilateral organizations.

Public international bodies to provide for peaceful change appeared in embryo in the 19th century to deal with specialized problems of international communications and public health. During the life of the League of Nations, 1918-39, a number of conventions affecting international economic relations were signed, mostly under the International Labor Office. From 1939-45, limited international bodies brought about collaboration to control scarce raw materials and some fabricated goods (e.g., the Combined Boards, which were collaborative bodies of the U.S.A., Britain, and later Canada). But the most ambitious efforts to improve international relations, both political and economic, were made after 1945 through the United Nations and associated bodies. These bodies possess no coercive powers comparable to those of national states. Their influence must be exerted through persuasion (backed by the prestige of their more important members) and any resources they adminster. The failure of Russia and its satellites to participate in most of the economic organizations severely limits the effectiveness of multilateral bodies.

International regulation of trade has taken the form of efforts to reduce import duties and reduce the restrictive effect of international commodity agreements. The U.S.A. initiated efforts to reduce the barriers to international trade in 1945. Inter-allied bodies allocating materials, food and some manufactured goods were dismantled soon after the end of hostilities. To modify the older restrictive policies of national states, the U.S.A. proposed an International Trade Organization under the U.N. The charter for the organization (drawn up in Havana in 1948) was not confirmed by the U.S. Congress. But two international conferences in 1947 and 1949 negotiated reductions in trade barriers, and an Interim Commission for the International Trade Organization was established. The U.S.A. and most western European countries gave effect in 1949 and 1950 to the reduced duties agreed in the General Agreement on Tariffs and Trade (GATT) (signed at Geneva in 1947) and in further agreements at Annecy in 1949. At Torquay in 1951, 38 nations in 147 pairs of negotiations agreed on 55,-000 tariff rates, to remain stable for three years. The negotiations, being multilateral, could take account of the aggregate direct and indirect effects of tariff reductions. All countries accepted the unconditional most-favored-nation principle, and a code of administrative practices reducing the hardships and uncertainties resulting from changing controls of trade and foreign exchange. But a number of countries were permitted restrictions (regarded as temporary) to enable them to deal with balance of payments problems. Russia and the eastern European countries did not participate. In 1953, 31 nations agree to continue the agreed rates until 1955, Australia, Brazil, and Peru, however, failing to do so.

The U.N. also established in 1947 an Interim Coordinating Committee for International Commodity Agreements. The Economic and Social Council adopted the principles laid down in the Havana Charter for the International Trade Organization: namely, that (1) any country interested in a particular commodity may request international consideration of the problems involved; (2) both consuming and producing countries should participate in the operation of commodity agreements; (3) study groups and conferences should precede such agreements; (4) resort to agreements regulating prices or restricting output should be limited; (5) there should be full publicity as to proposed operating agreements; (6) operations affecting different commodities should be coordinated.[48] The objection to restriction of output without the participation of buying countries expressed a more balanced international view of such arrangements than prewar agreements had. A number of study groups has been set up, and the principal agreements have related to wheat and sugar (p. 565). A committee of experts appointed by the U.N. remarked that the prospects of success for commodity agreements of a less restrictive type than in the past were improved by the increasing chance of avoiding world depression and by anticipated increases in world production. Although commodity arrangements for the 25 most important primary commodities (by value) would cover only one-third of world trade, the stabilization of world commodity markets would contribute notably to general economic stability.[49]

The European Coal and Steel Community[50] was established in 1952 as a step toward the integration of the European economy. Based on the Schuman Plan proposed by the Foreign Minister of France in 1951, it is limited as to products, and as to countries (France, Western Germany, Belgium, Luxembourg, the Netherlands, and Italy, but not Britain). To "substitute for age-long rivalries a fusion of their essential interests," these countries made a fifty-year agreement to establish a single market among the members by eliminating import and export duties, quantitative controls on trade, subsidies, discriminatory selling and buying, and restrictive practices for sharing or exploiting markets. Within this common market, however, the High Authority administering the treaty may, in the event of a crisis (actual or imminent) establish minimum prices and production quotas, make levies on production in excess of quotas, and use the proceeds to subsidize firms producing less than their quotas. It may also set maximum prices for any coal or steel products (apparently intended to apply where production is highly concentrated), and its prior consent is necessary to mergers of producers. The treaty also prohibits (after 5½ years) restrictions on the migration of qualified labor among the subscribing countries, and nationality restrictions on the employment of labor. German and Dutch collieries were also to pay about half the subsidies to producers in Belgium and Italy, their governments paying the remainder.

This regulated free competition does not extend to non-member countries. Producers are not clearly restricted in combining in selling to and buying from non-member countries, nor prohibited from using unfair competitive practices and discrimination in non-member countries. Member governments may also impose import duties and the High Authority

---

[48] U.N., *Review of International Commodity Problems*, 1951, 4. This program was based on the suggestions of the U.S. State Department in *Proposals for the Expansion of World Trade and Employment*, Ch. IV.

[49] U.N., *Measures for International Economic Stability*, 1951, 19, 25, Ch. II.

[50] Mendershausen, H., "First Tests of the Schuman Plan," *Rev. of Econ. and Stat.* Nov. 1953, 269.

may fix minimum and maximum export prices, impose quantitative export restrictions (unless member governments unanimously oppose them), and protect the producers in the single market against imports from non-member countries threatening serious damage to production in member countries.

The common market for coal, iron ore, scrap, and steel was declared in 1953. The import duties on iron and steel then abolished were fairly important in all but the Benelux countries, but there were no duties on coal or iron ore, and only in Italy on coke (where the duties were continued under a transitional clause in the treaty). But import quotas were imposed to protect iron and steel producers in the Benelux countries. The Authority also proceeded against discriminatory transport rates, but it approved continuance of special subsidies to, or levies on, producers by national governments, on a transitional basis and a declining scale. The Authority had set no minimum prices by 1953, but had set maximum prices for coal and scrap, but not for iron ore or steel. It has also allowed producers in the member countries to participate in a combination under its control to purchase scrap, to assist them to compete in the world market. It also approved an agreement among producers in four member countries on the price of rolled steel products exported to non-members.

The High Authority has power to veto investments by members, except when made out of the funds of the enterprise. It can itself assist investments by loans or guarantees to increase production, reduce costs, or facilitate marketing, and in 1954 obtained a loan in the U.S.A. for such purposes. Thus it is not yet clear how far the Community will lower barriers to trade and reduce monopoly. It has agreed to price fixing in dealing with non-members. Within the common market it was fairly successful in eliminating discrimination in the sale of coal in 1953, but the market for steel appears to have been traditionally monopolistic.[51]

International organization to deal with monetary policy was born of the experience of currency warfare during the inter-war years, which made it evident that the exchange value of a country's currency is too much a matter of international concern to be determined satisfactorily by unilateral action. The international conference at Bretton Woods drew up a charter for the International Monetary Fund in 1944. The members agreed to maintain the exchange value of their currencies within 1% of the parity agreed to by the Fund, by buying and selling currencies within this range of prices. They also agreed not to alter this parity by more than 10% without the consent of the Fund, and to subscribe to a fund from which members could purchase foreign currencies, within prescribed limits, to enable them to meet temporary deficits in their balance of payments. Their contributions were to be provided 75% in their own currency and 25% in dollars,

---

[51] U.N., *Econ. Surv. of Europe in 1953*, 14.

the fund's initial supply of dollars being $3.6 billion.[52] They also agreed not to engage in currency practices leading to economic warfare (such as rationing foreign exchange, currency discrimination and multiple exchange rates), subject, however, to permission to restrict capital transfers, make transitional use of controls and ration "scarce currencies." The Fund may decide which transactions are "current" and which are "capital." After 1952 the Fund may expel members continuing restrictions when the Fund holds that the member is in a reasonable position to end them. If the Fund is in danger of running out of a currency (e.g., dollars) it may attempt to borrow that currency from the member whose currency is scarce. The member is not obliged to lend, but is obliged to sell its currency for gold. If all measures to increase the supply of the scarce currency fail, the Fund must formally declare it "scarce" and ration it to its members, who may then ration imports from the scarce-currency country. There were 35 original member countries and 48 members in 1951 (approximately all the members of the U.N. excluding Russia and its satellite countries, although including Czechoslovakia).

The Fund began to organize at the end of 1945, when the agreement was ratified by governments with 80% of the total subscriptions. In December 1946 it announced the exchange rates at which it would begin to operate, which were all the rates then in effect, and mostly below their dollar value in 1936. But changes in prices and wages in the various countries since the pre-war period differed markedly from changes in the exchange values of their currencies. Judged in terms of relative changes in prices since pre-war, the currencies of Britain and most of the Commonwealth countries were undervalued from 6 to 37% and most others overvalued.[53] Consequently, the members could balance their international payments only by (1) adjusting internal prices and costs to these exchange rates, (2) adjusting their exchange rate to existing internal price levels (in either of which events controls could be abandoned), or (3) retaining controls over trade and capital movements. At first controls were retained. But, under pressure from the U.S.A. to remove barriers to international trade, and to meet the problem of balancing trade with the U.S.A. (a pre-war problem that reappeared), countries began to reduce the exchange value of their currencies.

France reduced the franc 44.4% in January 1948, in virtual defiance of the Fund, in the hope of increasing exports. It permitted a freer market in gold and dollars but continued import controls and promised the Fund that the new devices would be only temporary. The Fund urged the British to devalue to facilitate freer trade, and in October 1949 the pound was reduced about 30% (from $4.05 to $2.805). Between September and December 1949 import prices rose but few export prices rose in Britain, the imports obtainable from a given volume of exports falling 10%. Retail prices

[52] Hart, op. cit., 405.
[53] Metzler, Triffin, and Haberler, International Monetary Policies, 5, 24, 39.

and wages tended to rise.[54] A number of countries (including South Africa, Australia, New Zealand, India, Ceylon, Burma, Eire, Iraq, Egypt, Iceland, Israel, Holland, Denmark, Finland, Norway, Sweden, and Greece) reduced the foreign exchange value of their currency by the same amount as Britain. The price of British imports was not changed in these countries, but the local price of imports from the U.S.A. was increased, with the result that the British could compete more effectively with the U.S.A. and reduce the demand upon the sterling area for dollars. Other countries (including Canada, Belgium, France, Italy, Portugal, Siam, and West Germany) reduced the value of their currency, but less than sterling. A further list of countries (including all the Latin American countries, Pakistan, Switzerland, and a number of east European countries) maintained the former value of their currency in dollars. In exporting to these countries, the British were in the same position as in exporting to the U.S.A.[55]

The gold-producing countries urged an increase in the price of gold, the Union of South Africa at least twice recommended that the Fund raise uniformly and simultaneously the gold equivalent of all member currencies.[56] The Fund refused, but later agreed not to object to domestic transactions at prices above official parities unless they in fact established new rates of exchange or undermined the rates of other members, and finally permitted exports at premium prices for industrial purposes. South Africa, Southern Rhodesia, Canada, U.S.A., and Australia have exported gold under this provision. In 1951 South Africa exported 40% of its gold in the industrial market, and between 1949 and 1953 received about $42 million in premiums on sales above the U.S.A. price. It denied that in joining the International Monetary Fund it had agreed to support the U.S. price of $35 per ounce for gold (which it held to be unrealistic), and denied that the consent of the Fund was necessary to premium sales for commercial purposes. South Africa was naturally concerned because world prices were rising while the value of gold in dollars was not. Canada preferred to subsidize its gold mining. But the premium sales increasingly diverted gold (both newly mined and from existing monetary stocks) to free markets for hoarding, thus virtually nullifying the Fund's Articles and undermining the gold parity of the various currencies. But the price of gold, which reached a peak of $56 in 1950, was back to the U.S.A. price of $35 in 1953.

The International Monetary Fund has not succeeded in acting like a world central bank providing movements of short-term funds to facilitate the settlement of trade balances at reasonably stable exchange rates. It had made available to its members by July 1951 $729 million in U.S. dollars (after allowing for repayments) and small amounts of other currencies. But countries have been unwilling or unable to make the necessary adjustments

54 U.N., *Econ. Surv. of Europe*, 1949, 8.
55 *Economist*, Feb. 4, 1950.
56 U.N., *Measures for International Economic Stability*, 1951, 34.

in domestic prices and wages to balance their international accounts, and have continued direct controls of trade and financial transactions. Its initial supply of dollars ($3.6 million) is below what is likely to be needed to assist its members to tide over a temporary lack of balance on international account, and far below what is likely to be needed in the event of a recession in the major countries. It can supplement national reserves only to the extent of about 2.5% of the imports of its members, and even minor lapses from full employment in the U.S.A. may cause reductions in the dollars becoming available far in excess of the resources of the Fund. A United Nations Committee therefore suggested less restriction on the drawings of member countries on the Fund in time of recession, increases in the total sums available to the Fund, and more liberal loans to the Fund by countries experiencing recession.[57] "Reserves of countries other than the United States," even when supplemented by recourse to the Fund, "are, in general, barely sufficient to meet the unforeseen emergencies (such as crop failures, political changes and rumors, and foreign exchange speculation) that arise in the affairs of most countries from time to time even in periods of general world prosperity."

International organization to provide long-term capital also developed after 1945 in anticipation of a great need for capital in many developed countries for postwar reconstruction, and in underdeveloped countries for development at a time when the private international capital market was paralyzed. The Bretton Woods international conference in 1944 drafted a charter for the International Bank for Reconstruction and Development that began to organize in 1946. In 1953 there were 54 members (including China, Japan, and Czechoslovakia, but not Russia). The Bank has obtained funds partly from the subscriptions of member countries to the Bank's capital which amounted to $9.036 billion on June 30, 1953. Members are required to pay in only 20% (2% in U.S.A. dollars and 18% in their own currency), the remainder being subject to call to meet the obligations of the Bank. The Bank may itself borrow to relend, and by 1953 had borrowed $556.4 million ($500 million in U.S.A. dollars, $13.6 million in Canadian dollars, $14 million in British pounds, and $28.8 million in Swiss francs). It may obtain funds for new loans by selling to the public securities representing past loans, with or without its guarantee, and by 1953 had sold $70 million of borrower obligations (Figure 22). Its loans may not exceed 20% of its subscribed capital, and it may guarantee loans up to the remaining 80%. The 18% subscribed in member currencies may be lent only with the consent of the member, and in 1953 about 17% of its disbursements had been made in other than U.S. dollars.

The Bank was intended not as a substitute for the private market in voluntary savings, but as a supplement to assist projects that fail to appeal

---

[57] *Ibid.*, 8, 12, 28, 33, Ch. IV.

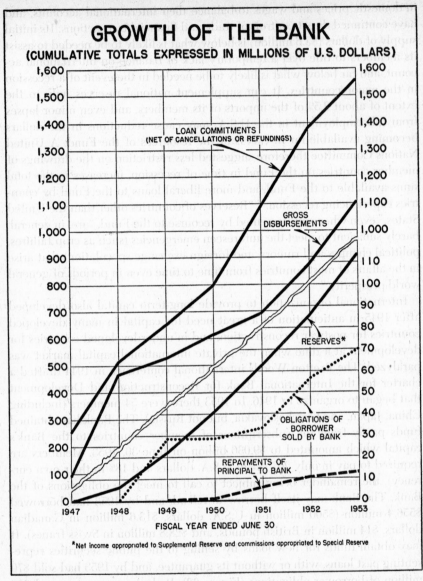

Fig. 22. Growth of the International Bank for Reconstruction and Development, 1947-1953. (Source: International Bank for Reconstruction and Development *Annual Report, 1952-3,* p. 6.)

to the private investors and yet appeared to the Bank to be worthy of support. It was expected to lend for specific projects of reconstruction and development (and not for relief and rehabilitation), and was required to check the costs of proposed projects and the borrower's ability to pay. It was further required to act through the government of the country where the project was located and to lend only with the guarantee of that government.

In its early years the Bank was relatively inactive. Its funds were not large (and their purchasing power was seriously reduced by rising dollar prices). It could borrow only with the consent of the government of the country where it borrowed. The U.S.A. was the chief potential source of funds, but borrowing there was restricted by U.S. government policy, and for a time by the hesitant attitude of investors toward the Bank's bonds. Although the U.S. government was itself making funds available for European reconstruction, and there was a shortage of capital goods for export, the chief loans by the Bank until about 1950 were for reconstruction. By 1953 such loans to France, the Netherlands, Denmark, and Luxembourg were about 30% of the total loans of the Bank ($1.560 billion). Loans to underdeveloped countries increased after 1950, and by 1953 were about 70% of all loans. About 40% were for electric power, 24% for transportation, 2.6% for communications, 15% for agriculture, 15% for industry, and the remainder for general development. About 17% went to Asia and the Middle East, 13% to Africa, 15% to Australasia, 22% to Europe, and 33% to the western hemisphere.

The Bank has been prepared to lend only to cover the foreign exchange requirements of projects, which has caused an uneconomic bias in favor of projects requiring little foreign exchange. Local development projects require some diversion of local resources (labor for constructing roads, ports, buildings, and the like) as well as imported equipment. The financing of either from foreign loans is equally reasonable. The Bank must, however, determine how much of the total cost of the project can be borne by the country, and it may be that the foreign loan should exceed or fall short of the immediate foreign exchange requirements of the project. The Bank must also take account of the country's later ability to service the loan; projects which increase internal production and consumption do not necessarily increase available exports to service the loan. But in 1951 the Bank stated that it was considering loans intended to cover indirect as well as direct foreign exchange requirements arising out of expenditures in the borrowing country.

A Bank requirement that it lend only for specific projects simplified its task of ensuring that funds were spent in accordance with the loan agreement, but prevented it from financing the many small projects that must be important in the early stages of industrialization. In 1950, however, it made loans to the Industrial Bank of Turkey and to a consortium of eight Mexican banks and the *Nacional Financiera*. Both loans were to finance private enterprises individually small but collectively capable of contributing significantly to development, and to attract local funds into investment. Though retaining power to ensure that the loans conformed to its general standards, the Bank delegated the screening of projects to a local organization.

The Bank has repeatedly emphasized in recent years that its loans are limited chiefly by the dearth of good projects, partly because underdevelopment "connotes an insufficiency of talents necessary to translate development projects into practical propositions ready for execution." It has stated that "the resources of most underdeveloped areas are adequate, if effectively used, to support a substantially higher level of production and income" and that capital equipment is available for export, but that there are political and economic obstacles to economic growth.[58] The Bank could contribute to world economic stability if it expanded loans greatly in time of recession to help to offset fluctuations in private international investment, and to avoid sharp setbacks in development programs due to a fall in export proceeds. It might also help by financing "buffer stocks of commodities." But the Bank's resources are inadequate to these purposes, partly because of its dependence on the private capital market as the main source of funds for its loan and guarantee operations, a deficiency that might be remedied if member governments would lend more funds to the Bank directly or through central banks.[59] As the Bank is not authorized to make equity investments, an International Finance Corporation has been suggested as an affiliate of the International Bank to make loans to private enterprise without government guarantee, and participate with private capital in equity investment. But by 1953 the governments on whom the corporation would have to rely for capital had not agreed to provide it.

Underdeveloped countries need not only capital but also technicians from the developed countries to formulate programs for foreign financing, to adapt the methods of production in developed countries for use under the conditions in the underdeveloped, and to maximize the incomes yielded by local resources. In January 1949 President Truman announced as point four in American foreign policy "a bold new program for making the benefits of our scientific advances and industrial progress available for the improvement and growth of underdeveloped areas" and for fostering (in cooperation with other nations) investment in areas needing development. The U.N. initiated a small program of technical aid, and in 1950 the Congress appropriated $34.5 million to effectuate "point four," of which $12.007 million was contributed to the U.N. program costing $20 million. By December 1950 there were 350 American technicians in 36 foreign countries, and during 1950 the U.N., in cooperation with the Technical Assistance program of the U.S.A., arranged for about 110 experts to visit 17 countries to assist development projects, and nine countries to aid social welfare projects. It also provided training for the nationals of underdeveloped countries abroad or in regional seminars.

---

58 Inter. Bank for Reconstruction and Development *Annual Report*, 1952-3.
59 U.N., *Measures for International Economic Stability*, 1951, 11, 25, 30, Ch. III.

No public international body has been established to deal with the general migration of persons, although international organizations were established after 1945 to deal with refugees. National states regard the control of movements of people into and out of their countries as an essential political function. In consequence, the present tendency is to deal with inequality of incomes among nations by bringing technical knowledge and capital to the people where they are, rather than to allow them to move to places where production is more efficient and resources are more plentiful.

Chapter 27

The Nature and Measurement
of Consumption

A. Relation of Consumption to Production

Total consumption exceeds total production if a society lives on inventories of consumer goods or receives net contributions from outside, expenditure on the armed forces being regarded as collective consumption. A country that fails to maintain its capital does not consume more than it produces, but consumes at the expense of its future capacity to produce. Total consumption falls short of production because of saving and investment, net contributions to other countries, or goods being allowed to rot or being destroyed. The components of aggregate consumption differ from those of aggregate production because of international trade.

Consumption and production are also related over time. Investment in one period increases production and permits increased consumption (or investment) in subsequent periods. Durable consumer goods like houses yield satisfaction over a period after production is completed. Imports of capital at one time may be followed by increased production and exports to service the loans. Countries exporting capital may later receive imports to cover loan service.

B. The Measurement of Consumption

1. Problems of Measurement

The impossibility of measuring consumption in terms of welfare has already been discussed (Ch. 1). We are, therefore, compelled to use money values of incomes in goods and services. These vary among individuals, but we cannot consider all such variations; we can here discuss only the more general outlines of variation.

National averages of consumption suggest the broad pattern of consumption throughout the world. Comparison of intranational patterns of consumption provides further information. Inequality of incomes (although less inequality of consumption) is universal, but there is no one method of comparing unequal distributions, and the methods in use differ in their emphasis. The significance of information on the size of the largest incomes depends on the proportion of all income thus accounted for. The significance of information about the amount of the national income going to the group receiving the largest incomes depends on the number of people receiving such incomes, the definition of "largest" incomes, and the distribution of the remainder. The information available permits only partial statements in any of these forms. National income is not known for many countries (Ch. 1) and data as to intra-national distribution are less common. Information about consumption as distinct from income (i.e., allowing for savings) is still less common.

2. National Averages

International comparisons of average incomes for any considerable number of countries are usually based on average production rather than consumption. It has already been shown (Ch. 1) that national averages vary widely (Table 1), 85% of the world's population having only 38% of world production, this inequality being relatively recent and increasing. Consumption per head appears to have declined in western European countries between 1939 and 1949 except in Czechoslovakia, and the Scandinavian countries (Table 54). In the U.S.A. personal consumption expenditures per person (in 1953 prices) fell about 20% between 1929 and 1933, but rose about 44% between 1929 and 1953.[1]

3. Intra-National Distribution among Persons

Comparisons of intra-national distribution of incomes can be made for only a few countries. The Pareto coefficient of inequality is obtained by plotting on a double logarithmic scale the cumulative number of incomes at or above a series of income levels. The position of the line joining the points depends on the size of the population and its average income. The

---

[1] U.S.A., *Economic Report of the President*, 1954, 168, 178.

TABLE 54

CONSUMPTION PER HEAD IN SELECTED EUROPEAN COUNTRIES IN 1949
AND BEFORE THE WAR OF 1939-45*

Country	Pre-war Year Used as Base	1949 Index
Czechoslovakia	1937	130†‡
Sweden	1938-9	113
Denmark	1938	104
Norway	1938	103
Belgium	1938	100§
United Kingdom	1938	99
Netherlands	1938	98
France	1938	97
Finland	1938	97‡
Italy	1938	92
Austria	1937	86
Germany (western zone)	1936	85
Bulgaria	1939	80‡§

* U.N., *Econ. Surv. of Europe in 1949*, 26. Based generally on prewar prices.
† Probably overestimated about 10%.
‡ 1948.
§ Approximate.

slope of the line depends on the pattern of distribution; the steeper the
line (when income is plotted on the horizontal axis), the less is the difference between the highest and lowest incomes and the higher is the coefficient. Such coefficients as are available (Table 55) suggest less inequality

TABLE 55

PARETO COEFFICIENTS OF DISPERSAL OF INCOMES IN SELECTED COUNTRIES*

Country	Period	Coefficient†
New Zealand	1938-9	2.35
Palestine: Arab	1944	2.20
Sweden	1944	2.15
Finland	1942	2.13
Australia	1943-4	2.12
Russia	1924	1.96
U.S.A.	1945	1.95
Denmark	1935	1.94
Canada	1944	1.92
Palestine: Jews	1944	1.90
Hungary	1935	1.86
Netherlands	1935	1.83
France	1934	1.82
India	1945-6	1.79
Britain	1944-5	1.75
Germany	1936	1.67
Japan	1930	1.66
Brazil	1942	1.27-2.0
Venezuela	1945	1.24
Argentina	1942	1.2-1.3

* Clark, *Conditions of Economic Progress* 2d ed., 534.
† More equal distribution is indicated by a higher coefficient.

in New Zealand, Australia, and some Scandinavian countries than in the U.S.A. and Canada. Greater inequality appears in Britain, France, Germany, and India, and still greater in Brazil and Argentina. But the figures are not all for the same years. In the U.S.A. the largest number of income receivers was in the class receiving $603 to $1207 per year in 1941, and $3000 to $3999 in 1950. But the proportion of all income receivers receiving incomes of $2000 or less (in dollars of 1950 purchasing power) fell from 41% in 1941 to 26% in 1950. This group received 13% of all incomes in 1941 and 7% in 1950 (Table 56). Alternatively, the fifth of income receivers

TABLE 56

DISTRIBUTION OF MONEY INCOMES (BEFORE TAXES) IN THE
UNITED STATES 1941 AND 1950*

1950			1941		
Money Income Before Taxes (dollars)	Percent of Families & Individuals	Percent of Total Money Income	Money Income Before Taxes (dollars)	Percent of Families & Individuals	Percent of Total Money Income
Under 1000 ..	11	1	Under 603 ...	20	4
1000-1999 ...	15	6	603-1207	21	9
2000-2999 ...	16	10	1208-1810 ...	19	15
3000-3999 ...	18	16	1811-2413 ...	15	17
4000-4999 ...	13	14	2414-3017 ...	11	15
5000-7499 ...	18	26	3018-4525 ...	9	16
7500 and over	9	27	4526 and over	5	24
	100	100		100	100

* U.S., Joint Committee on the Economic Report, *Report on the January 1952 Economic Report of the President* (82nd Congress, 2nd Session, Sen. Rep. 1295), 71. Income classifications in 1941 have the same purchasing power as the corresponding classifications for 1950.

receiving the lowest incomes received about 4% of total incomes in 1935-6 and in 1949, but the share of the highest fifth fell to 45% in 1949 (from 53% in 1935-6). (Table 57.) The share of total income received by the top 1% of incomes fell from 12% in 1939-40 to 8.5% in 1947-8. In Britain in 1948, 28.5% of all income (not incomes) was in incomes of under £250 a year, and 62.8% in incomes of less than £500 a year (Table 58). In Italy the 40% of families with lowest incomes received 16.6% of all income, and the 10% with the highest incomes 34.1% (in 1948). In Denmark, however, the 40% of tax returns with the lowest incomes received 15.3% of all income and the 10% with the highest incomes received 29.4% of all income in 1948.[2] In South Africa less than 3% of Europeans received over £1000 a year (averaging £2000), and about 1% of the total population received about

[2] U.N., *National Income and its Distribution in Underdeveloped Countries*, 1951, 27, 29, 31.

TABLE 57

Spending Units Arranged by Size of Income	Percentage of Net Income Accounted for by Each Fifth of the Population			
	1935-6	1941	1948	1949
Lowest fifth	4	3	4	4
Second fifth	9	9	11	11
Third fifth	14	16	16	17
Fourth fifth	20	22	22	23
Highest fifth	53	50	47	45
	100	100	100	100

* U.S., Council of Economic Advisors, *Annual Economic Review,* Jan. 1950, 144, Jan. 1951, 299. Incomes are reported for "spending units," including as such units families, individuals who do not pool their incomes with their family although living with it, and individuals living alone.

TABLE 58

Range of Income (£ per Year)	Percentage of Income within the range
Under 250	28.5
250 to 499	34.3
500 to 999	17.9
1000 to 1999	8.5
2000 to 9999	8.5
10,000 and over	2.3
	100.0

* U.K., *National Income and Expenditure of the United Kingdom 1946-49* (Cmd. 7933). About £1213 million of income could not be allocated to income ranges. A married couple is counted as one individual.

12.5% of the total money income of the country.[3] In general, farm incomes are probably less unequal than urban incomes, but the more agrarian countries (e.g., Denmark and Norway) have lower average incomes than the more industrialized.[4]

In underdeveloped countries the highest incomes may be high but the great majority of all incomes are very low. In the Middle East 90% of the population lives almost at a subsistence level, and the middle-income group is small, with the result that there is a striking gap between the standards of life of the rich and the poor.[5] In Egypt the gap between the lowest and highest wage and salary incomes was higher than anywhere in

[3] Franklin, *Economics in South Africa,* 46.
[4] Clark, *op. cit.,* 538.
[5] U.N., Econ. Surv. Mission for the Middle East *Final Report,* I, 1.

western Europe in 1939.[6] In India about 5% of the population is wealthy or comfortable, 33% enjoy tolerable conditions, and 62% are poverty-stricken. In fact, Indians are among both the richest and the poorest individuals in the world. Urban incomes are about three times as high as rural, and both are highly unequally distributed.[7] In Puerto Rico the 40% of all families with the lowest incomes received 10.8% of all income and the 10% with the highest incomes received 40.8% of all income (in 1946-7).

Socialist countries provide no information regarding income distribution. In Russia and eastern Europe, prohibitions on the accumulation of large amounts of private property eliminate the major source of the larger inequalities in incomes in capitalist countries, but in capitalist countries much of the larger incomes has been saved, whereas Russian incomes are largely net of saving, heavy investment in development having kept down consumption. The higher incomes in Russia are received in some of the professions and by officials, and by those who receive rewards for high achievements. But there has been some private trade in agricultural produce since 1934, and the wartime decentralization of food control favored private trade. Some of the private donations toward the defense of the country in 1943 amounted to several hundred thousand rubles, made possible by price inflation, but they represented considerable inequality of incomes that, however, was largely eliminated by the currency reform of 1947.

In countries beginning to develop, labor incomes rise unless prevented by population increases (as in Japan and India in the past). Incomes from capital are usually lower than in the more developed countries, because (a) there has not been sufficient time for big industrial fortunes to accumulate, (b) investment may also have been made from outside the country, and (c) some kinds of property may be state-owned (particularly public utilities). But as development progresses, inequality appears to increase for a time, and later to fall. In the U.S.A. income distribution was highly unequal in the 1870s and in 1929, but subsequently inequality has declined. In Britain incomes were less equally distributed in 1812 than in the 17th century. The Pareto coefficient was about the same in 1909 as in 1812, but inequality has since been reduced, as it has in France since 1894. In Germany, inequality increased during the 19th century and thereafter decreased. In Japan inequality increased from 1911 to 1935.[8] But in capitalist societies there has been a considerable disparity between consumption and income in the upper income groups who did most of the saving. During the 20th century, distribution shifted in favor of the lower income groups in Europe between 1939 and 1949, as a combined result of (a) increases in the general level of wages in relation to other in-

---

[6] Issawi, *Egypt: An Economic and Social Analysis*, 54.

[7] Thakurdas, *et al.*, *A Plan of Economic Development for India*, Penguin Edition, 67.

[8] Clark, *op. cit.*, 2nd, 537.

comes, (b) changes in distribution within the wage earning class raising the lower incomes, and (c) food and housing subsidies, rent control and expansion of social services, government expenditures for many of these purposes being financed by progressive taxation.[9]

4. Intra-National Distribution among the Factors of Production

Interpersonal distributions of income are influenced by the payments to the main contributors to production, namely labor, capital, and land. Payments of wages, interest, dividends, and rent do not directly indicate consumption by separate groups because individuals often receive incomes of more than one sort. Even if individuals receive incomes of only one sort, their incomes would depend not only on the share of national income going to labor, capital, or land, but also on the number of recipients sharing each class of income and the way it was shared. Furthermore, the proportion of income saved and paid in taxes varies among persons whose incomes come predominantly from each of the principal sources.

The distribution of total income among the factors of production is not calculated everywhere in the same way. It is predominantly influenced by the economic organization of the society. In primitive societies land is the principal factor of production (other than labor) but usually no rent is paid. In all countries, prior to about the 18th century, national incomes were shared mainly among landowners, merchants, and cultivators in proportions largely dependent upon the pressure of population upon the land. These conditions still prevail in most underdeveloped countries. It is alleged that this distribution is often based on a customary charge for the use of land. But when the ratio between labor supply and land changes, the customary payment often changes. Increases in income per acre of land may attract more acres into use, and to that extent increase the absolute income of landowners. If the number of receivers of labor incomes increases, but their unit income falls less than the labor supply increases, the share of labor increases. In Kenya, Rhodesia, Chile, Peru, and Japan compensation of employees accounts for less than 50% of all income, and total incomes from property are correspondingly high. (Table 59.)

The use of more highly capitalized methods of production introduces industrial capital as a new participant in the national income. In the more developed countries property incomes are a little less than 20% of all income (this, however, is a lower percentage than in some predominantly agrarian countries). The compensation of employees ranges from about 66% in the U.S.A. and Britain to 45.8% in Japan (Table 59), but the relative importance of unincorporated enterprises differs widely, and methods of classifying incomes are not uniform. Nevertheless, a high proportion of incomes may go to labor in a predominantly agricultural society where

---

[9] U.N., *Econ. Surv. of Europe in 1949*, 22.

TABLE 59

PERCENTAGE DISTRIBUTION OF NATIONAL INCOME BY TYPES OF PAYMENT
IN SELECTED COUNTRIES*

Country	Year	Percentage of All Income in Form of:		
		Compensation of Employees	Income of Unincorporated Enterprises	Property Income
Africa				
Kenya	1949	34.8	65.2†	
Northern Rhodesia	1949	37.7	19.4	42.9
Southern Rhodesia	1949	48.9	29.1	22.0
America, North				
Canada	1949	58.8	21.5	19.7
Cuba	1949	60.8	20.6	18.6
Puerto Rico	1948-9	56.8	43.2†	
U.S.A.	1949	65.1	16.0	18.9
America, South				
Chile	1948	46.0	27.9	26.1
Colombia	1948	51.9	31.7	16.4
Peru	1947	42.2	33.7	24.1
Asia				
Japan	1949	45.8	48.6	5.6
Europe				
Belgium	1949	56.1	34.5	9.4
Czechoslovakia	1948	68.3	22.9	8.8
Finland	1948	60.9	24.8	14.3
France	1949	49.3	50.7†	
Netherlands	1948	56.3	43.7†	
Norway	1948	58.9	41.1†	
Switzerland	1949	59.4	21.2	19.4
United Kingdom	1949	67.2	12.4	20.4
Oceania				
Australia	1948-9	54.0	29.1	16.9
New Zealand	1948-9	54.3	27.3	18.4

* U.N., *National Income and its Distribution in Underdeveloped Countries*, 1951, 17.
† Includes property income (total not broken down).

there is a large number of poor cultivators, little capital, and a generally low national income; or in an industrial country where the wages of workers are relatively high. A low proportion of wage incomes may indicate a large number of small enterprises (as, probably, in France).

The historical background of these figures is far from clear. During periods of rapid industrialization the share of income going to profits and interest must have risen from a previously low figure. In the U.S.A., interest, dividends and rent together accounted for about 18.9% of the national product in 1850; 20.4% in 1900; 22.3% in 1910.[10] Total employee com-

[10] U.S., Bureau of Census, *Historical Statistics of the United States*, 15.

pensation was about 60% from 1899 to 1918, but had risen to 65.1% in 1919 to 1928, and 75% in 1953.[11] In Britain wages (excluding salaries) were 38.6% of national income in 1870 and 41.9% in 1950. Changes over long periods have been due chiefly to changes in the relative number of wage earners. The proportion of wage earners rises in the early stages of industrialization, at the expense of the self-employed and of family workers in agriculture and the crafts. Later the proportion of salaried technicians and administrators rises, which tends to reduce the share of wages, but the long-run downward trend of salaries offsets the tendency for the share of wages to fall. The share of rents has also fallen.[12] In Australia labor's share has risen only slightly since 1900 (under compulsory arbitration of wage disputes), but the share of property fell and the share of entrepreneurial incomes (including agriculture) rose between 1928 and 1948.[13] Labor's share increased in France from 62% in 1886 to 81% in 1938, and it rose slightly in Germany from 1913 to 1937, although it remained unusually low.[14]

Between 1938 and 1951 in Britain, incomes from agriculture increased more than those from wages and salaries or profits, and profits and rents increased least (Table 60). About half the increase in real wages was due to a shift in distribution that favored wage earners. In the Netherlands, agricultural incomes also rose more than any other class, but other profits rose more than wages and salaries. In the Scandinavian countries all classes of income (except rent from dwellings) increased about the same amount (Table 60). The shift in favor of labor was probably greatest in eastern Europe, where inequality of incomes was greatest before the war. But although the share of wage earners has risen in Czechoslovakia and Poland, the proportion of wage earners in the population has risen faster, with the result that wages have risen less than average income.[15] In France, however, labor's share in the national income fell from 48% to 43% between 1938 and 1948, although most of this fall is eliminated if employers' contributions to social insurance are included.

The proportion of the national income going to labor is influenced by the proportion of wage earners in the various sectors of production. Of the product of non-rural activity, over 80% went to labor in Canada and France, about 75% in Britain and the U.S.A., and less than 75% in Japan and Germany before 1939 (Table 61). These percentages depend partly upon the quantity of capital provided per worker. In manufacturing, the proportion of output going to capital remained fairly stable at 25% in the

---

11 U.S., *Econ. Rep. of President*, 1954, 16.

12 E. H. Phelps-Brown and Hart, P. E., "The Share of Wages in National Income," LXII *Ec. Jour.* (1952), 253, 273, 276; Prest, "National Income of the United Kingdom 1870 to 1946," LVIII, *Ec. Jour.* (1948), 57; Clark, *op. cit.*, 524.

13 H. P. Brown, "Composition of Personal Income," *Economic Record*, June 1949, 35.

14 Clark, *op. cit.* (2nd), 524.

15 U.N., *Econ. Surv. of Europe in 1949*, 25.

TABLE 60

CHANGES IN THE DISTRIBUTION OF INCOME BEFORE TAXATION IN
SELECTED COUNTRIES 1938 TO 1951*

	Index Number (1938=100) in 1951				
	United Kingdom	Norway	Netherlands (1950)	Sweden	Denmark
Wages and Salaries	264	337	320	320	320
Agriculture	460	373	635	324	345
Non-Farm Profit	269	395			
Interest, Dividends, and Rent	108	75			
Profit interest and dividends excluding agriculture and ownership of dwellings	...	...	410	300	329
Ownership of Dwellings	...	...	127†	171	149

* U.N., *Econ. Surv. of Europe Since the War*, 1953, 71 (adapted).
† Includes dwellings and land.

TABLE 61

LABOR'S SHARE OF THE NON-RURAL NET PRODUCT IN SELECTED COUNTRIES*

Country	Date	Labor's Share of Total Non-Rural Net Product
		%
Canada	1938	83.2
France	1938	81.5
Australia	1938-9	79.7
United Kingdom	1930	76.3
Eire	1938	75.6
U.S.A.	1938	75.5
Japan	1934	70.3
Germany	1937	59.5

* Clark, *Conditions of Economic Progress* 2d ed., 522. Agricultural and pastoral incomes and their recipients are omitted. The average wage of an "adult male equivalent" is imputed to employers and working proprietors (women, juveniles, and old men being equivalent to half an adult male).

U.S.A. from 1899 to 1922, although the quantity of capital per worker greatly increased.[16]

5. INTRA-NATIONAL DISTRIBUTION AMONG THE MAJOR SECTORS OF PRODUCTION

The net contribution of the major sectors of production (e.g., agriculture, industry, and services) varies widely among countries (Ch. 4), and it has changed in developing countries. Realized net farm income fell from 7% of national income in 1935-9 (average) to 4.6% in 1952[17] in the U.S.A., but the farmer's share of the national income doubled in Britain between 1938 and 1949.[18] The share of any sector changes as the proportion of total

[16] Paul Douglas, *The Theory of Wages*, Ch. 5.
[17] U.S.A., *Econ. Rep. of President*, 1954, 175, 181.
[18] Seers, *Levelling of Incomes*, 49.

resources devoted to it changes. Thus the share of agriculture falls when the resources devoted to it increase more slowly than those devoted to other sectors. But the sector shares depend also on the relative values of the produce of each (or the terms of trade among the sectors), which are influenced by elements of monopoly in industries selling to farmers (Ch. 12) or in agencies marketing agricultural products (Ch. 7) by government action and by the relative slowness and difficulty with which sector output is adjusted to changes in demand (Ch. 5).

This sector classification cuts across the distribution among factors of production since all factors are used in all sectors. But shifts in the relative size of the sectors affect the remuneration of the factors of production. The growth of industry raises agricultural wages, unless the tendency is offset by population increases or increased imports of agricultural products. Rising wages (within a limited range), however, somewhat improve the market for agricultural products. But as incomes rise further, expenditure on services increases, and services compete with both industry and agriculture for labor. Distribution among sectors affects the interpersonal distribution of incomes after allowance for the number of persons sharing the income from each sector and the pattern of distribution among them. It affects the interpersonal distribution of consumption only after allowance for the incidence of saving and taxation.

C. Influences Affecting Consumption

The foregoing methods of analyzing the distribution of national incomes suggest a number of approaches to the major forces influencing personal incomes. The simplest approach, however, is by way of the major sources of income, namely the various kinds of property and labor. Gross incomes from these sources depend in varying degrees in different countries on the operation of markets and on government action. International trade, loans, and grants, which affect these incomes, also depend on the operation of markets and on authoritarian control. But authoritarian elements are important also in determining redistributions of real income through the family and through taxation and socially provided incomes and services. Even the resulting disposable incomes must be adjusted for saving and dissaving to arrive at consumption. In the U.S.A. from 1901 to 1950, 75% of the gross national product was needed for the support of the population in each decade at the level of living of the previous decade, and for the maintenance of the capital stock. Of the remaining 25%, 26% was used for war and defense and 23% for net capital increase, leaving 51% for increases in consumption per head in each decade over the previous one.[19] The influences affecting saving have, however, already been discussed (Ch. 21).

---

[19] Mills, F. C., National Bureau of Economic Research, *Occasional Paper 38*, 9, 14.

Chapter 28

International Economic Relations and Consumption

International economic transactions affect consumption through their effect on national incomes per person and on the intra-national interpersonal distribution of national incomes.

A. National Incomes per Person

The chief types of international transactions affecting national incomes per person arise out of trade, capital movements, and international levies and grants.

1. INTERNATIONAL TRADE

International trade increases national income to the extent that the satisfactions yielded by imports exceed those obtainable if the resources used to produce export goods were used to produce goods and services for home consumption. But there is no means of measuring this excess. At any time the value of a country's exports may exceed or fall short of the value of its imports, but the balance may be due to services, capital transfers, levies or grants, and in no way measures the gain from foreign trade. But it is possible to obtain indications of *changes* in the terms of trade. The "net barter terms of trade," obtained by dividing a price index for imports by a price index for exports, shows the changes in the amount of a constant mixture of imports obtained in exchange for a constant mixture of exports. The "gross barter terms of trade," calculated by expressing the total value of imports as a ratio of the total value of exports, takes into account changes in the volume of trade as well as in prices, but treats credit and capital transactions as free gifts. Indexes of terms of trade are, however, very approximate indicators of change. If the prices used are those in exporting countries, importing countries gain from

601

foreign trade when the cost of international transport falls, even when the "terms of trade" do not change. If the landed prices in importing countries are compared with their export prices, a fall in transport costs causes the terms of trade to move in favor of the importing country, without any loss to the exporting country. Price indexes are unreliable over long periods because of changes in the composition of imports and exports and because manufactured goods change more in quality than primary goods. Finally, a fall in export prices equivalent to a fall in production costs involves no loss to the exporting country (see p. 603).

The net barter terms of trade depend in the short run on the bargaining position of each country, that is, on the relative price elasticities of demand for its exports and of its demand for imports. If a slight rise in the price of its exports causes a sharp fall in demand, or if its imports fall little when their price increases, the country is in a weak bargaining position. The price elasticity of demand for exports may be high because the ultimate demand in importing countries is elastic, or because the exporting country supplies only part of the world market and a slight rise in prices brings out large supplies from competing sources. The price elasticity of demand for imports is high where a slight rise in import prices brings out considerable increased supply from domestic sources or a notable fall in final demand. Generally the more dependent a country is on foreign supplies, the less elastic is its demand for imports. In a processing economy (importing raw materials and exporting finished products) the elasticity of demand for the imported raw materials depends partly on the elasticity of demand for exports of the finished product.

In periods of time long enough to take account of changes in the geographical distribution of production, and in national incomes, the terms of trade depend on influences that lie behind these price elasticities— namely, what goods and services countries can export, and what they desire and are able to import. If resources were completely mobile, the production of each good and service would be distributed throughout the world so as to maximize the net satisfactions yielded by world production (accepting existing income distributions) and result in uniform marginal returns to each factor of production everywhere. Division of labor throughout the world would be dominated by immovable natural conditions of climate, soil, and mineral supply, and the costs of transport. The terms of trade would depend on elasticities of demand and supply under these conditions. The benefits of improved methods of production in any location or occupation would be distributed among countries through price reductions. But in fact resources have been far from mobile, and world development has not followed this pattern.[1]

The terms of trade in fact have depended on the extent to which international exchange is guided by attempts to maximize satisfactions,

[1] U.N., *Econ. Surv. of Latin America*, 1949, 14, 55, 74.

and by government intervention. Attempts to get all one can in bargaining with another member of the same society have often been condemned in the past, but the condemnation has rarely applied to dealings with "foreigners." Governments have regulated foreign trade from the beginning of history. They have made levies on conquered territories and imposed taxes on imports. In western Europe in medieval times governments sought to protect the national food supply. Under the mercantile system they controlled trade to increase the military and economic power of nations (Ch. 23). Industrialization greatly changed international bargaining power by causing sharp changes in demand for means of production (especially structural minerals and energy sources) and consumer goods (due to rising standards of living). But the unevenness of the adoption of new methods of production created two types of economy, the industrialized and the primary producing country, the terms of trade between which were dominated by the differences in their economic organization.

Movements in the terms of trade in the early stages of industrialization primarily affected British foreign trade. The net barter terms of trade moved against Britain from 1798 to 1882 (from an index of 197 to 96).[2] The index of the prices of exports fell chiefly because of declining prices for cotton yarn and cotton cloth (which was displacing wool as the main export). The cotton industry was shifting from fine to coarse goods, and the price of imported raw cotton was falling. The prices of other exports fell less than the prices of imports. From 1816 to 1835 the terms of trade deteriorated less than in the later stages of the Napoleonic war;[3] the volume of trade was expanding rapidly and the index of gross barter terms of trade (allowing for changes in both prices and quantities) rose from 12 in 1815 to 21 in 1842, 100 in 1880 and 291 in 1931.[4] But between about 1870 and 1910 the net terms of trade moved some 10% to the disadvantage of countries trading with Britain.[5] Japan transmitted the gains from its development to the rest of the world in low prices for its exports to a greater extent than other industrial countries (except Britain), and it achieved a notable increase in income that probably would not have occurred without this expansion of exports.[6]

The consequences of these movements in indexes of the terms of trade are far from clear. The "adverse" movement in the net barter terms of British trade until 1880 did not mean that British gains from foreign trade were shrinking; the cost of producing export goods was falling. For about a century Britain passed on at least some of the cost reductions in

[2] Imlah, A. H., "The Terms of Trade of the U.K., 1798-1913," X *Jour. Econ. Hist.*, 1950, 183.

[3] Ashton, T. S., "The Standard of Life of the Workers in England, 1790-1830," IX *Tasks of Economic History*, 1949, 25 ff.

[4] Imlah, *op. cit.*, 183.

[5] U.N., *Econ. Surv. of Latin Am.*, 1949, 30.

[6] *Ibid.*, 77.

falling prices. The non-industrial areas benefited from these reductions until the 1880s. The industrial countries turned increasingly to the non-industrial for food and raw materials, for which they paid in manufactured goods. But by 1938 sellers of primary products were, in terms of relative prices, about one-third less well off than between 1876 and 1880,[7] a significant change when it is remembered that the underdeveloped countries typically trade little with each other.[8] But again the cost of producing many primary exports and the cost of transport were both falling during the period.

The reasons for changes in the contribution of foreign trade to the welfare of individual nations are complex. Competition, especially in the cotton textile industry, must have been the major compulsion for Britain to translate falling costs into falling prices (Ch. 30) during the first hundred years of the industrial revolution. As internal purchasing power grew little more than population until the middle of the century, the domestic market was restricted. The increasing output was exported at prices that undercut foreign handicraft industries (notably textiles in India). Japan's terms of trade moved in her favor from an index of 100 in 1873 to 140.7 in 1892, largely because of rising prices for raw silk, which was over one-third of all exports.[9] But after 1892 the terms of trade moved adversely when Japan, like Britain, appeared as a competitor in foreign markets in the early stages of its industrialization, partly because the low level of wages limited domestic demand.

After the middle of the 19th century, a continued decline in British textile prices was offset by increases in the export prices of other manufactures.[10] Free trade facilitated exports to Britain (especially of food) and, therefore, payments for British exports; British investment abroad also improved the market for exports. The U.S.A., Germany, and other western European countries accelerated their industrialization, which improved the demand for British exports of capital goods. These countries' influence as buyers of British capital goods was felt before their influence as competitors in the export markets. Germany invaded export markets toward the end of the century, and later Japan did likewise. For some time, however, Germany's increasing industrial output was absorbed within Germany. The U.S.A. similarly absorbed most of its rapidly increasing industrial output until recent years, largely because of increases in labor incomes. Increases in labor incomes in Britain also provided an expanding market. But these influences are not the whole cause of changes in the terms of trade "adverse" to the primary exporting countries.

The underdeveloped countries encountered increasing competition in

---

[7] U.N., *Relative Prices of Exports and Imports in Underdeveloped Countries,* 1949, 23.

[8] Hirschman, *National Power and the Structure of Foreign Trade,* 107.

[9] Oriental Economist, *Foreign Trade of Japan,* 698.

[10] Imlah, *loc. cit.*

the sale of primary products to the industrial countries after 1870. New lands were opened where production per head was greater than in the older regions. Relocations of the production of particular commodities affect the bargaining power of countries producing them. Argentina, Canada, and Australia competed successfully in grain production with Hungary, Russia, and other European sources. Cotton production, virtually a U.S.A. monopoly until the end of the 19th century, has expanded in Brazil, Russia, Egypt, the Sudan, and other countries. Brazil is no longer the chief source of exports of cacao and rubber. Coffee and tea production are becoming more widely distributed.

The discovery and exploitation of new sources of minerals has had similar effects, notably in recent years in petroleum, potash, and copper. The discovery of methods for making synthetic substitutes for agricultural and mineral products has reduced the bargaining power of Chile in exporting nitrate, Java in exporting quinine, Japan in exporting naptha, the Dutch East Indies and Malaya in exporting rubber.

Falling costs of transport also increased competition by increasing the types of products that enter into trade, the distances over which they can be economically traded, and, therefore, the relative bargaining power of particular countries. Changes in the cost of operating transport, and in competition in transport, affect each country according to its location in relation to sources of supply and markets. The more distant it is from these supplies and markets the greater is the significance of the cost of trading, and the greater is the number or products that it cannot economically export and import, and the less benefit it can obtain from trade. In parts of China and Latin America (particularly Brazil) the cost of internal transport is almost prohibitive, and restricts the benefits such areas can obtain from international trading. Some products rarely enter into international trade because the cost of transport is so high, because differences in the local cost of production are not great, or because demand for them is very elastic.

The fact that rising incomes due to technical progress generate a more than proportionate increase in demand for manufactures and a less than proportionate increase in demand for agricultural consumers' goods,[11] also contributed to the fall in the price of primary goods. But the low costs were in part due to low wages owing to increases in population. Similar conditions in Britain before 1870 had accompanied similar movements in the terms of trade. But in the course of time, population increase decelerated and the absorption of labor released from primary activities accelerated and real wages rose, but the primary producing countries remained primary producers. The gains from technical progress were increasingly retained in the industrial countries, partly because such gains

---

[11] Singer, H. W., "The Distribution of the Gains between Investing and Borrowing Countries," *Proc. Am. Econ. Assn.*, 1949, 478.

were increasingly distributed through the mechanism of rising wages rather than through falling prices,[12] whereas the primary producing countries distributed such gains more through price changes and thus shared them with importing countries.[13] But, insofar as the movement of the terms of trade unfavorable to these countries merely reflected differential cost reductions in industrial and primary activities, the price mechanism operated to distribute the gains of progress.

In fact the supply of primary goods did not increase sufficiently to reduce their price so much as to absorb all their increases in productivity,[14] and output did not fall because of unremunerative prices. Exports from Russia and Hungary fell, but resources have remained in primary production. In the underdeveloped countries, largely for lack of alternatives, a relative abundance of potential labor in primary occupations keeps down wages and the prices of primary goods. In the industrial countries, surpluses of agricultural workers (indicated by relatively low agricultural incomes) have in the course of time been absorbed into other activities, where their productivity has been higher and their purchasing power has increased. But such surplus workers in underdeveloped areas have had no opportunity (if they had the desire) to enter the developed countries and be absorbed there,[15] and have been insufficiently absorbed in industry in their own countries.

Industrialization requires capital goods, the production of which has absorbed labor in industrial countries, but an underdeveloped country has no capital-goods industries. To import such goods, it must pay in exports, which is difficult unless more developed countries increase their imports. Otherwise efforts to increase exports to pay for capital goods cause a further deterioration in the terms of trade, and can even reduce national income.[16] The labor needed to produce additional goods to be exported at lower prices may be less productive than it would have been in producing for the domestic market without the aid of the additional capital goods. The improvement of conditions in these countries depends on the deceleration of population growth, an increase in the demand for primary products, or a reduction in their supply. The last requires the development of industrial and collateral activities to absorb part of the now overcrowded labor in primary activities. Present trends in population growth, and the difficulty of finding further and equally effective agricultural areas, may cause a rise in agricultural prices, but most of these countries look to industrial development. If development absorbs labor now in primary activities and reduces the supply of primary goods, it will enable

---

12 U.N., *Econ. Surv. Lat. Am.*, 1949, 57.

13 *Ibid.*, 49; Singer, H. W., "The Distribution of Gains Between Investing and Borrowing Countries," *Proc. Am. Econ. Assn.*, 1949, 478.

14 Singer, *loc. cit.*

15 U.N., *Econ. Surv. of Latin America, 1949*, 13, 49.

16 *Ibid.*, 65.

these countries to obtain a greater share in world progress (and the new activities will also add to the national product).

Fluctuations in the terms of trade have sharply affected relative national welfare, especially between primary goods exporting and industrial countries. The proceeds of exports (volume multiplied by prices) largely determine the import capacity of primary goods exporting countries. The yearly fluctuations in these proceeds between 1901 and 1950 averaged 23% (on the average, such countries experienced a drop in proceeds from 100 to 77, or a rise from 77 to 100). Cyclical fluctuations with an amplitude of 37% had a period of four years. Changes in the quantity of exports were the major factor in the instability of proceeds, annual fluctuations in volume averaging about 18% and annual fluctuations in price about 14%. Cyclical declines in prices averaged 27% in four-and-one-half-year cycles.[17] Furthermore, the fluctuations in export proceeds in many individual countries are widened by their dependence on exports of one or very few products. Egypt obtains 90% of its foreign exchange from exports of cotton, Columbia 80% from coffee. Malaya and Java are predominantly dependent upon exports of rubber and copra, Malaya on tin, West Africa upon cocoa, Brazil on coffee, Uganda and the Sudan upon cotton, Canada on wheat, Argentina on wheat, linseed, and meat. Venezuela obtains 97% of its exchange from petroleum, Chile 70% from copper, and Bolivia the major part from tin.

After the outbreak of war in Korea in 1950, rising prices for primary goods moved the terms of trade sharply in favor of the countries producing raw materials, and against the industrial countries. But the primary producers could not greatly enlarge their imports because the industrial countries were already producing nearly to their full capacity. The change in the terms of trade, however, increased the difficulties of Britain and many western European countries (other than Sweden) in meeting their international obligations. In 1951 Europe as a whole expected to have to pay about $3 billion more than in 1950 for the same imports.[18]

Much of the fluctuation in terms of trade is due to fluctuations in production and income in the more developed countries. Between 1925 and 1950, U.S. imports from Latin America were dominated by fluctuations in real income in the U.S.A., but British imports did not show the same relation to British income, probably because of the import restrictions during the 1930s.[19] The price terms of trade usually move in favor of the industrial countries in time of depression, since the prices of food and raw materials fall more than those of manufactured goods. Because the industrial countries reduce their imports at the same time, the effect of de-

---

[17] U.N., *Instability in Export Markets of Underdeveloped Countries*, 1952, *passim*.
[18] Federal Reserve Bank of New York, *Monthly Review of Credit and Business Conditions*, June 1951.
[19] U.N., *Ec. Surv. Lat. Am.*, 1949, 22, 26, 31.

pression on the incomes and import capacity of the primary producing countries is intensified, whereas the industrial countries obtain their imports with a smaller proportion of their money income.[20] Furthermore, reductions in export proceeds during recessions encourage the restriction of imports or the devaluation of currencies which may cause inflationary pressure. Such devaluations occurred in Latin America during the 1930s. Rapid increases in the money incomes of exporters when prosperity returns may generate inflation and be spent on goods that contribute little to economic development. Thus the underdeveloped country is threatened with inflation in both depression and prosperity.[21]

The distribution among countries of the benefits of mineral exploitation depends on the physical distribution of minerals and the terms on which minerals are sold (royalty arrangements and taxes being part of these terms). In general, Europe prospered and developed during the 19th century with the aid of the resources of other and larger areas,[22] but many countries supplying minerals were in no position to use them. There is, however, no basis for appraising the international distribution of these benefits. It is not obviously morally right, for instance, for the benefits from the production of oil in Bahrein or Kuwait to go either to individuals with political power there, or even to the whole population. But it is also difficult to say to whom the benefits should go, and the human race is not yet civilized enough at the international level even to consider the problem.

Private monopolies influence the terms of trade. Private groups able to control particular products seek benefits for sellers at the expense of buyers by control of prices and of entry into the business. The effects of such controls upon each country depend on the extent to which it is able to participate in each controlled market, the number of such markets in which it shares, and the actual power of the regulators (which is often far from clear).

Government regulation of international trade has generally been aimed at improving the economic position of one country at the expense of others. Such efforts have a long history even before the regimes of mercantilism. But whether they succeed depends in the short run on the relative elasticities of demand for exports and imports.

To maintain their advantage in the longer run some developed countries have discouraged industrialization in countries buying manufactures from them. The British discouraged industrialization in China and in India. During their occupation of Egypt, they encouraged agriculture

---

20 *Ibid.*, 34.
21 U.N., *Instability of Export Markets of Underdeveloped Countries*, 1.
22 Clark, J. M., "Common and Disparate Elements in National Growth and Decline" in *Problems in the Study of Economic Growth*, Universities-National Bureau Committee, 1949.

(especially cotton growing), but not industry. Germany discouraged industrialization in customer countries as an integral part of foreign economic
policy.[23] But some underdeveloped countries have denied themselves
part of the gains of economic progress by taxes on imports,[24] partly,
however, in the effort to redress the inequality of economic development
by encouraging industrialization. Developing countries almost universally
protect their new industries against foreign competition. Although, in
the short run, prices may be higher than if foreign competition had free
play, this loss may be temporary. But, within limits, if such industries
employ labor more productively than the primary goods industries, they
add to income, although they would add more if they were as efficient as
competing foreign industries.[25] The U.S.A. has used import duties and
agricultural parity prices to protect its high income level obtained from
technical progress.[26]

Socialist countries gain from international trade under the same ultimate
limitations as others. The terms of trade depend on the same elasticities
of demand for exports and imports. Since their trade is organized as a
national monopoly, export prices are not affected by competition among
domestic exporters, but the country must still compete with foreign exporters. Until 1945 the Russian policy of minimum reliance on foreign
trade involved a sacrifice of short-run gains from trade. Such imports as it
bought were those for which its price elasticity of demand was low, and
probably lower than the price elasticity of demand for its exports. But no
information is published regarding Russian foreign trade.

Before 1939 the mutual trade of Russia and the east European countries
was unimportant. Since 1945 the Soviet Council for Economic Mutual
Assistance has aimed at binding the satellites severally to Russia to the
advantage of the latter. It is reported that satellite countries (e.g., Poland,
Czechoslovakia, and Hungary) have been required to drop projects for
their own development or for closer economic relations with other satellites. Trade treaties are aimed at making the satellites dependent on
Russia, making some of them (e.g., Czechosolovakia) process Russian
materials and return the product to Russia. Practically all Rumanian trade
is with Russia. Although the economies of the satellites are too similar to
that of Russia to be complementary, political considerations are powerful,
and the policies of the western powers have discouraged trade with
communist countries and forced them into trade among themselves.

---

[23] Voeglien, P., "Old China Hands and the Foreign Office," 16 *Soc. Res.* 103;
Hirschman, *op. cit.,* 149.

[24] U.N., *Relative Prices of Exports and Imports in Underdeveloped Countries,* 1949,
23.

[25] U.N., *Econ. Surv. of Lat. Am., 1949,* 85.

[26] *Ibid.,* 75, 76.

2. Influence of International Capital Movements

International movements of capital, and the servicing of past debts, influence the terms of trade at the time the transactions occur, and later insofar as they influence the distribution of productive capacity among countries.

Borrowing countries increase their capacity to import goods and services while the loan is being spent. They thus avoid the necessity for forcing exports to increase imports and thus deteriorating their terms of trade. The subsequent payment of interest and amortization necessitates increased exports, and tends to deteriorate the terms of trade. But if the loan is spent in ways which increase productivity (e.g., on capital equipment and know-how) the national income is raised. If the additions to the national income displace former imports, or permit increased exports that still leave in the economy more goods and services than before, there is a net gain to the country. But the outcome depends on the increase in productivity and the terms of trade.

A country may postpone the achievement of a net export balance to service its foreign debt by continued imports of capital. Britain was borrowing abroad in excess of debt service at the end of the 18th century; the U.S.A. and much of Europe in the earlier part of the 19th century, and countries like Australia, Canada, and Japan, and much of Latin America in the later 19th century were doing likewise. But interruption of the flow of foreign capital places great pressure on borrowing countries. If they force exports to maintain their debt service, the prices of their exports may fall intolerably, as happened when the major capital exporting countries almost ceased their foreign lending after 1929. Some countries were compelled to suspend debt service. But, in the longer run, development may continue, and capital importers transform themselves into exporters (as did Britain early in the 19th century, Germany and France later, and the U.S.A. in about 1900). India, Argentina, and a number of Scandinavian countries became net exporters during the war of 1939-45 (often by buying back debts held abroad).

Lending countries export capital by exporting goods and services in excess of imports, usually increasing exports rather than reducing imports. The terms of trade are little changed, but there is a cumulative effect on employment, income, capital, technical progress, and external economies.[27] After about 1840 much of British exports of capital was spent on railroad and utility equipment, which built up these and subsidiary industries in Britain, particularly steel and coal. Exports of capital from Germany after 1890 had much the same effect. This stimulation of industral efficiency in industrial countries widened the gap between them and the underdeveloped.

---

[27] Singer, H. W., "The Distribution of Gains Between Investing and Borrowing Countries," *Proc. Am. Econ. Assn.*, 1949, 474.

While loans are being serviced, the lending country acquires currently unrequited imports that tend to improve its terms of trade but depress employment and production (unless offset by continued capital exports). From 1874 to 1914 capital exports from Britain, France, and Germany about equalled their income from foreign investments. Britain only occasionally between 1840 and 1900 received in loan service more than it re-lent abroad. But during the wars of 1914-18 and 1939-45, commodity imports were partly paid for by selling foreign assets.[28] Exports from Germany generally exceeded imports during the 1880s because Germany was beginning to invest abroad but had little return flow for interest and principal, and paid for the use of foreign shipping. But the flow reversed after 1890 because of payments of interest on past loans and receipts for the use of German ships. France between 1850 and 1876 was exporting capital but paying a heavy shipping bill to Britain. In the U.S.A. imports generally exceeded exports during the 19th century because of foreign borrowing. Between 1900 and 1914 there was an export surplus because of payments of interest and principal. Between 1914 and 1929 the export surplus continued spasmodically but it was increasingly due to capital exports. After 1929, although the annual interest due the U.S.A. on foreign loans exceeded net foreign lending by the U.S.A., the export surplus continued because of tourist expenditures abroad and foreign remittances.

Capital inflow has usually fluctuated more widely than the proceeds of exports. In 19 underdeveloped countries, average year-to-year fluctuations in net capital inflow were three times as wide as those in export proceeds between 1946 and 1950, and the two often fluctuated in the same direction. Thus capital inflow destabilized rather than stabilized their foreign purchasing power. Before 1939, capital inflow rarely amounted to more than 10% of export proceeds in six countries, and from 1946 to 1950 many underdeveloped countries had a net capital outflow (partly because they retired foreign debts and resumed debt service).[29]

In general the significance of indexes of terms of trade is far from clear, but the long-run effect of foreign loans on productive capacity employment and income is more important than the short-run effect on terms of trade. But these long-run effects also influence trade terms, as explained on p. 604. Russia has pioneered in the effort to industrialize with little importation of capital.

3. Influence of International Levies and Grants

International levies and grants, which are subtractions from or additions to the resources of a country arising out of other than market

[28] U.N., *International Capital Movements in the Inter-War Period*, 15.
[29] U.N., *Instability in Export Markets of Underdeveloped Countries*, 7.

considerations, affect the resources available for consumption or investment. Levies are coercive and grants voluntary.

International levies, far more ancient than grants, go back to the beginnings of war, which is a long time. The size of these transfers depends more on political than on economic factors. The term "booty" suggests a right to what can be seized by force, and the term was reintroduced into international economic relations after 1945. For a time "reparations" displaced "booty," implying that the transfer did not exceed the cost of achieving victory. But during the 20th century the cost of war has increased far beyond any feasible levy on the defeated country. Feasibility, however, is as much a political as an economic concept. A defeated country could be deprived of all excess production above a biological subsistence. It is doubtful that the yield could be further increased even if the victor were prepared to starve part of the population. But victors have not gone to the subsistence limit for fear of the political reactions in the defeated country (and sometimes in their own).

Since ancient times victors have not only seized booty but also occasionally destroyed means of agricultural production to reduce a country's capacity to fight in the future, or impose political control involving continuing economic transfers. After 1945 the allied powers again adopted a disarmament policy aimed at reducing the military power of the defeated. But actual transfers by defeated countries have been small or negative during the 20th century. Germany paid about $2 billion in war reparations, but received about twice that amount in foreign capital between 1922 and 1929.[30] By 1950 Germany had provided reparation for the war of 1939-45 amounting to about $1 billion (1949 dollars), mostly in foreign assets, industrial equipment, and ships. The largest reparation ($205 million) was received by the U.S.A., owing to the large amount of German assets in the U.S.A. Other large receipts were Britain ($168 million), France ($136 million), the Netherlands ($69 million), and Yugoslavia ($60 million). But Germany received from the U.S.A. direct and indirect benefits (above occupation costs) of $3.25 billion between the end of hostilities and June 1951, and Britain also contributed to the maintenance of the German population. Russia claimed $10 billion in reparation, and has received unknown amounts of industrial equipment, about one-third of German shipping, and considerable amounts of current output from eastern Germany. Estimates of the reparation taken from Germany up to 1951 varied from $9 to $17 billion. In 1951 Russia was taking about $2 billion a year from eastern Germany through seized mines and factories (accounting for 20 to 30% of the productive wealth of the Soviet zone) and through trade agreements. Russia also claimed reparation from Finland and Hungary. The U.S.A. government also spent about $1.7 billion to

---

[30] U.N., *International Capital Movements During the Inter-War Period*, 16.

cover the import surplus of necessities for consumption and production in Japan between the end of hostilities and June 1950.[31]

International grants have appeared only in the 20th century on any large scale. U.S.A. transfers of goods and services to its allies during the war of 1939 to 1945 were intended to increase their military effectiveness without giving rise to a mass of postwar international debts such as had caused severe political and economic difficulties after 1918. Grants and low interest intergovernment loans continued after 1945 and by 1952 totalled $36 billions. By 1952, however, about half of the $5.2 of grants and loans in that year were for military purposes. Britain, France, the Netherlands, and other countries have also made grants, and the United Nations has provided technical aid.

Such grants enable the recipient to increase the standard of living or investment. The grants through the European Cooperation Administration were intended to facilitate the replacement of wartime losses of equipment and to modernize production beyond what would have been possible out of internal saving, without a politically undesirable (if economically feasible) reduction in the standard of living. While such grants represent subtractions from the current incomes of the granting country, reducing consumption and saving capacity there, they also stimulate production and may be made out of resources that would otherwise be partly or wholly unemployed. But their actual incidence in receiving countries varies according to the method of administration. If they are used to reorganize production and reduce costs without the benefits being passed on in either higher wages or lower prices, they remain to increase profits. Or they may be used to finance ordinary government services and thus relieve local taxpayers.

Ultimately these grants have continued in times of relative peace because the international distribution of welfare determined by the market, and by commercial policies of the national interest type, have proved unacceptable. Politically, this distribution may encourage either communism or capitalism. Ethically, there are lurking doubts whether the international distribution of the burden of the war of 1939-45 is defensible. Economically, the virtual cessation of private international investment threatens economic breakdown in a world in which a number of developed countries are in urgent need of redevelopment and many underdeveloped countries clamor for development.

B. Interpersonal Distribution of National Incomes

The changing incidence of the gains from international trade on the different parts of an economy is difficult to trace. The cheapening of food and other goods of wide consumption is progressive in incidence. Such goods, however, were not generally falling in price in terms of

[31] Feary, R. A., *The Occupation of Japan: Second Phase*, 218.

money wages (i.e., real labor incomes were not rising much) during most of the first century of the industrial revolution in Britain. The terms of trade moved against Britain, but costs of production were falling. The terms of trade moved most adversely when the volume of trade was rising, but the condition of the workers did not deteriorate when trade was good, because opportunities for earning were improved and increases in incomes from exports generated other increases in incomes.[32] The general free-trade policy benefited the mass of the population by reducing the cost of living and increasing the demand for labor to produce exports, but depressed wages and rents in agriculture. The repeal of the Corn Laws was expected to reduce the cost of living, keep down money wages, and assist exports of manufactures, and probably did so. The favorable change in the terms of trade after 1870 in Britain and most other countries exporting manufactures probably contributed to rising standards of living among workers, because the gains of progress were partly distributed in rising money wages while the prices of imported food and raw materials rose less or fell. If the gains had continued to be distributed through falling prices, part of the gains would have gone to countries importing manufactured goods at falling prices.[33]

The underdeveloped countries have gained from foreign trade chiefly through the prices received for primary exports and those paid for imported manufactures. Increasing demands for agricultural products, due both to the expansion of the industrial countries and the decline in transport costs, have caused increases in land rents, most notably in countries newly opened (e.g., Australia, New Zealand, and Latin America).[34] Those controlling reserves of minerals for which there was increasing demand, or which could be produced more cheaply than from older sources, have also gained. Exports tend to raise the price of the exported product by reducing the local supply. Many of the exported products, however, entered little into local consumption. But some countries exported food, and rising food prices are regressive in incidence. Real wages are often low. But ultimately it is not the foreign trade that reduces real wages. Low real wages reduce the effective demand in local markets and leave a surplus for export which is facilitated by low labor costs of production. Before 1939, for instance, Hungary exported wheat, although Hungarian peasants were inadequately fed. Medieval countries, however, limited exports of food to prevent higher foreign prices from raising the domestic cost of living, and a number of countries (e.g., Australia, New Zealand, and South Africa) have restricted some exports for the same reason since 1939. Labor incomes are low in underdeveloped countries, usually because of high population

---

[32] Ashton, T. S., "The Standard of Life of the Workers in England, 1790-1830," IX *Tasks of Econ. Hist.*, 1949, 25.

[33] Singer, H. W., "Economic Progress in Underdeveloped Countries," 16 *Soc. Res.*, 1949, 3.

[34] U.N., *Econ. Surv. of Lat. Am., 1949*, 53.

increase and restricted opportunities for labor outside primary production. The provision of alternative opportunities has, however, been hampered by the fact that the capital goods for industry could not be produced in these countries and have been bought at prices reflecting high wages in the more developed countries. If such imports could have been obtained at prices reflecting a stationary standard of living in developed countries, the under-developed countries would have paid about one-third the prices they in fact paid, and would not have been compelled to rely so much on precarious capital imports.[35]

International movements of capital tend to reduce inequalities in returns from capital in different countries. In the importing country, the increase in output resulting from the additional capital (after deducting the cost of servicing the foreign capital) is distributed between management and labor in proportions that depend on the net effect on the demand for and supply of each factor. Capital exports retard the tendency in the exporting country for capital to increase faster than labor, and somewhat increase the bargaining power of labor in relation to capital. Capital exports increase property incomes if the foreign investment yields a higher income than the most profitable new investment available at home. But, in fact, the yield on foreign loans has often been much less than the anticipated yield. Britain, France, the U.S.A. and Germany have all incurred heavy losses on foreign loans. Furthermore, countries like Holland, Britain, and France, having reinvested abroad when the loans fell due for servicing, have deferred receipt of real returns, piling up increasing claims on the rest of the world that may or may not be honored. Britain after 1939 was able to meet the first costs of defense by presenting some of these claims (selling some of its foreign investments).

International migrations of labor tend to reduce inequalities in the net satisfactions of labor in different parts of the world. Migrations have occurred throughout recorded history, and in the 19th century there were large migrations from Britain and western Europe and, later, eastern Europe. But widening differences in levels of living, while increasing the inducement to migrate, have also induced the establishment of increasingly effective barriers that are one of the major causes of the unequal distribution of gains from world production. Differences in rates of population increase, supplies of capital and knowledge, and desire for material improvement are also important. There is, however, much basis for the argument that the levelling down of the highest incomes by free migration would, in the long run, involve losses to the human race in excess of the gains. The world as a whole might in time be on a mere subsistence level whereas the present inequality at least provides a demonstration of the possibility of higher levels.

---

[35] Singer, *op. cit.*, 3.

Chapter 29

Incomes from Property

The distribution of incomes from property depends on the distribution of its ownership and on incomes per unit of property.

A. The Distribution of Ownership of Property

Differences in the quantity of property owned provide the chief explanation of the distribution of incomes from property and of the largest incomes in most countries.

1. The Measurement of Property Ownership

The best measure of property would be the present capitalized value in money of the anticipated income from ownership, after discount for risk. But this value is unknown for property not often sold. The money value of land is especially difficult to ascertain. In capitalist countries a good deal of property is held through corporate securities, for many of which market values are ascertainable, but there remains much property not so valued.

2. The Actual Distribution of Property Ownership

In primitive societies, land is the chief source of income other than labor, but it is typically owned in common. Cattle are often individually owned (e.g., in East Africa), holdings being unequal because of access to grazing (often determined by the state), marriage customs, skill, and luck. In the ancient world also, the larger incomes were attributable to inequalities in the ownership of land or some form of right to its produce. But slaves were also property in the ancient world as well as in some primitive societies. Again in medieval Europe non-labor incomes were chiefly determined by rights to land or its produce.

In contemporary agrarian societies in the Middle East, the Far East, and Latin America land is the major source of property incomes, but information regarding the distribution of ownership is generally in physical rather than economic terms, and it is often not clear whether information regarding the size of "holdings" refers to those of owners or of tenants (Ch. 6). In general, however, ownership is unequal except where land has been recently redistributed. There are usually some small owners and in some countries they are increasing in number while their average and total holdings may be falling. In other countries their numbers and total holdings may be falling. But larger holdings account for most of the largest incomes.

In Russia before 1917, 30,000 landlords had average holdings of over 6000 acres. In Egypt in 1949 about 33% of the privately owned cultivated land was owned by .4% of all owners (in average holdings of about 166.6 acres), about 33% by 7% of all owners (in average holdings of 10.7 acres), and about 33% by 92.6% of all owners (in average holdings of .83 acres). In Syria most of the state and privately owned land is owned or controlled by large owners, but in Lebanon there are a number of family owned farms averaging 10 acres. In Saudi Arabia in the few areas cultivated, the land is mostly owned by small farmers.[1] In Mexico in 1923 there were some 300 haciendas, each over 25,000 acres. and 11 over 250,000 acres, but many of the large estates have since been redistributed.[2] In Chile in 1926, 2.4% of all privately owned land was held by 72% of all owners (in holdings of less than 50 acres). In Argentina most of the good land had been parcelled out in large private estates by 1880. By 1937, 70% of all farm land was in holdings of 3087 acres or more, and less than 10% in holdings of 247 acres or less.[3] In Uruguay, the average landholding for cattle and sheep in 1900 was 158 acres but the few hundred largest holdings were vast.[4] In China before the revolution, 4% of the owners owned 50% of the land.

Minerals are important as a potential source of income in some of these countries, but in many they are vested in the state, although the right to exploit has been granted to concessionaires in the Middle East and Latin America[5] (Ch. 15). Commercial capital has been important for many centuries in the Middle East, India, and China. It provides some large incomes, and numerous small incomes from small stores and the like. There is also considerable foreign ownership of mines, plantations, or merchant capital concerned mainly with foreign trade (e.g., in the Middle East, India, China, Indonesia, and African colonial territories). Industrial property is typically of small importance.

---

[1] Warriner, Land and Poverty in the Middle East, 14, 22, 34, 57, 63, 77, 87; La Revue d'Egypte Economique et Financière, March 3, 1951.

[2] McBride, The Land Systems of Mexico, 25.

[3] U.S. Tariff Commission, Agricultural, Pastoral, and Forest Industries in Argentina, 10, 94.

[4] Hanson, S. G., Utopia in Uruguay, 5.

[5] U.N., Econ. Surv. of Latin America in 1948, 81.

In capitalist industrial countries land ownership has declined as a proportion of all property as a result of the industrial revolution, and is usually widely enough distributed to be a relatively unimportant source of large incomes. In Britain, Canada, Australia, New Zealand, and South Africa the family farm is the prevailing type, some being rented. In the U.S.A., conditions are broadly similar, although large landholdings have appeared during the 20th century. In 1934, 25 owners owned 70,400 farms, 15 owned 10,011, and 84 owned 17,207.[6] In Australia, 58% of the area of rural holdings, but only 1% of all holdings, is in holdings of more than 100,000 acres, but these are in semi-arid regions suitable only for extensive sheep and cattle production. In the higher rainfall areas the majority of holdings are about 300 acres.[7] In northwestern and central Europe, peasant ownership (a small version of the family farm in Britain and the U.S.A.) is widespread (Ch. 6). But there are large holdings in parts of southern Europe. In Italy in 1946 35% of the total farm area (in holdings of over 125 acres) was held by .6% of all owners, and 4.1% of the area (in holdings of under 1.25 acres) was held by 93% of all owners.[8] In some parts of Spain and Portugal large families live on small farms that they own. In northern Portugal the average land holding is less than 1.25 acres.

Mineral rights are a considerable source of property incomes in Britain (for coal until 1938) and the U.S.A. (notably for petroleum). In continental Europe, however, mineral rights are often claimed by the state (Ch. 15). But industrial property has become the most important source of property incomes and of all large incomes, although there is no comparative statistical information on the distribution of ownership. The scope of such ownership has been somewhat reduced in Britain and France since 1945 by nationalization (Ch. 13), but compensation reduces the effect of such transfers on the general distribution of property incomes.

In socialist countries the confiscation of most forms of property largely eliminates incomes from property. Interest is paid on savings bank deposits and government bonds in Russia but is a small part of the national income.

3. Influences affecting the Distribution of Ownership

Individual property holdings are influenced by government policies, marriage customs, inheritance, saving, and changes in the capital value of property.

All states influence the distribution of property ownership by their decisions as to the scope of private property and often also by distributions of property (e.g., land) among individuals or by seizures of property.

In primitive societies where land is held communally, individual bene-

---

[6] U.S., *Payments made under Agricultural Adjustment Programs,* 74th Congress, Second Session, Senate Document 274, 1936.

[7] U.N., *Progress in Land Reform,* 2.

[8] *Ibid.,* 13, 17 ff.

fits from the use of land depend upon the distribution of the right to use it, which is usually controlled by the chief acting within tribal tradition. In the ancient world the distribution of land ownership was frequently much influenced by state donations of conquered and seized lands for public services (notably in war). In Rome, particularly in the Empire, conquered lands were often awarded to veterans of the Roman armies. The citizens of Athens had silver mines at Laurium that were worked by contractors, the proceeds being distributed like a dividend among the full citizens until Athens began to build a fleet. In China and Japan land ownership has been redistributed more than once. Under the Chow dynasty (1122-256 B.C.) in China the *tsing tien* system required land and taxation to be apportioned according to estimates of the fertility of the land and the working capacity of the family to which the land was allotted. But after 659 B.C., the empire was broken into warring states, and in Chin (one of these states) land was given as private property to those willing to cultivate it (partly because land was plentiful in relation to population, possibly because of war). After 246 B.C., when the empire was reunited, this private property system was applied throughout the empire. After 220 A.D., *tsing tien* was restored, but only after wars that reduced the peasantry (according to some estimates) to 20 to 30% of their former number. From 618 to 905 A.D., and 960 to 1276 A.D., the *tsing tien* system again prevailed[9] Similar arrangements for periodic redistributions of land prevailed in Japan in the 7th century A.D., but increases of population reduced the size of family allocations, and redistributions became less frequent. Local feudalism had become established by the 10th century.[10]

In medieval Europe the state dominated the distribution of incomes under the feudal regimes. Rights to land were different from the property rights of modern western countries, but they provided for the distribution of incomes from the land. The cultivator received as income the produce from the land he cultivated for his own use. The produce of the lord's land, which was also worked by serfs, represented the surplus above the payment for labor. The size of the surplus depended partly on the relation between the population and the cleared (and defended) land, as is evidenced by the fact that when about 25 to 50% of the population in England died in the Black Death in 1348, competition for labor resulted in better terms for the cultivators.[11] This surplus was distributed among the king, ecclesiastical authorities, and lay lords, through the distribution of manors. This distribution was made by the king, although the lords sometimes acquired considerable bargaining power. But the feudal lords

---

[9] Wrench, G. T., *The Restoration of the Peasantries*, 27-31.

[10] Taeuber, "Population Growth and Economic Development in Japan," XI *Jour. of Econ. Hist.*, 1951, 419.

[11] Turner, "Economic Discontent in Medieval Western Europe," *Tasks Econ. Hist.*, 1948, 86.

were required to provide for the maintenance of order and military service. When the need for this service was reduced by local tranquilization, or the services were taken over by the state, the lords continued to receive part of the produce of the land, and as a result of enclosure, they emerged as property owners. They became liable to money taxes, but as their lands continued to have a value, the taxes must have been less than the economic rent of the land.

In predominantly agrarian societies today, the distribution of land ownership is partly traceable to state grants of land in the past. In Latin America the transfer of land rights to the invading Spanish was originally made through the *encomienda* (or *repartimento*), under which the Spanish Crown granted the invading Spanish a number of Indians with the land they inhabited. First utilized in the West Indies as a temporary means of giving the invading forces time to adjust to their new conditions, these grants were used to levy tribute and transfer part of it to soldiers who had aided in the conquest. As the Indian population could not pay in money, it was required to contribute services. The native population, unaccustomed to ideas of property, did not protest. These grants developed into a form of serfdom, and attempts by the Spanish Crown to ameliorate the system and even to cancel *encomiendas* (in 1542) were frustrated. By the end of the 17th century the grants had become virtually heritable property. In the early 18th century *encomiendas* were abolished in Mexico and later in Chile, but by then they were unimportant.[12]

In the Islamic states of the Middle East, generals and former tax farmers were granted land in the 13th century when the state ceased to be able to pay its troops in cash. Although these feudal titles were abolished at the beginning of the 19th century in the Ottoman Empire, large land holdings reappeared during the century.[13] In North Africa (Algeria, Tunisia, and Libya) considerable grants of land have been made to European colonists.

In India, private property in land emerged out of taxation policy, including methods of collecting taxes. The East India Company took over the established tradition that the state was the ultimate owner of land. It therefore aimed at taking over all the produce of land in excess of what had to be left to the cultivator. In 1793 the Company recognized tax farmers and others as virtual owners (*zamindari*) of large estates in some parts of India, subject to tax payments equal to ten-elevenths of what had previously been collected from the cultivators (*ryots*) as rent. At the outset many *zamindari* defaulted in their payments, and their lands were sold off to others.[14] It seems probable, therefore, that one-eleventh of these rents about covered the cost of rent collection. The *zamindari* in general had no equity in the land, and the East India Company was the real

---

12 MacBride, G. M., *Chile: Land and Society*, 65; *For. Agric.*, Sept. 1951.
13 Bonné, *State and Economics in the Middle East*, 123, 186.
14 U.K., Indian Statutory Commission *Report*, I, 339.

recipient of land rent. But the tax liability was fixed in money in perpetuity with a specific provision that the taxes payable by the *zamindari* and their heirs would not be increased in consequence of any improvement of the land, presumably to encourage improvements (which in general have not occurred). Many of these lands have increased in value and some (especially urban lands in towns like Calcutta) greatly. Consequently the *zamindari* pay a very small proportion of the present income from these lands in taxes, and have now a valuable property right in the land. These "permanent settlements" were made in most of Bengal and Bihar, about one-half of Orissa, about one-third of Madras, and parts of Assam and the United Provinces.[15] But in other parts of India only "temporary settlements" were made, and taxes are reassessed about every 30 years. In theory the government was to take half the produce of the land, but in fact it has taken considerably less.[16] In view of the widespread sharing of the produce of land equally between owners and cultivators in sharecropping areas, the government's 50% share of the net produce of the land more or less represented the full economic rent leaving little room for private equities in land. But, by claiming less than 50% of the net produce, and by abjusting taxes only infrequently, the government made room for such equities; private ownership therefore exists but under less profitable conditions than in the permanently settled areas.

The state also determines who shall receive incomes from minerals. In Iran, Iraq, and Mexico, for instance, the state itself takes these incomes. In some of these countries, however, this income is used partly or wholly to meet current government expenses. The ultimate benefits, therefore, accrue to those who would otherwise pay higher taxes, namely the wealthier, who are mainly the larger landowners. Industrial property is relatively unimportant, but some of it is the property of the state (e.g., in Iran, Turkey, and parts of Latin America).

In western Europe the present distribution of land is influenced by past government policies. In Britain the government seized and redistributed most of the monastic lands under Henry VIII, and the Enclosure Acts of the 16th century and later during the 18th and 19th centuries influenced the distribution of land when feudal tenures were abolished. The transition from feudal tenures to private property was also regulated by governments in western Europe. In Denmark 66% of the peasants owned their land by 1834 (and about 100% by 1900).[17] In Ireland the government assisted in the transfer of about 66% of all the land to the tenants of the estates after 1869, and under the Irish Free State government the transfer has been virtually completed. Owners were compen-

---

[15] U.K., Indian Statutory Commission *Report*, I, 1930, Cmd. 3568, 339; Wadia and Merchant, *Our Economic Problem*, 242, 248, 253.
[16] Wadia and Merchant, *op. cit.*, 239 ff.; Wrench, *op. cit.*, 51.
[17] *For. Agric.*, Sept. 1951.

sated and purchasers were financed by the government, which was repaid by instalments.[18]

In the U.S.A., Canada, Australia, New Zealand, and South Africa much of the land was taken over by invading governments, which determined the subsequent ownership of land by their policies of distribution. The British crown made grants of land in the eastern part of the U.S.A. during the colonial period, and all vestiges of feudal tenures had gone by the time of the Revolutionary War. Land ordinances of 1785 and 1787 broadened the free lands to include all unsettled land and the Preemption Act of 1841 and the Homestead Act of 1862 made public land freely available to settlers at low prices.[19] Some lands, however, were conveyed to railroads (often in large grants). Government policy regarding minerals fluctuated during the 19th century. But during the 20th century some minerals have passed into the hands of the government in Britain and France (Ch. 15). Industrial property was generally permitted to become private property without any restraint on acquisition, in accordance with the general theory of *laissez-faire*.

The terms of the transfer affect the distribution of property incomes. Seizure without compensation clearly reduces the incomes of the previous holders, whereas seizure with full compensation does not. If the property is redistributed, the method of redistribution also affects the distribution of incomes. When Henry VIII seized the endowments of the religious houses in Britain they were not compensated. The proceeds of the sale of the properties went into the public funds. A little of the property was used to endow new public institutions and very little was distributed among courtiers. Most of it was sold and the property included much of the land that has subsequently become the major source of coal in England.[20] Since that time the precedent has been followed in many countries in Europe, and in Russia and Latin America. This method of disposal had no necessary effect on the general distribution of property, especially on the size of holdings.

In eastern Europe after 1918, 50% of the farm land was redistributed in Greece, 35% in Rumania, 42% in Latvia, 18% in Lithuania, 25% in Esthonia, 10% in Hungary, and 6% in Poland (mostly from the larger holdings)[21] In Czechoslovakia about 11% of all land was redistributed. The German Weimar government attempted to redistribute the large estates in eastern Germany, but the Hitler seizure of power (supported by the large landowners) terminated the effort. Landowners were well compensated in Poland and Czechoslovakia, partially in Greece, and not at all in the Baltic

---

18 "Land Legislation, Irish," Article in *Palgrave's Dictionary of Political Economy; For. Agric.*, Sept. 1951.
19 U.N., *Progress in Land Reform*, 4.
20 Trevelyan, *English Social History*, 106.
21 Brandt, *Reconstruction of World Agriculture*, 41.

states (where the former owners were German). The recipients usually paid for the land in instalments.

The Mexican government has passed a series of laws since 1915 aimed at the restoration of the former communal holding of agricultural land. Groups of cultivators (*ejido*) may apply for land if their holdings are inadequate, the rights to newly granted land being conveyed partly to the group and partly to its members (*ejidatarios*). The grants are made from public lands or nearby estates in excess of the maximum size prescribed by law. Private owners may be compensated in cash or bonds. Between 1916 and 1944 nearly half of all cultivated land has been so transferred, as well as arid and pasture lands. The Bolivian government in 1953 enacted reforms similar to the Mexican.[22] In Puerto Rico some of the holdings by corporations in excess of 500 acres are being redistributed in small farms, to be paid for by instalments. But by 1952 only 7200 acres had been distributed, owing to difficulties of financing and administration. Some of these excess holdings are also made available for Proportional Profits Farms (Ch. 6) and for government-operated estates.[23] By 1950 the government Land Authority had purchased about 50% of the excess holdings.[24] In Russia, the land was taken by the state without compensation at the 1917 revolution, and a large part of the produce of the land previously paid as rent now passes to the state.

After 1945, a second and more serious wave of land redistribution passed over eastern Europe.[25] Since 1944, when the Polish government decreed the redistribution of all land holdings over 125 acres (in some provinces 250 acres), about 29% of the agricultural land has been redistributed. In Hungary all holdings over 137 acres (and some smaller holdings) aggregating about 30% of the land have been redistributed. In Czechoslovakia the government prescribed a maximum holding of 125 acres of arable land and redistributed about 7% of the land in addition to 23% confiscated as enemy property, making 41% of all agricultural land redistributed since 1920. In Finland part of all holdings above 62 acres (the proportion increasing with the size of holding) was taken for redistribution. Yugoslavia in 1945 began to expropriate without compensation all estates over 112 acres cultivated by tenants, all estates owned by banks and corporations, and all land beyond 25 acres belonging to religious institutions. Land beyond 112 acres held by other owners was taken, with compensation. Much of this land was redistributed in very small holdings.[26] In eastern Germany all larger holdings have been expropriated. In western Germany legal provision has been made for redistributing large holdings, but they are not numerous and the area affected is small. In Italy no general

---

[22] U.N., *Progress in Land Reform*, 82.
[23] *Ibid.*, 87; U.N., *Land Reform*, 59.
[24] U.N., *Land Reform*, 23; *Econ. Devel. in Selected Countries*, 1950, 188, 196.
[25] U.N., *Progress in Land Reform*, 16, 66, 73.
[26] *Ibid.*, 77.

land reform has yet been enacted, but laws applying to specified localities (in some of which the peasants had seized land) have been passed. They are expected to affect only 3% of the area of privately owned land and 40% of the area of holdings of over 500 hectares, mostly uncultivated or thinly cultivated. The government pays the landowners in bonds at the tax assessment value.[27]

In general landowners have received little compensation. In Czechoslovakia and Finland, the price was based on pre-inflation land values and paid in post-inflation money or bonds, and enemy property was not paid for. But in Italy owners are being compensated. The new proprietors, however, pay for the land in instalments, and it is not clear whether their incomes were raised by the redistribution. But by 1949 these new small landlords were being displaced in eastern Europe by pressures to collectivize farming. Generally the land has not been nationalized, and those contributing their land to producers' cooperatives receive a share of the cooperative income for their land in addition to compensation for their labor (Ch. 6).

After 1945 the land redistribution movement spread to other parts of the world in spite of the active opposition of land owners. In Burma the Land Nationalization Act of 1948 authorized the government to take possession of agricultural land held by non-agriculturalists and all holdings above a prescribed size (50 acres for rice), and redistribute it in amounts capable of cultivation by one yoke of oxen (10 to 15 acres) per family. Some transfers were made in 1950. In China the communist government avoided seizures of land so long as it was fighting Japan, but it reduced land rents and interest on loans. After 1945, during the conflict with the Nationalist government, it confiscated all land which landlords and rich peasants could not till themselves, and redistributed it among tenants, landless, and land-poor peasants, according to the size of their families. Property other than agricultural land and cattle was not to be seized, and the new owners were to be given title deeds. The Land Law of 1950 continued this policy, partly to avoid discouraging production. By mid-1951, the land reform had affected about 50% of the rural population.[28] In North Korea land was seized and redistributed, but the peasants obtained no title and their subsequent condition (allowing for taxation) appears to have been little better than before the reform. In South Korea a similar reform was enacted, but no actual redistribution occurred.[29]

In Japan a law of 1945 required landowners to sell to the government for resale to tenants all land owned by absentees from the village and cultivated by tenants, and all land in excess of 2.5 acres (10 acres in Hokkaido) owned by residents and rented to tenants, and most owner-

---

[27] *Ibid.*, 66, 71.
[28] U.N., *Land Reform*, 55.
[29] *For. Agric.*, Oct. 1950.

operated land in excess of 7.5 acres (with some exceptions). The limits varied in different parts of Japan. Local land commissions (on which tenants were represented) selected the land to be purchased, selected purchasers, settled transfer prices, and arranged payments to the previous owners and from the purchasers. Payments were limited to 40 times the 1938 rentals for paddy fields, but inflation reduced the payments received by owners far below market value. By the end of 1949 about 4.5 million acres had been acquired and resold, with the result that the percentage of the cultivated area under tenancy was reduced from 46% to 8%.[30] Landowners were paid partly in cash and partly in bonds. Tenants could pay in not more than 30 annual instalments, but 70% of the tenants paid in full. In Burma compensation was provided at one to twelve times the annual land tax (according to tenure).

In India the federal government announced in 1949 that 75% of the property and fortunes of the native princes (who formerly ruled 25% of India) were to be handed over to the new provincial governments in the areas concerned. All princely holdings of land were confiscated unless ancestral ownership could be proved, the total property involved amounting to about $330 million. Some landowners have voluntarily surrendered land without compensation as part of the Land Gift (*Bhoodan Yagna*) movement.[31] A number of states have introduced legislation eliminating intermediaries (such as *zamindari*), irrespective of the size of their estates. Some states sell rights of ownership to the tenants, and others retain ownership; the tenants become tenants of the state until they have paid the full purchase price for their land. Maximum holdings have been prescribed in some states to restrict future concentration of ownership. Not all states have legislated, and progress varies in those that have. In 1952 some 2.2 million intermediaries and 160 million acres had been affected. Delays have been due to lack of information and administrative organization, the inability of tenants to pay, difficulties in assessing compensation to former owners, and opposition of landowners who resorted to litigation. In general, compensation is a multiple of previous net income, in some states a flat multiple, and in others a declining multiple for larger holdings. Some states, however, compensate on the basis of the assessed value of the land for taxes. The multiples of the base are as low as two in some states and as high as 12 in others.[32]

In East Pakistan the government is nationalizing all rent-receiving interests in land, but all tenants will be owners with power to sell or bequeath but without the power to sublet or to retain the land if they do not cultivate it. Land cultivated by the owner beyond a specified amount

---

[30] Feary, R. A., *The Occupation of Japan: Second Phase 1948-50*, 87, 91; U.N., *Land Reform*, 54; U.N., *Progress in Land Reform*, 62.

[31] U.N., *Progress in Land Reform*, 91.

[32] *Ibid.*, 22, 54; U.N., *Land Reform*, 52.

is to be acquired by the government and redistributed. In parts of West Pakistan tenants may acquire the land they occupy by paying a specified multiple of the annual rent, and share tenants may become owners of a share of the land corresponding to their share of the produce from the land they have cultivated. The maximum area of land that may be retained by the owner for cultivation is also prescribed.[33]

In Latin America little land has been redistributed outside Mexico and Bolivia. In Argentina government policies of breaking up large estates and aiming at farms of not less than 250 acres for crops and 4000 to 5000 acres for cattle have been announced. But by 1949 little progress had been made. Tenants have little interest because they are virtually secure from eviction, grain prices are unfavorable, and rents have been reduced by law. But the government has also found difficulty in raising funds to compensate owners. The provincial governments have, however, taken over a few *estancias*.[34] In Chile there are large land holdings, but interest in land reform has been waning since 1946.[35]

Land redistribution is beginning in the Middle East. In Turkey provision was made for a limited redistribution in 1946, with compensation for landowners. Among other lands, all estates over 1250 acres were to be redistributed. By the end of 1950, 1.361 million acres had been distributed among private owners.[36] In Iran a law has been passed setting forth procedures for redistributing the lands ceded to the state by the previous Shah and other state and crown lands in lots of not more than 24 acres,[37] but actual redistribution has been slow because of vigorous opposition by landowners. In Egypt the government decreed in 1952 that agricultural land ownership was to be limited to a little over 200 acres, excess holdings being taken over by the government within five years and distributed to small farmers so that they will own not less than two or more than five acres. Owners are being compensated in government bonds at ten times the annual rental value of the land, and recipients pay for the land.[38] Laws have also been passed in Iraq providing for the distribution of land in a few small irrigated areas. In Saudi Arabia the government proclaimed in 1948 its willingness to grant state land to whomever would cultivate it.

Governments have also taken over industrial property, but not to redistribute it. In Russia all such property was expropriated without compensation after the revolution. Subsequently, in 1947, when the currency was revalued, part of the value of bank accounts and government bonds was written off. The governments of eastern Europe under Russian influence have also seized such property, sometimes with formal provision

---

[33] U.N., *Progress in Land Reform*, 59.
[34] *For. Agric.*, Aug. 1950.
[35] *Ibid.*, May 1952.
[36] U.N., *Land Reform*, 58; U.N., *Progress in Land Reform*, 80.
[37] U.N., *Econ. Devel. in Selected Countries*, 186.
[38] U.N., *Progress in Land Reform*, 79.

for the compensation of foreign owners (e.g., in Bulgaria) and sometimes establishing a fund for the compensation also of domestic owners. In Rumania (where 85% of industry was foreign owned) former owners were to receive bonds of the "Nationalized Industries Fund" to be redeemed out of the net profits of nationalized undertakings.[39] But in 1950, the government nationalized without compensation all fixed property owned by industry, rural landowners, bankers, big commercial concerns, and "other elements of the major bourgeoisie."[40] In Poland, the former domestic owners of nationalized businesses were to be compensated in amounts to be determined by a commission taking account of the decrease of national wealth as a result of the war, the extent of war damage, and investments made since 1939. Former enemy owners receive no compensation, but allied owners were to be compensated. In Czechoslovakia foreign owners were to receive the same treatment as Czechoslovak citizens, but citizens of Germany and other enemy states were not to be compensated. Collaborators were dispossessed without compensation, and there was no compensation for unexploited mineral wealth. In Yugoslavia, a considerable amount of property, particularly mines, has been taken over by the government without compensation, because it was formerly owned by Germans or collaborators.

Governments have also taken over mineral deposits (Ch. 15), some claiming future discoveries but some taking over already proven resources, usually with compensation. The potash deposits in Alsace passed to the French government after 1918. The coal deposits in Britain were nationalized in 1938. Toward the end of the 19th century and mostly during the 20th century (when the coal industry ceased to prosper in Britain) the payment of royalties for the right to mine coal was the subject of a long dispute, royalties being regarded as more than usually unearned income. Petroleum reserves in Mexico were nationalized in 1917. Constitutional rights were recognized in 1928, but both oil deposits and oil processing properties were nationalized in 1930. Compensation was paid to the former American owners in 1947, and payments to British owners began in 1948.[41]

In Britain and France only some industries have been nationalized since 1945. Compensation is then necessary to avoid inequity among holders of different kinds of property. In Britain two general bases of compensation have been used: the previous owners may be guaranteed the same income as they have received in the immediate past, or they may be given securities of about the same capital value as their previous property. The first principle (of "net maintainable revenue"), which involves little change in incomes, was applied in compensating the previous stockholders in the

[39] I.L.O., *Ind. and Lab.*, March 1949, 219.
[40] *Economist: Records and Statistics*, May 6, 1950.
[41] U.N., *Ec. Surv. Lat. Am.*, 1948, 228.

Bank of England. The government gave, in exchange for stock in the Bank of England, 3% government stock in an amount which would maintain the incomes of stockholders on the same level as for the preceding 22 years. But as the yield on Bank stock had also been 3%, both principles of compensation would have produced the same result. The same principle was used by the special arbitration tribunal in 1946, which set a global sum as compensation for coal properties taken over by the Coal Board, but not including securities (which were not taken over). This sum was distributed among recipients by Valuation Boards. Subsidiary assets were taken over at their estimated value in a free sale. The government paid in stock that was inalienable but is redeemable when the former coal companies are liquidated or seek cash to develop their remaining business activities. The same principle was applied when the government took over the companies holding shares in Cables and Wireless, Limited (foreign telegraphs).

The principle of giving government securities of an estimated capital value equal to that of the securities of the enterprises nationalized was applied to transport, electricity, gas, and iron and steel. Before the Transport Bill was published in 1946, the government announced that stockholders in railroad, canal, and London Transport undertakings would receive government stock equal in value to the average stock market value of the securities for the six business days November 1-8, 1946, or the average mid-monthly quotations from February to July, 1945, if that were higher.[42] Most canal stocks were already held by railroads. The property of trucking concerns was taken over at a valuation. Electricity and gas securities were taken over on a market value basis but special provision was made for concerns that had suffered war damage or loss of population. Local authorities receive annual payments equal to their net debt charges attributable to enterprises taken over from them. Holders of securities in iron and steel companies received 3½% government bonds, also on a similar basis. Holders of securities in all the other industries received 3% government stock.

This method of transfer maintains the capital value of private property holdings, but insofar as the securities received carry a lower rate of yield than those surrendered, the incomes (and risks) of former owners are reduced. Compensated owners might maintain their income by selling the new government stocks and buying securities with a rate of yield equal to that on the securities surrendered. But because many of such investments have disappeared from the market, and the supply of government bonds carrying lower yields has increased, the former owners have not been able to avoid a reduction in income. It has been argued that the market price of securities is not a good measure of their value, because stock market values were depressed by the threat of nationalization and

---

[42] *Ind. and Lab. in Britain,* Dec. 1949, 189.

by government control of dividends.[43] But where the threat of nationalization reduced the market value of securities, the loss fell upon holders at that time, who are not necessarily identical with the holders who surrendered securities or the holders of the government securities received in compensation.

In France government securities have generally been exchanged for private securities of equal capital value. The Bank of France, the Coal Board (*Charbonnages de France*) and the *Caisse Nationale d'Equipment de L'Electricite et du Gaz*, issued bonds carrying 3% interest (except those of the Bank of France, which paid 2%) or a minimum of 3% plus an additional sum depending on the income of the companies. The shareholders in about fifty of the larger insurance companies also received 3% government bonds in exchange for their stock. The former securities were valued at their market value during specified periods or by special commissions. Bank of France stock was converted at its average market value for twelve months prior to August 31, 1945. But the Swiss stockholders in the electricity and gas industries complained that the stock market values used had been depressed by proposals to nationalize, and the government agreed to compensate them on the basis of market values prior to the discussion of nationalization, and to issue to them a more favorable type of government bond than it issued to its own nationals. When the four largest deposit banks were nationalized, their stockholders received new scrip, resulting in a government guarantee of their 1944 dividends. The U.S.A. has not nationalized private property, but it destroyed it without compensation when the slaves were emancipated and the sale of alcoholic liquor prohibited. When slavery was abolished throughout the British Empire in 1832 the slave owners were awarded £20 million in compensation.

The economic quantity of property owned can be reduced by government limitations on the income derived from it, such as those prescribing maximum rents for land. Agricultural rents are controlled in the Scandinavian countries, Belgium and Switzerland, but not in Britain, the U.S.A., Canada, Australia, or New Zealand.[44] They are now also controlled in most provinces in India and Pakistan. In Japan, the Agricultural Land Adjustment Law of 1945 prescribed maximum rents equivalent to 25% of the crop for paddy land and 15% for upland (the previous shares having been respectively 50 to 70% and 30 to 35%). The payment of share rents was virtually prohibited.[45] In Formosa, where rents had been 55% of the crop, a legal maximum of 37.5% was set in 1949.[46] In the Philippines a law

---

[43] *Economist*, Jan. 31, 1948; Nov. 6, 1948.
[44] U.N., *Progress in Land Reform*, 139.
[45] Feary, R. A., *op. cit.*, 89.
[46] *For. Agric.*, June 1950.

of 1946 provided that the landowner's share must be reduced to 30%, but the law has been widely evaded and ignored.[47] There is little control in the Middle East, except in Egypt where the Agrarian Reform Law of 1952 prescribes a maximum cash rent of seven times the basic land tax and a maximum share rent of half the produce, net of all expenses. In Israel, where the government and the Jewish National Fund are the only lessors, rents are nominal. Nor are agricultural rents widely controlled in Latin America. In Cuba rents are limited to 6% of the assessed value of the land, and in Argentina, the Leasing and Share Cropping Law of 1948 required a 20% reduction in share rents.[48] Such laws are often evaded or not enforced, but where they are effective the capital value of the land is reduced (and the incomes of tenants increased) and landowners may cease to maintain improvements to the land. Similar limitations on the rent of buildings or on profits have a similar effect.

Savings influence the distribution of property ownership in capitalist countries. Where a larger proportion of income is saved out of high than out of low incomes, the rich tend to get richer. And as high incomes generally come from property, increases in property due to saving depend on the inequality in property ownership, the rate of return on property and the propensity to save.

In primitive societies, and the ancient and medieval worlds, private saving was relatively unimportant. In predominantly agrarian societies today, high rates of return on property facilitate saving by larger property owners who use their savings to take over the land of the smaller holders, thus increasing the inequality of property ownership. But low propensities to save limit this tendency. In the capitalist countries inequality in property ownership, high rates of return and a high propensity to save increased inequality in property ownership in the 19th century. Dissaving or living on principal, being more likely to be indulged in by the poorer, generally reduces the chance of rising from small to large property ownership. In Japan, the rapid increase of population during the period of most rapid development kept down both urban and rural wages, and raised profits that were the source of accumulation. But more recently high progressive taxation in western capitalist countries has reduced ability to save. In Russia, individual saving is small.

Changes in the capital value of property also change the distribution of property. They occur because of changes in property incomes and in the capitalization ratio applied to such incomes. If the anticipated income from an asset rises, its capital value is reassessed and the prospective change in income expresses itself in an increase in the quantity of property owned. If the interest rate declines, the right to receive the same income as before increases in capital value.

---

[47] *Ibid.*, Jan. 1951; U.N., *Economic Devel. Sel. Co.*, II, 75.
[48] *For. Agric.*, Aug. 1950.

Increases in land values are especially important in agrarian societies. Where savers buy land they raise the capital value, but not necessarily the income from land. Increasing population increases both capital value of land and its income. In areas opened to agricultural or mining development, land rents increase,[49] but where new lands are opened because of improvements of transportation part of the gains flow to the urban centres in lower prices. The more economical use of land tends, however, to reduce its value by reducing the demand for it. Furthermore special taxes on increases in the value of land (e.g., in Denmark, Portugal, and Formosa) reduce increases in property from this source.[50]

In the capitalist countries, increases and decreases in the value of industrial property are common. Where there are market facilities for speedy purchase and sale of this kind of property, some individuals aim to hold securities while they rise in value, and then to dispose of them. Or they may owe securities while they fall in value, and purchase them when they believe the fall is ended. The purchase and sale of investments have an important influence on inequality of incomes in the U.S.A.[51] Changes in the capital value of property are unimportant in Russia because there is little private property. The government controls the price of government bonds.

Marriage customs influence the distribution of property because of methods of choosing mates, and property transfers at marriage. In almost all societies the parties to a marriage come from two different families. This practice affects the economic assets and liabilities of each family. In some societies the husband transfers property to the parents of the bride and in others, the parents of the bride transfer property to the new family.

Where wives are economic assets, the bridegroom or his family are likely to transfer property to the bride's family. In many African tribes where women perform most of the agricultural labor, the bridegroom or his family transfers cattle to the bride's parents (*lobola*), the amount of the transfer varying with the attractiveness of the bride. This practice often results in considerable debt, for the *lobola* is sometimes paid on the instalment plan, and the instalments may even run over more than one generation. This *lobola* induces the parents to persuade the wife to be good, work well, and look after her husband lest the husband return the bride and ask for repayment of the *lobola*. It also limits polygamy, as husbands cannot have more wives than they can pay the *lobola* for. Herodotus records a more complex procedure in an ancient Scythian community where there was an annual auction of brides. The more attractive were put up first and as the less attractive came under auction, prices

---

[49] U.N., *Ec. Surv. Lat. Am.*, 1949, 53.
[50] U.N., *Progress in Land Reform*, 307.
[51] Clark, *Conditions of Economic Progress* 2d, 540.

diminished, until finally a number were auctioned at negative prices. Husbands were paid to take them, the payments being made out of the sums received for the more attractive.[52]

Knowledge of marriage arrangements in other countries chiefly concerns the upper classes, where for many centuries the bride's family has contributed property (a dowry) to the new family, partly because wives were not economically productive. Such arrangements existed in ancient Greece and Rome. In Rome, something like a bride price existed in very early times, but became nominal and finally gave place to payments in the opposite direction (dowries). These dowry payments may have originated out of efforts to protect the bride from ill-treatment in her new home; the dowry being a conditional gift, was voidable on the ill-behavior of the husband, or if the wife was divorced or childless. They were fairly common among the wealthier classes in Europe during the period of commercial capitalism. Where women could not hold property, dowries were frequently placed in trust. On the death of the husband the dowry returned to the wife, or those who would use it for her, and it took the place of a compulsory share in inheritance from the family. On the death of the wife, the dowry passed to the children, but not to the husband. Dowries were, however, not common in Britain. They almost invariably accompany monogamy. A bride's family is likely to object to setting up junior wives. In capitalist countries customs in these matters are less rigid than formerly, and there is considerable variety of practice.

The choice of mates has often been influenced by considerations of property. If one party to every marriage were rich and one poor, marriage would tend to reduce inequality of ownership. In most countries the children of the wealthy intermarry, which helps to preserve the concentration of property, but the selection of mates for their property is not unknown.

Inheritance permits the ownership of property without resort to saving, speculation, marriage, or a government grant. By increasing the ability of beneficiaries to save and, therefore, extending the process of accumulation over more than one lifetime, it tends to magnify inequality. Inheritance also transmits the effects of the marriage customs of property owners to the next generation. But the effect of inheritance depends on the degree of freedom of bequest allowed by the state, and upon customary ways of using this freedom.

In primitive societies inheritance is unimportant because property is unimportant. Furthermore, tools and other personal possessions are often regarded as part of the individual and buried with him, sometimes in the belief that he will need them in the next world. Houses are sometimes destroyed upon the death of the head of the family (although usually where they are fairly easy to construct). But land is regarded as the source

---

52 Herodotus, *History: On the Persians* I, 196.

of livelihood of the family, not to be disposed of at the will of the deceased person, but rather according to custom, and those who have been dependent on the land usually have customary rights to it.

In the ancient world property could be inherited and generally passed in the male line, except where women were permitted to hold property. In ancient Egypt women could inherit, but in ancient Greece property was generally inherited by male children, except in Sparta where women could inherit. In Rome, property was generally inherited by males. In medieval Europe serfs had no right to make wills disposing of their property. The lord was, however, usually willing (if not anxious) to accept their children as successors on the land (for a customary fee). Transfers of the feudal rights of lords were dependent on the will of the king who exacted a fee comparable with a death duty. But custom solidified into law restricting the freedom of testators. The Christian Church, which administered wills, urged testators to leave at least part of their property to the Church, and in the absence of a will, part of the property passed to the Church.

In agrarian countries inheritance is permitted, but restricted by law and custom based on religious doctrine. In most Islamic countries and among Hindu peoples, property is divided among the males (although some large estates in India are heritable only by the eldest son; this provision has kept such estates together). Among the poorer, inheritance by all males in an expanding population has reduced the smaller landholdings (Ch. 16). The Indian Famine Inquiry Commission rejected proposals to change the inheritance law to prevent this subdivision of land on the ground that there is no evidence that the small holder produces less per acre than the medium-sized holder, and that the possession of land provides social security; India may have the choice between an increase in the number of small holdings and an increase in the number of landless laborers, and public opinion might not tolerate the disinheritance of younger sons.[53] Any tendency for sharing among all sons to widen the distribution of property in general is offset by the fact that the wealthy intermarry. In Japan inheritance of the land by the eldest son retarded the subdivision of land (and drove other sons into the urban proletariat in recent decades.) The entailment of estates, which preserves them against subdivision, has been practiced in the past by some of the leading families in Britain and South America. In Chile entailment began at the end of the 17th century, but was abolished in 1857. It was abolished in Mexico in 1823.[54]

In continental Europe the principle that property vests partly in the whole family has long been expressed in laws restricting the right of the male head of the family to dispose of property, and vesting in the widow

---

[53] Famine Inquiry Commission *Report*, 259.
[54] McBride, G. M., *Chile: Land and Society*, 111.

and children a legally enforceable claim to part of the property. These restrictions vary in detail but exist in most European countries other than England. They also exist in many states in the U.S.A. and in Latin America, but often apply more rigidly to land than to investments. Primogeniture is one form of restriction, and it impedes the wider distribution of ownership, but it has not been common and has usually applied only to real estate. More frequently land must be distributed equally among children, subject to the rights of a widow. In the U.S.A. and in Britain in the past, the law often provided a "dower right" to a widow, of a life-interest in one-third of the husband's heritable land. In the U.S.A. this requirement has sometimes been extended to all property, and is sometimes absolute rather than for life, but this type of restriction is going out of use. Such a rule has little effect if it requires people to distribute their property as they would in the absence of the law. Insofar as it does change the conduct of testators, it tends to require relative equality within the family. Its effect on distribution in general depends on the size of families and on marriage customs. In France, where families have been small, little effect is to be expected, but in French Canada where families have been larger, land holdings have diminished in size.

Unrestricted rights to dispose of property by will developed mostly in the earlier part of the 19th century in England (but not in Scotland) as an expression of individualist philosophy,[55] although it was also believed that freedom might increase the inducement to accumulate. A large measure of freedom of bequest exists in most parts of the U.S.A., England, and Russia (where, however, it can apply only to private property, which is insignificant). Even where testamentary disposition is free, the state typically prescribes a short list of near relatives as beneficiaries where a property owner dies without a will. Where disposition is unrestricted, property is often kept in the family. Thus it remains concentrated, but concentration increases because inheritance increases the ability of beneficiaries to save. Even bequests outside the family are often made to people in the same economic class as the testator. If testators distributed their property widely at death, the inequality of the ownership of property would be reduced as it is when the wealthy leave property to charitable foundations, who use the income for wide distribution, or distribution among lower income groups. But in most countries, the majority of people bequeath little or no property because they own little or none. In Britain, for instance, about 50% of all estates liable to death duties were in the net capital value class £2000 to £4999, and accounted for about 13% of the total value of all such estates in 1947-8. Large numbers left no property, or property valued less than £2000. The effect of inheritance depends partly on the amount of property in a society. In older countries, with considerable accumulations of property, inheritance markedly increased

[55] Mill, *Political Economy*, Book II, Ch. 2, Sect. 4.

inequality until recent years when taxes on inheritance (Ch. 32) have severely reduced its effects. In more recently developed countries inherited wealth is a smaller proportion of all wealth, because inheritance has not operated on any scale over a long period.

Changes in the value of money greatly influence incomes from different kinds of property. In capitalist countries price increases favor holders of equity securities because selling prices rise faster than costs and industrial equipment is usually more fully used as such times. But they reduce the real incomes of receivers of fixed money incomes from bonds or land rents. In general, this redistribution favors the more active element in the property-owning class. Falling prices favor the less active property-owning class, and permit the dead hand of the past to hinder the entrepreneur.[56] But in the course of time landowners can adjust their money rents. In underdeveloped countries where land is the principal form of property, and landowners receive a share in the crop as rent, they are thereby protected from reductions in real income due to rising prices.

B. Incomes per Unit of Property

Incomes from property depend on the income per unit of property as well as on the amount of property owned. This income is usually expressed as a percentage of the capital value of the property.

Rates of yield vary from one kind of property to another and one country to another. The gross rate of return on risky investments is higher than on the safer, although the average net rate of return (after allowing for losses) may be no higher or even lower than on safer investments. For example, the over-all returns on gold mining in South Africa from 1887 to 1932 averaged about 4.1% a year.[57] Individuals may take risks in the same spirit as gamblers who realize that total winnings paid out in the long run fall short of sums risked, although some individuals win. General preferences for some types of investment cause lower rates of return on them than on other types. In many underdeveloped countries the preferences for land as an investment (Ch. 16) results in higher rates of return on commercial and industrial property (usually also higher on commercial than industrial). But the general level of return on property is higher in the underdeveloped than in developed countries.

Incomes per unit of property depend ultimately upon the supply of cash offered for prospective incomes (the supply of investment funds) and the supply of prospective incomes offered for cash (the demand for investment funds).

The demand for investment funds depends upon calculations by borrowers as to the profitableness of using the funds (the marginal efficiency of investment, which is the amount another dollar of investment would

---

[56] Keynes, *Tract on Monetary Reform*, 44.
[57] Frankel, *Capital Investment in Africa*, 91.

add to the value of output). Investors in the less developed countries have been disinclined to make such calculations, or make them with undue pessimism (although this is not the only reason for small investment in industry). In more developed countries the demand for funds has been greatly increased by the fact that so much new knowledge of production methods has required capital for its use. Canals, railroads, and subsequent industrial techniques in general, have all demanded more capital than previous methods of production. "Capital saving" innovations reduce the need for capital for a given output. The destruction of capital goods during the wars creates a demand for capital even to utilize previously existing knowledge of methods or production. Finally, the opening of new areas throughout the world provides new demands for capital in the same way as new technical knowledge.

The supply of investment funds depends on the amount of savings (voluntary or forced). It has already been shown (Ch. 21) that domestic savings vary widely among countries, owing to differences in average income, distribution of income, and mores. But the funds seeking investment in a country consist of these domestic savings, after deducting capital exports or adding capital imports.

The rates of return in different countries differ with differences in the relation between supply and demand, although differences in net rates of return must be less than differences in gross returns. The international mobility of capital has not sufficed to eliminate differences in return, although it must have reduced them. Ignorance or distrust of conditions in the high-return countries limits imports of capital and often even induces exports. Government policies regarding the protection or seizure of property, taxation, public investment, and monetary policy all affect the relation between supply and demand.

The great long-run increases in the demand for capital have not, however, caused great changes in rates of return in capitalist countries. Industrial methods of production have called for large amounts of capital, but they have helped to meet the demand. High productivity has meant high profits unequally distributed, and high ability to save and a high propensity to save has largely prevented great changes in the net rate of return over long periods of time.

Chapter 30

Incomes from Labor

Incomes from labor account for most incomes, and usually 50% of the national income (considerably more if the labor component in the incomes of small agricultural and other enterprises is included). Labor incomes are sharply contrasted with incomes from property in that differences in labor incomes are due mainly to differences in the value of units of labor rather than to differences in the amount of labor performed. The only available measure of the quantity of labor is in units of time, which are very relevant from the worker's point of view, and some of the lowest incomes are paid for the longest hours of work. Although hours of work vary among countries, times, and occupations (Ch. 19), we are here mainly concerned with the incomes obtained from whatever periods of labor are supplied. These can be discussed in terms of national averages and intra-national differences in incomes from different kinds of labor.

A. The Measurement of Labor Incomes

The ideal measure of labor incomes would be the net satisfactions resulting from labor, which depend on the satisfactions resulting from working and from the goods and services obtained as a result of working, less the dissatisfactions resulting from work. But no such measures are available. Existing statistical information usually concerns money rewards, with little or dubious allowance for non-monetary rewards and none for the satisfactions and dissatisfactions of work. Even if non-monetary rewards are valued in money, the resulting satisfactions depend on differences in the purchasing power of money between town and country, different countries, and different times, and on differences in felt needs that are sometimes correlated with differences in climate and culture. Differences in the dissatisfactions of labor do not appear in comparisons of annual or weekly income. Rewards per hour take some account of leisure as a consumption good if information is also available on hours of labor. If hourly incomes are unequal

637

and hours are equal, the group with higher hourly incomes is the better off. If hourly incomes are equal but hours unequal, the group working longer hours is better off in goods and services but worse off in leisure, and it is impossible to strike a balance unless it can be assumed that each arrangement was freely chosen by workers. Similarly, differences in money incomes from different jobs are influenced by, but do not measure, differences in their relative attractiveness. The same occupation is less attractive to some individuals than to others, and individuals are often attracted to occupations which they are unable to enter. Finally, incomes from labor cannot always be separated from incomes from property and risk (especially in agriculture). Nevertheless, there is no alternative to taking the available information and endeavoring to allow for its shortcomings.

B. National Average Labor Incomes

1. Actual National Average Labor Incomes

Comparisons of national averages of labor incomes provide a first broad approach to differences in these incomes. Such information is available, however, for only a small part of the working population of the world, and in local currencies. The difficulty of converting these curriencies into a single unit for comparison has already appeared (Ch. 1). Comparisons over time are equally difficult since all available methods allowing for changes in prices and the composition of consumption are valid at best only over short periods.

The conversion of hourly industrial earnings into the quantities of food (alone) that they will purchase makes some allowance for differences in price levels. In Canada, Australia, New Zealand, Scandinavia, Britain, and Israel, an hour's industrial labor purchased more than half as much food as in the U.S.A. in 1950; in France 31%, Italy 24%, and in Russia only 14% (Table 62). In some of these countries food was subsidized, subsidies per person in 1948 or 1949 being: Norway $42.7, Britain $32.3, Denmark $12.5 and Netherlands $8.8.[1] But the figures do not measure the consumption level of workers because they are before taxes (which differ among countries) and family allowances. Non-food items in workers' budgets differ in cost in different countries. Mass-produced consumer goods are generally cheaper in the U.S.A., but services and rent dearer than in most other countries. The purchasing power of agricultural labor is more difficult to appraise. There is little comparative information about labor incomes in underdeveloped areas, partly because much income from agriculture is not in money, and not always separable from incomes from land ownership. Labor incomes are known, however, to be very low, but probably less unequal within the labor group, than in industrial countries.

Present differences among countries in labor incomes are much greater than in the past, owing to differences in rates of increase. In the ancient

---

[1] U.S., *Monthly Lab. Rev.*, Feb. 1950, 153.

Mediterranean world real labor incomes may have sometimes been higher than those of much of the world's labor force at present. In the early sixth century B.C. in Greece "the average production per man year of the whole working community was . . . a good deal higher than that of present day Greece or of most southern and eastern European countries" and "comparable with the real incomes per head of countries like the

TABLE 62

INDEXES OF THE PURCHASING POWER OF HOURLY EARNINGS IN INDUSTRY IN TERMS OF FOOD IN SELECTED COUNTRIES IN 1937-8 AND 1950[*]
(U.S.A.=100)

Country	1937-8	1950
Australia	92	107
Norway	68	84
Canada	86	78
Denmark	73	73
Sweden	60	63
Israel	52	63
Great Britain	46	62
Czechoslovakia	34	46
Ireland	44	46
Switzerland	49	46
Finland	49	39
Germany	51	38
Netherlands	45	38
Chile	26	37
France (Paris)	68	31
Austria (Vienna)	38	28
Hungary	29	27
Italy	26	24
U.S.S.R.	24	14

[*] U.S., *Monthly Lab. Rev.*, Feb. 1951, 143. Earnings are before taxation, exclude family allowances, and are converted at current exchange rates.

Baltic states, Italy, Japan or Chile at the present time, of Britain in the 1850s and of Germany or France in the 1870s." In the fourth century B.C. real wages may have been comparable with those of unskilled workers in the 19th century. In Egypt in the fourth century B.C., the standard of living is estimated to have been comparable with that in Asiatic countries at the present time.[2]

In Europe after the tenth century labor incomes from agriculture were generally low, although measurement is impossible. They fluctuated with the weather and with changes in labor supply. Labor incomes must have risen after the plague in 1348 because almost every Parliament from 1350 to 1380 tried to fix wages at the pre-pestilence level.[3] But in general the rigidity of feudal organization that regulated incomes, and the lack of change in methods of cultivation, suggest stability of income (at a low

[2] Clark, *Condns. of Econ. Progress*, 2d, 543, 561, 562.
[3] Clapham, *A Concise Economic History of Britain*, 118.

level), the effect of slow increases in population being offset by taking in more land. But incomes rose after the 12th century in the expanding city crafts that attracted serfs from the manors and presumably improved labor incomes in agriculture (or offset any tendency for them to deteriorate). Wage employment increased in towns in the 13th century, when master craftsmen began to employ journeymen at daily wages. Formerly self-employed craftsmen became merchant capitalists and (as liverymen) regulated full membership in the guilds, the training of apprentices, the civil liberties of journeymen, and agricultural incomes. Where rural populations passed under the control of town governments in Italy and the Netherlands, peasants were forbidden to export food, their wages were regulated, and they were prohibited from home industries (which would conflict with urban crafts). Pressures for rising incomes were evident in almost every part of Europe from about 1250 to 1500, and where they were frustrated workers revolted. Artisans rose in 200 to 300 towns, especially in the centers of cloth industry in Flanders, northern France, west Germany and central Italy, and improved their conditions. Revolts among peasants were even more continuous and widespread (in Switzerland, Flanders, Denmark, and France in the 14th century and in the Peasants' War in 1525).[4]

The underdeveloped countries provide little information about past labor incomes. There is no evidence of any general trend for many centuries, but famine and war and occasional redistributions of land in China and Japan (Ch. 29) have caused temporary increases. But in recent years real labor incomes have fallen in some of these countries (e.g., North Africa and Java). In parts of India both the share of the crop going to cultivators and the amount of land available to each has fallen. The real wages of field labor in Bengal fell from 20 to 50% between 1842 and 1922, and real wages in general fell between 1939 and 1949.[5]

Industrialization has not usually caused much increase in labor incomes for a considerable time, although all indexes of real wages more than a few decades ago are highly dubious. In Britain all economists from Malthus to Mill doubted that industrialization had improved the condition of the poor. Real wages appear to have fallen from the middle of the 18th century until after the Napoleonic wars (Table 63). During the wars employment was high but the level of comfort was low. Obstacles to the import of food raised rents and farming profits, but wages did not rise as fast as prices. The population was increasing, and, also, the cost of housing and the tax system was highly regressive. All these changes were adverse to the worker but favorable to property owners and entrepreneurs.[6] After

---

[4] Turner, "Economic Discontent in Medieval Europe," *Tasks of Economic History,* 1948, 90, 94.

[5] Wadia and Merchant, *Our Economic Problem,* 259.

[6] Ashton, T. S., "The Standard of Life of the Workers in England 1790-1830," IX *Tasks of Economic History,* 1949, 19.

1820 fiscal reforms lightened the burden of the national debt, rents and prices fell, and real wages rose slightly, but by 1850 they seem to have been no higher than a century earlier (Table 63). What evidence is available for France suggests that wages probably declined outside agriculture from the middle of the 17th century until the revolution in 1789; there was no trend from 1800 to 1850[7] (Table 64). In Japan real wages rose little from 1875 to 1895, although measurement is complicated by payments supplemental to wages.

The major increases in real wages in developing capitalist countries occurred after 1850, and by 1900 wages had increased about 100% in Britain and France (Tables 63 and 64) and some 60% in the U.S.A. (Table 65). Thus during this period a considerable part of the gains from de-

TABLE 63

REAL WAGES IN THE UNITED KINGDOM, 1759 TO 1903[a]

Decades and Trade Cycles	Index (1900=100)
1759-68	62
1769-78	60
1779-88	60
1789-98	58
1799-1808	50
1809-18	43
1819-28	47
1820-26	47
1827-32	48
1833-42	51
1843-49	53
1849-58	57
1859-68	63
1869-79	74
1880-86	80
1887-95	91
1895-1903	99

[a] J. Kuczynski, *A Short History of Labor Conditions in Great Britain, 1750 to the Present Day*, 54. The figures are based on a very small sample.

velopment were distributed among workers. Since 1914 real wages have been affected by wars and have followed no uniform pattern in these countries. In Britain net real wages per full week fell somewhat during the war of 1914-1918 and rose above their 1900 level between 1930 and 1938.[8] In France, they probably fell slightly between 1914 and 1939,[9] and had fallen further by 1950.[10] In the U.S.A. the composite cash wage index rose from 66 in 1899 to 242 in 1920, but fell to 167 by 1930.[11]

[7] Kuczynski, *A Short History of Labor Conditions in France, 1700 to the Present Day*, 54.

[8] Kuczynski, *A Short History of Labor in Britain*, 120.

[9] Kuczynski, *A Short History of Labor in France, 1700 to the Present Day*, 170.

[10] U.N., *Inflationary and Deflationary Tendencies*, 17.

[11] U.S. Bureau of the Census, *Historical Statistics of the U.S.*, 68, 70.

TABLE 64

REAL WAGES IN FRANCE, 1789-1939[*]

	Index (1900=100)
1789	54
1800-09	62
1810-19	55
1820-9	70
1824-33	68
1833-9	65
1840-51	59
1852-8	55
1859-69	75
1868-78	76
1879-86	82
1887-95	89
1895-1903	87
1903-8	104
1909-14	105
1914-23	96
1924-34	99
1934-9	95

[*] Kuczynski, *A Short History of Labor Conditions in France, 1700 to the Present Day*, 170. Includes agriculture after 1859. After 1895 net real wages (allowing for loss of wages due to unemployment).

TABLE 65

CHANGES IN MONEY WAGES IN THE U.S.A., 1860-1899
Daily Wages in All Non-agricultural Employments in the U.S.A.[*]

	Index of Average Money Wages Per Day
1860	100
1865	143.1
1870	162.2
1875	158.4
1880	141.5
1885	150.7
1890	158.9

Farm Wage Rates in the U.S.A.[†]

	Composite Index of Farm Wage Rates in Money (1910-14=100)
1866	53
1869	52
1874 or 5	57
1880 or 81	60
1884 or 5	63
1889 or 90	64
1895	59
1899	66

[*] U.S. Bureau of the Census, *Historical Statistics of the United States*, 66.
[†] *Ibid.*, 70.

During the war of 1939-45 and subsequently, both prices and money wages rose. Real earnings of manual workers, including payment for overtime and increases in hours of labor, rose more than 25% in Sweden, Norway, Hungary, Britain, Switzerland, Finland, and Poland (Table 66).[12]

TABLE 66

REAL EARNINGS IN SELECTED EUROPEAN COUNTRIES
(1938 to 1949)*

	Real Earnings in 1949 as Per Cent of 1938
Sweden	135
Hungary	133
Norway	132
United Kingdom	129
Switzerland	127
Finland†	126
Poland	126
Czechoslovakia†	125
Denmark	119
Italy	
Married	115
Unmarried	99
Netherlands	101-112
France	80-104
Germany (U.K.-U.S. zone)	67

* U.N., *Econ. Surv. of Europe in 1949*, 24. The figures relate mainly but not wholly to manual workers and exclude family allowances where possible.
† 1948.

In Britain the increase was due mainly to shifts of labor to higher paid jobs and changes to incentive methods of payment yielding higher incomes.[13] But in France, Belgium and Italy the real wages of single (but not married) manual workers were lower in 1949 than in 1938. In Czechoslovakia and Poland average labor incomes rose, partly because of an increase in the proportion of workers in urban areas where incomes were higher than in rural areas.[14] In Spain real wages (including social security payments) fell 10 to 30% between 1935 and 1952.[15] In the U.S.A. income per worker was 330% higher in 1944 than in 1850.[16] In Russia real wages and salaries of (mainly) urban workers fell 18% to 42% between 1928 and 1937, but rose some 25% between 1937 and 1952.[17]

The purchasing power of hourly industrial earnings in terms of food alone increased between 1937-8 and 1950 about 17% in the U.S.A. In gen-

[12] U.S. Dept. of Labor, *Wage Trends and Wage Policies in Various Foreign Countries*, Bulletin 934, 1948.
[13] Seers, *The Levelling of Incomes since 1938*, 57.
[14] U.N., *Econ. Surv. of Europe, in 1949*, 24.
[15] U.N., *Econ. Surv. of Europe in 1953*, 141.
[16] Dewhurst, *et al., America's Needs and Resources*, 23.
[17] Janet Chapman, "Real Wages in the Soviet Union," *Rev. Econ. and Stat.*, May 1954.

eral the countries at the top and the bottom of the scale changed little, but the differences between them widened (Table 62). The countries where hourly industrial earnings purchased less than 40% as much food as in the U.S.A. rose from 5 in 1937-8 to 9 in 1950, and the countries above 60% rose from 5 in 1937-8 to 7 in 1950. The position in Norway, Israel, and Britain notably improved, but that of France and Germany seriously deteriorated, and Russia remained very low. In Britain the purchasing power of hourly industrial earnings rose over 50%, when allowance is made for the increase of 17% in the U.S.A. But consumption per head did not increase (Table 54) because food rose much less in price than most other consumer goods, and tax payments increased considerably. In addition, the proportion of the whole population at work and the number of hours worked both fell somewhat.

2. Influences Affecting National Average Labor Incomes

Average labor incomes depend on total output, the remuneration of property and the number of workers, but only in an arithmetic sense, for labor incomes are no more residual than property incomes. The chief influences affecting labor incomes are the supply of labor, the demand for it, and government policies.

a. The Supply of Labor

Changes in the supply of labor in relation to other resources must have been the chief cause of changes in labor incomes until a few centuries ago. In primitive societies the remuneration for labor cannot always be segregated. The total income of the individual depends on the amount and productivity of the land to which he is allowed access (often without payment), the amount of labor applied to it, and techniques of cultivation. Incomes are low partly because technology is primitive. In some such societies they are low because land is scarce, but often because less than the full potential supply of labor and land is used. Leisure is preferable to more of the small variety of goods they consume.

In the ancient world, labor incomes probably rose when population declined after war, pestilence, and famine, and when new land became available, but subsequent increases in labor supply reduced incomes again leaving little trend. In medieval Europe the population rose slowly, but when plagues greatly reduced the population, the condition of workers improved. The growth of city crafts after the 12th century somewhat reduced the supply of rural labor, but the craft guilds regulated the number of craftsmen, terms of apprenticeship, hours of work, and conditions of competition in order to maintain their incomes.

In underdeveloped countries predominantly engaged in agriculture, the ratio of population to land is high and labor incomes are low. The reward of the agricultural worker depends on the terms on which he obtains access to land, its fertility, and the worker's skill in using it. The income of a sharecropping cultivator depends on the size of his share of the crop and the amount of land he can lease. In the last century or so population increases have accelerated in most such countries, owing to the reduction of death rates because of the reduction of fighting and the improvement of health measures. Increased population means increased competition for land and a smaller amount for the average worker. Although the basis of sharing crops with landowners is somewhat customary, the worker's share also falls (as it has in parts of India) and there may be chronic unemployment or underemployment little of which is due to individual preference for leisure over consumption. Labor incomes in such countries are also reduced by ill-health and low vitality that makes the worker relatively unproductive. Poverty in one generation breeds poverty in the next.

In developing countries populations have also increased (100% in Britain from 1801 to 1850, 340% in the U.S.A., 24% in France), because of declining death rates and migration, but the decline in the amount of land per person can be offset by transfers of population to non-industrial production. The failure of real wages to rise much suggested to Malthus and Ricardo that incipient increases in wages raised birth rates, which increased the supply of labor and reduced its price. Marx came to a similar conclusion, arguing that employers were enabled to annex part of the output of labor by increases in population whenever wages rose above the vital needs of the worker (as well as by the continuous introduction of labor-saving devices that fed the "reserve army" of the unemployed.) But he admitted that the definition of "vital needs" depended on historical and moral factors that did not preclude increasing wages under capitalism. Nevertheless, he asserted that in the long run the condition of the workers steadily worsened (which has hitherto not happened). In fact, the increase of population was caused mainly by declining death rates, not rising birth rates. Age-old habits of procreation persisted in the presence of new health conditions. The decline in death rates was, however, assisted by development. But the failure of real wages to rise facilitated accumulation, which meant that the gains from development were not all absorbed in maintaining the increased population. Accelerated accumulation partly or wholly offset any tendency for increases in population to reduce the capital stock per worker and reduce his productivity. Lower rates of population increase would have improved the bargaining power of workers and raised wages, but these forces would have been partly offset by a slower rate of accumulation. Wages were also held down, however, by the almost continuous displacement of workers at a time when the labor force was increasing and labor unions hardly existed. Taxation of food imports (notably in Britain until 1844) maintained or raised the cost of the principal item in the worker's budget. In Japan events followed a similar course in the early decades of development. Population rose 100% from 1873 to 1935, wages rising little until 1900, 16 to 20% from 1900 to 1915, and little thereafter.[18]

The rise in real wages in the developing countries after 1850 accompanied a further rise in population, which increased about 100% in Britain between 1850 and 1900 (compared with 100% between 1800 and 1850), 230% in the U.S.A. between 1850 and 1900 (compared with 340% in the earlier period), and about 7% in France between 1860 and 1899 (compared with 24% in the earlier period). Any tendency for the increased supply of labor to reduce its bargaining power was evidently offset by other influences. Wages rose by similar percentages in the different countries while population increases were unequal. In the subsequent period population rose about 80% in the U.S.A. between 1900 and 1945, while labor income also rose.[19] But in western Europe rates of population increase declined while labor incomes followed no uniform pattern of change. Thus although the supply of labor was apparently the dominant influence on labor incomes for many centuries, other influences have so increased in importance during the past century that real wages have increased while populations have also increased (although at a declining rate).

b. The Demand for Labor

An increased labor supply is also a source of demand for the produce of labor. If other resources remain fixed, average product may rise or fall as population increases (Ch. 18), but the power of labor to bargain for a share in the product is likely to fall in comparison with that of the owners of other resources. If other resources increase in relation to labor supply, average product is likely to rise and the bargaining power of labor to improve. These combinations of forces produce a variety of results.

In predominantly agrarian countries the slowness of the increase of non-labor resources prevents much rise in average product or any tendency to a fall in the bargaining power of the non-labor factors. In fact, labor-saving devices, reducing the demand for labor, reduce real wages unless alternative labor demands are increasing. In the Middle East, for instance, mechanization of agriculture has apparently raised rent without helping the farmer.[20] Industrialization increases average product by increasing the importance of capital among the means of production. But the increasing supply of capital tends to reduce its power to bargain for a share in the increasing product, although increases in the quantity of capital may prevent any deterioration in its total reward. Labor-saving devices reduce the demand for some kinds of labor per unit of product, but, as

18 Allen, A Short Economic History of Modern Japan, 57, 106 ,163.
19 U.S. Bureau of the Census, Historical Statistics of the United States, 26.
20 Warriner, Land and Poverty in the Middle East, 126.

labor incomes have risen most in countries using such devices most extensively, the long-run effect cannot be to reduce labor incomes. There must, therefore, have been countervailing forces tending to increase the demand for labor. If the price of consumer goods is reduced and the demand for them is elastic, there is a countervailing increase in demand for labor in the same industry. If the demand is inelastic, purchasing power is freed to be spent on other goods and services, causing an increased demand in the industries supplying them. If wages are raised there is an increase in demand (unless wage earners hoard). If profits rise there is an increased demand for consumer or producer goods (unless profit receivers hoard). Furthermore the increased use of capital goods increases the demand for labor to construct and maintain capital goods. In fact, 70% to 80% of non-agricultural output goes in remunerating labor (Table 67),

TABLE 67

AVERAGE WAGES PER ADULT MALE EQUIVALENT* IN NON-AGRICULTURAL WORK AS A
PERCENTAGE OF AVERAGE TOTAL INCOME PER ADULT MALE EQUIVALENT
FROM NON-AGRICULTURAL PRODUCTION†

Country	Period	Average wage income as percentage of all income
U.S.A.	1938	75.5
Canada	1938	83.2
Eire	1938	75.6
United Kingdom	1930	76.3
France	1938	81.5
Germany	1937	59.5
Japan	1934	70.3
Australia	1938-9	79.7

* Assuming all men aged 20-59 are seeking work. Women and males of other ages equated to half an adult male. Salaries included with wages. The average wage of an adult male equivalent is imputed to each employer and working proprietor.

† Clark, *Conditions of Economic Progress* 2d ed., 523. These figures compare "what the wage earner gets" with "what he would get if the remuneration of all the other factors of production were zero" (after imputing to the employer and working proprietor the average wage of an adult male equivalent).

and the percentage has tended to increase. These forces must explain much of the increase in labor incomes in the later stages of development, and they must have been strong enough to overcome any tendency of increases in population to reduce wages.

Exports of capital affect real wages through their effect on productivity and the bargaining power of labor in the exporting country. By tending to reduce domestic investment they maintain interest and profits and reduce the bargaining power of labor. But they also improve the market for exports, and possibly the terms upon which imports are obtained. Capital invested abroad may set to work populations living under social and economic systems with low wages, and induce exports that undercut products made in the investing country where wages are higher. Although workers in the investing country benefit from the reduced cost of living, some may lose their jobs. In Britain, however, the export of capital during the 19th century accompanied the emigration of workers to the U.S.A., Canada, Australia, and New Zealand, which reduced the bargaining power of non-labor factors in Britain. In importing countries the influx of capital raises average productivity, but may reduce the bargaining power of capital.

Increases in labor incomes themselves affect the demand for labor, adversely or favorably insofar as they reduce or increase the demand for activities in which labor is relatively important as a factor in production. Any tendency for increments in income to be spent in diminishing proportions on the consumption of manufactured goods and in increasing proportion on the products of tertiary activities, such as commerce and other services, may cause a relative increase in the demand for labor as against capital. But some tertiary activities such as railroad transportation are heavy users of capital, and even the service industries apparently use a considerable amount of capital in relation to labor.

c. Labor Organizations

Labor incomes depend not only on the larger forces affecting the relation between the supply of and the demand for labor, but also on organizations affecting the free operation of these forces in each of the many situations in which wages are set.

Competition for labor is usually imperfect on a national scale because of the imperfect mobility of workers. In some local markets wages below the marginal value product of labor yield a monopsony profit to employers. But in longer periods any large profits of this sort attract more employers. In fact the great transfers of labor within and among capitalist countries indicate considerable competition for labor and considerable response by labor. Employers' organizations sometimes cooperate in wage policy, although the extent of their influence is unknown. In Britain in 1943, there were about 1900 employers' associations dealing with labor conditions. The British Employers' Federation covered about 75% of the industrial population. Similar associations exist in most western European countries and the U.S.A. In South Africa the gold mines obtain labor through two recruiting organizations; this arrangement not only reduces the cost of recruiting but also eliminates competition among the mines for labor. The Transvaal Chamber of Mines allocates the native workers arriving in Johannesburg, sometimes favoring the low-grade mines. Nevertheless, the Native Wages Commission failed to find "anything which can fairly be called a monopoly of recruiting" because other industries were also recruiting native labor. The Transvaal Chamber of Mines sets a maximum average wage per day on all mines (which may be exceeded only on payment of a penalty) to prevent mines from competing "unfairly" with each other for native labor.[21]

Competition for employment is influenced by labor organizations. Individual workers are often too weak in dealing with employers to exact wages equivalent to their marginal value product. They may be ignorant of alternative opportunities to work under better conditions, or unable or loth to move to these jobs. They are often unable to strike for long enough to force employers to raise wages. Workers in union can threaten a stoppage of work by all workers. They can employ specialized bargaining agents, and accumulate strike funds (which have been more important in Britain than in the U.S.A.). The power of unions depends on their control over labor supply and the productivity of labor.

In western Europe craft guilds maintained the incomes of their members from the 12th century by regulating entry to the craft. But they were undermined when competing production was organized outside the cities, to which the guild monopolies were restricted. Most of them finally collapsed under the impact of industrial competition, although some remain in continental Europe (and in some underdeveloped countries). After the collapse of the medieval system, there was a long period of *laisser faire* in which labor was organized hardly at all. Modern labor unions and employers' associations appeared first in Britain, and there only after industrialization was well under way.[22]

In Britain labor organizations were reborn in the 1830s when industrialization had caused severe dislocations in agriculture and craft production and offered desperate conditions of work in industry. Most of the early unions opposed the new industrial methods and sought to introduce worker-controlled production units, using the strike of all labor as their instrument. But general strikes are difficult to organize, they are militantly opposed by governments, and producers' cooperatives have not been a success (Ch. 11). The unions were poorly financed and failed to retard industrialization or raise labor incomes. The Grand National Consolidated Trade Union was formed in Britain in 1833 to be one big union using the general strike as its major weapon. In 1834, the agricultural members of the union were prosecuted for administering secret oaths, and the "Tolpuddle Martyrs" were transported for seven years. The Union gave up the administration of oaths, but it collapsed because employers refused to employ union members, and the Union had no funds. The ideas of the Grand National Union reappeared as part of the Chartist movement from 1839 to 1848.

Labor unions accepting industrial methods of production appeared in Britain, the U.S.A., and Scandinavia in the second half of the 19th century

[21] South Africa, Witwatersrand Mine Natives' Wages Commission *Report*, 1943, 3, 4, 6.

[22] Galenson, W., (ed.), *Comparative Labor Movements*, x.

when labor incomes were increasing. Their primary object was to make the best possible bargain for their members within the existing framework of production. There can be little doubt that these unions had some influence on wage increases after the middle of the century, but the influence cannot be measured. Their membership was limited, and in the U.S.A. too limited to have much influence on wages.

In Britain "business unionism" appeared after the collapse of the Chartist movement in 1848. The first unions were in the building and engineering trades, and were at the peak of their activity from 1850 to 1880. Administration was highly centralized, they favored cooperation with employers, and disavowed any militant strike policy. After about 1870 skill began to decline in importance and, although the unions of skilled workers continued to be powerful, unskilled industrial workers were organized in the 1880s (e.g., coal miners, dock workers, and gas workers). Unable to control the supply of workers by controlling the acquisition of skill, these unions were more aggressive than the craft unions, and adopted a fighting strike policy. Agricultural workers were slow to organize (as in all countries). They exercised most of the votes in the rural constituencies, which were returning the anti-labor candidates to Parliament. They were unionized only after 1918. Professional workers also slow to organize now have powerful unions, although non-manual civil servants may not belong to unions which are affiliated with the Trades Union Congress. By 1947 there were about 9.1 million members of labor unions, about 7.5 million of whom were in unions affiliated with the Trades Union Congress. The total membership of the unions has more than doubled since 1933. Unions have been growing in size and diminishing in number, more than two-thirds of the total membership being in 17 large unions. Their total funds increased from £20 million at the end of 1938 to £50 million at the end of 1947.

Labor unions appeared later in the U.S.A. Unions of craftsmen existed in the larger cities from the beginning of the 19th century. As early as 1820 they sought to use their newly won political franchise by forming local labor parties in the eastern cities. But their less radical proposals were taken over by other parties and they fell into disrepute. Again in the 1880s the Knights of Labor (the last of a series of labor organizations with general labor programs) began the organization of the unskilled, and attempted to substitute self-employment for capitalist employment. National and international craft unions with a business policy developed after 1850 with the acceleration of industrial development. After the collapse of the Knights of Labor, the business union was dominant, although it affected only a minority of workers almost entirely in the skilled crafts. These unions developed little and remained non-radical, partly because of legislation restricting union activity and concessions by large corporations beyond what unions could get by bargaining. The high mobility of workers, and the hope of each worker to rise in the world, minimized the importance attached to union activity, free land in the West provided an outlet, immigration and regional shifts of production and the presence of non-union colored workers complicated the job. These craft unions remained almost the only labor unions until the Congress of Industrial Organizations was formed in 1935. There were .44 million members of labor unions in 1897, 1.058 million in 1901, and 2.064 million in 1914.[23] But after changes in the law and the organization of the unskilled, there were in 1945 about 6.9 million members of unions affiliated with the American Federation of Labor, 6 million in those affiliated with the Congress of Industrial Organizations and 2.1 million in unaffiliated unions. There are virtually no labor unions in agriculture in the U.S.A., although some cooperative marketing associations perform analogous functions (Ch. 7), and only a few professional unions (e.g., among teachers).

Labor organization in general, although it began on a craft basis, each union consisting of members doing the same kind of work, has been shifting to an industrial basis, each union consisting of workers employed in the same industry. Developments in industrial technology have reduced the importance of skills and upset the old demarcation of jobs (and caused jurisdictional conflicts between craft unions). Employers, exasperated with the necessity of negotiating with many unions (often in conflict with each other) have sought industrial organization. New industries have grown up in which relatively few skilled craft workers are needed. In Britain, where the union movement is organized on both a craft and industry basis, it seems to be gradually passing to an industrial base. In the U.S.A., the unions belonging to the American Federation of Labor are in the main craft unions, and those belonging to the Congress of Industrial Organizations are mainly industrial unions. In France the typical unions are industrial, and in Sweden and Belgium industrial unions were increasing prior to 1939. In Russia the whole union movement is industrial.

Labor organization is western Europe also appeared later than in Britain and, because mercantilism never entirely disappeared, there is more continuity with the guilds than in Britain. In France and Germany, unions were hampered by legislation, the hostility of employers, and conflicts between revolutionary and gradualist policies. In France labor unions of some sort existed from about 1825, but were not officially recognized and had no legal right to strike until 1864, and no clear right to form unions until 1884. Moderate unions of various types appeared after about 1871, and affiliated with various of the Socialist parties. In 1875 they repudiated socialism as a bourgeois utopia, but by 1879 were again passing socialist resolutions. After 1884, when the law was liberalized, unions developed more rapidly in affiliation with a variety of Socialist parties. There have been unions in agriculture, but only where it is organ-

---

[23] U.S. Bureau of Census, *Historical Statistics of the United States,* 72.

ized on a large scale. Civil servants, postal workers, teachers, and the like are now organized. The unions were severely damaged during the German occupation after 1939, and union membership has fluctuated greatly since 1945 owing to destructive schisms over political policy, induced by employer and middle-class resistance to concessions to workers. By 1953 only 17% to 25% of workers belonged to unions. In Germany the revolutionary movement of the 1840s stimulated tentative efforts to form unions, most of which were wiped out in the 1850s. They appeared again in the 1860s, but legal restrictions hampered them seriously and they had only 3 million members in 1909. The new Weimar constitution after 1918 consolidated the enhanced status of the unions achieved during the war. It provided for the abandonment of company unions, the abolition of discrimination against union workers, the eight-hour day, shop committees, and joint administration of employment offices. Works councils were set up in 1920 as part of a hierarchy of councils culminating in the Federal Economic Council (which was merely advisory to the Government). But the movement was destroyed by the Nationalist Socialist government after 1933, and recovered slowly after 1945 although almost all its former leaders had been lost.

In most European countries unions have organized in over-all labor federations for much the same reasons that manufacturers in general have organized (Ch. 12). They seek to obtain benefits for workers by entering politics to modify the social framework where it restricts the gains to be obtained from business unionism. By the exercise of political power they may reduce inequality of incomes. In Britain practically all labor unions belong to a single federating organization, the Trades Union Congress, formed in 1868. The Independent Labor Party, formed in 1893, supported left-wing liberal candidates for Parliament until 1899 when it began promoting labor candidates. In 1906, the Labor Party formed to promote Fabian (gradualist socialist) and not Marxist policies was controlled by the Labor unions. The Labor Party was the dominant party in a coalition government in 1931 to 1935, and after 1945 it formed the first wholly Labor Government. The communists sought to capitalize on the Trades Union Council policy of a stop on wage increases, and acceptance of government pressure to increase productivity, but they have declined in power since 1948. The Trades Union Congress urged all ranks to fight communist infiltration, and the fight was successful. Nevertheless, there is a number of communist members of unions, and some communist union officers (for example, in the miners' union).

Labor organization in Australia and New Zealand has had a somewhat vigorous past. Short-lived labor unions appeared in Australia in the 1850s. Led by sheep shearers and waterside workers, they were aggressive and reacted to government efforts to repress them by forming a labor party in the 1890s. Early in the 20th century they pronounced in favor of the nationalization of industry (which they have never pursued). The Labor Party was in power from 1910 to 1913, and, after 1914, from 1929 to 1931, and from 1941 to 1950, but the Senate was Liberal until 1944. There have also been Labor governments in some states but not usually in all. After 1945, there was a not inconsiderable Communist party, which is now relatively unimportant. In New Zealand, relations between employers and workers were also violent in the late 19th century, and the unions relied on collective bargaining of a forceful sort. Compulsory arbitration was introduced early in the 20th century to reduce the wastage due to strikes, most of which occurred in mining and among waterside workers. There was a wave of syndicalist unionism after 1910, and a split in labor union ranks in the early days of the war in 1914, which (like that among the workers in France and Germany) was concerned with pacifism versus cooperation with the state in wartime. But the labor movement has now a flavor similar to the British, and was in power in the government from 1935 to 1950.

In western continental Europe no such unity exists. Union movements are divided between gradualist and revolutionary policies, and often also along religious lines. Workers' organizations accept industrial methods of production (as does the Russian government) but the anarcho-syndicalist tradition has never died out. Mostly in France, Italy, and Spain there have been groups basically opposed to the capitalist organization of society and aiming ultimately at revolution against the state. The struggle for higher wages and shorter hours is a means of intensifying class consciousness and developing techniques of class warfare, to come to fruition in the last act of the class struggle, namely, the general strike, which is to end the capitalist system. The new society is to be a free federation of classless productive and distributive organizations with collective ownership operating in accord with the needs of society; that is, each industry is to be run by its workers, the state, as we know it, being non-existent. This revolutionary socialism persisted from the First International of 1868-72 until 1914.

In France the leaders of the *Confederation Générale du Travail* translated this policy into modern form in the course of the revision of Marxist policy, and the labor movement was revolutionary-syndicalist until 1914. It refused collaboration with the government, its ultimate aim being to take over plants and factories by a general strike and arrange for the workers to operate them. As the C.G.T. had little funds, it was compelled to use methods with a dramatic appeal. But in 1914 French workers abandoned the anti-war policies of the Second International and agreed to cooperate with the government by accepting mobilization orders and cooperating in production during the war. Union membership rose from about 500,000 to 2 million. The unions adopted a gradualist reform policy and sought legislation to raise the standard of living of workers, and reached the high point of their power in the Popular Front Government of Leon Blum in 1936 to

1937. There was, however, a Communist movement (the *Confederation Générale du Travail Unitaire*) from 1919 to 1936. When the policies of the Nazi Government in Germany revealed the dangers of a disunited union movement, the popular front in politics, (including Communists, Socialists, and Radicals) was paralleled by a reformation of the union movement, which was again united in one federation. The membership of labor unions rose rapidly to about six million workers in 1937. In 1939, however, on the eve of war, the Communist unions pronounced in favor of the German-Russian pact, and were expelled from the C.G.T.

During the occupation of 1940-45, the Vichy government dissolved the labor unions and formed a labor front comparable to that in Germany. The members of the former labor movement became the backbone of the resistance movement, the most vigorous being the Communists. When the C.G.T. was reestablished in 1945, the Communists, being the dominant group took control, and maintained it until 1950. But after the failure of a general strike in November 1947, about one-fifth of the members seceded from the C.G.T. and formed a separate federation, the *Force Ouvière*, which rejected political strikes. But, failing to obtain wage concessions from the government (which continued to insist upon stabilization of wages), it was greatly weakened and by 1948 it included only a few clerical workers and old syndicalists. Most of the membership drifted back to the C.G.T. (which remained communist) or abandoned the union movement. By 1949 the C.G.T. contained about 3 million members; the *Force Ouvière*, .8 million or less; the Christian unions, .8 million or less; the Anarchist, .08, and others .019 million.

In Germany the labor movement was generally revisionist before 1914, and converted the Social Democratic Party to its policy. Unions were rigidly opposed by employers, who emphasized the benefits accruing to workers from Bismarck's policies and the desirability of a personal relation with workers. Collective bargaining was not very effective. The organized workers supported the government war policy from 1914-18 and departed from the Second International. An independent Socialist Party split off from the main movement on the war issue, and later developed into the Communist Party. Between 1918 and 1933 a Social-Democratic Government achieved considerable gains for workers, and was the first German government sympathetic with labor. But by 1935, the unions were all suppressed and replaced by the government *Arbeitsfront,* which was virtually the government organization for the mobilization and utilization of the labor force. Labor organization is similarly divided in Italy. In all these countries the vigor of the revolutionary wing is largely due to the uncompromising attitudes of governments, employers, and the middle class.

In France, Italy, Belgium and Holland, the movement is also divided along religious lines. In Italy, there are three central labor organizations. In France, there is a confederation of Christian workers, which is Catholic, as well as a Communist and a nominally non-political central organization. In Holland, there are central organizations for Catholic, Protestant, moderate Socialist and Left-wing unions.

In the U.S.A. also there are two central labor organizations. The American Federation of Labor, consisting predominantly of craft unions, has generally opposed the political organization of workers, and often opposed social legislation (believing that it weakened the hold of the unions). The Congress of Industrial Organizations, formed in 1935, has initiated political action but operates through the existing parties. The U.S.A. is almost unique in having no political labor organization. Even so, however, real wages have risen to higher levels than elsewhere. After 1945, there was a conflict between communist and business union policies, but the influence of communist views in unions declined after 1948. Unions whose officers fail to take oath that they are not Communists under the Taft-Hartley Act are denied recourse to the machinery of the National Labor Relations Board. In 1951 the American Federation of Labor withdrew from general cooperation with the Congress of Industrial Organizations. Nevertheless, the increased coverage of the labor movement has stimulated interest in problems of labor in general, such as social security and tax policies, and the labor movement is now in a position to enforce wage policies leading to inflation. These central national labor organizations are further federated into international organizations that also reflect the political divisions in most national organizations (Ch. 26).

The effects of labor union activities are difficult to appraise. The influence of labor union operations cannot be separated from the effect of other forces influencing labor incomes, and the scope for combined action, the policies pursued and the comprehensiveness of labor organization. In Britain the increase in business union activity synchronizes fairly closely with the period of rising real wages. So long as unions were mainly craft, apprenticeship control and entrance fees could be used to restrict the supply of labor at a time when the demand was rising. But it is much more difficult to control the supply of unskilled labor, the wages for which also rose. In fact, increases in real labor incomes in different countries show no close correlation with union membership. After 1933 depression restricted the economic power of unions, and since 1939, war and reconstruction have hampered them in countries which suffered severe war losses. In the U.S.A. wages rose while labor union membership was relatively small and largely confined to skilled workers (until 1935).

A labor union can push wages in any occupation up to the value of the marginal product of the worker provided it can achieve uniform action among all potential workers. If it can also control the inflow of workers (by control of apprenticeship or union membership and prevention of the employment of non-union workers), it may raise incomes above a competitive level. Higher wages raise costs, and if prices also rise, the value of the product of labor rises. But the industry is smaller than it would be under free competition, and the national product lower. One group of workers benefits at the expense of the remainder of the society. Workers forcing wages beyond the existing marginal product of their labor may, however, increase productivity. The marginal productivity of labor may vary among firms, and wages forced above the marginal value of product for some employers may cause them to reorganize production and increase their efficiency. Or such wage increases may drive the less efficient users of labor out of business and shift the demand for labor to more efficient users. Wages forced beyond the general marginal product in an industry may compel employers to use labor more efficiently, thus increasing the efficiency of the industry. Success of this sort in one line of production tends (in the absence of obstacles to entry) to attract workers from other occupations, raising wages elsewhere and spreading the pressure for greater efficiency. Efficiency may be increased by substituting capital for labor, which may either increase or reduce the demand for labor in the long run. But if employers cannot raise the marginal product of labor to the price they have to pay for it, they make a subnormal profit, and leave the industry. Even so, labor may restrict the number of workers, and thus keep the industry smaller than is economical in the general interest. When new methods of production become available in particular industries (possibly as a result of union pressure) unions may make "feather-bedding" rules which keep the demand for labor above what is necessary with new technology, preventing the full benefits of improved technology from being achieved and passed on to consumers.

Within shorter periods labor organizations have only a limited power to raise labor incomes in times of less than full employment, but they may be able to limit wage reductions that, although they hold up labor costs, limit reductions in payroll disbursements and, in general purchasing power and employment. For instance the National Industrial Recovery Act in the U.S.A. was based partly on the belief that increased disbursements on payrolls in time of depression would stimulate activity. But in times of full employment they may force up wages, payrolls, and prices without increasing output, and generate an inflationary spiral.

When labor is widely organized, it must have regard for the interests of workers in general. Even though unions pursuing the interests of particular groups of workers may benefit at the expense of the remainder of the society (including other workers), organizations of all or most workers may gain only at the expense of recipients of property incomes. If they reduce the general level of profits, they may drive investment abroad except where exports of capital are restricted (as they have been in many countries in recent years), or reduce accumulation.

General wage policies are determined in some countries by negotiation between over-all workers' and employers' organizations (usually with the government more or less in the background). In Italy representatives of the three principal labor federations and the General Confederation of Italian Industry negotiate basic wages for the various skills and regions and also family allowances. Subsequently, unions bargain for the application of these standards.[24] In Sweden, the central organizations of workers and employers made a basic agreement to stabilize wages, during the war of 1939-45, that was taken into account in collective agreements. Wage increases were to vary with the cost of living, although not taking full account of price changes. Prices were fairly effectively stabilized after 1942, until 1947.[25] A new agreement stabilized wages from 1948 to 1950. Wages are also the subject of general agreements between employers and unions in Denmark and Norway.

Labor organizations entering politics operate on a broader front as to policy. In Britain, Sweden, Norway, Denmark, Australia, and other countries, they publish newspapers to popularize their policies. In the 20th century, they have operated the government in Britain, Germany, Norway, Sweden, Denmark, Australia, New Zealand, and a number of other countries, sometimes with the support of agricultural parties. Some of their policies have been aimed at the redistribution of the existing national product (through taxation, social security benefits, widening the legal scope of labor union action, and the like) (Ch. 31). Some have promoted the nationalization of industry. In both France and Britain nationalization was urged by workers dissatisfied with conditions of employment. Discouraged by the outcome of collective bargaining, suspicious of restrictionism by employers and suspecting that lack of progressiveness had limited their ability to pay higher wages, workers turned to nationalized industry for a better deal than they had obtained from private industry.

Government policies as employers will influence general labor incomes in these countries in a variety of ways. If the government pays wages in excess of the marginal product, it may stimulate increased productivity and lift labor incomes in general; it may raise the prices of nationalized products and reduce productivity in general, throwing part of the burden on workers in non-nationalized industries; or it may incur losses in nationalized industries which involve subsidies out of taxation or inflation, thus throwing part of the burden of the rise in wages on higher incomes but reducing productivity. But workers also hoped that nationalization would reduce costs in key industries, thus raising efficiency in others and increase their ability to pay higher wages. But these two objectives conflict. Insofar as other industries are to be aided by lower charges for energy and transport, improvements in efficiency in these industries cannot be wholly trans-

---

[24] U.S. Dept. of Labor, *Labor Abroad*, Dec. 1952; I.L.O., *Ind. and Lab.*, May 1951, 387.

[25] U.S. Dept. of Labor, *Wage Trends and Wage Policies in Various Foreign Countries*, 1948, 24.

mitted to workers in higher wages. Furthermore, it remains to be seen how far labor unions will accept methods of increasing efficiency that require reallocations of labor.

As governments extend controls of economic life over-all labor organizations participate in these controls. In Europe since 1939 many governments, having intervened to divert economies to war and subsequently to recovery from war, have been compelled to make decisions affecting levels of consumption. The wage level in Britain and Belgium has been largely determined by political agreement between the labor unions and the government. The British labor government did not control wages in general by law, but attempted to avoid inflation and to divert goods from domestic consumption to export. The Trades Union Congress influenced the policies of its member unions in collective bargaining and in December 1949, the General Council of the Congress approved a policy of stabilizing wage scales and suspending sliding scales unless the index of retail prices rose or fell by six points; this was to assist the Government to close the "dollar gap" and avoid an upward spiral of wages and prices. But the Union movement insisted on stabilization of the cost of living and restriction of profits. In effect, there was a wage standstill, except for the purpose of increasing output, raising "unduly low" wages, and attracting additional workers. Since 1947 real wages have fallen slightly, and probably also labor's share of the national income. In Belgium, the *Conseil Générale de l'Economie*, established in 1948 and consisting of representatives of owners, managers, and workers, has cooperated with the government in making general economic policy. But general wage agreements are not always effectively enforced by employers, and earnings tend to rise in spite of agreements in times of full employment, e.g., in Britain, Italy, the Scandinavian countries, and Belgium.[26] Where the labor movement is divided between revolutionary socialism and gradual reform (Fabianism), it exerts less power than where it is united. It may be divided because employers are uncompromising in their attitude even to gradualism. In France, for instance, the labor movement has achieved little, in part at least because it is divided.

In the underdeveloped countries only a small proportion of all workers is organized. In Latin America the only important unions are in large-scale industries such as railroad and port organizations (in Mexico, Argentina, Chile, and Brazil) and mining (in Mexico, Chile, and Bolivia). Nitrate activities and copper mining have been organized in varying degrees in Chile for about 50 years. The labor organization in the petroleum industry in Mexico played a decisive part in bringing about nationalization. The textile industry has provided the core of union activities in Peru, and has been important in union organization in Brazil. Unionization has been somewhat facilitated where industry is foreign-owned, such ownership

26 U.N., *Econ. Surv. of Europe since the War*, 1953, 72.

modifying middle-class opposition. Such unions as existed before 1914 in Argentina, Chile, and Brazil were mostly affiliated with anarchist groups in Spain, although there were socialist unions. But union movements in these countries have since suffered from complex and changing cleavages between gradualist and communist views (as in France and Italy). Between 1914 and 1944 unions in Argentina were mainly socialist; in Chile and Cuba, communists and socialists shared leadership. In Peru, unions were more or less socialist but with some communist influence; in Costa Rica mostly communist; and in Colombia the communist group was the strongest. Often nationalist and anti-foreign, they have typically avoided political repression by making agreements with political parties, sometimes becoming virtually part of the government administration. But during the war of 1939-45 they moderated their antagonism to Americans and British, and lined up against the Axis countries. In Brazil the government has encouraged unions, but used them as an instrument for controlling labor. In Peru reactionary governments have experimented with government-aided unions to counteract the more or less socialist dominated "aprista." In Chile and Cuba the administrations have been much more sympathetic to union organization. In Argentina, President Peron has undermined the political influence of the land-owning group and the army by strengthening the labor unions, although in 1954 business opposition increased. Collective bargaining is also increasing in the West Indies.

In India, craft guilds (especially in the south) and some castes have for long performed some of the functions of fraternal orders. Unions of the modern western type appeared after the war of 1914-18 in the textile industry, where wages failed to rise with the cost of living while some mills paid dividends of 100% or more. Union membership never rose above about 300,000 members (mostly seamen, railwaymen, and textile workers) during the 1930s. In Bombay the unions followed an aggressive strike policy, but elsewhere they were conciliatory. But after 1947 membership grew from 1.6 millions to 3.3 millions in 1950.[27] There is a great number and variety of unions, many very small, often consisting of the workers in one mill, and the allegiance of individual unions is not always clear because of the struggle for power among aspirant labor leaders. There are three central organizations; the All India Trade Union Congress, formerly the principal one, became communist and its leaders were imprisoned by the government (which represented the Indian National Congress); the Indian National Labor Congress, established by the Congress party when India became independent, is recognized by the government; an organization allied to the socialist party also exists. The labor union movement did not follow Mahatma Ghandi in opposing the war, and it rallied anti-Japanese sentiment in 1942. The Famine Inquiry Commission[28] recommended that

[27] U.N., *Prelim. Rep. on World Social Situation, 1952*, 176.
[28] Famine Inquiry Commission *Report*, 272, 324.

the provincial governments assist agricultural laborers to organize to improve their economic and social condition and enable them to cooperate in the improvement of agriculture, contending that higher wages would improve the efficiency of the worker. It also suggested that the terms upon which tenants obtained access to land should be improved "in the same way in which improvement of labor conditions has been secured in industry; that is, by developing the principle of collective bargaining." No such action has been taken. In Pakistan, union membership rose from 79,000 to 320,000 between 1947 and 1950, during which period membership rose in Burma from 41,000 to 260,000, in Ceylon from 169,000 to 179,000, and in the Philippines from 33,000 to 370,000.[29] In Japan before 1945, labor union membership never exceeded 7% of the labor force. But suggestions by the military occupation authorities that labor unions be formed appealed to a people reputed to dislike standing alone. Workers were rapidly organized and a number of strikes (some unconventional) followed.

In the Middle East, labor unions are now appearing but are generally weak,[30] except in Israel where workers are actively organized. The largest sector in the *Histadrut* comprises 40% of the Jewish population, but is primarily concerned not with improving labor conditions of workers but with "the creation of a permanent Jewish agricultural proletariat." The organization operates a wide variety of enterprises and runs its own schools. Labor union members must belong to the *Histadrut*. Its enterprises (both agricultural and industrial) are cooperative in form and controlled through a kind of holding company. *Histadrut* dominates mixed agriculture, contract construction, road transport, and has central credit and finance institutions. Many of its activities are subsidized. It remains to be seen how much self-determination the worker achieves in this type of organization. Industry under Arab control is only now appearing, and there are no Arab trade unions.

In Africa, labor unions of white workers have been powerful in improving their conditions. But African labor unions are embryonic, although they have increased in number in the British colonial territories since 1939.[31] The increase has been especially notable in Nigeria, although unions are not always of the European type. In Southern Rhodesia only European labor unions are recognized (except on the railways). In the Union of South Africa, African labor unions are not illegal, but they are denied any power.[32] Unionization of the African workers in the gold fields has been opposed by the employers, but there have been disorganized and spontaneous strikes of African workers, suggesting that united action

---

[29] U.N., *Prelim. Rep. on World Social Situation, 1952*, 176.

[30] Issawi, *Egypt: an Economic and Social Analysis*, 95.

[31] U.K., *The Colonial Empire (1939-47)*, 73.

[32] Union of South Africa, Department of Native Affairs *Report of the Interdepartmental Committee on the Social, Health, and Economic Conditions of Urban Natives*, 1942, 3.

could be effective if it were not hampered by the law. Poor educational facilities also prevent the development of skilled and competent labor organizers in South, East, and central Africa.

In these underdeveloped countries, labor organization is limited to a small part of the labor force, most of which is engaged in agriculture (which is everywhere difficult to organize). Unions do, however, exist on plantations producing hennequin in Mexico, sugar in Cuba, rubber in Malaya, and bananas in Central America. Subsistence farmers and share croppers might organize to obtain better terms from landowners, but do not. Industrial employment typically engages a small proportion of the labor force, but the availability of alternative labor from often over-crowded agriculture necessarily reduces the bargaining power of unions in industry. Many of the population prefer to stay on the land rather than leave for urban areas or mines where conditions are unfamiliar, but usually the number ready to move is sufficient to hold down efforts to raise industrial wages much above the low incomes obtainable on the land. Organization is also impeded by lack of education and of leaders experienced in union organization. Looking to the west for experience, incipient unions see conflict over basic objectives. In socialist countries all union activities are regulated by the state.

d. The State

The state influences labor incomes through its policies regarding property and labor union activities, by direct and indirect regulation of wages and conditions of labor, and through monetary policy.

The state indirectly regulated labor incomes under the feudal system in medieval Europe. Regulation of the amount of land to which the worker had access, and the amount of labor time he was required to apply to the lord's land, determined the sharing of the total produce between the military and priestly classes on the one hand and the cultivators on the other. The numerous sporadic uprisings, which were brutally suppressed, indicate the extent to which the system depended on the state.[33]

Many governments regulate labor union activities to restrict their economic or political power. The more developed capitalist countries formerly prohibited labor organizations, but now grant them considerable though not unlimited freedom. In Britain laws against monopolies, before industrialization, forbade journeymen (or employers) to combine to control a trade, which was also contrary to common law. In 1799 and 1800 the Combination Acts strengthened and consolidated the prohibition, and forbade workers to combine to raise wages and reduce hours of work. All laws against combinations were repealed in 1824, and membership in a union ceased to be a criminal offense. But in 1825 further legislation,

---

[33] Turner, "Economic Discontent in Medieval Europe," *Tasks of Economic History*, 1948, 86.

though retaining the right of workers to form unions, virtually prohibited strikes by prohibiting resort to threats, intimidation, molestation, and obstruction. Beyond the belief that unions obstructed the free operation of the labor market and might become monopolistic, the government was haunted by fear of the workers, and remained so until 1850. The French Revolution, the rebellion in Ireland, the naval mutiny at the Nore in 1797, and unrest due to rising prices and industrialization, all contributed to this fear and hardened the attitude of the state toward organizations of workers known to be discontented because they were suffering from the violent economic changes of the time.

In 1859 the Molestation of Workmen Act authorized the peaceful persuasion of workers to cease working in an effort to raise wages. The Trade Union Act of 1871 withdrew the common law restrictions against unions, permitted them to register as benefit societies, and gave legal protection to their funds. The Criminal Law Amendment Act, passed at the same time, provided for the prosecution of unions molesting, intimidating, and obstructing workers, but was largely repealed in 1875 and 1876. In 1875, the law was changed to prevent interference with the actions of unions unless they would be illegal if committed by an individual, and to authorize peaceful picketing. The law continued to be liberalized until 1926, often in order to reverse judicial decisions. In 1906, the Trade Disputes Act placed the funds of unions beyond damage suits for tortious acts of their members. In 1913 the Trade Union Act authorized unions to raise political funds from their members, provided the objectives were determined by secret ballot and the contributions were not compulsory. Thus they were enabled to engage in politics. But in 1926, when the government withdrew a subsidy to coal mining, and the coal miners struck, the Trade Union Congress authorized a sympathetic strike of practically all unions. The government used the army and volunteers to keep the economy going and asserted that labor was using its organized power against the state, which was a revolutionary act (which was only formally true).

The Trade Union Act of 1927 prohibited strikes designed or calculated to coerce the Government either directly or by inflicting hardship on the community. "Contracting out" of contributions to the political funds of unions was replaced by "contracting in" to hamper political activities. The Act also prohibited non-manual civil service workers from joining unions with other workers, or affiliating with the Trades Union Congress, prohibited strikes with objects other than the furtherance of a trade dispute, and forbade mass picketing. This legislation, bitterly resented by workers in general, was repealed as soon as the Labor Party controlled the government in 1945.

In France, all associations of masters or men were prohibited in 1791. In 1803 Napoleon restored the *livret* (a book carried by workers, bearing the names of all their employers), and no man could be employed unless his record with his previous employer was satisfactory. In 1834, the law forbade associations of twenty or more persons, if they were part of some larger association. Until 1865 the word of the master was decisive as to wages due, and strikes and picketing were illegal. Nevertheless, there were a few unions between 1815 and 1845 (particularly among the weavers in Lyon and the printers in Paris). Unions were tolerated after 1868 and restrictions on them finally removed in 1884. The Vichy government, at the behest of the German occupation authorities, abolished all unions of the pre-war type during the war of 1939-45. It required membership in unions, but deprived them of most of their previous rights, including the right to bargain and strike. The right to form unions was restored after 1945, but collective bargaining only in 1950.

In Germany the right to collective bargaining was restricted until 1869, although the right to form a union was not. The anti-socialist laws passed in 1878 hindered the political activities of unions. Anti-union legislation was abrogated in 1890, the social security measures introduced by Bismarck being intended to weaken the unions. But they were still seriously hampered. Unions could be sued, but could not sue. Strikes were dealt with by the police. Many employers, increasingly antagonistic to the unions under the Weimar Republic, supported the National Socialist Party, which after 1933 prohibited membership in labor unions, seized their property, made past membership punishable, and established the *Arbeitsfront* to take over union property and administer government policy regarding the utilization of labor. The unions recovered their rights and much of their property after 1945.

In the U.S.A. labor union activities probably encountered more legal obstruction until 1933 than in any other democratic country.[34] Employers contended that all unions were illegal under the law of conspiracy taken over from Britain. But juries were loth to convict, and the doctrine was finally abandoned in a Massachusetts court decision in 1842. Between 1860 and 1880 several states specifically authorized unions in an effort to improve working conditions. But the status of unions depended on state law and judicial interpretation (partly of the federal constitution). For long the courts held that workers not only had the right to, but also must, bargain individually, although they might join a union if the employer did not object. The courts enforced "yellow dog" contracts between workers and employers not to join a union, such contracts having appeared in the 1880s. They also held that state laws forbidding such contracts were an unconstitutional interference with the right of an employer to choose his workers. In 1917 the Supreme Court held that a union may not seek to organize workers who have made such contracts (Hitchman Coal and Coke Co. v. Mitchell, 245 U.S. 229, 1917), but in 1921, it condemned only the methods used to organize and held that injunctions to prevent any

---

[34] Marquand, *Organized Labor in Four Continents*, XI.

attempts to organize were improper (American Steel Foundries v. Tri Cities Central Trades Council, 257 U.S. 184, 1921), and later accepted the state and federal laws (including the Norris-LaGuardia Act of 1932) holding such contracts unenforceable.

Strikes were not illegal, but in applying the law of conspiracy, the courts appraised the objectives and methods of the strike. Violence and threats of violence were illegal, but not non-violent picketing. In 1921 a state statute condemning noisy, abusive, but non-violent picketing was held unconstitutional (Truax v. Corrigan, 257 U.S. 312, 1921) and in 1932 the Norris-LaGuardia Act sought to enlarge the legal scope for peaceful picketing under the Clayton Act. A strike lawful in method might be unlawful in purpose. Higher wages, shorter hours, and better conditions were legal objectives, but injury of the employer, the closed shop (in some states), and, generally, the sympathetic strike were not. Whether or not a strike was illegal, it might (until 1932) be prevented in practice by an injunction.

The injunction in general prevents one party to a dispute from destroying the remedy that the other might have, but in labor cases it was a speedy means of obstructing a strike. The continuance of a strike after an injunction was punishable as contempt of court. The issuance of an injunction was frequently, therefore, more important than the outcome of the suit. The injunction could be obtained from a judge chosen by the employer or his representative, without a public hearing. But in 1932 the Norris-LaGuardia Act abolished federal injunctions against conspiracies to instigate a strike if instigation was without fraud or violence. By requiring jury trial it also delayed trials for violation of an injunction. A number of states have laws similar to the Norris-LaGuardia Act.

Legislation against monopolies and restraint of trade (e.g., the Sherman Act of 1890 and the Clayton Act of 1914) were more speedily used against labor unions than against monopolies among sellers of goods. The Danbury Hatter's case (Loewe v. Lawlor, 208 U.S. 274, 1908) in which union funds were held to be liable for damage resulting from the boycott of a non-union employer to induce him to recognize the union, aroused fear of a broader attack on the unions under the Act, and the Clayton Act in 1914 declared labor not to be a commodity, that unions of workers for mutual assistance were not conspiracies in restraint of trade, and attempted to restrict the use of injunctions. But judicial interpretation largely frustrated the efforts of Congress. In 1922 the courts decided that labor unions, although unincorporated, may be sued in their own names—which renders funds collected to finance strikes subject to execution for torts (Coronado Coal Company v. United Mine Workers, 259 U.S. 344, 1922). In fact, a heavy fine was imposed on John L. Lewis and the United Mine Workers in 1946.

The labor unions were not emancipated until the depression of the

1930s. In 1932 the Norris-LaGuardia Act restricted the use of injunctions. In 1933 the National Industrial Recovery Act provided (among other things) that every code of fair competition under the Act must include a provision recognizing the right of workers to bargain collectively through any organization of their own choosing. The National Labor Relations Act, passed in 1935 after the National Industrial Recovery Act had been held unconstitutional, preserved the right of collective bargaining by establishing a list of unfair labor practices, including the obstruction of labor organization, victimization of workers, and refusal to engage in genuine collective bargaining. In 1947, however, the Taft-Hartley Act continued the list of unfair labor practices but forbade the "closed shop" (one in which none but union members may be employed), restricted the "union shop" (in which all employees must join a union), prohibited contributions by unions to political activities, and obstructed the appointment of members of the Communist Party to high offices in labor unions. The union shop is permitted if a majority of all workers in the bargaining unit (not of those voting) request the employer to bargain about it, and if he agrees to it. The list of unfair union practices includes the coercion of workers, secondary (and possibly all) boycotts, and jurisdictional strikes. Both unions and employers may sue for damage resulting from breach of collective bargaining contracts (the significance of which provision against employers has not yet become clear). Officers of unions wishing to use the National Labor Relations Board procedures must file detailed financial statements with the Secretary of Labor, and affidavits that they are not members of the Communist Party. In the event of a strike causing a national emergency, the President may appoint a Board of inquiry. If the Board finds that there is a national emergency, an injunction can be obtained against the strike for 90 days, at the end of which the President can refer the matter to Congress.[35]

In other capitalist countries, restrictions on discrimination against union members and requirements of collective bargaining are uncommon because employers have voluntarily accepted unions. In Sweden, however, employers and workers can be required to negotiate in good faith, and the right of association is guaranteed. In Canada, seven of the nine provinces in 1937 and 1938 granted the right of workers to organize for lawful purposes without employer interference. Employers must bargain with representatives of the majority of the employees. In 1939 the Dominion Government established penalties for discrimination against union members. In some countries (Sweden, Norway, and Denmark) strikes and lock-outs during the life of an agreement are illegal. Machinery for applying a collective bargain in part of an industry to the whole of it, or to the whole of the industry in a particular region, has been provided by the government

---

[35] Witte, "Labor Management Relations under the Taft-Hartley Act," XXV, *Harvard Business Review*, 1947, 554.

in Britain, France, the Netherlands, Belgium, Switzerland, New Zealand, some Australian states, and some Canadian provinces. The British Cotton Manufacturing Act of 1934 applied the principle to weaving, in which there were many small shops. In 1936 the Minister of Labor in France was empowered to transform collective agreements into a legalized code for the whole of an industry or region, only on the request of both parties; the government in 1950 refused the request of the labor unions that wage contracts be automatically extended to all shops and factories in an industry, but authorized such extension by the Minister of Labor. The 1936 law in Belgium and the 1937 law in Holland are similar to the French law of 1936, except that the Belgian law is limited to agreements about hours of labor. In New Zealand, wage fixing by the Court of Arbitration permits collective agreements affecting the majority of workers in an industry, to be made binding on all employers in the industry. In Switzerland since 1941 both the cantonal and federal governments may extend agreements.[36] In New Zealand all workers are required by law to belong to a union. If a worker refuses to join, the union finds a worker who will join, and the employer is compelled then to fire the non-unionist. This provision results in a large proportion of inactive union members, and in power to vigorous organizers largely free from member control. In Japan labor unions were seriously hampered until 1945. Both the Trade Union law of that year and the constitution of 1946 guarantee the right of organization and collective bargaining.[37]

In the less industrialized countries the formation of labor unions in fact, if not in law, usually waits upon the consent of the state. This consent is slowly forthcoming and often limited. In Chile labor unions cannot exist without specific authority to acquire a legal personality (which permits the acquisition of property and making of contracts). Only recognized unions can legally bargain collectively (although, in fact, others do), and appear before government conciliation authorities. Collective bargaining takes place within a framework of government mediation and sometimes arbitration. But the government does not always exercise its full powers. Many unions are fairly wealthy. They engage in collective bargaining and mutual benefit and social service work. Unions are active in Mexico and Argentina. In India employers are required by law to recognize unions, and they have achieved a place in tripartite conferences among government, employers, and labor. In Iran a law of 1946 permits workers in the same factory or trade to form unions. But if they exceed their rights or disturb the public peace, the government may require them to select new officers, or dissolve, or it may suspend the union. In 1939 the international

[36] U.S. Dept. of Labor, *Wage Trends and Wage Policies: Various Foreign Countries,* 46.

[37] Reubens, Beatrice G., "Social Legislation in Japan," *Far Eastern Survey,* 1949, 269.

Penal Sanctions (Indigenous Workers) Convention, providing for the progressive abandonment of penal sanctions for specified breaches of contract, was ratified by the British government, and considerable progress has been made with its application to colonial territories.[38]

In Russia the revolution occurred in a primarily agrarian country without unions. Such unions now exist in Russia and east Europe. Membership is not compulsory but the unions constitute the personnel department of the state (Ch. 20) and may not strike or bargain collectively over labor conditions. In China, however, a new trade union law in 1950 provided for the establishment of labor unions in all enterprises, public, cooperative, and private. In private enterprises they negotiate collective agreements, but in public and cooperative enterprises they merely sign them. All unions are directed to assist in fulfilling the production plan. They are financed by dues, allocations by employers, and state subsidies.[39]

Direct government interference with conditions of work, now common in industrialized countries, generally increases the net satisfactions from work. Inhumane conditions in the early stages of industrialization were often defended on the ground that conditions of labor, like wages, should be determined by free bargaining between workers and employers. But sooner or later these conditions have generated a public sense of guilt, and governments have regulated them. Such legislation often increases productivity by lightening the physical burden of work, reducing invalidity, and preventing the health of women and children from being undermined. Much of such legislation has been first limited to women and children, on the ground that they are weak negotiators (partly because they do not organize effectively) and that society is interested in protecting the productive power of workers. But humanitarian feeling, and fear of disgruntled workers, have both been important. In some countries, in some industries, legislation regarding hours of work has been applied to men, although hours of labor have often been left to union bargaining.

Governments do not customarily directly control wages in general in capitalist countries. Organized workers insist on bargaining over wages. The French government, however, controlled wages from 1939 to 1950 in order to obtain resources to rehabilitate and modernize the economy. Having suspended collective bargaining over wages in 1939, wages were placed under the control of the Minister of Labor, who continued to exercise this power under the Vichy government. Wages were held down to force workers into war production industries (particularly in Germany). After the liberation in 1945 the government decreed a basic minimum wage, with adjustments for geographic and cost of living zones, and for five job classifications in which the wages were fixed in relation to the lowest category. The legislation of 1945 also set a percentage by which the

[38] U.K., *The Colonial Empire* (1939-47), 78.
[39] I.L.O., *Ind. and Lab.*, Nov. 1, 1950, 365.

average maximum wage could exceed the minimum wage. The wage policies pursued under this arrangement threw much of the burden of postwar rehabilitation on workers. In 1945 real wages were about 50% of 1938. Inflation raised the cost of living in the absence of effective price control, and wages and family allowances were not increased as fast as prices. In 1947 hourly wages were 60 to 65% of 1939, but labor incomes had not fallen by this amount because workers were working longer hours, there was less unemployment, and they were receiving family allowances. Some French economists asserted that the whole share of labor (including government transfer payments) was about the same in 1947 as in 1939, although this is improbable.[40] But by 1949 real earnings, net of taxes and contributions, were 80-104% of 1938, but 92-119% if family allowances are included.[41]

The government has also controlled wages in the Netherlands since 1945, and real wages have been reduced since 1948.[42] In Belgium the National Labor conference (representing employers and labor unions) advised the government on wage changes after September 1944, and the government usually made the recommended changes by decree.[43] It has been agreed that wages shall be adjusted to the cost of living index. In Denmark also, the government has controlled wages.[44] In Finland and Norway wages are adjusted to changes in the cost of living, and in Canada the government directly controlled wages from 1941 to 1946. Real weekly earnings in 1945 were 37% above 1939, but in 1946 about 22%.[45]

Compulsory arbitration in Australia and New Zealand has virtually required the arbitration courts to regulate wages and the share of labor in the national product, although there is little legislative definition of the policies to be pursued. Labor disputes almost prostrated the Australian economy in the 1890s. Compulsory arbitration appealed to the middle class as a just device for recognizing the principle of collective bargaining without surrender to powerful unions or to the intransigence of employers. Boards were established to control wages in Victoria in 1896 and later in other provinces, and the Commonwealth Court of Conciliation and Arbitration was operating by 1905. In 1907 the Court set a minimum wage for unskilled workers about 27% above the lowest wage then paid. Since that time the minimum wage has been periodically adjusted for changes in the cost of living. The minimum real wage was reduced 10% in 1931 as an antidepression measure, but raised again in 1937 to about the level in 1907.

40 U.N., *Inflationary and Deflationary Tendencies*, 17.

41 U.N., *Econ. Surv. of Europe in 1949*, 24; U.S. Dept. of Labor, *Wage Trends and Wage Policies in Various Foreign Countries*, 1948, 16 ff.

42 U.N., *Econ. Surv. of Europe since the War*, 1953, 72.

43 U.S. Dept. of Labor, *Wage Trends and Wage Policies: Various Foreign Countries*, 32.

44 *Ibid.*, 28.

45 *Ibid.*, 49.

Most other wages, being expressed as percentages of the minimum, rise and fall with it, although not always by the same amount. Under this system between 1911 and 1948 real wages rose 43% while weekly hours of labor fell 18% and average hourly real wages rose 75%. Between 1914 and 1939 real wages rose 34% in Australia, compared with 100% in the U.S.A. and 50% in Britain.[46]

The New Zealand arrangements have been somewhat similar to the Australian. After 1930 the Court reduced cash wages less than prices fell. After 1932 the powers of the Court were curtailed, but restored again in 1936 by the Labor government. In 1936 all reductions in wages were restored, and real wages were about 9% above 1929. The Court establishes a "basic wage" based on the needs of a man with a wife and three children. By an order of the Court in 1936 this wage became the minimum for all male workers governed by awards of the Court. By an act of 1945, however, Parliament established specific minimum wages for males and adult females, differing from and superseding those of the Court. These minima, which apply whether an award exists or not, were amended in 1947 and 1949. The Court also makes pronouncements as to "standard rates" for the principal grades of labor (unskilled, semi-skilled, and skilled) that merely guide the Court in making awards and in appraising voluntary industrial agreements (which become subject to the sanctions available to the Court, if it accepts them). The Court makes specific awards, based in general on the "standard rates." It also makes general orders amending simultaneously all rates of wages under its jurisdiction. In 1950 the government abolished the power of the Court to set maximum wages, and the Court issued a general order raising by 5% all rates of pay in awards and industrial agreements accepted by it to take account of the reduction of subsidies on consumer goods. Separate authorities, however, regulate the wages of agricultural workers, waterside workers, coal miners, employees on public works and government railroads, postal workers, public officials, and hospital board employees.[47] Wages in Brazil, are also fixed by labor courts.

In socialist countries, wages are determined by the government as part of the general economic plan. Money wages are determined in outline in the five-year and more frequent plans. The five-year plans include a table of basic wage rates for major sections of the economy. In successive plans, however, these tables have become less detailed. All proposals for changes in wage payments must be approved by a sub-committee of commissars on relations between wages and prices. In Hungary wages are determined by a National Wage Fixing Board functioning under the Prime Minister through the Secretary General of the Superior Economic Council.[48] In

[46] Wood (ed.), *Australia: its Resources and Development,* 236; Galenson (ed.), *Comparative Labor Movements,* 179, 216, 222.

[47] I.L.O., *Ind. and Lab.,* Nov. 15, 1951.

[48] I.L.O., *Ind. and Lab.,* Mar. 1949, 179.

Czechoslovakia all wage contracts must be approved by the Minister of Social Assistance in agreement with the labor union organization. The Minister may modify rates of pay and other benefits and introduce piece work.[49] In Yugoslavia in 1946 wages and salaries were fixed by the government, but unions might request higher wages. They were not forbidden to strike, although few strikes have occurred. Some 80% of the workers belong to unions.

In these socialist countries wages and the prices of consumer goods are controlled in the short run to ensure that disbursements on payrolls and other sources of consumer demand about equal the value of the supply of consumer goods at the prices fixed. Periodic shortages, however, indicate that this objective is not always attained. Thus real wages can be raised by government decisions to reduce prices. Since 1947 the Russian government has announced a wide range of price reductions in the spring, those in 1953 being larger than any since 1950, adding about 12% to consumer purchasing power.[50] In 1954 it was announced that the average price of goods bought by workers had fallen 57% since 1947, although the average price of foodstuffs was 14% above 1940, and of consumer goods generally 27% above 1939. The real wages and salaries of urban workers rose some 25% between 1937 and 1952, when they were 72% to 103% of 1928 (according to the index of cost of living used).[51] The U.S. Bureau of Labor Statistics calculated that the average worker in Russia had to work 43% longer in 1954 than in 1928 to purchase a constant amount of the seven basic foods.[52] Ultimately labor incomes depend on the volume of production of consumer goods as there are virtually no non-labor incomes. In most of these countries under the dictatorship of the proletariat, labor incomes are lower than in capitalist societies and in some in Eastern Europe lower than under the previous political organization of the same society. In some (e.g. Russia) productivity has been low because previous economic development had been small. In all such countries labor's share of total output is low because of relatively large allocations of resources to development and armament.

In Yugoslavia production decisions were decentralized in 1952, and each enterprise was authorized to dispose of its profits (after taxes) as the workers' council for the enterprise decided. Many chose to distribute them as bonuses on wages, but in 1953 the taxes paid by enterprises were increased and the distribution of profits among workers was severely restricted.[53]

Some governments have set minimum wages for some sections of the labor force, during the 20th century on the ground that the poorest paid

[49] *Ibid.*, Apr. 1, 1949, 283.
[50] U.N., *Econ. Surv. of Europe in 1953*, 49.
[51] Chapman, "Real Wages in the Soviet Union," *Rev. Econ. and Stat.*, May 1954.
[52] *N.Y. Times*, Apr. 28, 1954.
[53] U.N., *Econ. Surv. of Europe in 1953*, 115, 118.

workers are too ignorant, poor, or otherwise repressed to be able to bargain for the marginal value of their product. Where the marginal value of their product is low, it is argued that it should be raised by improved methods of production or workers should be diverted into other occupations. In Britain minimum wages were first prescribed for "sweated industries" in which wages were "unreasonably low." The unionization of unskilled workers in the 1890s, and the strikes organized by the new aggressive unions, acquainted the public with the poor conditions in some industries and led to the Trade Boards Act of 1909. This act permitted the establishment of Trade Boards (consisting of representatives of employers and workers in equal numbers, and three government representatives) to establish minimum wages in the industry. Between 1918, when the act was extended to poorly organized trades, and 1937, 37 new boards were set up, but few have appeared since 1937. By 1944, there were Trade Boards for fifty-two trades covering 1.2 million workers. In the earlier period enforcement proved difficult because the courts were antagonistic to attempts to enforce the decisions of the Boards. Boards similar to Trade Boards have been established in other industries where wages are not necessarily low or workers unorganized.[54] In 1945 the Trade Boards gave place to Wages Councils with power to fix not only minimum but also actual wages, as well as a guaranteed workweek, and to recommend on any matters affecting the welfare of workers. The Councils are appointed by the Minister of Labor on application by representatives of workers and employers, or on his own initiative if he is satisfied that there is no adequate voluntary machinery for fixing wages and conditions of work.[55]

In France the government continued to set minimum wages after collective bargaining was restored in 1950. A High Commission for Collective Bargaining (consisting of 15 representatives of labor unions, 15 of employers, 3 of the government, and 3 of family organizations) determines the cost of living of an unmarried unskilled laborer in Paris, but the minimum wage is determined by the Minister of Labor. Arrangements were made to adjust the minimum automatically with changes in the cost of living. Most other European countries have minimum wage regulations.

Some state governments sought to prescribe minimum wages in the U.S.A. but the Supreme Court (in Adkins v. Children's Hospital, 261, U.S. 525, 1923) held such legislation unconstitutional because a socially desirable minimum might deprive the employer of property by compelling him to pay more than the value of the labor. But in 1935, the Court rejected this precedent and held that low wages could be a social evil, employers

---

[54] The Road-Haulage (Wages) Act 1938, the Agricultural Wages (England and Wales) Act 1924, the Agricultural Wages (Scotland) Act 1937, the Cotton Manufacturing Industry (Temporary Provisions) Act of 1934, and the Catering Wages Act of 1943.

[55] U.S. Dept. of Labor, *Wage Trends and Wages Policies in Various Foreign Countries*, Bulletin 934, 1, 7.

were not entitled to complete freedom from the exercise of the police power, the police power could be used to relieve one class of the oppressed (for example, women), without being discriminatory because it failed to eliminate all oppression, and that the state had a special interest in the protection of women.

Until 1937 minima were set only for women, but in that year the Federal Fair Labor Standards Act established a minimum wage for a week of prescribed duration of work in occupations within the reach of the federal government, namely, employment in interstate commerce and in the production of goods for interstate commerce (which includes about 24 million workers). The law established a standard work week of 40 hours, work in excess of which must be paid at one-and-one-half times the regular rate. The minimum wage was 30 cents an hour from 1939 to 1945, 40 cents an hour from 1945 to 1950, and 75 cents an hour after 1950. The Administrator may, however, permit a lower minimum for particular industries. Children under 16 are not permitted in manufacturing and mining, or in occupations where the work is declared particularly hazardous to their health or well-being. State laws affecting a further 4.5 million workers prescribe minima from 60 to 75 cents an hour.[56]

State minimum wages are beginning to appear in newly developing countries. In Chile there has been a minimum wage for white collar workers since 1937, prescribed by regions and adjusted annually to take account of changes in the cost of living.[57] In Uruguay a minimum was prescribed for port workers in 1926, packing plant employees loading and unloading ships in 1930, and employees on public works in 1927.[58] But a proposal to set a general minimum was defeated. Minimum wages are also beginning to be prescribed in British colonial territories where labor is not extensively organized. Tripartite wage boards are empowered in some colonies to fix wages in some occupations, with the consent of the governor.[59] In Southern Rhodesia, minimum wages aimed at protecting European workers sometimes prevent African workers from being employed on the same work at a lower wage. Finally, there is a minimum wage in Russia, but in 1928 average wages in large-scale industry were nine times the minimum.[60]

Some Latin American countries require employers to share profits with workers. In Chile, where there are industrial unions (consisting of all workers in a mine or industrial establishment), all profit over 10% on capital is shared with workers. The employer may pay the workers 10% of the profit or 6% of the wage bill in the previous year, including all payments to workers. One-half of the profit participation is paid direct to the workers, and

---

56 U.S., *President's Economic Report*, 1954, 100.
57 Ellsworth, *Chile: an Economy in Transition*, 100.
58 Hanson, *Utopia in Uruguay*, 141.
59 U.K., *The Colonial Empire* (1939-47), 74.
60 Bergson, A., *The Structure of Soviet Wages*, 163.

the other half to the union, the government controlling the expenditure of the union's share. Of the half paid direct to the workers, one-half is distributed in proportion to daily wages and the other half on the basis of attendance records. In Peru companies whose profits exceed 10% must pay workers an annual bonus, depending on their rate of pay and length of service.

Monetary policy affects real labor incomes because rising prices generally accompany increased employment and some reduction in real wages, whereas falling prices accompany increased unemployment but rising real wages. But it is difficult to segregate the effect of monetary policy, and there have been no very reliable figures regarding the cost of living and real wages until recent years. In Britain and France real wages fell between 1750 and 1815, the cost of living rising more than money wages. After 1818 real wages rose some 10% in Britain, money wages falling less than prices. But in France there was little trend in real wages, the cost of living, or money wages. From 1850 to 1891 real wages rose some 85% in Britain, France, and the U.S.A., while the cost of living trended slowly downward. Between 1900 and 1939, real wages rose little in England, while prices rose. But in France real wages rose 8%.[61] Real wages and prices changed little in the U.S.A. between 1900 and 1929, but in the depression, from 1929 to 1933, real wages rose somewhat as wages fell less than prices, but unemployment was severe.

During the war of 1939-45 all the capitalist countries at war suffered from inflationary pressures, and attempted to restrict price increases by price control and rationing. In general, incomes from labor (and agriculture) increased during this period. After 1945 prices rose in most countries, but labor unions have probably secured increases in money wages more nearly in step with increases in the cost of living, with the result that inflation has had less effect on real wages than formerly. In the U.S.A., Britain, and Chile prices and real wages rose between 1945 and 1948. In France, Japan, and Holland real wages fell.[62]

In predominantly agrarian countries, changes in the purchasing power of money affect labor incomes according to the extent to which contracts are made in money. Agricultural producers often hold produce rather than money in times of rising prices, and sharecroppers gain, at least from the increasing value of their share of the crop. Since 1939, however, prices have risen more rapidly in many of these countries than cash incomes. In India, for instance, rising prices between 1939 and 1945 seriously reduced real wages in agriculture (in Bengal about 27% between 1939-40 and 1942-3).[63] Per capita food consumption in calories fell nearly 15% from 1934-8 to

---

[61] Kuczynski, *A Short History of Labor Conditions in Britain*, 18, 53, 92; Kuczynski, *A Short History of Labor Conditions in France*, 42, 77, 169; Clark, *op. cit.* 1st, 170.
[62] Harris, *Economic Planning*, 83.
[63] Famine Inquiry Commission *Report*, 473.

1949. Rationing was partial, the price of rationed supplies was not much below black market prices, and income distribution shifted in favor of profits.[64] In Brazil between 1914 and 1938, the cost of living rose 218% and wages 215%, but until 1930 real wages were below those in 1914, and between 1930 and 1935 they were higher.[65]

Fluctuations in business activity, accompanied by recurrent unemployment, have caused complete loss of labor incomes for some workers in most capitalist countries (Ch. 19). This loss has been serious during the 20th century in most capitalist countries, and most serious in the U.S.A. Furthermore, fluctuations in the more developed capitalist countries have been transmitted to the less-developed countries through falling prices and shrinking demand for their exports, e.g., Argentina (meat, wheat), Australia (meat, wool), New Zealand (dairy products, wool, and meat), South Africa (fruit), Cuba (sugar), Brazil (coffee), Malaya (rubber), Chile (copper), and Bolivia and Malaya (tin). The impact upon workers comes partly in unemployment (sometimes concealed) and partly in reductions in real wages.

C. The Structure of National Labor Incomes

The foregoing national averages depend on the labor incomes received in different activities, and on the number of workers in each activity. If everyone had equal access to every job, there would be more uniformity in labor incomes within a country than there is. Differences in income in different activities would cause shifts in supply from the lower to the higher paid occupations. In fact, about half the rise in earnings in Britain from 1880 to 1910 was caused by workers moving into better-paid jobs.[66] But people may believe that there is less difference in net satisfactions from jobs (including non-monetary satisfactions and dissatisfactions) than in money incomes. People differ in their productive qualities, and there may be a smaller supply in relation to demand in some kinds of labor than in others. This shortage may be temporary (owing to lack of training), or biological. People differ in their attitudes to different kinds of jobs. If enough people are repelled by a job, a wage differential is necessary to obtain the necessary supply. There are often obstacles to movement due to personal inertia, the cost of movement, lack of knowledge of opportunities, legal obstacles to physical movement, and control over entry into jobs (e.g., by labor unions). All these conditions obstruct any tendency to uniform money incomes. And at any time the tendencies to uniformity may be only partly worked out. Differences are, therefore, likely to be especially important in countries in process of reallocating their labor supply (Ch. 20).

---

[64] U.N., *Inflationary and Deflationary Tendencies*, 25.
[65] Spiegel, *op. cit.*, 97.
[66] Bowley, *Wages and Income in the U.K. since 1860*, App. C.

1. Differentials Between Agricultural and Other Labor Incomes

Labor incomes from agriculture are usually lower than those in most other sectors.[67] But the differences are difficult to measure because agricultural incomes often combine incomes from labor and property. The difference between agricultural and other wages is wider than that between agricultural labor incomes in general and other labor incomes, where agricultural wage earners are worse off than agricultural entrepreneurs. But agricultural incomes may include income from the work of more than one member of the family, and it is difficult to allow for produce consumed by the producer and differences in the cost of housing, clothing, and the like.

Agricultural wages were only 25% of non-agricultural in pre-war years (Table 68) in the U.S.A., but in 1948 average net income from all sources

TABLE 68

Average Annual Wage of Farm Workers as a Percentage of Average Annual Wage of Non-Agricultural Workers in Selected Countries*

Country	Period	Percentage
U.S.A.	1937	25
Canada	1937	26
Great Britain	1937	36
France	1932	52
Italy	1938	43
Germany	1932	35
Norway	1937	30
Sweden	1937	30
Finland	1938	39
Hungary	1934	43
India	1931	54
Japan	1936	22
Australia	1937	62
New Zealand	1937	49
Spain	1937	16

* Clark, *Conditions of Economic Progress* 2d, 456. Agricultural wages include income in kind. Non-wage incomes from agriculture not included in agricultural wages.

per person for people living on farms was about 60% of that of the non-farm population. Agricultural earnings were falling in relation to industrial earnings during the 1930s but there was more visible unemployment in industry, and by 1953 realized net income from farming per farm family worker was about 70% above the 1935-9 average (after allowing for price changes).[68] Agricultural wages were also low, compared with non-agricultural, in pre-war years in Canada, Britain, Japan, and Spain, but relatively high in Australia, India, and France (Table 68). The differential may be low in the early stages of industrialization, when non-agricultural wages

[67] U.N., *National Income and its Distribution in Underdeveloped Countries*, 7.
[68] U.S., *President's Economic Report*, 1954, 181.

are also low (e.g., in India). In Russia the real incomes of farmers compared favorably with those of industrial workers, although payments for agricultural labor in labor days results in considerable differences in agricultural incomes.[69]

Industrialization withdraws labor from agriculture, but technical progress in agriculture may reduce the labor needed per unit of output[70] (e.g., in the U.S.A., Britain, and recently France). Mechanization also reduces the demand for labor to produce fodder for animals that provide power in agriculture. Increases in population increase the demand for food that, however, may be imported. Agricultural exports maintain the demand for agricultural labor, although competition from other source of supply may reduce export markets (e.g., for the U.S.A.). Changes in food habits also affect the demand for agricultural labor. The greater proportion of the diet taken in animal protein, the greater is the labor component in the agricultural output. During the 1930s this component somewhat declined in the U.S.A., and since 1939, it has declined in a number of countries (largely because economic pressures resulting from war have necessitated reduced meat consumption). On the supply side the population has increased faster in rural than in urban areas.

Changes in the differences between agricultural and non-agricultural labor incomes depend, therefore, on the importance of these forces affecting relative supply of and demand for labor in the two sectors, and the speed with which the labor supply is reallocated. In Britain the outflow of workers from agriculture after 1860 reduced the absolute number of workers almost enough to keep pace with falling demand for them. But in most countries, excepting Australia and New Zealand, the outflow was not sufficient to prevent a widening gap between agricultural and non-agricultural wages.[71] In the U.S.A. there was for long a great demand for labor in agriculture to bring new lands into use (partly to produce exports). Nevertheless, agriculture has taken a diminishing proportion of all new labor coming on to the market (42% between 1870 and 1880, 17% between 1890 and 1900, and none between 1900 and 1930). Between 1929 and 1937 labor flowed out of industry into agriculture.[72] Since 1938 wages in agriculture, forestry, and coal mining have generally risen in Europe in relation to other wages. In Denmark and Britain wages in agriculture are higher in relation to those in industry than at the beginning of the century. In Britain increased demands for domestic agricultural production and the unionization of agricultural labor since 1939 had doubled the farmers' share of the national income by 1949.[73]

Labor unions have appeared in agriculture in almost all west European

69 Bergson, *op. cit.*, *Quar. Jour. Econ.*, Aug. 1950, 424.
70 U.N., *Econ. Bull. for Europe*, Vol. II, No. 5, 1950, 53.
71 Clark, *op. cit.* 1st, 230.
72 Clark, *Economics of 1960*, 96.
73 Seers, *op. cit.*, 55.

countries during the 20th century. By collective bargaining they determine the welfare of agricultural workers in Scandinavian countries, Britain, western Germany, Australia, and Portugal. They have been important in the Netherlands since 1900 (they organized a six-months strike in the 1930s), but in Britain only since 1939. In the Netherlands a Protestant, a Catholic and a general union (with a total membership of 80,000) are co-ordinated in the Agricultural Workers' Union Council, which participates with farm employers in a General Council for Agriculture; workers are said to have achieved very considerable gains in wages, vacations, and old-age insurance.[74] In some of these countries unions participate in making government policy for agricultural workers.

Governments influence labor reallocations when they seek to maintain the price of agricultural produce which tends to maintain the demand for agricultural labor but does not always keep agricultural incomes up. Wage earners may be encouraged to remain in agriculture, or even to enter it, or those in agriculture may be encouraged to maintain a high rate of production. But part of the benefits of such state activity goes to landowners. In the past, governments have sometimes sought control of mobility directly. In Britain when the towns began to attract workers from agriculture, and agricultural wages tended to rise in spite of an increase in sheep raising, the Statute of Artificers of 1562-3 was passed to suppress the rise in agricultural wages by compelling all persons between the ages of 12 and 60, not engaged in manufacturing, commercial, or maritime pursuits, and not having independeont means, to engage in agriculture. The attempt was in general abortive, "but the combined pressures of a growing population and the law kept enough on the land to rob their labor of the scarcity value which their predecessors had enjoyed in the later fourteenth century."[75] Governments may also seek to hold down agricultural wages, as the British parliament did for 30 years after the plague of 1348. The Statute of Artificers above mentioned may have been intended to regulate wages according to the cost of living. But the local Justices of the Peace who were empowered to regulate wages were closer to employers than to workers, and often failed to raise wages when prices rose.[76] The Spanish government in 1932 forbade agricultural workers to leave their villages (to prevent an increase in urban unemployment) and prohibited mechanization in agriculture.[77]

But in recent years governments have more actively sought to keep workers in agriculture by bringing their conditions of work more nearly in line with those in urban employment.[78] In Norway, where wages are linked to the cost of living, the government agreed in 1950 that, if no

---

[74] *For. Agric.*, April 1950.
[75] Clapham, *op. cit.*, 214.
[76] *Ibid.*, 213.
[77] U.N., *Econ. Surv. of Europe in 1953*, 146.
[78] U.N., *Progress in Land Reform*, Ch. 4.

other means were available to link farm incomes and industrial wages, agricultural prices would be regulated to increase farm incomes by 4.25 million Norwegian kroner for every *ore* increase in hourly wages for industrial workers. In Finland, where wages are also linked to the cost of living, it was decided in 1951 to maintain a fixed relation between agricultural and other incomes. In Britain a tripartite board fixes minimum wages for a prescribed number of hours of work, fixes overtime rates, evaluates non-monetary benefits, and regulates paid holidays. Somewhat similar arrangements exist in Belgium. In Norway and Sweden hours of labor, paid holidays, and limitations on the employment of women and children are all regulated by law. Recent legislation in West Germany provides for works councils on farms with a minimum of ten workers. In Spain the government regulates wages and working conditions. In Australia and New Zealand, supply and demand conditions have favored agricultural workers, but decisions by the Arbitration Courts have been of limited influence. In Canada and the U.S.A. there is little union organization and governments do not actively regulate conditions in agriculture. There are minimum wages for immigrants in Canada and for Mexican workers temporarily in the U.S.A., where some state minimum wage laws apply to agriculture. Thus any tendency for industrialization to close the gap between agricultural and non-agricultural incomes operates, at best, alongside a great many other forces, not all of which operate in the same direction.

In predominantly agrarian countries these factors operate with different force and sometimes in a different direction from those in industrializing countries. There is little demand for labor in industry, and little mechanization of agriculture, to expel people from agriculture. But imports of industrial goods from developed countries compete with native craft goods and force former craftsmen into agriculture. Imports (especially of textiles) into India expelled many craft workers into agriculture; the number of agricultural laborers is reported to have been about 25.879 million in 1911, and 31.480 in 1931.[79] Many crafts were similarly destroyed in England during the late 18th and early 19th centuries, but rising demands for labor in industry had an offsetting effect, whereas in India displaced craft workers were compelled to enter an already overcrowded agriculture. These forces combine to prevent any increase in (or to depress) agricultural incomes, and population increases typically magnify these effects. But development abroad creating a demand for agricultural exports (of tropical fruits, coffee, tea, cotton, jute, sisal, and the like) have somewhat offset these tendencies.

Labor unions are of little importance except on plantations, and government regulation can achieve little in the face of heavy competition for work even at low wages. Nevertheless, some Latin American countries

---

[79] Wadia and Merchant, *op. cit.*, 256.

include some agricultural workers in their general labor legislation (e.g., Cuba, the Dominican Republic, Ecuador, and Haiti). Minimum wages are set for the larger agricultural enterprises in Puerto Rico, Cuba, Argentina, and Venezuela.[80] In Uruguay a minimum wage was prescribed in 1923 for agricultural workers on estates, varying with the tax value of the estate, but was not enforced.[81] In India the Minimum Wages Act of 1948 required the provincial governments to set minimum wages by the end of 1953, and a number of provinces have done so. Such minimum wages are also authorized in Burma and the Philippines (where they are widely evaded), and are contemplated in Pakistan. In the Middle East, Israeli legislation regarding minimum wages and other conditions of labor applies to agriculture, and the Egyptian government authorized minimum-wage fixation in 1952 as part of the agrarian reform.

In socialist countries differentials between agricultural and industrial labor incomes are explicitly determined in the production plan with a view to achieving the allocation of labor necessary to fulfill the plan. In Russia the standard of living of agricultural workers depends on the volume of their production, the amount of compulsory deliveries to the state (partly for tractor service), the amount of money received from the state, the market for crops, and the price charged for consumer goods. The distributional pattern of labor incomes within the collective farm is influenced by the "labor day" system of payment, which results in some inequality (Ch. 20). From 1939 to 1945, however, considerable monetary rewards were offered for special efforts in agriculture, and some farmers became wealthy until they were largely dispossessed by the currency reform in December 1947 (Ch. 25). The reductions in the prices of many consumer goods in 1950 improved the real incomes of industrial workers more than those of peasants because industrial wages remained stable while the prices of some agricultural goods sold in the free collective farm market fell 25% to 30%. But in the end, because the socialist governments rely largely on pecuniary incentives to allocate labor, differentials depend partly on supply and demand.

2. Other Differentials in Labor Incomes

Within industry, occupations involving strenuous labor or skill generally receive the highest incomes (apart from management). Mining has been an exception, partly because of immobility and isolation from the rest of the labor force. In Britain, for instance, when the demand for coal began to decline in the 20th century, the low mobility of miners pressed heavily on coal mining incomes. But coal miners have recently moved to a more advantageous position in the wage structure in most countries. In Britain their weekly average earnings rose 200% between 1938 and 1948, but their

[80] U.N., *Progress in Land Reform*, Ch. 4; *Prelim. Rep. on World Social Situation*, 1952, 102.

[81] Hanson, *Utopia in Uruguay*, 141.

real earnings much less. In Russia, coal mining, once one of the lowest paid, is now almost the highest paid activity. Coal mining wages have also increased, relatively to other wages, in Poland, Australia, New Zealand, and the U.S.A., as a result of increases in the power of unions, increased mobility, or the necessity to expand mining.[82]

The differential paid in skilled occupations is usually wider in less than in more developed countries, but it has been declining.[83] In Britain real wage rates for laborers in 1949 were at or above their level in 1938, but those for skilled workers had fallen substantially.[84] Between 1913 and 1920 this differential shrank in most countries and rose again after 1920, but not to the 1913 level.[85] New methods of production or new products have reduced the demand for skill in some occupations; at the same time the spread of education increases the supply of skilled workers, except where labor unions and others can limit the number of persons acquiring skill.

Fluctuations in production have also affected the differential for skill. In depressions new workers are compelled to enter the occupations where there are jobs. Demand, rather than the relative attractiveness of conditions of labor, determines labor allocation, and relative wages during such periods are often determined by historical accidents. But in times of full employment, relative wages are more closely geared to the net advantages of different kinds of work. In Europe, unemployment obstructed occupational changes, and wages in strenuous occupations fell relatively to others between 1918 and 1939, but had returned to the 1914 relation by 1950.[86] Inflationary conditions after 1914 generally improved the relative position of lower-paid workers in Europe (except in France). In some European countries (e.g., Norway and Sweden) labor unions have explicitly sought in recent years to improve the relative position of lower paid workers. But in France the government, through restricting the upward movement of wages between 1945 and 1950, specifically preserved most previous differentials.

In socialist countries margins for skill and strenuous work have been increased to stimulate the supply of these types of labor. Marx regarded inequalities in incomes as inevitable in the first stages of a post-capitalist world, and inequality in the rewards of different workers is the essence of soviet distribution of incomes.[87] Government policy was influenced by equalitarian attitudes until about 1928, when inequalities among industrial wage earners were less than in 1914. But they increased between 1928 and 1934, although still not to the 1914 level. After 1935, inequality increased further, owing to the revision of wage scales and the increased use of

82 U.N., *Econ. Bull. for Europe*, Vol. 2, No. 2, 1950, 57.
83 Clark, *Conditions of Economic Progress* 2d, 458.
84 Seers, *op. cit.*, 57.
85 U.N., *Econ. Bull. for Europe*, Vol. 2, No. 2, 1950, 54, 56.
86 *Ibid.*, 53, 58.
87 Schwartz, *op. cit.*, 82 ff.

progressive piece-rates.[88] In fact, inequality among wage earners may be as great in Russia as in the U.S.A.

The differential paid to white collar workers has also been shrinking, mainly because of the spread of education. In fact, average white collar earnings in the U.S.A. during the 1930s were at or below the average of wages in general.[89] In Britain non-wage labor incomes fell from 7.5 to 4.5 times wage incomes between 1880 and 1938 because of the increased proportion of low non-wage labor incomes.[90] In Russia this differential is also relatively small, but creative workers have been highly favored. The royalty earnings of the 14 highest-paid authors were about 43 times the average earnings of all soviet workers in 1936, and the margin for authors may have been still greater in 1947.[91]

Wage differentials in male labor as against female have also narrowed since 1938, partly because more occupations are open to women in times of full employment.[92] In Britain the absolute difference between the wages of adult males and adult females was the same in 1938 and 1948, after allowing for taxes and price changes, but it had fallen in relation to real income.[93] Where incomes are controlled by law, as in Australia, New Zealand, and South Africa, the wages of male workers are typically considerably above those of females but the margin is narrowing. In Australia the wages of unskilled women are 75% of those of unskilled men.

In some countries incomes have been increasingly differentiated by size of family in recent years (Ch. 31). Though allowances for children may not be regarded as incomes from labor, such payments may reduce the incomes of childless workers below what they would otherwise be, particularly where the whole cost of the allowances falls on the employer, as it does in France, Belgium, and some other European countries. In France and Belgium, such allowances have provided a way of making the cost of living increases more adequate for those with families than for others, thus increasing net labor income differentials. In France in 1949 the average real wages of a single worker were 81% of his wages in 1938, whereas those of a worker with a wife and two children were 109%.

In countries in which the labor force consists of workers of more than one national or racial origin, their incomes may differ, especially between white and indigenous workers. In South Africa in 1948 the average annual incomes of Europeans were about 14 times, and those of Indians about three times, those of Africans. In Southern Rhodesia in 1946 the incomes

[88] Bergson, op. cit., 106, 207.

[89] Clark, op. cit., 1st, 8.

[90] Phelps-Brown and Hopkins, "The Course of Wage Rates in Five Countries," Oxford Econ. Papers, June 2, 1950.

[91] Bergson, "On Inequality of Incomes in the U.S.S.R.," X American Slavic and East European Review, 1951, 95.

[92] U.N., Econ. Bull. for Europe, Vol. 2, No. 2, 1950, 56; U.S. Dept. of Labor, Wage Trends and Wage Policies in Various Foreign Countries, 14, 22, 29, 32, 43, 48.

[93] Seers, op cit., 57.

of non-Africans were about 33 times those of Africans (including the imputed value of subsistence production); in Northern Rhodesia about 60 times, and in Kenya 33 times.[94] In Java in 1939 more than 25% of all income went to 2.5% of the population, largely European but including some Chinese. But the wage differential is narrower, because the European incomes include non-wage and property incomes. In South Africa the wages of Europeans are 380% greater than those of Africans in industry, and about 1000% greater in gold mining, although African wages are considerably higher in the Union of South Africa than in other areas south of the Sahara.[95] Wide differentials also exist in Malaya, and existed formerly in India.

These differentials are largely due to the different groups being in different occupations, in which the labor supply and demand relations differ. In the typically "white" occupations, the labor of officials, technicians, and entrepreneurs can be obtained only in competition with other countries in which they can obtain employment (i.e., at a sort of international rate of pay). To reduce their incomes to those obtained by the average native worker would almost completely cut off the supply. Mining could be developed in South Africa only with the aid of skilled white workers who had to be paid sufficient to attract them to that country, but native labor, particularly when "assisted" by government pressure, could be obtained far more cheaply.[96] Differentials also extend to manual work (e.g., in the U.S.A., South Africa, and many colonial areas). Lack of education and training prevent indigenous workers from entering the higher-paid occupations and reducing the differential. Exclusion from apprenticeship and white labor unions effectively bar native workers from many occupations in South Africa,[97] and African labor unions, though not illegal, are rendered impotent by law. The government helps to maintain the differential by establishing a list of jobs in mines that may not be performed by Africans, and by setting a high level of education for apprentices while supplying few educational opportunities for Africans.[98] For instance, an African may not run a car carrying passengers underground at 8 miles an hour, but may drive an automobile on the surface carrying passengers at 50 miles an hour. Consequently, African workers have low productivity and are crowded into the unrestricted occupations. Until they are provided with education and training, it cannot be known whether Africans are "naturally" less suited to various occupations than white workers (as is often alleged), but the existing barriers to their entry into various occupations suggests that those who make the allegation are none too confident that it will stand the test of the market.

---

[94] U.N., *National Income and its Distribution in Underdeveloped Coustries*, 21.

[95] U.N., *Rev. Econ. Condns. in Africa 1949/50*, 79.

[96] Union of South Africa, *Economic and Wages Commission*, 1925.

[97] Franklin, *Economics in South Africa*, 167, 198.

[98] *Ibid.*, 196; De Kiewiet, *A History of South Africa*, Ch. VIII.

Chapter 31

The Relation Between Consumption and Incomes from Property and Labor

Incomes from labor and property, although they are the primary influence affecting consumption, are not the only one. Decisions by individuals and by groups, such as the family, private groups, and the state, are everywhere important.

A. Individual Decisions

Individuals invariably have some power to determine their own consumption, and often also that of others. In widely varying degrees, they choose between work and leisure, consumption and saving, the kind of work they do, and the form of their consumption. Their decisions are influenced by personal qualities but also by social influences, the two being difficult to separate. Social environment affects the importance attached to the material aspects of life, attitudes toward saving and the form of consumption (in some countries as a result of advertising). Finally, individuals influence the operations of group organizations such as the family, private groups, and the state.

B. The Family

For much of the population of the world, family decisions determine the distribution of economic well-being among husbands, wives, children, the aged and sometimes remote relatives. The scope of family influence depends largely on custom. But most governments regulate marriage. Polygamy is permitted in some primitive societies. In most parts of Africa, where it is permitted by native law or custom, it is restricted in practice by the requirement of transfers of property from the husband's to the wife's family (Ch. 29). Plural marriage is permitted in Islamic countries, but is unusual. In the wealthier families in the Middle East, it may be an

683

alternative to divorce. But peasants occasionally take a second wife in a good crop year (e.g., in Syria or Iran). Plural marriage is prohibited in all the more developed societies, the Mormon communities in the U.S.A. being an exception until 1890, when it was prohibited there. Governments also define the obligations of parents to children and, often, to poor relatives who are sick or aged.

Power to allocate consumption among the members of a family has resided in the male head, in most societies, until recently. The subordination of women is typically reflected in restrictions on their power to hold separate property. There have, however, been a few scattered examples of matriarchy among primitive peoples, and in some, a wife has separate property in the produce of her agricultural activities, subject to an obligation to feed her husband (or to share this responsibility in polygamous families).

Patriarchy prevailed in the ancient Mediterranean world. In Babylon, however, women could engage in business and could sometimes dispose of property, but they seem never to have achieved full legal personality. In ancient Egypt, women had considerable economic status, including full rights of property. In ancient Greece the father was the religious and legal head of the family. Women had only the right of maintenance and dowry, and it was difficult for them to obtain education. In Sparta, however, women managed the land while the men were fighting, and women could inherit and retain landed estates as their own. Plato argued that women ought to be admitted freely to all the duties and rights of men, and that society suffered considerable loss because of its restriction of the activity of women. But Aristotle believed that men were by nature superior to women and should, therefore, rule them. In Rome in the 5th century B.C., a woman passed at marriage under the control of her husband, but in the course of time the bride remained under at least the nominal guardianship of her father and did not become a member of her husband's family. She acquired complete control over her own property, and divorce was the free choice of either party. The freedom of women began to be restricted, however, under the Roman Empire, although wives were more independent legally and socially than in any civilization until recent times.

The early Christian fathers, under the influence of the law of the Old Testament and of the Germanic tribes, established the patriarchal family under canon law, and women lost some of the freedom obtained under Roman and Anglo-Saxon law. Women enjoyed no legal rights or independent existence, except that free courtship and consent to marriage were recognized. In the feudal period, women were also subject to the feudal powers. The marriage of nobles was controlled by the king and of peasants by the manorial lord. The Reformation in England liberalized views of marriage, but the husband remained the absolute head of the family.

The patriarchal family prevails also in most of the less developed countries, e.g., in Latin America and the Islamic Middle East. In India and China women have had little economic status, but in the tropical Far East (the Philippines, Burma, Siam, Cambodia, and Java) they have enjoyed a higher status.[1] In India until recently the "joint family" was a large group of relatives descended from a common ancestor, the male head of which administered all the property and income of the family. Adult sons with wives and children had no power to dispose of incomes from their economic activity; these went into the family purse controlled by the patriarch. Debts incurred by the head of the family were a charge on the family property passing from father to son. These families formerly remained together for a number of generations, but they are now often dissolved on the death of the father and the property divided among the sons, who set up their own families.[2] The joint family has continued least changed among artisans and in agriculture, but has been disintegrating in cities and towns. Increasing pressure on the land, however, has compelled some members of the family to leave the land to seek an income elsewhere. Furthermore, in recent years the sharing of family income has caused disputes where some members of the family feel that they have been more energetic than others.

The legal right of women to own separate property and participate in the management of the family in modern times dates from the latter part of the 19th century. The improvement in the status of women derives partly from a rationalistic equalitarian philosophy, but has been reinforced by industrialization. Women working outside the home and augmenting the family income achieved more influence in family counsels. The wider social contacts of women in developing societies also undermined male dominance. American women were entitled to own separate property, however, in Mississippi in 1839, and most states have since followed this example, although the status of women still differs among the states. But in Britain the property of married women was at the absolute disposal of their husbands except where it was vested in trustees (often in ante-nuptial settlements) until 1870, when wives obtained separate property in the earnings of their own labor. In 1882 they obtained separate legal personality and the right to own property in their own names, and, in 1886, equal rights with husbands over the control of children. In France wives have an absolute right to half the husband's earnings, but they may not alienate their property without their husband's consent. Nor may a wife sue, or contract independently, even if she is engaged in trade. Furthermore, she may not exercise parental power. In Germany the civil code of 1900 placed single women on an equal footing with men. A husband, however, had powers of decision in all matters affecting the com-

---

[1] Furnival, *The Tropical Far East*, 15.
[2] Wadia and Merchant, *Our Economic Problem*, 43.

mon married life. Except where a marriage contract prescribed otherwise, the husband controlled the property of the wife as well as the property acquired by their common labor. This code was further strengthened under the Nazi government. In Russia (which had a long tradition of male dominance), the Soviet legal code provides for equality between the sexes in all economic matters.

The nature of family decisions as to the disposition of the resources of the family among its members is known only in broad outline.[3] Nor is the significance of law and custom regarding the power to dispose at all clear. In nominally patriarchal families, women often have more influence than is suggested by their legal position. The fact that women often live longer than men often enhances their influence in family affairs. Where husbands and wives are legally coequal, it is not always clear who in fact decides, or how decisions are made. Much depends on individual personality. But family decisions are operative only within a restricting framework. The size of the family income often leaves only a narrow scope for choice. In market economies, the pattern of prices influences consumption. Law and custom often regulate the allocation of consumption goods to wives, children, the dependent, aged, and unemployed, although family responsibility for education, health, the destitute, and unemployed has been reduced in most developed countries. But a sample survey of rural families in Egypt indicated that they received 10% of their income from relatives.[4] Where the state provides monetary distributions (e.g., payments on behalf of children or the aged or in time of unemployment), discretion as to their expenditure remains within the family. But where the state provides services, such as education and health services, it supplements the family income without leaving discretion to the family as to the form of the supplement. Over long periods of history, and still for a large part of the population of the world, however, the family has evidently provided sufficient consumption by children to permit large numbers to survive, and has been the chief agency providing for the maintenance of the sick and the aged.

C. Private Groups

Individual consumption is influenced by transfers of property or income to private groups who provide consumption goods and services. The influence of such groups on the interpersonal distribution of consumption depends on the size of the income of the groups, its sources, and the way in which it is distributed.

The amount of their income depends on the attitudes of individuals and the state to private charity. The state may levy taxes for the benefit of private groups, grant them property, confiscate their property, or ex-

---

[3] Zweig, *Labor Life and Poverty*, passim.
[4] U.N., *Prelim. Surv. of World Social Situation*, 1952, 161.

empt private contributions to them from taxation. At least two thousand years ago, many states in Europe and the Middle and Far East required the payment of tithes to religious institutions (e.g., the ancient Jews, ancient Greece, and Egypt). European feudal societies typically provided for tithes, which are still paid in many parts of the Middle East.[5] In many parts of medieval Europe, religious institutions were also granted considerable amounts of manorial land that yielded further income to the church, and considerable amounts of land are held for religious purposes in the Middle East. But many of these ecclesiastical lands were confiscated at the Reformation in England and later in many other countries, especially in France, Mexico, Russia, and eastern Europe. Religious institutions have also obtained income from private donations. The giving of "alms" has typically been enjoined as a religious duty. Islam enjoins the giving of alms in cash or kind according to well-defined rules that require at least 2.5% of annual savings to be so used, poor relatives having a priority.[6] Similar injunctions have been made by the Christian church and among Hindus. There was also strong religious pressure upon individuals to bequeath at least part of their property to the church. But the influence of religious institutions over the disposition of the national income is much less than it was, in developed countries.

Secular charitable groups appeared in England in the 16th century[7] and increased in importance in most western countries, notably in the 19th century. But the proportion of all social services provided by them has declined greatly during the present century. Nevertheless private charity remains important. Philanthropic gifts (by contribution, bequest or from corporations) in the U.S.A. totalled about $1.206 billion in 1929, and $.715 billion in 1933, after which time they rose continuously until 1949, when they reached $4.032 billion.[8] In the socialist societies there are virtually no private groups affecting the distribution of consumption.

Private group activities would not much affect the distribution of consumption if they obtained their contributions from the people whom they serve, but they usually do not. The widespread use until recent times of the tithe to support religious activities suggests proportional taxation, at least in intention. But tithes have often fallen largely or wholly on the cultivator, and have ceased to be proportional to incomes in general. Gifts by living persons and through bequests are progressive where the rich give a larger proportion of their incomes than the poor. In the U.S.A., however, there appear to be considerable ranges of income over which the incidence is proportional and occasionally regressive. In 1943 philanthropic contributions by living persons were 12% of incomes over $5

[5] Bonné, *State and Economics in the Middle East*, 119.
[6] U.N., *Prelim. Surv. of World Social Situation*, 1952, 161.
[7] Andrews, *Philanthropic Giving*, Ch. 2.
[8] *Ibid.*, 72.

million, and 3% of those over $100,000. The lowest proportion (1.9%) was for incomes of $10,000 to $20,000. Incomes below $3,000 provided 60% of all contributions by living persons, and the percentage of income contributed (2.8%) was higher than for incomes in the next higher bracket.[9]

The incidence of the benefits provided by these groups depends on the nature of their activities. Religious organizations have spent a considerable part of their resources on the maintenance of buildings and personnel to provide religious services not usually regarded as part of consumption in an economic sense. But from the earliest times, and in most countries, they have also provided poor relief. Some have distributed food. The ancient Jewish temples distributed sacrificial meats. Greek temples acted as redistributive agencies and provided shelter to travellers. The ancient Egyptian temples made similar charitable distributions. In the Middle Ages the Christian church was the principal poor relief agency in Europe. As early as about 800 A.D. Charlemagne commanded that tithes be used partly for the relief of the poor. In 1014 Ethelred decreed that one-third of the proceeds of tithes be devoted to the relief of the needy in England.[10] The confiscation of most of the property of the religious houses in England reduced the income of the church at a time when the need for poor relief was increasing. The alms of the devout fell short of the needs of the poor and the government sought to increase alms-giving. In 1532 the City of London provided for collections by aldermen at the doors of churches for the relief of the needy. An act of 1535 made each parish responsible for its poor, and ordered the clergy and local officials to collect charitable offerings for the poor. In 1551 and 1552 collectors of alms were ordered to exhort the giving of alms and to bring recalcitrants before the bishop.[11] But all these measures failed to produce the desired results, and in 1601 the Poor Rate Act authorized taxation to finance poor relief. In the 19th century, private groups provided poor relief in industrial countries, but left a considerable residual burden to be borne by the state. Some such charity comes from religious sources in India and in Islamic countries, but the amount is small, especially in relation to the need.

Private groups have also distributed educational service. In medieval Europe the Christian Church was for some centuries the bearer of literate tradition and the main source of education. Secular private groups became interested in the 16th century, but finally, like poor relief, education passed mainly into the hands of the state, although there remains a considerable amount of financing through private groups. Of current annual giving in the U.S.A., 50% is for religion, 8% for higher education, and 15% for health and welfare.[12] Provision for the sick, insofar as it is not made by

---

9 *Ibid.*, 53, 55.
10 *Ibid.*, 36.
11 *Ibid.*, Ch. 2.
12 *Ibid.*, 73.

the family, appears to have run a similar course, through attempts to provide service by religious groups, then by secular groups, and, finally, in many developed countries, in the main by the state. Higher and more widely applicable standards of minimum well-being call for administrative machinery and financial resources beyond those of private groups, and workers have insisted on emancipation from reliance on private charity.

D. The State

The state also influences consumption by taking over from individuals and business units part of the incomes obtained from property and labor and providing goods and services.

In non-monetized economies transfers to the state are in kind. In many countries for many centuries part of the crop was due to the state directly or through intermediaries. Alternatively workers were required to work on land, the produce of which accrued to the state or its representatives (e.g., under the feudal system in Europe, and in the Inca economy). The produce thus obtained supported the governmental machine, civil and military. In some societies the bureaucracy, inadequate to the task of collecting this income, delegated the function to tax farmers who engaged to make specified deliveries to the state in return for the right to collect prescribed taxes, an arrangement which has typically been corrupt and oppressive. Even when the obligation was converted into money taxes, collection continued in the hands of these private contractors in many countries (including pre-revolutionary France). Tax farmers sometimes developed into landowners (e.g., India and the Middle East) or merchants (Japan). In the Ottoman Empire attempts to eliminate tax farming in 1839 and 1879-80 proved abortive, and the state began direct collection of taxes only in 1917-18.[13] In Syria tax farming was abolished only in 1925.

Frequently the state combined the collection of taxes and the provision of service into one operation by imposing taxes in labor and using the work for public projects such as roads, water works, or pyramids. Under the feudal system lords were required to provide military service on demand. But, as economies become monetized, the relations between the state and individuals are typically converted into money taxes. The obligation to provide military service, however, survives and has been extended, but the increase in recent years in the financial remuneration for military service in the more developed countries has reduced the net contribution to the state by members of the armed forces. States also provide military protection, police, health, education, and other services in kind. But the power to levy directly upon the national product is separated from the performance of service (e.g., military). Governments have, however, reverted to taxes in kind in times of rapid inflation (e.g., after the currency

---

[13] Bonné, *op. cit.*, 56.

breakdown in the Roman Empire under Diocletian,[14] after the revolution in Russia (from 1917 to 1924), and in the early years of communist government in China.

The effect of state policies on the interpersonal distribution of consumption depends on how the state raises its income and distributes benefits. Progressive taxes, taking a greater proportion of large than of small incomes, reduce inequality of disposable income. Proportional taxes, taking an equal proportion of incomes of all sizes, leave inequality unchanged; regressive taxes, taking a greater proportion of the smaller than of larger incomes, increase inequality. Expenditures may be similarly classified: progressive expenditures tend to reduce inequality. The net effect of the fiscal activities of the state is the net effect of all taxes and all disbursements by the state, both in money and services.

1. Influences Affecting Distributive Policies

The redistributive policies of states depend upon the classes of individuals able to exercise state power, their interest, and the limits set by the necessity for defense and internal order.

In many countries, at many times, military groups have dominated state policy, using their power to take over part of the national product to pay for military operations and to provide for their own consumption (Ch. 29). Even after monetization, the military class may greatly influence government policy (e.g., in Germany, Japan, Spain, many Latin American and Middle East countries). Those who formerly took over part of the produce of agriculture and were responsible for military service often emerged after monetization as landowners subject to money taxes. These landowners exercise primary control over the state in predominantly agrarian countries (e.g., in western Europe until the 17th and 18th centuries, and at the present time in much of the Middle East (outside Israel), in India and much of Latin America). For the most part they have used their power to minimize their contribution to the state and enhance their benefits from it.

The emergence of classes with other interests has modified state policy. The mercantile classes in western Europe espoused mercantilism (Ch. 23). Their power derived from their ability to finance the government and their knowledge of the effects of various kinds of economic intervention (although their opinions were not unbiased). Industrialists had other interests. British industrialists urged *laisser faire* (or the minimization of state redistribution). In countries industrializing later (the U.S.A., Germany, and France) industrialists sought *laisser faire* internally but tariffs against foreign competition. Farmers seek to obtain redistribution in their favor (Ch. 8). Workers have used political power to reduce the inequality of consumption (Ch. 30). Socialist economies are too young to reveal the

---

[14] Clark, *Conditions of Economic Progress* (2d), 566.

ultimate determinants of state policy. Russian policy is presently determined by an élite, whose power derives, at least in part, from its control
of the means of defense and internal police. Its policies are directed toward military strength and economic development.

The extent and pattern of redistribution depends, however, on the cost
of state activities. These may be enlarged with the deliberate purpose of
distributing economic welfare more equally. But increases (for instance, in
the cost of military activities) may have to be borne more by the upper
than the lower income groups because of the inability of the latter to pay
more. It is, however, impossible to measure the extent of redistribution in
a country taxing to pay for military activities, because it is impossible to
measure the distribution of the benefits of military services.

2. Distributive Policies

a. Past Non-Industrial Societies

In primitive societies the state has little influence over distribution of
consumption (apart from its power over access to land). There is, usually,
some taxation in kind. Individuals may be required to deliver food to the
chief when festivals are announced, but they are entitled to participate
in the feast, with the result that there is often no important redistribution.
Communal work may be ordered, but its incidence is often fairly equal.
Individuals may be required to participate in the hunt, but they also share
in the results. In some such societies the produce of agriculture is placed
in communal granaries to be shared by all, but in many produce is private
property.

Taxes in labor have often been continued or imposed by colonial powers
and much criticized, although in non-monetary economies there may be
no other way of providing some local services. But such taxes have been
much abused. In the Dutch East Indies, labor taxes continued into the
20th century. They applied to all able-bodied men up to 60 years of age
except non-natives, workers on plantations or in industry, and students
in school, which meant to about 25% of the population. The tax could be
paid in money, and about one-third of those liable did so pay. The maximum number of days of labor payable was 20 a year, although in some districts more was exacted. The tax was finally abolished in the last districts
in 1941. In about 1830 the Dutch government also introduced the "culture
system" of taxation, the native population being required to cultivate part
of its land for the benefit of the government. Later this system was extended to require unpaid labor in sugar refineries and factories, and was
abused.[15]

In the ancient Mediterranean world, state redistribution was often important. Part of the produce of the land was commonly due to the state

---

[15] J. S. Furnival, *Netherlands India*, 182, Ch. V.

and used to support the military and civil services (which provided large personal incomes to some individuals). But individuals were often entitled to support according to their status, citizens being those mainly cared for. In Babylon the state had great storehouses of grain and the like throughout the country, and made distributions to the needy. Athenian citizens had rights to food, and "bread and circuses" were furnished by the Roman Republic. Levies were also made in labor for the building and maintenance of public works (where they were not constructed by slaves), the incidence of such levies being mainly on the lower income groups. Money taxes appeared in the Greek world soon after the introduction of coinage in the 6th century B.C.

In medieval Europe the pattern of feudal rights and duties was the primary regulator of consumption (Ch. 29). Other levies were made (e.g., on inheritance and occasionally on commodities), and the obligation to grind grain at the lord's mill was a form of tax. Taxation in money of modern types appeared mostly in the cities, which were required to pay the central government for incorporation and other privileges. Expenditures were largely for military purposes.

In 17th century Europe, particularly England and Holland, monetary levies increased. There were taxes on land. The merchant classes successfully urged taxes on many imports and some exports. Inheritance taxes were introduced during the 17th century in the Dutch provinces and German principalities, and by the end of the 17th century in England, France, Spain, and Portugal. Excise taxes also were many and varied.

b. Contemporary Underdeveloped Countries

i. Incidence of Benefits

In contemporary underdeveloped societies, governments typically play a small, though increasing, redistributive role. Total government expenditures are small. In India they were about 10% of net national product in 1948-9. They are mostly for military purposes and administration. Military expenditures are more than 30% of all government expenditures in a number of countries in Asia and the Far East, and 60% in Pakistan (Table 69). They are over 20% in most of the Middle East (Table 70). Welfare expenditures have typically been small, and are around 15% of total government expenditures in the Middle East (Table 70). Poor relief has generally been meagre. Small amounts of cash relief were given on a poor-law basis in Ceylon and Singapore before 1939.[16] In India poor relief has been mainly provided on a family, caste, or village basis. Land is still set aside in some villages for poor relief, artisans are taxed for the maintenance of their less fortunate brethren, and a part of the crop is set aside for the poor.[17]

---

16 Peacock (ed.), *Income Distribution and Social Policy*, 281.
17 Wrench, *The Restoration of the Peasantries*, 101.

But much has taken the form of famine relief. Between 1870 and 1880 India spent about £15 million on famine relief (obtaining the funds out of additions to the national debt), and a Famine Commission in 1880 proposed work on public projects as a condition of relief to the able-bodied. Nevertheless deaths from starvation have been numerous (Ch. 1). Some countries, however, have subsidized food in recent years. Such subsidies were 11% of the Indian budget in 1948, and a further 11% was for the support of refugees resulting from the partitioning of the country in 1947. In Egypt 4% of the state expenditures in 1947 were for the reduction of the cost of living (mainly bread subsidies).

Expenditure on education is small but increasing in some countries. In Egypt about 12% of government expenditures was for education between 1929 and 1939, and 11% in 1946-7, a further 2.5% being for the alleviation

TABLE 69

MAJOR COMPONENTS OF GOVERNMENT EXPENDITURE IN SELECTED COUNTRIES
IN ASIA AND THE FAR EAST IN 1949-50*

Country	Percentage of Total Government Expenditures on:			
	Defense	Interest on Public Debt	Other Current Expeditures	Investment, Loans & Advances
Burma	26	...	59	15
Ceylon	1	...	71	28
China (1950)	39	...	37	24
India	37	7	26	30
Indonesia (1949)	29	17	49	5
Pakistan	60	3	15	22
Thailand (1950)	14	...	59	27

* U.N., Econ. Surv. of Asia and the Far East, 1949, 154.

TABLE 70

MAJOR COMPONENTS OF GOVERNMENT EXPENDITURE IN SELECTED
COUNTRIES IN THE MIDDLE EAST IN 1950*

Country	Percentage of Total Expenditures on:				
	Military Purposes (Revenue and Capital)	Social Services (Including Education and Public Health)	Public Works	Public Debt	Civil Administration and Other
Egypt	27	17	15	3	38
Iran	22	11	14	4	49
Iraq	22	13	9	...	56
Jordan	32	4	11	...	53
Lebanon	18	15	25	...	42
Syria (1947)	19	16	25	...	40
Turkey (1948)	34	14	7	15	30

* U.N., Rev. Econ. Condns. in the Middle East, 1951, 80. Figures are budget estimates and allocations are somewhat arbitrary.

of sickness, poverty, and illiteracy. In Brazil 7% of federal, state, and local expenditures was for education in 1944.[18] Expenditure on health is similarly small. In Egypt health conditions among the mass of the population are deplorable, and the need for clean water supplies, health services, and housing is tremendous. Yet it is estimated that "to bring clean water to the villages . . . would cost about £200 million at 1943 prices—about twice the pre-war annual gross income from agriculture."[19] In the years from 1929 to 1939 about 8% of government expenditures was on public health, and in 1946-7 about 6.5%, with an additional 1.5% for "social affairs." In China 4.1% of government expenditures was for health and education in 1950. Even where these expenditures are a fairly important part of all public expenditures, they are low because total public expenditures are low; and these are low partly because national income per person is low.

Social security programs are beginning to appear in these countries in an attempt to follow the lead of the more developed countries, where, however, they were introduced only after considerable development, and as a way of reaping the fruits of progress. In the underdeveloped they often affect only a small proportion of the population, but insofar as they are effective they may stimulate population increase and hinder development.[20] In Latin America all 18 countries have some provision regarding accidents at work. Eleven have old-age, survivors, and invalidity insurance, and 11 health and maternity insurance, the old-age programs being the most advanced. The oldest wage earners' health and maternity benefits system in the hemisphere is in Chile;[21] it covers agriculture and domestic service as well as industrial workers, who receive medical aid, through dispensaries maintained by the fund, and income payments (which decline after the first week of sickness). Working mothers receive medical attention during pregnancy and children receive medical care for the first two years of life. Mothers receive income payments equal to 50% of wages for two weeks before and two weeks after childbirth. Chile also has unemployment insurance, but only for salaried workers. Uruguay has contributory workmen's compensation and unemployment insurance in a few activities. Family allowances are provided in Uruguay and in Chile for salaried employees only.[22] In 1952 a health and social welfare program was established in Peru. It is financed out of increased taxes on alcohol and a 3% tax on salaries and wages paid by larger corporations. Industrial workers in Chile have obtained children's allowances by collective bargaining.

Little of this legislation affects the native Indian population, or, indeed,

---

[18] Spiegel, *The Brazilian Economy*, 65.

[19] Warriner, *Land and Poverty in the Middle East*, 40.

[20] H. W. Singer, "Economic Progress in Underdeveloped Countries," XVI *Soc. Res.*, 1949, 4.

[21] I.L.O., *Ind. and Labor*, 1953, 52.

[22] S. G. Hanson, *Utopia in Uruguay*, Ch. X.

much of the total population. It concerns mostly urban groups, seamen, and railroad personnel. In Uruguay retirement systems cover employers, agricultural workers, domestic servants, and industrial workers, and in Uruguay and Argentina non-contributory pensions on a needs test basis supplement insurance programs. These programs are typically administered through a "fund" or "institute" not part of the executive branch of the government, although under government supervision.

In the Middle East social security legislation is almost restricted to work accident legislation, and even this is recent and does not cover all countries. In Iran workers and employers contribute. Maternity insurance was enacted in Turkey in 1945, and old age, invalidity, and survivors' insurance in 1950. Voluntary mutual funds have been set up in Israel to deal with sickness. In Asia social security programs of the western type are almost restricted to Japan, where meagre poor relief was provided by law in 1874 and workmen's compensation existed before 1939. Subsidized voluntary health insurance began in 1938 as a supplement to a compulsory scheme that had been in operation for many years. The Daily Life Security Act of 1946 provided cash payments to the unemployed, aged, sick, mothers, and vagrants, and for assistance to vocational training and for funeral expenses. Old age, invalidity, and survivors' benefits are payable at the age of 55 at about one-third of the average annual earnings over the whole period of employment. In 1947 Japan introduced the first compulsory unemployment insurance law in Asia, national in organization and requiring contributions from workers, employers, and the state. In part it was intended to eliminate the traditional practice of keeping redundant workers on the payroll.[23] In India new workmen's compensation and health insurance laws were passed in 1948, the workmen's compensation requiring contributions by workers and employers. Generally in India and Burma there is little more than workmen's compensation,[24] which is also provided in the Philippines.

Government expenditures on economic development have been unimportant until recently in underdeveloped countries. In the Ottoman empire expenditures on trade, education and public works together accounted for less than 1% of all government expenditures in 1860.[25] In Egypt and Indonesia, however, the government provides irrigation water without direct charge. In Egypt about 3.6% of all government expenditure was on irrigation in 1948 to 1951; in 1946-7 about 1.1% was for commerce and industry, 9.9% for public works, and 2.6% for agriculture. But not all these expenditures were calculated to promote production. In Iran expenditures

---

[23] Reubens, *Far Eastern Survey*, 1949, 274.

[24] A. N. Agarwala, "The Social Security Movement in India," LVI *Ec. Jour.*, 1946, 568. In 1952 health programs for industrial workers on a contributory basis were introduced in the states of Delhi and Kampur.

[25] Bonné, *op. cit.*, 58.

on development projects were 30 to 40% of all public expenditures from 1930 to 1941, 7% in 1945-6, and 12% in 1947-8.[26] In Brazil in 1944, 4.3% of the expenditures budgeted by the federal government were for labor, industry, and commerce, 12.7% for roads and public works, and 2.9% for agriculture.[27] In Asia and the Far East budget provision for development is greater in all countries than before the war of 1939-45.[28] Development plans now provide for increased expenditures in India, Egypt, Syria, Iran, and Turkey, but they vary in scope and some have encountered serious opposition. In general, expenditures in these countries have been regressive in their incidence.

ii. Incidence of Cost

The agrarian countries have generally obtained their revenues by regressive taxation, notably in the Middle East where the "exceedingly narrow tax base . . . exempts a broad area of non-monetary income and covers only a relatively minor portion of monetary income. Existing fiscal techniques which have not succeeded in taxing the incomes of the wealthy are grossly inadequate to finance any large scale program of economic development."[29]

Taxes on land or the income from it are the chief potential means of taxing the wealthier classes where land is the major source of larger incomes. Such taxes have been almost universal for many centuries, and are sometimes hardly distinguishable from land rents payable to the sovereign, notably in India.[30] Such taxes can be heavy and progressive, but they have recently been neither in most underdeveloped countries. Rates of tax are often low, and such taxes have provided a declining proportion of all government income since 1938 (Tables 71, 72), partly because government budgets have increased (especially under the impact of inflation) and land assessments are infrequently adjusted. Where the capital or rental value of the land for tax purposes is raised only at long intervals, and where prices rise, the price of produce and rents rise but tax payments do not, and the real burden of taxation on landowners falls.

The "permanent settlement" of land taxes collected by provincial governments in parts of India has pegged money taxes for 150 years while the population has pressed increasingly on the land.[31] In parts of the country where land taxes are "temporarily settled," the tax varies from 40 to 70% of the rental value of the land. Where the settlement is made with individual owners (ryotowari system) the tax was originally one-third of the net produce, until 1855, and thereafter one-half. But settlements are made

---

26 U.N., *Public Finance Information Papers: Iran*, 21.

27 Spiegel, *op. cit.*, 65.

28 U.N., *Econ. Surv. of Asia and the Far East, 1949*, 149.

29 U.N., Econ. Surv. Mission for the Middle East *Final Report*, I, 3, 35.

30 Nanavati and Anjaria, *The Indian Rural Problem*, Ch. 29.

31 India Famine Inquiry Comission *Report*, 449.

every 20 or 30 years, the tax being recalculated in money on the basis of the average yield of the type of soil and average prices during the preceding period (excluding famine years) and various deductions to arrive at the net profit of the cultivator. Between settlement dates the money tax is fixed irrespective of actual returns. But the government often claims less than 50% of the net yield, and no share in the increase in profits due to the improvements made by the cultivator, although it does claim a share in profits due to general improvements such as the introduction of a railway. It is alleged that "every periodical revision is utilized as an occasion for enhancement" and therefore "the system of peasant proprietorship has not brought in all the glorious results attributed to it by econ-

TABLE 71

MAJOR COMPONENTS OF GOVERNMENT TAX REVENUE IN SELECTED
COUNTRIES IN THE MIDDLE EAST IN 1950*

Country	Percentage of Government Tax Revenue Derived from:				
	Taxes on Incomes of Businesses and Persons	Taxes on Property	Excises, Turnover Taxes and Monopolies	Customs	Other
Egypt	15	7	24	34	20
Iran	17	..	47	31	5
Iraq	10	3	51	34	2
Israel	31	6	22	28	3
Jordan	16	4	11	56	13
Lebanon (1948)	8	4	32	43	13
Syria (1947)	10	2	47	33	8
Turkey (1947)	34	2	...	...	19

* U.N., Rev. of Econ. Condns. in the Middle East, 1951, 82. Excludes oil royalties and profits of enterprises. Budget estimates (except Turkey and Jordan).

TABLE 72

PROCEEDS OF LAND TAXES AND TAXES ON GENERAL CONSUMPTION AS
PROPORTION OF TOTAL TAX REVENUE IN SELECTED COUNTRIES*

	Land Tax		Taxes on General Consumption (About 1949-50)
	1938	1949-50	
India	17	4	50
Philippines	..	3.4	50
Brazil (1940)	1.4 (1948)	0.6	40
Egypt	21	5.0	70
Iran	5	4	75
Iraq	19	21	66
Syria	25 (1947-8)	17	75
Turkey	7	2	50

* U.N., unpublished materials. These figures differ from those in Table 70 because taxes on agricultural produce are included above.

omists and land reformers."[32] By historical accident, "permanent settlement" has been associated with the *zamindari* system of tenure and temporary settlement with the *rytowari* system. Permanent settlements with
individual peasants are conceivable, and were in fact contemplated by the
originators of the system. Similarly temporary settlements could have been
made with the *zamindari*, and some were made.[33] The inflations since 1945
have reduced the burden of these taxes in India and Pakistan, and they
have provided a declining proportion of government revenues.

In Egypt, where the tax is imposed on the rental value of the land, the
average value for taxation was prescribed in 1889 and the tax set at
28.64%. Both remained unchanged until 1939, when the rental valuation
was raised, but the rate of tax was reduced sufficiently to leave the tax
yield unchanged. During the fifty years before 1950 the yield of the tax
remained stable at about 5 million Egyptian pounds, although as a percentage of government revenue, it fell from 50% to 14%.[34] During this period
actual rents rose greatly, owing to improvements in irrigation and inflation.
In 1951, however, the rate of tax was doubled (retroactively for two years).
Land taxes have also generally been low and slow to be adjusted to increases in land values in Latin America, but some states in Brazil and
Argentina have made them progressive with the amount of land held.
Some states in Argentina impose surtaxes on absentee owners and some
in Brazil on unused land. In the state of Goiaz in Brazil the tax is regressive, the rate decreasing with increases in the value of the land (to encourage development). In Chile, Iran, and Iraq, somewhat the same result
is achieved by exemptions on newly reclaimed lands.

Some Middle East governments have recently replaced the land tax
with a tax on the produce of the land when it is marketed or processed,
but these taxes have proved expensive and difficult to collect. They exempt unused land and produce consumed by the cultivator. In Turkey
the land tax was discontinued in 1935, but the tax on agricultural produce
introduced in 1943 lasted only about three years. A tax on animals
marketed is the only tax on land revenues. In Iran the land tax law was
codified in 1925, and the major tax on land was 3% on the value of gross
output before division between landowner and tenant. This tax was
abolished in 1933 when a 3% tax was imposed on agricultural produce
when marketed. In 1946 the tax on gross output was reinstated at 150% of
its level in 1925. In Syria and Lebanon until 1944 the tithe was the principal tax on land (originally 10% but raised to 12½%) and was levied on the
villages as units with the result that influential landowners are said to
have borne less than a reasonable share. Beginning slowly in 1940 this tax
was replaced with a tax of 7.5% of the value of all agricultural produce

---

[32] Nanavati and Anjaria, *op. cit.*, 118, 125.
[33] *Ibid.*, Ch. 8.
[34] Issawi, *Egypt: an Economic and Social Analysis*, 140.

destined for sale. Tithes are reported still to be illegally collected in some parts of the country. There is also a tax on animals marketed. In Iraq a land tax existed only between 1936 and 1939. The basic tax is a tithe (increased to 11.5% in 1943). Crops are valued at official prices and the tax is not at a uniform rate on all crops. The provision in the Income Tax law of Iran in 1949 requiring the landowner to sell part of the output of wheat and barley to the state at a fixed price is equivalent to a tax.

Income taxes, generally the most progressive element in fiscal systems, have been introduced into some of these countries, but in general the rates are neither high nor steeply progressive and the tax yields a relatively small proportion of all government revenue. An income tax was introduced in India in the 1860s, but by 1950 it yielded 35% of all tax revenues (Table 73), and the income and corporation tax yield more than half the revenues of the central government. The highest rate of 77% applied to incomes over 3 million rupees in 1951. Income and corporation taxes are levied in most countries in Asia and the Far East, but they generally provide less than 25% of tax revenues (Table 73), although the rates were

TABLE 73

Types of Taxation as a Proportion of Government
Revenues in Selected Countries in Asia and the
Far East in 1949-50[*]

Country	Yield as percentage of all tax revenues		
	Direct Taxes	Customs Duties	Other Indirect Taxes
Burma	14	52	34
Ceylon	23	64	13
India	35	40	25
Japan	56	0	44
Malaya	—	76	—
Pakistan	15	58	27
Philippines	19	10	71
Thailand (1950-51)	5	36	59

[*] U.N., *Econ. Surv. of Asia and the Far East*, 1949, 155.

increased in some countries in 1951.[35] But they were reduced in Pakistan in 1951-2 because of high export prices, mainly for cotton. Japan, however, raised 56% of all its tax revenue from income taxation in 1949-50 (Table 73). In Malaya and the Philippines, agricultural incomes are subject to income tax. In India incomes from land are not subject to the central government income tax, except that plantations are taxed as industrialists. But a number of provinces have imposed progressive taxes on incomes from land.

In Israel and Turkey, income taxes provide about 30% of government

[35] U.N., *Econ. Surv. Asia and Far East*, 1951, 257.

revenues, and in other Middle East countries about 10 to 15% (Table 71). In many of these countries incomes from land have not been liable to income tax, but this position is being reversed, although such incomes are difficult to measure and tax. In Iran incomes from land are subject to income tax, but not in Egypt. The income tax rates introduced in Egypt in 1949 rose from 5% on incomes from 1001 to 1500 Egyptian pounds to 50% on incomes over 100,000 Egyptian pounds. Some Latin American countries raise a considerable proportion of their tax revenue from income taxes (e.g., Chile 30 to 40%, and Brazil about 33%). In Mexico, Chile, and Argentina, income from agriculture is subject to income tax. In Africa there is an income tax in the British colonial territories applicable equally to native and white persons. A few Africans have a sufficiently high income to pay the tax.

Taxes on commodities are generally the major source of revenue in these countries. Taxes on imports provide about one-third of government revenues in most countries in the Middle East (Table 71) and more than one-half in many parts of Asia and the Far East (except Japan). (Table 73). In the Philippines import duties yielded only 5% of all government revenue before 1951, when the government imposed a tax of 17% on all foreign exchange transactions. Indonesia imposed heavy import duties in 1951.[36] In Brazil import duties have provided 14% of all federal government revenues,[37] but in Uruguay, 60%. Excises, sales, or turnover taxes, and profits on government monopolies generally, provide a further 25 to 50% of government revenues in the Middle East (Table 71). In Iran there are sales taxes on almost all basic products, some of which are collected through government monopolies of manufacture. The government takes the profit margin between the cost of production and selling price for products like tobacco, sugar, tea, and opium. In India the central government alone obtained 37% of its income from customs and excise duties in 1948. In Asia and the Far East generally taxes are levied on alcohol, tobacco, and luxuries, and general sales taxes (which have recently been introduced in Pakistan, Vietnam, Cambodia, and Burma) often exempt necessities.[38] In Brazil excise duties have provided about 40% of federal revenues.

The incidence of import duties, internal taxes on commodities, or profits from government monopolies of sale depends on the income groups who pay the resulting higher prices. Taxes on luxury and semi-luxury goods are progressive. But many commodity taxes are on goods of wide consumption and, therefore, are regressive. A large part of the taxes on imports into Egypt apply to commodities of wide consumption (e.g., tobacco,

---

[36] *Ibid.*, 252.
[37] Spiegel, *op. cit.*, 70.
[38] U.N., *Econ. Surv. of Asia and Far East*, 1949, 15; 1951, 255.

kerosene, sugar, alcohol, and matches).[39] In Brazil excise taxes were levied on matches (63% of their value), tobacco (44%), beverages (25%), salt (24%), and a number of other products of general consumption;[40] policy in Uruguay is similar. Internal taxes on commodities such as salt and tobacco and matches are regressive, but taxes on luxury products are not. In general, taxes (import, excise, or government monopoly profits) on commodities of general consumption (typically tobacco, sugar, tea, alcoholic beverages, petroleum, and cotton piece-goods) provide about 50 to 65% of all tax income in agrarian countries (Table 72), and in some this percentage is as high as 80.

Export duties are frequently imposed by underdeveloped countries with a comparative advantage in the export of mineral or agricultural products. Burma, North Borneo, Ceylon, India, Indonesia, Malaya, and Pakistan have all imposed such taxes to hold down internal prices. Malaya and Indonesia tax exports of rubber and Pakistan of cotton (Ch. 13). The same end can be achieved by government export monopolies. Burma and Thailand have held down the internal price of rice in this way.[41] The resulting government income was intended to be used for development, but has in fact been used for current government expenses. The Burmese government also has a timber-export monopoly. Chile taxes exports of copper. Bolivia taxes a long list of agricultural and mineral exports, but 70% of the value of its exports consists of tin, and 90% of minerals.[42] Brazil has taxed exports of coffee. The incidence of these taxes and monopoly profits is difficult to trace. Where demand is inelastic, the tax may fall partly or wholly on foreign buyers. But it may fall partly or wholly on the domestic economy (including foreign or domestic investors in the enterprises affected) or ultimately on landowners.

Governments indirectly tax exports and imports when they control foreign exchange and set different exchange rates for different goods and obtain revenue from the operation. In Argentina the proceeds of exports of some agricultural produce are converted into local currency at a rate only about 33% of the fluctuating market rate, and foreign exchange to pay for imports affecting agriculture is sold at relatively unfavorable exchange rates. But in Venezuela exchange rates are controlled to promote exports of cocoa and coffee, the proceeds of the sale of products at world prices below a specified level being converted into *bolivares* at favorable rates. In Indonesia until 1952 the government in fact sold foreign exchange at a higher price than it paid for it, thus imposing a tax of 33% on exports (in addition to duties of about 8%).[43] Governments may achieve similar results by trading monopolies in exports and imports, as in Turkey and

[39] Issawi, *op. cit.*, 142.
[40] Spiegel, *op. cit.*, 270.
[41] U.N., *Econ. Surv. of Asia and Far East*, 1951, 250.
[42] U.S. Tariff Commission, *Economic Controls and Commercial Policy in Bolivia*.
[43] U.N., *Econ. Surv. of Asia and the Far East*, 1951, 252.

Argentina. The marketing boards in Nigeria and the Gold Coast make profits partly intended for disbursement in years of low world prices, but partly in the nature of a tax to finance development (Ch. 8). The incidence of these taxes and profits is difficult to trace.

Governments in the Middle East and Latin America have obtained revenue from petroleum by a variety of devices, such as charging royalties, taxing exports, taxing imports of goods needed for petroleum production, and through the price charged for foreign exchange. Petroleum provided 15% of all government revenues in Iran from 1943 to 1949, 11.5% in Iraq in 1949, 51% in Lebanon in 1949, 49.3% in Saudi Arabia in 1948, and 54.6% in Bahrein in 1946.[44] Some of the proceeds of petroleum in Iran have been invested, and the five-year plan of development was to have been financed from this source. In Iraq oil royalties were used to finance consumption imports and the ordinary running expenses of the state until the new agreement in 1951, which increased the government's share in income from oil and provided for all the increase to be earmarked for the National Development Board. Some countries in the Middle East have too few other resources to permit much development, even if petroleum profits were segregated for the purpose, and political conflicts will probably prevent the royalties from being used to develop neighboring countries with large depressed populations.[45] Apart from differential exchange rates, about 63% of government revenues were from mining in Venezuela in 1946-48, 54% in Bolivia in 1944, and 5 to 12% of federal revenues in Mexico in 1938 to 1945.[46] The Venezuelan government plans to use petroleum revenues for economic development. Where these revenues are used in relief of taxation for current administration, the benefit mainly accrues to those who would otherwise have had to pay higher taxes.

c. Capitalist Industrial Countries

The proportion of the national income passing through the government fiscal system has steadily increased in capitalist countries, although policies of *laisser faire* would minimize government activitity. In 1938 taxes were about 12% of national income throughout western and southern Europe, though by 1948 central government revenues were about 40% in Britain and 30% in the Netherlands, Belgium, and France, and less in the Scandinavian countries (Table 74). But in southern Europe the proportion had changed little, and had fallen to about 9% in Spain and Portugal in 1952.[47] It is difficult to tax away as high a proportion of low as of high incomes. In the U.S.A. government (federal, state, and local) purchases of

44 U.N., *Econ. Rev. of the Middle East, 1949-50*, 29, 62.
45 Warriner, *Land and Poverty in the Middle East*, 137.
46 U.N., *Econ. Surv. of Latin America, 1948*, 65.
47 U.N., *Econ. Surv. of Europe in 1953*, 189.

TABLE 74

CENTRAL GOVERNMENT REVENUES AS PERCENTAGE OF NET NATIONAL
INCOME IN SELECTED EUROPEAN COUNTRIES IN 1948[*]

Country	Total Government Revenue	Direct Taxes[†]	Indirect Taxes (including turnover taxes)	Social Security Contributions[‡]	Other Current Revenue
United Kingdom (1948-9)[0]	40.8	19.1	16.9	3.5	1.3
Netherlands[0]	31.9	11.7	13.6	4.3	2.3
Czechoslovakia[0] . .	30.6	6.8	11.5	7.2	5.1
Belgium	30.2	9.5	13.3	5.2	2.2
France[0]	29.2	8.4	13.0	6.7	1.1
Hungary (1947-8) .	28.4	6.6	14.9	3.2	3.7
Norway (1947-8)[0] .	26.1	5.5	14.8	2.9	2.9
Sweden (1947-8)[0] .	22.3	10.4	10.1	1.1	2.5
Finland[0]	19.8	6.7	8.6	1.1	3.4
Denmark[0]	19.7	8.1	8.7	1.4	1.5
Italy (1947-8)	17.8	2.7	9.3	4.1	1.7
Austria[0]	17.4	5.6	9.5	1.6	0.7
Ireland (1947-8) .	17.0	5.1	9.2	0.6	2.1
Poland[0]	13.3	5.1	2.9	1.7	3.6

[*] U.N., *Econ. Surv. of Europe in 1948*, 41.

[†] "Direct Taxes" include death duties and extraordinary taxes on capital and profits (capital levies, excess profits except where capital levies are tied to loan schemes).

[‡] Includes both employer and employee contributions.

[0] Based on budget estimates.

goods and services and transfer payments were about 26% of gross national product in 1953.[48]

i. Incidence of Benefits

Military services have long been regarded as inappropriate for provision by private enterprise. But until the present century they absorbed only a small part of national income. In many European countries such expenditures were less than 3% of the gross national product in 1938, but more than 5% in 1951 (Table 75). In France and Britain the percentage changed little, and in Italy it fell. In the U.S.A. government purchases of goods and services for national security were 3.2% of the gross national product in 1939, and 14% in 1953.[49]

Government expenditure on economic development was also small in the 19th century; it went mostly for roads, bridges, railroads, posts, telegraphs, telephones, and the like. But these expenditures have increased during the 20th century, partly as a result of the establishment of national enterprises (Ch. 22). In France investment expenditures rose from 5% of the government budget in 1938 to 40% in 1949 and 30% in 1951.

Expenditures on the welfare of the population, mitigating the effect

[48] U.S., *Economic Report of the President*, 1954, 167, 175.
[49] *Ibid.*, 167, 169.

of inequalities in incomes from property and labor, increased during the 19th century, and more rapidly during the 20th. Industrialization and urbanization necessitated increased public health services, unlikely to be provided through the market. Industrial accidents and diseases increased in importance. The conditions of labor, properly criticized for their inhumanity and sometimes for their inefficiency, led to increasing expenditure on the administration of protective labor legislation. The growing political power of the mass of the population (recognized in the extension of the suffrage) necessitated payments for public education.

TABLE 75

Defense Expenditures as a Percentage of Gross National Product in European Countries in 1951*

Greece	7.7
United Kingdom	7.3
France	6.9
Italy	5.3
Western Germany	5.2
Turkey	4.9
Belgium	4.9
Netherlands	4.5
Spain	4.1†
Sweden	3.8
Norway	3.5
Portugal	3.2†
Switzerland	3.0
Denmark	2.2

* U.N., *Econ. Surv. of Europe since the War*, 1953, 60.
† 1950.

Poverty due to intermittence of labor incomes increased in the 17th century, owing to changes in methods of agricultural production and the rise of the domestic system, and relief became a public responsibility in Britain in 1601. The introduction of the factory destroyed craft and domestic industries, causing unemployment and political unrest that was further stimulated by the French revolution. The burden of poor relief increased. In Britain, as in most other countries, it was the financial and administrative responsibility of local authorities. It was generally assumed that poverty was largely the fault of the poor and could be remedied if sufficient pressure were applied to them. Vagabonds were whipped, or branded, and the right to use their labor was sold off by auction. It was more difficult to blame the aged and orphans for their poverty, and policy was aimed at barely keeping them alive. When the factories appeared, the orphans were frequently sold off into indentured labor in cotton mills and sometimes coal mines. The ruling classes were fearful of revolt, and fearful that poor relief would undermine the incentive to work, thereby increasing the cost of relief.

Commissions of inquiry in various countries produced few constructive recommendations. The British Poor Law Commission of 1832-4 laid down the principle of "less eligibility," whereby the economic position of the "pauper class" should always be less than that of the lowest paid independent worker. It also stressed the importance of uniformity of national policy to reduce the movement of paupers from one parish to another, and recommended that relief in the home (outdoor relief) be replaced by indoor relief (the workhouse test) for able-bodied persons. The latter principle was never thoroughly applied because of its inherent inappropriateness to some types of poor, and the cost of establishing the necessary institutions. Far from being solved, the problem increased as successive changes in methods of production continued to generate technological unemployment, and as the industrial system engendered cyclical unemployment. Toward the end of the 19th century, falling birthrates and increasing longevity increased the problem of caring for the needy aged. A growing humanitarian sentiment focused first upon the welfare of children, later included the aged and the handicapped (especially the blind), and finally encompassed the entire "low-income group."

Wages were often inadequate to permit the individual to carry these risks even if he knew how to make the necessary arrangements, and private charitable groups were able to carry only a small part of the burden. The increasing proportion of industrial workers in the population and their growing political power made better treatment of the poor the price of the political coherence necessary for continued industrial production and social stability. In Germany Bismarck explicitly sought to head off socialism by legal provision for the aged and sick, coupled with repression of socialism and labor union activities.

The first steps toward a "welfare state," accepting responsibility for a minimum of economic well-being for the mass of its population, were taken in western Europe in the late 19th century and in the 20th century. Since that time, the scope of welfare activities has widened. After each world war, the social forces which accelerated the redistribution of land and the nationalization of industry produced increasingly comprehensive "social security programs." The Atlantic Charter of the Allied Powers included among the aims of the war of 1939-45 "freedom from want." Soon after the beginning of the war many countries enacted legislation either creating new systems or (more frequently) enlarging and liberalizing existing ones.[50] The great publicity given by the allied powers to the social security proposals contained in the Beveridge Report (p. 707) reflects the belief that this type of activity would enlist the active support of the working population in the conduct of the war. In the countries overrun by Germany, extensive social security legislation assimilated systems to those

---

[50] Federal Security Agency, *Social Security Legislation Throughout the World*, 1949, 165-6.

in Germany. By 1950, therefore, most capitalist governments accepted responsibility for the maintenance of the labor force (and in some the entire population) as a social overhead charge, and devoted a significant proportion of the national income to the purpose.

By 1948 social service expenditures by national governments alone, in western Europe, accounted for from 6% to 9.4% on net national income (Table 76). In many of these countries these payments had about doubled

TABLE 76

CENTRAL GOVERNMENT EXPENDITURES ON SOCIAL SECURITY[*]
AS A PERCENTAGE OF NET NATIONAL INCOME IN
SELECTED EUROPEAN COUNTRIES IN 1948[†]

France	9.4
Belgium	8.0
Czechoslovakia	7.9 (est)
Netherlands	6.5 (est)
United Kingdom (1948-9)	6.1 (est)
Italy (1947-8)	6.1
Norway (1947-8)	5.4 (est)
Sweden (1947-8)	5.0
Denmark	4.6 (est)
Austria	4.2 (est)
Hungary (1947-8)	3.1 (est)
Ireland (1947-8)	2.8
Poland	1.4 (est)
Finland	1.3 (est)

[*] Includes expenditures by national governments as well as payments from national insurance funds. Includes both transfer payments (including war pensions) and expenditures on goods and services.

[†] U.N., *Econ. Surv. of Europe in 1948*, 40. The above figures differ from those in Table 74 because the proceeds of "social security contributions" may exceed or fall short of expenditure on social security.

between 1939 and 1948 in spite of lower levels of unemployment in 1948. Substantial expenditures are also made at subsidiary governmental levels, though the proportion varies greatly. State (or provincial) and local expenditures in 1948 to 1950 were 56.5% of all welfare expenditures in the U.S.A., 36.6% in Norway, 33% in Canada, 30% in Denmark, 24% in Britain, 22.7% in Sweden, and 16.6% in Finland. In Britain in 1949-50 welfare expenditures by all levels of government were 16.6% of national income and 46.1% of total government expenditures: the corresponding figures for the U.S.A. were 10.4% and 35.0% (Table 77), and for Canada 7.9% and 21.8%.[51] In 1948 welfare expenditures (excluding education) were 9% of net national income in Denmark, 10.2% in Finland, 8.3% in Norway, and 10.9% in Sweden.[52] In Britain about 30% and in the U.S.A. about 40% of these costs

[51] U.S., *Social Security Bulletin*, July 1952, 15. The totals include income-maintenance programs, health, education, housing, food subsidies, other welfare services.

[52] G. Holmstedt, "De sociala utgifterna i de nordiska länderna," *Sociala Meddelanden*, 1951, VI, 416-17.

TABLE 77

SOCIAL SERVICE EXPENDITURES IN BRITAIN AND THE U.S.A.*
1949-50

	Britain		U.S.A.	
	As percent of National Income	As percent of Total Government Expenditures	As percent of National Income	As percent of Total Government Expenditures
Income Maintenance Program	5.7	15.9	4.2	14.2
Health Services	3.7	10.2	1.4	4.7
Education	2.6	7.3	4.2	14.2
Housing	0.7	1.9	0.1	0.4
Other Welfare	0.1	0.4	0.4	1.2
Food Subsidies	3.7	10.4	0.1	0.2
Total	16.6	46.1	10.4	35.0

* U.S., *Social Security Bulletin,* July 1952, 14-15.

represented cash disbursements to maintain incomes, and the remainder partly or wholly subsidized benefits in kind.

Income maintenance payments were very general in 1950. Public relief or assistance for the destitute, on individually demonstrated need, continues, but income security payments have been increasingly designed during the 20th century to deal with poverty according to its immediate origin in ways adapted to each cause.[53] Since 1940, governments have increased the risks covered and consolidated social security legislation. The "Beveridge Plan" is the best-known integrated series of income security programs. While outlining a detailed system of income maintenance, the Beveridge Report emphasized its relation to programs concerning health, education, and housing, without making detailed proposals.[54] The income maintenance programs encompassed the risks of old age, short- and long-term sickness, survivorship, unemployment, industrial injury, maternity, children's allowances, and death benefits. In principle all benefits were to be equal (except for differentials for youth and sex and for industrial injuries). Coverage was in principle universal, with the population grouped into three categories for the purpose of assessing contributions, the categories reflecting different risk exposures. Contributions calculated separately for each risk were to be collected as a single weekly levy on employers and workers, with the general taxpayer meeting a substantial part of the cost. A comprehensive integrated income security system had been inaugurated by New Zealand in 1938, and similar programs were enacted in France in 1945 and Australia from 1947 to 1949. Income main-

[53] For the classic statement of this approach, see the Reports (especially the Minority Report) of the British Royal Commission on the Poor Laws, 1905-9.

[54] W. H. Beveridge, *Social Insurance and the Allied Services,* Cmd 6404, 1942.

tenance payments increasingly provide payments dependent on prior contributions to a social insurance scheme (or on defined demographic characteristics, such as age or youth) irrespective of proof of individual need. British workers suffered for more than a century from the stigma of poor law or charity when normal sources of income failed, and emphasize this right and the abolition of the "means test," although there is still a means test for a few benefits in Britain.

The proportion of the population covered by income security measures varies from risk to risk and country to country. The New Zealand and British income security measures cover the entire population and almost all risks: in Canada and Sweden old-age pensions are universal as are children's allowances in Britain, Australia, Canada, New Zealand, and Scandinavia. The many schemes based on employment fail to provide for the self-employed or those in agriculture or small business, but there is a general tendency to widen coverage and also to include more risks. In the U.S.A., however, public protection against loss of income due to ill-health is only fragmentary. The proportion of income loss covered also varies. Practically all schemes leave the beneficiary worse off than he would have been had the risk not materialized. But governments increasingly attempt to provide a minimum standard of living without requiring the worker to meet the full actuarial cost of his benefits.

The broadening of state responsibility to cover an increasing number of risks of lapse of income follows a somewhat uniform pattern, although there are still notable differences among countries.[55] In general governments first provide against accidents while at work, then for income maintenance in old age, invalidity, and for survivors (or some of them), and, later, the maintenance of income during sickness (often accompanied by health service), unemployment insurance, and allowances to finance the cost of rearing children. In principle all the more developed countries accept responsibility for all these major sources of poverty, but they have not all acted in all fields.

Occupational accidents and disease caused increasing loss of income as production was mechanized. By 1950, of 45 member states (excluding Soviet Russia, Japan, and Germany) replying to a questionnaire from the International Labor Organization, 41 had workmen's compensation legislation providing for income in the event of occupational accident, and most of these included compensation for some or all occupational diseases (particularly silicosis). Four additional states have legislation that does not provide for compulsory insurance by the employer, so that payment of benefits is not guaranteed.[56] This type of legislation developed out of efforts to define the liability of an employer for accidents to his employees

---

55 I.L.O., *International Survey of Social Security*, 1950; International Social Security Association, *Recent Developments in the Field of Social Security*, 1951.

56 I.L.O., *International Survey of Social Security*, 1950, *passim.*

and, later, to ensure that the liability would be met. In the early stages of industrialization in England, the risk of accident fell mainly on the worker. The law of Master and Servant assumed that the worker took risks with his eyes open and allowed for them in striking an employment bargain. The employer was liable for his own neglect but not for the effect on the worker of neglect by his co-workers.

The first law making employers liable for all accidents, even when the fault of the employee, was passed in Germany in 1884. But it excluded occupational diseases, covered only serious and fatal accidents, and was restricted to specified industries. Employers were grouped into mutual trade associations for insurance purposes. Austria followed Germany's example in enacting workmen's compensation in 1887, Norway, Finland, France, and Denmark in the nineties, and many other European countries, certain Canadian provinces and Australian and American states in the first decade of the 20th century.[57] In England the worker's chances of compensation were improved by the Employer's Liability Act of 1880, but after 1897 the employer was liable for any accident to a worker arising "out of and in the course of his employment." The employer could (but was not required to) insure the risk. Compensation was based on the rate of pay of the worker, with a rather low maximum. The Industrial Injuries Act of 1946 retained the phrase "arising out of and in the course of work" as the test of liability, but divorced the amount of compensation from the amount of wage loss (the extent of incapacity being the only test). It also changed the incidence of the burden, by requiring contributions from workers as well as employers, and providing a state subsidy. Although the typical law requires the employer to insure, only about half the countries require insurance with a state fund. Elsewhere, the employer can insure with a private company or choose between private and state insurance funds. Coverage is often restricted occupationally or to firms in excess of a specified size. Benefits for temporary and permanent incapacity and death, and often for specific injuries, are typically based on the worker's previous earnings, and are sometimes payable for a limited time only. Denmark and Venezuela (as well as Britain) provide a state subsidy.

Lack of income due to old age, invalidity (of non-occupational origin), and death of a breadwinner was widely met by contributory insurance schemes by 1950. In Australia, Canada (for persons 65-69), Denmark, Norway, Spain, and the Union of South Africa, however, pensions were subject to an income test. In Belgium, France, Britain, Netherlands, New Zealand, Sweden, Switzerland, U.S.A., and a few Latin American countries, means or income test programs supplement the social insurance system.[58] In the U.S.A. old age and survivors' insurance, established in 1935, and a special program for railroad workers (the only social insurance

---

[57] B. M. Armstrong, *Insuring the Essentials*, 1932, 223-83.
[58] U.S., *Social Security Bulletin*, March 1950, 3, 4.

schemes wholly administered on a national basis) provide benefits after ten years of covered employment, although more lenient provisions apply to those already elderly when the Act was passed, and to survivors' benefits. The rates of benefit depend on average earnings in covered employment. This insurance system covers five-sixths of the working population and is complemented by federally aided state payments to the needy aged (whether or not in receipt of insurance benefits).[59] Sweden and Canada pay pensions to all persons above a specified age, irrespective of need. New Zealand has established a universal scheme to provide old age pensions at 65 without an income test. The annual payment, initially set very low, is to be slowly raised to a standard figure. But few of the aged now benefit substantially from this scheme, and most draw the income-test pension.

Provision of income in old age and for invalids has for long been made by various industrial groups. Austria in 1854, Belgium in 1868, and France in 1884 organized into compulsory systems of old age and invalidity insurance mining funds that dated back to the middle ages. The German old-age and invalidity insurance act of 1889 provided pensions at the age of 70, ranging from the equivalent of 50 cents to one dollar a week, according to previous contribution. It required contributions in equal shares by employers and workers and benefited only those in regular employment. This legislation, originally opposed by the socialists, was supported by them ten years later.[60] Other countries thereafter subsidized voluntary old-age and invalidity insurance funds, but in 1910 France provided compulsory insurance for the aged (but with little effect). Luxembourg followed in 1911, Rumania in 1912, the Netherlands and Sweden in 1913, and subsequently many other countries. Britain provided insurance against invalidity in 1911 as part of the health insurance system, but not against old age until 1925. The U.S.A. waited until 1935, and Switzerland (on a national basis) until 1948. By 1949 such schemes, with varying coverage, existed in 37 countries.

The old-age insurance programs (which frequently also provide benefits for invalidity and for survivors) typically vary the amount of the benefit with the worker's previous earnings, and often with the number of years of covered employment. There is usually a minimum benefit, and benefit formulae are weighted in favor of the lower paid workers. Benefits are often provided for dependents, although Britain and the Scandinavian countries provide a uniform benefit. Most social insurance plans were initially restricted to urban workers (occasionally with special schemes for white-collar employees), but increasingly legislation includes the self-employed and agricultural employees. To receive benefits the insured must usually have been in covered employment for a specified period, but is not required to prove need. The cost of these schemes is variously dis-

---

[59] E. M. Burns, *The American Social Security System*, Ch. 4, 5, 11, 12, Supplement.
[60] Armstrong, *op. cit.*, 399-403, 418-421.

tributed among employers, workers, and the state, and is usually one of the largest social service expenditures. Pensions for the aged and occasionally also for the permanently disabled, separate from the poor law system but payable only if the claimant has less than a prescribed income, were initiated in Denmark in 1891. New Zealand initiated a true pension system of this type in 1898 by setting out in the law the precise amount of the benefit. It was followed in two Australian states in 1901, in France in 1905, and in Britain and the Australian Commonwealth in 1908. The Canadian and American state old-age programs, however, which do not define in the law the eligibility conditions and amount of the benefit, are analogous to public assistance. By 1950, seven countries provided benefits, typically at flat rates to all residents whose incomes fell below a prescribed level, meeting the costs from general taxation.

Loss of income due to ill-health, whether invalidity, temporary sickness, or maternity (as distinguished from the cost of medical care) was provided for in varying degree by almost 40 governments in 1950. Maternity benefit was granted to workers in four countries that did not provide sickness benefit, and was absent in only two that granted sickness allowances. Workers in many parts of Europe had endeavored to deal with this problem through cooperative benevolent associations. Mutual insurance pools of miners provided a precedent for more general pools encouraged in Prussia by Frederick the Great. A Prussian law of 1845 allowed local authorities to set up compulsory pools for handicraftsmen, and in 1849 they were permitted to require factory owners to insure workers against sickness. In 1879 an imperial German law regulated friendly societies and restricted them to sickness and funeral benefits, and in 1883 Germany set a pattern by passing a compulsory sickness insurance law under which the benefit societies, sick guild clubs, a few local associations, and communal insurance funds were used for administrative purposes. This example was followed by Austria (1888), Hungary (1891), Luxemburg (1901), Norway (1909), Serbia (1910), Russia (1911), Britain (1911), and Rumania (1912).[61] Sweden, however, set a different precedent in 1891 by subsidizing approved voluntary sick funds. This example was followed by Denmark (1892), by relatively ineffectual schemes in Belgium (1894) and France (1898), by New South Wales (1908), and Switzerland (1911). But by 1950 most of these subsidy arrangements had given place to compulsory insurance.

Cash payments during sickness are usually proportionate to the earnings of the beneficiary, although flat rates are not uncommon and benefits for dependents are frequent. Benefits are typically paid for less than a year, but some countries prolong them for diseases such as tuberculosis, or continue payments indefinitely. Many provide indefinite payments in effect

---

[61] *Ibid.*, 303-30.

by paying invalidity benefit where incapacity to work extends beyond
the period for which sickness benefit is available. The costs are usually
shared among employer, worker, and the state.

Unemployment became so serious a cause of loss of income as industrialism spread that it exceeded or heavily strained the resources of workers
(individually or in unions), of private charity, and of the local jurisdic-
tions administering poor relief. As with other risks, the first state action to
assist the unemployed took the form of subsidies to out-of-work benefit
funds maintained by labor unions, although some countries established
public employment exchanges to assist workers to find jobs (Ch. 20).
The city of Ghent (Belgium) in 1900 subsidized, and in some degree
supervised, the administration of labor union unemployment funds, setting
a pattern shortly followed by a number of cities in Switzerland, France,
Norway, Denmark, and Belgium. Britain in 1911 established an insurance
fund, financed by contributions from employers, workers, and the central
government, out of which benefits were paid for short periods of unemployment in a few occupations, as a matter of right and irrespective of
income. Coverage, duration, and amount of benefit were greatly liberalized
after the war of 1914-18. Italy followed the British example in 1919, Germany only in 1927, and U.S.A. in 1935.

In the U.S.A. compensation during unemployment was left until 1933
almost wholly to private charity and poor relief. In some cities and states
the public payment of out-relief in cash was legally prohibited. After
1929 "drives" to increase charitable gifts to carry the burden proved inadequate, and the federal government then took steps to provide relief, or
work. Of these, the most permanent was the Social Security Act of 1935,
which, by imposing a federal tax on all employers of eight or more workers, which could be offset to the extent of 90% if an employer paid contributions to a state for unemployment insurance, stimulated all states
to enact unemployment insurance laws. The state funds are invested in a
federal unemployment trust fund and used only for benefit payments, the
federal government meeting all costs of administration. The American
systems are almost unique in that in all but two states the entire cost
falls upon the employer, and all states have adopted experience rating
systems whereby the individual employer's rate of tax varies with the extent of benefits paid to his former employees.[62] By 1950, some 17 countries
operated unemployment funds, while Denmark, Finland, Sweden, and
Switzerland subsidized private funds; in Denmark the government subsidy
may not exceed 75% of the members' contributions, but municipalities
are authorized to pay an additional subsidy.[63] Australia and New Zealand
provide legally specified unemployment benefits, subject to proof of income below a prescribed level for unlimited periods of unemployment.

[62] Burns, E. M., *op. cit.*, Ch. 7.
[63] U. S., *Social Security Bulletin*, March 1950, 4.

There is no unemployment insurance in France, where former arrangements were destroyed during the wartime occupation, although some assistance is paid to registered unemployed. In the U.S.A. publicly provided work played a major role in maintaining the unemployed during the depression of the 1930s, and such works have been utilized in other countries from time to time.

Unemployment benefits are at a flat rate (sometimes varying with age and sex, and usually accompanied by payments to dependents) in nine countries. Elsewhere they are a prescribed fraction of earnings, usually approximating 50%. Most insurance plans limit duration to three or six months. Britain, however, pays benefits for unlimited periods of unemployment without the income test applied in Australia and New Zealand, and some other countries provide special assistance to unemployed who have exhausted insurance benefits. All schemes test the beneficiary's attachment to the labor market and the involuntary character of his unemployment. The cost of these schemes, ranging from 1% to 4% of taxable earnings, is variously shared among workers, employers, and government. Coverage is often less extensive than for other risk programs, agriculture and domestic service being frequently excluded.

The incidence of the cost of maintaining children has increasingly been redistributed by governments. In 1939, seven countries (Belgium, Chile, France, Hungary, Italy, New Zealand, and Spain) made cash payments to families (frequently to the mother), irrespective of (a) whether the parents were employed, (b) their other sources of income, or (c) the size of their income. In addition, the family was relieved of much of the cost of education and health service, of meals at school, and part of the cost of housing. By 1950 these children's or family allowances were paid in 27 countries,[64] the U.S.A. being almost unique among highly industrialized nations in making no such provision.

Schemes vary as to the children covered and the numbers of children in a family for whom payments are made. The British Commonwealth and the Scandinavian countries cover all children in principle, although there are occasionally residence or nationality requirements. In France and Belgium payments are limited to gainfully occupied persons, and elsewhere to employees. Australia, Canada, Finland, New Zealand, and Sweden pay such allowances for every child including the first; France pays for the first child if there is only one earner in the family. Britain and Norway pay for the second and subsequent children, and Brazil pays only for the eighth and subsequent children. In most countries the allowance is at a flat rate. But in Canada the rate varies with the age of the child, and in some countries it varies with the worker's previous earnings. In France

[64] U. S. Federal Security Agency, *Social Security Legislation throughout the World*, 5; I.L.O., *International Survey of Social Security, passim;* U.N., *Economic Measures in Favor of the Family*, 1952, 3-27.

the payment is related to the basic wage and reflects geographical differences in living costs.[65] The children's allowance for three children is 84% of the wage without the allowance in France, but less than 30% in all other countries (and only 6% in Britain) (Table 78). Alternatively, the al-

TABLE 78

THE SIZE OF CHILDREN'S ALLOWANCES IN SELECTED EUROPEAN
COUNTRIES IN 1950*

Country	Ratio of Average Wage of Adult Man in Industry to National Income Per Head		Family Allowance for Three Children as Percentage of Average Wage Without Family Allowance
	Excluding	Including	
	Family Allowance for 3 Children		
France	1.3	2.4	84
Italy	2.7	3.5	30
Belgium	1.6	2.0	25
Netherlands	1.8	2.1	17
Sweden	1.7	1.9	12
Switzerland	1.7	1.9	12
Austria	2.6	2.9	12
United Kingdom	1.8	1.9	6
Norway	2.2	2.3	4.5
Denmark	1.8	1.9	6

* U.N., *Econ. Bull. for Europe*, Vol. 4, No. 2, 27.

lowance for two children raises the purchasing power of hourly industrial earnings in food alone 35% in France, 16% in Italy, 13% in the Netherlands, 6.4% in Canada, 5.6% in Australia, and 3.2% in Britain.[66] These allowances are financed wholly by the state in Canada, Finland, Ireland, Norway, Sweden, and Britain; by contributions from protected persons and employers, plus a state subsidy in Australia and New Zealand; and elsewhere by employer contributions. In many countries they are the largest or the second largest public income security expenditures. In addition, most governments make allowance for children in calculating taxable income. In Britain these allowances reduced tax payments by about 1.2% of all personal incomes before tax in 1949-50.

Governments modify the consumption pattern that would result from incomes from property and labor by distributing subsidized goods and services as well as cash payments. Military services, public health, and much education are fully subsidized, and all have increased in scope. Many states meet the needs of children by providing free school meals,

[65] Direction Générale de la Securité Sociale au Ministère du Travail, *Social Security in France* (n.d.), 32.
[66] U.S., *Monthly Lab. Rev.*, Feb. 1950, 143.

free protective foods, payment of vacation travel expenses, special clothing subsidies and the like.[67] Similar special grants or subsidies are also often paid to the aged and the blind.

All the more highly industrialized societies have long accepted responsibility for providing medical care, or subsidizing its cost in whole or in part, for at least the destitute poor, the mentally ill, and veterans disabled in military service. The quality and extent of care given to the poor has varied widely and, until recently, has included little rehabilitation. The medical care provided for veterans is often extensive, and, in view of the high proportion of adults drawn into the armed services since 1940, represents a significant form of income redistribution in some countries (notably in the U.S.A., where free medical care for veterans is not restricted to service-connected injuries). For other categories of persons, state intervention was first limited to persons suffering from occupational disability. Even in 1950 many workmen's compensation laws provided for cash payments in compensation for medical costs rather than the assurance of adequate medical service including rehabilitation. Attention to rehabilitation has, however, increased in recent years, the law in Ontario, Canada, being outstanding.

Germany made the first attempt to cover part of the cost of medical care for a large part of the population. The compulsory Sickness Insurance Law of 1883 provided for meeting part of the cost of medical attention (as well as for income maintenance payments above mentioned).[68] This example was followed in 1888 by Austria, in 1891 by Hungary, and in the first decade of the 20th century by a number of other countries. Britain enacted a compulsory Health Insurance law in 1911 to provide medical care to workers (but not to their families). All these schemes restricted medical care to insured persons and often limited the types of care provided and the duration of medical benefit. In 1938, however, New Zealand made medical care a free public service theoretically available to the whole population (following a precedent set in Russia in 1922). The New Zealand system was to come into full effect over 15 years. Britain introduced the most comprehensive public medical service in 1946; the state not only meets the costs of needed medical care but also undertakes to allocate resources to ensure an adequate supply of medical personnel and facilities. After 1948, the National Health Service provided medical, hospital, and dental care and medicines, and appliances to all persons resident in the country irrespective of income or coverage by the special insurance schemes. During the first year of the operation of the scheme, 95% of the population were registered with medical practitioners (over 90% of whom agreed to provide service). Slightly more than one-tenth of the employer and employee contribution for national insurance goes toward the health

---

[67] U.N., *Economic Measures in Favor of the Family*, 1952, *passim*.
[68] Armstrong, *op. cit.*, 303-312.

service, and it meets about one-ninth of the total cost.[69] Hospital care is similarly provided in Sweden, and in British Columbia and Saskatchewan in Canada.

In 1950 at least 43 countries were making some public provision for medical care. Five protected all residents or nationals, but the majority protected only employees (and often their families), or some groups of employees. They varied in the extent of medical service available, free or on a subsidized basis, ranging from the full extent of care that modern science can provide, to limited care in the event of maternity or specified illnesses, or excluding certain specialist services.[70] In some, the patient receives free treatment and, in others, he is reimbursed for all, or more usually, a part of the cost. In Britain, at the outset, medical advice and treatment, medicines and medical aids, dental service, hospital and specialist service, care of the eyes, hearing aids, health visitors and home nursing, vaccination and immunization were free,[71] but in 1949 a charge of one shilling per prescription was introduced, and in 1951 a few other charges. In New Zealand, whereas some kinds of medical care are free, physicians are entitled to charge patients for general practitioner and specialist services, the patient being reimbursed by the government at a fixed flat rate that does not necessarily cover the entire cost. In France in 1949, medical service was provided by state reimbursement of the cost of medical treatment to insured persons, their wives or husbands, and their dependent children, according to a table of refunds for each type of service; these refunds generally amount to 60 to 80% of the fee paid to the medical practitioner. In Sweden, the patient is reimbursed for two-thirds of the doctor's fee, according to an official schedule of charges; hospital care (ward care) is free.

Almost all countries provide for free choice of doctor and freedom to the doctor to participate or not in the public plan, but the methods of remunerating the doctor vary. In some plans he is paid a fee for service, in some he receives a capitation fee, an annual payment for each insured person he has accepted as a patient; in other plans he is a salaried employee. Doctors receive a fee for service in New Zealand, France, and in many of the voluntary subsidized plans. Britain utilizes all three methods of payment. The general practitioner is paid on a capitation basis, receiving a fixed sum per annum for each patient on his list, regardless of the amount of service given. The doctor also receives a mileage payment for visiting. Special inducements have been offered to attract doctors into under-doctored areas. Dentists are paid a fee for service according to a prearranged price list. There has been much criticism of the high incomes of some dentists; these have been due partly to the price list being high,

---

[69] U.S., *Social Security Bulletin*, March, 1950, 4.

[70] I.L.O., *International Survey of Social Security*, Ch. II, 110-23.

[71] National Council of Social Service, *Public Social Services Handbook, passim.*

but also to the very long hours worked by many dentists. Specialists are paid by salary, but not necessarily on a full-time basis.

Some countries seek to improve access to medical service by subsidizing voluntary health insurance plans and making grants for the construction of hospitals and other medical institutions, and for training medical personnel. The former have been of especial significance in Europe, where voluntary sick benefit societies, often organized by trade unions, had become widespread during the 19th century.[72] In 1891 Sweden began to subsidize these societies to enable them to extend their coverage, especially to lower income groups, and to increase their medical benefits. Denmark and Belgium almost immediately followed this example, and later France and Switzerland. Many of these schemes have since been taken over by the state as compulsory systems, and most of those remaining in 1950 were heavily subsidized if they covered any substantial part of the population. In Sweden in 1949 the state subsidized 46% of the expenditure of the voluntary funds, and provided hospital care. Canada and Australia have paid considerable subsidies to increase the supply of medical facilities and personnel since 1945.

Housing was provided by private enterprise in industrial countries in the 19th century, but during the 20th century governments have accepted increasing responsibility for housing in most European countries, the U.S.A., Australia, New Zealand, and parts of Latin America. Sweden was granting loans and subsidies early in the 1900s. This change in government policy has been due in part to the fact that the kind of housing many workers have been able to buy or rent out of their labor incomes has adversely affected their productivity, and that of future workers. Housing conditions have been blamed for social unrest and crime. But the change has been more due to inflation during two wars. To hold down the cost of living and wages, most governments prohibited rent increases. In Italy rent as a proportion of all family expenditure in 1947 was 5% of what it had been in 1938; in France it was 16% of what it had been in 1928, and in most other European countries about 50% of pre-war.[73] This policy discouraged private investment in housing. The economic rent of new houses was far in excess of the frozen rents of old houses at the end of each war, and investors in housing must anticipate that their rents will be held down in any future emergency and will fall with any fall in building costs.

Britain began to subsidize the building of new small dwellings in 1919, and some states in the U.S.A. (notably New York) in 1920. The U.S. federal government entered the field in 1932, and in 1937 provided loans and subsidies to publicly sponsored housing developments. Similar policies were followed in a number of north European countries. After 1945 the supply of dwellings was seriously inadequate. War destruction and dam-

---

[72] Armstrong, *op. cit.*, 316-22, 330-39.
[73] U.N., *Econ. Bull. for Europe*, Fourth Quarter, 1951, 27.

age was generally less important than the virtual suspension of new building during the war. Consequently in 1949, and in the immediately succeeding years, 80% of the new dwellings were government-assisted in the
Netherlands, Norway, and Britain, about 40% in France, and 33% in
Sweden and Switzerland.[74] In Britain 90% of the new dwellings until 1951
were built by local authorities for renting at less than a market rent, and
public authorities have been active in Sweden. Non-profit cooperative
building societies have been subsidized in Scandinavia, Switzerland, the
Netherlands, Belgium, and France. Most countries also assist individuals
and cooperatives to buy houses. Britain has granted annual subsidies,
originally covering half the loan charges and annual maintenance costs
calculated at 1945 prices, although subsequent increases in building costs
have reduced the subsidy from one-half to about one-third. The Netherlands, France, and Italy have also paid annual subsidies. Switzerland paid
a lump sum subsidy until 1949. Most countries also grant mortgage loans
on terms more favorable than could be obtained in the market (notably
Scandinavian countries, West Germany, and Britain). In Britain, housing
subsidies were .5% of the national income in 1951-2. Some governments
grant tax exemptions on new housing (Argentina, Belgium, Brazil, Denmark, and France). Some charge rents for public housing which discriminate in favor of families with children.[75]

Food subsidies are generally also progressive in incidence. Such subsidies hardly existed before 1939, and were subsequently introduced in
many countries to stave off increases in the cost of living and wages in
wartime. By 1948 they were about 25% of consumer expenditures on food
in Norway, 20% in Britain, and 13% in New Zealand. They were reduced
in 1948 in Austria, Belgium, the Netherlands, and Finland, and in 1950
in Norway, New Zealand, and Britain. In Britain, food subsidies take
the form of trading losses by the Ministry of Food, which buys food at
home and abroad and resells it. Part of these losses may be the result of
poor buying, but most of them represent subsidies that keep down the
cost of living. Food subsidies were about 15% of government expenditures
in New Zealand in 1950, and 4% in the Netherlands in 1951. Governments
also subsidize goods and services when they are provided by nationalized
industries operated at a loss.

ii. The Incidence of Costs

The taxes most likely to be regressive are those on commodities and
wages. Taxes on commodities fall only on expenditure, which is a smaller
proportion of large than of small incomes. But the effect of such taxes
depends also on the type of commodity taxed. Taxes on commodities
bought mainly out of higher incomes are progressive in relation to incomes

---

[74] *Ibid.*, 29.
[75] U.N., *Econ. Measures in Favor of the Family*, 75-116.

in general. Taxes on tobacco, matches and liquor (which are very common) are generally regressive. Some import duties have little effect on prices. But where they have an effect, they raise prices and their progressiveness or regressiveness depends on the sort of commodity affected. And they may have their maximum price-raising effect when they yield no income to the government (when they keep out all taxable imports). Income taxes are generally progressive in incidence.

Customs duties yield less than 9% of government income in the more developed countries in Europe; this is generally much less than in 1929 (owing to greater increases in the proceeds of other taxes, especially those on income, rather than to a fall in import taxation). But in less developed countries like Iceland, Greece, and Portugal, import duties provided more than 20% of government revenue in 1949 (Table 79). Taxes on specific con-

TABLE 79

THE DISTRIBUTION OF CENTRAL GOVERNMENT TAXES
IN SELECTED EUROPEAN COUNTRIES IN 1929 AND
1949* (EXCLUDING SOCIAL SECURITY CONTRIBUTIONS)

| | Taxes on: | | | | | | | | | |
| Country | Real Estate | | Income, Capital and Enterprise | | Turnover | | Consumption | | Imports† | |
	1929	1949	1929	1949	1929	1949	1929	1949	1929	1949
United Kingdom ...	...	...	59	57	...	8	39	33	2	2
Ireland	...	...	30	38	...	...	64	57	6	5
Denmark	3	2	34	44	...	...	47	51	16	3
Finland	...	2	30	24	...	34	36	37	34	5
Iceland	3	...	25	27	...	7	37	35	35	31
Norway	...	...	35	35	...	22	47	39	18	4
Sweden	...	...	37	49	...	...	43	46	20	5
Austria	...	...	36	53	19	23	25	22	20	2
Germany‡	11	..	46	42	13	28	24	28	6	2
Luxembourg ..	...	...	31	58	18	20	28	8	23	14
Netherlands ..	4	...	55	60	...	20	29	12	12	8
Switzerland ..	...	...	55	51	.	22	24	19	21	8
Belgium	4	1	43	49	21	28	15	18	17	4
France	3		46	34	19	45	29	20	3	1
Greece	4	2	30	20	...	22	29	32	37	24
Italy	2	1	43	23	4	24	41	46	10	6
Portugal	12	8	34	48	9	2	15	21	30	21
Spain	11	9	40	48	...	36	28	36	21	7
Turkey	14	3	16	40	11	22	39	24	20	11

* U.N., *Econ. Bull. for Europe*, Vol. 2, No. 3, 1950, 60.
† For some countries "consumption taxes" includes customs duties on imported commodities of general consumption (which are excluded from "customs duties").
‡ For pre-war territory in 1929 and three western zones only in 1949.

sumption goods have also yielded a declining proportion of government revenue since 1929 in many European countries, although their contribution has increased in some of the less developed (Italy, Portugal and Spain) and in Denmark and Sweden (Table 79). Restrictions on consumption reduced the yield of some taxes (e.g., on gasoline) but the percentage contribution of taxes on alcohol and tobacco to government revenues has generally increased.[76] As a percentage of total personal outlays on consumption, such taxes range from 15% in Britain to 4% in the Netherlands, and have been increasing in Britain and the Scandinavian countries. In Britain "purchase" taxes have been used since 1939 to divert resources from luxury goods into war production, later into exports, and still later into war production again. The tax on tobacco has been increased greatly since 1939, because tobacco must be imported and the demand for it is highly inelastic (especially when many other commodities are not obtainable). Federal excise taxes in the U.S.A. (e.g., on automobiles, gasoline, perfumes, luggage, and amusements) accounted for 3.4% of personal incomes in 1948 (Table 83).

This decline in the importance of taxes on specific consumption goods has been more than offset by the increasing importance of sales or turnover taxes (on the production, sale, or distribution of a wide range of commodities). These taxes (which did not exist in many European countries in 1929) now account for more than 20% of tax revenue in many (and 45% in France) (Table 79). The frequent exemption of food and other necessities makes these taxes mildly progressive. Sales taxes have also been increasingly used in the U.S.A. to finance municipal (and occasionally state) expenditures. All indirect taxes (including turnover taxes) in Europe ranged from 16.9% of net national income in Britain to 8.6% in Finland in 1948 (Table 74).

Taxes on income and property consisted chiefly of taxes on land until the 19th century. When the ownership of real estate was a rough index of individual wealth, such taxes were somewhat adjusted to ability to pay. But as other types of property (especially industrial and commercial capital and government bonds) increased in importance as sources of income, taxes on land or the income from it ceased to be closely related to ability to pay. Taxes on real estate have for 20 years been an insignificant source of central government incomes in Europe, and remain most important in the less developed countries (e.g., Portugal and Spain). But they account for 100% of the tax revenues of local government units in Britain, 44% in Germany, and 24% in Denmark.[77] Taxes on personal property are levied in most west European countries except Britain, but they declined as a percentage of all taxes on income, capital, and enterprise from 1928-9 to

---

[76] U.N., *Econ. Bull. for Europe,* Vol. 2, No. 3, 1950, 67.
[77] *Ibid.,* 62.

1948-9, from 26 to 8% in Denmark, 17 to 4% in Norway, 9 to 2% in Germany, and 12 to 3% in the Netherlands.[78]

Personal income taxes yielded 52% of all the proceeds of taxes on incomes, property, and enterprise in Britain in 1949, about 40% in Norway and Denmark, 72% in Germany, 65% in the Netherlands, but 8% in Belgium, 28% in France, 9% in Italy, 3% in Spain, and 1% in Greece.[79] The highest yields are obtained where a highly progressive tax is levied on all personal income regardless of source, as declared in compulsory annual declarations. But some countries tax each type of income separately, the tax varying with the amount of income from each source rather than with the total income of the individual. The income from each source is, furthermore, often based not on actual income but on estimates of "normal" yields or crude valuations based on outward indices of wealth or consumption. In these countries the yield is usually lower than where the tax is levied on total personal income.[80] Income taxes also account for an increasing proportion of all tax revenues in western Europe. The proportion of tax revenue obtained from taxes on income, capital, and enterprise together have increased in many European countries (Table 79), (but not in Britain, Germany, France, and Italy). It is over 50% in the Netherlands, Switzerland, Austria, Luxembourg, and Britain and 35% or less in Norway, France, Greece, and Italy. "Direct taxes" (approximately the same as taxes on income, capital, and enterprise) in 1948 absorbed about 19.1% of net national income in Britain, 11.7% in the Netherlands, 10.4% in Sweden, and ranged down to 2.7% in Italy (Table 74).

This shift of taxation from property to income began in Europe at the end of the 18th century, although the commercial democracies in medieval Italy appear to have invented the income tax. At first, the income tax was an occasional resort in time of war. France levied a "compulsory loan" in 1793, and Britain imposed an income tax in 1798 that was abolished in 1816, and the U.S.A. levied an income tax during the Civil War, between 1864 and 1872. Later income taxes were levied temporarily in peacetime. Britain reintroduced an income tax in 1842 for three years to compensate for the loss of the customs revenue when the Corn Laws were repealed. Income taxes were also levied in Austria in 1849 and Italy in 1864. Finally, in 1874, the tax became a permanent part of the British system. Thence it spread to South Australia in 1884, New Zealand in 1891, Tasmania in 1894, Japan in 1887, Prussia and the German Commonwealths in 1891, and the Netherlands in 1893. The U.S.A. enacted an income tax in 1894, but it was declared unconstitutional in 1895 and reenacted in 1913 after the constitution had been amended. The primitive general property tax of the states began to disintegrate in the 20th century, and in 1911 Wisconsin

---

[78] *Ibid.*, 64.
[79] *Ibid.*, 64.
[80] *Ibid.*, 62.

experimented with an income tax. In 1919 New York State replaced its property tax as a chief source of income with an income tax, and by 1948 state income taxes (corporate and individual) provided 16% of all state tax revenues. Most of the new states established in Europe at the end of the war in 1918 established income taxes, owing to their increased fiscal burdens and their democratic and socialist sentiments. An income tax was adopted in France in 1917 and modernized in 1948. Turkey adopted a tax of the modern type in 1949.

These taxes generally exempt a basic amount of income and apply at progressively increasing rates to increasing amounts of taxable income. They sometimes differentiate the rate of tax according to the source of income. Lower taxes have been imposed on incomes from work than on incomes from property in Britain, the U.S.A. (in the 1920s), Italy, France, and Germany. The tax liability often depends also on the method of disposing of income. Many states increase the exemption to married persons, and, further, according to the number of children, and sometimes to varying classes of dependents. In Britain allowance is made for children in college, and in Germany for medical and maternity expenses. Some countries also exempt life insurance premiums. Many countries allow charitable benefactions to be deducted from income for tax calculation. Some European countries have imposed increased rates on bachelors, divorced persons, and childless couples.

The incidence of income taxes is invariably progressive. For a time, they were increased in progressiveness to increase their yield, notably during the war of 1914-18. The highest rate of tax imposed in the U.S.A. at that time was 77% (on incomes over $2 million). Later the rate of progression was reduced, but in the war of 1939-45 high rates of progression were restored; in 1944 the highest individual surtax rate was 91%, which applied to income over $200,000. But further increases have been obtained by increasing taxes on the middle- and lower-income groups. In Britain since 1938-9, the tax has increased as a percentage of gross income at all levels, but most in the range from £250 to £499 a year, thus reducing its progressiveness (Table 80). But between 1938-9 and 1947-8, the number of incomes (after tax) of more than £6000 was reduced from 7000 to 70, and those from £4000 to £6000 from 12,000 to 3430. In fact there is almost a ceiling of £5000 on net disposable incomes. In 1948-9, of taxable incomes of £12,000, £3950 was left after taxation, of incomes of £30,000, £4675, and of those of £100,000, £6425. In the U.S.A., the federal personal income tax changed very little the share of money incomes going to those with incomes less than $7500 in 1949 (Table 81), although there must have been changes within the higher income brackets.

Taxes on property continue in the form of inheritance taxes, and have recently increased in amount. These taxes existed in ancient Rome, and fees for permission to succeed to the property and rights of deceased

TABLE 80

INCIDENCE OF INCOME TAXES IN THE UNITED KINGDOM
IN 1938-9 AND 1947-8*

Range of Income Before Payment of Income Taxes	Income Tax as Percentage of Income Before Tax	
	1938-9	1947-8
£ 250 to £ 499	2.6	8.2
500 to 999	8.9	19.0
1000 to 1999	15.0	29.0
2000 to 9999	29.1	46.4
10000 and up	56.7	76.6

* Calculated from U.K., *National Income and Expenditure of the United Kingdom,*
1946-8, Cmd. 7649. See also *Economist: Records and Statistics,* April 29, 1950, 405.

persons were common in feudal Europe. In Britain a small uniform tax
was imposed on estates irrespective of size in 1779, and in 1780 taxes varying with the size of estates and of legacies were introduced, but were applicable only to personal property. Finally, in 1853, real property was
included. France introduced death duties in 1796 and Italy soon after.
Germany imposed a national inheritance tax in 1906. The federal government in the U.S.A. imposed such taxes during the civil war and again in
1894. The tax was held unconstitutional and became a permanent part of
the federal tax system only in 1916 after the constitution had been
amended. In 1902, however, 26 states taxed inheritances in some way.
Since payments of state inheritance tax can be offset against a large proportion of the federal tax, almost all states impose such taxes at rates that
take full account of the credit against the federal tax (which reduces the
yield of the federal tax).

TABLE 81

DISTRIBUTION OF MONEY INCOMES AND THE FEDERAL
INCOME TAX IN THE U.S.A. IN 1949*

Annual Money Income Before Taxes	Total Money Income Per Cent	Federal Personal Income Tax Per Cent	Money Income Less Federal Personal Income Tax Per Cent
Under $1000	2	. . .	2
1000 to 1999	9	3	9
2000 to 2999	16	9	17
3000 to 3999	19	13	20
4000 to 4999	15	13	15
5000 to 7499	19	23	19
7500 and over	20	39	18
All income groups	100	100	100

* U.S. Joint Committee on the Economic Report *Report on the January 1951 Economic Report of the President,* 82nd Congress, 1st Session Report No. 210, 52.

The rates of tax were relatively low in the 19th century, but have been increased and applied to personal as well as real estate. Many countries (e.g., Britain) tax the estate progressively according to its net value. They also tax the amounts received by beneficiaries, according to the amount received and the relation of the legatee to the deceased (e.g., France, Italy, and most American states). In the U.S.A. inheritances in the direct line are usually not taxed. Some countries rebate part of the tax if the same property has been taxed within a stated number of years previously. Some adjust tax rates to the number of children (e.g., France and Belgium) in an effort to increase the birth rate. Taxes on inheritances and gifts, however, yielded considerably less than 10% of all taxes on income, property and enterprise in most European countries in 1949 (15% in Ireland, 14% in Portugal, 9% in Britain, 6% in Italy, 5% in France, and less in the remaining countries).[81]

Taxes on wages have increased with the extension of contributory social security. Contributions by both employers and workers in 1948 accounted for 6.7% of national income in France, 5.2% in Belgium, 4.3% in the Netherlands, 4.1% in Italy, 3.5% in Britain and lesser proportions in other European countries (Table 74). In the U.S.A. federal payroll taxes were 1.7% of all incomes in 1948 (Table 83). The frequent association of social security benefits with particular new taxes suggests the possibility of calculating the incidence of the cost of these schemes apart from other government taxes. Their immediate incidence varies widely. Insured persons carry 67% of the cost in Australia, and 40% in New Zealand and Switzerland, but only 5% in Italy. Employers carry 75% in Turkey and 64% in France, but only 11% in Sweden, 12% in Denmark, 13% in New Zealand, and 14% in Canada and Finland. The share borne by the state ranges from 77% in Sweden, 74% in Canada, 72% in Denmark and Finland, to 6% in Italy and Turkey (Table 82). Taxes proportional to wages are regressive in relation to all incomes. If the cost of a social security program is paid mainly by the same group that benefits from it, the distribution of incomes in general is not changed. Even so, the group may be compelled to redistribute its spending over time and among its individual members. Unemployment insurance schemes to which workers contribute compel them to save in times of employment to deal with times of unemployment, but every individual does not save enough to deal with the cost of his own unemployment. But the final incidence of the cost of these programs is impossible to calculate. The share immediately paid by the employer may be added to the price of his product. The cost of family allowances may be shifted to workers without families. The shares immediately paid by workers may be ultimately shifted through collective bargaining or otherwise. Finally, part of the cost of most schemes falls upon the state, which means upon the general tax system.

---

81 U.N., *Econ. Bull. for Europe*, Vol. 2, No. 3, 1950, 64.

TABLE 82

The Distribution of the Cost of Social Security Programs in Selected Countries in 1949*

Country	Insured Persons Per Cent	Employers Per Cent	State Per Cent
Australia	67	15	17
Austria	29	40	30
Belgium	18	38	40
Canada	7	14	74
Denmark	13	12	73
Finland	9	14	73
France	15	64	16
Germany	24	40	35
Greece	32	44	—
Iceland	28	16	50
Ireland	6	22	70
Italy	5	83	6
Netherlands	18	50	24
New Zealand	40	13	46
Norway	30	18	50
Sweden	10	11	77
Switzerland	40	30	17
Turkey	18	75	6
Union of South Africa	14	20	55
United Kingdom	19	16	60
U.S.A.	14	28	52

* "The Cost of Social Security," *Intern. Lab. Rev.*, June, 1952. Distributions do not add to 100 because of other sources of income (e.g., Interest, fines, etc.).

The figures refer to calendar 1949 or the financial year ending in 1949. They cover all public systems for all governmental levels whose objective is to grant curative or preventive medical care, income maintenance (including payments to veterans) and family allowances. Some figures are estimated.

The distributive effect of tax systems as a whole in these capitalist countries is far from clear. In the U.S.A. the federal tax system is regressive up to incomes of $2000 a year before tax, and only slightly progressive from $2000 to $5000. State and local taxes are generally regressive. The whole system is regressive up to $2000, and thereafter almost proportional up to $5000 (Table 83). In Britain, the top 1% of incomes (and indeed the top 50%) accounts for a smaller proportion of all private income after taxes than before (Table 84). If changes in prices as well as taxes are allowed for, the top sixth of income receivers (receiving more than about £250 a year in 1938 and £500 a year in 1948) received average real incomes about 350% of the average of the other five-sixths in 1938, and only 200% in 1948. In 1938 they received 40% of all post-tax income at 1938 prices, and in 1948 only 28%.[82] Since the lower incomes are mainly from labor, the share of all private income paid in wages, salaries, and pay of the armed forces

[82] Seers, *The Levelling of Incomes*, 56.

was 59.8% before tax and 65.1% after tax in 1949, whereas the share of property and mixed incomes was 33.8% before and 27.1% after tax.[83]

The net effect of both government expenditures and income on the various income groups is extremely difficult to calculate. In general in recent decades expenditures on the armed services and individual welfare have greatly increased. The incidence of defense expenditures is unknown, but that of welfare expenditures is progressive. But turnover, income, and wage taxes have also increased. Turnover taxes are regressive, income taxes are progressive but have been reaching further down the

TABLE 83

TAX PAYMENTS AS PERCENT OF INCOME BY INCOME BRACKETS
IN THE U.S.A. IN 1948*

	Spending Unit Income Bracket, Before Tax, in Dollars							
	Under 1,000	1,000 to 1,999	2,000 to 2,999	3,000 to 3,999	4,000 to 4,999	5,000 to 7,499	7,500 and up	Total
Federal Government:								
Personal income taxes	0.2	2.8	4.4	5.5	7.0	9.3	12.3	7.8
Corporation income taxes .	6.1	4.3	3.8	3.7	3.7	3.8	9.9	5.6
Excises	5.1	4.3	4.0	4.0	3.5	3.4	2.3	3.4
Payroll taxes	2.5	2.1	3.3	2.5	1.9	1.2	.5	1.7
Estate and gift taxes	—	—	—	—	—	—	1.4	.4
Total	13.9	13.5	15.5	15.5	16.1	17.7	26.3	18.8
State and Local Government: Total	9.7	6.8	6.1	6.0	5.6	5.4	5.5	5.8
All levels of government Total	23.6	20.3	21.6	21.8	21.7	23.1	31.7	24.7
Percent of spending units	12.2	17.7	22.9	20.1	11.6	10.2	5.3	100.0
Percent of income	1.9	7.0	14.8	17.9	13.4	16.3	28.8	100.0

* Musgrave, et al., cit., U.S. Joint Committee on the Economic Report *Report on the January 1951 Economic Report of the President* 82nd Congress, 1st Session, Senate Report No. 210, 56.

income scale, and wage taxes are regressive. In the U.S.A. in 1950 money incomes (minus governmental transfers) of less than $5000 were 55.24% of all incomes. After these same incomes are adjusted for taxes paid and benefits in cash and kind received from the government, they were 62.3% of all such adjusted incomes. There was, therefore, a net transfer from the class receiving $5000 or more to the class receiving less. The net transfer was, moreover, progressive among the income brackets below $5000.[84] In Britain in 1950-51 there was a net transfer through the social services

---

[83] *Ibid.*, 52, 49.
[84] A. T. Peacock (ed.), *Income Redistribution and Social Policy*, 197, 238.

TABLE 84

CUMULATIVE DISTRIBUTION PERCENTAGES OF ALL PRIVATE
INCOMES BEFORE AND AFTER TAXES IN THE UNITED
KINGDOM IN 1938 AND 1947[*]

	1938		1947	
Number of Incomes	Pre-tax Income Percent	Post-tax Income Percent	Pre-tax Income Percent	Post-tax Income Percent
Top 1%	19	14	17	11
2½%	27	22	24	16
5%	33	28	30	21
10%	42	38	38	30
25%	58	54	55	48
50%	75	73	74	70

[*] Seers, D., *The Levelling of Incomes Since 1938*, 39.

from incomes over £500 to lower incomes amounting to about 5.3% of
the national income. In general since 1945 the low income groups have
paid about as much in taxes as they have received in social services, and
thus have contributed little to the cost of other government services.[85]
In Denmark in 1949 workers and the self-employed made a net contribution to the remainder of the population (chiefly the aged). Such transfers
were about 35% of all the incomes of the aged, but the younger employed
population was relieved of its former responsibility for providing for the
aged and for their own old age.[86]

d. *Socialist Societies*

The proportion of the national income passing through the government
fiscal organization was about 30% in Czechoslovakia and Hungary (which
was similar to the proportion in western Europe) and 13% in Poland
(which is comparable with the proportion in Southern Europe) (Table 74).
But in Russia the proportion was about 36% in 1937, and 50% in 1947.[87]
Calculation is difficult, however, because the official figures for net national income must be adjusted to include government, professional, and
personal services, which are not included in national output, and to allow
for the fact that much of the national product in Russia was valued until
1949 at 1936-7 prices, which by 1945 were probably about 50% of current
prices. Government revenues, on the other hand, are in current rubles.

Since 1939 the state budget of the U.S.S.R. has included the budgets of
the Union, the allied and autonomous republics (of which there were fif-

---

[85] Weaver, "Taxation and Redistribution in the United Kingdom," *cit.*, Peacock
(ed.), *op. cit.*, 156, 206.

[86] Peacock (ed.), *op. cit.*, 83.

[87] Bergson, "Soviet National Income and Product in 1937," *Quar. Jour. of Econ.*
May 1950, 236.

teen in 1941), local soviets, and the social insurance system. The budget of the Union includes the cost of financing enterprises and economic measures of all-union importance such as large-scale industry, transportation, communication, and foreign trade. It also includes the net receipts of state railway and communication facilities. Most of the capital expansion for collective farms is provided from their own resources, but the remainder is included in the federal budget. The federal budget also includes social and cultural institutions of all-union importance, such as higher education, scientific research, medical training, and the like. It includes defense and all-union administrative agencies and the cost of servicing government loans, which, however, is small. The budgets of the local republics are similar to that of the Union government, except that they do not include defense, and are restricted mainly to services of local importance, such as local industries including transport, local services such as education and health, and local administrative expenses. Social and cultural expenditures represent the larger part of their expenditures. Most of their expenditures, furthermore, are made through even more local bodies. These local republics collect some taxes, of which they remit a prescribed percentage to the Union government, but receive grants from the Union government in support of their activities.

i. Incidence of Benefits

These socialist economies came into being at a time of generally increasing armament expenditures. Of the national budget in Russia, about 22% was explicitly for defense in 1938, 22% in 1946, and 20.8% in 1953 (Table 85). In addition, expenditures on the "national economy" include considerable but unknown sums for capital equipment for armament plants and other military establishments. Of the total national product, about 14% is estimated to have been for defense in 1948 (compared with 6 to 8% in the U.S.A. and Britain).

TABLE 85

EXPENDITURES OF THE GOVERNMENT OF THE U.S.S.R. IN
1938, 1946, 1950, 1953*

	Billions of Rubles			
	1938	1946	1950†	1953†
Military Services	23.1	73.6	79.4	110.2
National Economy	51.7	106.2	164.4	192.5
Social Services	35.3	80.4	120.7	139.5
Administration and Justice	5.4	11.8	13.9	
Total expenditures‡	124.0	307.5	427.9	543.4

* 1938-50. Schwartz, op. cit., 415.
† Planned, not actual.
‡ Total includes items not enumerated in table.

Expenditures on social and cultural development accounted for 28% of all government expenditures in 1938, 26% in 1946, and 25% in 1953 (Table 85). Half of this sum is for education (Table 86), which includes political propaganda, newspaper and book publishing, orchestras, and expositions,

TABLE 86

EXPENDITURES ON SOCIAL AND CULTURAL DEVELOPMENT
IN RUSSIA, 1938-1953*

	Billion Rubles			
	1938	1946	1950†	1953‡
Education	18.7	38.1	59.5	na
Health and physical culture	7.6	13.8	22.0	na
Social insurance	6.0	7.3	na	na
State aid to widows and mothers of many children	na	3.6	4.0	na
Social security (mainly veterans)	na	17.6	22.4	na
Total	35.3	80.4	120.7	139.5

* For 1938-1950 from Schwartz, *Russia's Soviet Economy*, 428. (Totals do not always add.)
† Planned.
‡ Details not available. Planned, not actual.

as well as schools, research institutes, and museums. In 1922 Russia made medical care a free public service available (in principle) to the whole population. Health and physical culture includes not only medical personnel, hospitals, and the like, but also the maintenance of kindergartens and children's homes. Health service is provided to all persons without payment of doctors' fees (with a few exceptions). Other services apply mainly to workers in industry, although in agriculture 2% of the incomes of collective farms is set aside for the care of the aged and other welfare services. Social insurance expenditures provide payment to persons unable to work because of illness, accident, or related cause, and for funeral expenses, pensions to permanently incapacitated, aged and retired workers, sanatoria, rest homes, parks, and the like. Children's allowances are paid on a sliding scale, beginning with the fourth child and rising from 480 rubles a year for four children to 1800 rubles for eleven or more. Social security payments are primarily to or for persons invalided in military service. There has been no unemployment insurance since unemployment was officially declared to have been liquidated in about 1931.[88] Funds for social and cultural development are also provided from the social insurance fund, surcharges on wage bills (to meet the cost of training personnel), the profits of social and cultural organizations run for profit

[88] Schwartz, *op. cit.*, 442.

(spas, dispensaries, the press, and the like), the funds of labor unions and cooperatives, directors' funds (for cultural needs), the funds of business institutions (for training and research work), and from special funds of collective farms (for cultural and welfare needs). Most of these sums are spent locally but are coordinated with the central plan.

In eastern Europe social security laws similar to those in force in Russia were passed in Yugoslavia in 1946, Albania 1947, Rumania 1948, and Bulgaria 1948.[89] Integrated income maintenance programs were introduced in Bulgaria, Czechoslovakia, and Rumania in 1948, and in Poland in 1949. Unemployment insurance existed in Poland and Bulgaria in 1950, but not elsewhere. Family allowances are universal (except in Albania), and the provision of medical care has increased. The family allowance for a wife and two children raised the food purchasing power of industrial earnings 3.6% above those without a family allowance in Hungary in 1950, and 6.6% in Czechoslovakia.[90] Coverage has been widened, but benefits were generally no higher in 1950 than in 1940.

The socialist countries seek to minimize the tendency of social security to reduce production and maximize the achievement of the desired allocation of labor. Old age pensions, for instance, are payable whether or not the beneficiary works, disability benefits depend on length of service in the same undertaking, and trade union members receive twice the benefits of non-union members, except for temporary disability. Old age pensions are payable at an earlier age in heavy industry and dangerous occupations, and invalidity benefits are more generous to those in these occupations.

The remaining important group of expenditures by the Russian government consists of grants to the "national economy," which accounted for 46% of the national budget in 1938, 32% in 1946, and 36% in 1953. These grants provided 72% of the additions to fixed and working capital in 1953, the remaining 28% being provided from profits, amortization reserves, and other resources of productive enterprises and other institutions. In communist China about 25% of all government appropriations in 1950 was for the development of public enterprises.

ii. Incidence of Costs

The Russian government financed itself until 1924 by currency issues and taxes in kind. From 1917-1921, the pre-revolutionary system broke down, and the government experimented with literal communism. Rising prices and disorganization rapidly reduced the revenue from taxes on commodities and currency issues. The output of nationalized enterprises was taken over by the government without payment, and urban food supplies were obtained by requisitions of agricultural produce, which were taxes in kind. In 1921 the government resumed money payment for the

[89] U.S., *Soc. Sec. Bull.* March, 1950, 10.
[90] U.S., *Monthly Lab. Rev.*, Feb. 1950, 143.

products of government enterprises and excluded the current financial operations of the enterprises from the national budget. Issues of currency remained a substantial source of revenue until 1924. The 12 taxes payable in kind up to 1921 were gradually consolidated and made payable at prescribed rates in money, and after 1924 were payable only in money. Since that time, taxes have been payable in money, except that compulsory deliveries of farm produce are taxes in kind (Ch. 8). In Bulgaria, however, a law of 1948 required (in principle) ten days of labor from all adults (subject to specified exemptions), but individuals were released from the obligation on payment of a specified sum of money.[91]

A large part of the income of the state in Russia comes from its management of the socialized sector. Production units charging prices that approximately equate supply and demand (except in times of rationing or shortage of supply at current prices) take in more purchasing power from the sale of goods and services than they pay in costs, where the production plan diverges from consumer choice. Turnover and profit taxes transfer most of this excess to the government. Turnover taxes were introduced in 1930, although excise taxes payable in money had been reintroduced in 1921. They have provided about 60% of all government income in time of peace (Table 87). They are levied at the time of fabrication, and also upon

TABLE 87

REVENUES OF THE GOVERNMENT OF THE U.S.S.R. IN SELECTED YEARS
(1938-51)*

Source	Billions of Rubles					
	1938	1940	1946	1948	1950†	1951†
Turnover tax	80.4	105.9	190.9	247.3	239.1	244.7
Profit tax	10.5	21.7	16.2	27.2	40.0	47.2
Direct taxes on population	5.1	9.4	22.7	33.2	36.4	43.4
Loans and gifts to state	7.6	11.5	24.7	23.9	31.8	na
Income from social insurance levies	7.2	8.5	na	16.2	na	na
Total Revenue‡	127.5	180.2	325.4	410.5	433.2	458.7

* 1938-50 from Schwartz, op. cit., 415.
† Planned, not actual.
‡ Totals include items not enumerated in the table.

government purchases at low prices of compulsory deliveries of agricultural produce. In 1939 requisitioned agricultural produce yielded 34.4% of all turnover tax revenue, the food industry about 30%, and the textile industry 13%, and all consumer goods about 90%.[92] On many items the tax was over 70% of the selling price (90% for alcohol), and in 1934 it was 48%

[91] I.L.O., Ind. and Lab., March 1949, 174.
[92] Schwartz, op. cit., 416.

of the entire trade turnover.[93] In 1941 there were 2500 different rates of tax. On industrial goods the tax is typically a percentage of the wholesale transfer price, and on agricultural products a fixed money amount per physical unit of product. Where the wholesale prices are zoned, the tax is graded according to the zone in which the goods are to be sold. The tax also depends on whether the goods are to be consumed by industry or by the general market. Typically once a commodity has been taxed, it subsequently moves free of tax toward ultimate consumption. But a second tax may be levied at a reduced rate on goods manufactured from products already taxed.[94]

The profits tax, also introduced in 1930, yielded only 8% of all state revenues in 1938, less than 5% in 1946, and about 10% in 1951. The rate of tax differs from industry to industry and year to year, partly according to the needs of each industry to increase its capital. Enterprises whose incomes equal or fall short of their operating costs (and their needs for fixed or working capital to carry out the plan of future production) are allowed to retain most of their profits. A minimum 10% rate of tax is applied to provide an opportunity of checking their performance. But enterprises whose income exceeds their needs for capital to carry out future production plans pay higher rates. In 1940 the rate was 25% of profits in the iron and steel industry, and 35% in petroleum, and ranged up to 51.9% in transport, 63.8% in machinery, 84.1% in food, and 90% in light industry and textiles.[95] These turnover and profits taxes differ from sales and corporation taxes in capitalist countries in that they provide practically all the savings of the economy, as well as the usual government expenditures.

Income and property taxes were reimposed in 1922. Land taxes are unusual (although the Chinese communist government has introduced such a tax). Direct taxes provided about 4% of Russian state revenue in 1938, 7% in 1946, and 9% in 1951 (Table 87). Incomes are taxed according to their origin. Wage earners receiving more than 150 rubles a month pay a progressive tax that rises to 13% of the income in excess of 1000 rubles (which is well above the average wage in 1949, but not above the highest). Members of industrial cooperatives pay 110% of the rates applicable to wage workers. Writers, artists, and the like pay higher rates than wage workers on their income in excess of 1000 rubles per month. Agricultural cooperatives were first taxed in 1936, and pay 4% of the value of produce used for their own needs (for seed, farm insurance funds, and the like), 8% of the value (at the price paid by the government for non-obligatory sales) of grain and other produce distributed among their members as part of their remuneration, 4% of the money income received from sales to the

---

[93] Baykov, *op. cit.*, 372.

[94] Bergson, "Soviet National Income and Production in 1937," *Quar. Jour. Econ.*, May 1950, 228.

[95] Schwartz, *op. cit.*, 418.

government of "technical crops" (sugar beets, flax, cotton, and the like), and 8% of the proceeds of sales in the free market. These taxes do not yield a great deal, but provide an opportunity for control of the operations of the cooperatives. The income tax payable by the farm population discriminates in favor of cooperative operation. The collective farmer pays no tax on his income from the collective as payment for labor days. His income from non-collective production is assessed according to the number of acres available to him and their use. Since 1948 he has paid 11% on imputed incomes of under 2000 rubles from this source, the rate rising to 30% on income in excess of 8000 rubles a year. The non-collective farmer is taxed on his sales in the open market, and the methods of assessing his taxable income are the same as for collective farmers, but the tax rates are twice as high.[96]

Most of the special honors awarded to workers exempt them from taxes. Urban employees who are unmarried adults, or married but without children, pay an additional tax of 6% of their income, those with only one child 1%, and those with only two children .5%. These progressive taxes on incomes depend for their importance on the degree of inequality of income distribution, but their effect is unknown. Creative workers are among the highest income receivers, and the ratio between the income of the group receiving the highest royalties in 1936 and the average wage was 43:1 before income tax and 27:1 after tax.[97] Inheritances are taxed at sharply progressive rates. Loans and gifts to the state, which are included in the income of the state, have accounted in recent years for about 6% of state income (Table 87). Insofar as there is strong pressure on workers to devote three or four weeks' wages to bond purchases, these partake somewhat of the nature of a tax.

Taxes on wages are not common in socialist countries because in general the total cost of social security services is met out of the general tax funds. Government enterprises, however, contributed about 4 to 6% of government revenues in Russia between 1938 and 1948, the contributions varying from 4 to 11% of payroll, according to the risk in each industry. In Poland these contributions are 22.3% of payrolls plus the cost of work accident insurance, and in Rumania 10% of payrolls plus the cost of family allowances. But workers contribute in some east European countries. In Czechoslovakia, 8.4% of payroll is paid by the insured and 13.4% by the employer, in Hungary 1% is paid by the insured and 17% by the employer, the state paying all family allowances. In Yugoslavia 6.5% is paid by the insured and 14.2% plus the cost of family allowances by the employer.[98] Contributions

---

[96] *Ibid.*, 420.
[97] A. Bergson, "On Inequality of Incomes in the U.S.S.R.," *American Slavic and Eastern European Review*, 1951, 95.
[98] U.S., *Soc. Sec. Bull.*, March 1950, 10.

by employers and workers in Czechoslovakia in 1948 were 7.2% of national income, in Hungary 3.2%, and in Poland 1.7% (Table 74).

The distribution of consumption has not always been determined in Russia by money incomes after adjustment for government financial operations and the provision of services. Consumer goods were rationed before 1922 and on an expanding scale from 1928 to 1936, and again from the Nazi attack until 1947. This rationing was not equalitarian, but was devised to support the production plan of the government (by providing preferential treatment for "more important" industries and plants and more productive workers).[99] But since 1947, emphasis has been placed on money and prices as the means of regulating individual consumption. Piece and bonus methods of payment for work are intended to provide greater monetary reward for greater production, and freedom to expend money is intended to permit greater real reward. Food has also been rationed in most of the east European countries (including Yugoslavia until 1951). In Russia and Poland, house rents vary with income and number of dependents. Furthermore, periodic reductions in the prices of consumer goods have raised the purchasing power of the ruble in recent years.

The over-all effect of government income and expenditures on the distribution of consumption is unknown. The incidence of defense expenditures, which were about 21% of government expenditures in 1953, is incalculable. In 1953, 86% of government income came from industry, agriculture, and other branches of the national economy, and 36% of expenditures were for further development, the incidence of which is also incalculable. The population in general provided, through taxation, compulsory deliveries, and loans, about 12% of government income, and received in social welfare payments and services and price reductions 36% of all government expenditure.[100] The difference represented mainly a transfer of part of the net result of productive operations to consumers, somewhat resembling a dividend. But the interpersonal distribution of gains and burdens remains unknown.

---

[99] Bergson, "Soviet National Income and Production in 1937," *Quar. Jour. of Econ.*, Aug. 1950.

[100] Speech by Premier Georgi M. Malenkov, *cit.*, *N.Y. Times*, Aug. 10, 1953.

List of References

I. Government Publications

AUSTRALIA, COMMONWEALTH (CANBERRA)

Rural Reconstruction Commission:
Commercial Policy in Relation to Agriculture (10th report), 1946.
Irrigation, Water Conservation and Land Drainage (8th report), 1943.
Land Utilization and Farm Settlement (3rd Report), 1944.
Rural Land Tenure and Valuation (9th report), 1946.

FRANCE

Ministère du Travail, Direction Générale de la Securité Sociale:
Social Security in France (no date)

INDIA

Advisory Planning Board:
Report (New Delhi, 1947)

Cooperative Planning Committee:
Report (Bombay, 1946)

Famine Inquiry Commission:
Final Report (Delhi, 1945)

Ministry of Industry and Supply:
Conference on Industrial Development in India (New Delhi, 1947)

INDONESIA

Departments of Economic Affairs and Agriculture and Fisheries:
The Economic Review of Indonesia (Jakarta, Java, current)

KENYA, COLONY AND PROTECTORATE (NAIROBI)

The Agrarian Problem in Kenya (1947)
The Kikuyu Lands (1946)
Development Committee
Report (2 vols.) (1946)

LEAGUE OF NATIONS (GENEVA)

Condition of Private Foreign Investment (1946)
International Currency Experience (1944)
Network of World Trade (1942)
Raw Material Problems and Policies (1946)

735

QUEENSLAND (AUSTRALIA)

Bureau of Industry:
Review of Economic Progress (Brisbane, 1949 to 1952)

SOUTHERN RHODESIA (SALISBURY)

Report on a visit to Certain African Colonies to study Native Production and Cooperation (Mimeo, 1948) ("Pendered Report")

Secretary of Native Affairs, Chief Native Commissioner and Director of Native Development:
Report for Year 1946 (1947)

UNION OF SOUTH AFRICA (PRETORIA)

Commissioner of Inland Revenue:
Annual Report, 1946-7.

Committee on Deep Level Mining:
Report, 1945

Committee on Gold Mining Taxation:
Report, 1946

Department of Native Affairs:
Report for Years 1945-7, 1948.

Industrial and Agricultural Requirements Commission:
Third Interim Report; Fundamentals of Economic Policy in the Union, 1941.

Interdepartmental Committee on the Social, Health and Economic Conditions of Urban Natives:
Report, 1942.

Mine Workers Union Commission of Inquiry:
Report, 1946.

National Marketing Council:
Report on the Marketing Boards 1938-46, 1947.

Social and Economic Planning Council:
Report No. 11, 1947.

Wheat Commission:
Report, 1941.

Witwatersrand Mine Natives' Wages Commission:
Report on the Remuneration and Conditions of Employment of Natives in Witwatersrand Gold Mines and the Regulation and Conditions of Employment of Natives at Transvaal Undertakings of the Victoria Falls and Transvaal Power Company Limited, 1943.

UNITED KINGDOM (LONDON)

Board of Trade, Overseas Economic Surveys:
Argentina (1947)
Brazil (1948)
Egypt (1947)
Turkey (1947)

British Electricity Authority:
Reports and Accounts (Annual, 1949-)

British Information Service:
Britain Speeds the Plough (New York, 1949)
British Development and Welfare Acts (1949)

From Darkness to Light (1949)
Labor and Industry in Britain (Quarterly)
Town and Country Planning in Britain (1949)
"Trade Unions in Britain," *Labor and Industry in Britain*, Dec. 1949

Colonial Office:
Colonial Mining Policy (Colonial No. 206, 1946)
Labor Conditions in East Africa (Report by Major G. St. J. Orde Browne, 1946)
Northern Rhodesia, Annual Report for the year 1946 (1948)
Uganda, Annual Report for the year 1946 (1948)

Indian Statutory Commission:
Report (1930)

Ministry of Health:
The National Health Service (n.d.)

National Coal Board:
Annual Report and Statement of Accounts (Annual 1947-)

Overseas Food Corporation:
Report and Accounts for 1948-9

Parliamentary Papers:
Coal Mining, Report of Technical Advisory Committee (Cmd 6610, 1945)
Colonial Development, Fifth Report from the Committee on Estimates (1948)
Colonial Empire (1939-1947) (Cmd 7167, 1947)
Company Law Amendment Committee Report (Cmd 6659, 1945)
Economic Survey for 1950 (Cmd 7915, 1950)
Employment Policy (Cmd 6527, 1944)
Industry and Trade Committee Report (Cmd 3282, 1929)
Mechanised Production of Ground Nuts in East and Central Africa, Plan for (Cmd 7030, 1947)
National Income and Expenditure of the United Kingdom 1946-9 (Cmd 7933, 1950)
Overseas Food Corporation, Future of (Cmd 8125, 1951)
Steel Industry, Report of the Import Duties Advisory Committee on the Position and Future Development of (Cmd 5507, 1937)
Trusts, Committee Report on (Cmd 9236, 1918)

Royal Commission on Population:
Report (1949)

UNITED NATIONS (LAKE SUCCESS AND NEW YORK)

Conciliation Commission for Palestine:
Final Report of the United Nations Economic Survey Mission for the Middle East (2 vols.) (1949)

Department of Economic Affairs:
Current Inflationary and Deflationary Tendencies (1947)
Economic Bulletin for Europe (Geneva, quarterly, 1949-)
Economic Development in Selected Countries (1947, and 1950)
Economic Development of Latin America and its Principal Problems (1950)
Economic Survey of Asia and the Far East (Annually, 1948-)
Economic Survey of Europe (Annually, 1948-)
Economic Survey of Latin America (Annually, 1948-)
European Steel Trends in the Setting of the World Market (1949)

Inflationary and Deflationary Tendencies in 1946-8 (1949)

Instability in the Export Markets of Underdeveloped Countries (1952)

International Capital Movements during the Inter-War Period (1949)

International Flow of Private Capital (1954)

Land Reform; Defects in Agrarian Structure as Obstacles to Economic Development (1951)

Maintenance of Full Employment (1949)

Major Economic Changes in 1948 (1949)

Measures for the Economic Development of Underdeveloped Areas (1951)

Measures for International Economic Stability (1951)

Methods of Financing Economic Development in Underdeveloped Countries (1949)

Mobilization of Domestic Capital in Certain Countries of Asia and the Far East (Bangkok 1951)

National and International Measures for Full Employment (1949)

National and Per Capita Income in Seventy Countries (1949)

National Income and its Distribution in Underdeveloped Countries (1951)

National Income Statistics 1938-48 (1950)

Problems of Unemployment and Inflation, 1950 and 1951 (1951)

Progress in Land Reform (1954)

Public Finance Information Papers:
    Egypt
    Iran
    Iraq
    Italy

Relative Prices of Exports and Imports of Underdeveloped Countries (1949)

Review of Economic Conditions in Africa (1951)

Review of Economic Conditions in the Middle East (1951)

Review of International Commodity Problems, 1951 (1952)

Rural Progress through Cooperatives (1954)

Survey of the Economic Situation and Prospects in Europe (Geneva, 1948)

Technical Assistance for Economic Development (1949)

World Economic Report (annually 1948-)

World Energy Supplies in Selected Years, 1929-1950 (Statistical Paper Series J, No. 1), 1952

World Iron Ore Resources and their Utilization (1950)

Department of Social Affairs:

Economic Measures in Favor of the Family (1952)

Preliminary Report on the World Social Situation (1952)

Food and Agriculture Organization:

Food Balance Sheet 1948 (1949)

Rice Report (1950)

Year Book of Food and Agricultural Statistics, 1948 (Washington 1949)

Year Book of Food and Agriculture, 1950 (1951)

International Labor Office:

Industry and Labor (current)

International Survey of Social Security (Geneva, 1950)

Year Book of Labor Statistics, 1947-8

Scientific Conference on Conservation and Utilization of Resources:

World Resources and Population

Statistical Office:

Demographic Year Book (annually 1948-)

Monthly Bulletin of Statistics (1947-)
Statistical Year Book (1948-)

UNITED STATES OF AMERICA (WASHINGTON)

Bureau of the Census:
Historical Statistics of the United States (1949)
Irrigation of Agricultural Lands: Sixteenth Census of the U.S.A., 1940

Council of Economic Advisors:
Economic Review (annual)

Congress:
Joint Committee on the Economic Report, *Report on the January 1952 Economic Report of the President*, Senate Report 1295 82nd Cong., 2nd Sess. (1952)
Payments made under the Agricultural Program Senate Doct. 274 74th Cong., 2nd Sess. (1936)

Department of Agriculture:
Agricultural Statistics, 1947
Crop Production, 1948
Foreign Agriculture (current)
Foreign Crops and Markets (current)
Graphic Summary of World Agriculture (Miscellaneous Publication 705, 1949)

Department of Agriculture and Department of Commerce:
Graphic Summary of Farm Tenure in the United States (1948)

Department of Commerce:
Survey of Current Business (current)

Department of Interior:
Minerals Year Book (current)

Department of Labor:
Wage Trends and Wage Policies: Various Foreign Countries (Bulletin 934, 1948)

Department of State:
Energy Resources of the World (1949)
Proposals for the Expansion of World Trade and Employment (1945)

Federal Security Agency:
Social Security Legislation throughout the World (1949)
Summary of International Vital Statistics, 1937-44 (1947)
"World Developments in Social Security Legislation" 13 *Social Security Bulletin* (1950), 3.

Federal Trade Commission:
Prices, Profits and Competition in the Petroleum Industry (1928)
The Copper Industry (1947)

President:
Economic Reports (semi-annual)
Water Resources Policy Committee *Summary of Recommendations* (1950)

S.C.A.P.:
Summation of Non Military Activities in Japan and Korea

Tariff Commission:
Agricultural, Pastoral and Forest Industries of Argentina (1947)
Agricultural, Pastoral and Forest Industries of Brazil (1946)

Agricultural, Pastoral and Forest Industries in Cuba (1947)
Economic Controls and Commercial Policy in Bolivia (1946)
Economic Controls and Commercial Policy in Brazil (1948)

Temporary National Economic Committee:
Competition and Monopoly in American Industry (Monograph No. 21, 1941)

II. Books and Periodical Articles

Acton Society Trust, *Accountability to Parliament*, Claygate, Surrey, England. Acton House, 1950.

Adler, J. H., *The Underdeveloped Areas; their Industrialisation*, New Haven: Yale Institute of International Studies, 1949.

Agarwala, A. N., "The Social Security Movement in India," *Economic Journal*, 1946, LVI, 568.

Allen, G. C., *A Short Economic History of Modern Japan*, London: Allen and Unwin, 1946.

Andrews, Frank E., *Philanthropic Giving*, New York: Russell Sage Foundation, 1950.

Anjaria, J. J., *Indian Land Tenure Systems*.

Anjaria, J. J. and Sir M. B. Nanavati, *Indian Agricultural Problems*, Bombay: Indian Society of Agricultural Economics, 1945.

Armstrong, B. N., *Insuring the Essentials*, New York: Macmillan Co., 1932.

Arnold, A. Z., *Banks, Credit and Money in Soviet Russia*, New York: Columbia University Press, 1937.

Ashton, T. S., "The Standard of Life of the Workers in England 1790 to 1830" *Tasks of Economic History*, 1949, IX, 19.

Baine, J. S., *Pacific Coast Petroleum Industry* (3 vols.), Berkeley: University of California Press, 1945.

Baran, P. A., "National Income and Product of the U.S.S.R.," *Review of Economic Statistics*, 1947, 29: 226.

Bauer, P. T., *The Rubber Industry*, Cambridge: Harvard University Press, 1948.

———, "The Working of Rubber Regulation," *Economic Journal*, 1946, LVI, 391.

Baykov, A., *The Development of the Soviet Economic System*, New York: Macmillan Co., 1947.

Bennett, M. K., "International Disparities in Consumption Levels," *American Economic Review*, 1951, XLI, 632.

Bergson, A., "On Inequality of Incomes in the U.S.S.R.," *American Slavic and East European Review*, 1951, X, 95.

———, "Post War Reconstruction and Development in Russia," *Annals of American Academy of Political Science*, May, 1949.

———, "Soviet National Income and Product in 1937," *Quarterly Journal of Economics*, 1950, LXIV, 208, 408.

———, *The Structure of Soviet Wages*, Cambridge: Harvard Univ. Press, 1944.

Bergson, A. (ed.), *Soviet Economic Growth: Conditions and Perspectives*, White Plains: Row Peterson and Co., 1953.

Bergson, A. and H. Heymann, *Soviet National Income and Product, 1940-48*, New York: Columbia University Press, 1954.

Beveridge, Sir William H., *Social Insurance and the Allied Services*, London: H.M. Stationery Office (Cmd. 6404), 1942.

Bonné, A., "Land and Population in the Middle East," *Middle East Journal*, 1951, V, 55.

——, *State and Economics in the Middle East*, London: Kegan Paul, 1948.

Brady, R. A., *Business as a System of Power*, New York: Columbia University Press, 1943.

——, *The Rationalization Movement in German Industry*, New York: Columbia University Press, 1933.

Brandt, K., *Reconstruction of World Agriculture*, New York: Norton & Co., 1945.

Brebner, J. B., "Laisser Faire and State Intervention in Nineteenth Century Britain," *Tasks of Economic History*, 1948, VIII, 59.

Brown, H. G., "The Challenge of Australian Tax Policy," *American Journal of Economics and Sociology*, 1949, 8: 377.

Brown, W. A., "Gold as a Monetary Standard," *Tasks of Economic History*, 1949, IX, 39.

Buck, J. L., *Land Utilization in China*, Shanghai: Commercial Press, 1947.

Burns, A. R., *Money and Monetary Policy in Early Times*, London: Kegan Paul, 1926.

——, *Decline of Competition*, New York: McGraw Hill, 1936.

Burns, Eveline M., *The American Social Security System*, Boston: Houghton Mifflin, 1951.

Chapman, Janet, "Real Wages in the Soviet Union," *Review of Economics and Statistics*, May 1954.

le Cheminant, K., *Colonial and Foreign Banking Systems*, London: Routeledge, 1924.

Chen, Ta., *Population in Modern China*, Chicago: Chicago University Press, 1946.

Chester, D. N., "Organization of Nationalized Industries," *Political Quarterly*, 1950, XXI, 122.

Cheyney, E. P., *The Dawn of a New Era*, New York: Harper Bros., 1936.

Chossudowsky, E. M., "Derationing in the U.S.S.R.," *Review of Economic Studies*, 1941, 22.

Clapham, Sir John, *A Concise Economic History of Britain*, Cambridge: Cambridge University Press, 1949.

Clark, C., *Conditions of Economic Progress*, London: Macmillan Co., 1st Ed. 1940, 2nd Ed. 1951.

Clark, J. M., "Common and Disparate Elements in National Growth and Decline," *Problems in the Study of Economic Growth*, New York: Universities-National Bureau Committee (mimeo), 1949.

Clegg, H., *Labor in Nationalized Industry*, London: Gollancz, 1950.

Cohen, R., "The New British Law on Monopoly," *American Economic Review*, 1949, 39: 485.

Cooper, M. R. and G. T. Barton, "A Century of Farm Mechanization," *The Agricultural Situation*, 1948, 82:9.

Creech-Jones, A., *Labor's Colonial Policy*, London: 1947.

Crouchley, A. E., *The Economic Development of Modern Egypt*, London: Longmans, Green & Co., 1938.

Davies, E., "Ministerial Control and Parliamentary Responsibility of Nationalised Industries," *Political Quarterly*, 1950, XXI, 150.

Davis, K., "Population and the Further Spread of Industrial Society," *Proceedings of the American Philosophical Society*, 1951, 95: 8.

——, *The Population of India and Pakistan*, Princeton: Princeton University Press, 1951.

Deane, Phyllis, *The Measurement of Colonial National Incomes: an Experiment*, Cambridge: Cambridge University Press, 1948.

De Kiewiet, C. W., *A History of South Africa, Social and Economic,* London: Oxford University Press, 1941.

Dewhurst, J. F. *et al, America's Needs and Resources,* New York: Twentieth Century Fund, 1947.

Dobb, M. H., *Soviet Planning and Labor in Peace and War,* New York: International Publishers, 1943.

Douglas, Paul, *The Theory of Wages,* New York: Macmillan Co., 1934.

Dupriez, L. H., *Monetary Reconstruction in Belgium,* New York: King's Crown Press, 1947.

Eckstein, A., "Conditions and Prospects for Economic Growth in Communist China," *World Politics,* 1954, VI, 1.

Ellsworth, P. T., *Chile: an Economy in Transition,* New York: Macmillan Co., 1945.

Elizari-Volcani, I., *Planned Mixed Farming,* 1938.

Fabricant, S., *Employment and Manufacturing, 1899 to 1939,* New York: National Bureau of Economic Research, 1942.

Feary, R. A., *The Occupation of Japan: Second Phase 1948-50,* New York: Macmillan Co., 1950.

Fellner, W. J., *Monetary Policies and Full Employment,* Berkeley: Univ. of California Press, 1947.

Frankel, S. H., *Capital Investment in Africa,* London: Oxford University Press, 1938.

Franklin, N. N., *Economics in South Africa,* Cape Town: Oxford University Press, 1948.

Furnival, J. S., *Netherlands India: a Study of Plural Economy,* New York: Macmillan Co., 1944.

———, *The Tropical Far East,* London: Oxford Pamphlets on World Affairs, 1945.

Galbraith, J. K., *American Capitalism,* Boston: Houghton Mifflin, 1952.

Gerschenkron, A., "The Soviet Indices of Industrial Production," *Review of Economic Statistics,* 1947, 29: 217.

Giblin, L. F., *The Growth of a Central Bank,* Melbourne: Melbourne University Press, 1951.

Granick, D., *Management of the Industrial Firm in the U.S.S.R.,* New York: Columbia University Press, 1954.

———, "Initiative and Independence of Plant Management," *American Slavic and East European Review,* 1951, 191.

Greenshields, E., "Farms are Getting Larger and Fewer," *The Agricultural Situation,* 1947, 1.

Griffith, J. A. G., "The Voice of the Consumer," *Political Quarterly,* 1950, XXI, 171.

Hamilton, Alexander, *The Encouragement and Protection of Manufactures,* 1791.

Hamilton, E. J., "Profit Inflation and the Industrial Revolution," *Quarterly Journal of Economics,* 1942, LVI, 256.

———, "American Treasure and the Rise of Capitalism, (1500 to 1700)," *Economica,* 1929, 338.

———, "Prices and Progress," *Jour. Econ. Hist.,* 1952, XII, 325.

Hanson, S. G., *Utopia in Uruguay,* New York: Oxford University Press, 1938.

Harris, S. E., *Economic Planning,* New York: Alfred Knopf, 1949.

Harrod, R. F., *Towards a Dynamic Economics,* London: Macmillan Co., 1951.

Hart, A. G., *Money Debt and Economic Activity,* New York: Prentice-Hall, Inc., 1948.

Hirschman, Albert O., *National Power and the Structure of Foreign Trade*, Berkeley: University of California Press, 1945.

Hoffman, *Studien und Typen der Industrialisierung*, Jena: 1931.

Horowitz, D. and R. Hendon, *Economic Survey of Palestine*, 1938.

Hunter, H., "Planning of Investment in the Soviet Union," *Review of Economic Statistics*, 1949, XXXI, 54.

Hurst, H. E., *A Short Account of the Nile Basin*, Cairo: Ministry of Public Works, 1944.

Imlah, A. H., "The Terms of Trade of the United Kingdom, 1798 to 1913," X, *Journal of Economic History*, 1950, 170.

International Cooperative Alliance, *International Cooperation 1930-1936*, London: Cooperative Printing Society, 1938.

International Social Security Association, *Recent Developments in the Field of Social Security*, Geneva: 1951.

Issawi, C., *Egypt; an Economic and Social Analysis*, New York: Oxford University Press, 1947.

——, "Population and Wealth in Egypt," *Milbank Memorial Fund Quarterly*, January 1949.

Jacks, G. V. and R. O. Whyte, *The Rape of the Earth: a World Survey of Soil Erosion*, New York: Doubleday Doran, 1939.

Johnson, E. and Bachman, A. L., "How Many Farms; How Big," *The Agricultural Situation*, 1948, 32:2; *ibid*, 1949, 33:14.

Kaser, M. C., "Soviet Planning and the Price Mechanism," *Economic Journal*, 1950, LX, 81.

Keen, B. A., *The Agricultural Development of the Middle East*, London: H. M. Stationery Office, 1946.

Kemmerer, E. W., *Gold and the Gold Standard*, New York, McGraw-Hill, Inc., 1944.

Kessler, W. C., "The German Corporation Law of 1937," *American Economic Review*, 1938, XXVIII, 653.

Keynes, J. M., *The Economic Consequences of Sterling Parity*, New York: Harcourt Brace, 1925.

——, *Indian Currency and Finance*, London: Macmillan Co., 1913.

——, *Treatise on Money*, London: Macmillan Co., 1930.

Klein, L. R., "Planned Economy in Norway," *American Economic Review*, 1948, XXXVIII, 795.

Knorr, K. E., *World Rubber and its Regulation*, Palo Alto: Food Research Institute, Stanford University, 1945.

Kris, M. A., "Central Banks and the State Today," *American Economic Review*, 1948, XXXVIII, 565.

Kuczynski, J., *A Short History of Labor Conditions in France, 1700 to the Present Day*, London: Frederick Muller, 1946.

——, *A Short History of Labor Conditions in Great Britain, 1750 to the Present Day*, London: Frederick Muller, 1942.

Kuznets, S., *National Income: a Summary of Findings*, New York: National Bureau of Economic Research, 1946.

Ladejinsky, W., "Collectivization of Agriculture in the Soviet Union," *Political Science Quarterly*, 1934, IL 1, 207.

——, "Soviet State Farms," *Political Science Quarterly*, 1938, LIII, 60, 207.

Landes, D. S., "French Entrepreneurship in the Nineteenth Century," *Journal of Economic History*, 1949, IX 45.

Large, E. C., *The Advance of the Fungi*, New York: Holt and Co., 1940.

Leavens, D. H., *Silver Money*, Bloomington, Indiana: Principia Press, 1939.

Lee, Shu Ching, "The Heart of China's Problem: the Land Tenure System," *Journal of Farm Economics*, 1948, XXX, 259.

Levy, Hermann, *Monopoly and Competition*, London: Macmillan Co., 1911.

Lewis, W. A., *Overhead Costs*, London: Allen and Unwin, 1949.

Lille, W. S., *India and its Problems*.

List, Friedrich, *Das Nationale System der Politischen Oekonomie*, 1841.

Lucas, A. F., *Industrial Reconstruction and the Control of Competition*, London: Longmans, Green, 1937.

MacFadyean, Sir A. (ed.), *The History of Rubber Regulation, 1934-43*, London: Allen and Unwin, 1944.

Mackenzie, K., *The Banking Systems of Great Britain, France, Germany and the United States of America*, London: Macmillan Co., 1947.

McBride, G. M., *Chile: Land and Society*, New York: American Geographical Society, 1936.

———, *The Land Systems of Mexico*, New York: American Geographical Society, 1923.

Mandelbaum, D. G., "Population Problems in India and Pakistan," *Far Eastern Survey*, Nov. 30, 1949.

Marquand, H. A., *Organized Labor in Four Continents*, New York: Longmans, Green, 1939.

Mason, E. S., *Controlling World Trade*, New York: McGraw-Hill, Inc., 1946.

Mauldon, F. R. E., "The Australian Coal Industry," *Economic Record*, 1948, XXIV, 234.

Miller, J., "Some Recent Developments of Soviet Economic Thought," *Soviet Studies*, 1949-50, I, 119.

Minc, Hilary, *Poland's Economy, Present and Future*, New York: Polish Research and Information Service, 1949.

Mitchell, H., "The Impact of Sudden Accessions of Treasure on Prices and Real Wages," *Canadian Journal of Economics and Political Science*, 1946, XII, 1.

Morgan, O. S. (ed.), *Agricultural Systems of Middle Europe*, New York: Macmillan Co., 1933.

Mukerjee, K. M., "The Problem of Rural Indebtedness in Bengal," *Indian Journal of Economics*, 1949, 375.

Myers, M. G., "The Nationalization of Banks in France," *Political Science Quarterly*, 1949, LXIV, 189.

Myrdal, Alva, "Population Trends in Densely Populated Areas," *Proceedings of the American Philosophical Society*, 1950, 95:1.

Myrdal, G., "Industrialization and Population," in *Economic Essays in Honor of Gustav Cassel*, London: Allen and Unwin, 1933.

Nanavati, M. B. and Anjaria, J. J., *The Indian Rural Problems*, Bombay: Vora and Co., 1947.

National Council of Social Service, *Public Social Services: Handbook of Information on Services provided by the State*, London: 1949.

Nazmy, "The Land as a Bottomless Sink for Egyptian Capital," *L'Egypte Contemporaine*, 1948, XXXV, 239.

de Neumann, A. M., *Consumer Representation in the Public Sector of Industry*, Cambridge, Eng.: no pub., 1950.

New South Wales Fabian Society, *The Case for Bank Nationalisation*, Sydney: n.d.

Nobutaka, I., "The Development of Capitalism in Japan," *Pacific Affairs*, June, 1949.

Nurkse, R., "Some International Aspects of the Problem of Economic Development," *Proceeding of the American Economic Association*, 1951, 571.

Nussbaum, A., *Money in the Law*, New York: Brooklyn Foundation Press, 1950.

Owen, Henry, *Steel: the Facts about Monopoly and Nationalization*, London: Lawrence and Wishart, 1946.

Peacock, Alan T. (ed.), *Income Redistribution and Social Policy*, London: Jonathan Cape, 1954.

Pelzer, K. J., "Tara Sabrang and Java's Population Problem," *Far Eastern Quarterly*, 1946, V, 133.

Pim, Sir Alan, *Colonial Agricultural Production*, London: Oxford University Press, 1946.

Piotrowski, R., *Cartels and Trusts*, London: Allen and Unwin, 1933.

Prest, A. R., "National Income of the United Kingdom, 1870 to 1914," *Economic Journal*, 1948, LVIII, 31.

——, *War Economies of Primary Producing Countries*, Cambridge: Cambridge University Press, 1948.

Punekar, D. S., *Trade Unionism in India*, Bombay: New Book Company, 1948.

Rao, V. K. R. V., *National Income of British India, 1931-2*, London: Allen and Unwin, 1939.

Reubens, Beatrice G., "Social Legislation in Japan," *Far Eastern Survey*, 1949, 269.

Robinson, Joan, *The Economics of Imperfect Competition*, London: Macmillan Co., 1946.

——, "Mr. Harrod's Dynamics," *Economic Journal*, 1949, LIX, 68.

Robson, W. A., "The Governing Board of the Public Corporation," *Political Quarterly*, 1950, XXI, 135.

Rosenstein-Rodan, P. N., "The Problems of Industrialization of Southern and South Eastern Europe," *Economic Journal*, 1943, LIII, 203.

Rostas, L., *Comparative Productivity in British and American Industry*, Cambridge: Cambridge University Press, 1948.

Rostow, E. V., *A National Policy for the Oil Industry*, New Haven: Yale University Press, 1948.

Rostow, W. W., "Government and Private Enterprise in European Recovery," *Tasks of Economic History*, 1950, X, 105.

Rowan, D., "Banking and Credit under the Labor Government," *Journal of Politics*, 1950, 12:290.

Roy, M. N., *People's Plan for the Economic Development of India*, Delhi: Indian Federation of Labor, 1944.

Royal Institute of International Affairs, *The Middle East*, New York: Royal Institute of International Affairs, 1950.

Russell, Sir John, "World Population and World Food Supplies," *Proceedings of the British Association for the Advancement of Science*, 1949.

Schultz, T. W., *Agriculture in an Unstable Economy*, New York: McGraw Hill, Inc., 1945.

Schwartz, H., *Russia's Soviet Economy*, New York: Prentice-Hall, Inc., 1950.

Scitovsky, T., "The State of Welfare Economics," *American Economic Review*, 1951, XLI, 303.

Seers, D., *The Levelling of Incomes since 1938*, Oxford: Basil Blackwell, n.d.

Sharp, S. L., *Nationalisation of Key Industries in Eastern Europe*, Washington: Foundation for Foreign Affairs, 1946.

Shaw, A. G. L., *The Economic Development of Australia*, New York: Longmans, 1944.

Shoup, C. S., *The Principles of National Income Analysis*, Boston: Houghton Mifflin, 1947.

Singer, H. W., "Economic Progress in Underdeveloped Countries," *Social Research*, 1949, 16:1.

——, "Trade and Investment in Underdeveloped Areas: the Distribution of Gain between Investing and Borrowing Countries," *Proceedings of the American Economic Association*, 1949, 474.

Spengler, J. J., "Aspects of the Economics of Population Growth," *Southern Economic Journal*, 1948, 26:248.

——, "Economic Factors in the Development of Densely Populated Areas," *Proceedings of the American Philosophical Association*, 1951, 50.

——, "Note on France's Response to her Declining Rate of Demographic Growth," *Journal of Economic History*, 1951, XI, 104.

——, "The World's Hunger; Malthus, 1948," *Proceedings of the Academy of Political Science*, 1949, 65.

Spiegel, H. W., *The Brazilian Economy: Chronic Inflation and Sporadic Industrialization*, Philadelphia: Blakiston, 1949.

Staley, Eugene, *World Economic Development*, Montreal, International Labor Office, 1944.

Stockder, A. H., *Regulating an Industry: The Rhenish Westphalian Coal Syndicate 1893 to 1929*, New York: Columbia University Press, 1932.

Subercaseaux, G., *Monetary and Banking Policy of Chile*, New York: Oxford University Press, 1922.

Sweezy, Paul, M., "The Transition from Feudalism to Capitalism," XIV *Science and Society*, 1950, XIV, 134.

Taeuber, I., "Population Growth and Economic Development in Japan," *Journal of Economic History*, 1951, XI, 424.

Takizawa, M., *The Penetration of Money Economy in Japan*, New York: no. pub., 1927.

Thakurdas *et al.*, *A Plan for the Economic Development of India*, "Bombay Plan," New York: Penguin Books, 1944.

Thompson, Warren, S., *Population and Peace in the Pacific*, Chicago: Chicago University Press, 1946.

Tirana, R., "Government Financing of Economic Development Abroad," *Tasks of Economic History*, 1950, X, 192.

Titmuss, R. H., *Poverty and Population*, London: Macmillan Co., 1938.

Tothill, J. D., *Agriculture in Uganda*, London: Oxford University Press, 1940.

Transvaal Chamber of Mines, *The Native Workers on the Witwatersrand Gold Mines, Johannesburg*, Transvaal Chamber of Mines, 1947.

Trevelyan, G. M., *English Social History*, New York: Longmans, Green, 1942.

Turner, R. E., "Economic Discontent in Medieval Europe, VIII, *Tasks of Economic History*, 1948, 85.

Usher, A. P., "The Balance Sheet of Economic Development," *Journal of Economic History*, 1951, XI, 331.

Veblen, Thorstein, *Imperial Germany and the Industrial Revolution*, New York: Viking Press, 1939.

Wadia, P. A., and K. T. Merchant, *Our Economic Problem*, Bombay: New Book Co., 1946.

Walker, Sir E. W., *Canadian Banking*, Toronto: Canadian Bankers' Association, 1923.

Walker, G., "The Economics of British Transport," *Westminster Bank Review*, August 1950.

Warriner, Doreen, *Land and Poverty in the Middle East,* London: Royal Institute of International Affairs, 1948.

Weber, Max, *The Protestant Ethic and the Spirit of Capitalism,* (tr. T. Parsons), New York, Scribner's, 1950.

Weinryb, B. D., "The Industrialisation of the Near East," *Quarterly Journal of Economics,* 1947, LXI, 474.

Welles, C. B., "The Economic Background of Plato's Communism," *Tasks of Economic History,* 1948, VIII, 101.

Wickizer, V. D., *Tea under International Regulation,* Palo Alto: Food Research Institute, Stanford University, 1945.

Wilson, J. S. G., "The Future of Banking in Australia," *Economic Journal,* 1949, LIX, 208.

Witte, E. E., "Labor Management Relations under the Taft-Hartley Act," *Harvard Business Review,* 1947, XXV, 553.

Wood, G. L. (ed.), *Australia: its Resources and Development,* New York: Macmillan Co., 1947.

Woodbury, R. M., "The Incidence of Industrial Disputes: Rates of Time Loss 1927-47," *International Labor Review,* 1949, LX, 451.

Wrench, Guy T., *The Restoration of the Peasantries,* London: C. W. Daniel Co., 1939.

Zauberman, A., "Economic Law and the Theory of Value," *Review of Economic Studies,* 1948-9, XV, 1.

Zweig, F., *Labor, Life and Poverty,* London: Victor Gollancz Ld., 1948.

——, *Poland between Two Wars,* London: Secker and Warburg, 1944.

Index

749